D1556926

THE PAPERS
OF
JOHN MARSHALL

Sponsored by
The College of William and Mary
and
The Omohundro Institute of Early American History and Culture
under the auspices of
The National Historical Publications and Records
Commission

JOHN MARSHALL
Oil on canvas by Edward F. Peticolas, ca. 1824.
Courtesy of Lafayette College, Easton, Pennsylvania.

THE PAPERS
OF
JOHN MARSHALL

Volume IX

Correspondence, Papers, and Selected Judicial Opinions
January 1820–December 1823

CHARLES F. HOBSON, *Editor*

LAURA S. GWILLIAM   SUSAN HOLBROOK PERDUE

ROBERT W. SMITH

The University of North Carolina Press, Chapel Hill
in association with the
Omohundro Institute of Early American History and Culture
Williamsburg, Virginia

The Omohundro Institute of Early American History and Culture
is sponsored jointly by
The College of William and Mary in Virginia
and The Colonial Williamsburg Foundation.
On November 15, 1996, The Institute adopted the present
name in honor of a bequest from Malvern H. Omohundro, Jr.

The paper in this book meets the guidelines for permanence and durability of the Committee on
Production Guidelines for Book Longevity of the Council on Library Resources.
The ornament on the title page is based upon John Marshall's personal seal, as it appears on a gold
watch fob that also bears the seal of his wife, Mary Willis Marshall. It was drawn by Richard J.
Stinely of Williamsburg, Virginia, from the original, now owned by the Association for the
Preservation of Virginia Antiquities, Richmond, Virginia, and is published with the
owner's permission.

Library of Congress Cataloging-in-Publication Data

Marshall, John, *1755–1835.*
  The papers of John Marshall.
  Vol. 5–   : Charles F. Hobson, editor.
  "Sponsored by the College of William and Mary and the Institute of Early American History and
Culture under the auspices of the National Historical Publications Commission."
  Includes bibliographical references and indexes.

  CONTENTS: v. 1. Correspondence and papers, November 10, 1775–June 23, 1788. Account
book, September 1783–June 1788. [etc.] v. 8. Correspondence, papers, and selected judicial opinions,
March 1814–December 1819. v. 9. Correspondence, papers, and selected judicial opinions, January
1820–December 1823.
  1. Marshall, John, 1755–1835 — Manuscripts.   2. United States — Politics and government —
1775–1783 — Sources.   3.   United   States — Politics   and   government — 1783–1865 —
Sources.   4.   Statesmen — United   States — Manuscripts.   5.   Judges — United   States — Manu-
scripts.   6. Manuscripts, American.   7. Judicial opinions.   I. Johnson, Herbert Alan, ed.
II. Cullen, Charles T., 1940–   , ed.   III. Hobson, Charles F., 1943–   , ed.   IV. Title.
E302.M365   347.73'2634   347.3073534   74-9575
ISBN-13: 978-0-8078-1233-4 (v. 1)   ISBN-10: 0-8078-1233-1 (v. 1)
ISBN-13: 978-0-8078-1302-7 (v. 2)   ISBN-10: 0-8078-1302-8 (v. 2)
ISBN-13: 978-0-8078-1337-9 (v. 3)   ISBN-10: 0-8078-1337-0 (v. 3)
ISBN-13: 978-0-8078-1586-1 (v. 4)   ISBN-10: 0-8078-1586-1 (v. 4)
ISBN-13: 978-0-8078-1746-9 (v. 5)   ISBN-10: 0-8078-1746-5 (v. 5)
ISBN-13: 978-0-8078-1903-6 (v. 6)   ISBN-10: 0-8078-1903-4 (v. 6)
ISBN-13: 978-0-8078-2074-2 (v. 7)   ISBN-10: 0-8078-2074-1 (v. 7)
ISBN-13: 978-0-8078-2221-0 (v. 8)   ISBN-10: 0-8078-2221-3 (v. 8)
ISBN-13: 978-0-8078-2404-7 (v. 9)   ISBN-10: 0-8078-2404-6 (v. 9)

To the memory of
LAURA S. GWILLIAM

*Publication of this volume has been assisted by grants from the
National Endowment for the Humanities, the National Historical Publications
and Records Commission, and the William Nelson Cromwell Foundation.*

CONTENTS

Illustrations	xiv
Preface	xv
Acknowledgments	xix
The Plan of the Volume and Editorial Policy	xxiii
Editorial Apparatus	xxvii
Editorial Method	xxvii
Textual Notes	xxix
Descriptive Symbols	xxx
Location Symbols	xxxi
Record Groups in the National Archives	xxxi
Abbreviations for Court and Other Records	xxxii
Abbreviations for English Courts	xxxii
Short Titles	xxxiii
Marshall Chronology	xxxvii

JANUARY 1820–DECEMBER 1823

1820

To William Bainbridge, 3 January	3
From William Wirt, 17 January	3
John Williams to Justices of the Supreme Court, 10 February	4
United States v. Wiltberger, Opinion, 18 February	5
To [Smith Thompson], 23 February	12
To John George Jackson, 25 February	12
Loughborough v. Blake, Opinion, 10 March	13
Notes on Arguments, 10–11 March	17
From William Wirt, 11 March	25
To Samuel F. Jarvis, 26 March	29
From William Wirt, 11 April	29
To Bushrod Washington, 13 April	30
The Brig Wilson v. United States, Opinion, ca. 22 May	31
Gallego, Richard & Company v. United States, Opinion, ca. 22 May	40
United States v. Smith, Sentence, 29 May	44
To John Quincy Adams, 30 May	46
To William Wirt, 30 May	46
From William Wirt, 1 June	47
To St. George Tucker, 2 June	47

Wilson v. LeRoy, Bayard & McEvers, Opinion, 7 June   48
Anderson & Wilkins v. Tompkins, Opinion, 12 June   53
To Bushrod Washington, 26 June   58
Memorandum concerning Leeds Manor, 29 June   59
To [Agatha Marshall], 1 July   61
To Louis Marshall, 1 July   61
From Walter L. Fontaine, 21 July   62
To John C. Calhoun, 1 August   63
To George A. Ward, 2 September   63
To Bushrod Washington, 2 September   64
To George A. Ward, 18 September   66
To Bushrod Washington, 7 November   68
To St. George Tucker, 22 November   69
Robertson v. Miller, Opinion, 27 November   69
Thompson and Dickson v. United States, Opinion,
    11 December   76
The Santissima Trinidad and St. Ander,
    Opinion, 20 December   89

1821

To Bushrod Washington, 8 February   101
To Smith Thompson, 13 February   102
From Smith Thompson, 15 February   103
To [James Monroe], 20 February   103
To Mary W. Marshall, 26 February   104
To James K. Marshall, [26 February]   105
Cohens v. Virginia, Editorial Note   106
    Opinion, 3 March   113
From Gales and Seaton, 3 March   142
To Gales and Seaton, [3 March]   143
Cohens v. Virginia, Opinion, 5 March   143
To Richard Rush, 16 March   147
To Henry Wheaton, 24 March   147
To Henry Wheaton, 2 June   150
Coates v. Muse, Opinion and Decree, 4 June   150
Backhouse v. Jett's Administrator, Opinion and Decree,
    6 June   156
To Joseph Story, 15 June   167
To Bushrod Washington, 15 June   168
United States v. P. T. Shelton & Company, Opinion and
    Decree, 15 June   169
To Edward C. Marshall, 24 June   172

CONTENTS [xi]

To William S. Cardell, 25 June 173
From Joseph Story, 27 June 174
To Joseph Story, 13 July 178
To Bushrod Washington, 13 July 180
To Charles Miner, [15] July 181
To John Quincy Adams, 6 September 182
To Joseph Story, 18 September 183
To Daniel Raymond, 25 September 185
To Walter L. Fontaine, 27 September 186
To Walter L. Fontaine, 20 November 187
To Walter L. Fontaine, [8 December] 188
Jacob v. United States, Opinion, 11 December 188
From John Quincy Adams, 12 December 193
To Walter L. Fontaine, 13 December 194
To John Quincy Adams, 18 December 194
To Bushrod Washington, 27 December 195

1822

From Philip Slaughter, 28 January 196
To [John C. Calhoun], 16 February 197
To Jedidiah Morse, 21 February 197
From James A. Hamilton, 8 March 200
To James A. Hamilton, 9 March 200
To Bushrod Washington, 15 April 201
To Littleton W. Tazewell, 19 May 202
To Bushrod Washington, 28 May 203
Furniss, Cutler, & Stacey v. Allan & Ellis,
    Opinion, 1 June 204
From William Gaston, 12 June 210
Coates v. Muse, Opinion, 12 June 210
Hopkirk v. Page, Opinion, 12 June 217
United States v. Mann, Opinion, 12 June 232
To James Monroe, 13 June 236
To Bushrod Washington, 17 June 237
To Bushrod Washington, 6 July 238
To James M. Marshall, 9 July 239
To Martin Marshall, 23 September 241
To St. George Tucker, 23 November 242
To [Hugh Mercer?], 4 December 243
Pendleton v. United States, Opinion, 16 December 243
To Joseph Gales, 19 December 248
Scott and Lyle v. Lenox, Opinion, 26 December 249

Gaines v. Span, Opinion, [28 December?]   253
United States v. Nelson and Myers, Opinion, 28 December   263

1823

To Jaquelin A. Marshall, 15 January   270
To Robert Mayo and William A. Bartow, 26 January   272
To Mary W. Marshall, 4 [February]   273
Notes on Arguments, 12–13 February   275
Johnson v. McIntosh, Editorial Note   279
     Opinion, 28 February   284
To Jaquelin B. Harvie, 8 March   302
To Mary W. Marshall, 11 April   302
To Bushrod Washington, 3 May   303
United States v. Maurice, Opinion, 22 May   304
To St. George Tucker, 27 May   321
To Bushrod Washington, 28 May   322
To Joseph Story, 1 June   323
Bank of the United States v. Dandridge, Report, 6 June   324
From Joseph Story, 22 June   327
To Bushrod Washington, 25 June   328
To Joseph Story, 2 July   330
To St. George Tucker, 7 July   331
United States v. Manuel Catacho, Order, 11 July   332
To Bushrod Washington, 12 July   332
To Bushrod Washington, 6 August   334
To Bushrod Washington, 12 August   336
To Stephen Girard, 25 September   337
To Joseph Story, 26 September   338
To Caleb P. Wayne, 29 September   339
From Stephen Girard, 6 October   340
To Bushrod Washington, 11 October   340
To Joseph Story, 12 October   341
From John Lowell, 25 October   341
United States v. Manuel Catacho, Charge to
     Grand Jury, 27 October   344
To Mary W. Marshall, 31 October   344
To [John Lowell], 6 November   345
To Joseph Story, 24 November   346
Mankin v. Chandler & Company, Opinion, 5 December   347
To Bushrod Washington, 6 December   352
To James Monroe, 9 December   353
To Joseph Story, 9 December   353
Maxwell v. Call, Opinion, 16 December   355

Coates v. Muse, Opinion, 18 December   360
To Henry Clay, 22 December   365
To Charles Hammond, 28 December   367

Appendices   369
   I: Opinions Delivered by Chief Justice John Marshall in
      the U.S. Supreme Court, 1820–1823   371
  II: Calendar of Miscellaneous Papers and Letters Not Found   374
Index   381

ILLUSTRATIONS

JOHN MARSHALL   FRONTISPIECE

WILLIAM WIRT   26

HENRY WHEATON   149

U.S. HOUSE OF REPRESENTATIVES   198

BUSHROD WASHINGTON   335

Preface

The chronology of Volume IX of *The Papers of John Marshall* begins in January 1820 and proceeds through December 1823. During these four years, straddling the first and second administrations of President James Monroe, the Supreme Court of the United States maintained the high public profile it had earned at the eventful 1819 term. Cases in which the claims of national power and state sovereignty came into collision continued to appear on the Court's docket. These cases attracted the public's attention because they bore directly on the great issues of the day: state taxation of branch banks of the Second Bank of the United States, the power of Congress to prohibit slavery in the territories (raised in the debate over the admission of Missouri to statehood), and the authority of Congress to appropriate money for "internal improvements."

The most important case of this period was *Cohens* v. *Virginia* (1821), in which a prosecution for the sale of lottery tickets became the occasion for expounding federal judicial power. Chief Justice Marshall delivered the opinion in *Cohens*, but disqualified himself in another prominent case, *Green* v. *Biddle* (1821, 1823), which involved the validity of certain Kentucky land laws. In addition to *Cohens* and *Green*, several other constitutionally significant cases were on the docket and ready for argument by the end of 1823. These included *Gibbons* v. *Ogden* (1824), which would bring forth the Court's first exposition of the commerce clause. Aside from *Cohens*, Marshall delivered one other major Supreme Court opinion during these years, *Johnson* v. *McIntosh* (1823). Although not a constitutional case in the strict sense, *Johnson* affirmed the federal government's exclusive right to extinguish Indian titles to lands not within any state. In so doing, it defined for the first time the legal relationship between the government and Indian tribes within the territorial boundaries of the United States.

Cohens v. *Virginia*, like *McCulloch* v. *Maryland* two years earlier, subjected the Supreme Court to intense public scrutiny and condemnation in Virginia. There the controversy occasioned by the bank case had scarcely subsided when the brothers Philip and Mendez Cohen of Norfolk brought their case to the federal Supreme Court. Members of a flourishing family enterprise whose specialty was vending lottery tickets, the Cohens sought redress for a fine levied against them for unlawfully selling tickets to a lottery drawn in the city of Washington. The appeal, which went directly from the local Norfolk court to the Supreme Court, alarmed the zealous guardians of states' rights. To them *Cohens* appeared to be a more direct and dangerous assault on the commonwealth's sovereignty and independence than the decision in the bank case. Very quickly the jurisdictional issue — whether a state could be called to the bar of the federal Supreme

Court for enforcing its own penal laws—overshadowed the merits of the case. A thorough public airing of Virginia's case against the jurisdiction took place in the state legislature and in the newspapers well in advance of the Supreme Court's hearing (see Cohens v. Virginia, Opinion, 3 March 1821, editorial note).

On 3 March 1821 Chief Justice Marshall for a unanimous Court sustained the jurisdiction in an opinion that constitutes the most comprehensive judicial statement of the scope and extent of the Supreme Court's appellate jurisdiction. Two days later he again spoke for the Court in upholding the fine assessed against the Cohens, a decision that scarcely assuaged the ire Virginia republicans directed against the Court for presuming to entertain jurisdiction in this case. In a reprise of their campaign against McCulloch two years earlier, Richmond newspaper editor Thomas Ritchie and Judge Spencer Roane orchestrated their party's response to Cohens. Marshall easily identified Roane as the author of the "Algernon Sidney" essays, which appeared in Ritchie's newspaper in May and June of 1821. "There is probably but one man in the United States who could or would write such pieces," wrote the chief justice, who recommended them "as being an excitement to stagnating spirits as powerful as the essence of chian to a palate which has lost its discriminating power" (to Bushrod Washington, 15 June 1821). Irritated as he was by Roane's relentless tirade against the Court, the chief justice did not on this occasion undertake an anonymous defense as he had done two years earlier in response to the attacks on McCulloch. In private correspondence he confided his suspicions that the malign influence of Thomas Jefferson, "the great Lama of the mountains," was working to undermine the independence of the federal judiciary (to Joseph Story, 18 September 1821).

Marshall was deeply concerned that anti-Court sentiment in Virginia and elsewhere would translate into attempts to curb the power of the Supreme Court. Proposals came before Congress to repeal the twenty-fifth section of the Judiciary Act, to amend the Constitution by giving the Senate appellate jurisdiction in cases where a state was a party, and to require a supermajority of the Supreme Court justices to pass on the constitutionality of state and federal acts. This last proposal elicited a private communication (recently discovered and hitherto unpublished) to the influential Senator Henry Clay, in which the politically astute chief justice warned of the danger of enacting "a general law of great and extensive influence to effect a particular object." Pointing out that such legislation would in effect prevent the Supreme Court from exercising judicial review, Marshall reaffirmed his conviction that the intention of the Constitution was "to provide a tribunal for every case of collision between itself and a law, so far as such case can assume a form for judicial enquiry" (to Henry Clay, 22 December 1823).

The death of Justice Brockholst Livingston in March 1823 marked the first change in the personnel of the Supreme Court since 1811. Amid rumors concerning Livingston's successor, Marshall fretted that "our Presidents" would "never again seek to make our department respectable." In truth, President Monroe had quickly offered the nomination to a worthy candidate, Smith Thompson, then serving as secretary of the navy and who like Livingston was a New Yorker. Some months later Thompson finally agreed to the nomination after concluding that his presidential aspirations for 1824 were unlikely to be realized. A relieved chief justice was "truly rejoiced" to learn of Thompson's appointment (to Story, 2 July 1823; to Washington, 6 August 1823).

Circuit court cases kept Marshall busily employed, as evidenced by two dozen opinions he wrote. Many of these opinions were in complicated equity suits brought by or against a decedent's estate for the recovery of a long-standing debt. Other circuit opinions were in admiralty and prize causes appealed from United States District Court. In one such opinion the chief justice offered his first judicial commentary on the extent of the commerce clause of the Constitution, a subject he would soon take up at large in *Gibbons* v. *Ogden* (see The Brig Wilson v. United States, Opinion, ca. 22 May 1820). Another category of opinions embraced cases brought against debtors to the United States, including officials or agents employed by the federal government who had defaulted on performance bonds. One of these cases also gave rise to constitutional exposition, in this instance the president's power of appointment (see United States v. Maurice, Opinion, 22 May 1823).

Marshall consulted with brother Justices Joseph Story and Bushrod Washington when confronted with new or perplexing questions on circuit. He particularly sought such advice when the case for various reasons could not be brought to the Supreme Court for ultimate resolution. Legal matters the chief discussed with his brethren concerned the respective liabilities of the creditors of an insolvent debtor to the United States, a demurrer to evidence in a case against a whiskey distiller, the sufficiency of process served on the president of a state bank, a motion for a mixed jury composed of citizens and foreigners, and a claim for salvage on a vessel recaptured from pirates. Regarding the salvage case, Marshall confided to Story: "I know that you are more *au fait* on these questions than I am" (to Story, 9 December 1823). The chief justice gave advice, too, as shown by his reply to Washington's query about a case on a bill of exchange (to Washington, 13 July 1821).

In two of his doubtful circuit cases, Marshall predicted his decision would "be reversed by your Honors" (to Washington, 28 May 1822). The more important of these was a case brought by the Bank of the United States against the cashier of the Richmond branch. The principal issue concerned the evidence necessary to prove the bank's acceptance of a performance bond. The chief justice ruled that such acceptance had to be recorded in the minutes of the board of directors (Bank of the United States v. Dandridge, Report, 6 June 1823). Acknowledging "that the practice of banks" probably did not conform to his "construction of the law," he remarked that the judge who overruled him "must have more ingenuity than I have." To Story (who subsequently delivered the Supreme Court's reversing opinion), Marshall declared he would "bow with respect to the judgement of reversal but till it is given I shall retain the opinion I have expressed" (to Story, 2 July 1823).

In token of their deepening friendship, Story sent Marshall a quintal of New England codfish with instructions on how to cook them. The chief justice promised "to feed on the fish with an appetite which would not disgrace a genuine descendant of one of the Pilgrims." He in turn sent Story "two barrels of our family flour" (to Story, 18 September 1821; 12 October 1823). When Marshall sent his youngest son, Edward Carrington Marshall, to Cambridge to enter Harvard College, Story kindly undertook to help the young scholar get settled and to advance funds on his behalf. Although the father had given Edward money, he purposely restricted the amount so as not to "encourage expensive habits." A subsequent advance of money went directly to Story, Marshall explaining that "my sons, in the north, have such an aptitude for spending money, that I am unwilling to tempt Edward by placing too much in his hands" (to Story, 1 June 1823; 26 September 1823). Edward's Cambridge experience would prove to be much happier than that of his older brothers John and James.

Apart from conferring on judicial business, Marshall and Bushrod Washington continued their close collaboration on two projects, the publication of a second edition of the *Life of Washington* and an edition of General Washington's correspondence. By the end of 1821 Marshall had finished revising the *Life* and abridging it to four volumes. Negotiations for printing the work then got underway. To make the undertaking more attractive to the printer, the chief justice at length proposed to publish the "introduction," essentially a history of the colonies, as a separate volume and incur the expense of printing it. There could be no objection, he said, since that part was "considered rather as an incumbrance on the residue of the work." He had in mind an edition of a thousand copies to be published first, he explained, "because (excuse this vanity & keep it to yourself) I think it is so much improved that its publication may probably be useful to what is to follow." He was willing to take on the risk of publication, he added, because "my object" was "to do justice to my own reputation in this work" (to Washington, 12 July 1823; 12 August 1823). Abraham Small, a Philadelphia printer, agreed to this proposition and published Marshall's *History of the Colonies* in 1824. Eight more years would pass, however, before publication of the second edition of the main body of the *Life*.

Meanwhile, Marshall and Washington proceeded with the copying of General Washington's correspondence, evidently having in view a simultaneous publication with the second edition of the *Life*. Problems arose with the copyist, who "plays the devil by beginning almost every word with a capital." The chief justice set out to erase the capitals with his knife, "but found the task so laborious that I would really prefer copying over the whole again." As originally organized, the letters were arranged according to the letterbook from which they had been copied, but Marshall preferred a strict chronological presentation. His other editorial principles included avoiding repetitions, omitting uninteresting letters, and correcting "apparent inaccuracies." Whether the errors were the fault of his secretary or were committed by "the General in the hurry of writing, is perhaps not very material" (to Washington, 6 July 1822; 12 July 1823; 11 October 1823).

Family life continued to revolve around home in Richmond, the farm on the Chickahominy River just northeast of town, and extended summer sojourns in the upper country. When absent from home, Marshall anxiously inquired after Mary Marshall's health, a perennial concern. Unable to tolerate loud noise, she fled to the farm during the "noisy rejoicings" of General Washington's birthday celebration. Even there she could hear the drum, and the "Cannon shook the house," which must have interrupted her "mornings nap" (to Mary W. Marshall, 26 February 1821). All of their children were now married, except Edward, who was preparing for college. In June 1821 Marshall advised Edward (then fifteen) that he would "derive great benefit" from studying an extra year at a school in Fauquier before going off to Harvard (to Edward C. Marshall, 24 June 1821). As it turned out, Edward's college career was postponed for two years. Thomas, the oldest son and proprietor of the family's Oak Hill estate in Fauquier, ran unsuccessfully for Congress in 1823, the father attributing his defeat in part to losing federal votes that had been committed "before his being known as a candidate" (to Mary W. Marshall, 11 April 1823). Outside his immediate family, Marshall continued to look after the affairs of his widowed sister, Jane Marshall Taylor, and to console her on the death of her only son.

While continuing to profess his detachment from party politics, Marshall remained an interested observer of the political scene. As the presidential election of 1824 approached, he went so far as to circulate a letter written to him on behalf of Henry Clay's candidacy. He considered Clay to be "an enlightened Statesman" who was "entitled to particular credit" for resolving the Missouri crisis. At the same time he stated he would "be perfectly content with the choice of the nation whoever he may be" (to Charles Hammond, 28 December 1823).

Acknowledgments

The research for this volume was made easier by the courteous assistance of the staffs of the Earl Gregg Swem Library and the Marshall-Wythe Law

Library, College of William and Mary. Special thanks are owed to Margaret C. Cook of Swem and to James S. Heller and Petra Klemmack of Marshall-Wythe. Conley Edwards and his staff at the archives division of the Library of Virginia, Richmond, greatly facilitated the search for materials at that institution. Timothy Connelly and Michael T. Meier of the National Historical Publications and Records Commission promptly responded to requests for documents in various record groups of the National Archives. The following persons also supplied information or documents used in preparing this volume: Beth Carroll-Horrocks of the American Philosophical Society, Philadelphia; Philander D. Chase of the Papers of George Washington, University of Virginia; Jeanne K. Cross of the Papers of James Madison, University of Virginia; Patrice Donoghue of the Harvard University Archives, Pusey Library, Cambridge; Margaret Kulis of the Newberry Library, Chicago; Barry L. McGhee of Research Services, Port Royal, Virginia; Sandra O'Keefe of Lloyd House, Alexandria Library, Alexandria, Virginia; Daniel Preston of the James Monroe Papers, College of William and Mary; and Sandra F. VanBurkleo of the history department at Wayne State University, Detroit.

This edition continues to enjoy the benefits of sponsorship by the College of William and Mary and the Omohundro Institute of Early American History and Culture. The college contributes generous monetary and in-kind support; the Institute contributes the services and editorial expertise of its highly regarded book publishing program. The editors thank Fredrika J. Teute and Gilbert Kelly of the Institute publications staff for their wise counsel. The National Endowment for the Humanities provided major funding for the preparation of this volume. Additional support was supplied by grants from the National Historical Publications and Records Commission and the William Nelson Cromwell Foundation.

Laura Gwilliam

Volume IX is dedicated to the memory of Laura S. Gwilliam, who died on 9 October 1995. Laura's name graces the title page of this and three preceding volumes of this edition, and her editorial hand will be evident in volumes to come. Laura joined the Marshall Papers in October 1986 as secretary and administrative assistant. With no professional background or training, she made herself into an accomplished documentary editor. Endowed with a sense of perfectionism, a passion for organization, discipline, and accuracy, Laura was temperamentally suited to the exacting work of preparing a scholarly edition. She was devoted to her work and took great pride in her craftsmanship.

We have lost a professional colleague and dear friend. Laura liberally shared her abundant gifts of charm, good humor, and empathy. Her radiant personality delighted and animated all who came within her presence. She was a tonic whose restorative powers continually worked a magical cure for the doldrums. She remained true to her character well into the advanced stages of illness. She faced this challenge with rare courage and self-possession. We watched with awe as she negotiated the terms of her own surrender.

The Plan of the Volume
and
Editorial Policy

Volume IX is composed of 138 documents published in full and another 71 that are either calendared or listed. Most of the documents fall into two broad categories, correspondence and judicial papers, which together record Marshall's public and private activities through December 1823. The greater part of the volume consists of judicial opinions given in the Supreme Court and the U.S. Circuit Court for Virginia.

CORRESPONDENCE

Large portions of Marshall's correspondence have been lost or destroyed. What survives does not form a continuous record and consists overwhelmingly of letters Marshall wrote to others. Of a total of 99 letters published in full in Volume IX, 84 are from Marshall to various recipients. Twenty of these are to Bushrod Washington. The next most frequent correspondent is Joseph Story, with whom Marshall exchanged 9 letters. Aside from judicial business, correspondence in this volume yields information about Marshall's private pursuits and family concerns. Eleven letters are addressed to family members.

JUDICIAL PAPERS

Over the course of his long judicial tenure, Marshall delivered nearly 700 reported opinions in the Supreme Court and in the U.S. Circuit Courts for Virginia and North Carolina. From 1801 on, judicial opinions constitute an ever-increasing proportion of the documentary record of his career. The editors have adopted the following policy with respect to this voluminous material.

This edition is not a documentary history of the Supreme Court from 1801 to 1835. Nor does its scope entail reproducing all 550 opinions Marshall delivered on the Supreme Court, the full texts of which are accessible in the official *United States Reports*. The original drafts of the great majority of his opinions have not survived, and their loss precludes rendering more accurately the texts that we now have. Only 88 of Marshall's manuscript opinions (16 percent of the total) are extant, most of them dating from his last years in office. (For a fuller description of the sources documenting Marshall's Supreme Court career, see the *Papers of John Marshall*, VI, 69–73.) Yet an edition of Marshall's papers cannot omit altogether such a large and important group of documents. As a workable compromise between total inclusion and total exclusion, this edition is publishing in full most of the constitutional opinions (about 30) and a small but representative selection of nonconstitutional opinions. It also presents calendar entries for all the opinions given by the chief justice during the years covered by a volume. (See Appendix I for a list of the opinions from 1820 through 1823.)

Selecting from the huge mass of nonconstitutional opinions presents an editorial problem that admits of no fully satisfactory solution. Even eliminating many relatively insignificant cases that were disposed of in a brief opinion still leaves a sizable body of judicial literature. From this corpus the editors have attempted to provide a sampling of Marshall's jurisprudence in the several fields that occupied the major share of the Court's attention, including procedure, real property, contracts and commercial law, admiralty, and international law. With this general purpose in mind, they have flexibly applied several other criteria to shorten the list of potential choices. Priority is given to opinions that illuminate Marshall's broader views on politics, society, and economy; that reflect an important public issue or policy of the time; and that can be amply documented from the official case file and other sources, especially if the supplementary materials provide new information about the case not found in the printed report. Another important consideration is the availability of the original manuscript opinion, though this criterion will not often come into play until the last seven years of Marshall's chief justiceship. There is an unavoidable element of arbitrariness in the selection process. For every opinion chosen for inclusion, many others could equally suffice as examples of the chief justice's style, mode of reasoning, and learning in a particular field of law.

Although publishing in full only a small fraction of the Supreme Court opinions, this edition presents complete texts of all extant opinions given in the U.S. Circuit Courts for Virginia and North Carolina. Marshall spent much the greater part of his judicial life on circuit, yet this side of his career is relatively unknown, and the documents are less accessible. His circuit court papers include more than 60 autograph opinions delivered in the Virginia court. The one previous edition of Marshall's circuit opinions, prepared by John W. Brockenbrough in 1837, is extremely rare. Although Brockenbrough's reports have been reprinted in *Federal Cases*, the alphabetical arrangement of that work scatters Marshall's opinions over many volumes. Brockenbrough also took certain liberties with Marshall's drafts, regularizing his spelling and punctuation, for example, and occasionally improving what he regarded as infelicitous phrasing. The editors believe that bringing these opinions together and presenting texts that more faithfully adhere to the original drafts serve a sound documentary purpose. By comparison with the Virginia materials, judicial papers from the North Carolina court are scanty—no manuscript opinions and only a handful of published reports of cases. (Marshall's circuit court papers are described at greater length in the *Papers of John Marshall*, VI, 126–29, 142–44.)

Five Supreme Court opinions are published in the main body of Volume IX. They deal with questions of federal criminal law, statutory construction, constitutional law, and the nature of Indian land title. Other Supreme Court documents (besides opinions) include Marshall's notes on arguments of cases heard at the 1820 and 1823 terms. The volume presents 23 circuit opinions given in cases brought in the U.S. Circuit Court for Virginia. Most of them fall into the categories of prize and admiralty, suits against federal officials, and equity suits brought against decedents' estates.

OMITTED PAPERS

As a general editorial policy, dinner invitations and routine documents arising from Marshall's financial transactions — bills of exchange, promissory notes, bank drafts, and the like — are omitted entirely, though they may be referred to in the annotation. The same holds true for land deeds, even though in previous volumes these have been calendared and sometimes printed in full.

Editorial Apparatus

Editorial Method

The editors have applied modern historical editing standards in rendering the texts of documents. Transcriptions are as accurate as possible and reflect format and usage as nearly as is feasible, with the following exceptions. The first letter of a sentence is capitalized, and redundant or confusing punctuation has been eliminated. Superscript letters have been brought down to the line, and thorns ("ye," "yt," "yn") have been expanded. Words abbreviated by a tilde ($\sim$) have not been expanded, but the tilde has been omitted and a period added. Layout and typography attempt to replicate the appearance of the originals. The location of the dateline in letters, however, has been standardized, placed on the first line of the letter, flush to the right margin. The salutation has been set flush to the left margin. The complimentary closing has been run into the last paragraph of letters. Signatures, regardless of whether they are autograph, have been set in large and small capital letters and indented one space from the right margin. Other names at the foot of a document (for example, those of witnesses, sureties, and pledges) are rendered in the same distinctive type as signatures and are placed approximately where they appear in the originals.

Obvious slips of the pen, usually repeated words, have been silently corrected, as have typographical errors in printed sources. Words or parts of words illegible or missing because of mutilation are enclosed in angle brackets; letters or punctuation added by the editors for clarity's sake are set off by square brackets. If the editors are uncertain about their rendition, the words are enclosed within brackets followed by a question mark. If a portion of the manuscript is missing, the lacuna is shown by ellipsis points within angle brackets. Undecipherable words or phrases are indicated by the word "illegible" set in italics within angle brackets. Official and corporate seals are designated by the word "seal" set in capital letters and enclosed within square brackets. Wafer, or signature, seals are denoted by the initials "L.S." (*Locus Sigilli* [place of the seal]) within square brackets.

This volume follows the format first adopted in Volume V. Footnotes follow immediately at the end of the document, and identification of the source occurs in an unnumbered provenance note (referred to as "n." in cross-references) preceding the first numbered footnote. This note also supplies information on other copies, endorsements, dating, description, or peculiarities of the original. The provenance contains a full citation for the source of each document, except that National Union Catalog Symbols for depositories are used throughout. Elsewhere the editors have employed abbreviated titles for the most frequently cited public collections of manuscripts and secondary sources. These appear below in the lists of symbols and short titles. For other publications, a full citation is given the first time a source is cited in a document.

For books, periodicals, and articles, the editors follow the style of citation used in standard academic history. Reports of cases, however, are given in legal citation form. The name of the case is followed by the volume number and abbreviated title (usually the reporter's last name); the page number on which the case begins; and, if needed, the court and year within parentheses. For the old English cases, the volume number and page of the reprint of the case in the *English Reports* (abbreviated "Eng. Rep.") are also given. Full titles of all reports cited in this volume are provided in the short-title list. References to statutes also follow the historical style. In citing English statutes, the editors use the standard abbreviated form giving the regnal year, chapter and section (if appropriate), and year of enactment (if not otherwise indicated), e.g., 13 Edw. I, c. 31 (1285); 4 and 5 Anne, c. 3, sec. 12 (1705).

Annotation consists of footnotes to documents, occasional editorial notes preceding a document or group of documents, and short contextual notes preceding Marshall's court opinions. The guiding principle is to supply enough information and explanation to make the document intelligible to the general reader. The editors prefer to let the documents speak for themselves as much as possible. This laissez-faire policy is more easily followed in the case of personal correspondence. Legal materials by nature require denser annotation. Without presuming any knowledge of law on the reader's part, the editors attempt to strike a balance between too little and too much commentary.

The provenance note is followed, if needed, by one or more numbered footnotes that address matters arising immediately from the document: identifications of persons, places, technical words and phrases, statutes, authorities, cases, pamphlets, newspaper articles, and the like. If the information is available in a standard reference or secondary work, the note is brief, often no more than a citation to that source. Three standard reference works are not cited: *Dictionary of American Biography*, *Dictionary of National Biography*, and *Biographical Directory of Congress*. If the source is a manuscript collection or archival record group that is relatively inaccessible, the information derived from it is reported in greater detail. Cross-references to other documents or notes in the same volume are kept to a minimum, relying on the index to bring them all together. Editorial notes provide more extensive information or interpretation than can be conveniently included in footnotes. They serve to introduce documents of unusual significance or important subjects or episodes that are reflected in a number of documents. In Volume VII the editors adopted the practice of supplying brief contextual notes to introduce court opinions. Unlike editorial notes, these notes are concerned only with setting the immediate context of the opinion to follow. They typically provide the full names of the parties, the essential facts of the dispute (including, in the case of Supreme Court appellate opinions, the history of the case in the lower federal court or in the state court), and the particular point or motion addressed by the opinion.

Textual Notes

Marshall's manuscript drafts of judicial opinions receive special editorial treatment. With these documents, Marshall's intent as author takes on additional importance, for he meant them to be officially promulgated. In his opinions, Marshall made many deletions and insertions, which reveal his thought process at work; his choice of words and redrafting of phrases show a careful consideration of meaning. The final result was what he intended the public to hear, and, in keeping with that object, the editors have followed their standard rules of transcription and editorial method in presenting nearly clear texts of these documents as the main entries. In order to provide an inclusive list of Marshall's alterations in the manuscript, however, they have appended a set of textual notes, following the annotation, to each of these autograph opinions and drafts. By this means, a genetic text can be reconstructed, and a complete record of Marshall's revisions is preserved.

Marshall made changes in his text in a variety of ways: he struck through words, erased them, wrote over them, added words above the line, or indicated by means of a superscript symbol an addition to be inserted from the margin or a separate sheet. In recording Marshall's alterations, the editors have not distinguished among his various modes of deleting words, or between words inserted above the line as opposed to altered on the line. Marshall made many of his changes on the line, indicating that he amended as he was writing. The editors believe that the alterations were part of his process of refining his opinions and that he incorporated them into his final statement from the bench. He apparently did not go back later and revise his opinion as delivered orally in court.

Deletions are indicated by canceled type (~~ease~~), and insertions are surrounded by up and down arrows (↑court↓). Deleted punctuation will appear below the strike-through rule (~~,~~ appeal). Illegible erasures or deletions are denoted by "*erasure*" within square brackets. Uncertain renderings are followed by a question mark within square brackets. Insertions within insertions are not indicated, but deletions within insertions are. Insertions within a deletion appear in canceled type and are set off by arrows.

Characteristically, in changing a preposition, article, indefinite pronoun, or verb ending, Marshall wrote over the end of the existing word to alter it to a new form. For instance, he transformed "that" to "this" by writing "is" over "at" and "on" to "in" by writing "i" over "o." Rather than placing internal marks within words to replicate Marshall's process of altering them, the editors have represented the change in substance by entering complete words. Canceled type shows his first version; up and down arrows indicate his substitution. Thus, a change from "that" to "this" will appear in the text notes as ~~that~~ ↑this↓, rather than ~~that~~ ↑is↓. Although this method sacrifices the exact recording of how Marshall entered a change, it does make clear the alteration of the content of what he wished to say. Marshall's intentions are not always self-evident; irregularities in pen, ink, and manuscript preclude certainty in some instances. Sometimes it is not possible to know whether he added or erased a word, or whether he had crowded words on a line or blotted a drop of ink. Where Marshall inadvertently repeated a word or words, the repetition is left out in the main text but is recorded verbatim in the textual notes.

All deletions and insertions, as the editors have been best able to determine from appearance and context of the manuscript, are listed by paragraph and line numbers of the printed document. (Paragraph numbers appear in the margin of the main text to facilitate use.) A word or two before and after the alteration is included to aid the reader in finding the phrase and following the change. The succeeding designations indicate alterations made in places other than in the middle of the text: "Title," in the title of an opinion; "mar.," in a marginal note; "footnote," in a note at the bottom of the manuscript page; "beg.," at the beginning of a paragraph before the first word of the main text. To avoid confusion, footnote numbers in the document have been dropped from words appearing in the textual notes.

Descriptive Symbols

AD   Autograph Document
ADS   Autograph Document Signed
ALS   Autograph Letter Signed
Df   Draft
JM   John Marshall
MS   Manuscript
Tr   Transcript

All documents in an author's hand are designated as autograph items (e.g., ALS). If the attribution of autograph is conjectural, a question mark within parentheses follows the designation. Documents can be in the hand of someone else but signed by persons under whose names they are written (e.g., DS). If the signature has been cropped or obliterated, the "S" appears within square brackets (e.g., AL[S]). Copies are contemporary replications of documents; if they are made by the author, the type of document will be indicated by one of the above symbols followed by "copy" or "letterbook copy" within parentheses. For instance, an unsigned copy of a letter retained by the writer will be described as AL (copy). Thomas Jefferson's letterpress copies are designated as ALS (press copy). Transcripts are transcribed versions of documents made at a later time by someone other than the author.

Location Symbols

CtHi	Connecticut Historical Society, New Haven, Conn.
DLC	Library of Congress, Washington, D.C.
DNA	National Archives, Washington, D.C.
ICN	Newberry Library, Chicago
InU-Li	Lilly Library, Indiana University, Bloomington, Ind.
KyLoF	Filson Club, Louisville, Ky.
MH-Ar	Harvard University, Archives, Cambridge, Mass.
MHi	Massachusetts Historical Society, Boston, Mass.
MiU-C	University of Michigan, Law Library, Ann Arbor, Mich.
MoSW	Washington University, St. Louis, Mo.
NcU	University of North Carolina, Chapel Hill, N.C.
NHi	New-York Historical Society, New York, N.Y.
NjMoHP	Morristown National Historical Park, Morristown, N.J.
NjP	Princeton University, Princeton, N.J.
NNPM	Pierpont Morgan Library, New York, N.Y.
OHi	Ohio Historical Society, Columbus, Ohio
PHi	Historical Society of Pennsylvania, Philadelphia, Pa.
PP	Free Library of Philadelphia, Philadelphia, Pa.
PPAmP	American Philosophical Society, Philadelphia, Pa.
PWbH	Wyoming Historical and Geological Society, Wilkes-Barre, Pa.
Vi	Library of Virginia, Richmond, Va.
ViHi	Virginia Historical Society, Richmond, Va.
ViU	University of Virginia, Charlottesville, Va.
ViW	College of William and Mary, Williamsburg, Va.

Record Groups in the National Archives

RG 15	Records of the Veterans Administration
RG 21	Records of the District Courts of the United States
RG 24	Records of the Bureau of Naval Personnel

RG 45	Naval Records Collection of the Office of Naval Records and Library
RG 59	General Records of the Department of State
RG 60	General Records of the Department of Justice
RG 94	Records of the Adjutant General's Office, 1780's–1917
RG 156	Records of the Office of the Chief of Ordnance
RG 267	Records of the Supreme Court of the United States

Abbreviations for Court and Other Records

App. Cas.	Appellate Case RG 267, National Archives
U.S. Circ. Ct., N.C. Min. Bk.	U.S. Circuit Court, N.C. Minute Book RG 21, National Archives
U.S. Circ. Ct., Va. Ord. Bk. Rec. Bk.	U.S. Circuit Court, Va. Order Book Record Book Library of Virginia
U.S. Dist. Ct., Va. Ord. Bk.	U.S. District Court, Va. Order Book Library of Virginia
U.S. Sup. Ct. Minutes Dockets	U.S. Supreme Court Minutes Dockets RG 267, National Archives
Va. Ct. App. Ord. Bk.	Virginia Court of Appeals Order Books Library of Virginia

After the first citation of legal papers in a case, the court reference is omitted, and the suit record is designated simply by the names of plaintiff v. defendant. The exception is the provenance note, where complete depository information will be given for the document printed.

Abbreviations for English Courts

Ch.	Chancery
C.P.	Common Pleas

Crown   Crown Cases
K.B.   King's Bench
N.P.   Nisi Prius

Short Titles

The expanded titles for the English reports are taken chiefly from W. Harold Maxwell and Leslie F. Maxwell, *A Legal Bibliography of the British Commonwealth of Nations* (7 vols.; London, 1955).

Amb.

> Charles Ambler, *Reports of Cases Argued and Determined in the High Court of Chancery, with Some Few in Other Courts* (Dublin, 1790).

ASP

> *American State Papers. Documents, Legislative and Executive, of the Congress of the United States* . . . (38 vols.; Washington, D.C., 1832–61).

Bacon, *Abridgment*

> Matthew Bacon, *A New Abridgment of the Law* (1st Am. ed. from 6th London ed.; 7 vols.; Philadelphia, 1811).

Blackstone, *Commentaries*

> William Blackstone, *Commentaries on the Laws of England* (4 vols.; 13th ed.; Dublin, 1796).

Black. W.

> William Blackstone, *Reports, Courts of Westminster-Hall, 1746–1779* (2 vols.; London, 1780).

Bos. & Pul.

> John Bernard Bosanquet and Christopher Puller, *Reports of Cases Argued and Determined in the Courts of Common Pleas and Exchequer Chamber, and in the House of Lords* (3 vols.; London, 1800–1804).

Brock.

> John W. Brockenbrough, *Reports of Cases Decided by the Honorable John Marshall . . . in the Circuit Court of the United States for the District of Virginia and North Carolina, from 1802 to 1833 [1836] Inclusive* (2 vols.; Philadelphia, 1837).

Burr.

> James Burrow, *Reports, King's Bench, 1756–1772* (5 vols.; London, 1766–80).

Call

> Daniel Call, *Reports of Cases Argued and Adjudged in the Court of Appeals of Virginia* (6 vols.; Richmond, Va., 1830–33). Beginning with vol. IV, the title reads: *Reports of Cases Argued and Decided.* . . .

Camp.
> John Campbell, Baron Campbell, *Reports of Cases Determined at Nisi Prius: In the Courts of King's Bench and Common Pleas* (4 vols.; London, 1811).

Cowp.
> Henry Cowper, *Reports, King's Bench, 1774–1778* (London, 1783).

Cranch
> William Cranch, *Reports of Cases Argued and Adjudged in the Supreme Court of the United States* (1801–15) (9 vols.; New York and Washington, D.C., 1804–17).

C. Rob.
> Chr. Robinson, *Reports of Cases Argued and Determined in the High Court of Admiralty; Commencing with the Judgments of the Right Hon. Sir Wm. Scott from 1798–1808, with the Orders of the Court* (6 vols.; London, 1799–1808).

Cro. Eliz.
> George Croke, *Reports of Cases in King's Bench and Common Bench.* Part 1, Elizabeth (London, 1661).

Cro. Jac.
> George Croke, *Reports of Cases in King's Bench and Common Bench.* Part 2, James (London, 1657).

Dall.
> Alexander J. Dallas, *Reports of Cases Ruled and Adjudged in the Several Courts of the United States, and of Pennsylvania* . . . (4 vols.; Philadelphia, 1790–1807).

Doug.
> Sylvester Douglas, *Reports, King's Bench* (London, 1782).

East
> Edward Hyde East, *Reports of Cases Argued and Determined in the Court of King's Bench* (16 vols.; London, 1801–14).

Eng. Rep.
> *The English Reports* (176 vols.; reprint of all the early English reporters).

Evans.
> Charles Evans, ed., *American Bibliography* . . . *1639* . . . *1820* (12 vols.; Chicago, 1903–34).

Fed. Cas.
> *Federal Cases* (1789–1880) (30 vols.; St. Paul, Minn., 1894–97).

Gall.
> John Gallison, *Reports of Cases Argued and Determined in the Circuit Court of the United States, for the First Circuit* (2 vols.; Boston, 1815–17; S #34758).

Hening, *Statutes*
> William Waller Hening, ed., *The Statutes at Large; Being a Collection of All the Laws of Virginia, from the First Session of the Legislature* . . . (13

vols.; 1819–23; Charlottesville, Va., 1969 reprint: vols. I–IV from 2d ed.; vols. V–XIII from 1st ed.).

Leach

Thomas Leach, *Cases in Crown Law* (4th ed.; 2 vols.; London, 1815).

Lev.

Creswell Levinz, *Reports of Cases in the Court of King's Bench and Common Pleas, during the Time of Sir R. Foster, Sir R. Hyde and Sir J. Kelyng Were Chief Justices: Also Cases in Other Courts during that Time* (2 vols.; London, 1722).

Mason

William P. Mason, *Reports of Cases Argued and Determined in the Circuit Court of the United States, for the First Circuit* (5 vols.; Boston, 1819–31; S #49945).

Mass.

Massachusetts, *Reports of Cases Argued and Determined in the Supreme Judicial Court of the Commonwealth of Massachusetts* (100 vols.; Boston, 1837–78).

Moo. K.B.

Sir Francis Moore, *Cases Collect and Report* (London, 1663).

Mosely

William Mosely, *Reports of Cases Argued and Determined in the High Court of Chancery: During the Time of Lord Chancellor King* (London, 1803).

Munf.

William Munford, *Reports of Cases Argued and Determined in the Supreme Court of Appeals of Virginia* (6 vols.; New York, Philadelphia, Fredericksburg, Richmond, 1812–21).

Paxton, *Marshall Family*

W. M. Paxton, *The Marshall Family* . . . (1885; Baltimore, 1970 reprint).

PJM

Herbert A. Johnson et al., eds., *The Papers of John Marshall* (9 vols. to date; Chapel Hill, N.C., 1974–).

Revised Code of Va.

The Revised Code of the Laws of Virginia . . . (2 vols.; Richmond, Va., 1819).

Richmond Portraits

Richmond Portraits in an Exhibition of Makers of Richmond, 1737–1860 (Richmond, Va., 1949).

S

Ralph R. Shaw and Richard H. Shoemaker, eds., *American Bibliography* . . . *1801–1819* (22 vols.; New York, 1958–66).

Shepherd, *Statutes*

Samuel Shepherd, ed., *The Statutes at Large of Virginia, from October Session 1792, to December Session 1806, Inclusive* (3 vols.; 1835; New York, 1970 reprint).

Story, *Life and Letters*
William M. Story, ed., *Life and Letters of Joseph Story* . . . (2 vols.; Boston, 1851).

T.R.
Charles Durnford and Edward Hyde East, *Term Reports in the Court of King's Bench* (8 vols.; London, 1787–1800).

Tucker, *Blackstone's Commentaries*
St. George Tucker, *Blackstone's Commentaries: With Notes of Reference, to the Constitution and Laws, of the Federal Government of the United States; and of the Commonwealth of Virginia* (5 vols.; Philadelphia, 1803).

U.S. *Statutes at Large*
The Public Statutes at Large of the United States of America, 1789–1873 (17 vols.; Boston, 1845–73).

Vent.
Ventris, P., *Reports in Two Parts* (London, 1696).

Ves. jun. or Ves. (after vol. II)
Francis Vesey, Jr., *Reports of Cases Argued and Determined in the High Court of Chancery* . . . (20 vols.; London, 1795–1822).

VMHB
Virginia Magazine of History and Biography.

Wash.
Bushrod Washington, *Reports of Cases Argued and Determined in the Court of Appeals of Virginia* (2 vols.; Richmond, Va., 1798–99).

Wheat.
Henry Wheaton, *Reports of Cases Argued and Adjudged in the Supreme Court* (1816–27) (12 vols.; Philadelphia, 1816–27).

Wils. K.B.
George Wilson, *Reports of Cases Argued and Adjudged in the King's Courts at Westminster* (2 vols.; London, 1770–75).

MARSHALL CHRONOLOGY
7 February 1820–18 December 1823

1820

7 February–17 March	At Washington, attends Supreme Court.
8 February	At Baltimore, attends wedding of son John.
14 April	Sets out for upper country.
12–13 May	At Raleigh, attends U.S. Circuit Court.
Ca. 22 May–ca. 15 June	At Richmond, attends U.S. Circuit Court.
28 June	At Petersburg, visits Jane Marshall Taylor.
2 September	Returns to Richmond from mountains.
Late October	Injured in fall from horse.
13–14 November	At Raleigh, attends U.S. Circuit Court.
22 November–23 December	At Richmond, attends U.S. Circuit Court.

1821

7 February–16 March	At Washington, attends Supreme Court.
3 March	Delivers opinion in *Cohens* v. *Virginia*.
12 May	At Raleigh, attends U.S. Circuit Court.
22 May–15 June	At Richmond, attends U.S. Circuit Court.
5 September	Returns to Richmond from mountains.
12–14 November	At Raleigh, attends U.S. Circuit Court.
22 November–19 December	At Richmond, attends U.S. Circuit Court.

1822

4 February–22 March	At Washington, attends Supreme Court.
13–15 May	At Raleigh, attends U.S. Circuit Court.
4–5 April	At Richmond, attends adjourned session of U.S. Circuit Court.
22 May–12 June	At Richmond, attends U.S. Circuit Court.
Ca. 6 August	At Happy Creek (Frederick County) with James Marshall.

12–14 November	At Raleigh, attends U.S. Circuit Court.
22 November–28 December	At Richmond, attends U.S. Circuit Court.

1823

3 February–14 March	At Washington, attends Supreme Court.
11 April	At Warrenton (Fauquier County) on personal business.
2 May	Returns to Richmond from upper country.
12–13 May	At Raleigh, attends U.S. Circuit Court.
22 May–14 June	At Richmond, attends U.S. Circuit Court.
Late September	Returns to Richmond from mountains
27 October–1 November	At Norfolk, attends special session of U.S. Circuit Court.
5 November	Returns to Richmond from Norfolk.
12–13 November	At Raleigh, attends U.S. Circuit Court.
22 November–18 December	At Richmond, attends U.S. Circuit Court.

CORRESPONDENCE, PAPERS,

AND

SELECTED JUDICIAL OPINIONS

January 1820–December 1823

To William Bainbridge

Dear Sir   Richmond Jany. 3d. 1820

I have just received a letter from my brother expressing his most earnest wish that his son John Marshall may be transferred from the Guerriere on board which he now is, to your ship.[1] There will, we beleive, be no indelicacy in making this request, as Commodore McDonaugh, we understand, no longer commands that vessel.[2] We therefore hope that we may without impropriety indulge the wishes which both my brother & myself entertain on this subject. The favorable disposition you expressed towards my Nephew when I formerly made an effort to place him in your ship encourages me to make this application.[3] With great respect & esteem I am dear Sir, Your Obedt. Servt

J MARSHALL

My brother desires me to say that his sons drafts on him will be honored to any extent you may think proper for him.

ALS (advertised for sale by Gallery of History, Inc., Las Vegas, Nev., 1993). Addressed to Bainbridge in Washington; postmarked Richmond, 3 Jan. Endorsed.

1. Letter not found. Bainbridge had taken command of the uncompleted battleship *Columbus* in Nov. 1819 in his new capacity as commander of U.S. naval forces in the Mediterranean (Thomas Harris, *The Life and Services of Commodore William Bainbridge, United States Navy* [Philadelphia, 1837], 220–21).

2. Thomas Macdonough (1783–1825) had recently been relieved of command of the *Guerrière*.

3. JM to Benjamin Crowninshield, 21 Feb., 13 Mar. 1818 (*PJM*, VIII, 180–81, 186).

From William Wirt

Dear Sir   Washington. Jan 17th. 1820.

Colo. Allen Mc.Lane, of the revolution, of whom honourable mention is made in the life of Washington, conceives himself entitled to land bounty from the state of Virginia, on account of his services in Lee's legion during the war.[1] His name, I understand, was not returned by Genl. Lee as one of his officers; but he has a certificate of his services from Genl. Washington; of which I enclose a copy.[2]

Colo: Mc.Lane flatters himself that you will take sufficient interest in behalf of an old brother officer, to inform him, whether according to the practical construction of the laws of Virginia, providing for the payment of revolutionary services, he is not entitled — & whether his claim should be presented to the Executive Council, or the Legislature of the State.

I beg you to be assured that I wd. have no participation in giving you this trouble, but on the supposition that your familiarity with the subject will enable you to answer his questions without difficulty & that you would have no objection to gratify so far an old gentleman who seems to have been a favorite with Genl. Washington. I am dear sir, with very great respect & esteem, Your devotd. servt.

WM. WIRT

ALS (copy), Wirt Papers, DLC. Inside address to JM in Richmond.

1. McLane, of Delaware, had a distinguished record as an officer during the Revolution, as JM noted in the *Life of Washington*. At the outbreak of the war he joined Virginians (including JM) who fought against Lord Dunmore's forces at the battle of Great Bridge, near Norfolk. His later service included a brief but unhappy stint in "Lee's Legion," a corps of partisans commanded by Henry ("Lighthorse Harry") Lee during the Southern campaign in 1780–81. JM evidently intervened successfully on his behalf, for the commonwealth issued two land warrants to McLane in June and Sept. 1820 (*PJM*, VI, 346, 347 n. 3, 358, 359 nn.; Gaius Marcus Brumbaugh, *Revolutionary War Records*, Volume I: *Virginia* [Washington, D.C., 1936], 108).

2. This was probably a copy of a certificate dated 4 Nov. 1783, which noted that McLane "served with great reputation in Lees legion, till March, 178⟨1⟩" (copy of certificate on behalf of Maj. Allan McLane, 4 Nov. 1783, NjMoHP. The editors are grateful to Philander D. Chase of the Papers of George Washington for supplying a copy of this document).

John Williams to Justices of the Supreme Court

Gentlemen,   Senate Chamber, Feb: 10th 1820.

Most of the law books on the list you furnished last year have been purchased by our library committe.[1] I understand some of them have not been procured becau⟨se⟩ they were not in the bo⟨ok⟩ stores to which application ⟨was⟩ made. Permit me to di⟨rect⟩ your attention to this subj⟨ect⟩ as soon as it suits your con⟨v⟩enience, and to request tha⟨t⟩ you will furnish an other list of such books as wil⟨l⟩ be of service to the Sup: Cou⟨r⟩t. And I will take pleasure in urging the library commit⟨tee⟩ to purchase them.[2] Your Hum: Servt.

JOHN WILLIAMS

ALS, RG 267, DNA. Addressed to "Judges of the Supreme Court / Washington City."

1. John Williams (1778–1837) represented Tennessee in the Senate from 1815 to 1823 and was also a member of the Supreme Court bar.

2. Williams enclosed a "List of Law Books purchased by the Comee. last year." It contained thirty titles, most of which were state law reports.

United States v. Wiltberger
Opinion
U.S. Supreme Court, 18 February 1820

Peter Wiltberger, master of the American ship *Benjamin Rush*, was indicted
in the U.S. Circuit Court at Philadelphia for committing manslaughter "on
the high seas" against John Peters, a seaman. The alleged manslaughter
occurred in February 1819, while the ship was anchored in the Tigris River
in the empire of China at a point thirty-five miles above the river's mouth
and within the ebb and flow of the tide. In October 1819 a jury returned a
verdict of guilty, subject to the court's opinion on the question of jurisdiction. Judges Washington and Peters were divided on this question and certified the case to the Supreme Court. Argument was heard on 14 February
1820, with Charles J. Ingersoll, U.S. Attorney for Pennsylvania, and Attorney
General Wirt representing the United States and John Sergeant representing Wiltberger. In his opinion for the Court on 18 February Marshall presented an important statement of the rules for statutory construction (U.S.
v. Wiltberger, App. Cas. No. 1018; U.S. Sup. Ct. Minutes, 14 Feb. 1820).

The indictment in this case is founded on the 12th section of the act,
entitled, "an act for the punishment of certain crimes against the United
States."[1] That section is in these words: "And be it enacted, that if any
seaman, or other person, shall commit manslaughter on the high seas,
or confederate," &c. "such person or persons so offending, and being
thereof convicted, shall be imprisoned not exceeding three years, and
fined not exceeding one thousand dollars."

The jurisdiction of the Court depends on the place in which the fact
was committed. Manslaughter is not punishable in the Courts of the
United States, according to the words which have been cited, unless it be
committed on the high seas. Is the place described in the special verdict a
part of the high seas?

If the words be taken according to the common understanding of
mankind, if they be taken in their popular and received sense, the "high
seas," if not in all instances confined to the ocean which washes a coast,
can never extend to a river about half a mile wide, and in the interior of a
country. This extended construction of the words, it has been insisted, is
still farther opposed, by a comparison of the 12th with the 8th section of
the act. In the 8th section, Congress has shown its attention to the distinction between the "high seas," and "a river, haven, basin, or bay." The well
known rule that this is a penal statute, and is to be construed strictly, is
also urged upon us.

On the part of the United States, the jurisdiction of the Court is sustained, not so much on the extension of the words "high seas," as on that
construction of the whole act, which would engraft the words of the 8th
section, descriptive of the place in which murder may be committed, on

the 12th section, which describes the place in which manslaughter may be committed. This transfer of the words of one section to the other, is, it has been contended, in pursuance of the obvious intent of the legislature; and in support of the authority of the Court so to do, certain maxims, or rules for the construction of statutes, have been quoted and relied on. It has been said, that although penal laws are to be construed strictly, the intention of the legislature must govern in their construction. That if a case be within the intention, it must be considered as if within the letter of the statute. So if it be within the reason of the statute.

The rule that penal laws are to be construed strictly, is perhaps not much less old than construction itself. It is founded on the tenderness of the law for the rights of individuals; and on the plain principle that the power of punishment is vested in the legislative, not in the judicial department. It is the legislature, not the Court, which is to define a crime, and ordain its punishment.

It is said, that notwithstanding this rule, the intention of the law maker must govern in the construction of penal, as well as other statutes. This is true. But this is not a new independent rule which subverts the old. It is a modification of the ancient maxim, and amounts to this, that though penal laws are to be construed strictly, they are not to be construed so strictly as to defeat the obvious intention of the legislature. The maxim is not to be so applied as to narrow the words of the statute to the exclusion of cases which those words, in their ordinary acceptation, or in that sense in which the legislature has obviously used them, would comprehend. The intention of the legislature is to be collected from the words they employ. Where there is no ambiguity in the words, there is no room for construction. The case must be a strong one indeed, which would justify a Court in departing from the plain meaning of words, especially in a penal act, in search of an intention which the words themselves did not suggest. To determine that a case is within the intention of a statute, its language must authorise us to say so. It would be dangerous, indeed, to carry the principle, that a case which is within the reason or mischief of a statute, is within its provisions, so far as to punish a crime not enumerated in the statute, because it is of equal atrocity, or of kindred character, with those which are enumerated. If this principle has ever been recognized in expounding criminal law, it has been in cases of considerable irritation, which it would be unsafe to consider as precedents forming a general rule for other cases.

Having premised these general observations, the Court will proceed to the examination of the act, in order to determine whether the intention to incorporate the description of place contained in the 8th section, into the 12th, be so apparent as to justify the Court in so doing. It is contended, that throughout the act the description of one section is full, and is necessarily to be carried into all the other sections which relate to place, or to crime.

The 1st section defines the crime of treason, and declares, ["]that if any person or persons owing allegiance to the United States of America shall levy war," &c. "such person or persons shall be adjudged guilty of treason," &c. The second section defines misprision of treason; and in the description of the persons who may commit it, omits the words "owing allegiance to the United States," and uses without limitation, the general terms "any person or persons." Yet, it has been said, these general terms were obviously intended to be limited, and must be limited, by the words "owing allegiance to the United States," which are used in the preceding section.

It is admitted, that the general terms of the 2d section must be so limited; but it is not admitted, that the inference drawn from this circumstance, in favour of incorporating the words of one section of this act into another, is a fair one. Treason is a breach of allegiance, and can be committed by him only who owes allegiance either perpetual or temporary. The words, therefore, "owing allegiance to the United States," in the first section, are entirely surplus words, which do not, in the slightest degree, affect its sense. The construction would be precisely the same were they omitted. When, therefore, we give the same construction to the second section, we do not carry those words into it, but construe it as it would be construed independent of the first. There is, too, in a penal statute, a difference between restraining general words, and enlarging particular words.

The crimes of murder and of manslaughter, it has been truly said, are kindred crimes; and there is much reason for supposing, that the legislature intended to make the same provision for the jurisdiction of its Courts, as to the place in which either might be committed. In illustration of this position, the 3d and 7th sections of the act have been cited. The 3d section describes the places in which murder on land may be committed, of which the Courts of the United States may take cognizance; and the 7th section describes, in precisely the same terms, the places on land, if manslaughter be committed in which, the offender may be prosecuted in the federal Courts.

It is true, that so far as respects *place*, the words of the 3d section concerning murder, are repeated in the 7th, and applied to manslaughter; but this circumstance suggests a very different inference from that which has been drawn from it. When the legislature is about to describe the places in which manslaughter, cognizable in the Courts of the United States, may be committed, no reference whatsoever is made to a prior section respecting murder; but the description is as full and ample, as if the prior section had not been in the act. This would rather justify the opinion, that in proceeding to manslaughter, the legislature did not mean to refer us to the section on murder for a description of the place in which the crime might be committed, but did mean to give us a full description in the section on that subject.

So, the 6th section, which punishes those who have knowledge of the commission of murder, or other felony, describes the places on land in which the murder is to be committed, to constitute the crime, with the same minuteness which had been before employed in the 3d, and was, afterwards, employed in the 7th section.

In the 8th section, the legislature takes up the subject of murder, and other felonies, committed on the water, and is full in the description of place. "If any person or persons, shall commit upon the high seas, or in any river, haven, basin or bay, out of the jurisdiction of any particular State, murder," &c.

The 9th section of the act applies to a citizen who shall commit any of the offences described in the 8th section, against the United States, or a citizen thereof, under colour of a commission from any foreign Prince or State.

It is observable, that this section, in its description of place, omits the words, "in any river, haven, basin, or bay," and uses the words "high seas" only. It has been argued, and, we admit, with great force, that in this section the legislature intended to take from a citizen offending against the United States, under colour of a commission from a foreign power, any pretence to protection from that commission; and it is almost impossible to believe that there could have been a deliberate intention to distinguish between the same offence, committed under colour of such commission, on the high seas, and on the waters of a foreign State, or of the United States, out of the jurisdiction of any particular State. This would unquestionably have been the operation of the section, had the words, "on the high seas," been omitted. Yet it would be carrying construction very far to strike out those words. Their whole effect is to limit the operation which the sentence would have without them; and it is making very free with legislative language, to declare them totally useless, when they are sensible, and are calculated to have a decided influence on the meaning of the clause. That case is not directly before us, and we may perhaps be relieved from ever deciding it. For the present purpose, it will be sufficient to say, that the determination of that question in the affirmative, would not, we think, be conclusive with respect to that now under consideration. The 9th section refers expressly, so far at least as respects piracy or robbery, to the 8th; and its whole language shows that its sole object is to render a citizen who offends against the United States or their citizens, under colour of a foreign commission, punishable in the same degree as if no such commission existed. The clearness with which this intent is manifested by the language of the whole section, might perhaps justify a latitude of construction which would not be allowable where the intent is less clearly manifested; where we are to be guided, not so much by the words in which the provision is made, as by our opinion of the reasonableness of making it.

But here, too, it cannot escape notice, that the legislature has not referred for a description of the place to the preceding section, but has inserted a description, and by that insertion has created the whole difficulty of the case.

The 10th section declares the punishment of accessories before the fact. It enacts, "that every person who shall either upon the land or the seas, knowingly and wittingly, aid and assist, procure, command, counsel, or advise any person or persons to do or commit any murder or robbery, or other piracy, aforesaid, upon the seas, which shall affect the life of such persons, shall," &c.

Upon this section, also, as on the preceding, it has been argued, that the legislature cannot have intended to exclude from punishment those who shall be accessories before the fact to a murder or robbery committed "in a river, haven, basin, or bay, out of the jurisdiction of any State"; and now, as then, the argument has great weight. But it is again to be observed, that the legislature has not referred for a description of place to any previous parts of the law, but has inserted a description, and by so doing, has materially varied the obvious sense of the section. "Every person who shall, either upon the land or the seas, knowingly and wittingly aid," &c. The probability is, that the legislature designed to punish all persons amenable to their laws, who should, in any place, aid and assist, procure, command, counsel, or advise, any person or persons to commit any murder or piracy punishable under the act. And such would have been the operation of the sentence, had the words, "upon the land or the seas" been omitted. But the legislature has chosen to describe the place where the accessorial offence is to be committed, and has not referred to a description contained in any other part of the act. The words are, "upon the land or the seas." The Court cannot reject this description. If we might supply the words "river, haven," &c. because they are stated in the 8th section, must we supply "fort, arsenal," &c. which are used in the 3d section, describing the place in which murder may be committed on land? In doing so, we should probably defeat the will of the legislature. Yet if we depart from the description of place given in the section, in which Congress has obviously intended to describe it, for the purpose of annexing to the word "seas," the words "river, haven, basin, or bay," found in the 8th section, there would be at least some appearance of reason in the argument, which would require us to annex also to the word "land," the words "fort, arsenal," &c. found in the 3d section.

After describing the place in which the "aid, assistance, procurement, command, counsel, or advice," must be given, in order to give to the Courts of the United States jurisdiction over the offence, the legislature proceeds to describe the crime so to be commanded or procured, and the place in which such crime must be committed. The crime is, "any murder or robbery, or other piracy, aforesaid." The place is "upon the seas."

In this section, as in the preceding, had the words "upon the seas" been omitted, the construction would have been that which, according to the argument on the part of the United States, it ought now to be. But these words are sensible and are material. They constitute the description of place which the legislature has chosen to give us; and Courts cannot safely vary that description, without some sure guide to direct their way.

The observations made on this section apply so precisely to the 11th, that they need not be repeated.

The legal construction of those sections is doubtful, and the Court is not now, and may perhaps never be, required to make it. It is sufficient to say, that should it even be such as the Attorney General contends it ought to be, the reasons in favour of that construction do not apply conclusively to the 12th section. They both contain a direct reference to the 8th section. They describe accessorial offences, which from their nature are more intimately connected with the principal offence, than distinct crimes are with each other.

The 12th section takes up the crime of manslaughter, which is not mentioned in the 8th; and, without any reference to the 8th, describes the place in which it must be committed, in order to give jurisdiction to the Courts of the United States. That place is "on the high seas." There is nothing in this section which can authorize the Court to take jurisdiction of manslaughter committed elsewhere.

To prove the connection between this section and the 8th, the attention of the Court has been directed to the other offences it recapitulates, which are said to be accessorial to those enumerated in the 8th. They are admitted to be accessorial; but the Court draws a different inference from this circumstance. Manslaughter is an independent crime distinct from murder, and the legislature annexes to the offence, a description of the place in which it must be committed in order to give the Court jurisdiction. The same section then proceeds to enumerate certain other crimes which are accessorial in their nature, without any description of places. To manslaughter, the principal crime, the right to punish which depends on the place in which it is committed, Congress has annexed a description of place. To the other crimes enumerated in the same section, which are accessorial in their nature, and some of which at least may be committed any where, Congress has annexed no description of place. The conclusion seems irresistible, that Congress has not in this section inserted the limitation of place inadvertently; and the distinction which the legislature has taken, must of course be respected by the Court.

It is the object of the law, among other things, to punish murder and manslaughter, on land, in places within the jurisdiction of the United States; and also to punish murder and manslaughter, committed on the ocean. The two crimes of murder and manslaughter, when committed on land, are described in two distinct sections, as two distinct offences; and the description of place in the one section, is complete in itself, and makes no reference to the description of place in the other. The crimes of murder and manslaughter, when committed on water, are also described

as two distinct offences, in two sections, each containing a description of
the place in which the offence may be committed, without any reference
in the one section to the other. That section which affixes the punishment
to manslaughter on the seas, proceeds to describe other offences which
are accessorial in their nature, without any limitation of place. In every
section throughout the act, describing a crime, the right to punish which
depends on place, and in some instances where the right of punishment
does not depend upon place, the legislature has, without any reference to
a preceding section, described the place in which it must be committed,
in order to bring the offender within the act. This characteristic feature of
the law now to be expounded, deserves great consideration, and affords a
powerful reason for restraining the Court from annexing to the description contained in one section, parts of the description contained in another. From this review of the examination made of the act at the bar, it
appears that the argument chiefly relied on, to prove that the words of
one section descriptive of the place ought to be incorporated into another, is the extreme improbability that Congress could have intended to
make those differences with respect to place, which their words import.
We admit that it is extremely improbable. But probability is not a guide
which a court, in construing a penal statute, can safely take. We can
conceive no reason why other crimes which are not comprehended in
this act, should not be punished. But Congress has not made them punishable, and this Court cannot enlarge the statute.

    After giving the subject an attentive consideration, we are unanimously
of opinion, that the offence charged in this indictment is not cognizable
in the Courts of the United States; which opinion is to be certified to the
Circuit Court for the district of Pennsylvania.[2]

Printed, Henry Wheaton, *Reports of Cases Argued and Adjudged in the Supreme Court of the United States . . .* , V (New York, 1820), 93–105.

    1. See *U.S. Statutes at Large*, I, 112–15, for the relevant sections of the 1790 act for the
punishment of crimes discussed throughout this opinion.
    2. JM's opinion reaffirmed the Court's refusal to assume jurisdiction for federal courts in
criminal cases unless the crime was expressly provided for by statute. In a learned note on
the criminal jurisdiction of admiralty appended to this decision, Wheaton maintained that
there was no inconsistency between JM's opinions in Wiltberger and in U.S. v. Bevans (3
Wheat. 386–91; *PJM*, VIII, 181–85) and Story's claims for broad admiralty jurisdiction
urged on circuit in De Lovio v. Boit (7 Fed. Case 418 [U.S. Cir. Ct., Mass., 1815]) and in his
unpublished opinion in Bevans. Wheaton informed Story that he would prepare this note
by reworking the justice's De Lovio and Bevans opinions, adding: "I think there is nothing
in the Ch: Justice's Op: in the U.S. v. Wiltberger which contradicts our notions of the extent
of the Admiralty jurisdiction in criminal cases. As in the U.S. v. Bevans, the only question
was whether Congress had exercised the entire Admiralty & maritime jurisdiction given by
the Constitution. I would make the note very guarded & cautious" (5 Wheat. 106–16;
Wheaton to Story, 14 Apr. 1820, Wheaton Papers, NNPM).

To [Smith Thompson]

Sir[1]   Washington Feb. 23d. 1820
    I take the liberty to solicit a midshipmans warrant for one of my Nephews Mr. Wilson Duke, a young gentleman who lives with his Father in Washington, Macon county, Kentucky.[2] He is about sixteen, of good dispositions, & his education has not been neglected. I persuade myself, should his application be successful, that he will not disgrace our navy. With very much respect, I am Sir your Obedt

J MARSHALL

ALS, Butler Collection, CtHi.

1. Smith Thompson (1768–1843) served as secretary of the navy from 1819 until 1823, when he accepted an appointment as associate justice of the Supreme Court.
2. Nathaniel Wilson Duke (1806–1852), son of Basil Duke and the late Charlotte Marshall Duke, entered the navy in May 1822 and during a thirty-year career rose to the rank of captain (Paxton, *Marshall Family*, 180; abstract of service record, Nathaniel Wilson Duke, RG 24, DNA).

To John George Jackson

Dear Sir   Washington Feb. 25th. 1820
    I have received yours of the 15th. & shall with much pleasure satisfy the enquiry you have made.[1]
    The uniform practice of the courts of the United States has been to commit to a jury such cases as those you mention. The act of Congress has been construed to be designed to expedite the trial but not to vary the constitutional mode of trial. Very respectfully I am dear Sir, Your obedt. Servt

J MARSHALL

ALS, InU-Li. Addressed to Jackson in Clarksburg, Harrison County, Va. (now W.Va.); postmarked Washington, 26 Feb. Endorsed by Jackson.

1. Letter not found. John George Jackson (1777–1825) was a prominent Virginia Republican who had served in the state legislature and in the U.S. House of Representatives. In 1819 he was appointed the first judge of the U.S. District Court for Western Virginia, where he sat until his death. This district encompassed the region west of the Alleghenies (*U.S. Statutes at Large*, III, 478–79).

Loughborough v. Blake
Opinion
U.S. Supreme Court, 10 March 1820

This was evidently an arranged case, brought in the U.S. Circuit Court for
the District of Columbia to test the constitutionality of a direct tax imposed
by Congress on the District. Nathan Lufborough brought an action of re-
plevin against James H. Blake for the recovery of cattle distrained by Blake as
collector of direct taxes for the District. Lufborough contended he was not
constitutionally bound to pay the direct tax enacted by Congress in 1815
and 1816. The circuit court gave judgment for Blake in December 1817,
and an appeal was filed at the ensuing Supreme Court term. The case was
argued on 7 March 1820 by Walter Jones for the plaintiff and William Wirt
for the defendant (Lufborough v. Blake, App. Cas. No. 921; *U.S. Statutes at
Large*, III, 216, 255–56; U.S. Sup. Ct. Minutes, 7 Mar. 1820).

This case presents to the consideration of the Court a single question.[1]
It is this: Has Congress a right to impose a direct tax on the District of
Columbia?

The counsel who maintains the negative has contended, that Congress
must be considered in two distinct characters. In one character as legislating for the States; in the other, as a local legislature for the district. In the
latter character, it is admitted, the power of levying direct taxes may be exercised; but, it is contended, for district purposes only, in like manner as
the legislature of a State may tax the people of a State for State purposes.

Without inquiring at present into the soundness of this distinction, its
possible influence on the application in this district of the first article of
the constitution, and of several of the amendments, may not be altogether unworthy of consideration. It will readily suggest itself to the gentlemen who press this argument, that those articles which, in general
terms, restrain the power of Congress, may be applied to the laws enacted
by that body for the district, if it be considered as governing the district in
its character as the national legislature, with less difficulty than if it be
considered a mere local legislature.

But we deem it unnecessary to pursue this investigation, because we
think the right of Congress to tax the district does not depend solely on
the grant of exclusive legislation.

The 8th section of the 1st article gives to Congress the "power to lay
and collect taxes, duties, imposts and excises," for the purposes thereinafter mentioned. This grant is general, without limitation as to place. It,
consequently, extends to all places over which the government extends.
If this could be doubted, the doubt is removed by the subsequent words
which modify the grant. These words are, "but all duties, imposts, and
excises, shall be uniform throughout the United States." It will not be
contended, that the modification of the power extends to places to which

the power itself does not extend. The power then to lay and collect duties, imposts, and excises, may be exercised, and must be exercised throughout the United States. Does this term designate the whole, or any particular portion of the American empire? Certainly this question can admit of but one answer. It is the name given to our great republic, which is composed of States and territories. The district of Columbia, or the territory west of the Missouri, is not less within the United States, than Maryland or Pennsylvania; and it is not less necessary, on the principles of our constitution, that uniformity in the imposition of imposts, duties, and excises, should be observed in the one, than in the other. Since, then, the power to lay and collect taxes, which includes direct taxes, is obviously co-extensive with the power to lay and collect duties, imposts and excises, and since the latter extends throughout the United States, it follows, that the power to impose direct taxes also extends throughout the United States.

The extent of the grant being ascertained, how far is it abridged by any part of the constitution?

The 20th section of the first article declares, that "representatives and direct taxes shall be apportioned among the several States which may be included within this Union, according to their respective numbers."

The object of this regulation is, we think, to furnish a standard by which taxes are to be apportioned, not to exempt from their operation any part of our country. Had the intention been to exempt from taxation those who were not represented in Congress, that intention would have been expressed in direct terms. The power having been expressly granted, the exception would have been expressly made. But a limitation can scarcely be said to be insinuated. The words used do not mean, that direct taxes shall be imposed on States only which are represented, or shall be apportioned to representatives; but that direct taxation, in its application to States, shall be apportioned to numbers. Representation is not made the foundation of taxation. If, under the enumeration of a representative for every 30,000 souls, one State had been found to contain 59,000, and another 60,000, the first would have been entitled to only one representative, and the last to two. Their taxes, however, would not have been as one to two, but as fifty-nine to sixty. This clause was obviously not intended to create any exemption from taxation, or to make taxation dependent on representation, but to furnish a standard for the apportionment of each on the States.

The 4th paragraph of the 9th section of the same article will next be considered. It is in these words: "No capitation, or other direct tax, shall be laid, unless in proportion to the census, or enumeration herein before directed to be taken."

The census referred to is in that clause of the constitution which has just been considered, which makes numbers the standard by which both representatives and direct taxes shall be apportioned among the States.

The actual enumeration is to be made "within three years after the first meeting of the Congress of the United States, and within every subsequent term of ten years, in such manner as they shall by law direct."

As the direct and declared object of this census is, to furnish a standard by which "representatives, and direct taxes, may be apportioned among the several States which may be included within this Union," it will be admitted, that the omission to extend it to the district or the territories, would not render it defective. The census referred to is admitted to be a census exhibiting the numbers of the respective States. It cannot, however, be admitted, that the argument which limits the application of the power of direct taxation to the population contained in this census, is a just one. The language of the clause does not imply this restriction. It is not that "no capitation or other direct tax shall be laid, unless on those comprehended within the census herein before directed to be taken," but "unless in proportion to" that census. Now this proportion may be applied to the district or territories. If an enumeration be taken of the population in the district and territories, on the same principles on which the enumeration of the respective States is made, then the information is acquired by which a direct tax may be imposed on the district and territories, "in proportion to the census or enumeration" which the constitution directs to be taken.

The standard, then, by which direct taxes must be laid, is applicable to this district, and will enable Congress to apportion on it, its just and equal share of the burthen, with the same accuracy as on the respective States. If the tax be laid in this proportion, it is within the very words of the restriction. It is a tax in proportion to the census or enumeration referred to.

But the argument is presented in another form, in which its refutation is more difficult. It is urged against this construction, that it would produce the necessity of extending direct taxation to the district and territories, which would not only be inconvenient, but contrary to the understanding and practice of the whole government. If the power of imposing direct taxes be co-extensive with the United States, then it is contended, that the restrictive clause, if applicable to the district and territories, requires that the tax should be extended to them, since to omit them would be to violate the rule of proportion.

We think, a satisfactory answer to this argument may be drawn from a fair comparative view of the different clauses of the constitution which have been recited.

That the general grant of power to lay and collect taxes, is made in terms which comprehend the district and territories as well as the States, is, we think, incontrovertible. The subsequent clauses are intended to regulate the exercise of this power, not to withdraw from it any portion of the community. The words in which those clauses are expressed import this intention. In thus regulating its exercise, a rule is given in the 2d section of the first article for its application to the respective States. That rule declares how direct taxes upon the States shall be imposed. They shall be apportioned upon the several States according to their numbers. If, then, a direct tax be laid at all, it must be laid on every State, conformably to the rule provided in the constitution. Congress has clearly no power to exempt any State from its due share of the burthen. But this regulation is expressly confined to the States, and creates no necessity for extending the tax to the district or territories. The words of the 9th section do not in terms require, that the system of direct taxation, when resorted to, shall be extended to the territories, as the words of the 2d section require that it shall be extended to all the States. They, therefore, may, without violence, be understood to give a rule when the territories shall be taxed, without imposing the necessity of taxing them. It could scarcely escape the members of the convention, that the expense of executing the law in a territory might exceed the amount of the tax. But be this as it may, the doubt created by the words of the 9th section, relates to the obligation to apportion a direct tax on the territories as well as the States, rather than to the power to do so.

If, then, the language of the constitution be construed to comprehend the territories and district of Columbia, as well as the States, that language confers on Congress the power of taxing the district and territories as well as the States. If the general language of the constitution should be confined to the States, still the 16th paragraph of the 8th section gives to Congress the power of exercising "exclusive legislation in all cases whatsoever within this district."

On the extent of these terms, according to the common understanding of mankind, there can be no difference of opinion; but it is contended, that they must be limited by that great principle which was asserted in our revolution, that representation is inseparable from taxation.

The difference between requiring a continent, with an immense population, to submit to be taxed by a government having no common interest with it, separated from it by a vast ocean, restrained by no principle of apportionment, and associated with it by no common feelings; and permitting the representatives of the American people, under the restrictions of our constitution, to tax a part of the society, which is either in a state of infancy advancing to manhood, looking forward to complete equality so soon as that state of manhood shall be attained, as is the case with the territories; or which has voluntarily relinquished the right of representation, and has adopted the whole body of Congress for its legitimate government, as is the case with the district, is too obvious not to present itself to the minds of all. Although in theory it might be more congenial to the spirit of our institutions to admit a representative from the district, it may be doubted whether, in fact, its interests would be rendered thereby the more secure; and certainly the constitution does not consider their want of a representative in Congress as exempting it from equal taxation.

If it were true that, according to the spirit of our constitution, the power of taxation must be limited by the right of representation, whence is derived the right to lay and collect duties, imposts, and excises, within this district? If the principles of liberty, and of our constitution, forbid the raising of revenue from those who are not represented, do not these principles forbid the raising it by duties, imposts, and excises, as well as by a direct tax? If the principles of our revolution give a rule applicable to this case, we cannot have forgotten that neither the stamp act nor the duty on tea were direct taxes.

Yet it is admitted, that the constitution not only allows, but enjoins the government to extend the ordinary revenue system to this district.

If it be said, that the principle of uniformity, established in the constitution, secures the district from oppression in the imposition of indirect taxes, it is not less true, that the principle of apportionment, also established in the constitution, secures the district from any oppressive exercise of the power to lay and collect direct taxes.

After giving this subject its serious attention, the Court is unanimously of opinion, that Congress possesses, under the constitution, the power to lay and collect direct taxes within the District of Columbia, in proportion to the census directed to be taken by the constitution, and that there is no error in the judgment of the Circuit court.

Judgment affirmed.

Printed, Henry Wheaton, *Reports of Cases Argued and Adjudged in the Supreme Court of the United States . . .*, V (New York, 1820), 317–25.

1. Wheaton spelled the plaintiff's name "Loughborough," though it is spelled "Lufborough" in the official records of the case. The newspaper rendered it as "Luffborough" (Washington *Daily National Intelligencer*, 9, 11 Mar. 1820).

Notes on Arguments
U.S. Supreme Court, 10–11 March 1820

EDITORIAL NOTE

To supplement the formal record and written briefs of cases that came before the Supreme Court, Chief Justice Marshall and his brother justices took notes of oral arguments. The document below is one of a few surviving sets of such notes in Marshall's hand. It contains notes of three cases heard in the Supreme Court on 10 and 11 March 1820: *United States* v. *Lancaster*, *Bussard* v. *Levering*, and *Lyle* v. *Rodgers*.

The bulk of the notes pertain to *United States* v. *Lancaster*, an embargo case that had come up from the U.S. Circuit Court for Pennsylvania in 1818. Thomas Lancaster, a Philadelphia merchant, was part owner of the brig *Eliza*, which had been libeled in the U.S. District Court for Delaware in 1808 for violating the embargo laws. In consequence the United States in May 1811 obtained a judgment against him on a forfeited embargo bond in the amount of $75,000. In these legal proceedings the vessel had been restored to Lancaster after he gave a bond for its appraised value of $2,001. He was liable for this amount if the vessel were ultimately condemned. Both the district court and circuit courts decreed restitution of the *Eliza*, but the Supreme Court in 1813 reversed this decree.

In 1816 Lancaster successfully petitioned the secretary of the treasury for a remission of the forfeiture on the embargo bond. In the meantime the United States had brought suit on the bond for the appraised value of the *Eliza*. Lancaster then petitioned President Monroe, who in April 1817 issued a pardon remitting all claim and interest of the United States in both bonds and directing all legal proceedings by the United States against Lancaster to be discontinued. The question was whether the remission and pardon could affect the vested rights of the collector of customs who had originally seized the vessel. The case was argued on 10 March 1820 by Charles J. Ingersoll for the United States and by John Sergeant for Lancaster. Because the Supreme Court ultimately dismissed the case for want of jurisdiction, Wheaton's brief report omits the arguments. Marshall's notes thus provide the only record of the hearing of the case on the merits.[1]

Bussard v. *Levering*, which came up from the U.S. Circuit Court for the District of Columbia in 1818, concerned a protested inland bill of exchange. Daniel Bussard of Georgetown, the defendant below, drew the bill on a Baltimore merchant in October 1816, payable to Aaron Levering of the Bellona Gunpowder Company. The bill was accepted for payment but was later protested for nonpayment. The question was whether Bussard had received due notice of the nonpayment and protest. The circuit court ruled against Bussard, who brought the case to the Supreme Court on a writ of error. The appeal was argued on 10 March 1820 by Walter Jones for Bussard and Francis Scott Key for Levering. Again, Wheaton did not report the arguments in this case.[2]

Lyle v. *Rodgers* originated in the U.S. Circuit Court for the District of Columbia in December 1816. It was an action of debt on a bond given by Jerusha Dennison, widow and administratrix of Gideon Dennison, and John Rodgers to James Lyle and Joshua B. Bond of Philadelphia in November 1815. The bond was in the amount of $12,000, with a condition to perform an award of persons chosen to arbitrate all differences between the plaintiffs and Jerusha Dennison, either as administratrix of her late husband or in any other capacity. The arbitrators awarded $8,700 plus interest to Lyle and Bond, who sued for this amount when it was not paid. The defendant contended that no award had been made since it left certain matters in dispute unsettled. After the circuit court ruled in favor of the defendant in December 1817, the plaintiffs brought the case to the Supreme Court by writ of error. The appeal was argued on 11 March 1820 by Walter Jones for the plaintiffs and by William Pinkney and Francis Scott Key for the defendant. Wheaton fully reported the case.[3]

1. U.S. v. Brig Eliza, 7 Cranch 113 (1812); U.S. v. Lancaster, App. Cas. No. 949; U.S. Sup. Ct. Minutes, 10 Mar. 1820; U.S. v. Lancaster, 5 Wheat. 434–35 (1820); U.S. v. Lancaster, 26 Fed. Cas. 859 (U.S. Cir. Ct., Pa., 1821).

2. Bussard v. Levering, App. Cas. No. 950; 6 Wheat. 102–3; U.S. Sup. Ct. Minutes, 10 Mar. 1820.

3. Lyle v. Rodgers, App. Cas. No. 951; 5 Wheat. 394–405; U.S. Sup. Ct. Minutes, 10 Mar. 1820.

The United States ⎫
    v   ⎬
Lancaster   ⎭

Mr. Ingersol

v.4.p 131.151. The embargo laws.[1]

Question is had the President or secretary of the Treasury after final judgement a right to remit an interest vested in a citizen.

Remission by the secretary

This applies only to the bond in the petition

Sec. 6 of these acts adopts the previous acts respecting forfeitures & remissions[2]

2.V.48. The act organizing the Treasury department[3]

2.v.103 confers it. Proviso that it shall not affect the vested rights &c[4]

    299. continued—

    481.585—Power to remit &c on terms—& before judgement[5]

    3.v.304 proceedings to be discontinued.[6] 3 v. p 221. Sec. 89.91. The interests vest in severalty[7]

1. Whe. 470.4. 1st. Gal.195.205. 2 Gal. 516. 1st. Mason 431.[8]

    1st. Ruth B.1 ch 18 Sec. 14. ch.18. & sec 17. 1 Chitty 398. on crim. law 467. 742. 763.4 2 Browns chy. cases 304. Hales treatise on the customs Hargraves law tracts p 226.[9]

The pardon or remission of the President. This a remission & the constitution gives the power to pardon not to remit

---

Const.2.Art.2d.Sec.p67.

1.Gal.186

2.inst 233.ch105

3.Inst.237.

2.H.P.C.B.2.Ch37.Sec.34⟨. . .⟩

5.B.ab. Tit.pardon.l.1⟨. . .⟩

4.Bl.398.9

It is confined to the interest of the United States in terms "Power to grant reprieves & pardons for offences against the United States." He could not give away even the share of the US

Certainly not the vested right of the private individual The King of England cannot do it.[10]

Mr Sergeant.

The remission by the Secretary & the first remission by the President apply to the cargo bond.

That of the 25th. of April 1815 were intended to apply to the bond for the vessel & for its value—after suit but before judgement on bond.

Remission by P.

The U.S. have the exclusive right to prosecute for offences & forfeitures under the embargo act.

2. The P. has by the constitution the right to relinquish whether before or after

3. Has been duely exercised to the whole extent of the penalty

1st. The penalty given to a certain extent in the individual who sues

2. v. p 81. laws relative to Marshalls &c half to informer[11]

Embargo & The laws relative to duties &c pursue a different course
2.v.7.sec 36.38 & retain the exclusive right to conduct the business to
3.v.p136   its termination is reserved to the US. & to its officers.
89th.sec.p221. adopts the act of 99. as to duties No qui tam action or
4th.v.p132.   any action in which an individual can appear is allowed.

The Government can at any time withdraw the proceeding so as to withhold the money.[12]

The power given to the collector is meerly ministerial—He has no power to suspend or discontinue—That belongs to the P. or S. of the T. wherever that power is lodged it must remain until the money be recovered.

Denies that the interest is vested in the officer by the Judgement. Either vested long before or not till the money be paid.

The record exhibits no other name nor interest than the U.S. After judgement the U.S. give what portion they please. These laws of distribution apply solely to the time of distribution.

The offence is purely public & concerns no individual.

It may be committed under circumstances which give the full claim of innocence to the remission of the penalty. These circumstances may not be shown until the moment before a judgement.

In this case Lancaster was acquitted by the district & circuit courts & could not know his danger till it was too late to get relief.

---

1 Wh. 462 71 The case of Jones v Shore assumes the time of seizure as the basis of the judgement.[13] The question then was not when? but to whom? It vests by relation.

That case does not decide that the penalty so vested as to preclude the power to remit.

The power inefficacious unless it be coextensive with the penalty.

The officer has his share in the penalty in its original grant subject to this power of remission.

It is of the essence of the pardoning power for an offence against the Government that the pardon be co-extensive with the offence.

The prosecution is at the expence of the U.S. Is not this enough without the ungracious power of asserting the power of pardons.

He cannot prevent a dismission or take out an execution.

There is no separation of interest.

But suppose he can proceed in the name of the U.S. what must he do with the money? — Divide it. Till the actual recovery of the money nothing is said of any right but that of the U.S.
The constitutional power of the P to remit not limited by law
    There was a condemnation of the vessel but no judgment on the bond.

2. V. 299. The saving superfluous. Congress could not limit the right.[14]

This disposes of the English cases where Parliament is unlimited.

The import of the word pardon is to releive from the offence.

The practice has been to pardon partially — to pardon conditionally.

The whole power might be destroyed by Congress by vesting the penalty in an individual.
The power has been duely executed.
    A pardon is to be liberally construed.

"All the interest of the United States." Did this comprehend the whole penalty?

The recital shows the intention to remit entirely as he is declared to be innocent. No other interest is known to the law until the money is levied.

2. Gal. 522. The claim of the Collector is attendant on that of the U.S. It is contingent, has no separate existence. It is to receive half what maybe recovered.[15]

There is in the pardon no saving of the rights of the collectors.
Ingersol
    The court will percieve in the language of the remission by the Secretary what the language of the pardon would have been had the President intended to remit the whole or the rights of the collector.

———

It is admitted that the President cannot pardon a vested interest. Is an interest vested by the judgement?

The collectors have inadequate salaries without the extraordinary reward of forfeitures. The collectors run the whole risk & the U.S. divide the forfeitures.

———

Reads the paragraph & shows that according to the argument the interest of the United States does not vest until the money is received.

———

If there is no vested interest until the money is received the Secretary of the Treasury may remit after judgement as well as the President.[16]

Bussard ⎤
 v   ⎬
Levering ⎦

Mr. Jones

The court was of opinion that the notice of protest was irregular but that other circumstances supplied the want of notice.

———

1. Term. 167 No knowledge of insolvency can discharge from the
11. East. 114 necessity of regular notice of dishonor. Nor will any irregular notice.[17]

Mr. Key

The draft was drawn & accepted on the express promise of the drawer to provide funds.

———

The uniform course in Baltimore where this bill was drawn & accepted is to demand & give notice on the last day of grace.

———

Jones

Nothing in the record to dispense with notice or distinguish it from any other case of a bill. The man who purchases goods & gives a bill in payment which is accepted is in the common situation of the drawer of a bill.[18]

Lisle & Bond
 v
Rodgers

Jones for plfs in Error. The letter referred to is No. 2 p 12 addressed by Mr. Lisle to Mr. Hollingsworth his attorney.

———

1st. Obj. The arbitrators have no[t] determined all the subjects in controversy & the only evidence produced is a letter written 20 years past.

———

But the arbitrators have done enough if they decide all that the parties submit to them.

———

2d. Obj.   That an Admx. cannot submit differences relative to her
Toler 465   intestates estate to arbitration[19]

———

1. Term 691   The right is established to submit to arbitration & the sub-
5. T. 7. 7T   mission is evidence of assetts. Cowper 284.9.[20]
453 —

3d. Obj.Uncertainty in what Lisle & Bond are awarded to do. Insists that the universality is advantageous to Rodgers. A general release is the best release for the defendents.

———

It is objected that the arbiters use the words all lands.

———

In the old cases the Judges have employed all their astuteness to defeat awards. In the progress of society they have been viewed with more favor & many things are now deemed certain which were formerly bad.

———

It is not necessary that every thing should be stated certainly — it may be rendered certain by reference Aliunde. The question is whether the party has a certain & definite remedy. Here defendent may show that certain deeds have been executed & are not released. If he should attempt to sue on those securities the award would bar.

———

It is sufficiently certain what bonds &c may be delivered up. It is within the knowledge of the parties.

———

If the whole be summed up it is a general release to which is superadded a particular recital also in general terms.

———

How does it appear that the defendants knew that these several documents were known to the arbitrators so as to be specified by them.

———

The alternative part of the award to deliver up the papers or account for them on oath.

———

An alternative award is good if certain — Oath.

———

Were the Arbitrators bound to have the goods brought in
Might they not direct a discovery on oath.
Kidd on award 101 191[21]

———

Pinkney

The rules relative to awards are drawn from the civil law
This award decides nothing — it decides what was unimportant & leave all that was material ad referendum

———

It does not state in what character Mrs. Dennison owes this money. This is a material uncertainty. It is impossible to charge the debt on the estate. The award itself ought to show the character in which he is chargeable.

———

This award is no proof of assets. That question is referred to arbitrators. If they say the money shall be paid it finds assets, otherwise if it meerly finds that so much is due.[22]

AD, Wheaton Papers, NNPM.

1. The citation is to the embargo laws of 9 Jan. and 12 Mar. 1808 (*U.S. Statutes at Large*, II, 453, 473). Here and below the edition of laws cited in JM's notes is *Laws of the United States of America, from the 4th of March, 1789, to the 4th of March, 1815* (5 vols.; Philadelphia and Washington, 1815).

2. *U.S. Statutes at Large*, II, 454, 475.

3. Ibid., I, 65.

4. Ibid., 122–23. This act empowered the secretary of the treasury to remit forfeitures and penalties accruing under the revenue laws, provided that nothing in the act should "be construed to affect the right or claim of any person, to that part of any fine, penalty or forfeiture, incurred by breach of either of the laws aforesaid."

5. Ibid., 275, 425, 506.

6. Ibid., II, 7.

7. The 1799 act to regulate the collection of duties, secs. 89 and 91 (ibid., I, 695–96, 697).

8. The cases cited are Jones v. Shore's Executor, 1 Wheat. 462, 470–74 (1816); The Mars, 1 Gall. 192, 195–205, 16 Fed. Cas. 784 (U.S. Cir. Ct., Mass., 1812); The Margaretta, 2 Gall. 515, 516, 16 Fed. Cas. 719 (U.S. Cir. Ct., Mass., 1815); The Hollen, 1 Mason 431, 12 Fed. Cas. 344 (U.S. Cir. Ct., Mass., 1818).

9. T[homas] Rutherforth, *Institutes of Natural Law* . . . (3d ed.; 2 vols.; Philadelphia, 1799), bk. I, chap. 18, secs. 14, 17, pp. 432–36, 448–50; Joseph Chitty, *A Practical Treatise on Pleading* (2d Am. ed.; 2 vols.; New York, 1812; S #25064), I, 398; Joseph Chitty, *A Practical Treatise on the Criminal Law* (1816; 4 vols. in 5; New York, 1978 reprint), I, 467; II, 742, 763–64; Clarke v. Hackwell, 2 Bro. C.C. 304, 29 Eng. Rep. 166 (Ch., 1788); Francis Hargrave, *A Collection of Tracts Relative to the Law of England* (Dublin, 1787), 226. The citation to Hargrave is Matthew Hale's, "A Treatise in Three Parts," of which the third part is entitled "Concerning the Custom of Goods Imported and Exported."

10. U.S. v. Mann, 1 Gall. 177, 186, 26 Fed. Cas. 1153 (U.S. Cir. Ct., Mass., 1812); Edward Coke, *The Third Part of the Institutes of the Laws of England* . . . (London, 1797), 233, 237 (the first citation to Coke should also be to the "Third Part"; both are from chapter 105, "Of Pardons"); William Hawkins, *A Treatise of the Pleas of the Crown* (1724; New York, 1972 reprint, from 2d ed.), bk. II, chap. 37, sec. 34, p. 392; Bacon, *Abridgment*, V, 286–89 (s.v. "Pardon," sec. B: "In what Cases, and for what Offences it may be granted"); Blackstone, *Commentaries*, IV, 398–99.

11. The citation is to the census act of 1790, sec. 3, relating to penalties against marshals for failing to file returns within a specified time (*U.S. Statutes at Large*, I, 102).

12. The act to regulate the collection of duties of 31 July 1789, secs. 36 and 38; the act to regulate the collection of duties of 2 Mar. 1799, sec. 89; the embargo act of 9 Jan. 1808 (ibid., 29, 47, 48, 627, 695–96; II, 453–54).

13. Jones v. Shore's Executor, 1 Wheat. 462, 471 (1816).

14. The reference is to the 1792 act continuing in force the act providing for mitigating or remitting penalties and forfeitures accruing under the revenue laws. It contained a proviso that "nothing in the said act shall be construed to limit or restrain the power of the President . . . to grant pardons for offences against the United States" (*U.S. Statutes at Large*, I, 275).

15. The Margaretta, 2 Gall. 522, 16 Fed. Cas. 719 (U.S. Cir. Ct., Mass., 1815).

16. The case had come to the Supreme Court by certificate of division. On 17 Mar. 1820 JM declared that the Court did not have jurisdiction, "as the District Judge could not sit in the Circuit Court on a writ of error from his own decision, and consequently there could be no division of opinion to be certified to this Court." It was accordingly remanded to the U.S. Circuit Court for Pennsylvania, where at the Apr. 1821 term Judge Washington ruled that the customs collector was entitled to a moiety of the penalty on the bond (5 Wheat. 434–35; 26 Fed. Cas. 859–61).

17. Tindal v. Brown, 1 T.R. 167, 99 Eng. Rep. 1033 (K.B., 1786); Esdaile v. Sowerby and Meller, 11 East 114, 103 Eng. Rep. 948 (K.B., 1809).

18. The Court on 7 Feb. 1821 affirmed the circuit court's judgment, ruling that Bussard had received sufficient notice of the nonpayment (6 Wheat. 103).

19. Sir Samuel Toller, *The Law of Executors and Administrators* (3d ed.; New York, 1815; S #36100), 465.

20. Atkins v. Hill, 1 Cowp. 284, 98 Eng. Rep. 1088 (K.B., 1775); Hawkes v. Saunders, 1 Cowp. 289, 98 Eng. Rep. 1091 (K.B., 1782). The cases cited in the margin are Barry v. Rush, 1 T.R. 691, 99 Eng. Rep. 1324 (K.B., 1787); Pearson v. Henry, 5 T.R. 6, 7, 101 Eng. Rep. 3–5 (K.B., 1792); Worthington v. Barlow, 7 T.R. 453, 101 Eng. Rep. 1072–73 (K.B., 1797).

21. Stewart Kyd, *A Treatise on the Law of Awards* (1st Am. ed.; Philadelphia, 1808, from 2d London ed.; S #15384), 101, 191.

22. On 15 Mar. 1820 JM for the Court upheld the circuit court's judgment for the defendant Rogers (5 Wheat. 405–11).

From William Wirt

Dear Sir   Washington March 11. 1820

Since the argument of the question propounded by the Bench, as arising under the spanish treaty, in the case of the Isabella,[1] my reflections on the bearing of that question on the belligerent rights of this nation, connected with the doubts which the court expressed on the subject have led me to forget the individual interests involved in the controversy, and to consider the construction of the Spanish treaty as one of the most serious national questions which has been ever raised before the Supreme tribunal of the Nation. Under this impression I have thought it my duty to bring the pendency of this question to the knowledge of the federal executive and to receive their instructions as to the course which it was their wish I should pursue. I beg leave to enclose a copy of my communication to the President together with his answer; and to request, if any doubts still remain on the mind of the court, that the court will be pleased to hear a more full & solemn argument on that

[26]

WILLIAM WIRT
Oil on canvas by Charles Bird King, 1820. *Courtesy of Redwood Library and Athenæum, Newport, Rhode Island.*

single branch of the case of the Isabella which involves the construction of the Treaty. I hope that the request is perfectly compatible with the sacred respect which is felt for the independence of the judiciary — the government asking only to be heard, if the doubts of the Court still remain, on a question which they consider as replete with the most serious consequences to our nation. Because the decision of the Supreme Court in this case must of necessity give the law to the prize Courts of our country, in any future war in which we may be involved, and if the decision be favorable to the construction set up on the part of the claimant, it is very easy to fore:see the use which may and will be made of it by any enemy with whom it may be our misfortune to be hereafter engaged in a war.

Should there be nothing indelicate or improper in this request, as I trust there is not, I will take the liberty to move the subject in Court to day, in presence of the opposite counsel. But if, in the estimation of the Court, there should be the slightest impropriety in such a motion (which I confess, I am not able to discern) my respect for the Court will certainly restrain me from making it. I have the honor to be, Dear Sir, very respectfully, Your most ob. &c.

WM WIRT

[Enclosure]

Sir.   Office of the Attorney Genl U S.

The case to which I adverted in conversation, is the case of a merchant ship called the Amiable Isabella under the spanish flag, captured by one of our Privateers, during our late war with Great Britain, & condemned in the circuit court of North Carolina as prize of war. On appeal by the Spanish claimant to the Supreme Court, several questions have arisen on the construction of the 17th. article of our treaty of 1795, with Spain, which strike me as being of great importance to the nation, & which therefore I deemed it my official duty to bring to your notice. These questions are First, whether certain papers, offered by the claimant as being the passport & certificate required by that article (of which, you will observe, no form is given by the treaty, altho' intended to have been given) be in truth, the documents thereby required; & Secondly: whether, if they be, & it be made apparent to the Court from the other documentary evidence of the Ship, the preparatory examination of the witnesses, & the farther proof which has been allowed in the cause, that the alleged passport, & certificate has been obtained by collusion between the enemy owners & a Spanish subject in Havanna, & by an imposition on the spanish officers who granted those papers, a court of the U.S. is bound to respect them, and to restore the Ship & cargo to the claimant. I was engaged in this case, as one of the counsel for the captors. My duty to my clients is discharged, & the cause is in the hands of the Court. How, or when, it may be decided I know not. In the private practice of my profession I have nothing more to do with it. Since the argument, however, I have been reflecting on it, *officially* & the consequences of the decision have presented themselves to me as being of such serious consequences to the belligerent rights of the nation, in case of any future war, that I should have considered myself as failing criminally, in my duty to the Government whose officer I am, to have omitted the communication I have made to you. We have other treaties — with Holland & sweaden for example, which contain the provision that free ships make free goods: should the Supreme Court of our own Government fix the principle by their decision, that any belligerent who can possess himself of the flag & pass of any one of those nations, by whatsoever means, shall be protected thereby against our right of capture, it is manifest that we can never make war with a maritime power, which has no such treaty, on equal terms, & that as a belligerent nation, we shall be shorn of half our strength.

The case being fraught with these serious national consequences I submit it to You Sir, whether it would be improper on the part of the Government that I, as their officer should be instructed to suggest that if the decision of this cause shall necessarily involve the decision of these momentous national questions, & if the Court entertain doubts upon them, they will permit a more extended & solemn argument upon them.

I cannot myself conceive that they would consider the application as otherwise than respectful, or that they could fail to see the serious & vital connexion which those two questions have with the interests of the nation. I at least, have done my duty in bringing them to your view; & I submit it myself entirely to Your direction.[2] I am &c &c.

WM WIRT

ALS (letterbook copy), RG 60, DNA; letterbook copy, RG 60, DNA.

1. The Amiable Isabella was a prize case originating in the U.S. Circuit Court for North Carolina. JM on circuit had condemned the Spanish vessel as prize of war in May 1817. The case was appealed to the Supreme Court and argued from 22 Feb. through 29 Feb. 1820. On 4 Mar. the Court requested reargument "upon the point as to the form and effect of the passport." The claimant claimed exemption from capture and condemnation on the ground that he possessed a valid passport according to the form prescribed by the treaty of 1795 between Spain and the U.S. In fact, however, no form of a passport had been annexed to the treaty. The case presented the delicate question of whether strict adherence to the terms of a national treaty might undermine the government's ability to prosecute its belligerent rights (6 Wheat. 1, 47; U.S. Sup. Ct., Dockets, App. Cas. No. 900; U.S. Sup. Ct., Minutes, 22–29 Feb. 1820).

2. On 15 Mar. the case was reargued, "upon the application of the executive Government, to the Court, on the question of the construction of the Spanish treaty, and the form and effect of the passports." The cause continued under advisement until the next term, when Story (on 22 Feb. 1821) for the Court affirmed the decree of condemnation (6 Wheat. 50, 65–81; U.S. Sup. Ct., Minutes, 15 Mar. 1820).

To Samuel F. Jarvis

Sir   Richmond March 26th. 1820

I have deferred making my acknowledgements for your polite atten-
tion in favoring me with a copy of your "Discourse on the religion of the
Indian tribes of North America" until I could give it an attentive perusal.[1]
I have now had that gratification.

The subject is interesting, & furnishes much matter for reflection. The
religion of these untaught children of the forest partakes less of gross
idolatry than has been generally supposed. It is matter of curious observation that the original theory or creed of these ignorant savages approaches so nearly that of the most polished & enlightened nations, while
unaided by revelation. Man, left to himself, seems, at all times, to have
formed nearly the same system respecting the creator of all things, &
some future state of rewards & punishments. There seems to be some
sentiment impressed on our minds by the divine hand which produces
nearly the same results in all created beings.

Accept Sir my thanks for the pleasure I have received from the very
interesting view you have taken of this subject, and believe me to be with
great respect. Your Obedt.

J MARSHALL

ALS (advertised for sale by The Scriptorium, Beverly Hills, Calif., 1974). According to
Parke-Bernet Catalog No. 3605 (28 Feb. 1974), item 301, the letter had an integral address
leaf with postmark, which is now missing.

1. Jarvis (1786–1851), a Connecticut native and Yale graduate (class of 1805), had a
distinguished career as an Episcopal clergyman and theologian. At this time he was a
professor at the newly established General Theological Seminary in New York City and had
just received a call to become first rector of Saint Paul's Church, Boston. Among his many
published works was *A Discourse on the Religion of the Indian Tribes of North America. Delivered
before the New-York Historical Society, December 20, 1819* (New York, 1820; S #1782). See
Franklin Bowditch Dexter, *Biographical Sketches of the Graduates of Yale College* (6 vols.; New
York, 1885–1912), V, 770–79.

From William Wirt

Dear Sir,   Washington. April 11. 1820.

You gave me leave to remind you of the discrimination among the
pirates, with the view of enabling the President to select two, who were
most fit to be made examples of. Will you be so good, at your convenience
to give the necessary information.[1] Yours most respectfully

WM. WIRT.

ALS (letterbook copy), RG 60, DNA; letterbook copy, RG 60, DNA. Inside address to JM
in Richmond.

1. The attorney general referred to the piracy case, U.S. v. Smith, which had been tried at a special term of the U.S. Circuit Court at Richmond in the summer of 1819. The case was certified to the Supreme Court for its opinion whether the offense committed by Smith and others was piracy and thus punishable by an 1819 act of Congress. The Court at the Feb. 1820 term ruled that the offense was piracy. The case then went back to the circuit court for sentencing. JM replied to Wirt's request after sentencing the pirates to death at the May term (*PJM*, VIII, 370–72; U.S. v. Smith, Sentence, 29 May 1820 and nn.; Wirt to JM, 1 June 1820 and n. 1).

To Bushrod Washington

My dear Sir   Richmond Apl. 13th. 1820

I have received your letter requesting to know whether I had formed an opinion on the case which was remanded to the circuit court of Pennsylvania.[1] I regret that I had not formed one. It would give me pleasure to communicate it to you.

I congratulate you on the prospect of a full docket in Jersey & congratulate myself on the prospect of an empty one in North Carolina. The difference is that I come home as soon as the court in North Carolina rises & that you loiter away the whole time between the rising of the court in Jersey & the sitting of that in Pennsylvania.

I called on Mr. Blair the President of the Bible society who promised me to enquire into your accounts with the Bible society.[2] I told him that you supposed yourself not to be a permanent member. I saw him again the other day & he told me that you were a permanent member & were in arrears for the years 1816, 1817, 1818 & 1819. I requested him to strike your name from the list & to give me the amount of your account, that you had placed money in my hands to discharge it. At the same time I told him that you were a member of the parent society & of one other branch. He thought it perfectly reasonable that you should retire from this.

I was so frozen on the 2d. of april that I am scarcely thawed by the mild breezes of yesterday & to day; yet I set out tomorrow for the upper country. Farewell, I am your

J MARSHALL

ALS, Marshall Papers, ViW. Addressed to Washington in Philadelphia; postmarked Richmond, 14 Apr. Endorsed by Washington.

1. Letter not found. Two cases were remanded by the Supreme Court at the 1820 term to the U.S. Circuit Court for Pennsylvania: Conn v. Penn, 5 Wheat. 424; U.S. v. Lancaster, 5 Wheat. 434; Notes on Arguments, 10–11 Mar. 1820.

2. The Bible Society of Virginia had been established in June 1813 and was modeled on similar societies in Philadelphia and in other U.S. cities. The purpose of this charitable organization was to distribute "Bibles and Testaments to the poor of our country, and to the Heathen." The Rev. John D. Blair of Richmond had been president of the Virginia society since 1814. He was one of the "two parsons" (the other was John Buchanan) who were fellow members with JM of the Barbecue Club (*Address of the Managers of the Bible Society of Vir-*

ginia to the Public [Richmond, Va., 1814; S #30910], 3, 7, 9; George Wythe Munford, *The Two Parsons; Cupid's Sports; The Dream; and The Jewels of Virginia* [Richmond, Va., 1884], 326–41).

The Brig Wilson v. United States
Opinion
U.S. Circuit Court, Virginia, ca. 22 May 1820

The brig *Wilson* was libeled in the U.S. District Court at Norfolk in November 1819. The first four counts of the libel claimed forfeiture under the act regulating the collection of duties of a quantity of brandy, gin, and other merchandise found on board the vessel. The fifth count claimed forfeiture of the brig itself for having brought in "three persons of Color," contrary to a federal law preventing the importation of such persons into states whose laws prohibited their admission. Ivory Huntress, master of the *Wilson*, claimed that the brig was a privateer commissioned by the United Provinces of Venezuela and New Grenada; that the spirits and other goods on board had been captured as prize of war and were intended to be used as sea stores, not as merchandise; that the vessel had intended to refit at Norfolk, with no intention of unloading; that there was no attempt to conceal any articles; and that the three persons of color had not been imported into the state but were part of the crew of a foreign armed vessel. At a special court held in Williamsburg on 22 December 1819, Judge Tucker issued a decree forfeiting the brandy, gin, and other merchandise, along with the vessel itself, to the United States. The owner of the *Wilson*, Joseph Almeida of Baltimore, appealed to the U.S. Circuit Court. Marshall's opinion brought forth some commentary on the extent of the commerce power (proceedings in U.S. District Court [copy], 22 Dec. 1819, Brig Wilson [Ivory Huntress, claimant] v. U.S., U.S. Cir. Ct., Va., Ended Cases [Unrestored], 1820, Vi).

Huntress

v

The U.S.

The 4 first counts of this case present for the consideration of the court a general question of considerable importance. It is this   ¶1

Does the act "To regulate the collection of duties on imports & tonnage," apply to Privatiers, not engaged in the importation of goods?   ¶2

Sec. 31. The Sec. enacts "That it shall not be necessary for the master or person having the command of any ship or vessel of war &c to make such report & entry as aforesaid."[1]   ¶3

If the word ship or vessel of war be construed to comprehend a privatier, there is an end of this part of the case, because, if no report or entry is required, it cannot be pretended that any of the provisions of the act extend to a privatier demeaning herself in her military character & not performing the office of a merchant vessel.   ¶4

¶5   The counsel for the appellant has certainly urged many reasons which have great weight in favor of the construction for which he contends. The term "Ship or vessel of war" has been considered, & I think properly considered, as a generic term, including both national ships & private armed ships. When it is used generally, it comprehends both unless the context or the subject matter should exclude the one or the other. The authorities cited at the bar show that courts & writers on public law, have used the term in this general sense.

¶6   If either the objects or the language of this law be consulted, I think they strengthen this natural & comprehensive construction of these words.

¶7   The object of the law is professedly & obviously to raise a revenue from commerce & consumption, not to regulate the conduct of the ships of war, whether public or private, of foreign nations. All the regulations are obviously calculated for merchant vessels & not one calculated for privatiers who might come into our ports, altho a totally distinct provisions for them would certainly be necessary.

¶8   The language of the law applies it to vessels destined for the United States, not to vessels destined for a cruize on the high seas. The form of the manifest requires that the importer should state to what port the vessel is bound & to whom the goods are consigned, Regulations not adapted to goods captured at sea by a cruizer.

¶9   If this act applies to privatiers the tonnage duty would be demandable. But it cannot be supposed that this duty is imposed on privatiers employed in cruizing & not in the conveyance of merchandize.

¶10   It is also an argument which deserves consideration that the policy of the United States has been unfriendly to the sale in our ports of prizes made by foreign privatiers on nations with whom we are at peace. Some of our treaties contain express stipulations against it; & the course of the government has been to prohibit the practice even where no specific engagements bind us to do so. Were the revenue laws applicable to privatiers & to their prizes & prize goods, they would give a right to introduce those goods in opposition to the avowed & uniform policy of the government. The doctrine that the validity of prizes could not be adjudged in our ports would be of little importance if they could be brought in & sold.

¶11   I think then that our revenue laws do not apply to Privatiers unless they take up the character of merchant men by attempting to import goods. When they do so they attempt under the garb of their military character to conceal real commercial transactions. This would be a fraud on the revenue laws which no nation will or ought to tolerate. The privatier which acts as a merchant vessel must be considered & treated as a merchant vessel.

¶12   In this case there is no evidence that any goods were landed or that more were brought in than were intended to be carried out. The only evidence which I think at all important is that of the pilot. His testimony certainly excites suspicion.[2] Opposed to it however is the testimony of the witnesses belonging to the vessel who say that the spirits were designed for the crew to be used as stores.

I[3] proceed now to the 5th. count in the libel.   ¶13

The first question which will be considered in this part of the case is the   ¶14
constitutionality of the act of Congress under which this condemnation has been made.[4]

It will readily be admitted that the power of the legislature of the Union   ¶15
on this subject is derived entirely from the 3d. clause of the 8th. section of the 1st. article of the constitution. That clause enables Congress "to regulate Commerce with foreign nations, & among the several states, & with the Indian tribes."

What is the extent of this power to regulate commerce? Does it not   ¶16
comprehend the navigation of the country? May not the vessels, as well as the articles they bring, be regulated? Upon what principle is it that the ships of any foreign nation have been forbidden under pain of forfeiture to enter our ports? The authority to make such laws has never been questioned, & yet it can be sustained by no other clause in the Constitution than that which enables Congress to regulate commerce. If this power over vessels is not in Congress, where does it reside? Certainly it is not annihilated, &, if not, it must reside somewhere. Does it reside in the States? No American politician has been so extravagant as to contend for this. No man has been wild enough to maintain that although the power to regulate commerce gives Congress an unlimited power over the cargoes, it does not enable that body to controul the vehicles in which they are imported. That while the whole power of commerce is vested in Congress, the state legislatures may confiscate every vessel which enters their ports & Congress is unable[5] their entry. Let it be admitted for the sake of argument that a law forbidding a free man of any colour to come into the United States would be void, & that no penalty imposed on him by Congress ⟨c⟩ould be enforced. Still the vessel which should bring him into the United States might be forfeited, & that forfeiture enforced; since even an empty vessel, or a packet employed solely in the conveyance of passengers & letters may be regulated or forfeited. A [There is not, in the Constitution, one syllable on the subject of navigation. And yet, every power that pertains to navigation has been uniformly exercised, and, in the opinion of all, been rightfully exercised, by congress. From the adoption of the Constitution, till this time, the universal sense of America has been, that the word commerce, as used in that instrument, is to be considered a generic term, comprehending navigation, or, that a control over navigation is necessarily incidental to the power to regulate commerce.][6]

I could feel no difficulty in saying that the power to regulate commerce   ¶17
clearly comprehended the case, were there no other clause in the constitution showing the sense of the convention on that subject. But there is a clause which would remove the doubt if any could exist.

¶18   The first clause of the 9th. Sec. declares that "The migration or importation of such persons as any of the States now existing shall think proper
to admit, shall not be prohibited by the Congress prior to the year 1808."

¶19   This has been truely said to be a limitation of the power of Congress to
regulate commerce, & it will not be pretended that a limitation of a
power is to be construed into a grant of power. But though such limitation be not a grant; it is certainly evidence of the extent which those who
made both the grant & limitation attributed to the grant. The framers of
our constitution could never have declared that a given power should not
for a limited time be exercised on a particular object, if in their opinion it
could never be exercised on that object.

¶20   Suppose the grant & the limitation to be brought together. The clause
would read thus. Congress shall have power to regulate commerce &c
"but this power shall not be so exercised as to prohibit the migration or
importation of such persons as any of the states now existing may think
proper to admit prior to the year 1808." Would it be possible to doubt
that the power to regulate commerce in the sense in which those words
were used in the constitution included the power to prohibit the migration or importation of any persons whatever into the states except so far
as this power might be restrained by other clauses of the constitution? I
think it would be impossible.

¶21   It appears to me then that the power of Congress over vessels which
might bring in persons of any description whatever was complete before
the year 1808 except that it could not be so exercised as to prohibit the
importation or migration of any persons whom any state in existence at
the formation of the constitution might think proper to admit. The act of
congress then is to be construed with a view to this restriction on the
power of the legislature; and the only enquiry will be whether it comprehends this case.

¶22   The case is, that the brig Wilson a private armed cruizer commissioned
by the government of Buenos Ayres[7] came into Norfolk navigated by a
crew some of whom were people of colour. They were however all free
men & all of them sailors composing part of the crew. While in port some
of them were discharged & came on shore.

¶23   The libel charges that three persons of colour were landed from the
vessel whose admission or importation was prohib⟨ite⟩d by the laws of
Virginia, contrary to the act of Congress, by which the vessel was
forfeited.

¶24   Is this case within the act of Congress passed the 28th. of Feby. 1803?

¶25   The 1st. sec., which is the prohibitory part of the act, is in these words.
"From & after the first day of April next no master or Captain of any ship
or vessel, or any other person, shall import or bring, or cause to be
imported or brought any negroe, mulattoe, or other person of colour"
&c. There are nice shades or gradations in language which are more
readily percieved than described, & the mind, impressed with a particu-

lar idea, readily employs those wo⟨r⟩ds which express it most appropriately. Words which have a direct & common meaning, may also be used in a less common sense, but we do not understand them in the less common sense, unless the context, or clear design of the person using them, requires that they should be so understood. Now the verbs "to import" or "to bring in" seem to me to indicate, & are most commonly employed as indicating, the action of a person on any thing animate or inanimate, which is itself passive. The agent, or those who are concerned in the agency or importation are not in common language said to be imported, or brought in. It is true that a vessel coming into port is the vehicle which brings in her crew, but we do not in common language say that the mariners are "imported, or brought" in by a particular vessel; we rather say they bring in the vessel. So too if the legislature intended to punish the captain of a vessel for employing seamen of a particular description, or for allowing those seamen to come on shore, we should expect that this intention would be expressed by more appropriate words, than "to import" or "bring in." These words are peculiarly applicable to persons not concerned in navigating the vessel. It is not probable then that in making this provision, a regulation respecting the crew of a vessel was in the mind of Congress. But it is contended on the part of the prosecution that the succeeding words of the sentence, exempting certain descriptions of persons from the general prohibition, show that the prohibition itself was intended to comprehend the crew as well as those who did not belong to the vessel. Those words are "not being a native, a citizen, or registered seaman, of the United States, or seaman natives of count⟨rie⟩s beyond the Cape of Good Hope."

That this limitation proves the prohibition to have been intended to   ¶26
comprehend freemen as well as slaves, must I think be admitted; but it does not follow that it was also intended to comprehend the crew of a vessel actually employed in her navigation, & not put on board in fraud of the law. A person of colour, who is a registered seaman of the United States, may be imported or brought into the United States in a vessel in which he is not employed as a mariner. The construction therefore which would extend the prohibitory part of the sentence to the crew of the vessel in consequence of the language of the exception, is not a necessary construction though I must admit that it derives muc⟨h⟩ strength from that language.

The forfeiture of the vessel is not in this section of the act, but I have   ¶27
noticed its construction because it is not reasonable to suppose that it was intended to forfeit a vessel for an act which was not prohibited. The 2d. Sec. enacts "that no ship or vessel arriving in any of the said ports or places of the United States, & *having on board* any negroe mulattoe or other person of colour, not being a native, a citizen, or registered seaman of the United States, or seamen natives of countries beyond the Cape of Good Hope, as aforesaid, shall be admitted to an entry."

¶28   It is obvious that this clause was intended to refuse an entry to every vessel which had violated the prohibition contained in the first section; & that the words "having on board" were used as coextensive with "import or bring." We had at that time a treaty with the Emperor of Morocco & with several other Barbary powers. Their subjects are all people of colour. It is true they are not so engaged in commerce, as to send ships abroad. But the arrival of a moorish vessel in our ports is not an impossibility; and can it be beleived that this law was intended to refuse an entry to such a vessel? It may be said that an occurrence which has never taken place; & which in all probability never will take place, was not in the mind of Congress; and consequently the omission to provide for it ought not to influence the construction of their acts. But there are many nations with whom we have regular commerce who employ coloured seamen. Could it be intended by congress to refuse an entry to an english, a french, a spanish, or a portuguese, merchant vessel, in whose crew there was a man of colour? I think this construction could never be given to the act. The words "*having on board* a negroe mulattoe or other person of colour," would not I think be applied to a vessel, one of whose crew was a person of colour.

¶29   The section then proceeds "And if any such negroe &c shall be landed from on board any ship or vessel" & "the said ship or vessel &c shall be forfeited."

¶30   The words "shall be landed," seem peculiarly applicable to a person or thing which is *imported or brought in*, & which is landed, not by its own act, but by the authority of the im⟨porter⟩, not to a mariner going on shore voluntarily, or on the business of the ship. The words "*such* negroe" &c refer to the preceding passages describing those whom a Captain of a vessel is forbidden to import, & whose being on board a vessel excludes such vessel from an entry, and no others. If then the commentary which has been made on those passages be correct, the forfeiture is not incurred by a person of colour coming in as part of a ship's crew, & going on shore.

¶31   Although the powers of Barbary do not send merchant ships across the Atlantic, yet their treaties with us contemplate the possibility of their cruizers entering our ports. Would the cruizer be forfeited should one of the crew come on shore?

¶32   I have contended that the power of Congress to regulate commerce comprehends necessarily a power over navigation, & warrants every act of national sovereignty which any other sovereign nation may exercise over vessels foreign or domestic which enter our ports. But there is a portion of this power, so far as respects foreign vessels, which it is unusual for any nation to exercise, & the exercise of which would be deemed an unfriendly interference with the just rights of foreign powers. An example of this would be an attempt to regulate the manner in which a foreign vessel should be navigated in order to be admitted into our ports; and to subject such vessel to forfeiture if not so navigated. I will not say that this is beyond the power of a government; but I will say that no act ought to have this effect given to it, unless the words be such as to admit of no other rational construction.

I will now take some notice of that part of the act which has a reference to the state law. ¶33

The language both of the constitution & of the act of Congress show that the forfeiture was not intended to be inflicted in any case but where the state law was violated. In addition to the words in the first & second sections of the act which confine its operation to importations into "a state which by law has prohibited or shall prohibit the admission or importation of such negroe["] &c the third section enjoins it on the officers of the United States in the states having laws containing such prohibitions "to notice & be governed by the provisions of the laws now existing of the several states prohibiting the admission or importation of any negroe, mulatto, or other person of colour as aforesaid.["] This is not inflicting a penalty for the violation of a state law, but is limiting the operation of a penal law of the United States by a temporary line of demarcation given in the constitution. The power of Congress to prevent migration or importation was not to be exercised prior to the year 1808 on any person whom any of the states might think proper to admit. All were admissible who were not prohibited. It was proper therefore that the act of Congress should make the prohibitory act of the state the limit of its own operation. The act of Congress does not necessarily extend to every object comprehended in the state law, but neither its terms nor the constitution will permit it to be extended farther than the state law. ¶34

The first section of the act to prevent the migration of free negroes ⟨&⟩ mulattos into this Commonwealth prohibits their coming voluntarily or being imported.[8] The 2d. sec. imposes a penalty on any master of a vessel who shall bring any free negroe or mulatto. ¶35

The 3d. sec. provides that "the act shall not extend to any masters of vessels who shall bring into this state any free negroe or mulatto employed on board & belonging to such vessel & who shall therewith depart." The act then does not prohibit the master of a vessel navigated by free negroes or mulattos from coming into port, & setting only part of his crew on shore provided they depart with the vessel. The state prohibition then does not commence until the vessel departs without the negroe or mulatto seaman. No probability however strong that the vessel will depart without the seaman can extend the act to such a case until the vessel has actually departed. If this be true, neither does the act of Congress extend to such a case. ¶36

But this is not all. The act of Assembly prohibits the admission of free negroes & mulattos only, not of other persons of colour. Other persons of colour were admissible into Virginia. ¶37

The act of Congress makes a clear distinction between negroes & mulattos, & other persons of colour. But so much of the act of Congress as ¶38 respects other persons of colour does not apply to Virginia because such persons were admissible into this state.

¶39   The libel charges the sailors landed to have been persons of colour, not negroes or mulattos.

¶40   If under this libel, it were allowable to prove that the sailors landed, were in fact negroes or mulattos, it is not proved. Mr. Bush does not prove that any were landed, but says that those discharged were "of different colours & nations."⁹

¶41   Andrew Johnson says that on the 29th. of october "the *people of colour* received their prize tickets & went on shore & of course took their own discharge."¹⁰

¶42   There is then no evidence that these people were negroes or mulattos.

¶43   Upon these grounds I am of opinion that no forfeiture of the vessel has been incurred & that so much of the sentence as condemns the brig Wilson ought to be reversed & restitution awarded.¹¹

AD, Marshall Judicial Opinions, PPAmP; printed, John W. Brockenbrough, *Reports of Cases Decided by the Honourable John Marshall...*, I (Philadelphia, 1837), 428–39. Insertion marked "A" missing (see n. 6). For JM's deletions and interlineations, see Textual Notes below.

1. *U.S. Statutes at Large*, I, 627, 651.
2. William P. Davis, commander of a pilot boat, testified on behalf of the U.S. that a person on the *Wilson* (then at anchor) had hailed him, inquiring whether there were any men-of-war in Hampton Roads and then requesting him to come on board and "take some goods out" (proceedings in U.S. District Court [copy], 22 Dec. 1819, Brig Wilson [Ivory Huntress, claimant] v. U.S.).
3. JM began this part of the opinion on a separate sheet and repeated the caption.
4. This was the act of Feb. 1803 "to prevent the importation of certain persons into certain states, where, by the laws thereof, their admission is prohibited." Under this law a vessel bringing in any "negro, mulatto, or other person of colour" to a state whose laws prohibited their admission was liable to forfeiture (*U.S. Statutes at Large*, II, 205–6).
5. JM omitted "to prohibit."
6. Text within brackets supplied from Brockenbrough.
7. The *Wilson* acted under a Venezuelan commission.
8. Shepherd, *Statutes*, I, 239.
9. JM referred to the deposition of Wilson Bush, a supernumerary customs inspector and witness for the U.S. (proceedings in U.S. District Court [copy], 22 Dec. 1819, Brig Wilson [Ivory Huntress, claimant] v. U.S.).
10. Andrew Johnson, who served as captain's clerk on the *Wilson*, was a witness for the claimant (ibid.).
11. Judge Tucker wrote the following note to his opinion in the U.S. District Court: "This Decree was reversed by Judge Marshal, in toto, & the Brigantine released & restored. She has since been cruizing off our Coast, from Virginia to South Carolina & Georgia, as appears by the papers. I am not inform'd of the Grounds upon which the Decree was revers'd, as none are assigned in the record" ("Cases in the Courts of the United States, 25 February 1813-November 1824," No. 3, p. 134, Tucker-Coleman Papers, ViW).
In June 1820 Judge Tucker ordered five seamen to be committed to jail in Norfolk for joining the *Wilson*, which was about to depart on a cruise against Spanish commerce in violation of U.S. law. The sailors were tried at the Nov. 1820 term of the U.S. Circuit Court and acquitted (Richmond *Enquirer*, 21, 24 Nov., 1 Dec. 1820; U.S. Cir. Ct., Va., Ord. Bk. XI, 1, 9–10).

Textual Notes

¶ 1 l. 1 beg.   ↑The 4 first counts of this↓ ~~This~~ case ~~presents~~ ↑present↓
¶ 2 l. 1   the ↑collection of↓ duties
¶ 3 l. 1   The ~~31st.~~ Sec. ~~of~~ enacts
¶ 4 l. 4   her ↑military↓ character
¶ 7 l. 6   would ↑certainly↓ be
¶ 9 ll. 1–2   demandable. ~~as well as~~ But
¶10 l. 5   practice ↑even↓ where
¶14 l. 1   this ↑part of the↓ case
¶15 l. 4   regulate ~~Congress~~ Commerce
¶16 l. 1   of ~~a~~ ↑this↓ power
    ll. 3–4   that ~~the tonnage duty is laid?~~ the
    l. 4   nation ~~are~~ ↑have been↓ forbidden
    l. 5   The ~~power~~ ↑authority↓ to
    ll. 16–17   ports ↑& Congress is unable their entry.↓ Let it be admitted ↑for the sake of argument↓ that
    l. 17   colour ~~from coming~~ ↑to come↓ into
    l. 21   solely ~~for~~ ↑in↓ the
¶19 l. 5   limitation ~~supposed~~ attributed
¶20 l. 10   impossible. ~~I app~~
¶23 l. 2   vessel ~~which were not admitted~~ ↑whose admission or importation was prohib⟨ite⟩d↓ by
¶25 l. 2   next ~~it shall~~ no
    l. 5   gradations ↑in language↓ which
    l. 8   Words ~~too~~ which
    l. 13   person ↑on any thing↓ animate
    l. 14   passive. ~~& not to indicate the~~ ↑The↓ agent,
    l. 17   in ~~the~~ her
    l. 18   are ↑"imported, or↓ brought"
    ll. 18–19   we ↑rather↓ say
    l. 27   words ~~in~~ ↑of↓ the
    l. 29   comprehend ~~seamen~~ ↑the crew↓ as
¶26 l. 5   A ↑person of colour, who is a↓ registered
    ll. 6–7   States ~~although not~~ ↑in in a vessel in↓ which
    l. 8   prohibitory ~~clause~~ part
¶28 ll. 3–4   with "~~imported~~ ↑import↓ or
    l. 6   not ↑so↓ engaged
    l. 13   who ~~have~~ ↑employ↓ coloured
    ll. 18–19   to ~~such~~ a vessel ↑, one of whose crew was a person of colour.↓
¶30 ll. 2–3   *in,* ↑& which is landed, not by its own act, but by the authority of the im⟨porter⟩,↓ not
    ll. 8–9   forfeiture ~~will~~ ↑is↓ not ~~extend to~~ ↑incurred by↓ a person of colour ~~being a~~ ↑coming in as↓ part
¶31 l. 3   Would ~~one of those cruizers~~ ↑the cruizer↓ be
¶32 ll. 5–6   unusual ↑for any nation↓ to
    ll. 9–10   to ~~subjugate~~ ↑subject↓ such
    ll. 12–13   other ↑rational↓ construction.
¶35 l. 1   prevent ↑the migration of↓ free
¶36 l. 4   prohibit ↑the master of↓ a vessel

l. 5   from ~~sending~~ coming into port, ~~sending?~~ ↑& setting↓ only

¶40 ll. 1–2   sailors ↑landed,↓ were in fact ~~sailors~~ ↑negroes↓ or

¶43 l. 1   that ~~an off~~ no

Gallego, Richard & Company v. United States
Opinion
U.S. Circuit Court, Virginia, ca. 22 May 1820

This case began in the U.S. District Court at Norfolk in December 1812 with a libel against the cargo of the ship *John & Adam* for an alleged violation of the nonintercourse laws. Joseph Gallego (1758–1818), John Richard, and Michael B. Poitiaux (1771–1854), Richmond merchants trading under the firm of Gallego, Richard & Company, petitioned the court for relief under an 1813 law that directed the secretary of the treasury to remit fines and forfeitures incurred under the nonintercourse laws in certain cases. This act provided for such remission where goods, wares, and merchandise owned by United States citizens had been imported from Great Britain and shipped on vessels departing from Britain between 23 June and 15 September 1812. In this instance the imported cargo was jointly owned by the petitioners and John Gilliat, a London merchant, with whom Gallego, Richard & Company had established a trade relationship in 1811. The district court ordered the petition and a statement of the facts of the case to be referred to the secretary of the treasury, who in November 1813 remitted the forfeiture so far as related to the interest of Gallego, Richard & Company. On receiving this notification, the court dismissed the libel as to the company's interest but ordered the petitioners to submit all their correspondence with Gilliat concerning the purchase and shipment of the merchandise so that the court could ascertain the exact extent of the company's interest. Neither Richard nor Poitiaux, the surviving partners, complied with this order, and in May 1819 the district court issued an interlocutory decree, which became final in November 1819, forfeiting the entire cargo as the property of Gilliat or of some other British subjects. The petitioners then appealed to the circuit court, where Marshall announced his opinion at the May 1820 term (proceedings in U.S. District Court [copy], 10 Nov. 1819, Gallego, Richard & Co. v. U.S., U.S. Cir. Ct., Va., Ended Cases [Unrestored], 1820, Vi; *U.S. Statutes at Large*, II, 789–90; *Richmond Portraits*, 71–73, 160–61).

Galliego Richard & Co.
v   ⎫ appeal from the District court
The United States   ⎭

¶1   A complection unfavorable to the appellants has been given to this case by their refusing or failing when required to exhibit to the District court any testimony whatever establishing the extent of their interest in the cargo of the John & Adam. This conduct is well calculated to impress on the mind a suspicion that their interest was in truth less than the moity which they now claim. If, at the time when the sentence of condemnation was pronounced, this enquiry was open for the District court, the Judge had certainly a right to expect, & it was his duty to require, full satisfaction upon it. If that subject was closed, then no enquiry ought to have been instituted; & the sentence of condemnation ought to have extended to that part of the cargo only which was not comprehended in the remission of forfeiture made by the secretary of the Treasury in pursuance of the act of Congress of the 2d. of Jany. 1813, the extent of which, in that view of the case, must be ascertained by the instrument itself.[1]

Upon examining the act of Congress, I felt much doubt whether it ¶2 applied to any case of a joint interest between American citizens & British subjects. The case described in the act is "goods wares & merchandise *owned by a citizen or citizens of the United States*"; not "goods &c. owned in whole or in part by a citizen." The act then speaks of the time of shipment & adds "and the person or persons interested in such goods &c or concerned in the importation thereof have incurred any fine" &c "on such person or persons petitioning for releif" &c "in all such cases wherein it shall be proved to his satisfaction *that said goods wares & merchandize*, at the time of their shipment, were bona fide *owned by a citizen or citizens of the United States*" &c ["]the secretary of the Treasury is directed to remit" &c. It might well be doubted whether the power of the secretary of the Treasury is extended to any case where the specific articles are not wholly owned by citizens of the United States. But the language of the act is not free from ambiguity, & it refers to an act passed the 3d. of March 1797 which in express terms applies to any interest the petitioner may have.[2] In construing the act no reason can be perceived for distinguishing between the interest of an American citizen when joint & when sole; & it is an act intended for the protection of the citizen which ought to be construed liberally so as to effect that intention. In addition to these considerations, the act has already been construed by the district Judges, I presume from the proceedings in this case, & certainly by the Treasury department, to embrace cases where American citizens are jointly concerned with British subjects. The construction put on the act by the department entrusted with the power of remission ought to be respected by the court. I shall therefore consider it as comprehending this case.

I am now to enquire whether the secretary of the Treasury has remit- ¶3 ted any ascertained portion of the cargo of the John & Adam, or has remitted an undefined interest in that cargo, leaving it to the court to ascertain its extent.

The act of 1813 directs the same proceedings in court on the petition ¶4 of the party applying for releif as are directed by the act of 1797. That act directs the District Judge to enquire into the circumstances of the case, & to "cause the facts which shall appear upon such enquiry, to be stated &

annexed to the petition, & direct their transmission to the secretary of the Treasury of the United States, who shall thereupon have power to mitigage [*sic*] or remit &c."

¶5   By this act the court is to put the secretary in possessio⟨n⟩ of all the facts of the case with the petition before he exercises the power given him by Congress.

¶6   The act of 1813 enacts, "and on the facts being shown on enquiry had by said Judge or court, stated & transmitted as by said act (the act of 97) is required; in all such cases wherein it shall be proved to his satisfaction" &c "The secretary of the Treasury is directed to remit all fines penalties & forfeitures that may have been incurred" on certain conditions in the act expressed, & to direct the prosecutions to cease.

¶7   The legislature seems to have intended that the act of the Treasury department should be final & conclusive & that all the facts should be placed before him before he performs that act. Those articles, the forfeiture of which is remitted, are of course restored to the proprietor. The prosecutions, if instituted, are to cease. It would seem to be a part, & an essential part, of the duty of the secretary, to define the articles on which this remission operates; or if it be only on a certain interest in those articles, to define that interest. If the statement of facts made by the court did not enable the Secretary to ascertain this interest, it would seem to be his duty to require a more full statement; & the case should go back to him for a final decision. It seems to be a part of his duty not only to say that the forfeiture shall be remitted, but to define with precision the objects on which this remission shall operate.

¶8   If this view of the law be correct, it would seem to follow that the remission granted by the Secretary of the Treasury ought to be construed to dispose entirely of the subject if it can fairly be so construed. Let the remission itself, with the papers to which it refers, be considered, for the purpose of determining whether it ascertains its own extent or refers that point to the court.

¶9   The petition states an application on the part of the petitioners to John Gilliat a merchant of London to ship goods some on the sole account of the petitioners, & some on joint account; & that, in consequence of this application, the cargo in question was purchased, which the pe[ti]tion avers to have been the sole property of Gilliat & the petitioners.[3] The statement transmitted by the Judge with this petition asserts "that the said goods wares & merchandize at the time of their shipment at the port of London in the Kingdom of Great Britain were the joint property of the said Joseph Gallego John Richard Michael Benedict Poiteaux & John Gilliat."[4] The secretary of the Treasury after reciting this petition & statement says, "And whereas it has been proved to my satisfaction," (How proved? Certainly by the statement. The instrument refers to no other testimony, nor does the law authorise him to receive any other.) "that part of the goods &c were bona fide owned by citizens of the United

States" &c "Now therefore Know ye that I &c do hereby remit to the petitioners aforesaid all the fines &c incurred as aforesaid on their several shares thereof or interest therein upon the costs & charges" &c being paid; "And do also direct the prosecution or prosecutions if any shall have been instituted for the recovery thereof to cease on payment of the costs["] &c.[5]

There is nothing in the statement of facts which shows any right in the ¶10 petitioners to any separate part of the cargo. The words therefore "their several shares thereof, or interest therein" must refer to their undivided shares or interest, not to any distinct property they might possibly hold in severalty. The remission is to take place, not on their ascertainment of their interest or shares, but on their paying charges & duties; and the prosecutions are to be discontinued, not on their proving to the court the extent of their interest, but on paying the costs. These circumstances as well as the view I have taken of the duty of the Treasury department lead to the opinion that the secretary considered the extent of the interest of the petitioners as already established & did not mean to institute a new enquiry into that subject. It was considered as established in the statement submitted to him by the court which represents them to have been jointly concerned with Gilliat.

Suppose the law to have required that the prosecutions should have ¶11 been instituted in one court, & the petition & statement to have passed through another. Could the court in which the prosecutions were depending have proceeded to an investigation of the extent of the interest of the petitioners after receiving this instrument of dismission from the treasury department. I believe it could not if by any construction the statement of the district court & the act of remission could be understood to define the extent of the remission. The whole subject passes, it is true through the same court; but that court is to exercise different powers in different stages of the proceeding. All which relates to the property is to be completed before the statement is submitted to the secretary of the Treasury. The Secretary acts on that statement & his act cannot be revised by the court.

Sentence reversed as to a moity.[6]   ¶12

AD, Marshall Judicial Opinions, PPAmP; printed, John W. Brockenbrough, *Reports of Cases Decided by the Honourable John Marshall . . .* , I (Philadelphia, 1837), 442–46. For JM's deletions and interlineations, see Textual Notes below.

1. *U.S. Statutes at Large*, II, 789–90.

2. Ibid., I, 506–7.

3. Proceedings in U.S. District Court (copy), 10 Nov. 1819, 4–6, Gallego, Richard & Co. v. U.S.

4. Ibid., 7–8, Gallego, Richard & Co. v. U.S.

5. Ibid., 8–10, Gallego, Richard & Co. v. U.S. The remission was granted by Acting Secretary of the Treasury J. William Jones.

6. The decree of reversal declared that the forfeiture should extend only to Gilliat's

interest, which was one-half (or a moiety) of the amount of the goods (draft of decree, Gallego, Richard & Co. v. U.S.).

Textual Notes

¶ 1 l. 2	failing ↑when required↓ to
ll. 4–5	This ~~failure~~ conduct ~~cannot fail~~ ↑is well calculated↓ to impress on the mind a ~~beleif~~ suspicion
l. 7	was ~~rendered~~ ↑pronounced,↓ this
¶ 2 ll. 16–17	In ~~addition~~ construing
¶ 4 l. 3	directs ~~that~~ the District Judge ~~shall cause~~ ↑to enquire into↓ the circumstances
¶ 6 l. 2	said ↑act↓ (the
¶ 8 l. 1	be ~~at al~~ correct,
l. 3	Let ~~the~~ the
l. 5	it ~~de~~ ascertains
¶ 9 l. 2	on ↑the sole↓ account
l. 16	aforesaid ↑all the fines &c↓ incurred
¶10 ll. 1–2	right [*erasure*] ↑in the petitioners↓ to
¶11 ll. 1–2	have ↑been↓ instituted in [*erasure*] ↑one↓ court,
l. 10	proceeding. [*erasure*] ↑All↓ which

United States v. Smith

Sentence

U.S. Circuit Court, Virginia, 29 May 1820

Yesterday, the Federal Court took up the case of the crew of the *Irresistable*, who were last year found guilty of piracy.[1] Mr. Stevenson, on behalf of the assigned counsel of the prisoners, stated to the Judge that he had examined the exception which he had intended to bring before the Court, but was satisfied upon deliberate investigation of it, that there was nothing in it.[2] He should therefore decline bringing the exception before the court. The Chief Justice then observed that he was aware of the point that the Counsel would have presented; that he had examined it both upon principle and authority; and he was satisfied, as far as the course of his own mind would permit him to decide, that the Counsel were correct in their decision. (It was, as we understand, that the prisoners were about being sentenced under a law, which would have expired by its own limitation, ere this time, though it has been continued by an act of the last Congress.)[3]

The Judge then ordered the prisoners to be brought to the bar; and asked them, one by one, whether they had any thing to say, why the sentence of the law should not be pronounced upon them. Some of them remained silent; most of them, however, gave a short narrative of the part which they had had in the acts of the Irresistable, contending, some that they had been *forced* to join in the enterprize; others, that they had been deceived into the belief of the vessel's being a lawfully commissioned privateer; and others, that they had got clear of the business as soon as they could. (One of them stated, that Black, a strong witness against them, had afterwards confessed he had given false testimony.[4] Mr. Stevenson suggested whether this was not a good cause for a new trial. But the Chief Justice stated that Black was only one out of three witnesses, and he the least creditable of the three, who had testified to the material facts of the case, and putting him aside, that there was sufficient evidence to support the verdict of the Jury.)

The Judge then addressed the prisoners; he told them that they had had a fair trial before an enlightened and impartial Jury, who had found the verdict of GUILTY, subject to a legal question, which had been decided against them — and he now therefore stood bound to pronounce the sentence of the law. He charged them to improve the short time which was still allowed them, and throw themselves upon the mercy of Him, who alone had power to *forgive their sins* — he then concluded by pronouncing their sentence, and fixing, Monday, the 19th June, as the day of execution.[5]

Printed, *Enquirer* (Richmond, Va.), 30 May 1820.

1. The sixteen crewmen of the *Irresistible* convicted of piracy were Thomas Smith, Samuel Poole, Bailey Durfey, William Chapels, Daniel Phillips, James Thomas, Daniel Levingston, Luke Jackson, Stephen Sydney, Peter Nelson, Isaac Sales, Peter Johnston, John Green, Henry Anry, John Fuller, and Francis Oglesby. The newspaper printed the names of Jackson, Sales, and Johnston in italics and noted that they were "men of colour" (ibid., 30 May 1820).

2. Andrew Stevenson (1784–1857), a lawyer and state legislator, was elected to Congress in 1821. He was Speaker of the House of Representatives from 1827 to 1834 and served as minister to Great Britain from 1836 to 1841. He then retired to his Albemarle County estate and engaged in agricultural pursuits.

3. Congress enacted a law to punish piracy on 3 Mar. 1819, which was to be "in force until the end of the next session of Congress." The "next session" was the first session of the Sixteenth Congress. On 15 May 1820, the last day of the session, Congress continued this act in force "as to all crimes made punishable by the same, and heretofore committed, in all respects as fully as if the duration of the said section had been without limitation" (*U.S. Statutes at Large*, III, 510, 513–14, 600).

4. James A. Black was a leader of the mutiny against the *Creola*, the privateer in which the crew of the *Irresistible* had originally signed up for service on behalf of the government of Buenos Aires. After the mutineers seized the *Irresistible*, Black (who held a lieutenant's commission in the navy of Buenos Aires) took command of the vessel and proceeded on a privateering cruise in the West Indies. At the ensuing trial at Richmond in July 1819, Black was granted immunity as a witness for the government (*PJM*, VIII, 370–72; Richmond *Enquirer*, 6 June 1820).

5. The fate of the convicted pirates aroused great sympathy in Richmond. A few days after sentence was pronounced, a writer in the *Enquirer* urged President Monroe to pardon them on account of various extenuating circumstances. Statements by Samuel Poole and James A. Black were included in this address. A draft of the formal sentence, in JM's hand, is in the case papers (Richmond *Enquirer*, 6 June 1820; U.S. v. Smith, U.S. Cir. Ct., Va., Ended Cases [Unrestored], 1820, Vi).

To John Quincy Adams

Sir   Richmond May 30th. 1820

I received yesterday morning the copy of the acts of the last Session of Congress which you transmitted to me.[1] Sentence was on the same day pronounced by the court on the prisoners who had been found guilty of Piracy. The District Attorney informs me that he will make you the communication respecting their cases which has been requested from him.[2] A similar request has been made to me by the Attorney General to whom I shall write to day. The communications made by the District Attorney & by my self will I presume be the same. With great respect I am Sir Your obedt

J MARSHALL

ALS, RG 59, DNA. Addressed to Adams in Washington and franked; postmarked Richmond, 30 May. Endorsed by Adams as "Recd 2nd."

1. See Adams to JM, 26 May 1820 (App. II, Cal.).
2. The U.S. Attorney for Virginia was Robert Stanard.

To William Wirt

Dear Sir   Richmond May 30th. 1820

Yesterday Sentence of death was pronounced on the prisoners who had been found guilty at the last term of Piracy. They are to be executed on monday the 19th. of June. As it was suggested that the Executive might suppose it most proper that they should be executed at Norfolk on board one of the national vessels, the place of execution is not mentioned in the sentence. The direction of the government will be obeyed by the officer. As it is not usual in Virginia for a warrant of execution to be signed by the Executive, it will be necessary to pardon or reprieve those who are not to be executed.

As the testimony against all the prisoners except Francis Oglevie was nearly the same I am unable to select & recommend for mercy any other than Oglevie & Samuel Pool a young man who I beleive has been trepanned. I requested the officers in whose custody they have been kept to give me a list of them in the order of their behavior placing last those who had behaved the worst. This list I now inclose you. Peter Johnson is a man of colour & Daniel Livingston a foreigner — I should think an Irishman. I am dear Sir with great respect & esteem, Your Obedt.

J MARSHALL

ALS, RG 59, DNA. Addressed to Wirt in Washington and franked; postmarked Richmond, 30 May. Endorsed by John Quincy Adams: "In Mr Wirts of 1 June 1820."

From William Wirt

Dear sir.   Washington June 1s 1820

I have the honor to acknowledge your letter of the 30th. Ulto. with its enclosure relative to the persons convicted of piracy at Richmond. The President will act immediately on the subject.[1] I am, &c &c &c &c

W WIRT

ALS (letterbook copy), RG 60, DNA; letterbook copy, RG 60, DNA. Inside address to JM.

1. Secretary of State Adams noted in his diary for 9 June: "It had been originally decided that two of those convicted at Richmond should also be executed; that if there were any circumstances of extenuation peculiarly favorable to any of them, they should be pardoned; if any circumstances of peculiar aggravation which could point to a selection of the two who should suffer, they should be attended to, and the rest should be reprieved for two months." Adams added that JM had mentioned Samuel G. Poole and Francis Oglesby as "meriting particular favor" but that he furnished no "ground for selecting any two of the other fourteen for execution." Since the execution was set for 19 June and President Monroe was then at his Albemarle County home, the secretary of state, after consulting with other cabinet members, directed that all fourteen should be reprieved. These reprieves, and the pardons for Poole and Oglesby, were issued under the president's name on 13 June (Charles Francis Adams, ed., *Memoirs of John Quincy Adams* . . . , V [Philadelphia, 1875], 146–47; Richmond *Enquirer*, 16 June 1820; Adams to Monroe, 15 June 1820, in Worthington C. Ford, ed., *Writings of John Quincy Adams*, VII [New York, 1917], 43–44).

To St. George Tucker

My dear Sir   Richmond June 2d. 1820

From an enquiry made yesterday by our friend Judge Coulter respecting your coming up to this term I fear I have been remiss in not answering your letter.[1] I beg you to excuse it & not to impute it to any inattention to what I understood to be your wish. I really considered your letter as giving me notice not to expect you unless there should be some cause which rendered your presence neccssary, & as requiring an answer only in case there was such a cause. There was no suit which would make it necessary that you should, at any inconvenience to yourself, come up to Richmond, & therefore I omitted to write. Indeed the lawyers had as usual been unprepared in every thing till I spoke of adjourning when they brought on so much business that my attention was wholly taken up with my official duty. I could however have stolen a minute to write to you had I not beleived that my silence would be understood as equivalent to information that the business of the court would not be delayed by your remaining in Williamsburg.

I congratulate you on ending your laborious term at Norfolk & am dear Sir with great respect & esteem, Your Obedt

J MARSHALL

ALS, Tucker-Coleman Papers, ViW. Addressed to Tucker in Williamsburg; postmarked Richmond, 2 June. Endorsed by Tucker.

1. Letter not found. John Coalter (1771–1838), a judge of Virginia's Court of Appeals, was Tucker's son-in-law (Mary Haldane Coleman, *St. George Tucker: Citizen of No Mean City* [Richmond, Va., 1938], 95–96, 133–34; Lyon Gardiner Tyler, ed., *Encyclopedia of Virginia Biography* [5 vols.; New York, 1915], II, 62–63).

Wilson v. LeRoy, Bayard & McEvers
Opinion
U.S. Circuit Court, Virginia, 7 June 1820

This suit began in the Virginia Superior Court of Chancery at Williamsburg in 1815. George Wilson of Norfolk, owner of the ship *Woodrop Sims*, sued the New York merchant firm of LeRoy, Bayard & McEvers, on a charter-party executed in January 1813. After obtaining an order in May 1816 for removing the suit to the U.S. Circuit Court, the defendants filed their joint answer in December 1817. Marshall's interlocutory decree of 7 June 1820 fully states the facts of the dispute (U.S. Cir. Ct., Va., Rec. Bk. XIV, 285–301; proceedings in Virginia Superior Court of Chancery, Williamsburg [copy], 30 May 1816; answer of Herman LeRoy, William Bayard, and Isaac Iselin [filed 4 Dec. 1817], Wilson v. LeRoy, Bayard & McEvers, U.S. Cir. Ct., Va., Ended Cases [Unrestored], 1821, Vi).

The bill states that, on the 21st of January, 1813,[1] the plaintiff, being owner of the Woodrop Simms, chartered her to James Dykes & Co. agents for Robert Pollard, who was agent for Le Roy, Bayard & M'Iver, to carry a load of flour from Norfolk, to Cadiz, for a freight of $3, per barrel, and five per cent primage. Having received a full cargo, 3407 barrels, he was about to despatch her, when on the 3d of March, he received a letter from Dykes & Co. forbidding him on the part of Le Roy, Bayard & M'Iver, from sending her to sea, under existing circumstances, (meaning the blockade,) and if he did, he would be held responsible. This letter was answered on the same day, expressing his readiness to prosecute his voyage, but that he should conform to the instructions he had received, holding Le Roy, Bayard & M'Iver, answerable for freight, &c. The blockade still continuing, the plaintiff on the 17th of June, 1813, wrote to Robert Pollard, proposing to change the voyage of the ship, on terms which he expressed. Robert Pollard rejected these terms, and insisted on the ship's going to sea so soon as she could sail, without violating the blockade. The blockade still continuing, and the warm weather commencing, the plaintiff was compelled to land the flour. The blockade appearing to be as lasting as the war, the flour was kept in store, and the plaintiff offered to abandon the voyage, on being paid a sum which he thought a reasonable compensation for his trouble and expense. On the 11th day of January, 1814, he received a letter from Moses Myers & Son, as agents, demanding the flour, and proffering their own responsibility, to comply with the decision of a court, as to the quantum of compensation. The flour was delivered, and this suit brought. It is prayed that a master may be decreed to report, what sum is due, and that it may be paid.

The charter-party lets the vessel, engages to receive the cargo to proceed with the first fair wind, and to deliver, &c. (excepting always "restraints of princes, and rulers,") for which the freighters covenant to pay, &c: the owner to allow 45 running days, for loading and delivery: and to receive demurrage at the rate of 10 guineas per day. The letter of 3d of March, 1813, forbidding Wilson to send the ship to sea, "under existing circumstances," was exhibited in evidence.

The answer admits the contract, &c., but alleges, that before she proceeded to sea, the blockade commenced. The ship was provided with a Sidmouth license, but the blockade embraced such vessels, as well as others, which fact became notorious, by the sending back of such vessels.[2]

Upon these facts, the plaintiff claims the full freight, as if the voyage had been performed, because he was stopped by the agent of the defendants, when ready to proceed upon it. If this be not allowed, then he claims compensation for his labour and expenses, performed and incurred at the request, and by the direction of the defendants.

The defendants insist, that they are responsible for nothing: that the plaintiff has not entitled himself to freight, because the voyage was not even commenced: and because, the whole contract was rendered so illegal, by the British license, with which the ship was furnished, that neither party can recover under it. The Woodrop Simms was furnished with a license, granted by the British government, then at war with the United States, to protect her in the voyage, mentioned in the charter-party. It is not denied, that if, by contract, Wilson had expressly stipulated, that the vessel should sail under the protection of such a license, the charter-party would have been vitiated, and the plaintiff would have been incapable of recovering on it. But it is insisted, that the fact of the license being on board, did not contaminate the charter-party, which contains no stipulation respecting it, nor annul the contract of which it is not an ingredient; the more especially as the voyage had not commenced, and the owner of the vessel might have parted with the license before she sailed.

This argument assumes a fact upon which its whole force depends. It is, that the license was not an ingredient in this contract. It is true, it is not mentioned in the charter-party. But if the consideration be contrary to law, it is not necessary that such illegal consideration should be expressed in the instrument. It may be pleaded and shown in evidence.

That this Sidmouth license did form an ingredient in the contract, that the plaintiff would have failed in his engagement, and, supposing the contract to sail under the protection of a license to be legal, would have been responsible in damages, had his vessel sailed without such protection during the war, is, I think, satisfactorily proved.

The contract itself, and the circumstances under which it was made, would go far in preparing us to believe the well and mutually understood views of the parties. I will not undertake to say what influence this mutual understanding might have been entitled to, had it not been communicated by the parties to each other; but if it was communicated, if the plaintiff declared, that his vessel was furnished with such a license, and the defendants chartered her on that declaration, the plaintiff was bound to make his vessel such as he described her to be, at least, so long as the license was material. I think the testimony shows, that these reciprocal communications were made by the parties. The defendants were about to make a voyage which required a British license, and a license for a particular port. They would, of course, inquire for a vessel furnished with such a license, and their inquiries would be answered, by any person disposed to make the contract, that his vessel was so furnished.

The letter from Robert Pollard to James Dykes & Co., authorizing the transaction on the part of his friends in New York, dated January 25th, 1813, contains these expressions: "I will thank you to charter a good vessel that will take from 3500 to 4000 barrels for Cadiz, if practicable, at a rate not higher than $2 75 a $3 per barrel, *having a Sidmouth license;* but if this cannot be done, to take up one for Lisbon, having such a license." In a letter, dated the 30th of the same month, James Dykes & Co., referring to a previous letter, say, "Dickson lately failed in exchanging his Sidmouth license to Lisbon, for one to Cadiz; in consequence, we have chartered the "Woodrop Simms," to load flour for you to Cadiz, at $3 per barrel, &c. Her Sidmouth is dated the middle of August, *which made her owner, Mr. George Wilson, very tenacious about time.*"[3]

The charter-party is dated the 31st of January, and is executed by James Dykes & Co., for Robert Pollard, agent for Le Roy, Bayard & M'Iver. Wilson, therefore, must be supposed cognizant of the authority, under which Dykes & Co. acted; and that authority contains the instruction to charter a vessel, furnished with a Sidmouth license, for Cadiz.

These papers, with the circumstances under which the contract was made, circumstances which, in themselves, are testimony never to be disregarded, prove, I think, that the possession of the Sidmouth license, was communicated, and was the inducement to the contract. If so, it has the same influence, as if it had been mentioned in the charter-party, so long as it was on board, and as it was material that it should be on board.

It has been insisted for the plaintiff, that, admitting the testimony to prove the fact, it is not alleged in the pleadings, and the proof must, therefore, be disregarded.

It is undoubtedly true, that a decree must be according to the allegations, as well as the proofs in the cause; but it is not necessary, that every circumstance attending a general fact, should be minutely alleged. In this case, the defendants say that the vessel was provided with a Sidmouth license, but do not aver, that this license formed an ingredient in the contract. If I should be of opinion, that the defendants could not, on this account, avail themselves of this defence, and that, in consequence thereof, the plaintiff would be allowed to claim the whole freight agreed on in the charter-party, so that the real justice of the cause would be defeated, I would certainly permit them to amend their answer on equitable terms; but not to amend it, so as to defeat the justice of the case. But I do not now think this part of the case material, because the blockade, having been imposed and declared, after the charter-party was signed, I do not think, the letter of the 3d of March, 1813, gave Wilson any right to claim freight, on the principle, that the voyage was arrested by Le Roy, Bayard & M'Iver. The blockade justified their interference. And as the voyage was never made, and the freight never earned, the owner of the vessel cannot recover on the charter-party, whether the parties to that instrument were bound by it or not. But as the view I take of the effect of the charter-party, has some influence on those circumstances, on which the decision of this Court may depend, I will observe, that in that contract there was nothing morally wrong. It is annulled by the law, upon principles of policy; and this operation of the law upon it, was unknown to the best informed among us, until the decision was made in the supreme court of the United States.[4] The parties, therefore, are, in fact, innocent. The contract was made with a belief that it was valid, and, therefore, I think, that although it could not have been enforced, it will not infect and vitiate any other contract between the parties. On the 3d of March, the defendants forbade the "Woodrop Simms" to proceed to sea, and afterwards, on the 19th of June, she was ordered by them, to continue ready to prosecute the voyage, so soon as the blockade should be removed, which, the letter says, was daily expected. The expenses, then, which were incurred, and the services which were rendered, perhaps, from the 3d of March, certainly from the 19th of June, were incurred and rendered by the direction of the defendants. Had the defendants, on understanding that the license would not protect the Woodrop Simms, from the effect of the blockade, allowed her owner to land his cargo, he might have employed his vessel, perhaps, in the bay navigation; certainly he would have been liberated from all the extra expenses of retaining his vessel in a state of preparation for sea.

While things were in this uncertain state, a proposition was made by Wilson, to vacate the contract, and abandon the voyage, on certain terms, which are stated generally, but as the proposition itself, is not before the Court, they cannot be particularly stated. This proposition was not accepted, but afterwards, on the 11th day of January, 1814, a proposition to abandon the voyage, was made on the part of the defendants, who demanded the delivery of the flour, offering to abide by the decision of a court. On this letter, the flour was delivered, and upon this part of the transaction, the claim of the plaintiff, in my opinion, rests.

He was in possession of the cargo, and had a right to hold that possession until he could perform his voyage. Whether he performed this voyage, with or without the license, he could have retained the flour at Cadiz, until the freight was paid. If the blockade should be of equal continuance with the war, he might at the expiration of the war, have made the voyage without the license; and I am not prepared to say, that in that case he might not have recovered the stipulated freight, even on the charter-party. In the mean time, the cargo might be, and, probably, would have been, totally lost to the defendants.

These advantages were given up with the flour. It could not have been expected by either party, that they should have been given up for nothing. The fair construction then of the contract, under which the flour was restored to the defendants, is, I think, that some equitable compensation should be made, with a view to all the circumstances of the case. This is rather a fit subject for the consideration of the parties themselves, or of friendly arbiters, than of a court. It is a case of hardship, and of loss on both. Each ought to concede something. If the court must decide it, I am not certain what will be my ultimate decision, but I shall now direct an account to be taken, of the expenses incurred by Wilson, from the date of the charter party, to the time of restoring the flour, stating separately those which were incurred, in taking the cargo on board, and prior to March 3d, 1813, those which were incurred between the 3d of March, and 19th of June, and those which were incurred after the 19th of June.

In addition to this report, I could wish to be informed how cases of this character have been generally settled by the parties.[5]

Printed, John W. Brockenbrough, *Reports of Cases Decided by the Honourable John Marshall . . .* , I (Philadelphia, 1837), 448–55.

1. The copies of the bill and the charter party in the record show the date to be 31 Jan. 1813, as JM himself states elsewhere in the opinion.

2. This was a license issued in Aug. 1812 by Viscount Sidmouth (Henry Addington [1757–1844]), then British secretary of state for the Home Department, permitting importation of the cargo into the port of Cádiz. An act of Congress of 2 Aug. 1813 prohibited the use of licenses or passports granted by the British government or its officers for protecting ships and cargoes on the high seas (U.S. Cir. Ct., Va., Rec. Bk. XIV, 308–10; *U.S. Statutes at Large*, III, 84–86).

3. For this correspondence, see U.S. Cir. Ct., Va., Rec. Bk. XIV, 304–6.

4. JM evidently referred to Patton v. Nicholson, 3 Wheat. 204, 207 and n. (1818). The reporter's note brings together several previous decisions by the Supreme Court on the subject of British licenses.

5. Pursuant to this interlocutory decree of 7 June 1820, Commissioner in Chancery John Cowper made a report on 3 Dec. 1820. Among the expenses stated in the account was $1,000 for a Sidmouth license. On 9 June 1821, JM issued a final decree, in which he disallowed the expense for the license and approved the remainder. The defendants were ordered to pay the plaintiff $2,816.95 (U.S. Cir. Ct., Va., Rec. Bk. XIV, 301–4; U.S. Cir. Ct., Va., Ord. Bk. XI, 131; decree [9 June 1821], Wilson v. LeRoy, Bayard & McEvers).

Anderson & Wilkins v. Tompkins
Opinion
U.S. Circuit Court, Virginia, 12 June 1820

The plaintiffs, partners in a British merchant firm, were creditors of Tompkins & Murray, a Virginia merchant firm. In May 1819, on the verge of bankruptcy, John Tompkins, one of the partners of the Virginia company, conveyed to trustees all the partnership effects as well as the separate property of the partners for the payment of company's debts. The deed of trust gave priority to certain named creditors and then to those other American and foreign creditors who stated their claims within a specified time period. Tompkins executed this deed without the knowledge or consent of his partner, Adam Murray, who had previously departed for Europe. In November 1819 Murray (then in England) executed a deed of trust conveying his share of the partnership property as well as all of his individual property for the benefit of certain creditors, including the plaintiffs. The purpose of the bill was to set aside Tompkins's deed and to establish the deed subsequently executed by Murray. According to Brockenbrough, Marshall gave his opinion and decree on 12 June 1820 (bill in chancery [filed in 1819], Anderson & Wilkins v. Tompkins, U.S. Cir. Ct., Va., Ended Cases [Unrestored], 1820, Vi).

Anderson & Wilkins

v

Tomkins & al

This suit is brought to establish a deed made by Adam Murray a partner ¶1 of the house of Tomkins & Murray, in Novr. 1819 while in England, conveying his moity of the property of that house to certain creditors of the firm.

On the 29th. of April 1819 Murray had embarked for England leaving ¶2 all the effects of the company in the hands of John Tomkins, the partner remaining in this country who continued for a short time to conduct the business of the concern. The pressure of their affairs was such that in May the house stopped payment & Tomkins for himself & his partner conveyed all the effects of the company & also the separate property of himself & partner to trustees for the payment first of certain creditors named in the deed, & then of those who should bring in their claims, the american creditors within sixty days, the foreign creditors within six months.

As the deed under which the plfs. claim can operate on that property ¶3 only which is not conveyed by the first, it will be proper first to enquire into the legal extent of the deed made by Tomkins.

That deed as has been already stated, purports to convey the whole ¶4 property of the concern & the private property of the partners.

That property consisted of the effects of the partnership for sale, of ¶5 real property, & of debts. I shall consider the deed in its application to each of these subjects.

¶6   1st. The goods in possession for sale.

¶7   The convenience of trade requires that each acting partner should have the entire controul & disposition of this subject. It would destroy co-partnerships entirely if the cooperation of all the partners were necessary to dispose of a yard of cloth. It is therefore laid down in all the books which treat on commercial transactions, that with respect to all articles to be sold for the benefit of the concern, each partner, tho the others be within reach, has, in the course of trade, an absolute right to dispose of the whole. "Each, says Watson, has a power to dispose of the whole of a part-nership effects."[1] This is a general rule, resulting from the nature of the estate & from the objects for which men associate in trade. They are joint tenents without the right of survivorship, they are seized *per mie & per tout*,[2] & they associate together for objects which require that the whole powers of the partnership should reside in each partner who is present & acting.

¶8   These general doctrines are universally admitted, & have not been controverted in this case; but it is contended that they do not authorize the deed made by Tomkins, because

   1st. This is not an act in the course of trade, but is a destruction of the whole subject, & a dissolution of the partnership.

   2d. It is a preference of particular creditors in making which Murray ought to be consulted.

   3d. It is by deed.

¶9   It will be readily conceded that a fraudulent sale whether made by deed or otherwise would pass nothing to a vendee concerned in the fraud. But, with this exception, I feel much difficulty in setting any other limits to the power of a partner in disposing of the effects of the company purchased for sale. He may sell a yard, a piece, a bale, or any number of bales. He may sell the whole of any article or of any number of articles. This power would certainly not be exercised in the presence of a partner without consulting him; & if it were so exercised slight circumstances would be sufficient to render the transaction suspicious, & perhaps, to fix on it the imputation of fraud. In this respect every case must depend on its own circumstances. But with respect to the power, in a case perfectly fair, I can percieve no ground on which it is to be questioned.

¶10   But this power it is said is limited to the course of trade. What is understood by the course of trade? Is it that which is actually done every day, or is it that which may be done whenever the occasion for doing it presents itself?

¶11   There are small traders who scarcely ever in practice sell a piece of cloth uncut, or a cask of spirits; they retail in small parcels. But may not a partner, in such a store sell a piece of cloth or a cask of spirits? His power extends to the sale of the article, & the course of trade does not limit him as to quantity. So with respect to larger concerns. By the course of trade is understood, dealing in an article in which the company is accustomed to deal; & dealing in that article for the company. Tomkins & Murray sold goods. A sale of goods was in the course of their trade & within the power of either partner. A fair sale then of all or of a part of the goods was within the power vested in a partner.

This reasoning applies with increased force when we consider the sit-   ¶12
uation of these partners. The one was on a voyage to Europe, the other in possession of all the partnership effects for sale. The absent partner could have no agency in the sale of them. He could not be consulted. He could not give an opinion. In leaving the country, he must have intended to confide all its business to the partner who remained for the purpose of transacting it.

Had this then been a sale for money, or on credit, no person I think   ¶13
could have doubted its obligation. I can percieve no distinction in law, in reason, or in justice, between such a sale & the transaction which has taken place. A merchant may rightfully sell to his creditor as well as for money. He may give goods in payment of a debt. If he may thus pay a small creditor, he may thus pay a large one. The *quantum* of debt, or of goods sold can not alter the right. Neither does it as I concieve affect the power that these goods were conveyed to trustees to be sold by them. The mode of sale must I think depend on circumstances. Should goods be delivered to trustees for sale without necessity, the transaction would be examined with scrutinizing eyes & might under some circumstances, be impeached. But if the necessity be apparent, if the act is justified by its motives, if the mode of sale be such as the circumstances require, I cannot say that the partner has exceeded his power.

This is denominated a destruction of the partnership subject, & a   ¶14
dissolution of the partnership. But how is it a destruction of the subject? Can this appellation be bestowed on the application of the joint property to the payment of the debts of the company? How is it a dissolution of the partnership? A partnership is an association to carry on business jointly. This association may be formed for the future before any goods are acquired & it may continue after the whole of a particular purchase has been sold. But either partner had a right to dissolve this partnership. The act however of applying the means of carrying on their business to the payment of their debts might suspend the operations of the company but did not dissolve the contract under which their operations were to be conducted.

2d It is said that Murray had a right to be consulted on giving a prefer-   ¶15
ence to creditors. It is true Murray had a right to be consulted. Had he been present he ought to have been consulted. The act ought to have been, & probably would have been a joint act. But Murray was not present. He had left the country & could not be consulted. He had by leaving the country confided everything which respected their joint business to Tomkins who was under the necessity of acting alone.

¶16   3d. It is said this transfer of property is by a deed, & that one partner has no right to bind another by deed. For this a case is cited from 7th D & E. which I beleive has never been questioned in England or in this country.[3]

¶17   I am not & never have been satisfied with the extent to which this doctrine has been carried. The particular point decided in it is certainly to be sustained on technical reasoning, & perhaps ought not to be controverted. I do not mean to controvert it. That was an action of covenant on a deed; & if the instrument was not the deed of the defendents, the action could not be sustained. It was decided not to be the deed of the defendents, & I submit to that decision. No action can be sustained against the partner who has not executed the instrument on the deed of his copartner. No action can be sustained against the partner which rests on the validity of such a deed as to the person who has not executed it. This principle is settled. But I cannot admit its application in a case where the property may be transferred by delivery under a parol contract. Where the right of sale is absolute, & the change of property is consummated by delivery I cannot admit that a sale so consummated is annulled by the circumstances that it is attested by, or that the trusts under which it is made are described in, a deed. No case goes thus far; and I think such a decision could not be sustained on principle.

¶18   The power of applying all the goods on hand for sale, to the payment of the partnership debts is I think a power created by the partnership, & the exercise of it must be regulated by circumstances. In extraordinary cases, an extraordinary use of power must be made. What is called the course of trade, is not confined to the most usual way of doing business in the usual state of things. In the absence of one of the partners, in a case of admitted & urgent necessity, the power to sell may be exercised by the partner who is present & who must act alone, in such manner as the case requires, provided it be exercised fairly. In this case, the fairness of the transaction is not impeached; & certainly upon its face, it is not impeachable.

¶19   So far then as respects the partnership effects which were delivered, I have never from the first opening of this cause entertained a moments doubt.

¶20   2d. The next subject to be considered is the real property comprehended in this deed.

¶21   Real property whether held in partnership or otherwise can be conveyed only by deed executed in the manner prescribed by statute. This deed can convey no more title at law than is in the person who executes it. Property conveyed to a firm, or to partners in trust for a firm is held by them as tenants in common, & neither party can convey more than his undivided interest.

¶22   In this case where the legal estate was in Tomkins, the whole property passes at law by his deed. Where the legal estate was in Murray, the whole property passes at law by his deed. Where the legal estate was in Tomkins & Murray the property passes in moities by their several deeds. I do not think the superior equity of either party is such as to controul the legal estate, or the disposition made by law of the subject.

Where the legal estate is in trustees for the use of Tomkins & Murray ¶23 the title does not pass at law by either deed; & I have greatly doubted whether the first deed ought not to be preferred. I have however come to the opinion that this trust ought to follow the nature of the estate at law & where the trustees have not conveyed before the subsequent deed was executed that the title to this property likewise should pass in moities.

The last subject to be considered is the debts due to the partnership. ¶24 The right of one of the partners to assign debts which are assignable at law, is admitted provided that assignment be made in the usual way. The assignment then of these debts is as valid a transaction as the sale of the goods on hand if it be not contaminated by the seal. I should not suppose, on the principle settled in 7 D & E. that an action could be maintain⟨ed⟩ on this assignment. But I am not satisfied that it does not pass the assignable paper which the partner had a legal right to assign. I rather think it does.

A question of more difficulty respects the book debts. This is a part of ¶25 the subject on which I have entertained & still entertain great doubts. The deed does not pass these debts at law. They are not assignable at law, but they are assignabl⟨e⟩ in equity & a court of equity sustains their assignment. At law the assignment is only a power to collect & appropriate; and that power is revocable. So far as collections were made under it before it was revoked I can have no doubt that the money collected was in the trustees. With respect to debts not collected I have felt great doubts. I considered the power to collect as a contract which could not be enforced at law. But as Mr. Murray could not convey this property at law, & could only convey it in equity I have supposed that the prior equity must be sustained & that these debts also pass by the deed of Tomkins.

The opinion of the court then is that the plaintiffs have a right to a ¶26 decree for a sale of all the real property contained in the deed made by Adam Murray, the legal title to which was in Adam Murray, & to a moity of the real property the title to which was in Tomkins & Murray, or in trustees for their benefit; & that the residue of the property passes to the trustees in the deed executed by John Tomkins.[4]

AD, Marshall Judicial Opinions, PPAmP; printed, John W. Brockenbrough, *Reports of Cases Decided by the Honourable John Marshall . . .*, I (Philadelphia, 1837), 458–65. For JM's deletions and interlineations, see Textual Notes below.

1. William Watson, *A Treatise of the Law of Partnership* (1st Am. ed.; Philadelphia, 1807; S #14165), 91. JM paraphrased this sentence in Watson: "But with regard to all effects contributed, manufactured, or purchased, to be sold for the benefit of the partners, each partner in the course of trade has an absolute right to dispose of the whole."

2. Law French for "by the half and by the whole," describing the manner in which joint tenants hold the joint estate. For purposes of tenure and survivorship, each is holder of the whole; for purposes of alienation each has only his own share, presumed in law to be equal.

3. Harrison v. Jackson, 7 T.R. 207, 101 Eng. Rep. 935 (K.B., 1797). "D & E" stands for the editors (Durnford and East) of *Term Reports*.

4. The U.S. brought a separate suit against Tompkins and others, and Tompkins's trustees filed a cross bill against Anderson & Wilkins and others. The court's decree embraced all three suits (draft of decree, Anderson & Wilkins v. Tompkins).

Textual Notes

¶ 1	ll. 3–4	of [*erasure*] ↑the↓ firm.
¶ 3	l. 2	not ~~taken~~ conveyed
¶ 4	l. 1	deed ↑as has been already stated, [*erasure*] purports↓ to
¶ 6	l. 1beg.	~~It is admitted that~~ 1st. The goods in ~~the~~ possession
¶ 7	l. 3	partners ~~was~~ ↑were↓ necessary
	l. 5	on ~~p~~ ↑commercial↓ transactions,
	l. 5	articles [*erasure*] ↑to↓ be
¶ 9	l. 1	sale ~~would~~ whether
	l. 3	difficulty [*erasure*] ↑in↓ setting
	l. 5	bale, ~~a package~~ or any number of ~~packages~~ bales.
¶10	l. 3	done ~~every day~~ whenever
¶13	ll. 1–2	person ↑I think↓ could
	l. 7	the ~~ease~~ ↑right.↓ Neither
¶15	l. 2	true ~~murray~~ ↑Murray↓ had
¶17	ll. 7–8	sustained ↑against the partner↓ which
	l. 15	attested ↑by,↓ or
	l. 16	No ↑case↓ goes
¶18	ll. 3–4	In ~~the absence of one of the partners, in a case of admitted necessity~~ ↑extraordinary cases, an extraordinary use of power must be made. What↓ is
¶21	l. 1	whether ~~it belong~~ ↑held in partnership↓ or
¶22	l. 1	estate ~~is~~ ↑was↓ in
	l. 2	passes ~~by~~ ↑at↓ law
	l. 4	Murray ~~or in trustees for the use of Tomkins~~ the
	l. 4	deeds. ~~Where the~~ I
	l. 5	to ~~change~~ ↑controul↓ the
¶23	l. 2	the ~~estate~~ ↑title↓ does
¶24	ll. 1–2	to ↑the partnership.↓ The
¶25	ll. 1–2	a ↑part of the↓ subject
	l. 11	could [*erasure*] ↑only↓ convey
¶26	ll. 1–2	right to ~~obtain~~ a decree for ↑a sale of↓ all the ↑real↓ property
	l. 4	title [*erasure*] ↑to↓ which
	l. 5	that ~~with r~~ ↑the↓ residue

To Bushrod Washington

My dear Sir   Richmond June 26th. 1820

I received yesterday yours of the 26th.[1] I shall deeply regret the loss of any of the books or papers of Genl. Washington. I flatter myself however that you have all which do not remain with me. The last were sent by a

coal vessel of Alexandria & the impression on my mind is that you men-
tiond receiving them. It was to enable you to copy the correspondence
between Genls Washington & La Fayette.[2]

I have employed a person to copy the letters anterior to the war of our
revolution. I wish you would say what space they ought to occupy & what
number of volumes it is your desire to publish altogether. As soon as this is
accomplished I shall copy the military letters in my possession. The military letters are in books lettered **B**. Those to Congress & its members in
books marked **A**. I think those to distinguished foreigners are in books lettered **A. B.** or **C**. I forget which. I hope you will find that you have them all.

I shall also proceed to copy the letters between the close of the war &
the adoption of the constitution. I have retained no others. I shall be glad
to hear from you after making a full examination. Till then I shall continue to hope that none have miscarried. Yours truely

J MARSHALL

ALS, Marshall Papers, ViW. Addressed to Washington at Mount Vernon; postmarked
Richmond, 26 June. Endorsed by Washington.

1. JM evidently misdated Washington's letter, which has not been found.

2. JM and Bushrod Washington were working on an edition of General Washington's
correspondence (*PJM*, VIII, 82–83 and n. 3).

Memorandum concerning Leeds Manor

June 29th. 1820

Accounts between John Ambler & W Marshall respecting a purchase
made of part of the Manor of Leeds from J M M.[1]

Purchase money due 21st. Septr. 1799. —		£ 2762.19.5
	m d	
Int. to 21st. Jany. 1800 at 5 percent being	3.25	44. 2.4½
		£ 2807. 1.9½
Then paid John Hopkins		740.
		£ 2067. 1.9½
	y m	
Int. from the 15th.		
Jany. 1800 to the 1st. Jany. 1806 —	6. 4½	660.10.4
		£ 2727.12.3½
Deduct rents up to the 20th. Septr. 1806.		
supposed to be		350
		£ 2377.12.3½
Then sold a moity to W M[2] for	£2500	
£ 2500 with int at 5 per cent	y. m.	3332.10
from 21. Septr.	99. 6. 8. 832	
Over paid by Colo. Ambler —		£ 954.17.8½

He has since paid
     1807. March 12. to R. C.[3]   100
     1813. Septr. 30th. do.   1000
        Decr. 28th. do.   1167.25
                                 $ 2267.25 — in pounds £680.3.6

Colo. Ambler according to the above calculation had over paid on the 21st. May 1806 £954.17.8½ which remains on int. at 5 percent. He has since paid to Mr. Colston on the order of my brother James at the several dates mentioned above the sum above stated of £680.3.6 which also go on int. from the dates of payment. The receipts of rents since 1806 are to be adjusted between Colo. Ambler & the estate of my brother William.

On the 11th. of Aug. 1807 my brother gave a receipt to Colo. Ambler for his bond to Colo. Macon for £2192.9.8 payable with interest from the 3d. of July 1807 of which Colo. Macon had recd. £15 at the date. This bond is not calculated in the above account. By a decree of the court of appeals in the suit Ambler v Macon it is to be repaid to Mr. Ambler by Colo. Macon.[4] And Colo. Ambler is entitled out of it to the sum he has overpaid of the joint purchase. The residue is to be paid to my brother.[5]

                                                    J MARSHALL

ADS, Private Collection. Endorsed: "Mr. John Marshalls / Statement June 29. 1820."

1. John Ambler was a member of the syndicate that had contracted to purchase Leeds Manor. The transactions discussed in this document concern a contract between James M. Marshall and Ambler executed in 1798 or 1799 for one undivided sixteenth part of Leeds Manor, or ten thousand acres, for £5,000. This contract proved to be a source of contention, as James Marshall had difficulty collecting the money from Ambler. Marshall in turn counted on this money to pay Denny Fairfax (and afterwards, Philip Martin) and thereby obtain title to Leeds. Ambler eventually obtained two deeds covering his share of the manor, the first in 1815 for four thousand acres in Fauquier, the second in 1821 for six thousand acres in Frederick (PJM, II, 145; VII, 215; James M. Marshall to John Ambler, 5 Apr. 1806, ViU; Marshall to Ambler, 23 Oct. 1815, PP; Fauquier County Deed Book No. 21, 230–33; Frederick County Deed Book No. 44, 246–48).

2. William Marshall

3. Rawleigh Colston was also a partner in the purchase of Leeds. In a letter to Ambler in Oct. 1815, James Marshall included an extract of a letter from Colston to Marshall in which the former recounted his various efforts to collect the money from Ambler (James M. Marshall to John Ambler, 23 Oct. 1815, PP).

4. Ambler v. Macon was originally decided by the Virginia Court of Appeals in Oct. 1803 on appeal from a High Court of Chancery decree of 1800. The parties were the executors, administrators, and children of Edward Ambler and his wife Mary. William H. Macon brought the suit in the chancery court as administrator of his wife Sarah Macon (daughter of Edward Ambler) and of Mary Ambler (widow of Edward Ambler) against Edward Ambler's executors and John Ambler, the only surviving son of Edward Ambler. The Court of Appeals remanded the case to the Richmond Superior Court of Chancery for further proceedings and a final decree. That court decreed that John Ambler should pay Macon £3,860. Ambler applied for a bill of review, but the court in Mar. 1807 denied his motion. He then appealed to the Court of Appeals. The appeal was argued in 1817 and 1819 and finally decided in June 1820. In consequence of this decree Macon "had to return a very

large sum" that Ambler had paid to him (4 Call 605–26; Va. Ct. App. Ord. Bk. IX, 19, 260, 261, 501).

5. JM apparently drew this memorandum in his capacity as William Marshall's administrator.

To [Agatha Marshall]

My dear Sister   Richmond July 1st. 1820

On receiving the melancholy inteligence communicated in your letter[1] I immediately went to Petersburg to perform the painful task of communicating it to our sister Taylor.[2] A painful task indeed it was. I attempted to prepare her for the event, & to break it gradually to her, but the instant I mentioned Kentucky, & an epidemic, the whole dreadful truth flashed upon her at once, & I was under the necessity of telling her that her son was dead.[3] Afflicting as is, under any circumstances the loss of a child, deeply as I have felt it, & often as I have witnessed its effect on others, I could scarcely anticipate the depth of woe, the intensity of grief which was inflicted by this communication. The sudden & unexpected death of an only son, to a widowed mother who had been long dwelling with fond delight on the prospect of his future worth, is a blow which it is scarcely possible for fortitude to support, & which seems to blast every hope of happiness & to turn the future into one dark & gloomy waste.

I staid with her till the next day & then left with her your letter & that of my brother. As she becomes less agitated it will sooth⟨e⟩ her wounded mind to read the warm expressions of feeling for herself, & of affection & esteem for her lost son, which both letters contain.

Sincerely do I condole with you on the loss you have sustained.[4] My sister after some time enquired concerning the family & shuddered midst her own griefs at yours. I am my dear Sister, Your affectionate brother

J Marsha⟨ll⟩

ALS, NcU, Southern Historical Collection, Louis Marshall Papers. Enclosed in JM to Louis Marshall, 1 July 1820.

1. Letter not found. Agatha Marshall was the wife of JM's brother Louis.
2. Jane Marshall Taylor.
3. Thomas M. Taylor.
4. JM may have been referring to the death of an infant child of Louis and Agatha Marshall.

To Louis Marshall

My dear brother   Richmond July 1st. 1820

I returned two days past from Petersburg on a visit to our sister. She received the afflicting communication I went to make, as I feared she would. The shock overpowered her faculties, & she was for some time in a state of distraction. I stayed with her till the next day. The paroxysm of course had passed away, & I left her in deep dejection. Time will sooth⟨e⟩ her mind, but it will be very long, if ever, before it recovers its serenity & cheerfulness.

I wish my dear brother to know whether any thing, & if any thing, how much remains due for the board tuition & other expenses of our Nephew. It shall be immediately remitted. Mr. Leigh some time past enclosed you $200.[1] Will you either to him or me, acknowledge the receipt of it? A voucher is necessary for him in the settlement of his accounts as exr. Doctor Duk⟨e⟩ was to receive a sum of money from Mr. H. Marshall for my sister some time past.[2] We requested him to pay it to you. If these directions have not been complied with, & I suppose they have not, they will be countermanded, & a direct & immediate remittance will be made of whatever is due. My sister seems to experience what seems to me to be very unnatural treatment from some of her relations in Kentucky; but I suppose I am not well informed respecting those circumstances which certainly wound her feelings, & appear to me to be unjust & injurious.

Farewell my dear brother. I am with the best wishes for you & yours, Your affectionate

J MARSHA⟨LL⟩

ALS, NcU, Southern Historical Collection, Louis Marshall Papers. Addressed to Louis Marshall at Buckpond, Woodford County, Ky.

1. Benjamin Watkins Leigh and JM were coexecutors of George Keith Taylor.
2. Basil Duke and Humphrey Marshall (*PJM*, VIII, 315–16, 364).

From Walter L. Fontaine

Dear Sir,   Richmd. July 21st. 1820

Enclosed you will receve. by the hands of Mesrs. Fox's the sum of seven hundred dollars which you will please put to my credit, $550 in money & a recpt. from Isham Scruggs for $150 paid him according to your Letter to him some time past authorising him to call on me for that sum.[1] Your obedt. Servt.

W L FONTAINE

ALS (advertised for sale by Joseph Rubinfine, West Palm Beach, Fla., 1994). Addressed to Marshall in Richmond; noted as conveyed by "Mesrs. Fox's." Below signature and centered on page JM wrote: "Recd. J Marshall / July 25th. 1820." Endorsed by Fontaine.

1. Fontaine lived near New Canton, in the northeast corner of Buckingham County. This transaction was a partial payment for 421 acres of land on Randolph Creek in that county, which JM sold to Fontaine in 1816 for $4,215. JM took a mortgage from Fontaine, by which the latter was to make payments in three installments on 1 Mar. 1817, 1 Mar. 1818, and

1 Mar. 1819. The $700 received at this time was applied to the second of Fontaine's three bonds given to JM. Fontaine had previously made payments of $1,060 in Apr. 1817 and $1,050 in June 1818. Final payment in discharge of the mortgage took place on 1 July 1825. This property is probably the same as that on which the "Marshall Place," described as being "three miles east of Gold Hill," is situated (mortgage deed [in JM's hand], 18 June 1816 [advertised for sale by John Reznikoff, University Archives, Stamford, Conn., 1994]; account current [in Fontaine's hand], 1817–23 [owned by C. J. and Mary Ann Elder, Charlottesville, Va., 1990]; Margaret A. Pennington and Lorne S. Scott, *The Courthouse Burned: Buckingham County* [Waynesboro, Va., 1977], 127). JM corresponded further with Fontaine in the fall of 1821. For earlier references to JM's Buckingham land, see *PJM*, VI, 42, 44–45, 150–52, 198, 253–54.

To John C. Calhoun

Dear Sir   Richmond Aug. 1st. 1820

This will be presented to you by Mr. Harvie my near connexion and my friend.[1] He visits Washington for the purpose of making some propositions to the department over whi⟨ch⟩ you preside respecting a contract to furnish arms. It is a subject of which I am totally ignorant; & I take the liberty to write, only to inform you, that he is the proprietor of extensive iron works on James River in the neighborhood of this place, & that I beleive you may depend on his performing whatever engagements he may make.[2] With great respect, I am dear Sir your Obedt

J MARSHALL

ALS, RG 156, DNA. Addressed to Calhoun in Washington and noted as conveyed by "Mr. Harvie." Endorsed by Calhoun.

1. Jaquelin B. Harvie, JM's son-in-law.
2. JM's letter is part of a file of letters from prominent Virginians endorsing Harvie's proposal to manufacture small arms for the War Department. The proposal evidently did not come to fruition (Harvie to Calhoun, 10 Sept., 23 Oct., 19 Dec. 1820, RG 156, DNA).

To George A. Ward

Dear Sir   Richmond Septr. 2d. 1820

On my return to this place from a short excursion to our mountain country I had the pleasure of receiving your letter of the 15th. of August[1] transmitting copies of two letters written by Mr. Fairfax, & a salem paper containing extracts from the same letters with some commentaries on them.[2]

I thank you very sincerely for this communication.

The life of Washington was composed too precipitately, & it has therefore always been my wish to revise it deliberately, & to publish a corrected edition. Should I ever accomplish this wish, I shall certainly avail myself of every material incident of his life which may be communicated, & of which I was not previously informed. I cannot however beleive that the Major Washington mentioned in the letter of the 22d. of Feby. 49 was the same gentleman who afterwards commanded our armies & was so instrumental in establishing our independence. The services for which Major Washington sought compensation, for which he visited London, & for which he is said to have been placed on the half pay establishment, must have been performed during the war which was terminated in 1748 by the treaty of Aix la Chapelle. General Washington was but sixteen at the termination of this war, & was too young to have taken part in it, or to have sustained the losses to which the letter alludes. There is not only no account in the family of his having been engaged in this war, but there is an account of his having applied for a Midshipmans warrant & of his having been restrained from accepting it by the interference of his mother. There is not a trace of his having ever been on the half pay establishment, & several of his letters written during the war which commenced in 1755, contain unequivocal evidence of his never having been on the regular establishment, & of his never having received any adequate compensation for his military service. There are many other circumstances of his early life which show that this letter cannot refer to him. I am however extremely obliged to you for the polite & friendly attention manifested in this communication & shall make a point of enquiring farther into the subject. With great respect I am Sir, your obliged & obedt. servant

J MARSHALL

ALS, ICN. Addressed to Ward in Salem, Mass.; postmarked Richmond, 2 Sept. Endorsement in unknown hand below address: "Judge Marshall died July 1835."

1. Letter not found. The addressee was evidently George Atkinson Ward (1793–1864), who later published an edition of the journal and letters of Samuel Curwen, an American loyalist (*Journal and Letters of the Late Samuel Curwen* [1842; New York, 1973 reprint]).

2. The *Salem Gazette* (Mass.), 15 Aug. 1820, printed an article headed "General Washington," contributed by "W" (Ward?), containing extracts of two letters from William Fairfax to his relatives in Salem. A prefatory note explained that the original letters had long been in the possession of Fairfax's niece, who lived in Salem and had turned them over to "W."

To Bushrod Washington

My dear Sir   Richmond Septr. 2d. 1820

While at Mount Vernon I delivered you the affidavit of T. Marshall stating that he never received the certificate which you were so obliging as to obtain for him & I now enclose you mine that I have lost it. I have no doubt that they will be sufficient to obtain the renewal of the certificate;

but I beleive that some bond must be executed before it can issue. I do not know how this is to be filled up & suppose it must contain a description of the certificate which I cannot make. Will you excuse me for giving you the trouble of sending me from Philadelphia a bond to be executed?[1]

On my return home I found a letter from Mr. Ward of Salem enclosing the copy of a letter from Mr. Wm. Fairfax to Capt. Clarke of Salem dated Belvoir 22d. Feb. 1749 which contains this sentence "Please to acquaint our Sister Hannah that Mrs. Washington has lost all her children but Major Washington just returned from London whither he lately went to get his arrears of pay & be put on the establishment of half pay which he obtained & is in hopes of repairing his losses."

Mr. Wards letter is accompanied with a Salem paper in which this with another letter from Mr. Fairfax is published, & it is hinted that the biographers of General Washington have been remiss in omitting so material a circumstance as his voyage to London at so early an age & being placed on the half pay list.

I cannot doubt that this letter refers to some other Major Washington, who had claims in consequence of his services in the war which was terminated in 1748 by the treaty of Aix la Chapelle. General Washington was certainly too young to have been a major in that war; & I have never heard a syllable either of his visit to London or of his being on the half pay establishment.

Was General Washington born of a second Marriage? And were the other children of that marriage all dead in 49? If this letter does not refer to him, to whom does it refer? Probably to some of the Fairfax family who had married a Washington. I should suspect Mrs. Washington was the wife of the Generals eldest brother who devised Mount Vernon to him, but it is impossible that his son could have been the Major mentioned in this letter. What was the maiden name of the General's mother?

When you are in Philadelphia would it not be well to have some conversation with the Philadelphia editor of Langhornes Plutarch respecting his anecdote about Genl. Washingtons selling his old charger which he has inserted as a note in the life of the elder Cato?[2] I am my dear Sir your affection⟨ate⟩

J Marshall

ALS, Marshall Papers, ViW. Addressed to Washington at Mount Vernon, Fairfax County; postmarked Richmond, 2 Sept. Endorsed by Washington.

1. This matter apparently pertained to JM's transfer of stock in the Bank of the United States. On 5 Feb. 1819 he gave a power of attorney to Robert Adams to transfer twenty-five shares of stock to Thomas Marshall as trustee for the widow and heirs of William Marshall (*PJM*, VIII, 402).

2. *Plutarch's Lives. Translated from the Original Greek; with Notes Critical and Historical, and a Life of Plutarch, by John Langhorne and William Langhorne,* ed. Francis Wrangham (8 vols.; Philadelphia, 1811; S #23705), III, 196 n. 9, in which Cato is quoted as saying that a master of a family should sell off his old animals, farming implements, slaves, " 'and every thing

else that is useless. A master of a family should love to sell, not to buy.' " The editor (Langhorne) then comments: "What a fine contrast there is between the spirit of this old stoic,
and that of the liberal-minded and benevolent Plutarch!" At this point the Philadelphia
editor added: "Yet Washington, the *tertius Cato* of these latter times, is said to have sold his
old charger!" The publishers of the Philadelphia edition were Brannan and Morford.

To George A. Ward

Dear Sir   Richmond Septr. 18th. 1820
    I have received your favour of the 11th.[1] The more I have reflected on
the subject, the more am I confirmed in the opinion that Major Washington, mentioned in the letter of Mr. Fairfax, cannot be General Washington. This opinion is supported by many facts & circumstances in addition to his age. Had he been a major on the regular establishment, & on
half pay, he would not, when the first provincial troops were raised in
Virginia, have been placed under Colonel Fry, a private country gentleman without previous military rank;[2] nor could he, on the reduction of
that regiment, have been under the necessity of retiring from the service,
or of holding the rank of a Captain.
    When engaged with General Braddock, he would have been entitled to
the rank of Major independent of his situation as aid to that gentleman.
    His early letters show a desire to be placed on the regular establish-
ment, & his disappointment at not being so placed. There are many
expressions in them inconsistent with the idea of his receiving half pay or
of his ranking as a major in the regular service.
    After his being appointed to the command of the 1st. Virginia Regi-
ment, the regulation respecting the relative rank of British officers &
those in the temporary provincial corps was in force, by which the British
were to take rank of the provincials. Under this regulation a Captain
(Dagworthy I believe his name was) contested the rank of Colo. Washington.[3] This contest could not have existed had the Colonel been a
major in the British service. It seems to me too to be impossible that the
circumstances of his visiting England & being on half pay, had they existed, shou'd be unknown to all his friends; or if known should never have
been mentioned by any one of them, & should never have been alluded
to in any one of his letters.
    But what is conclusive on this subject is that, at the date of Mr. Fairfax's
letter, Mrs. Washington, the mother of the General, had not lost a single
child. She had then living three sons and one daughter.
    As Lawrence Washington the eldest son by the first marriage had actu-
ally been in the british service in the expedition against Carthagena, as
he had married Miss Fairfax the daughter of the writer & the niece of the
person to whom the information was given, & who of course would be

interested in knowing the situation of the family of that Mrs. Washington who was her niece, but would be indifferent to the family of that Mrs. Washington of whom she knew nothing, as Lawrence Washington bore generally the title of Major, I was strongly tempted to beleive that Lawrence Washington was the Major Washington of Mr. Fairfax's letter.[4] But the language of the letter, as printed in the newspaper, to which I referred after giving the manuscript a cursory reading, seemed entirely opposed to this conjecture.

As there was no other Major Washington than Lawrence who had then been in service, who could have visited England to claim compensation for that service, or who could have been on half pay, I determined to reexamine the manuscript letter; on doing so the difficulty was removed. The paper does not contain a correct copy of the manuscript letter sent to me. The words "who has" inserted in the printed paper after "Washington["] vary the sense materially. The manuscript is in these words. ["]Please to acquaint our sister Hannah that Mrs. Washington has lost all her children but Major Washington just returned from London whether he lately went to get his arrears of pay & be put on the establishment of half pay which he obtained, is in hopes of repairing his losses." What losses? clearly of his children. It is very natural after stating the loss, to state the hope of repairing it; but it would be a very strange & heterogeneous sentence if the word "losses" was to be referred to fortune which had not been stated, instead of children which had been stated. Place a comma after Washington, as there is after "obtained," or include the words "just returned from London whether he lately went to get his arrears of pay and be put on the establishment of half pay which he obtained?" within marks of parenthesis, which is clearly the sense, & the meaning will I think be apparent. This construction is strengthened by the fact that at that time Mrs. Washington the wife of Lawrence had lost all her children; & that she had one daught⟨er⟩ Sarah, born afterwards, who died in 1775.

If, as I doubt not, the certified manuscr⟨ip⟩t sent t⟨o⟩ me is a true copy from the original, I have as little doubt that Major Lawrence Washington is the gentleman of whom Mr. Fairfax speaks. I am dear Sir with great respect, Your Obedt

J MARSHALL

ALS, ICN. Addressed to Ward in Salem, Mass.; postmarked Richmond, 20 Sept.

1. Letter not found.

2. Joshua Fry (ca. 1700–1754) taught mathematics at the College of William and Mary, represented Albemarle County in the House of Burgesses, and in early 1754 took command of the Virginia militia to resist French encroachments in the upper Ohio Valley.

3. Capt. John Dagworthy (1721–1784) held a royal commission and claimed precedence over colonial militia officers, including Colonel Washington, during the French and Indian War. See George W. Marshall, *Memoir of Brigadier-General John Dagworthy of the Revolutionary*

War (Wilmington, Del., 1895), 6–14; James Thomas Flexner, *George Washington: The Forge of Experience, 1732–1775* (Boston, 1965), 142–44. JM discussed this incident in the *Life of George Washington* (2d ed.; Philadelphia, 1838), I, 12–13.

4. Lawrence Washington (1718–1752) served as a captain in an American regiment attached to the British regular army in the Anglo-Spanish War of 1739. Washington was entitled to a pension of half-pay for life because of his commission in the regular army and the disbanding of his regiment after the siege of Cartagena (Flexner, *George Washington,* 16, 121).

To Bushrod Washington

My dear Sir   Richmond Novr. 7th 1820

I thank you for the kind solicitude expressed in your letter of the 3d.[1]

I had imprudently mounted a young horse who started & threw me as I was riding him to my farm. I was much hurt but no bone was broken & I shall be able to attend the court at Raleigh to which place I shall set out the day after tomorrow.

The letters we agreed to copy are in progress; & I expect to carry them with me to Washington in February. I wish you would have some conversation with Mr. Wayne respecting a second edition of the life of Washington.[2] It would be well for Mr. Weems to have a subscription paper for the letters & the life at the same time.[3] I think we ought to reduce our charge on the life to half a dollar instead of a dollar per volume. I should hope with this reduction & the diminished expense which I suppose printing must experience, that the second edition might be sold for two dollars a volume, especially if the number of pages should be somewhat reduced. Talk with Mr. Wayne & write to me.[4]

I am much obliged both to you & Mr. Adams for the duplicate certificate. As soon as I could hold a pen I wrote to that gentleman & remitted him the money he had advanced for me.

I congratulate you on the recovery of you⟨r⟩ health & am dear Sir affectionately your

J MARSHALL

ALS, Marshall Papers, ViW. Addressed to Washington in Philadelphia; postmarked Richmond, 7 Nov. Endorsed by Washington "to be attended to."

1. Letter not found.

2. On the proposed second edition of the *Life of George Washington,* see *PJM,* VIII, 140–41 and n. 5. Caleb P. Wayne was publisher of the first edition.

3. Mason Locke Weems had served as subscription agent for the first edition (*PJM,* VI, 252–53 and n. 2).

4. Washington wrote to Wayne in Jan. 1821, asking him if he would be interested in undertaking the second edition. Washington also said that an edition of General Washington's private letters " 'to publick & some to private characters' " was nearly ready for the press and would run to three or four volumes (Washington to Caleb P. Wayne, 20 Jan. 1821, Dreer Collection, PHi).

To St. George Tucker

My dear Sir   Novr. 22d. 1820

I have just received your letter containing the unpleasant information
of your ill health.[1] I sincerely regret the unpleasant circumstance & condole with you on it.

There is one suit in court in which, a *near* connection of mine being
concerned, I cannot sit, that is in the name of a very old man whose death
would involve the parties plfs. in serious difficulties, about the trial of
which I am anxious; but I beg you not to think of coming upon that
account unless your health should be so improved as to enable you to
come without any danger or much inconvenience.[2] I hope there will be
no abatement between this & the spring. With my best wishes for your
health & happiness, I am my dear Sir truely yours &c

J MARSHALL

ALS, Tucker-Coleman Papers, ViW. Endorsed by Tucker "ansd. 25th" (not found).

1. Letter not found.
2. Martin v. Redd. See Special Verdict, 7 Dec. 1820 (App. II, Cal.). The "*near* connection"
was James M. Marshall, JM's brother. The "very old man" was Gen. Philip Martin (1733–
1821), brother and heir of the late Denny Martin Fairfax. He was a nominal party in a
number of suits involving the Fairfax title (Fairfax Harrison, *The Proprietors of the Northern
Neck, Chapters of Culpeper Genealogy* [Richmond, Va., 1926], 146).

Robertson v. Miller
Opinion
U.S. Circuit Court, Virginia, 27 November 1820

Archibald Robertson of Lynchburg filed his bill in the U.S. Circuit Court
seeking either to confirm his title to a house and lot in the town or, if the title
was defective, to obtain a refund of the purchase money. The defendants
were Boyd Miller, from whom Robertson purchased the property, the legatees and devisees of William Brown, who had been Miller's business partner,
and Samuel Garland, escheator of the commonwealth for Lynchburg. Marshall's opinion of 27 November 1820 fully states the facts of the case (U.S.
Cir. Ct., Va., Ord. Bk. XI, 8; proceedings in Va. Superior Court of Chancery,
Lynchburg [copy], 17 Oct. 1821, Robertson v. Miller, U.S. Cir. Ct., Va.,
Ended Cases [Unrestored], 1822, Vi).

Robertson
   v
Miller & al

William Brown, a citizen of Virginia, & Boyd Miller, a British subject,   ¶1
entered into partnership & carried on trade & commerce by the name of

William Brown & Co. During the partnership William Brown purchased a house & lott in Lynchburg with the funds & for the use of the company, but took the conveyance to himself. Some time in the year 1811 William Brown departed this life, having first made his last will in writing which was properly recorded in February 1812 by which, after certain legacies, his estate was devised to his relations in Scotland who are British Subjects. By this devise, the interest of William Brown to the house & lott in Lynchburg passes to the devisees subject to any claim Boyd Miller may have upon it as surviving partner. Boyd Miller became a resident of Virginia, & in Novr. 1815, while a resident, sold the house & lott in Lynchburg to Archibald Robertson the complainant for $8000. A suit was at that time depending in this court brought by the exrs. of William Brown against Boyd Miller & others, to which the legatees & devisees of William Brown were afterwards made parties, for a settlement of partnership transactions & a distribution of the partnership fund. In this suit, it is understood that the sum for which the house & lott in Lynchburg sold was considered as one item in the total amount of the fund. Boyd Miller was decreed as surviving partner, to pay to the exrs. of William Brown the sum of $225204.04 with interest & of course became entitled to the partnership effects.[1]

¶2   Archibald Robertson, the purchaser of the house & lott in Lynchburg, after paying the whole purchase money except $1717.78 became apprehensive that the property had become escheatable to the Commonwealth & that the title conveyed to him by Boyd Miller was not a good one. Under this apprehension he has filed this bill praying that the title may be considered, that if it is a good one the Escheator may be enjoined from instituting proceedings of escheat; and that; if it be not a good one, Boyd Miller may be decreed to refund the purchase money, & may be injoined from all proceedings to collect the residue.[2]

¶3   The answer of Boyd Miller admits the several allegations of the bill, & contends that the proceeds of the said house & lott have been rightly applied, under the orders of this court, to the payment of partnership debts.[3]

¶4   There has been no explicit direction of the court on this subject; nor has any question on it ever before been made. The only points decided by the court are that the debts of the company should be paid, and that the residue of its property should be divided according to the articles of copartnery which had expired, but under which the parties had continued to act. This question therefore is still open; & ought to be determined on the principles which would have applied to it, had it been made in November 1815.

¶5   William Brown having held the legal title to the property in question in trust for the firm, it will be considered in a court of equity, as if the conveyance had been made to the firm; and the enquiry will be what is the operation of the law of escheat upon such property where one of the partners is an alien?[4]

If an alien Merchant who is alone, purchases a house & lott for the purposes of trade either in fee [or] for life, that house & lott is escheatable; & I can percieve no reason, if he be a member of a firm, why his interest should not be equally escheatable. The commercial law does not extend its protection to real estate acquired by alien Merchants. The debts of the firm may attach on his interest, as his own private debts would attach on his private estate, but no farther; that is I presume, that what remained, after exhausting his personal estate, might charge his real. This would, I presume, be the rule, in the case of an estate at law; and a court of equity, in the absence of peculiar circumstances, would follow the rule of law. ¶6

In the life time of William Brown then, a court of equity would have subjected the interest of Boyd Miller to the claim of the Commonwealth, chargeable only with such debts as the personal fund of the company was insufficient to pay. ¶7

On the death of William Brown the whole legal estate passed to aliens and became escheatable. ¶8

Would the property, if then escheated, have been chargeable with the debts of the company? However this may be, had there been no other effects for the payment of debts, I know of no law or principle which would subject this real property to the payment of debts, in exoneration of the personal fund. ¶9

In this view of the subject, the fact that the escheat has not taken place can make no difference. If a court of equity would not interfere to subject the proceeds of escheated land to the payment of debts in exoneration of the personal fund; neither I presume would it interfere to order the sale of escheatable land & the application of the proceeds to the discharge of that fund. ¶10

If then there was nothing peculiar in the articles of copartnership, the real estate composing a part of the capital stock of the firm would, on the death of one of the partners, pass by the will of the decedent, or go in moities to the two partners subject to the title of the commonwealth, which, charged with the payment of debts, would act on each moity according to the law as applicable to that party. Both being aliens, both moities would be escheatable. ¶11

But it is contended by the defendent that the articles of copartnery, in this case, transfer the whole property to the survivor. ¶12

The articles of copartnership were entered into on the 14th. day of april 1803, between Boyd Miller, William Brown, & John MCredie; and were to continue in force for four years from the first day of September 1803; and might "be renewed by the joint consent of the whole in writing given one year before the expiration." The books were to be balanced in ¶13 the month of September in each year; and an inventory of all their effects, with a true state of all their affairs was then to be made out.[5]

¶14   In the 4th. article it is agreed that "In case of the death or bankruptcy of any of the said parties, in order to prevent any altercation with the heirs exrs. admrs. or assigns of the decd. or bankrupt; it is agreed that the shares of profits as well as capita⟨l⟩ of the deceased or bankrupt shall be paid by the survivors or solvents agreeable to the yearly statement of the company's affairs prior to his death or bankruptcy" &c.

¶15   It is very material to settle the extent of this article. If it be an agreement to transfer the real & personal estate of th⟨e⟩ company to the surviving or solvent partner or partners, entitling th⟨e⟩ representatives of the deceased or insolvent to his "share of the profits as well as capital" "agreeable to the yearly statement of the company's affairs prior to the death or bankruptcy" then it is equivalent to an agreement that the right of survivorship shall take place between the parties as to the subject itself, giving the assignees of the bankrupt, or the representatives of the deceased partner, his shar⟨e⟩ of the capital & profits according to the last yearly statement, instead of that interest to which, independent of special compact, he would be entitled by law. It is the substitution of a rule by the act of the partie⟨s⟩ for that rule which the law makes where the parties are silent.

¶16   After the best consideration I can give the subject, I am in favor of this construction for several reasons.

¶17   The article is professedly entered into "in order to prevent any altercation with the heirs, exrs., admrs., or assignees of the deceased or bankrupt.["] This object cannot be effected, unless the property be transferred to the survivor, or solvent, on the terms specified.

¶18   The rule for ascertaining annually the rights of the parties would be useless if the application of that rule were to be defeated.

¶19   The article contains also other provisions which demonstrate I think the intent with which it was made; & show a determination to leave nothing for discussion in the event provided for. Five per cent. is, in this annual statement, to be deducted from the cost and charges of the goods on hand; and no allowance is to be made for bad or doubtful debts. These goods then, and these debts, become the property of the surviving or solvent partner; and the representatives of the deceased or assignees of the Bankrupt, are entitled in lieu of all claims upon the subject, to the share allowed in the annual statement.

¶20   Is there any reason for withdrawing real estate, considered by the company as a part of its stock in trade, from the operation of this article? I can percieve no reason for the exception. The parties certainly have not made it, and the court could not be justified in doing what they have not chosen to do. Their language shows an intent to comprehend lands. The word "heirs" could be of no other use. To introduce the exception would defeat the object of the article. It would not only render the word heirs useless, but would reinstate those subjects of altercation which the article intended to remove. The real property must be withdrawn from the fund, its value ascertained by some rule to be agreed on by the parties or given by a court, & the residue be subjected to the rule stated in this article.

This construction is strengthened by the understanding of the parties as illustrated by an event which has taken place. ¶21

John McCredie, one of the partners, departed this life in the year 180 and his account was adjusted by the rule which has been stated, without an idea on either side that any other principle ought to prevail; and the court of chancery of the state has I percieve by its decree directing a conveyance of the real estate standing in his name, given this construction to the article. ¶22

I think then, had the event which has happened taken place during the four years for which the copartnership was originally prepared, it could not be doubted that the whole fund of the company, real & personal, would pass to the surviving partner; leaving the representatives of the deceased entitled to their testators share of the capital & profits of the company, according to the annual statement on the books. Putting alienage out of the question, I think it cannot be doubted but that a court of equity would, in such a state of things, decree a conveyance to Boyd Miller on his paying that share of capital & profits. ¶23

It remains to enquire whether the expiration of the time for which the articles were formed, produces any alteration in the law of the case. ¶24

I can percieve no reason for this opinion. Where two or more persons enter into a particular business for a stipulated time, under a special contract; & continue that business after the expiration of the time, without any change whatever of circumstances, or any expression of the terms on which the business is conducted, the natural conclusion seems to be that the business is still to be conducted on its original principles. The law I think would imply a contract that it shall be so conducted. Many examples might be adduced in illustration of this position. A tenent leasing a tenement for a year at a stipulated rent, & holding over with the consent of the LandLord, would be understood to hold under the original contract. If for some years he paid the same rent, and it was received by the LandLord, the law would certainly raise a tacit agreement binding on both parties, so long as the occupation of the land continued without any dissent expressed by either party. So with respect to the employment of an agent, or to an engagement of any other description. ¶25

The testimony in the cause shows that this general rule of reason is understood to apply to commercial companies. It also shows that the parties understood it to be applicable to them. Their declarations were to this effect, and their clerk proves that the annual statement required by the article was regularly made; and that the business continued to be conducted in the same manner & on the same principles, as before the expiration of the articles. ¶26

¶27   This court, in its decree in the original cause, without any view to the question of escheat, considered the articles as regulating all the subsequent transactions of the parties, & directed the settlement to be made in conformity with them. That opinion is still retained. Its application to the case before the court will now be considered.

¶28   The property in question though conveyed to William Brown singly, having been purchased with the money & held in trust for the company, must be considered in a court of equity as if the trusts had been expressed, or as if the legal estate had in terms conformed to the trust. As the property was acquired under the articles of copartnership, the trust must accord with those articles. The title then is to be considered as if the deed had been made to the firm; and, if either of the partners should die or become bankrupt during the continuance of the partnership, to the surviving or solvent partner, he paying the representatives of the deceased, or the assignees of the bankrupt partner his share of the capital & profits, including this property, as stated on the books at the last annual statement. Under such a limitation it cannot be doubted that the lott would pass to the surviving partner.

¶29   But the surviving partner is an alien, & this property was therefore, while held by him, escheatable. Has the right of the Commonwealth been released?

¶30   In 1813, the legislature passed an act which was reenacted in 1818, which contains the following clause Sec. 3. "And be it farther enacted" &c.[6]

¶31   Boyd Miller, in 1815 when this property was sold to the plaintiff, was an alien, residing within this commonwealth, in possession of, & claiming title to, the land in question, which had not then been escheated to the Commonwealth, and the sale is admitted to have been *bona fide*. The case is within the letter of the law, unless a distinction be taken between an equitable & a legal estate. I can percieve no ground for such a distinction. A court of equity will sustain the claim of the commonwealth to an equitable estate held by an alien; Why then sho⟨ul⟩d not the Commonwealth release its right to an equitable as well as to a legal estate? And what good reason founded in the principles of law or of policy can be assigned for not releasing to a citizen the right of forfeiture in lands of which he holds the equitable title, the meer legal title being in a foreigner, under circumstances in which that right would be released, had the legal title been conveyed?

¶32   I am entirely satisfied that the legislature intended to release the right of the commonwealth to all lands held by an alien, whatever his title might be, in every case in which that alien, being a resident, sells to a citizen, before the right of the Commonwealth has been asserted; and that the release is coextensive with the title of the alien.

¶33   I am therefore of opinion that the commonwealth has released its right to the land in the bill mentioned; and that the title is valid in equity.

Although upon a fair construction of the will of William Brown, I ¶34
doubt whether the legal estate would pass by it to his devisees, & am
satisfied he did not intend it should pass, it is proper that they should
release their right to the complainant & I shall direct them to do so.

This court has been under the necessity of considering incidentally the ¶35
title of the Commonwealth but cannot bind that title, since the commonwealth cannot be made a defendent either by serving process on its
escheator or otherwise. Of that part of the case the court has no jurisdiction & therefore the bill so far as it prays releif against the Escheator is
dismissed without prejudice.[7]

AD, Marshall Judicial Opinions, PPAmP; printed, John W. Brockenbrough, *Reports of
Cases Decided by the Honourable John Marshall . . .* , I (Philadelphia, 1837), 467–76. For JM's
deletions and interlineations, see Textual Notes below.

1. The decree in William Brown's Executors v. Boyd Miller et al. was rendered on 30 Nov.
1815 (U.S. Cir. Ct., Va., Ord. Bk. IX, 414–16).

2. A copy of Robertson's original bill in chancery (evidently filed in 1819) was attached as
"Exhibit B" to a subsequent bill brought by Robertson in the Superior Court of Chancery at
Lynchburg (proceedings in Va. Superior Court of Chancery, Lynchburg [copy], 17 Oct.
1821, Robertson v. Miller).

3. A copy of Miller's answer (sworn on 26 Jan. 1820) was attached as "Exhibit C" to
Robertson's subsequent bill in the state court (ibid.).

4. At common law aliens could not hold lands either by inheritance or by purchase. By
the law of escheats their lands were liable to revert back to the state. See St. George Tucker,
Blackstone's Commentaries (5 vols.; Philadelphia, 1803), II, App., Note C, 53–65.

5. A copy of the articles of copartnership is in the case file of the related suit of Brown's
Executors v. Miller et al., U.S. Cir. Ct., Va., Ended Cases (Unrestored), 1822, Vi.

6. This was an act "releasing the Commonwealth's right to lands, in certain cases."
Brockenbrough inserted the relevant passage at this point. It provided that citizens who
purchased bona fide the lands of an alien residing in the U.S. or who inherited the same
(which lands had not previously escheated to the commonwealth) should hold the lands
free of any claim accruing to the commonwealth (*Revised Code of Va.*, I, 354; II, 505).

7. Federal jurisdiction was precluded by the Eleventh Amendment. For the text of the
decree, see U.S. Cir. Ct., Va., Ord. Bk. XI, 8–9. A copy was annexed as "Exhibit D" to
Robertson's bill in the state chancery court. Robertson took his case to that court in order to
prevent the commonwealth from asserting its title by escheat. The defendant Miller, however, petitioned to have this suit removed to the federal court, where it was placed on the
docket in Dec. 1821. That order was set aside in Nov. 1822 (proceedings in Va. Superior
Court of Chancery, Lynchburg [copy], 17 Oct. 1821, Robertson v. Miller; U.S. Cir. Ct., Va.,
Ord. Bk. XI, 199, 285).

Textual Notes

¶ 1 l. 3   partnership [*erasure*] ↑William↓ Brown
  ll. 11–12   & ↑in Novr. 1815,↓ while
¶ 2 l. 8   may ↑be↓ decreed
¶ 4 l. 4   of ~~the~~ its property
¶ 5 l. 1   having ~~been~~ held
¶ 9 l. 4   this ↑real↓ property to the payment of [*erasure*] ↑debts,↓ in
¶ 11 l. 3   partners, ~~descend~~ ↑pass by the will of the decedent, or go↓ in

l. 5	which, ~~after~~ ↑charged with↓ the
¶15 ll. 2–3	the ~~survivor~~ ↑surviving↓ or
l. 5	or ~~year~~ ↑yearly↓ statement
l. 8	the ~~inso~~ assignees
¶17 l. 1. beg.	The [*erasure*] ↑article↓ is
l. 4	the ~~representa~~ ↑survivor, or↓ solvent,
¶20 ll. 5–6	do. ↑Their language shows an intent to comprehend lands. The word "heirs" could be of no other use.↓ To
ll. 7–8	would ↑not only render the word heirs useless, but would↓ reinstate
ll. 9–12	remove. ↑The real property must be withdrawn from the fund, its value ascertained by some rule to be agreed on by the parties or given by a court, & the residue be subjected to the rule stated in this article.↓
¶22 ll. 3–6	prevail ↑; and the court of chancery of the state has I percieve by its decree directing a conveyance of the real estate standing in his name, given this construction to the article.↓
¶23 l. 1 beg.	~~Suppose William~~ I
l. 3	not [*erasure*] ↑be↓ doubted ~~but~~ that
¶25 ll. 5–6	to ~~me~~ ↑be↓ that
l. 7	it ~~is to~~ ↑shall↓ be
¶26 l. 6	as ~~during~~ ↑before↓ the
¶27 ll. 1–2	cause, [*erasure*] ↑without any view to the question of escheat,↓ considered
l. 3	directed ~~Boyd~~ ↑the↓ settlement
¶28 l. 2	held ↑in trust↓ for
l. 12	a ~~conveyance~~ ↑limitation↓ it cannot be doubted that the ~~la~~ ↑lott↓ would
¶29 l. 1	property ~~is~~ ↑was↓ therefore,
¶31 l. 12	equitable ~~estate~~ ↑title,↓ the
l. 12	foreigner, ~~under~~ ↑under↓ circumstances
¶32 ll. 3–4	resident, ~~conveys~~ ↑sells↓ to a citizen, before the ~~titl~~ right

Thompson and Dickson v. United States
Opinion
U.S. Circuit Court, Virginia, 11 December 1820

The schooner *Patriot* was libeled in the U.S. District Court in the summer of 1812 for violating the nonintercourse laws. Judge Tucker rendered a final decree condemning the vessel and cargo on 16 November 1818. The claimants, William H. Thompson and Robert Dickson, citizens of the United States and part owners of the schooner's cargo, appealed to the U.S. Circuit Court. The facts of the case are fully set forth in Marshall's opinion, delivered on 11 December 1820 (proceedings in U.S. District Court [copy], 16 Nov. 1818, Thompson and Dickson v. U.S., U.S. Cir. Ct., Va., Ended Cases [Unrestored], 1820, Vi; U.S. Cir. Ct., Va., Ord. Bk. XI, 36).

The schooner Patriot, a British vessel then lying in the port of Norfolk ¶1 was purchased in Feby 1812 by Oswald Lawson a British subject, then & for some time before, a resident of the town of Norfolk. This purchase was made by Lawson at the instance of Henry Thompson & Robert Dickson citizens of the United States, whose object was a mercantile voyage to the West Indies; & who advanced the whole purchase money, & took a bottomree bond as security for the repayment thereof. The schooner sailed for the west Indies in Feby 1812 with a cargo owned by Thompson & Dickson which was placed under the controul of Oswald Lawson as super cargo.[1] He sold his cargo in the west Indies, & took on board at Guadaloupe a return cargo consisting of sugars belonging chiefly to Thompson & Dickson with which he sailed from Guadaloupe in May 1812 bound to Halifax in Nova Scotia, but with a determination to ly off the capes of Virginia until explicit instructions should be received from Mr. Thompson one of the owners of the cargo residing in Norfolk. She arrived off the capes of Virginia in June, immediately after the declaration of war was known in Norfolk. Lawson, the supercargo & owner of the vessel, being ignorant of that event, dispatched the mate with a letter of advice to Thompson & determined to await the return of his messenger off the coast. In this interval however he entered the capes but sailed out of them again without coming to anchor. The mate never returned, he being seized in Norfolk as a prisoner of war. Two days after the mate had been landed while the Patriot was plying off & on the coast about 10 miles from land & about 40 south of the capes, she fell in with a pilot boat & took a pilot on board. The super cargo says that he at first declined taking the pilot on board as the vessel was not bound inward, but was persuaded by the pilot to do so who represented the probability of an approaching storm from the east. To avoid this storm he determined to wait within the capes for instructions. The pilot taken on board who was an apprentice of the owner of the boat, denies that such advice was given. The vessel was brought within the capes with the knowledge of Lawson, the owner & super cargo.

On its being known in Norfolk that a British vessel was off the capes, ¶2 the revenue cutter was sent to take her; & fell in with her about three miles within the capes in the road heading to Lynhaven bay & also to Hampton roads. She was brought into Norfolk & libelled.

The first allegation of the libel is that she was a British schooner which ¶3 had come within the limits & territories of the United States of America having on board a cargo of the growth &c of a dependency of Great Britain to wit of the island of Guadaloupe.

The second allegation is that the cargo was imported into the United ¶4 States contrary, to the true intent & meaning of the acts of Congress. The third charge alleges that the cargo was taken on board for the purpose of being imported into the United States with the knowledge of the owner.

Before entering in to the consideration of the arguments belonging to ¶5 the cause it may not be altogether improper to notice some preliminary observations which were made on the union of the prize jurisdiction with that over municipal forfeitures in the courts of the United States.[2] As this union is not the act of the court, the only remark which will be made respecting it is that, in this case, it can have no possible operation on the claimants, unless it be one which is beneficial to them. By mingling the proceedings, ships papers which were obtained under the practice in prize causes, might be offered on a prosecution for a municipal forfeiture. How far the use of such papers might be allowed is a question which will be decided when the case occurs. In this case, those papers are not offered. Having been seized by the agents of the United States the owners are excused for their non production; & the voyage is admitted to be according to their own statement of it. The seizure of the ships papers therefore is either unimportant in this case, or an advantage to the claimants.

¶6   The forfeiture of the vessel & cargo is claimed under the 3d. Section of the act "to interdict the commercial intercourse between the United States & Great Britain & France & for other purposes" which was passed on the 1st. of March 1809, & was reenacted "against Great Britain her colonies & dependencies" on the 2d. of March 1811.[3]

¶7   By the 3d. Sect. of the act of the 1st. of March 1809, the entrance of the harbors & waters of the U.S. is interdicted to all ships or other vessels sailing under the flag of Great Britain or France, or owned in whole or in part by any subject or citizen of either. And if any such vessel shall "arrive either with or without a cargo, within the limits of the U.S. or of the territories thereof such ship or vessel together with the cargo if any which may be found on board shall be forfeited" &c.

¶8   Under this section the Patriot which was a British vessel, & her cargo part of which belonged to citizens of the U.S. were condemned in the District court.

¶9   The claimants have appealed, & contend that this sentence is erroneous; because

¶10   1st. The Patriot had not "arrived within the limits of the United States" at the time when she was seized by the revenue cutter.

¶11   The term arrival when applied to a vessel is said to be equivalent to the term "importation" when applied to goods; & a vessel cannot be properly said to have "arrived" within the meaning of this act, whose cargo might not at the same time with equal propriety be said to be imported.

¶12   Without denying or affirming that, in the laws of Congress, the term "importation" when applied to a cargo, is precisely equivalent to the term "arrival" when applied to a vessel, I will enquire whether the meaning of the word itself be in any manner ambiguous. "To 'arrive' is a neuter verb which when applied to an object moving from place to place designates the fact of 'coming to' or 'reaching' one place from another; or of coming to or reaching a place by travelling or moving towards it." If the place be designated then the object which reaches that place has arrived at it. A person who is coming to Richmond, has arrived when he enters the city.

But it is not necessary to the correct use of this term that the place at which the traveller arrives should be his ultimate destination, or the end of his journey. A person going from Richmond to Norfolk by water arrives within Hampton road when he reaches that place; or if he diverges from the direct course he arrives in Petersburg when he enters that town. This is I beleive the universal understanding of the term. Thus the duty law requires that the master of every vessel bound to Bermuda Hundred or City Point shall on his arrival in Hampton road or at Sewals Point deposit his manifest with the collector of Norfolk or of Hampton. It also requires that any vessel bound to any port of the United States shall on his arrival within four leagues of the coast, upon demand produce his manifest in writing to any officer of the customs who shall first come on board. No person can doubt that in the first case the vessel bound to City Point has arrived in Hampton road when she enters the road; & that a vessel bound to any port of the United States, say to Boston, has arrived within four leagues of the coast when she comes within that distance of land. It would be useless to multiply quotations on this point. The literal sense of the word seems too plain for controversy. When the law enacts that a British vessel which arrives within the limits of the United States shall be for-feited, the forfeiture attaches according to its letter, the instant that a vessel comes voluntarily within those limits. Now whatever doubt may exist respecting the application of this term to any part of the open sea, no doubt I beleive has ever been suggested respecting the Chesapeak bay. That bay is clearly within the limits of the United States; and the forfei-ture under the letter of the act is as complete as if it had attached by the words on her arrival within the Chesapeak bay.

Is the spirit of the law more favorable to the claim than its letter. I ¶13 understand by the spirit of the law, the intention of the legislature, to be collected from the general language of the act, the scope of its provisions, & the object to be attained.

The object of this section cannot be doubted. It is to exclude all vessels ¶14 owned by British subjects from the waters of the United States. Its lan-guage conveys this intention, & is obviously calculated to carry it into full effect. The other sections of the law which are designed to prohibit all intercourse with Great Britain & to exclude all British goods show a rigorous determination on this whole subject which forbids the suspicion that the intention of the legislature, or, in other words, the spirit of the law, is more favorable to the claimants than its letter.

If this be the object of the act, can we doubt that it would have been ¶15 completely defeated by allowing British vessels to come unmolested within the chesapeak & the other bays of the United States. If the Patriot might enter the chesapeak with impunity, where is the line drawn or who has drawn it, which she might not pass? Might she not pass the mouth of the James, the York, the Rappahanock, or the Potowmack? Are any of these points more certainly "within the limits of the United States" than this middle ground within the capes. And if British vessels laden with British goods might with impunity ly in the chesapeak & the other bays of the United States, what would become of the non intercourse act?

¶16   The Patriot being clearly within the enacting clause, it is scarcely necessary to say that she has not brought herself within the exception. She was not "forced in by distress or by the dangers of the sea." The only allegation which looks towards this subject is that the owner was advised to take a pilot on board, because a storm might be expected. No storm had commenced. All was fair. But the pilot said one might be expected. Even this is denied by the pilot who was put on board. But admitting the allegation to be true in its utmost extent, can this imagined fear, this apprehension of uncertain danger, satisfy the words "forced in by the danger of the sea"? If they may, language seems to have lost its use, & I am persuaded that non intercourse laws would do very little good or harm.

¶17   I think then it cannot be doubted that the Patriot, being stated in the claim to have belonged to a British subject, comes within the 3d. sec. of the act. This would be my opinion were it a case of the first impression. But the point is I think decided in the Penobscot.[4]

¶18   2d. The second point made for the claimants is that the non intercourse act of 1809 was not reenacted by the act of March 2d. 1811 so far as respected British vessels. Altho the 3d. section of that act is expressly reenacted, yet its reenactment is limited. It is to be carried into effect "against Great Britain, her colonies, & dependencies." So much of the act then as relates meerly to British vessels has been, it is said, permitted to expire. This strict exposition of the words is the more to be insisted on because the law is highly penal.

¶19   Let this argument be examined.

¶20   The original act respected equally the vessels of France & Britain & articles of their growth produce or manufacture. Its object was to interdict the entrance into the waters of the United States to the vessels of both nations & to forbid, all commercial intercourse with either of them. The 1st. & 2d. sections of the act relate solely to national ships. The 3d. Section is confined to vessels owned wholly or in part by the subjects of Great Britain or of France. The 4th. 5th. & other sections relate to the dominions &c of the two countries, & to articles which are the growth produce or manufacture of either; They also contain provisions calculated to secure the exclusion of those articles from the United States.

¶21   After making a painful experiment of this restrictive system against both nations, the law was permitted to expire, & the policy of the United States was in some degree varied. An act was passed on the 1st. of May 1810 promising that if either belligerent would so revoke or modify its edicts that they should cease to violate the neutral commerce of the United States the sections of the non intercourse law which have been recapitulated should three months thereafter be "revived & have full force & effect so far as relates to the dominions colonies & dependencies,

& to the articles the growth produce or manufacture of the dominions colonies & dependencies of the nation refusing or neglecting to revoke or modify her edicts in the manner aforesaid."[5]

The President having issued his proclamation on the 2d. of November 1810 announcing as a fact that the decrees of France were revoked as required by the act of the 1st. of May preceding,[6] Congress on the 2d. of March 1811 passed the act under which the Patriot & her cargo have been condemned. The case depends on the question whether the 3d. Section is reenacted so far as respects British vessels. ¶22

The language of the law certainly does not import a complete reenactment of the whole of those sections. They are in words reenacted only "against Great Britain her colonies & dependencies." The question whether these words comprehend the interdiction of our waters to vessels owned by British subjects is undoubtedly open for argument & for consideration. In deciding it we must search by legitimate means for the intention of the legislature & be guided by that intention. Was it the intention of the legislature to revive the whole act so far as it respected Great Britain, with perhaps the exception of its territorial operation which may be created by omitting its provision respecting her possessions? or only to revive those parts of the act which relate exclusively to those breaches of it which are connected with territory, such for example as importing a cargo from Great Britain, her colonies, or dependencies? ¶23

That the Act of 1809 is not revived generally is satisfactorily accounted for when we recollect that it was originally directed against both Great Britain & France; & that the legislature designed to reenact it against Great Britain only. If we advert to this fact, & recollect the history of the times, we shall be but little inclined to the opinion that Congress could have intended to leave our ports open to British ships when all commercial intercourse between the two countries was prohibited. It seems impossible to assign a motive for this particular relaxation. The policy of the United States was directed with at least as much earnestness against the navigation as against the manufactures of Great Britain. But what seems conclusive on this point is that the section is expressly revived & yet contains not one word which relates to the territory of Great Britain its colonies or dependencies. The section is limited to ships owned wholly or in part by British subjects. Consequently it applies to those vessels or to nothing. ¶24

The legislature might have revived the 3d. section only. Had this been done, could it have been said that it was not revived as to vessels because it was said to be revived against Great Britain her colonies & dependencies? Not a syllable in the section relates to colonies or dependencies; & not a syllable to Great Britain except the prohibition to her vessels. To have said in that case that the section was not revived as to vessels, would have been to ascribe to the legislature a declaration that a particular section should be revived in a manner to have no effect whatever: or to make a ¶25 law with an exception coextensive with its whole enactment. Such a construction must be totally inadmissible. The actual case is stronger than that supposed, because in the actual case other sections are revived which might suggest the propriety of adding the words "colonies & dominions," to Great Britain.

¶26   It cannot I think be necessary to add anything to this argument. Yet I will observe that the act of May 1st. 1810, which was perpetual, provided for the whole subject which was reenacted in March 1811. I can concieve no motive for the last law other than an apprehension, which I beleive was not well founded, that the courts might not have received the proclamation of the President as conclusive evidence that the fact had occurred on which the non intercourse was to be enforced as against Great Britain; or might have received other testimony than his proclamation to prove that Great Britain had modified her edicts so as not to affect the neutral commerce of the United States. Choosing to place it beyond doubt that this fact was to be decided by the President alone, Congress passed the Act of March the 2d. 1811. This being the sole conceivable motive for that act, it cannot be doubted that it was made, or at least intended to be made, coextensive with the act of May 1st. 1810. Yet there are very material variances in the language of the two acts. That of May 1st. 1810 enacts that if the one nation shall revoke her edicts, & the other shall not, then the 3d. 4th &c sections of the non intercourse act "shall be revived & have full force & effect so far as relates to the dominions, colonies & dependencies, & to the articles the growth produce or manufacture of the dominions colonies & dependencies of the nation so refusing &c.["] The act of March 2d. 1811 which carries this promise & threat into execution, omits the very material words "and to the articles the growth produce or manufacture," &c & declares only that the several recited sections of the original act "shall be carried into effect against Great Britain her colonies & dependencies." The omission of these very material words might be urged to prove that the non intercourse law was not reenacted with respect to articles of the growth produce or manufacture of Great Britain her colonies or dominions if imported from other than British territory with at least as much plausibility as the omission to declare, in reviving the 3d. section which relates only to British vessels, that it shall be enforced against British vessels.

¶27   To prove that the law was not revived as to British vessels, it has been urged that, if it was in force when the Patriot was seized, it is in force now, for which no person will contend; or at least remained in force until a commercial treaty was formed between the two nations, since it was certainly not repealed by the act of the 14th. Apl. 1814.[7]

¶28   This is true; but I do not think that an inadvertence of this kind; an inadvertence sufficiently ⟨accounted⟩ for by the existence of a war which of itself excluded British vessels when the repealing act passed, &, the oblivion into which the return of peace threw the whole subject can influence the construction of the acts of 1810 & 1811.[8]

An argument which produces the only serious doubt which can arise in this case remains to be noticed. It is that the 3d. section of the non intercourse act was repealed by the declaration of war.　¶29

It has been argued that all the provisions of that act were obviously adapted to a state of peace. That the declaration of war changed so entirely the relations of the two countries to each other as to render those provisions which were made for a state of peace totally inapplicable to that new state in which war placed the parties. This argument has been illustrated by showing the incompatibility of those provisions which respect the national ships of Great Britain with a state of war.　¶30

It is certainly true that the whole system of non intercourse was framed with a view to the continuance of a state of peace; But it does not follow that positive & general regulations formed in language equally adapted to peace & war shall, because they were particularly intended for a state of peace, expire on a declaration of war, unless there be something in war totally incompatible with their continuance. When this is the case, the declaration of war, being a national act of complete obligation, repeals all laws inconsistent with the state in which it places the nation, on the principle that posterior laws abrogate those which are anterior. But when the laws can exist & be executed together, I know of no principle which will authorize a court to say that the last law repeals the first. This principle is completely illustrated by different parts of the case now under consideration. The first section of the original non intercourse act forbids the national vessels of Great Britain to enter the waters of the United States, & authorizes the President to employ the military & naval force of the nation for the removal of any vessel which shall violate this provision of the act. The declaration of war makes it the duty of the President not to obey this mandate of the non intercourse law, but to capture the vessel as prize of war. It is obvious that this last law as entirely abrogates the first during its continuance, as if it had in terms commanded the President not to remove the offending vessel from the waters of the United States but to cause her to be brought in as prize of war. But those provisions of the act which prohibit the importation of goods of British manufacture &c, though framed in time of peace, for a state of peace, are not incompatible with a state of war. They may be continued or discontinued at the will of the legislature. I cannot then consider them as repealed by the meer declaration of war. British manufactures, the property of a friend, may be introduced or prohibited, in peace or in war, as shall seem wise to the legislature. A law then prohibiting them, which in its terms does not depend on peace or war, would seem to me not to be repealed by a declaration of war. The will of the legislature for its repeal must be more directly expressed, or the law continues in force.　¶31

¶32   But if we examine our course of legislation on this subject we shall find conclusive evidence that in the opinion of the legislature the law continued in force. Immediately after the declaration of war the Prize act was passed. The 14th. Sec. of this act repeals so much of all preceding acts as may prohibit the introduction into the United States of goods of British manufacture &c as may be captured from the enemy & made good & lawful prize of war.[9] There cannot be a stronger evidence of the opinion of the legislature that their declaration of war left their non intercourse act in full force.

¶33   Afterwards on the 14th. of April 1814, the act laying an embargo was repealed, & so much of every act as prohibits the importation of British goods, &c or as prohibits the importation of any goods from Great Britain &c is repealed.[10]

¶34   We observe that the embargo law is totally repealed. But the non intercourse law is repealed only in part. The language of the act shows the opinion of the legislature to have been that parts of the act still remained in force.

¶35   If then we respect the very inteligible opinion of the legislature; or are governed by those rules which generally prevail in the construction of statutes, I think we must be brought to the conclusion that the non intercourse laws, so far as respected goods &c imported from Great Britain or her dependencies, or articles of the growth produce or manufacture of Great Britain or her dependencies imported from any place whatever continued in force after the declaration of war.

¶36   That the act continued in force so far as respected vessels owned by British subjects is not quite so obvious. Since every vessel forfeited under the non intercourse law would also if captured be forfeited by the laws of war it may well be doubted whether the declaration of war does not suspend so much at least of the non intercourse act as applies to the very objects to which the laws of war apply. The Patriot for example, was a vessel belonging to the enemy, subject to capture according to the laws of war. The revenue cutters are a part of the naval force of the United States which may be employed by the President to prosecute the war & the 14th. sec. of the Prize act recognizes captures made by them. It may therefore admit of some doubt whether this so far as respects the vessel itself may not be a belligerent capture. But suppose this to be admitted, Does it follow that the non intercourse law may not apply to the cargo? The laws of war condemn the vessel but do not reach the cargo. The municipal law condemns both vessel & cargo. If the paramount operation of the law of war upon the subject overreaches the municipal forfeiture of the vessel, does it therefore discharge the cargo, to which its provisions do not extend. The declaration of war does not appear to me to affect the municipal forfeiture in any case in which it does not itself dispose of the subject.

The strongest point of view in which this question has been placed ¶37
remains still to be considered. The owner of the Patriot was an enemy. He
was on board & had the controul of the vessel. He brought her into the
chesapeake, & it is denied that his act can forfeit the goods of the American claimants. War, it is said, by way of illustrating this argument dissolves
all contracts between enemies; and, if the owner of the Patriot, instead of
bringing her into the chesapeake had carried her into the Thames, he
would not, even after the return of peace, have been responsible to the
owners of the cargo.

It will be admitted that war, if it does not dissolve contracts between ¶38
enemies, suspends their obligation, & enables the belligerent to annul
them. It is also admitted, as a consequence of this principle, that, if the
owner of the Patriot had carried her into the Thames, & there libelled
her cargo, he could not have been made responsible for it. The reason is
that those paramount duties which the war imposed upon him, would in
a legal sense, justify the act of carrying enemy property into the ports of
his country & protect him from the consequences of that act. The right of
property would have been changed by an act which the law had rendered
lawful; and however that act may wound the moral sense, the law cannot
punish it. But although the war would have justifyed the carrying the Patriot into the Thames it did not justify bringing her into the Chesapeak,
in violation of a statute of the United States. That act therefore remains
exposed to the same punishment as if war had not been declared.

It has been argued that the act of an enemy, to which the American ¶39
proprietor of the cargo has not consented, ought not to affect his property; & that the declaration of war having dissolved the connexion between the parties, the act of bringing the vessel into the waters of the
United States is to be considered as if it had been an act of violence by any
other person without authority.

But this argument is rather calculated to perplex than to satisfy the ¶40
mind. Lawson had in fact the direction of the voyage, & continued in that
direction. Altho he might with impunity have ceased to act as the agent of
the owners of the cargo, & have acted as an enemy, yet he did not divest
himself of the character of an agent, nor assume that of an enemy. Acting
under his original authority, he violated the laws of the United States; and
those who employed him must I think pay the penalty incurred by that
violation. The enemy character of an agent cannot I think exempt his
employer from the penalty attached by law to an offence. But the words
of the act subject to forfeiture the cargo of a citizen imported in a British
vessel. The terms of the law punish the act without enquiring into the
criminal intent. The cargo of a British vessel arriving within the limits of
the United States is exempt from forfeiture only if "forced in by distress,
or by the dangers of the sea." These are the only exceptions found in
the act. If any others can be introduced by construction, they must be

founded on the substantial principles of equity, not on the technical subtleties of law.

¶41   It has been also argued that had this vessel been captured & brought in by an American cruizer, or even by the owners themselves, the cargo could not have been forfeited.

¶42   This may be true. But in that case the captors would have been in the exercise of the rights of war; and the vessel with her cargo would have been brought in *jure belli.* In this case the act declaring war & the prize act might have operated on the municipal forfeiture & have suspended it. But in the case which has occurred, the act which created the forfeiture is not performed in the exercise of the rights of War, but is an act totally unconnected with war.

¶43   I have considered this case with no disposition favorable to the condemnation of this cargo. But according to the view I have taken of the subject the cargo is liable to forfeiture in consequence of being in a British vessel which has arrived within the limits of the United States while the non intercourse law was in force. I shall not regret it, if a higher tribunal shall be of a different opinion.

¶44   The sentence of the District court is affirmed with costs.

AD, Marshall Judicial Opinions, PPAmP; printed, John W. Brockenbrough, *Reports of Cases Decided by the Honourable John Marshall . . . ,* I (Philadelphia, 1837), 408–23. For JM's deletions and interlineations, see Textual Notes below.

1. A "supercargo" in maritime law is an agent specially employed by the owner of cargo to take charge of and sell to best advantage merchandise shipped and to purchase returning cargoes and receive freight as authorized.

2. By the Judiciary Act, U.S. District Courts had "exclusive original cognizance of all civil causes of admiralty and maritime jurisdiction, including all seizures under laws of impost, navigation or trade of the United States." The *Patriot* was subject to forfeiture as prize of war and as violating the nonintercourse laws (*U.S. Statutes at Large,* I, 77).

3. Ibid., II, 528–33, 651–52.

4. Brig Penobscot v. U.S., 7 Cranch 356 (1813).

5. *U.S. Statutes at Large,* II, 605–6.

6. For the president's proclamation of 2 Nov. 1810, see *ASP, Foreign Relations,* III, 392; J. C. A. Stagg et al., eds., *The Papers of James Madison,* Presidential Series, II (Charlottesville, Va., 1992), 612–13.

7. *U.S. Statutes at Large,* III, 123.

8. At a later time JM wrote: "This is a mistake. There is a repealing act which ⟨w⟩as not observed when this opinion was drawn." He probably referred to the repealing act of 3 Mar. 1815 (ibid., 226).

9. Ibid., II, 759, 763.

10. Ibid., III, 123.

Textual Notes

¶ 1 ll. 4–5   Dickson ↑citizens of the United States,↓ whose
ll. 11–12   consisting ~~chiefly~~ of sugars ↑belonging chiefly to Thompson & Dickson↓ with
l. 16   Virginia ~~soon~~ ↑in↓ June

ll. 18–19   to [*erasure*] ↑Thompson↓ &

l. 19   the ~~capes~~ ↑coast.↓ In

ll. 23–24   coast ↑about 10 miles from land & about 40 south of the capes,↓ she

ll. 27–29   east. ↑To avoid this storm he determined to wait within the capes for instructions.↓ The

l. 31   of ↑Lawson,↓ the

¶ 2 ll. 1–2   capes, ~~a~~ ↑the↓ revenue

ll. 3–4   road ↑heading↓ to Lynhaven bay ↑& also to Hampton roads.↓ She

¶ 3 l. 1   The ~~first count charges~~ ↑first allegation of the libel is↓ that

l. 4   Guadaloupe. ~~The second~~

¶ 5 l. 1   entering ~~ar~~ ↑in↓ to

l. 5   will ↑be↓ made

l. 8   obtained ~~by proceeding according to the rules~~ ↑under the practice↓ in

ll. 13–14   be ~~what~~ ↑according to↓ their own ~~testim~~ statement

¶ 6 l. 1   cargo ~~in this case~~ is

ll. 3–4   passed ↑on the 1st. of↓ March ~~1st.~~ 1809, & was reenacted ~~so far as respected~~ ↑"against ~~Grea~~↓ Great

¶ 7 l. 1 beg.   ↑By↓ the

l. 2   all ↑ships or other↓ vessels

l. 5   with ~~or with~~ or

¶ 9 l. 1 beg.   ~~It is contended by the~~ ↑The↓ claimants ~~who~~ have appealed, ↑& contend↓ that

¶11 l. 1   The ↑term↓ arrival

l. 3   "arrived" ~~under~~ ↑within the meaning of↓ this

¶12 l. 1   Without ~~enquiring whether~~ ↑denying or affirming that,↓ in

l. 2   cargo, ~~be~~ ↑is↓ precisely

ll. 6–7   of ↑coming to or↓ reaching

ll. 7–8   the ~~object~~ ↑place↓ be

ll. 12–13   Norfolk ↑by water↓ arrives

ll. 13–14   he ~~travels by land~~ & diverges

l. 20   demand ↑produce↓ his

l. 22   vessel ~~has ar~~ ↑bound to↓ City

ll. 26–27   point. ~~It~~ ↑The literal sense of the word↓ seems

l. 29   attaches ↑according to its letter,↓ the

l. 34   under ↑the letter of↓ the act [*erasure*] ↑is↓ as

l. 35   attached ↑by the words↓ on

¶13 ll. 1–2   letter. ~~The~~ ↑I understand by the↓ spirit of the law, ~~is~~ the

¶14 l. 1   this ~~law~~ ↑section↓ cannot

ll. 2–3   language ↑conveys this intention, &↓ is

l. 3   carry ~~this~~ it

l. 6   this ↑whole↓ subject

l. 7   or, ↑in other words,↓ the

¶15 l. 1   would ↑have↓ been

ll. 2–3   come ↑unmolested↓ within

ll. 6–7   Potowmack? ~~Is she more~~ ↑Are any of these points more certainly↓ "within

	ll. 7–8	than ~~the~~ ↑this↓ middle
	l. 8	if [*erasure*] ↑British↓ vessels
¶16	l. 1	being ↑clearly↓ within
	l. 3	not ~~in~~ ↑"forced in by↓ distress
	l. 3	sea." ~~nor was she a dispatch vessel.~~ The
	ll. 9–10	by ~~stress of weather?~~ ↑the danger of the sea"?↓ If
¶17	ll. 2–3	of [*erasure*] the act.
¶18	l. 1	the ~~act~~ non
	l. 4	limited. ~~to its effect on Great~~ ↑It is to be carried into effect↓ "against
	ll. 7–8	expire. ~~Let this arg~~ ↑This strict exposition of the words is the more to be insisted on because the law is highly penal.↓
¶20	l. 2	articles ~~the~~ ↑of their↓ growth
	l. 3	the ↑entrance into the↓ waters
	l. 4	intercourse ~~between the United Sta~~ with
	l. 5	to ↑national↓ ships. ~~of war~~ The
	l. 7	or ~~in~~ ↑of↓ France.
	ll. 7–8	to ↑the dominions &c of the two countries, & to↓ articles
	ll. 9–10	either; ~~country, & to~~ ↑They also contain provisions ↑calculated↓ to secure ~~their~~ ↑the↓ exclusion ↑of those articles↓ from
¶21	l. 2	nations, ~~it~~ ↑the law↓ was
	l. 4	so ~~repeal~~ ↑revoke↓ or
	ll. 5–6	neutral ~~rights~~ ↑commerce↓ of the United States ~~certain~~ ↑the↓ sections
	l. 7	should ↑three months thereafter↓ be
¶22	l. 2	announcing [*erasure*] ↑as↓ a
¶23	l. 5	owned [*erasure*] ↑by↓ British
	l. 9	exception ~~of~~ ↑of↓ its
	l. 10	omitting ~~the~~ ↑its↓ provision
	ll. 11–12	to ~~offence~~ ↑those↓ breaches of ~~the act~~ ↑it↓ which
	l. 12	territory, ? such
	l. 13	cargo ~~taken on board in~~ ↑from↓ Great
¶24	l. 2	that ~~the original act~~ ↑it was originally↓ directed
	l. 4	only. ~~When~~ ↑If↓ we
	l. 8	assign a ~~reason~~ ↑motive↓ for this ↑particular↓ relaxation.
¶25	l. 2	that [*erasure*] ↑it↓ was
	l. 7	to ~~declare~~ ↑ascribe↓ to
¶26	l. 11	alone, [*erasure*] ↑Congress↓ passed
	l. 13	that ~~the act of~~ it
	ll. 14–15	material ~~changes made~~ ↑variances↓ in
	ll. 28–29	dominions ↑if imported from ~~neutral~~ other than British territory↓ with
	l. 29	plausibility ↑as↓ the
¶27	ll. 2–3	now, ↑for↓ which
	l. 3	contend; ~~for~~ or at least ~~wa~~ remained
¶28	ll. 2–3	inadvertence ↑sufficiently ⟨accounted⟩ for by↓ ~~for~~ ↑which↓ the existence of a war ↑which of itself excluded British vessels↓ when

	ll. 3–4	the ~~chang~~ oblivion
	l. 4	subject ~~sufficiently accounts,~~ can
¶29	ll. 1–2	doubt ~~of~~ which ↑can arise in↓ this case ~~is susceptible~~ ↑remains to be noticed. It is↓ that
¶30	l. 6	illustrated ~~with considera~~ by
	ll. 6–7	of ~~that~~ those provisions which ~~respecting~~ ↑respect↓ the
¶31	l. 14	vessels ~~belonging to~~ ↑of↓ Great
	l. 16	nation t for
	l. 17	war [erasure] ↑makes↓ it
	l. 19	prize ~~to the nation.~~ ↑of war.↓ It
	l. 29	then ↑prohibiting them,↓ which
	l. 31	legislature ↑for its repeal↓ must
¶33	l. 3	goods ~~&c~~ from
¶36	l. 2	forfeited ~~be~~ under
	l. 3	also ↑if captured↓ be
	l. 4	the ~~no~~ declaration
	l. 5	much ↑at least↓ of
	l. 8	war. ~~Our Prize act in its~~ The
	l. 12	be ~~the fa~~ admitted,
	l. 15	the ↑paramount↓ operation
	l. 16	subject ~~suspends~~ ↑overreaches↓ the
¶37	l. 1	this ~~subject~~ ↑question↓ has
	l. 5	said, ↑by way of illustrating this argument↓ dissolves
¶38	l. 11	the ~~law~~ ↑war↓ would
	l. 13	States. ~~&~~ ↑That↓ act
¶40	l. 4	cargo, ↑& have ~~taken~~ acted as an enemy,↓ yet
	l. 9	an ~~act~~ ↑offence.↓ But
	l. 10	of ~~an~~ ↑a↓ citizen
¶42	l. 1	the [erasure] ↑captors↓ would
	ll. 3–4	the ~~declaration of~~ ↑act declaring↓ war ↑& the prize act↓ might
	l. 5	which ~~creates~~ ↑created↓ the
	l. 6	of ~~th~~ ↑War,↓ but
¶43	l. 2	according [erasure] ↑to↓ the

The Santissima Trinidad and St. Ander
Opinion
U.S. Circuit Court, Virginia, 20 December 1820

The official style of this prize case was Don Pablo Chacon, consul of Spain, v. Eighty-Nine Bales of Cochineal, Three Bales of Jalap, and One Box of Vanilla. The Spanish consul at Norfolk sought restitution of this merchandise on behalf of its owners, claiming that it had been unlawfully taken from two Spanish vessels, the *Santissima Trinidad* and the *St. Ander*. These goods were claimed as prize of war by James Chaytor, who called himself Don Diego Chaytor and acted as a commodore in the service of the government of the

United Provinces of Río de la Plata. Chaytor and his crew of the *Independencia del Sud* had captured this cargo early in 1817 and brought it into the port of Norfolk in March of that year. Soon thereafter the consul brought his libel in the U.S. District Court. The case raised important questions of international law, particularly with respect to preserving the neutrality of the United States in the wars for Latin American independence. In the district court, Littleton W. Tazewell for the libelant and Gen. Robert B. Taylor for the claimant each consumed twelve hours in arguing the case. On 25 May 1820 Judge Tucker decreed restitution of the cochineal and other articles. In the appeal to the circuit court Tazewell (assisted by Robert Stanard) and Taylor (assisted by John Wickham) again argued the case over several days. Marshall delivered his opinion and decree on 20 December 1820 (*Daily National Intelligencer*, 31 May 1820; Richmond *Enquirer*, 21 Dec. 1820; "Cases in the Courts of the United States, 25 February 1813-November 1824," No. 3, pp. 139–53, Tucker-Coleman Papers, ViW; U.S. Cir. Ct., Va., Ord. Bk. XI, 62; U.S. Cir. Ct., Va., Rec. Bk. XV, 93–275).

It is universally admitted, that the question of prize, or no prize, belongs solely to the courts of the captor. In no case, does a neutral assume the right of deciding it. But offences may be committed by a belligerent, against a neutral, in his military operations, which the neutral ought not to permit; and which give claims upon him, to the party injured by those operations, which he is not at liberty to disregard. In such a situation, the course to be pursued by the neutral, to assert his own rights, and perform his duties, by affording redress to the party injured by a violation of those rights, will vary with varying circumstances. If the wrong doer comes completely within his power, and brings that which will afford complete redress for the wrong done, the usage of nations, generally, as is believed, certainly the usage of this nation, is to restore the thing wrongfully taken. This act vindicates the offended dignity of the neutral, and gives to the injured party, the most ample redress, perhaps, which is attainable, or can reasonably be demanded. This ought to satisfy the sovereign, who claims reparation from the neutral, for his involuntary instrumentality in the war; and ought to be submitted to, by the sovereign of the offending party, whose duty it was, to restrain his officer from violating the rights of a friendly government, or to punish him for their violation. This usage, then, is recommended by the strong consideration of convenience and effectiveness.

This principle having been adopted by the American government, two questions arise in the case under consideration.

1st. Has the capturing vessel so violated the neutrality of the United States, as to give this government the right, and impose upon it the duty, of restoring to the original owners, when brought within its power, the property which has been taken?

2d. By what department is this right to be exercised? this duty to be performed?

Many points have been raised on both sides, and supported with great strength of argument, which on views, which might have been taken of the subject, by the court, it would have been necessary to consider and decide, but which, in the more narrow view that has been taken, need not be considered fully, because they are not necessary to the decision which will be made. These points, therefore, will be noticed very cursorily.

The right of Commodore Chaytor to make prizes, has been denied; because,

1st. He is an American citizen; and,

2dly. His commission does not authorize him to wage war.

1. The commodore, though a native American, insists, that he has expatriated himself, and has become a citizen of Buenos Ayres.

I deem it unnecessary, in this case, to discuss the abstract question of this alleged natural right to dissolve the connexion between an individual and his country, and will only observe, that the principle is often of more serious consequence to those who would shield particular acts by its assertion, than they suppose. The individual who divests himself of the obligations of a citizen, if this be within the power of an individual, loses the rights which are connected with those obligations. He becomes an alien. His lands, if he has any, are escheatable. He cannot recover these rights by residence, but must go through that process which the laws prescribe for the naturalization of an alien born. Would Commodore Chaytor wish to place himself in this situation? I decline inquiring whether he has done so, because I think, that an American citizen may, according to the modern usage of nations, engage in foreign service, without compromising the neutrality of his government.

I do not perceive any solid distinction between the land and naval service, in this particular. It is probable, that foreigners have less frequently obtained commissions in the marine than in the army; and for this it would not be difficult to account; but in cases where the subjects of the nation are supposed to be defective in maritime skill, as in the Russian service, foreigners are not unfrequently engaged.

It has been supposed, that the application of this general principle to Commodore Chaytor, is prevented by our treaty with Spain.

I do not think so; even admitting the Independencia del Sud to have been a privateer, and admitting the construction of the treaty, by the counsel for the libellant, to be right, (and I am very far from assenting to it,) the treaty may affect the individual, personally, but cannot affect the prize. Were it true, that a person holding a commission to cruize under the enemy of one of the contracting parties, might be prosecuted as a pirate, in their courts, he would not be deemed a pirate by the rest of the world. America and Spain may bind themselves, but they cannot bind foreign nations. They cannot bind the republic, if it be one, of Rio de la Plata. Pueyrredon had a right to grant this commission at his city of Buenos Ayres; and the world will respect it just as much as if the treaty between the United States and Spain had never been made.[1] As between the government granting the commission, and the person to whom it is granted, it is valid. Captures made under it, will be deemed valid by that government, and by all foreign nations. Such captures vest the prize in the belligerent sovereign, under whose commission it was made; and, however his prize acts, or his edicts, may dispose of it afterwards, the world considers it as his property, taken by himself. We may punish the instrument, personally, if our law directs it; but this does not authorize us to seize the property of a belligerent sovereign, taken *jure belli*. The only principle on which this can be done, is, that our neutral rights have been violated. Now, the grant of a commission to a neutral, while within the territory of a belligerent, has never been considered as a violation of neutral rights.

2. Neither do I think, the objections to the commission have been sustained.

Admitting that Rio de la Plata was not at war with Spain when it was granted, it is not doubted, that if a commission be given in contemplation of war, or in time of profound peace, that commission may be used when war shall break out. War existed at the time of the capture, and that is sufficient for the captor. The commission, in its terms, gives him the command of the Independencia, and so far as respects that vessel, is equivalent to a general commission in the navy; and the instructions authorize him to *cruize*, which term strongly indicates hostile operations. But I think that a commission to command a ship of war, authorizes the officer holding it, if not interdicted by other circumstances, to attack and capture an enemy.

It has also been contended that this vessel, which was originally the Mammoth of Baltimore, has not been transferred, with good faith, to the government of Rio de la Plata, but is, in truth, the property of an American citizen.

The circumstances in support of this proposition, are certainly entitled to consideration, although they do not outweigh the positive testimony of the transfer. I shall therefore consider the transfer as unimpeached.

The Court is now brought to the inquiry, whether the neutrality of the United States has been violated by any equipment, or augmentation of armament, or enlistment of seamen, within their territory?

These acts are forbidden to a belligerent, by the law of nations; and are also forbidden by an act of congress.

I will put out of the case the equipment in Baltimore, in 1815, for the voyage to Buenos Ayres, in January 1816, because I think the subsequent sale of the vessel authorised the purchaser, if unconnected with the original equipment, to make war upon the enemies of her flag.

I will consider the transactions of Commodore Chaytor, after his arrival in Baltimore, in October 1816, and will first inquire whether he has enlisted any part of his crew, in violation of the neutral character, and of the laws of the United States.

The act of 1794 enacts, "that if any person shall, within the territory or jurisdiction of the United States, enlist or enter himself, or hire, or retain, another person to enlist or enter himself, or to go beyond the limits, or jurisdiction of the United States, with intent to be enlisted or entered, in the service of any foreign prince or state as a soldier, as a marine, or seaman, on board of any vessel of war, letter of marque or privateer," &c. To this clause is added a proviso, which is understood to authorize the enlistment of a transient foreigner to serve on board a ship of war of his own sovereign, not equipped or armed within the United States.[2]

The history of the day informs us, that this act was considered as declaratory of the pre-existing law of nations, and was intended to aid the executive in the enforcement of that law. However serious may be the doubt, whether a section of a nation struggling for its independence, may come within the prohibitions of the act, there can be no doubt that such a people come within the more ample provisions of the law of nations. Whether Buenos Ayres be a state or not, if she is in a condition to make war, and to claim the character and rights of a belligerent, she is bound to respect the laws of war; and the government which concedes her those rights, is bound to maintain its own neutrality, unless it means to become a party to the war, as entirely as if she were an acknowledged state. She has no more right to recruit her navy within the United States, than Spain would have, and this government is as much bound to restrain her from using our strength in the war, as to restrain her enemy. If, therefore, Commodore Chaytor, has recruited any men within the United States, not being the subjects or citizens of Rio de la Plata, he has violated their neutrality.

The depositions of Henry, Irvine, and Pecker, are supposed by the counsel for the claimant, to have no bearing on the case, because they detail only what they have heard from others; and I readily admit, that their testimony, standing alone, would not be sufficient to establish the fact of an enlistment within the United States, prior to the capture of the cochineal, mentioned in the libel.[3] But they prove, unequivocally, that Commodore Chaytor did enlist American citizens, within the United States, for his subsequent cruize; and certainly, positive evidence of this fact, gives, in such a case as this, strong probability to other evidence, which asserts, that the same fact took place, previous to the preceding cruize. They prove also, the current declaration of the crew, that a great number of them were concerned in the preceding cruize, and were enlisted for that cruize, in the United States. I feel some difficulty in totally disregarding these declarations. The private communications of an individual, would certainly be entitled to no consideration; but the public conversation of a ship's crew, relative to the transactions of a ship, in a case where no motives exist for previous combination, will give some belief.

Of the same nature, is the testimony of the master of the captured vessel. He says, that the crew of the Independencia spoke English, and that the second officer told him, they had been equipped and fitted out in Baltimore.[4]

The testimony of John Davis, is positive; and, if true, establishes every thing for which the libellants contend.[5] This witness is supposed to be discredited by others, who, in some respects, are said to contradict him. Let us examine this subject.

Davis swears that he was born in New York, and that he was enlisted in Norfolk, by Hooper, for the Independencia. Currie swears that he is an Englishman, who deserted from an English merchantman, lying in the port of Baltimore, and secreted himself on board the Independencia, until she sailed.[6] It also appears, that Hooper recruited in Baltimore, not in Norfolk. But who is Currie? and what gives him superior credit to Davis? But I waive this inquiry, and will consider how far the repugnancy between their depositions, discredits either. Davis says he was born in New York; and if this be untrue, nothing he says ought to be believed, because, he knowingly asserts a falsehood. Currie says that Davis is an Englishman; and states facts, which may be presumed to be the foundation of his assertion. They are, that he deserted from an English merchantman, and that he had been employed during our war, under the British flag. But seamen, born in England, are found in American merchantmen, and seamen born in New York, may be found on board an English merchantman. The fact of his receiving prize-money, is much stronger, but not conclusive. We have the highest authority for saying, that many of our seamen were impressed, and Davis may be among them. The fact is susceptible of explanation, and might, perhaps, have been explained, had the deposition of Davis been taken, after the statements of Currie were known.

But he states, himself, to have enlisted in Norfolk, when it is proved, that he came on board in Baltimore; and Hooper, by whom he says he was engaged, was employed in Baltimore. But how often is it, that the memory errs with respect to unimportant circumstances, but is correct with respect to the principal subject. That Davis was enlisted, and by Hooper, were facts which would make a much stronger impression on his memory, than the place at which he enlisted. Baltimore and Norfolk were equal to him; he was, probably, at both, and might very well have the impression that he enlisted at the one place, when, in truth, he enlisted at the other. A mistake in such a circumstance, when the mind is not called particularly to it, would not, perhaps, invalidate the testimony of a witness whose moral character is not impeached.

But let it be, that Davis is to be rejected. The testimony which discredits him, must be believed. That testimony, as well as the admission implied in the questions put by Commodore Chaytor, shows, that Davis was enlisted within the United States; and shows, further, that he was not a subject of Buenos Ayres, but an Englishman.

Joseph Smith is proved to be unworthy of credit, but the testimony which discredits him, shows, that he was enlisted within the United States, and is a European Spaniard.[7]

Isaac Berry, also proves the whole case; but he is said to have destroyed his whole testimony, by the contradictions between his first and second depositions.[8] What are those contradictions? In his first, he says that he was shipped by M'Donnel; in his second, by James. Both these men may have kept sailors' houses; both have recruited for Buenos Ayres; both have communicated with Berry; and, certainly, his not recollecting distinctly with which he shipped, the act not always of a sober man, does not prove that he was not shipped at all. The commodore might shake his testimony, on this point, by his muster-roll, or by taking the deposition of those who are alleged to have shipped him, or of some of the crew who would prove, that no such man was on board. But no such testimony is adduced. One Wood, is said, in one deposition, to have been second mate, in another, a midshipman. He might, in the course of the voyage, have been both. But this does not prove that Wood was not on board. He varies in his estimate of the number of the crew. He does not profess to be exact.

I do not think these small variances affect the body of his testimony, especially, as he states a great number of facts which expose him to detection, if he spoke what was untrue.

John Harris, also, proves the whole case; but he, too, is said to be unworthy of belief, because he speaks of a forty-two pounder, which had no existence; and because he speaks of eighteen pounders, instead of twelves.[9]

There may have been some large piece on board, which was not brought in, though it is not probable; but this man, who has probably sailed in many cruizers, may have confounded what was on board one vessel, with the guns on board another. This mistake, if it be one, might affect very seriously his testimony respecting the armament, but does not destroy his testimony respecting his having been on board, when we recollect that he gives, completely, the means of contradicting him, if he could be contradicted. He names the officers and many of the crew, and says by whom he was enlisted. The muster-roll, or James, or any seaman on board the Independencia, could disprove any untruth he may assert. I cannot, therefore, reject his testimony.

John Lewis is discredited, because he says that he is a native American, and is proved to be a Frenchman.[10] I admit that his testimony is to be disregarded, but, still, he was enlisted in the United States, and is not a subject of Buenos Ayres.

Matthew Murray proves the case, but is said, in his second deposition, to speak only from hearsay.[11]

I disregard entirely the testimony of Edward M'Donnel.[12] His reputation is such as to discredit him completely.

I proceed, now, to the examination of the claimant's testimony.

Edward Currie was in the Independencia, while she lay in the port of Baltimore, in 1816, and could have contradicted the enlistments alleged to have been made there, had they been untrue. He speaks only of John Davis.

Daniel James discredits M'Donnel.[13] Why was he not examined as to the enlistment of the crew? It is said that he enlisted Berry; why was he not interrogated as to that fact?

James Barnes, commander of the Mangoree, says, that the Independencia was fitted, equipped, and manned, as he has understood, in Buenos Ayres, in May 1816; that the ships cruizing under the flag of that republic, of which the Mangoree was one, are manned chiefly by foreign seamen.[14] The Regent, another of these cruizers, he understood to be fitted out, and manned in the port of Baltimore. How the vessels of Buenos Ayres were manned, is, in some measure, stated by other witnesses.

Alexander Hunter, a native citizen of the United States, was a sailor on board the Mangoree.[15] Where did he enlist? He does not say, and it is of not much consequence in this case. But he enlisted in the Independencia, in Baltimore. How is this to be justified? He had served the republic in the Mangoree. But did this convert him into a subject of Buenos Ayres, who was not an inhabitant of the United States? Will it be contended that by enlisting on board one privateer, an American citizen acquires a right to enlist, within his own country, on board any other? The crew, he says, belonged to all nations. They did not belong exclusively to Buenos Ayres.

Hugh Cagne says, that he is a native of Ireland, and has been many years in the service of South America.[16] How in her service? He is a seaman, and the fair presumption is, that he served in her marine. What is her marine? We have no reason to presume that it consists of much more than such vessels as the Independencia, the Mangoree, the Altravida, and the Regent, fitted out in other countries, and manned by foreigners. At any rate, he does not state himself to have become a subject of Buenos Ayres, and he does not state himself to have enlisted in Baltimore.

He says, that among her crew, were many North Americans, and most of the crew, who came in her from Buenos Ayres. Where did those of her crew, who were North Americans, and who did not come in her from Buenos Ayres, enlist? We are left to conjecture. But what was the condition of that part of the crew, which came into port with her? The greater number of them sailed in her from Baltimore, and were, we must suppose, engaged for the voyage. On their return to port, their engagements terminated, unless others more extensive were made at Buenos Ayres.

William Amos has been examined, and gives us some information on this subject.[17] After the sale of the vessel, he says, Captain Chaytor came on board, and told them, they were at liberty to continue in the new service, or to be discharged. They chose to continue. Not one syllable is said of changing their political character, and throwing off their allegiance to the United States. Not one syllable is said of their engaging for a longer time, than till the vessel should return to the United States. We must, then, suppose that they continued citizens, and we have the more reason to believe, that their engagements expired on their return to the United States, because, Amos says he then left the vessel, and because Roe, who shipped at Buenos Ayres, also says that he left her at the same place.[18] The crew, then, which came in her from Buenos Ayres, were American citizens, who, most probably, re-enlisted in Baltimore. Such a re-enlistment, is equivalent to an original enlistment. If they engaged for a longer time in Buenos Ayres, I think it would have been stated.

Cagne goes, not to prove the enlistment of strangers, indiscriminately, but that they said they were in the service of the patriots. How in that service? He does not tell us. He does not say, admitting they spoke the truth, that every seaman, who had made a cruize in a privateer, said to be commissioned by any of the patriot governments, did not think himself in the service of the patriots. About fifteen of the crew of the Mangoree, shipped on board of her. All we know of this crew, would lead to the opinion, that they were American, and such other sailors as are found in our ports. They had been in the patriot service, and Captain Chaytor supposed himself authorized by that circumstance, to re-enlist them. But in this he was mistaken.

Cagne says, too, that when she left the capes, her crew consisted of about one hundred and twelve, among whom were twenty-eight or thirty new men. Who were they? Are they proved to be citizens of Buenos Ayres, transiently within the United States? He does not pretend that they were. The fair presumption from the whole testimony is, that they consisted of that class of sailors, who are usually employed in privateering. Whether those who had sailed in the Mangoree, were among the number of new men, is not certainly stated; it is probable they were.

Cagne states a fact, which is certainly material, in the inquiry, respecting the character of the Independencia. It is, that her crew was enlisted, not for the cruize, but for the year, and were on wages. But he entered the vessel in Baltimore, and does not say, that these were the terms on which the original crew were engaged. It gives some complexion to this transaction, that Cagne says, there were two brigs fitting out in Baltimore, which sailed about the same time with the Independencia, which were said to be intended as cruizers. It illustrates the practice of the place, and aids in informing us, what is understood by being in the patriot service.

John H. Speck appears also, to have entered the Independencia in

Baltimore, and he agrees in every thing with Cagne.[19] About thirty men
were enlisted in Baltimore, not one of whom is said to have been a subject
of Buenos Ayres; though they all said they had been in the patriot service.

I think, then, the evidence is more complete, than could have been
expected, in a case of violation of law, that nearly the whole crew of the
Independencia was enlisted within the United States, in violation of the
act of congress, and of the neutrality of this government. The prize goods
in question, have been taken by a neutral force. I must consider the men
who came in the Independencia from Buenos Ayres, and the thirty men
engaged in the Chesapeake, as enlisted within the United States, and as
being men who could not be lawfully enlisted.

It is unnecessary to extend the inquiry to the equipment, or the augmentation of the armament. The enlistment being established, the law is
the same, whether those charges be supported or not.

It is equally unnecessary to extend the inquiry to the Altravida.

The prize having been made, in truth, by neutral means, is it the duty
of the government to restore it to the original owner, when it is brought
within the power of the United States?

The reasoning in favour of an affirmative answer to this question, appears conclusive. The government is bound to maintain its neutrality;
and to prevent a foreign belligerent, from preparing a military force
within its territory, to operate against a nation with whom it is at peace. If
its means of prevention have been eluded, and its force against its will,
been employed by a belligerent, in a manner not authorized by public
law, if it has been thus made an instrument of war, the injured belligerent
has claims on the neutral government, which has corresponding claims
on the aggressing belligerent. If, under such circumstances, the means of
obtaining reparation from the one, and of making it to the other, are
placed within the power of the neutral, the strongest reasons of convenience, and of justice, seem to require that he should use those means.
When a ship of war, which has acquired her military capacities in a neutral country, brings her prize into that country, these plain principles
require, that the prize should be restored. In conformity with them, the
Grange, captured by the Ambuscade frigate, within the waters of the
United States, was restored by the government.[20]

A question of much more difficulty remains to be considered. By what
department of the government is this restitution to be made.

Without recapitulating much of what has been said at the bar, by stating
the reasons on which my opinion is founded, I will acknowledge, that in
my private judgment, this right, and this duty devolve on the executive, or
legislative, and not on the judicial department. The exercise must be regulated by a discretion, which courts do not possess, and may be controlled
by reasons of state, which do not govern tribunals acting on principles of
positive law. If, therefore, this was a case in which my own judgment was
alone to be consulted, I should, I believe, confine myself to the inquiry,

whether any act of congress authorized the restitution sought by the libellants. But this Court is not at liberty to decide for itself. It is bound, and ought to be bound, by the decisions of the supreme court, and its judgment must conform to those decisions. They are admitted to have settled the principle, that property captured by privateers, fitted out, armed, or manned, within the ports of the United States, and brought within the power of our courts, may be restored by them to the original owner.[21] It is, however, contended that the same principle does not extend to captures made by national ships.

That national ships are in many respects distinguishable from privateers, is not to be denied; is this a case in which a sound distinction can be taken between them?

Ships of war and privateers, both cruize under a commission from their sovereign, and both make prizes under the authority of that commission. In both cases, the sovereign is the captor, and the prize vests absolutely in him. The cruizer, in both cases, is a mere instrument of war employed by his sovereign, and the particular interest which the agent may have in the thing acquired, depends on municipal regulations, of which this Court can take no notice. The courts of the captor, will in both cases distribute the proceeds according to those municipal regulations, but foreign courts consider the property as the property of the sovereign, and the possession of the captor as the possession of the sovereign. In both cases, then, the foreign court which acts upon the prize, acts on property in the possession of a foreign sovereign, acquired by his authorized agent. In what then does the difference between the right of courts, to interfere with their prizes consist?

We are told that the national ship of war, carries upon its deck a portion of the sovereignty of his prince, and is, of course, inviolable.

I am not prepared to say that a privateer, commissioned for the purposes of war, is not equally inviolable, at least so far as respects its military operations. But I will not enter into this inquiry. I will ask, how is this inviolability acquired, and how far does it extend?

In the case of the Exchange, the supreme court laid down the principle expressly, that this exemption from the jurisdiction of the nation, in which the national ship of a foreign sovereign is found, is derived, where there is no express compact, from the assent implied in the admission of such vessel into port.[22] But the same case establishes this further principle: that this immunity is granted, on condition that the sovereignty of the place be respected. A breach of the condition, forfeits the immunity depending on it. A national ship, openly and grossly violating the laws of a neutral government, enlisting a full crew, in opposition to those laws, forfeits the condition on which an exemption from those laws was granted. On this principle, the Grange was restored. The government acts without being charged with a violation of faith. If the government acts, it acts by that department, which is entrusted with the power of inquiring, whether the belligerent has violated those neutral rights which forfeit his prize, and if the courts exercise this power rightfully, in the case of prizes made by privateers, they may, I think, exercise it in the case of prizes made by a national ship, and brought within our territory. If there is fallacy in this reasoning, I do not perceive it.

But, supposing it to be applicable to a capture made within our waters, and immediately arrested, it is contended, that it is inapplicable to a capture made on the high seas, and brought within our waters. The violation of neutrality gives, it is said, a claim on the sovereign, whose power is an unit, and cannot give rights to seize prizes made by one vessel, more than by another. When the offending vessel comes again into port, she comes in with all the immunities originally attached to her.

In theory, this argument is strong; but, practically, it would destroy the efficacy of the principle. It would deprive the neutral government of its power to give specific relief; and seems to me to be as applicable to prizes made by privateers, as by national ships.

Another idea was suggested by the counsel for the claimants, of which I feel the full force. It is, that this application to the neutral sovereign, to vindicate his neutral rights, and repair the wrongs done to a foreign sovereign, must be made by that foreign sovereign himself, through his authorized agent, and not by a private individual. Were I to admit this, the question immediately occurs — Does not this objection go as strongly to the restoration of prizes made by privateers, as to the restoration of prizes made by national ships?

I am not sure, that I am master of that train of reasoning, which has conducted the supreme court, to the assertion of that jurisdiction over prizes made by privateers, which has been exercised. If I were, I should not attempt to give it, because it will be stated more ably by those who are themselves convinced of its propriety. I content myself with saying, that I think the principles on which prizes made by privateers, have been restored, apply to prizes made by national ships, who have violated the neutrality of the United States, and I, therefore, hold myself bound to restore in this case. The sentence of the district court is affirmed.[23]

Printed, John W. Brockenbrough, *Reports of Cases Decided by the Honourable John Marshall . . .* , I (Philadelphia, 1837), 484–99.

1. Juan Martín de Pueyrredón was supreme director of the Buenos Aires government from 1816 to 1819. The commission in this case was actually signed by Antonio Gonzales Balcarce, who was acting supreme director before Pueyrredón's appointment (Charles Carroll Griffin, *The United States and the Disruption of the Spanish Empire, 1810–1822* [New York, 1937], 151–54, 258–59; Ricardo Levene *A History of Argentina*, ed. and trans. William Spence Robertson [Chapel Hill, N.C., 1937], 295, 327–28, 336; U.S. Cir. Ct., Va., Rec. Bk. XV, 114–15).

2. *U.S. Statutes at Large*, I, 381, 383

3. Depositions of John Henry, Hugh Irwin, and John Peckner (U.S. Cir. Ct., Va., Rec. Bk. XV, 150–57).

4. Deposition of Nariso Pares Oliver, commander of the *Santissima Trinidad* (ibid., 132–34).

5. Deposition of John Davis (ibid., 135–37).

6. Deposition of Edward Currie (ibid., 199–202).

7. Deposition of Joseph Smith (ibid., 139–41).

8. Deposition of Isaac Berry (ibid., 142–44, 163–65).

9. Deposition of John Harris (ibid., 165–68).

10. Deposition of John Lewis (ibid., 145–47).

11. Deposition of Mathew Murray (ibid., 148–49, 235).

12. Deposition of Edward McDonnel (ibid., 157–61).

13. Deposition of Daniel James (ibid., 216–17).

14. Deposition of James Barnes (ibid., 220–21).

15. Deposition of Alexander Hunter (ibid., 222–24).

16. Deposition of Hugh Cagne (ibid., 224–29).

17. Deposition of William Amos (ibid., 196–98).

18. Deposition of James Row (ibid., 236–37).

19. Deposition of John H. Speck (ibid., 230–32).

20. The *Grange*, a British ship, was captured on Delaware Bay and taken as prize in Apr. 1793 by *L'Embuscade*, a French privateer outfitted by Citizen Genêt. The cabinet determined this capture to be a violation of American neutrality and sought restitution (*ASP, Foreign Relations*, I, 147–49). JM discussed this incident in the *Life of George Washington* (2d ed.; Philadelphia, 1838), II, 262.

21. This principle had most recently been reaffirmed by the Supreme Court in La Amistad de Rues, 5 Wheat. 385, 389 (1820). See Benjamin Munn Ziegler, *The International Law of John Marshall* (Chapel Hill, N.C., 1939), 193–94, and cases cited there.

22. Schooner Exchange v. McFadon, 7 Cranch 116 (1812); *PJM*, VII, 306–15.

23. The case was appealed to the Supreme Court, which affirmed the circuit court's decree at the 1822 term, Story giving the opinion of the Court (7 Wheat. 283, 334).

To Bushrod Washington

My dear Sir   Washington Feby. 8th. 1821

I reached this place yesterday after a very fatiguing journey, & found all our brethren well, & all of them joining me in sincere regrets for your indisposition. However unwilling we may be to lose your aid, we all think that it would be madness to encounter the hazard of joining us, unless your health should be entirely restored. We hope, however, that you are improving, & will continue to improve, so that you may, after the earth & Atmosphere shall become dry, favor us with a short visit. Should you be well enough to remain with us a few days towards the end of the month we would avail ourselves of that time to deliver the opinion in the case of the Isabella[1] & in the case of the outstanding titles.[2] If your health should enable you to hear an argument, we might also hear one in the case of the statute of limitations from New Hampshire, upon which the court was divided & which is to be reargued in the presence of Judge Todd.[3] It is probable too that the case from Virginia, which has excited so much commotion in our legislature, will be set to some late day & it certainly is desirable that the court should be as full as possible when it is decided.[4] I mention these things as eventually to be wished, but as depending altogether on your being enabled to pass a few days in Washington with perfect safety to your self; for we all concur ⟨in advis⟩ing you not to encounter the slightest hazard to your health from any consideration whatever. In the progress of the term you will be enabled to form a better judgement of what you may do without danger; and more we all request that you will not think of attempting.

The wine is in fine order & we shall at dinner give a bumper to your better health.

I have brought with me the letters copied in Richmond, & hope I may see you & have some conversation on this subject before my return to Richmond.

My brethren all join me in sincere wishes for your better health. I am my dear Sir with esteem & affection, Your

J MARSHALL

ALS, Marshall Papers, ViW. Addressed to Washington at Mount Vernon; postmarked Washington, 10 Feb. Endorsed by Washington.

1. The opinion of the Court in The Amiable Isabella was delivered by Story on 22 Feb. (6 Wheat. 1, 65). See Wirt to JM, 11 Mar. 1820 and nn.

2. Possibly Clark v. Graham, 6 Wheat. 577.

3. Bullard v. Bell, an unreported case that had been certified from the U.S. Circuit Court for New Hampshire in 1818. It had been argued at the 1819 term and was ordered to be dismissed in 1824 (U.S. Sup. Ct. Dockets, Bullard v. Bell, App. Cas. No. 913).

4. Cohens v. Virginia.

To Smith Thompson

Dear Sir   Washington Feb. 13. 1821

On my arrival at this place I received a letter from my brother Mr. James Marshall of which I take the liberty to send you an extract.[1]

"My son John when he left Norfolk was informed by Capt. Warrington that by writing to him, he could get a renewal of his furlough.[2] He accordingly wrote early in November, but received no answer until the last post. Capt. Warrington now informs him that the Secretary of the navy requires that the application shall be made directly to him. I am desirous that John should make himself acquainted with the Mathematics, which I find he will have no opportunity of doing on board a ship. I must therefore request you to apply to the Secretary for a furlough for four months, or for such shorter time as the Secretary may think proper to grant. Capt. Warring[ton] says that, as there is nothing at present to do on board the Guerrier, he supposes the Secretary will have no objection to giving such leave of absence as John may require."

Will you have the goodness sir to take this application into consideration & to decide upon it? I wish to write to my brother, & he I presume is desirous of knowing whether his son is to return immediately to Norfolk or may engage in the studies adapted to his profession. With great respect, I am Sir your Obedt.

J MARSHALL

ALS, RG 45, DNA. Addressed to the secretary of the navy. Endorsed "Hon. John Marshall, / Washington, 13 Feb. 1821. / Respecting a furlough for his / nephew."

1. Letter not found.
2. Capt. Lewis Warrington (1782–1851), a native of Williamsburg, attended the College of William and Mary and entered the navy as a midshipman in 1800. His long and distinguished naval career included notable service during the War of 1812. He commanded the *Guerrière* in 1820 and 1821, the ship to which JM's nephew had been assigned.

From Smith Thompson

Sir   Navy Depmt 15th Febry 1821
Agreeably to your request I enclose you herewith a furlough for Midshipman John Marshall.[1] I find that no application of the Kind mentioned in your letter has been made directly to this Depmt. but a request for leave of absence which was granted by Capt. Warrington, as within his discretion as Commander of the Ship. Respectfully &c.

SMITH THOMPSON

ALS (letterbook copy), RG 45, DNA.

1. Midshipman Marshall was reassigned to the *Franklin* on 1 May 1821 (abstract of service record, John Marshall, RG 24, DNA).

To [James Monroe]

Sir   Washington Feb. 20th. 1821
I have conversed with my bretheren on the subject you suggested when I had the pleasure of seeing you, & will take the liberty to communicate the result.[1]

As the constitution only provides that the President shall take the oath it prescribes "before he enter on the execution of his office," and as the law is silent on the subject, the time seems to be in some measure at the discretion of that high officer. There is an obvious propriety in taking the oath as soon as it can conveniently be taken, & thereby shortening the interval in which the executive power is suspended. But some interval is inevitable. The time of the actual President will expire, and that of the President elect commence, at twelve in the night of the 3d. of March. It has been usual to take the oath at mid day on the 4th. Thus there has been uniformly & voluntarily an interval of twelve hours during which the Executive power could not be exercised. This interval may be un-avoidably prolonged. Circumstances may prevent the declaration of the person who is chosen until it shall be too late to communicate the inteli-gence of his elec⟨tion⟩ until after the 4th. of March. This occurred at the first election.

Undoubtedly, on any pressing emergency the President might take the oath in the first hour of the 4th. of March; but it has never been thought necessary so to do, & he has always named such hour as he deemed most convenient. If any circumstance should render it unfit to take the oath on the 4th. of March, and the public business would sustain no injury by its being deferred till the 5th., no impropriety is percieved in deferring it till the 5th. Whether the fact that the 4th. of March comes this year on Sunday be such a circumstance may perhaps depend very much on pub-lic opinion and feeling. Of this, from our retired habits, there are few perhaps less capable of forming a correct opinion than ourselves. Might we hazard a conjecture, it would rather be in favor of postponing the oath till Monday unless some official duty should require its being taken on Sunday. But others who mix more in society than we do, can give conjec-tures on this subject much more to be confided in than ours. With very great respect, I have the honor to be, Your obedt. Servt

J MARSHALL

ALS, RG 59, DNA. Note above salutation (hand of John Quincy Adams?): "J. Marshall."

1. Although this letter is in the State Department records, the addressee was probably President Monroe. Secretary of State Adams noted in his diary that Monroe had written to the chief justice requesting the Supreme Court's opinion about postponing the oath of office from Sunday, 4 Mar., to Monday, 5 Mar. (Charles Francis Adams, ed., *Memoirs of John Quincy Adams*, V [Philadelphia, 1875], 302).

To Mary W. Marshall

My dearest Polly   Washington March [February] 26th. 1821

I had the pleasure to day of receiving a letter from James of the 24th. informing me of your return from Chiccahominy.[1] I am very glad to hear that you have passed safely through the noisy rejoicings of the 22d & are as well as usual.[2] I hope care was taken to keep every thing quiet while you were at the plantation & that you slept better than you did at christmass. James informs me that you heard the drum distinctly & that the Cannon shook the house. Of course your mornings nap was interrupted but I hope you slept through the night.

Judge Washington still continues unwell at Alexandria & I have no hope of his joining us during the court. We continue very busy & have as much rain as heart could wish. We dine out too frequently & I think eating such late & hearty dinners disagrees with me. I watch myself, & resolve every day that I will be moderate but I cannot keep my resolution.

Washington is still very gay. There are continual parties but I make a point not to go to them. Farewell my dearest Polly, I am your ever affectionate

J MARSHALL

ALS, Marshall Papers, ViW. Addressed to Mrs. Marshall in Richmond; postmarked Washington, 27 Feb. Date assigned on basis of postmark and internal evidence. JM to James K. Marshall, 26 Feb. 1821, begins immediately below signature.

1. Letter not found. For JM's farm on the Chickahominy River, see *PJM*, VIII, 149, 150 n. 4, 179–80 and n. 3.

2. The celebration of Washington's birthday in Richmond was marked by "more than the usual honors—with salutations of Cannon, and military Parades" (Richmond *Enquirer*, 24 Feb. 1821). Because of her extreme nervous condition, Polly Marshall could not tolerate loud noises. She customarily left town at times of "noisy rejoicings" (see *PJM*, VIII, 146).

To James K. Marshall

My dear Son   [26 February 1821]

I have just received your letter of the 24th. & am very glad to hear that your mother has sustained no inconvenience from her visit to Chiccahominy.[1] I wish you would let me know what you think is the matter with young Jacob. Does he fall away much & lose his appetite? Does he stay in the house or go out? I wish to know whether you think him so seriously ill as to require a physician.

I wrote to you the other day to purchase five bushels of clover seed but I apprehend, if you should not get the money from Smith that you will not have enough to purchase th⟨a⟩t ⟨q⟩uantity.[2] I[n] that event purchase as far as t⟨he money⟩ will go.

I have heard nothing from D⟨. . . .⟩ John says he wrote to you concerning ⟨. . .⟩ before his leaving Fauquier.

I am obliged to you for sending me Mr. Murdocks letter.[3] I hope he received a letter from me about Christmass. I am my dear Son your affectionate Father

J MARSHALL

ALS, Marshall Papers, ViW. Letter begins immediately below JM to Mary W. Marshall, 26 Feb. 1821. MS torn.

1. Letter not found.

2. The reference is possibly to Thomas Smith, who leased part of the Oak Hill estate in Fauquier County (*PJM*, II, 195).

3. Letter not found. William Murdock of London was agent for the Marshalls in the Fairfax business (*PJM*, VI, 91 n. 4, 427 n. 6).

Cohens v. Virginia
Opinion
U.S. Supreme Court, 3 March 1821

EDITORIAL NOTE

Cohens v. *Virginia* elicited from Chief Justice Marshall a comprehensive inquiry into the constitutional foundations and extent of federal judicial power. "The judicial Power," declares the Constitution, "shall extend to all Cases, in Law and Equity, arising under this Constitution, the laws of the United States, and Treaties made, or which shall be made, under their Authority." In *Cohens* the chief justice read the "arising under" clause as conferring upon the Supreme Court broad jurisdiction to decide cases involving the conflicting powers of the general and state governments. Marshall had already announced in his extrajudicial and anonymous defense of *McCulloch* v. *Maryland* the theme he would develop in *Cohens*. Among the charges leveled against the bank decision, none cut more deeply than the contention that the Supreme Court was not a competent tribunal to decide that case or any controversy that brought into question the boundary between federal and state powers. In reply Marshall as "A Friend of the Constitution" briefly expounded the "arising under" clause.[1] *Cohens* provided the occasion for the chief justice to respond judicially to Spencer Roane and other states' rights champions who denied the Supreme Court's adjudicatory role in maintaining the federal system.

The brothers Philip and Mendez Cohen were members of a family that had settled in Baltimore in 1803 and established a successful mercantile business, specializing in the vending of lottery tickets. Jacob Cohen, the eldest brother, opened a lottery office in 1812, and seven years later Philip and Mendez Cohen moved to Norfolk to set up the company's first branch office. Subsequently, branches were established in Richmond, Philadelphia, New York, and Charleston.[2] The case against the brothers who ran the Norfolk branch began on 26 June 1820, when a grand jury of the borough court presented them for selling "National Lottery" tickets contrary to a Virginia law. At the succeeding term, on 2 September 1820, the court found them guilty and assessed a fine of one hundred dollars. A motion to appeal the judgment to a higher state court was refused on the ground that cases of this kind were "not subject to revision by any other Court of the Commonwealth." The brothers then obtained a writ of error to take their case directly to the federal Supreme Court, as provided by section twenty-five of the Judiciary Act. The appeal was filed on 6 February 1821, in time to be heard at that term of the court.[3]

The rapid and unimpeded progress of this cause from the local borough court to the Supreme Court suggests that it was designed to be a test case. It proceeded on an agreed statement of facts in which the defendants admitted selling the tickets. The remainder of the agreed case consisted of an act of the Virginia General Assembly that prohibited the sale of lottery tickets not authorized by the laws of the commonwealth, and three acts of Congress incorporating the city of Washington in the District of Columbia. The last of these acts, adopted in 1812, empowered the corporation to authorize the drawing of lotteries for public improvement projects. The Cohens maintained they had a legal right under these acts of Congress to sell "National Lottery" tickets notwithstanding the law of Virginia.[4]

From the outset the issue was whether the law authorizing lotteries in the District of Columbia had such extraterritorial operation as to override state laws that prohibited lotteries. Long before the case was argued in the Supreme Court, this question was thoroughly aired in the executive council and legislature of Virginia and in the public prints. Public discussion of the lottery issue, however, appears to have been initially prompted not by the legal proceedings in Norfolk but by an opinion signed by five prominent lawyers under a New York dateline of 27 June 1820. The first two signers were William Pinkney and David B. Ogden, who later represented the Cohens in the Supreme Court; the others were Thomas A. Emmet, John Wells, and Walter Jones. The lawyers emphatically declared that the state legislatures had no power to prohibit the sale of tickets in lotteries established in the city of Washington. A lottery authorized by Congress for the purpose of making improvements in the "national city" was a "national lottery," the opinion read, "and it would be monstrous if any state legislature could impede the execution of a law made for national purposes."[5]

The opinion was evidently prepared at the request of a New York vendor who was later indicted for selling national lottery tickets in that city.[6] Rumors about the opinion circulated in Richmond a month before editor Thomas Ritchie published it in the *Enquirer* on 5 September, a few days after the Norfolk judgment against the Cohens. In succeeding numbers Ritchie published essays refuting the lawyers' opinion.[7] Early commentary on the lottery question dealt with the merits — whether a state could prohibit the sale of tickets to lotteries authorized by the District of Columbia under acts of Congress. In October attention began to shift to broader constitutional issues raised by the Cohens' appeal of their case to the Supreme Court. On 27 October Ritchie published what he called the "singular Summons," signed by Chief Justice Marshall on 17 October, which "cited and admonished" the Commonwealth of Virginia to appear at the February 1821 term of the Supreme Court. In an accompanying editorial he predicted that the state would protest against the Supreme Court's jurisdiction "in dragging one of the United States to its bar."[8]

On receiving the summons Governor Thomas M. Randolph in consultation with his executive council appointed two members of the state's delegation in Congress to represent the commonwealth: Philip P. Barbour (1783–1841), who had served in the House of Representatives since 1814, and Alexander Smyth (1765–1830), a member of the House since 1817. In January 1821 a committee of the legislature responded to the summons by issuing a lengthy report and resolutions that rehearsed many of the arguments Barbour and Smyth soon after presented to the Supreme Court. Much of the report was devoted to demonstrating that the Supreme Court had no jurisdiction to hear the lottery case. In support of this conclusion the report restated the principles of states' rights republicanism that had become enshrined as political orthodoxy in Virginia: the Constitution as a compact in which the states as the constituent parties had surrendered only that portion of their sovereignty necessary for the general government to carry out its expressly enumerated objects. The general and state governments, according to this view, remained virtually separate and independent of each other, and the states were the rightful expositors of the extent of their own powers. Appended to the report were resolutions entering the legislature's "solemn protest" against the Supreme Court's jurisdiction and directing that copies of the report and resolutions be transmitted to the state's counsel.[9]

In addition to the "solemn protest," the General Assembly in its final action on this matter adopted a resolution declaring that the Supreme Court did "not possess appellate jurisdiction, in any case decided by a state court" and that a state could not be made defendant in any suit before a federal tribunal.[10] The lottery case had thus ripened into a full-blown constitutional controversy, with the legislature casting itself as the guardian of the rights and dignity of the commonwealth. That Virginia had been cited to appear at the bar of the Supreme Court was regarded as a monstrous invasion of state sovereignty and independence. The very right of the state "to protect and preserve the morals" of its own citizens was to be left to a tribunal that was manifestly disqualified from deciding impartially.[11] To what extent Chief Justice Marshall followed the progress of the controversy preceding the hearing of the appeal is not known, but he surely understood that *Cohens* v. *Virginia* presented the greatest test to date of the Supreme Court's authority to umpire disputes arising within the federal system.

The lawyers for Virginia argued the motion to dismiss the writ of error on 13 February. Barbour denied the Court's jurisdiction principally on the ground that a state was a party. He cited the political "axiom . . . that a sovereign and independent State is not liable to the suit of any individual, nor amenable to any judicial power, without its own consent." According to the doctrine of "sovereign immunity," a state could not be made a party to such a suit. Without parties there was no "case" to which the judicial power could extend — even though a state might have committed a clear violation of the Constitution.[12] Co-counsel Smyth asserted the proposition that the federal and state judicial systems were separate and independent of each other when acting within their respective spheres. This was a case arising upon Virginia's criminal laws, he insisted, the enforcement of which lay completely within the cognizance of the state's judiciary. Reopening a point supposedly settled by *Martin* v. *Hunter's Lessee*, Smyth further maintained that the Supreme Court's appellate jurisdiction extended only to revise judgments of inferior federal courts. State courts had exclusive power to judge of their own laws, he urged, for the states were "as properly sovereign now as they were under the confederacy."[13]

Nearly a week elapsed before Ogden and Pinkney, on 19 February, made the case for the Court's jurisdiction. It was sufficient for this jurisdiction, they argued, that a party claimed some right or privilege under the federal Constitution or laws. The claim might be absurd or frivolous, but this point was to be decided on the merits and had no bearing on the jurisdictional issue. The express language of the Constitution extended the judicial power to "all cases" arising under federal law. The principle of sovereign immunity did not create an exception where a state was a party, said Ogden, for "we deny, that since the establishment of the national constitution, there is any such thing as a sovereign State, independent of the Union."[14] Pinkney asserted that the Supreme Court must have appellate jurisdiction over the state tribunals if the "arising under" clause was to have any meaningful effect. Such jurisdiction was "indispensably necessary to the existence of the Union," he added, citing the "axiom of political science, that the judicial power of every government must be commensurate with its legislative authority."[15]

Marshall delivered the Court's unanimous opinion sustaining its jurisdiction on 3 March. The opinion was an extended exegesis of the judiciary article of the Constitution, in which the chief justice applied those rules of construction that judges traditionally employed to interpret written instruments. The governing rule of interpretation was to determine the "intention" of the document, and for Marshall the most reliable guide to intention was the literal meaning of the words. The "spirit" of a law no less than its strict letter was to be respected, but the spirit, too, was to be derived chiefly from the words.

In many of his notable constitutional decisions, Marshall rejected a restrictive reading of general words that qualified their meaning and introduced exceptions. The principal burden of proof, he contended, fell upon those who would depart from the plain meaning of words. More often than not the attempt to restrict the meaning to narrower limits than the words literally imported failed one or more tests laid down by the rules of construction. For example, the justification might rely on some supposed intention or spirit of the Constitution not grounded in the text. Strict construction might also fail the test of consequences, that is, it would in effect render the Constitution's provisions meaningless or subvert its objects and purposes. On the other hand, a restrictive reading of the words of one part of the Constitution was sometimes necessary to give full effect to those of another.

All of these elements of Marshall's method of constitutional interpretation were present in *Cohens*. The greater part of the opinion was devoted to showing that the words "all cases" in the "arising under" clause were to be understood literally as not admitting of any exception on the ground that a state was a party. The attempt to introduce such an exception, he concluded, rested on an abstract theory of state sovereignty that was applicable to the former Confederation but was not warranted by the words or spirit of the Constitution that had operated since 1789. The restrictive construction urged by Virginia, moreover, was to be rejected on account of its "mischievous consequences," namely, that it "would prostrate" the general government "at the feet of every state in the Union."[16]

A more difficult objection was that if the jurisdiction was conferred, it could only be original, not appellate. Here counsel for Virginia had pointed to an express provision of the Constitution. The "distributive clause" of the judiciary article declared that in "all cases" where a state was a party the Supreme Court "shall have original jurisdiction." Cases arising under the Constitution and laws were allocated to appellate jurisdiction. With respect to this clause, Marshall gave the words a narrower scope than their literal meaning. To rely on the latter in this instance, he observed, would produce inconsistency or repugnancy. A case in which a state was a party might also be a case arising under federal law. Construction was necessary to reconcile two seemingly contradictory rules supplied by the Constitution. To give effect to both the "arising under" and "distributive" clauses while preserving the "true intent" of the Constitution, the chief justice concluded that the "affirmative words" conferring original jurisdiction in cases where a state was a party should not be read "negatively" to deny appellate jurisdiction if the case also arose under federal law.[17]

In similar fashion Marshall restricted the scope of the Eleventh Amendment, which declared that federal judicial power should "not be construed to extend to any suit . . . commenced or prosecuted against" a state by citizens of another state or by foreigners. Both the history and language of that amendment, he argued, evinced a purpose merely to bar suits brought by individual creditors against the states. No intention could be read into it "to strip the government of the means of protecting, by the instrumentality of its courts, the constitution and laws from active violation."[18] The amendment, indeed, did not apply to this case, for the writ of error prosecuted by the Cohens was not a "suit" as defined by such eminent authorities on the common law as Coke, Bacon, and Blackstone.

Marshall read the words "all cases" in the "arising under" clause expansively, or more precisely, he did not read them restrictively. Although the words of that clause did not explicitly confer appellate jurisdiction over judgments of state courts in cases arising under federal law, he contended that such a construction was entirely consonant with the nature and objects of the Constitution. He buttressed this reading by taking into account "those considerations to which courts have always allowed great weight in the exposition of laws."[19] Here he invoked the historical circumstances that produced the Constitution, its "contemporaneous exposition" in the *Federalist* and in the Judiciary Act of 1789, and the long practice of hearing appeals under the twenty-fifth section of that act. Again, the weakness of the restrictive construction was that it was not founded on the letter of the Constitution but on its presumed "spirit" — a spirit derived not from the text but from some abstract hypothesis about the nature of the federal union.

In denying the motion for dismissing the writ of error, the Supreme Court affirmed its authority to adjudge the merits of the Cohens' claim. The Commonwealth of Virginia was already on record as refusing to argue the merits, but Cohens' counsel was likewise disinclined to pursue the case. However, since other lottery cases had arisen or were about to arise, the Court believed it should hear arguments on the merits. This argument took place on 2 March, the day before the Court handed down the opinion on the jurisdiction. Ogden and Attorney General Wirt stated the case for the lottery interests and were opposed by Webster, who let it be known that he appeared not as counsel for Virginia but as counsel for New York in a similar case.[20]

The opinion on the merits, delivered on 5 March, was decidedly an anticlimax. From expounding the Constitution to affirm a spacious view of federal judicial power, Marshall now undertook a relatively mundane exercise in statutory construction. Here, too, he applied the same rules of interpretation, though the result on this occasion was against an expansive reading of the act empowering the corporation of Washington to authorize the drawing of lotteries. Examining the words of that grant, the chief justice could discern no express or implied intent on the part of Congress to give the corporation's acts any extraterritorial obligation, certainly not to the extent of trumping a state's penal laws.

Chief Justice Marshall perhaps hoped the decision on the merits would forestall the anticipated outcry against the Court's assumption of jurisdiction. Besides calming suspicions that the Court was bent upon a career of federal aggrandizement and consolidation, the dismissal of the Cohens' claim would show the Court's good faith and moderation and inspire confidence that the federal judiciary could safely be entrusted with questions touching the respective powers of the general and state governments. A contemporary critic complained that the judgment on the merits was a " 'political maneuver' " to allay " 'apprehension that might be excited by sustaining the jurisdiction.' " Whether or not the second decision was contrived for this purpose, the chief justice, on being asked for a copy of the opinion on the jurisdiction for publication in the *Daily National Intelligencer*, informed the publishers that it would "be proper also to publish the opinion on the merits."[21]

If upholding the fine levied by Virginia against the Cohens made the decision on the jurisdiction more palatable to the public at large, it by no means mollified the partisans of state sovereignty in Virginia. Ritchie predicted that an opinion "so obnoxious in its doctrines" would "be thoroughly anatomised by some competent critics."[22] From mid-May through mid-July the pages of the *Enquirer* were filled with scathing reviews by "Somers," "Algernon Sidney," and "Fletcher of Saltoun." Each of these writers severely castigated the Supreme Court and its chief for misusing the rules of construction to impose their own political opinions in favor of federal consolidation. The sweeping assumption of federal judicial power was censured as a flagrant misreading, completely at odds with the principle of sovereign immunity and with the explicit constitutional language embodied in the Tenth and Eleventh Amendments. The Court's method of construction, "Somers" declared, was "a vampyre which sucks out the life-blood of the constitution."[23] "Fletcher" arraigned the Court for abandoning simplicity in construction in favor of "metaphysical refinements and philosophical subtlety."[24]

It was left to "Algernon Sidney" to launch the most comprehensive assault upon the principles and reasoning of *Cohens*. The author was widely known to be Judge Roane, Virginia's most vocal and passionate defender of state sovereignty, who had undertaken a similar assignment as "Hampden" in response to the Court's decision in *McCulloch* v. *Maryland*.[25] Roane's mission, as it had been in 1819, was to sound the clarion in defense of the liberties of the people, to rouse his fellow Virginians to take the lead once again in resisting federal usurpation. Characteristically, Roane cast his analysis in broad terms of political philosophy, restating themes set forth in his "Hampden" essays. Not content merely to provide a point-by-point refutation of the Court's construction of the judiciary article, he contended that the Supreme Court was disqualified from deciding this case by the very nature of the American union. The Constitution, he said, was "a confederation of free states," a compact between two parties, neither of which was "competent to settle, conclusively, the chartered rights of the other."[26]

Roane expressed his indictment with typical biting sarcasm, making no effort to suppress his disdain for the motives and reasoning of the Court. The opinion could "only be accounted for," he wrote, "from that love of power, which all history informs us infects and corrupts all who possess it, and from which even the high and ermined judges, themselves, are not exempted." Not only were its principles to be reprobated, but the opinion was defective in "form and structure"; it was "unusually tedious, and tautologous" and abounded in defects of logic and proof. That the opinion was unanimous could "only be ascribed to a culpable apathy in the other judges" or an inexcusable "confidence . . . in the principles and talents of their chief."[27]

"Algernon Sidney," like "Hampden" in 1819, succeeded in irritating Marshall, who complained of the author's "coarseness & malignity of invective" and his "calumnies & misrepresentations." Although lamenting that "in support of the sound principles of the constitution, & of the Union of the States, not a pen is drawn," the chief justice on this occasion confined his response to private correspondence. No doubt he was much relieved to learn that Henry Wheaton, styling himself "A Federalist of 1789," was at that very moment writing a reply to "Algernon Sidney." Wheaton's essays, said Marshall, were a "masterly answer."[28] Behind Roane's public tirade, Marshall detected the directing hand of Thomas Jefferson, whom the chief justice suspected of being both ideologically and personally hostile to an independent federal judiciary. Indeed, he attributed a large measure of this hostility to spiteful motives arising from *Marbury* v. *Madison* and *Livingston* v. *Jefferson*. The attack upon the judiciary department, "if not originating with Mr. Jefferson, is obviously approved & guided by him."[29]

Marshall's conjectures about Jefferson's involvement in Roane's project were not wholly unjustified, though the chief justice failed to appreciate the extent to which the former president was a reluctant participant. Besides privately endorsing Roane's essays and initiating steps to secure their republication, Jefferson yielded to pressure from Roane and Ritchie to publish an extract of a letter praising John Taylor's *Construction Construed, and Constitutions Vindicated*, a work highly critical of the Supreme Court. Although the extract did not mention *Cohens* or the judiciary, Ritchie's editorial introduction called upon good republicans to heed Jefferson's words and resist "yielding up the rights of the states at the feet of a *self-arrogated supremacy*."[30] Privately, Jefferson had spoken of the federal judiciary as "the subtle corps of sappers and miners constantly working under ground to undermine the foundations of our confederated fabric." Marshall's suspicions that his rival held such views were in some measure confirmed by Story, who happened to see a letter written by Jefferson that denied the Supreme Court's claim to be the arbiter of the federal system. The Massachusetts jurist accused Jefferson of seeking "to prostrate the judicial authority & annihilate all public reverence of its dignity." From the same source Marshall learned of Jefferson's efforts to have Roane's essays republished in a law journal.[31]

To Marshall the actions of Roane, Ritchie, and their allies, carried out with the blessing if not at the behest of "the great Lama of the mountains," had the appearance of a concerted campaign to dismantle the Union by first striking at its most vulnerable point, the federal judiciary. He saw "a deep design to convert our government into a meer league of States" and predicted an attempt to repeal section twenty-five of the Judiciary Act.[32] Indeed, Roane drafted a series of proposed amendments to the Constitution aimed at stripping away a large portion of federal judicial power. These were submitted to the Virginia legislature in February 1822, but that body adjourned without adopting them. Earlier, Senator Richard M. Johnson of Kentucky had introduced an amendment in Congress to give the Senate appellate jurisdiction in all cases where a state was a party or desired to become a party because its laws were in question. Nothing came of this proposal as well, but during the next several years anti-Court sentiment continued to be a source of concern to the chief justice.[33]

1. *PJM*, VIII, 356–57, 359–63.

2. W. Ray Luce, *Cohens v. Virginia (1821): The Supreme Court and State Rights, a Reevaluation of Influences and Impacts* (New York, 1990), 1–3.

3. 6 Wheat. 265–67, 289–90; Cohens v. Virginia, App. Cas. No. 1068.

4. 6 Wheat. 267–89.

5. *Niles' Weekly Register* (Baltmore), XIX (1820–21), 4.

6. Accounts of this indictment were reprinted from a New York newspaper in the Richmond *Enquirer*, 1, 7 Dec. 1820.

7. *Enquirer*, 8, 25 Aug., 5, 19, 29 Sept. 1820. The first publication of the opinion south of New York was in Baltimore editor Hezekiah Niles's paper of 2 Sept. 1820 (*Niles' Weekly Register* [Baltimore], XIX [1820–21], 3–5).

8. *Enquirer*, 27 Oct. 1820.

9. Ibid., 11 Jan. 1821.

10. Ibid., 11 Jan., 10, 20, 22 Feb. 1821.

11. " 'The last of the' Republicans," ibid., 25 Jan. 1821.

12. 6 Wheat. 290–312 (quotation at 303).

13. Martin v. Hunter's Lessee, 1 Wheat. 305 (1816); 6 Wheat. 312–44 (quotation at 327).

14. 6 Wheat. 344–51 (quotation at 347).

15. 6 Wheat. 351–75 (quotation at 354). Barbour on 20 Feb. spoke in reply to Ogden and Pinkney. Wheaton appears to have incorporated the reply with his report of Barbour's opening speech of 13 Feb.

16. Opinion, 3 Mar. 1821 (118, below).

17. Ibid. (123–24, below).

18. Ibid. (130, below).

19. Ibid. (134, below).

20. *Daily National Intelligencer*, 3 Mar. 1821.

21. Charles Hammond, writing as "Hampden" in the Washington *Gazette*, 20 Aug. 1821 (quoted in G. Edward White, *The Marshall Court and Cultural Change, 1815–1835* [New York, 1991], 520); JM to Gales and Seaton, 3 Mar. 1821.

22. *Enquirer*, 23 Mar. 1821. For a sampling of newspaper reaction, see Luce, *Cohens v. Virginia*, 157–87.

23. *Enquirer*, 12 June 1821. His seven numbers were published in the *Enquirer*, 15, 22 May, 1, 12, 19, 29 June, 13 July 1821. "Somers" has been identified as Peyton Randolph (1779–1828), a lawyer and son of the late Edmund Randolph. He was soon to be appointed official reporter for the Virginia Court of Appeals (Luce, *Cohens v. Virginia*, 166–69; R. Gaines Tavenner, "Peyton Randolph," in W. Hamilton Bryson, ed., *The Virginia Law Reporters before 1800* [Charlottesville, Va., 1977], 47–48).

24. *Enquirer*, 3 July 1821. Ritchie published the four numbers of "Fletcher" on 22, 26 June, 3, 6 July 1821. Without identifying him by name, JM spoke of him as "deeply concerned in pillaging the purchasers of the Fairfax estate" (JM to Story, 13 July 1821).

25. See *PJM*, VIII, 284–86. The five "Algernon Sidney" essays were published in the *Enquirer* on 25, 29 May, 1, 5, 8 June 1821. They have been reprinted in *John P. Branch Historical Papers of Randolph-Macon College*, II (June 1906), 78–183.

26. *Branch Historical Papers*, II (June 1906), 80, 97.

27. Ibid., 83, 88, 89.

28. JM to Story, 15 June, 13 July, 18 Sept. 1821 and n. 3.

29. JM to Story, 13 July, 18 Sept. 1821.

30. *Enquirer*, 17 July 1821; Dumas Malone, *Jefferson and His Time*, VI: *The Sage of Monticello* (Boston, 1981), 354–59.

31. Jefferson to Ritchie, 25 Dec. 1820, quoted in Malone, *Sage of Monticello*, 356; Story to JM, 27 June 1821; JM to Story, 18 Sept. 1821.

32. JM to Story, 18 Sept. 1821.

33. Luce, *Cohens v. Virginia*, 183–84; Charles Warren, *The Supreme Court in United States History* (2 vols.; Boston, 1926), I, 657–72.

OPINION

This is a writ of error to a judgment rendered in the Court of Hustings for the Borough of Norfolk, on an information for selling lottery tickets contrary to an act of the Legislature of Virginia. In the state court, the defendant claimed the protection of an act of Congress. A case was agreed between the parties, which states the act of Assembly on which the prosecution was founded, and the act of Congress on which the defendant relied, and concludes in these words: "If upon this case the court shall be of opinion that the acts of Congress before mentioned were valid, and, on the true construction of those acts, the lottery tickets sold by the defendants as aforesaid might lawfully be sold within the state of Virginia, notwithstanding the act or statute of the general assembly of Virginia prohibiting such sale, then judgment to be entered for the defendants: And if the court should be of opinion that the statute or act of the general assembly of the state of Virginia, prohibiting such sale, is valid, notwithstanding the said acts of Congress, then judgment to be entered that the defendants are guilty, and that the commonwealth recover against them one hundred dollars and costs."

Judgment was rendered against the defendants; and the court in which it was rendered being the highest court of the state in which the cause was cognizable, the record has been brought into this court by writ of error.[1]

The defendant in error moves to dismiss this writ, for want of jurisdiction.

In support of this motion, three points have been made, and argued with the ability which the importance of the question merits. These points are —

1st. That a state is a defendant.

2d. That no writ of error lies from this court to a state court.

3d. The third point has been presented in different forms by the gentlemen who have argued it. The counsel who opened the cause, said that the want of jurisdiction was shown by the subject matter of the case. The counsel who followed him, said that jurisdiction was not given by the judicial act.[2] The court has bestowed all its attention on the arguments of both gentlemen, and supposes that their tendency is to show that this court has no jurisdiction of the case, or, in other words, has no right to review the judgment of the state court, because neither the constitution nor any law of the United States has been violated by that judgment.

The questions presented to the court by the two first points made at the bar are of great magnitude, and may be truly said vitally to affect the Union. They exclude the inquiry whether the constitution and laws of the United States have been violated by the judgment which the plaintiffs in error seek to review; and maintain that, admitting such violation, it is not in the power of the government to apply a corrective. They maintain that the nation does not possess a department capable of restraining peaceably, and by authority of law, any attempts which may be made, either intentionally or inadvertently,[3] by a part, against the legitimate powers of the whole; and that the government is reduced to the alternative of submitting to such attempts, or of resisting them by force. They maintain that the constitution of the United States has provided no tribunal for the final construction of itself, or of the laws or treaties of the nation; but that this power may be exercised in the last resort by the courts of every state in the Union. That the constitution, laws, and treaties, may receive as many constructions as there are states; and that this is not a mischief, or, if a mischief, is irremediable. These abstract propositions are to be determined; for he who demands decision without permitting inquiry affirms that the decision he asks does not depend on inquiry.

If such be the constitution, it is the duty of the court to bow with respectful submission to its provisions. If such be not the constitution, it is equally the duty of this court to say so; and to perform that task which the American people have assigned to the judicial department.

1st. The first question to be considered is, whether the jurisdiction of this court is excluded by the character of the parties, one of them being a state, and the other a citizen of that State?

The second section of the third article of the constitution defines the extent of the judicial power of the United States. Jurisdiction is given to the courts of the Union in two classes of cases. In the first, their jurisdiction depends on the character of the cause, whoever may be the parties. This class comprehends "all cases in law and equity arising under this constitution, the laws of the United States, and treaties made, or which shall be made, under their authority." This clause extends the jurisdiction of the court to all the cases described, without making in its terms any exception whatever, and without any regard to the condition of the party. If there be any exception, it is to be implied against the express words of the article.

In the second class, the jurisdiction depends entirely on the character of the parties. In this are comprehended "controversies between two or more states, between a state and citizens of another state," "and between a state and foreign states, citizens, or subjects." If these be the parties, it is entirely unimportant what may be the subject of controversy. Be it what it may, these parties have a constitutional right to come into the courts of the Union.

The counsel for the defendant in error have stated that the cases which arise under the constitution must grow out of those provisions which are capable of self-execution; examples of which are to be found in the 2d section of the 4th article, and in the 10th section of the 1st article.

A case which arises under a law of the United States must, we are likewise told be a right given by some act which becomes necessary to execute the powers given in the constitution, of which the law of naturalization is mentioned as an example.

The use intended to be made of this exposition of the first part of the section defining the extent of the judicial power, is not clearly understood. If the intention be merely to distinguish cases arising under the constitution from those arising under a law, for the sake of precision in the application of this[4] argument, these propositions will not be controverted. If it be to maintain that a case arising under the constitution, or a law, must be one in which a party comes into court to demand something conferred on him by the constitution or a law, we think the construction too narrow. A case in law or equity consists of the right of the one party, as well as of the other, and may truly be said to arise under the constitution or a law of the United States, whenever its correct decision depends on the construction of either. Congress seems to have intended to give its own construction of this part of the constitution in the 25th section of the judicial act; and we perceive no reason to depart from that construction.

The jurisdiction of the court, then, being extended by the letter of the constitution to all cases arising under it, or under the laws of the United States, it follows that those who would withdraw any case of this description from that jurisdiction, must sustain the exemption they claim on the spirit and true meaning of the constitution, which spirit and true meaning must be so apparent as to overrule the words which its framers have employed.

The counsel for the defendant in error have undertaken to do this; and have laid down the general proposition, that a sovereign independent state is not suable, except by its own consent.

This general proposition will not be controverted. But its consent is not requisite in each particular case. It may be given in a general law. And if a state has surrendered any portion of its sovereignty, the question whether a liability to suit be a part of this portion depends on the instrument by which the surrender is made. If, upon a just construction of that instrument, it shall appear that the state has submitted to be sued, then it has parted with this sovereign right of judging in every case on the justice of its own pretensions, and has entrusted that power to a tribunal in whose impartiality it confides.

The American states as well as the American people, have believed a close and firm Union to be essential to their liberty and to their happiness. They have been taught by experience, that this Union cannot exist without a government for the whole; and they have been taught by the same experience that this government would be a mere shadow, that must disappoint all their hopes, unless invested with large portions of that sovereignty which belongs to independent states. Under the influence of this opinion, and thus instructed by experience, the American people, in the conventions of their respective states, adopted the present constitution.

If it could be doubted whether from its nature, it were not supreme in all cases where it is empowered to act, that doubt would be removed by the declaration that "this constitution, and the laws of the United States which shall be made in pursuance thereof, and all treaties made, or which shall be made, under the authority of the United States, shall be the supreme law of the land; and the judges in every state shall be bound thereby; any thing in the constitution or laws of any state to the contrary notwithstanding."

This is the authoritative language of the American people; and, if gentlemen please, of the American states. It marks, with lines too strong to be mistaken, the characteristic distinction between the government of the Union, and those of the states. The General Government, though limited as to its objects, is supreme with respect to those objects. This principle is a part of the constitution; and if there be any who deny its necessity, none can deny its authority.

To this supreme government ample powers are confided; and, if it were possible to doubt the great purposes for which they were so confided, the people of the United States have declared that they are given "in order to form a more perfect union, establish justice, ensure domestic tranquillity, provide for the common defence, promote the general welfare, and secure the blessings of liberty to themselves and their posterity."

With the ample powers confided to this supreme government, for these interesting purposes, are connected many express and important limitations on the sovereignty of the states, which are made for the same purposes. The powers of the Union on the great subjects of war, peace, and commerce, and on many others, are in themselves limitations of the sovereignty of the states; but in addition to these, the sovereignty of the states is surrendered in many instances where the surrender can only operate to the benefit of the people, and where, perhaps, no other power is conferred on Congress than a conservative power to maintain the principles established in the constitution. The maintenance of these principles in their purity, is certainly among the great duties of the government. One of the instruments by which this duty may be peaceably performed, is the judicial department. It is authorized to decide all cases of every description, arising under the constitution or laws of the United States. From this general grant of jurisdiction, no exception is made of those cases in which a state may be a party. When we consider the situation of the government of the Union and of a State, in relation to each other, the nature of our constitution, the subordination of the state governments to that constitution, the great purpose for which jurisdiction over all cases arising under the constitution and laws of the United States, is confided to the judicial department, are we at liberty to insert in this general grant, an exception of those cases in which a state may be a party? Will the spirit of the constitution justify this attempt to control its words? We think it will not. We think a case arising under the constitution or laws of the United States, is cognizable in the courts of the Union, whoever may be the parties to that case.

Had any doubt existed with respect to the just construction of this part of the section, that doubt would have been removed by the enumeration of those cases to which the jurisdiction of the federal courts is extended, in consequence of the character of the parties. In that enumeration we find "controversies between two or more states, between a state and citizens of another state," "and between a state and foreign states, citizens, or subjects."

One of the express objects, then, for which the judicial department was established, is the decision of controversies between states, and between a state and individuals. The mere circumstance that a state is a party gives jurisdiction to the court. How, then, can it be contended that the very same instrument, in the very same section, should be so construed as that this same circumstance should withdraw a case from the jurisdiction of the court, where the constitution or laws of the United States are supposed to have been violated? The constitution gave to every person having a claim upon a state, a right to submit his case to the court of the nation. However unimportant his claim might be, however little the community might be interested in its decision, the framers of our constitution thought it necessary for the purposes of justice, to provide a tribunal as superior to influence as possible, in which that claim might be decided. Can it be imagined that the same persons considered a case involving the constitution of our country and the majesty of the laws, questions in which every American citizen must be deeply interested, as withdrawn from this tribunal, because a state is a party?

While weighing arguments drawn from the nature of government, and from the general spirit of an instrument, and urged for the purpose of narrowing the construction which the words of that instrument seem to require, it is proper to place in the opposite scale those principles, drawn from the same sources, which go to sustain the words in their full operation and natural import. One of these, which has been pressed with great force by the counsel for the plaintiff[5] in error, is, that the judicial power of every well constituted government must be co-extensive with the legislative, and must be capable of deciding every judicial question which grows out of the constitution and laws.

If any proposition may be considered as a political axiom, this, we think, may be so considered. In reasoning upon it as an abstract question, there would probably exist no contrariety of opinion respecting it. Every argument, proving the necessity of the department, proves also the propriety of giving this extent to it. We do not mean to say that the jurisdiction of the courts of the Union should be construed to be co-extensive with the legislative, merely because it is fit that it should be so; but we mean to say that this fitness furnishes an argument in construing the constitution which ought never to be overlooked, and which is most especially entitled to consideration when we are enquiring whether the words of the instrument which purport to establish this principle, shall be contracted for the purpose of destroying it.

The mischievous consequences of the construction contended for on the part of Virginia are also entitled to great consideration. It would prostrate, it has been said, the government and its laws at the feet of every state in the Union. And would not this be its effect? What power of the government could be executed by its own means, in any state disposed to resist its execution by a course of legislation? The laws must be executed by individuals acting within the several states. If these individuals may be exposed to penalties, and if the courts of the Union cannot correct the judgments by which these penalties may be enforced, the course of the government may be, at any time, arrested by the will of one of its members. Each member will possess a *veto* on the will of the whole.

The answer which has been given to this argument does not deny its truth, but insists that confidence is reposed, and may be safely reposed, in the state institutions; and that, if they shall ever become so insane or so wicked as to seek the destruction of the government, they may accomplish their object by refusing to perform the functions assigned to them.

We readily concur with the counsel for the defendant in the declaration that the cases which have been put of direct legislative resistance for the purpose of opposing the acknowledged powers of the government, are extreme cases, and in the hope that they will never occur; but we cannot help believing, that a general conviction of the total incapacity of the government to protect itself and its laws in such cases, would contribute in no inconsiderable degree to their occurrence.

Let it be admitted, that the cases which have been put are extreme and improbable, yet there are gradations of opposition to the laws, far short of those cases, which might have a baneful influence on the affairs of the nation. Different states may entertain different opinions on the true construction of the constitutional powers of Congress. We know that, at one time, the assumption of the debts contracted by the several states, during the war of our revolution, was deemed unconstitutional by some of them. We know too that, at other times, certain taxes, imposed by Congress, have been pronounced unconstitutional. Other laws have been questioned partially, while they were supported by the great majority of the American people. We have no assurance that we shall be less divided than we have been. States may legislate in conformity to their opinions, and may enforce those opinions by penalties. It would be hazarding too much to assert that the judicatures of the states will be exempt from the prejudices by which the legislatures and people are influenced, and will constitute perfectly impartial tribunals. In many states the judges are dependent for office and for salary on the will of the legislature. The constitution of the United States furnishes no security against the universal adoption of this principle. When we observe the importance which that constitution attaches to the independence of judges, we are the less inclined to suppose that it can have intended to leave these constitutional questions to tribunals where this independence may not exist, in all cases where a state shall prosecute an individual who claims the protection of an act of Congress. These prosecutions may take place even without a legislative act. A person making a seizure under an act of Congress, may be indicted as a trespasser, if force has been employed, and of this a jury may judge. How extensive may be the mischief if the first decisions in such cases should be final!

These collisions may take place in times of no extraordinary commotion. But a constitution is framed for ages to come, and is designed to approach immortality as nearly as human institutions can approach it. Its course cannot always be tranquil. It is exposed to storms and tempests, and its framers must be unwise statesmen, indeed, if they have not provided it, as far as its nature will permit, with the means of self-preservation from the perils it may be destined to encounter. No government ought to be so defective in its organization as not to contain within itself the means of securing the execution of its own laws against other dangers than those which occur every day. Courts of justice are the means most usually employed; and it is reasonable to expect that a government should repose on its own courts rather than on others. There is certainly nothing in the circumstances under which our constitution was formed; nothing in the history of the times, which would justify the opinion that the confidence reposed in the states was so implicit as to leave in them and their tribunals the power of resisting or defeating, in the form of law, the legitimate measures of the Union. The requisitions of Congress, under the confederation, were as constitutionally obligatory as the laws enacted by the present Congress. That they were habitually disregarded, is a fact of universal notoriety. With the knowledge of this fact, and under its full pressure, a convention was assembled to change the system. Is it so improbable that they should confer on the judicial department the power of construing the constitution and laws of the Union in every case, in the last resort, and of preserving them from all violation from every quarter, so far as judicial decisions can preserve them, that this improbability should essentially affect the construction of the new system? We are told, and we are truly told, that the great change which is to give efficacy to the present system, is its ability to act on individuals directly, instead of acting through the instrumentality of state governments. But ought not this ability, in reason and sound policy, to be applied directly to the protection of individuals employed in the execution of the laws, as well as to their coercion. Your laws reach the individual without the aid of any other power; why may they not protect him from punishment for performing his duty in executing them?

The counsel for Virginia endeavor to obviate the force of these arguments by saying that the dangers they suggest, if not imaginary, are inevitable; that the constitution can make no provision against them; and that, therefore, in construing that instrument, they ought to be excluded from our consideration. This state of things, they say, cannot arise until there shall be a disposition so hostile to the present political system as to produce a determination to destroy it, and, when that determination shall be produced, its effects will not be restrained by parchment stipulations. The fate of the constitution will not then depend on judicial decisions. But, should no appeal be made to force, the states can put an end to the government by refusing to act. They have only not to elect Senators, and it expires without a struggle.

It is very true that, whenever hostility to the existing system shall become universal, it will be also irresistible. The people made the constitution, and the people can unmake it. It is the creature of their will, and lives only by their will. But this supreme and irresistible power to make or to unmake, resides only in the whole body of the people; not in any subdivision of them. The attempt of any of the parts to exercise it is usurpation, and ought to be repelled by those to whom the people have delegated their power of repelling it.

The acknowledged inability of the government, then, to sustain itself against the public will, and, by force or otherwise, to control the whole nation, is no sound argument in support of its constitutional inability to preserve itself against a section of the nation acting in opposition to the general will.

It is true, that if all the states, or a majority of them, refuse to elect Senators, the legislative powers of the Union will be suspended. But if any one state shall refuse to elect them, the Senate will not, on that account, be the less capable of performing all its functions. The argument founded on this fact would seem rather to prove the subordination of the parts to the whole, than the complete independence of any one of them. The framers of the constitution were indeed, unable to make any provisions which should protect that instrument against a general combination of the states, or of the people, for its destruction; and, conscious of this inability, they have not made the attempt. But they were able to provide against the operation of measures adopted in any one state, whose tendency might be to arrest the execution of the laws, and this it was the part of true wisdom to attempt. We think they have attempted it.

It has been also urged, as an additional objection to the jurisdiction of the court, that cases between a state and one of its own citizens, do not come within the general scope of the constitution, and were obviously never intended to be made cognizable[6] in the federal courts. The state tribunals might be suspected of partiality in cases between itself or its citizens and aliens, or the citizens of another state, but not in proceedings by a state against its own citizens. That jealousy which might exist in the first case, could not exist in the last, and therefore the judicial power is not extended to the last.

This is very true, so far as jurisdiction depends on the character of the parties; and the argument would have great force if urged to prove that this court could not establish the demand of a citizen upon his state, but is not entitled to the same force when urged to prove that this court cannot enquire whether the constitution or laws of the United States protect a citizen from a prosecution instituted against him by a state. If jurisdiction depended entirely on the character of the parties, and was not given where the parties have not an original right to come into court, that part of the 2d section of the 3d article which extends the judicial power to all cases arising under the constitution and laws of the United

States, would be mere surplusage. It is to give jurisdiction where the character of the parties would not give it, that this very important part of the clause was inserted. It may be true, that the partiality of the state tribunals, in ordinary controversies between a state and its citizens, was not apprehended, and therefore the judicial power of the Union was not extended to such cases; but this was not the sole, nor the greatest, object for which this department was created. A more important, a much more interesting, object was the preservation of the constitution and laws of the United States, so far as they can be preserved by judicial authority, and therefore the jurisdiction of the courts of the union was expressly extended to all cases arising under that constitution and those laws. If the constitution or laws may be violated by proceedings instituted by a state against its own citizens, and if that violation may be such as essentially to affect the constitution and the laws, such as to arrest the progress of government in its constitutional course, why should these cases be excepted from that provision which expressly extends the judicial power of the Union to *all* cases arising under the constitution and laws?

After bestowing on this subject the most attentive consideration, the court can perceive no reason founded on the character of the parties for introducing an exception which the constitution has not made; and we think that the judicial power, as originally given, extends to all cases arising under the constitution or a law of the United States whoever may be the parties.

It has been also contended that this jurisdiction, if given, is original, and cannot be exercised in the appellate form.

The words of the constitution are, "in all cases affecting ambassadors, other public ministers, and consuls, and those in which a state shall be party, the supreme court shall have original jurisdiction." In all the other cases before mentioned the supreme court shall have appellate jurisdiction.

This distinction between original and appellate jurisdiction excludes, we are told, in all cases, the exercise of the one where the other is given.

The constitution gives the supreme court original jurisdiction in certain enumerated cases, and gives it appellate jurisdiction in all others. Among those in which jurisdiction must be exercised in the appellate form are cases arising under the constitution and laws of the United States. These provisions of the constitution are equally obligatory and are to be equally respected. If a state be a party the jurisdiction of this court is original; if the case arise under a constitution or a law the jurisdiction is appellate. But a case to which a state is a party may arise under the constitution or a law of the United States. What rule is applicable to such a case? What then becomes the duty of the court? Certainly, we think, so to construe the constitution as to give effect to both provisions as far as it is possible to reconcile them, and not to permit their seeming repugnancy to destroy each other. We must endeavour so to construe them as to preserve the true intent and meaning of the instrument.

In one description of cases the jurisdiction of the court is founded entirely on the character of the parties; and the nature of the controversy is not contemplated by the constitution. The character of the parties is every thing, the nature of the case nothing. In the other description of cases, the jurisdiction is founded entirely on the character of the case, and the parties are not contemplated by the constitution. In these the nature of the case is every thing, the character of the parties nothing. When then the constitution declares the jurisdiction, in cases where a state shall be a party, to be original; and in all cases arising under the constitution or a law to be appellate; the conclusion seems irresistible, that its framers designed to include in the first class those cases in which jurisdiction is given because a state is a party; and to include in the second those in which jurisdiction is given because the case arises under the constitution or a law.

This reasonable construction is rendered necessary by other considerations.

That the constitution or a law of the United States is involved in a case, and makes a part of it, may appear in the progress of a cause, in which the courts of the Union, but for that circumstance, would have no jurisdiction, and which of consequence could not originate in the supreme court. In such a case the jurisdiction can be exercised only in its appellate form. To deny its exercise in this form is to deny its existence, and would be to construe a clause dividing the power of the supreme court in such manner as in a considerable degree to defeat the power itself. All must perceive that this construction can be justified only where it is absolutely necessary. We do not think the article under consideration presents that necessity.

It is observable that in this distributive clause no negative words are introduced. This observation is not made for the purpose of contending that the legislature may "apportion the judicial power between the Supreme and inferior courts according to its will." That would be, as was said by this court in the case of Marbury vs. Madison, to render the distributive clause "mere surplusage," to make it "form without substance."[7] This cannot, therefore, be the true construction of the article.

But, although the absence of negative words will not authorize the legislature to disregard the distribution of the power previously granted, their absence will justify a sound construction of the whole article, so as to give every part its intended effect. It is admitted that "affirmative words are often, in their operation, negative of other objects than those affirmed"; and that where "a negative or exclusive sense must be given to them, or they have no operation at all," they must receive that negative or exclusive sense. But where they have full operation without it, where it would destroy some of the most important objects for which the power was created, then, we think, affirmative words ought not to be construed negatively.

The constitution declares that, in cases where a state is a party, the Supreme court shall have original jurisdiction, but does not say that its appellate jurisdiction shall not be exercised in cases where, from their nature, appellate jurisdiction is given, whether a state be or be not a party. It may be conceded that, where the case is of such a nature as to admit of its originating in the Supreme Court, it ought to originate there; but where, from its nature, it cannot originate in that court, these words ought not to be so construed as to require it. There are many cases in which it would be found extremely difficult, and subversive of the spirit of the constitution, to maintain the construction that appellate jurisdiction cannot be exercised where one of the parties might sue or be sued in this court.

The constitution defines the jurisdiction of the Supreme Court, but does not define that of the inferior courts. Can it be affirmed that a state might not sue the citizen of another state in a circuit court? Should the circuit court decide for or against its jurisdiction, should it dismiss the suit, or give judgment against the state, might not its decision be revised in the Supreme Court? The argument is, that it could not; and the very clause which is urged to prove that the circuit court could give no judgment in the case, is also urged to prove that its judgment is irreversible. A supervising court, whose peculiar province it is to correct the errors of an inferior court, has no power to correct a judgment given without jurisdiction, because, in the same case that supervising Court has original jurisdiction. Had negative words been employed, it would be difficult to give them this construction if they would admit of any other. But, without negative words, this irrational construction can never be maintained.

So, too, in the same clause, the jurisdiction of the court is declared to be original, "in cases affecting ambassadors, other public ministers, and consuls." There is, perhaps, no part of the article under consideration so much required by national policy as this; unless it be that part which extends the judicial power "to all cases arising under the constitution, laws, and treaties, of the United States." It has been generally held that the state courts have a concurrent jurisdiction with the federal courts, in cases to which the judicial power is extended, unless the jurisdiction of the federal courts be rendered exclusive by the words of the 3d article. If the words "to all cases" give exclusive jurisdiction in cases affecting foreign ministers, they may also give exclusive jurisdiction, if such be the will of Congress, in cases arising under the constitution, laws, and treaties, of the United States. Now, suppose an individual were to sue a foreign minister in a state court, and that court were to maintain its jurisdiction, and render judgment against the minister, could it be contended that this court would be incapable of revising such judgment, because the constitution had given it original jurisdiction in the case? If this could be maintained, then a clause inserted for the purpose of excluding the jurisdiction of all other courts than this, in a particular case, would have the effect of excluding the jurisdiction of this court in that very case, if the suit were to be brought in another court, and that court were to assert jurisdiction. This tribunal, according to the argument which has been urged, could neither revise the judgment of such other court, nor suspend its proceedings: for a writ of prohibition, or any other similar writ, is in the nature of appellate process.

Foreign consuls frequently assert, in our prize courts, the claims of their fellow subjects. These suits are maintained by them as consuls. The appellate power of this court has been frequently exercised in such cases, and has never been questioned. It would be extremely mischievous to withhold its exercise. Yet the consul is a party on the record. The truth is, that where the words confer only appellate jurisdiction, original jurisdiction is most clearly not given; but, where the words admit of appellate jurisdiction, the power to take cognizance of the suit originally does not necessarily negative the power to decide upon it on an appeal, if it may originate in a different court.

It is, we think, apparent that, to give this distributive clause the interpretation contended for, to give to its affirmative words a negative operation, in every possible case, would, in some instances, defeat the obvious intention of the article. Such an interpretation would not consist with those rules which, from time immemorial, have guided courts, in their construction of instruments brought under their consideration. It must, therefore, be discarded. Every part of the article must be taken into view, and that construction adopted which will consist with its words, and promote its general intention. The court may imply a negative from affirmative words, where the implication promotes, not where it defeats the intention.

If we apply this principle, the correctness of which we believe will not be controverted, to the distributive clause under consideration, the result, we think, would be this: The original jurisdiction of the Supreme Court, in cases where a state is a party, refers to those cases in which, according to the grant of power made in the preceding clause, jurisdiction might be exercised in consequence of the character of the party, and an original suit, might be instituted in any of the federal courts; not to those cases in which an original suit might not be instituted in a federal court. Of the last description, is every case between a state and its citizens, and perhaps every case in which a state is enforcing its penal laws. In such cases, therefore, the Supreme Court cannot take original jurisdiction. In every other case, that is, in every case to which the judicial power extends, and in which original jurisdiction is not expressly given, that judicial power shall be exercised in the appellate, and only in the appellate form. The original jurisdiction of this court cannot be enlarged, but its appellate jurisdiction may be exercised in every case cognizable under the 3d article of the constitution, in the federal courts, in which original jurisdiction cannot be exercised; and the extent of this judicial power is to be measured, not by giving the affirmative words of the distributive clause a negative operation in every possible case, but by giving their true meaning to the words which define its extent.

The counsel for the defendant in error urge, in opposition to this rule of construction, some dicta of the court in the case of Marbury vs. Madison.

It is a maxim not to be disregarded, that general expressions, in every opinion, are to be taken in connection with the case in which those expressions are used. If they go beyond the case, they may be respected, but ought not to control the judgment in a subsequent suit when the very point is presented for decision. The reason of this maxim is obvious. The question actually before the court is investigated with care, and considered in its full extent. Other principles which may serve to illustrate it, are considered in their relation to the case decided, but their possible bearing on all other cases is seldom completely investigated.

In the case of Marbury vs. Madison, the single question before the court, so far as that case can be applied to this, was, whether the legislature could[8] give this court original jurisdiction in a case in which the constitution had clearly not given it, and in which no doubt respecting the construction of the article could possibly be raised. The court decided, and we think very properly, that the legislature could not give original jurisdiction in such a case. But, in the reasoning of the court in support of this decision, some expressions are used which go far beyond it. The counsel for Marbury had insisted on the unlimited discretion of the legislature in the apportionment of the judicial power; and it is against this argument that the reasoning of the court is directed. They say that, if such had been the intention of the article, "it would certainly have been useless to proceed farther than to define the judicial power, and the tribunals in which it should be vested.["] The court says that such a construction would render the clause dividing the jurisdiction of the court into original and appellate, totally useless; that "affirmative words are often, in their operation, negative of other objects than those which are affirmed; and, in this case, (in the case of Marbury vs. Madison,) a negative or exclusive sense must be given to them, or they have no operation at all." "It cannot be presumed,["] adds the Court, ["]that any clause in the constitution is intended to be without effect; and, therefore, such a construction is inadmissible unless the words require it."[9]

The whole reasoning of the court proceeds upon the idea that the affirmative words of the clause giving one sort of jurisdiction, must imply a negative of any other sort of jurisdiction, because otherwise the words would be totally inoperative, and this reasoning is advanced in a case to which it was strictly applicable. If in that case original jurisdiction could have been exercised, the clause under consideration would have been entirely useless. Having such cases only in its view, the court lays down a principle which is generally correct, in terms much broader than the decision, and not only much broader than the reasoning with which that decision is supported, but in some instances contradictory to its principle. The reasoning sustains the negative operation of the words in that case, because otherwise the clause would have no meaning whatever, and because such operation was necessary to give effect to the intention of the article. The effort now made is, to apply the conclusion to which the court was conducted by that reasoning in the particular case, to one in which the words have their full operation when understood affirmatively, and in which the negative, or exclusive sense is to be so used as to defeat some of the great objects of the article.

To this construction the court cannot give its assent. The general expressions in the case of Marbury vs. Madison must be understood with the limitations which are given to them in this opinion; limitations which in no degree affect the decision in that case, or the tenor of its reasoning.

The counsel who closed the argument, put several cases for the purpose of illustration, which he supposed to arise under the Constitution, and yet to be, apparently, without the jurisdiction of the court.

Were a state to lay a duty on exports, to collect the money and place it in her treasury, could the citizen who paid it, he asks, maintain a suit in this court against such state, to recover back the money?

Perhaps not. Without, however, deciding such supposed case, we may say that it is entirely unlike that under consideration.

The citizen who has paid his money to his state, under a law that is void, is in the same situation with every other person who has paid money by mistake. The law raises an assumpsit to return the money, and it is upon that assumpsit that the action is to be maintained. To refuse to comply with this assumpsit may be no more a violation of the constitution, than to refuse to comply with any other; and as the federal courts never had jurisdiction over contracts between a state and its citizens, they may have none over this. But let us so vary the supposed case, as to give it a real resemblance to that under consideration. Suppose a citizen to refuse to pay this export duty, and a suit to be instituted for the purpose of compelling him to pay it. He pleads the constitution of the United States in bar of the action, notwithstanding which the court gives judgment against him. This would be a case arising under the constitution, and would be the very case now before the court.

We are also asked, if a state should confiscate property secured by a treaty, whether the individual could maintain an action for that property?

If the property confiscated be debts, our own experience informs us that the remedy of the creditor against his debtor remains. If it be land, which is secured by a treaty, and afterwards confiscated by a state, the argument does not assume that this title, thus secured, could be extinguished by an act of confiscation. The injured party, therefore, has his remedy against the occupant of the land for that which the treaty secures to him, not against the state for money which is not secured to him.

The case of a state which pays off its own debts with paper money, no more resembles this than do those to which we have already adverted. The courts have no jurisdiction over the contract. They cannot enforce it, nor judge of its violation. Let it be that the act discharging the debt is a mere nullity, and that it is still due. Yet the federal courts have no cognizance of the case. But suppose a state to institute proceedings against an individual, which depended on the validity of an act emitting bills of credit: suppose a state to prosecute one of its citizens for refusing paper money, who should plead the constitution in bar of such prosecution. If his plea should be overruled and judgment rendered against him, his case would resemble this; and, unless the jurisdiction of this court might be exercised over it, the constitution would be violated, and the injured party be unable to bring his case before that tribunal to which the people of the United States have assigned all such cases.

It is most true that this court will not take jurisdiction if it should not; but it is equally true, that it must take jurisdiction if it should. The judiciary cannot, as the legislature may, avoid a measure because it approaches the confines of the constitution. We cannot pass it by because it is doubtful. With whatever doubts, with whatever difficulties, a case may be attended, we must decide it, if it be brought before us. We have no more right to decline the exercise of jurisdiction which is given, than to usurp that which is not given. The one or the other would be treason to the constitution. Questions may occur which we would gladly avoid; but we cannot avoid them. All we can do is to exercise our best judgment, and conscientiously to perform our duty. In doing this, on the present occasion, we find this tribunal invested with appellate jurisdiction in *all* cases arising under the constitution and laws of the United States. We find no exception to this grant, and we cannot insert one.

To escape the operation of these comprehensive words, the counsel for the defendant has mentioned instances in which the constitution might be violated without giving jurisdiction to this court. These words, therefore, however universal in their expression, must, he contends, be limited and controlled in their construction by circumstances. One of these instances is the grant by a state of a patent of nobility. The court, he says, cannot annul this grant.

This may be very true, but by no means justifies the inference drawn from it. The article does not extend the judicial power to every violation of the constitution which may possibly take place, but to "a case in law or equity," in which a right, under such law, is asserted in a court of justice. If the question cannot be brought into a court, then there is no case in law or equity, and no jurisdiction is given by the words of the article. But if, in any controversy depending in a court, the cause should depend on the validity of such a law, that would be a case arising under the constitution, to which the judicial power of the United States would extend. The same observation applies to the other instances with which the counsel who opened the cause has illustrated this argument. Although they show that there may be violations of the constitution of which the courts can take no cognizance, they do not show that an interpretation more restrictive than the words themselves import ought to be given to this article. They do not show that there can be "a *case* in law or equity," arising under the constitution, to which the judicial power does not extend.

We think, then, that, as the constitution originally stood, the appellate jurisdiction of this court, in all cases arising under the constitution, laws, or treaties, of the United States, was not arrested by the circumstance that a state was a party.

This leads to a consideration of the 11th amendment.

It is in these words: "The judicial power of the United States shall not be construed to extend to any suit in law or equity commenced or prosecuted against one of the United States by citizens of another state, or by citizens or subjects of any foreign state."[10]

It is a part of our history, that, at the adoption of the constitution, all the states were greatly indebted; and the apprehension that these debts might be prosecuted in the federal courts formed a very serious objection to that instrument. Suits were instituted; and the court maintained its jurisdiction. The alarm was general; and, to quiet the apprehensions that were so extensively entertained, this amendment was proposed in Congress, and adopted by the state legislatures. That its motive was not to maintain the sovereignty of a state from the degradation supposed to attend a compulsory appearance before the tribunal of the nation may be inferred from the terms of the amendment. It does not comprehend controversies between two or more states, or between a state and a foreign state. The jurisdiction of the court still extends to these cases; and in these a state may still be sued. We must ascribe the amendment, then, to some other cause than the dignity of a state. There is no difficulty in finding this cause. Those who were inhibited from commencing a suit against a state, or from prosecuting one which might be commenced before the adoption of the amendment, were persons who might probably be its creditors. There was not much reason to fear that foreign or sister states would be creditors to any considerable amount, and there was reason to retain the jurisdiction of the court in those cases, because it might be essential to the preservation of peace. The amendment therefore extended to suits commenced or prosecuted by individuals, but not to those brought by states.

The first impression made on the mind by this amendment is, that it was intended for those cases, and for those only, in which some demand against a state is made by an individual in the courts of the Union. If we consider the causes to which it is to be traced, we are conducted to the same conclusion. A general interest might well be felt in leaving to a state the full power of consulting its convenience in the adjustment of its debts, or of other claims upon it; but no interest could be felt in so changing the relations between the whole and its parts as to strip the government of the means of protecting, by the instrumentality of its courts, the constitution and laws from active violation.

The words of the amendment appear to the court to justify and require this construction. The judicial power is not "to extend to any suit in law or equity commenced or prosecuted against one of the United States by citizens of another state," &c.

What is a suit? We understand it to be the prosecution, or pursuit, of some claim, demand, or request. In law language, it is the prosecution of some demand in a court of justice. The remedy for every species of wrong is, says Judge Blackstone, "the being put in possession of that right whereof the party injured is deprived." "The instruments whereby this remedy is obtained are a diversity of suits and actions, which are defined by the Mirror[11] to be 'the lawful demand of one's right.' Or, as Bracton and Fleta express it, in the words of Justinian, '*jus prosequendi in judicio quod aliqui debetur.*'" The right of prosecuting &c.[12] Blackstone then proceeds to describe every species of remedy by suit; and they are all cases where the party suing claims to obtain something to which he has a right.

To commence a suit, is to demand something by the institution of process in a court of justice, and to prosecute the suit, is, according to the common acceptation of language, to continue that demand. By a suit commenced by an individual against a state, we should understand process sued out by that individual against the state, for the purpose of establishing some claim against it by the judgment of a court; and the prosecution of that suit is its continuance. Whatever may be the stages of its progress, the actor is still the same. Suits had been commenced in the supreme court against some of the states before this amendment was introduced into Congress, and others might be commenced before it should be adopted by the state legislatures, and might be depending at the time of its adoption. The object of the amendment was not only to prevent the commencement of future suits, but to arrest the prosecution of those which might be commenced when this article should form a part of the constitution. It therefore embraces both objects; and its meaning is, that the judicial power shall not be construed to extend to any suit which may be commenced, or which, if already commenced, may be prosecuted against a state by the citizen of another state. If a suit, brought in one court, and carried by legal process to a supervising court, be a continuation of the same suit, then this suit is not commenced nor prosecuted against a state. It is clearly in its commencement the suit of a state against an individual, which suit is transferred to this court, not for the purpose of asserting any claim against the state, but for the purpose of asserting a constitutional defence against a claim made by a state.

A writ of error is defined to be, a commission by which the judges of one court are authorized to examine a record upon which a judgment was given in another court, and, on such examination, to affirm or reverse the same according to law. If, says my Lord Coke, by the writ of error, the plaintiff may recover, or be restored to any thing, it may be released by the name of an action. In Bacon's Abridgement, title Error, letter L, it is laid down that "where by a writ of error, the plaintiff shall recover, or be restored to any personal thing, as debt, damage, or the like, a release of all actions personal is a good plea; and when land is to be recovered or restored in a writ of error, a release of actions real is a good bar; but where by a writ of error the plaintiff shall not be restored to any personal or real thing, a release of all actions, real or personal, is no bar." And for this we have the authority of Lord Coke, both in his Commentary on Littleton and in his Reports.[13] A writ of error, then, is in the nature of a suit or action when it is to restore the party who obtains it to the possession of any thing which is withheld from him, not when its operation is entirely defensive.

This rule will apply to writs of error from the courts of the United States, as well as to those writs in England.

Under the judicial act the effect of a writ of error is simply to bring the record into court and submit the judgment of the inferior tribunal to re-examination. It does not in any manner act upon the parties, it acts only on the record. It removes the record into the supervising tribunal. Where then a state obtains a judgment against an individual, and the court rendering such judgment overrules a defence set up under the constitution or laws of the United States, the transfer of this record into the supreme court for the sole purpose of enquiring whether the judgment violates the constitution or laws of the United States can, with no propriety, we think, be denominated a suit commenced or prosecuted against the state whose judgment is so far re-examined. Nothing is demanded from the state. No claim against it of any description is asserted or prosecuted. The party is not to be restored to the possession of any thing. Essentially it is an appeal on a single point; and the defendant who appeals from a judgment rendered against him, is never said to commence or prosecute a suit against the plaintiff who has obtained the judgment. The writ of error is given rather than an appeal, because it is the more usual mode of removing suits at common law; and because perhaps it is more technically proper where a single point of law, and not the whole case, is to be re-examined. But an appeal might be given, and might be so regulated as to effect every purpose of a writ of error. The mode of removal is form, and not substance. Whether it be by writ of error or appeal, no claim is asserted, no demand is made by the original defendant; he only asserts the constitutional right to have his defence examined by that tribunal whose province it is to construe the constitution and laws of the Union.

The only part of the proceeding which is in any manner personal is the citation. And what is the citation? It is simply notice to the opposite party that the record is transferred into another court where he may appear, or decline to appear, as his judgment or inclination may determine. As the party who has obtained a judgment is out of court, and may therefore not know that his cause is removed, common justice requires that notice of the fact should be given him. But this notice is not a suit, nor has it the effect of process. If the party does not choose to appear, he cannot be brought into court, nor is his failure to appear considered as a default. Judgment cannot be given against him for his nonappearance, but the judgment is to be re-examined and reversed, or affirmed in like manner as if the party had appeared and argued his cause.

The point of view in which this writ of error with its citation has been considered uniformly in the courts of the Union, has been well illustrated by a reference to the[14] course of this court in suits instituted by the United States. The universally received opinion is that no suit can be commenced or prosecuted against the United States. That the judicial act does not authorize such suits. Yet writs of error, accompanied with citations, have uniformly issued for the removal of judgments in favor of the United States into a superior court where they have, like those in favor of an individual, been re-examined and affirmed, or reversed. It has never been suggested that such writ of error was a suit against the United States, and therefore not within the jurisdiction of the appellate Court.

It is then the opinion of the court that the defendant who removes a judgment rendered against him by a state court into this court, for the purpose of re-examining the question whether that judgment be in violation of the constitution or laws of the United States, does not commence or prosecute a suit against the state, whatever may be its opinion where the effect of the writ may be to restore the party to the possession of a thing which he demands.

But, should we in this be mistaken, the error does not affect the case now before the court. If this writ of error be a suit in the sense of the 11th amendment, it is not a suit commenced or prosecuted "by a citizen of another state, or by a citizen, or subject of any foreign state." It is not then within the amendment, but is governed entirely by the constitution as originally framed, and we have already seen that in its origin, the judicial power was extended to all cases arising under the constitution or laws of the United States, without respect to parties.

2d. The second objection to the jurisdiction of the court is, that its appellate power cannot be exercised, in any case, over the judgment of a state court.

This objection is sustained chiefly by arguments drawn from the supposed total separation of the judiciary of a state from that of the Union, and their entire independence of each other. The argument considers the federal judiciary as completely foreign to that of a state; and as being no more connected with it in any respect whatever, than the court of a foreign state. If this hypothesis be just, the argument founded on it is equally so; but if the hypothesis be not supported by the constitution, the argument fails with it.

This hypothesis is not founded on any words in the constitution, which might seem to countenance it, but on the unreasonableness of giving a contrary construction to words which seem to require it; and on the incompatibility of the application of the appellate jurisdiction to the judgments of state courts, with that constitutional relation which subsists between the government of the Union and the governments of those states which compose it.

Let this unreasonableness, this total incompatibility, be examined.

That the United States form, for many and for most important purposes, a single nation, has not yet been denied. In war, we are one people. In making peace, we are one people. In all commercial regulations, we are one and the same people. In many other respects, the American people are one, and the government which is alone capable of controling and managing their interests in all these respects, is the government of the Union. It is their government, and in that character they have no other. America has chosen to be, in many respects, and to many purposes, a nation; and for all these purposes, her government is complete; to all these objects, it is competent. They[15] have declared, that, in the exercise of all powers given for these objects, it is supreme. It can, then, in effecting these objects, legitimately control all individuals or governments within the American territory. The constitution and laws of a state, so far as they are repugnant to the constitution and laws of the United States, are absolutely void. These states are constituent parts of the United States. They are members of one great empire—for some purposes sovereign: for some purposes subordinate.

In a government so constituted, is it unreasonable that the judicial power should be competent to give efficacy to the constitutional laws of the legislature? That department can decide on the validity of the constitution or law of a state, if it be repugnant to the constitution or to a law of the United States. Is it unreasonable that it should also be empowered to decide on the judgment of a state tribunal enforcing such unconstitutional law? Is it so very unreasonable as to furnish a justification for controling the words of the constitution?

We think it is not. We think that in a government acknowledgedly supreme with respect to objects of vital interest to the nation, there is nothing inconsistent with sound reason, nothing incompatible with the nature of government, in making all its departments supreme, so far as respects those objects, and so far as is necessary to their attainment. The exercise of the appellate power over those judgments of the state tribunals which may contravene the constitution or laws of the United States, is, we believe, essential to the attainment of those objects.

The propriety of entrusting the construction of the constitution, and laws made in pursuance thereof, to the judiciary of the Union, has not, we believe, as yet been drawn into question. It seems to be a corollary from this political axiom, that the federal courts should either possess exclusive jurisdiction in such cases, or a power to revise the judgments rendered in them, by the state tribunals. If the federal and state courts have concurrent jurisdiction in all cases arising under the constitution, laws, and treaties, of the United States; and if a case of this description brought in a state court cannot be removed before judgment, nor revised after judgment, then the construction of the constitution, laws, and treaties of the United States, is not confided particularly to their judicial department, but is confided equally to that department and to the state courts, however they may be constituted. "Thirteen independent courts," says a very celebrated statesman, and we have now more than twenty, "of final jurisdiction over the same causes, arising upon the same laws, is a hydra in government, from which nothing but contradiction and confusion can proceed."[16]

Dismissing the unpleasant suggestion that any motives which may not be fairly avowed, or which ought not to exist, can ever influence a state or its courts, the necessity of uniformity as well as correctness in expounding the constitution and laws of the United States, would itself suggest the propriety of vesting in some single tribunal the power of deciding, in the last resort, all cases in which they are involved.

We are not restrained, then, by the political relations between the general and state governments, from construing the words of the constitution defining the judicial power in their true sense. We are not bound to construe them more restrictively than they naturally import.

They give to the supreme court appellate jurisdiction in all cases arising under the constitution, laws, and treaties, of the United States. The words are broad enough to comprehend all cases of this description, in whatever court they may be decided. In expounding them, we may be permitted to take into view those considerations to which courts have always allowed great weight in the exposition of laws.

The framers of the constitution would naturally examine the state of things existing at the time; and their work sufficiently attests that they did so. All acknowledge that they were convened for the purpose of strengthening the confederation by enlarging the powers of the government, and by giving efficacy to those which it before possessed, but could not exercise. They inform us themselves, in the instrument they presented to the American public, that one of its objects was to form a more perfect union. Under such circumstances, we certainly should not expect to find, in that instrument, a diminution of the powers of the actual government.

Previous to the adoption of the confederation, Congress established courts which received appeals in prize causes decided in the courts of the respective states. This power of the government, to establish tribunals for these appeals, was thought consistent with, and was founded on, its political relations with the states. These courts did exercise appellate jurisdiction over those cases decided in the state courts, to which the judicial power of the federal government extended.

The confederation gave to Congress the power "of establishing courts for receiving and determining finally appeals in all cases of captures."

This power was uniformly construed to authorize those courts to receive appeals from the sentences of state courts, and to affirm or reverse them. State tribunals are not mentioned; but this clause in the confederation necessarily comprises them. Yet the relation between the general and state governments was much weaker, much more lax, under the confederation than under the present constitution; and the states being much more completely sovereign, their institutions were much more independent.

The convention which framed the constitution, on turning their attention to the judicial power, found it limited to a few objects, but exercised, with respect to some of those objects, in its appellate form, over the judgments of the state courts. They extend it, among other objects, to all cases arising under the constitution, laws, and treaties, of the United States; and, in a subsequent clause, declare that, in such cases, the supreme court shall exercise appellate jurisdiction. Nothing seems to be given which would justify the withdrawal of a judgment rendered in a state court, on the constitution, laws, or treaties, of the United States, from this appellate jurisdiction.

Great weight has always been attached, and very rightly attached, to contemporaneous exposition. No question, it is believed, has arisen to which this principle applies more unequivocally than to that now under consideration.

The opinion of the Federalist has always been considered as of great authority. It is a complete commentary on our constitution; and is appealed to by all parties in the questions to which that instrument has given birth. Its intrinsic merit entitles it to this high rank; and the part two of its authors performed in framing the constitution put it very much in their power to explain the views with which it was framed. These essays having been published while the constitution was before the nation for adoption or rejection, and having been written in answer to objections founded entirely on the extent of its powers, and on its diminution of state sovereignty, are entitled to the more consideration where they frankly avow that the power objected to is given, and defend it.

In discussing the extent of the judicial power, the Federalist says, "Here another question occurs: what relation would subsist between the national and state courts in these instances of concurrent jurisdiction? I answer, that an appeal would certainly lie from the latter, to the supreme court of the United States. The constitution in direct terms gives an appellate jurisdiction to the supreme court in all the enumerated cases of

federal cognizance in which it is not to have an original one, without a
single expression to confine its operation to the inferior federal courts.
The objects of appeal, not the tribunals from which it is to be made, are
alone contemplated. From this circumstance, and from the reason of the
thing, it ought to be construed to extend to the state tribunals. Either this
must be the case, or the local courts must be excluded from a concurrent
jurisdiction in matters of national concern, else the judiciary authority of
the Union may be eluded at the pleasure of every plaintiff or prosecutor.
Neither of these consequences ought, without evident necessity, to be
involved; the latter would be entirely inadmissible, as it would defeat
some of the most important and avowed purposes of the proposed government, and would essentially embarrass its measures. Nor do I perceive
any foundation for such a supposition. Agreeably to the remark already
made, the national and state systems are to be regarded as ONE WHOLE.
The courts of the latter will of course be natural auxiliaries to the execution of the laws of the Union, and an appeal from them will as naturally
lie to that tribunal which is destined to unite and assimilate the principles
of natural justice and the rules of national decision. The evident aim of
the plan of the national convention is, that all the causes of the specified
classes shall, for weighty public reasons, receive their original or final
determination in the courts of the Union. To confine, therefore, the general expressions which give appellate jurisdiction to the supreme court,
to appeals from the subordinate federal courts, instead of allowing their
extension to the state courts, would be to abridge the latitude of the
terms, in subversion of the intent, contrary to every sound rule of interpretation."[17]

A contemporaneous exposition of the constitution, certainly of not less
authority than that which has been just cited, is the judicial act itself.
We know that in the Congress which passed that act were many eminent members of the convention which formed the constitution. Not a
single individual, so far as is known, supposed that part of the act which
gives the supreme court appellate jurisdiction over the judgments of the
state courts in the cases therein specified, to be unauthorized by the
constitution.

While on this part of the argument, it may be also material to observe
that the uniform decisions of this court on the point now under consideration, have been assented to, with a single exception, by the courts of
every state in the Union whose judgments have been revised. It has been
the unwelcome duty of this tribunal to reverse the judgments of many
state courts in cases in which the strongest[18] state feelings were engaged.
Judges, whose talents and character would grace any bench, to whom a
disposition to submit to jurisdiction that is usurped, or to surrender their
legitimate powers, will certainly not be imputed, have yielded without
hesitation to the authority by which their judgments were reversed, while
they, perhaps, disapproved the judgment of reversal.

This concurrence of statesmen, of legislators, and of judges, in the same construction of the constitution, may justly inspire some confidence in that construction.

In opposition to it, the counsel who made this point has presented in a great variety of forms, the idea already noticed, that the federal and state courts must, of necessity, and from the nature of the constitution, be in all things totally distinct and independent of each other. If this court can correct the errors of the courts of Virginia, he says it makes them courts of the United States, or becomes itself a part of the judiciary of Virginia.

But, it has been already shown that neither of these consequences necessarily follows: The American people may certainly give to a national tribunal a supervising power over those judgments of the state courts which may conflict with the constitution, laws, or treaties, of the United States, without converting them into federal courts, or converting the national into a state tribunal. The one court still derives its authority from the state, the other still derives its authority from the nation.

If it shall be established, he says, that this court has appellate jurisdiction over the state courts in all cases enumerated in the 3d article of the constitution, a complete consolidation of the states, so far as respects judicial power is produced.

But, certainly the mind of the gentleman who urged this argument is too accurate not to perceive that he has carried it too far; that the premises by no means justify the conclusion. "A complete consolidation of the states, so far as respects the judicial power," would authorize the legislature to confer on the federal courts appellate jurisdiction from the state courts in all cases whatsoever. The distinction between such a power, and that of giving appellate jurisdiction in a few specified cases in the decision of which the nation takes an interest, is too obvious not to be perceived by all.

This opinion has been already drawn out to too great a length to admit of entering into a particular consideration of the various forms in which the counsel who made this point has, with much ingenuity, presented his argument to the court. The argument in all its forms is essentially the same. It is founded, not on the words of the constitution, but on its spirit, a spirit extracted, not from the words of the instrument, but from his view of the nature of our union and of the great fundamental principles on which the fabric stands.

To this argument, in all its forms, the same answer may be given. Let the nature and objects of our union be considered; let the great fundamental principles on which the fabric stands be examined, and we think the result must be, that there is nothing so extravagantly absurd in giving to the court of the nation the power of revising the decisions of local tribunals on questions which affect the nation, as to require that words which import this power should be restricted by a forced construction. The question then must depend on the words themselves; and on their construction we shall be the more readily excused for not adding to the observations already made, because the subject was fully discussed and exhausted in the case of Martin vs. Hunter.[19]

3d. We come now to the third objection, which, though differently stated by the counsel, is substantially the same. One gentleman has said that the judicial act does not give jurisdiction in the case.

The cause was argued in the state court, on a case agreed by the parties, which states the prosecution under a law for selling lottery tickets, which is set forth, and further states the act of Congress by which the city of Washington was authorized to establish the lottery. It then states that the lottery was regularly established by virtue of the act, and concludes with referring to the court the questions, whether the act of Congress be valid? whether, on its just construction, it constitutes a bar to the prosecution? and, whether the act of Assembly, on which the prosecution is founded, be not itself invalid? These questions were decided against the operation of the act of Congress, and in favor of the operation of the act of the state.

If the 25th section of the judicial act be inspected, it will at once be perceived that it comprehends expressly the case under consideration.

But it is not upon the letter of the act that the gentleman who stated this point in this form, founds his argument. Both gentlemen concur substantially in their views of this part of the case. They deny that the act of Congress, on which the plaintiff in error relies, is a law of the United States; or, if a law of the United States, is within the second clause of the sixth article.

In the enumeration of the powers of Congress, which is made in the 8th section of the first article, we find that of exercising exclusive legislation over such district as shall become the seat of government. This power, like all others which are specified, is conferred on Congress as the legislature of the Union; for, strip them of that character, and they would not possess it. In no other character can it be exercised. In legislating for the district, they necessarily preserve the character of the legislature of the Union; for, it is in that character alone that the constitution confers on them this power of exclusive legislation. This proposition need not be enforced.

The 2d clause of the 6th article declares, that "This constitution, and the laws of the United States, which shall be made in pursuance thereof, shall be the supreme law of the land."

The clause which gives exclusive jurisdiction is, unquestionably, a part of the constitution, and, as such, binds all the United States. Those who contend that acts of Congress, made in pursuance of this power, do not, like acts made in pursuance of other powers, bind the nation, ought to show some safe and clear rule which shall support this construction, and prove that an act of Congress, clothed in all the forms which attend other legislative acts, and passed in virtue of a power conferred on, and exercised by, Congress, as the legislature of the Union, is not a law of the United States, and does not bind them.

One of the gentlemen sought to illustrate his proposition that Congress, when legislating for the District, assumed a distinct character, and was reduced to a mere local legislature, whose laws could possess no obligation out of the 10 miles square, by a reference to the complex character of this court. It is, they say, a court of common law and a court of equity. Its character, when sitting as a court of common law, is as distinct from its character when sitting as a court of equity, as if the powers belonging to those departments were vested in different tribunals. Though united in the same tribunal, they are never confounded with each other.

Without enquiring how far the union of different characters in one court, may be applicable, in principle, to the union in Congress of the power of exclusive legislation in some places, and of limited legislation in others, it may be observed, that the forms of proceedings in a court of law are so totally unlike the forms of proceedings in a court of equity, that a mere inspection of the record gives decisive information of the character in which the court sits, and consequently of the extent of its powers. But if the forms of proceeding were precisely the same, and the Court the same, the distinction would disappear.

Since Congress legislates in the same forms, and in the same character, in virtue of powers of equal obligation, conferred in the same instrument, when exercising its exclusive powers of legislation, as well as when exercising those which are limited, we must enquire whether there be any thing in the nature of this exclusive legislation which necessarily confines the operation of the laws made in virtue of this power to the place with a view to which they are made.

Connected with the power to legislate within this district, is a similar power in forts, arsenals, dock yards, &c. Congress has a right to punish murder in a fort, or other place within its exclusive jurisdiction; but no general right to punish murder committed within any of the states. In the act for the punishment of crimes against the United States, murder committed within a fort, or any other place or district of country, under the sole and exclusive jurisdiction of the United States, is punished with death. Thus Congress legislates in the same act, under its exclusive and its limited powers.

The act proceeds to direct that the body of the criminal, after execution, may be delivered to a surgeon for dissection, and punishes any person who shall rescue such body during its conveyance from the place of execution to the surgeon to whom it is to be delivered.

Let these actual provisions of the law, or any other provisions which can be made on the subject, be considered with a view to the character in which Congress acts when exercising its powers of exclusive legislation.

If Congress is to be considered merely as a local legislature, invested, as to this object, with powers limited to the fort, or other place, in which the murder may be committed, if its general powers cannot come in aid of these local powers, how can the offence be tried in any other court than that of the place in which it has been committed? How can the offender be conveyed to, or tried in, any other place? How can he be executed elsewhere? How can his body be conveyed through a country under the jurisdiction of another sovereign, and the individual punished who, within that jurisdiction, shall rescue the body.

Were any one state of the Union to pass a law for trying a criminal in a court not created by itself, in a place not within its jurisdiction and direct the sentence to be executed without its territory, we should all perceive and acknowledge its incompetency to such a course of legislation. If Congress be not equally incompetent, it is because that body unites the powers of local legislation with those which are to operate through the Union, and may use the last in aid of the first, or because the power of exercising exclusive legislation draws after it, as an incident, the power of making that legislation effectual, and the incidental power may be exercised throughout the Union, because the principal power is given to that body as the legislature of the Union.

So, in the same act, a person who, having knowledge of the commission of murder or other felony on the high seas, or within any fort, arsenal, dock-yard, magazine, or other place or district of country within the sole and exclusive jurisdiction of the United States, shall conceal the same, &c. he shall be adjudged guilty of misprision of felony, and shall be adjudged to be imprisoned, &c.

It is clear that Congress cannot punish felonies generally; and, of consequence, cannot punish misprision of felony. It is equally clear that a state legislature, the state of Maryland for example, cannot punish those who, in another state, conceal a felony committed in Maryland. How, then, is it that Congress, legislating exclusively for a fort, punishes those who, out of that fort, conceal a felony committed within it?

The solution, and the only solution of the difficulty is, that the power vested, in Congress, as the legislature of the U. States, to legislate exclusively within any place ceded by a state, carries with it, as an incident, the right to make that power effectual. If a felon escape out of the state in which the act has been committed, the government cannot pursue him into another state, and apprehend him there, but must demand him from the Executive power of that other state. If Congress were to be considered merely as the local legislature for the fort or other place in which the offence might be committed, then, this principle would apply to them as to other local legislatures, and the felon who should escape out of the fort or other place, in which the felony may have been committed, could not be apprehended by the marshal, but must be demanded from the Executive of the state. But we know that the principle does not apply and the reason is, that Congress is not a local legislature, but exercises this particular power, like all its other powers in its high character, as the legislature of the Union. The American people thought it a necessary power, and they conferred it for their own benefit. Being so conferred, it carries with it all those incidental powers which are necessary to its complete and effectual execution.

Whether any particular law be designed to operate without the district or not, depends on the words of that law. If it be designed so to operate, then the question whether the power so exercised be incidental to the power of exclusive legislation, and be warranted by the constitution, requires a consideration of that instrument. In such cases the constitution and the law must be compared and construed. This is the exercise of jurisdiction. It is the only exercise of it which is allowed in such a case. For the act of Congress directs that "no other error shall be assigned or regarded as a ground of reversal, in any such case as aforesaid, than such as appears on the face of the record, and immediately respects the before mentioned questions of validity or construction of the said constitution, treaties," &c.

The whole merits of this case, then, consist in the construction of the constitution and the act of Congress. The jurisdiction of the court, if acknowledged, goes no farther. This we are required to do without the exercise of jurisdiction.

The counsel for the state of Virginia have, in support of this motion, urged many arguments of great weight against the application of the act of Congress to such a case as this; but those arguments go to the construction of the constitution or of the law, or of both; and seem therefore rather calculated to sustain their cause upon its merits, than to prove a failure of jurisdiction in the court.

After having bestowed upon this question the most deliberate consideration of which we are capable, the Court is unanimously of opinion that the objections to its jurisdiction are not sustained, and that the motion ought to be overruled.

Printed, *Daily National Intelligencer* (Washington, D.C.), 15 March 1821.

1. At JM's direction Wheaton here subjoined the following note in the volume of reports containing this case: "The plaintiff in error prayed an appeal from the judgment of the Court of Hustings, but it was refused, on the ground that there was no higher State tribunal which could take cognizance of the case" (JM to Wheaton, 2 June 1821; 6 Wheat. 376 n.).

2. Here and throughout Wheaton's text reads "judiciary" for "judicial."

3. The phrase "either intentionally or inadvertently" was dropped from Wheaton's subsequent report in accordance with JM's list of corrections (JM to Wheaton, 24 Mar. 1821; 6 Wheat. 377).

4. JM proposed "their" for "this," but the correction was not made (JM to Wheaton, 24 Mar. 1821; 6 Wheat. 379).

5. Wheaton has "plaintiffs."

6. The newspaper text has "organizable," an error that JM directed Wheaton to correct (JM to Wheaton, 24 Mar. 1821).

7. Marbury v. Madison, 1 Cranch 174 (1803); *PJM*, VI, 180.

8. JM directed Wheaton to replace "would" in the newspaper text with "could" (JM to Wheaton, 24 Mar. 1821).

9. 1 Cranch 174; *PJM*, VI, 180.

10. In defending the unamended judiciary article at the Virginia ratifying convention of 1788, JM remarked: "I hope no Gentleman will think that a State will be called at the bar of the Federal Court. . . . It is not rational to suppose, that the sovereign power shall be dragged before a Court." This passage was pointedly quoted in a report of a committee of the Virginia legislature in Jan. 1821 and in subsequent attacks on the Cohens opinion by Ritchie, Roane, and "Fletcher of Saltoun" (*PJM*, I, 279; Richmond *Enquirer*, 11 Jan., 23 Mar., 22 June 1821; *John P. Branch Historical Papers of Randolph-Macon College*, II [June 1906], 164).

11. The newspaper text reads "Minor," which JM corrected to "Mirror" (JM to Wheaton, 24 Mar. 1821).

12. Blackstone, *Commentaries*, III, 116. JM instructed Wheaton to complete the translation, but the report omitted the translation entirely (JM to Wheaton, 24 Mar. 1821). The full translation reads: "The right of prosecuting to judgment, which is due to everyone." The references in the quoted passage are to the ancient English legal treatises known as *Mirror of Justices*, Bracton, and *Fleta*. See Theodore F. T. Plucknett, *A Concise History of the Common Law* (5th ed.; Boston, 1956), 258–67.

13. Edward Coke, *The First Part of the Institutes of the Laws of England; or, A Commentary upon Littleton . . .* , II (16th ed.; London, 1809), 288b, cited in Bacon, *Abridgment*, II, 497. Bacon's marginal note also cites Edward Altham's Case, 8 Co. Rep. 150, 152, 77 Eng. Rep. 701, 704–5 (C.P., 1610).

14. Wheaton dropped "uniform" as directed by JM (JM to Wheaton, 24 Mar. 1821).

15. Wheaton replaced "They" with "The people."

16. *The Federalist* No. 80 (Hamilton), in Clinton Rossiter, ed., *The Federalist Papers* (New York, 1961), 476. Wheaton added "such Courts" after "twenty" in the parenthetical phrase. JM quoted this passage in his 1819 "Friend" essays (*PJM*, VIII, 357).

17. *The Federalist* No. 82 (Hamilton), in Rossiter, ed., *Federalist Papers*, 493–94. In the last sentence of the quoted passage, the newspaper text has "interest" instead of "intent." JM briefly quoted from this passage in his "Friend" essays (*PJM*, VIII, 357).

18. The newspaper text reads "strangest," which JM instructed Wheaton to correct (JM to Wheaton, 24 Mar. 1821).

19. Martin v. Hunter's Lessee, 1 Wheat. 304 (1816). Story delivered the opinion of the Court.

From Gales and Seaton

Respected Sir: Office of Natl. Intelligr, March 3, 1821.

We have heard much of the opinion of the Court delivered this morning, in the case Cohen & others, &c. We request that the Court will have the goodness to allow us to spread it on the columns of the National Intelligencer.[1] Very respectfully we have the honor to be, Your faithful servts

GALES & SEATON.

ALS, Endicott Autograph Collection, MHi. In hand of Joseph Gales. Addressed to JM. Above address JM wrote "Mr Gales."

1. Joseph Gales (1786–1860) was publisher of the Washington *Daily National Intelligencer*, which he owned from 1810 to his death.

To Gales and Seaton

[3 March 1821]

There are one or two verbal inacuracies observed in reading the opinion which I wish to correct. I shall have no objection myself to its being printed, but it is the property of the court & I shall ask the other Judges this evening whether they will part with the original; having no copy. If the opinion on jurisdiction be published, it will be proper also to publish the opinion on the merits. I am dear Sir your obedt

J MARSHALL

ALS, Endicott Autograph Collection, MHi. Written on verso of Gales and Seaton to JM, 3 Mar. 1821. Endorsed by Gales.

Cohens v. Virginia
Opinion
U.S. Supreme Court, 5 March 1821

This case was stated in the opinion given on the motion for dismissing the writ of error for want of jurisdiction in the court. It now comes on to be decided on the question whether the borough court of Norfolk, in overruling the defence set up under the act of Congress, has misconstrued that act. It is in these words:

"The said corporation shall have full power to authorize the drawing of lotteries for effecting any important improvement in the city, which the ordinary funds or revenue thereof will not accomplish: Provided, that the sum to be raised in each year shall not exceed the amount of 10,000 dollars: And provided, also, that the object for which the money is intended to be raised shall be first submitted to the President of the United States, and shall be approved of by him."[1]

Two questions arise on this act.

1st. Does it purport to authorize the corporation to force the sale of these lottery tickets in states where such sales may be prohibited by law? If it does,

2d. Is the law constitutional?

If the first question be answered in the affirmative, it will become necessary to consider the second. If it should be answered in the negative, it will be unnecessary, and consequently improper, to pursue any inquiries, which would then be merely speculative, respecting the power of Congress in the case.

In inquiring into the extent of the power granted to the corporation of Washington, we must first examine the words of the grant. We find in them no expression which looks beyond the limits of the city. The powers granted are all of them local in their nature, and all of them such as would, in the common course of things, if not necessarily, be exercised within the city. The subject on which Congress was employed when framing this act was a local subject; it was not the establishment of a lottery, but the formation of a corporate[2] body for the management of the internal affairs of the city, for its internal government, for its police. Congress must have considered itself as delegating to this corporate body powers for these objects, and for these objects solely. In delegating these powers, therefore, it seems reasonable to suppose that the mind of the legislature was directed to the city alone, to the action of the being they were creating within the city, and not to any extra-territorial operations. In describing the powers of such a being, no words of limitation need be used. They are limited by the subject. But, if it be intended to give its acts a binding efficacy beyond the natural limits of its power, and within the jurisdiction of a distinct power, we should expect to find, in the language of the incorporating act, some words indicating such intention.

Without such words, we cannot suppose that Congress designed to give to the acts of the corporation any other effect, beyond its limits, than attends every act having the sanction of local law, when any thing depends upon it which is to be transacted elsewhere.

If this would be the reasonable construction of corporate powers generally, it is more especially proper in a case where an attempt is made so to exercise those powers as to control and limit the penal laws of a state. This is an operation which was not, we think, in the contemplation of the legislature while incorporating the City of Washington.

To interfere with the penal laws of a state, where they are not levelled against the legitimate powers of the Union, but have for their sole object the internal government of the country, is a very serious measure, which Congress cannot be supposed to adopt lightly, or inconsiderately. The motives for it must be serious and weighty. It would be taken deliberately, and the intention would be clearly and unequivocally expressed.

An act, such as that under consideration, ought not, we think, to be so construed as to imply this intention, unless its provisions were such as to render the construction inevitable.

We do not think it essential to the corporate power in question that it should be exercised out of the city. Could the lottery be drawn in any state of the Union? Does the corporate power to authorize the drawing of a lottery imply a power to authorize its being drawn without the jurisdiction of a corporation, in a place where it may be prohibited by law? This, we think, would scarcely be asserted. And what clear legal distinction can be taken between a power to draw a lottery in a place where it is prohibited by law, and a power to establish an office for the sale of tickets in a place where it is prohibited by law? It may be urged, that the place where the lottery is drawn is of no importance to the corporation, and therefore the act need not be so construed as to give power over the place, but that the right to sell tickets throughout the United States is of importance, and therefore ought to be implied.

That the power to sell tickets in every part of the United States might facilitate their sale, is not to be denied; but it does not follow that Congress designed for the purpose of giving this increased facility to overrule the penal laws of the several states. In the city of Washington, the great metropolis of the nation, visited by individuals from every part of the Union, tickets may be freely sold to all who are willing to purchase. Can it be affirmed that this is so limited a market, that the incorporating act must be extended beyond its words, and made to conflict with the internal police of the states, unless it be construed to give a more extensive market?

It has been said that the states cannot make it unlawful to buy that which Congress has made it lawful to sell.

This proposition is not denied; and therefore the validity of a law punishing a citizen of Virginia for purchasing a ticket in the city of Washington might well be drawn into question. Such a law would be a direct attempt to counteract and defeat a measure authorized by the United States. But a law to punish the sale of lottery tickets in Virginia is of a different character. Before we can impeach its validity, we must enquire whether Congress intended to empower this corporation to do any act within a state which the laws of that state might prohibit.

In addition to the very important circumstance, that the act contains no words indicating such intention, and that this extensive construction is not essential to the execution of the corporate power, the court cannot resist the conviction, that the intention ascribed to this act, had it existed, would have been executed by very different means from those which have been employed.

Had Congress intended to establish a lottery for those improvements in the city which are deemed national, the lottery itself would have become the subject of legislative consideration. It would be organized by law, and agents for its execution would be appointed by the President, or in such other manner as the law might direct. If such agents were to act out of the District, there would be probably some provision made for such a state of things, and in making such provisions Congress would examine its power to make them. The whole subject would be under the control of the government, or of persons appointed by the government.

But in this case no lottery is established by law, no control is exercised by the government over any which may be established. The lottery emanates from a corporate power. The corporation may authorize or not authorize it, and may select the purposes to which the proceeds are to be applied. This corporation is a being intended for local objects only. All its capacities are limited to the city. This, as well as every other law it is capable of making, is a by-law, and, from its nature, is only co-extensive with the city. It is not probable that such an agent would be employed in the execution of a lottery established by Congress; but when it acts, not as the agent for carrying into effect a lottery established by Congress, but in its own corporate capacity, from its own corporate powers, it is reasonable to suppose that its act was intended[3] to partake of the nature of that capacity and of those powers; and, like all its other acts, be merely local in its nature.

The proceeds of these lotteries are to come in aid of the revenues of the city. These revenues are raised by laws whose operation is entirely local, and for objects which are also local; for, no person will suppose that the President's house, the Capitol, the Navy Yard, or other public institution, was to be benefitted by these lotteries, or was to form a charge on the city revenue. Coming in aid of the city revenue, they are of the same character with it; the mere creature of a corporate power.

The circumstances that the lottery cannot be drawn without the permission of the President, and that this resource is to be used only for important improvements, have been relied on as giving to this corporate power a more extensive operation than is given to those with which it is associated. We do not think so.

The President has no agency in the lottery. It does not originate with him, nor is the improvement to which its profits are to be applied to be selected by him. Congress has not enlarged the corporate power by restricting its exercise to cases of which the President might approve.

We very readily admit that the act establishing the seat of government, and the act appointing commissioners to superintend the public buildings, are laws of universal obligation. We admit, too, that the laws of any state to defeat the loan authorized by Congress, would have been void, as would have been any attempt to arrest the progress of the canal, or of any other measure which Congress may adopt.[4] These, and all other laws relative to the District, have the authority which may be claimed by other acts of the national legislature; but their extent is to be determined by those rules of construction which are applicable to all laws. The act incorporating the city of Washington is, unquestionably, of universal obligation; but the extent of the corporate powers conferred by that act, is to be determined by those considerations which belong to the case.

Whether we consider the general character of a law incorporating a city, the objects for which such law is usually made, or the words in which this particular power is conferred, we arrive at the same result. The corporation was merely empowered to authorize the drawing of lotteries; and the mind of Congress was not directed to any provision for the sale of the tickets beyond the limits of the corporation. That subject does not seem to have been taken into view. It is the unanimous opinion of the court that the law cannot be construed to embrace it. There is no error in the judgment, and it is to be affirmed with costs.

Printed, *Daily National Intelligencer* (Washington, D.C.), 16 March 1821.

1. This was an 1812 act further amending the charter of the city of Washington (*U.S. Statutes at Large*, II, 721, 726).

2. Wheaton has "separate" (6 Wheat. 442).

3. Wheaton has "acts were intended" (6 Wheat. 446).

4. JM referred to the Washington Canal, connecting the Potomac River with the Eastern Branch (Anacostia River), which opened in Nov. 1815 (Constance McLaughlin Green, *Washington: Village and Capital, 1800–1878* [Princeton, N.J., 1962], 28–29, 72).

To Richard Rush

Dear Sir   Washington March 16th 1821

I had the pleasure of receiving sometime past your favor of the 18th. of october.[1] I beg you to accept my acknowledgements for your kind & polite attention to the request I took the liberty to make, & to be assured that I am greatly obliged by it. I wrote to Mr. Murdock to make the necessary advances to counsel; &, having now all the information I can hope to obtain, I have given him instructions by which he will be governed.[2]

You will receive from others better information than I can give respecting our public affairs. Your old friends of the bench & bar are very much *in statu quo*. Time however is making on some of us more rapid advances than we would be willing to acknowledge. With very much respect & esteem, I am dear Sir your obedt. Servt

J MARSHALL

ALS, Richard Rush Papers, NjP. Addressed to Rush in London. Endorsed by Rush.

1. Letter not found. Rush (1780–1859), son of the Revolutionary patriot and physician Benjamin Rush, had a distinguished career as a statesman and diplomat. After serving as attorney general under James Madison, Rush acted briefly as secretary of state during the Monroe administration before being named minister to Great Britain, a post he held from 1817 to 1825. He was later secretary of the treasury and minister to France.

2. Letters not found. See JM to James K. Marshall, 26 Feb. 1821 and n. 3.

To Henry Wheaton

Dear Sir   Richmond March 24th. 1821

I did not thank you while in Washington for your Anniversary discourse delivered before the historical society of New York,[1] nor for your Digest of the decisions of the supreme court, because I had not liesure, while at that place, to look into either.[2] Since my return to this place I have read the first with a great deal of pleasure & have glanced over the Digest with much satisfaction.

However preeminent the antients may have been in some of the fine arts, they were, I think you very clearly show, much inferior to us, or a great way behind us, in the more solid & more interesting principles of international law; a law which contributes more to the happiness of the human race, than all the statues which ever came from the hands of the sculptor, or all the paintings that were ever placed on canvass. I do not, by this, mean to lessen the value of the arts. I subscribe to their importance, & admit that they improve as well as embellish human life & manners; but they yield in magnitude to those moral rules which regulate the connexion of man with man.

Old Hugo Grotius is indebted to you for your defence of him & his quotations. You have raised him in my estimation to the rank he deserves.

Your Digest is a work of great labor & utility. Without a compliment, it is I think, as far as I have looked into ⟨it well⟩ executed; & will I hope come into general use.

I have made a few memoranda below, to which I beg your attention when you prepare your next volume of reports for the press. With great regard & esteem, I am dear Sir your obedt

J Marshall

In the case of Cohens v The Commonwealth of Virginia as printed in the national Inteligencer.

In the first column of the first page in the paragraph succeeding that which states the 3d. point strike out "either intentionally or inadvertently" & commas.[3]

———

In the paragraph more than half way down the 2d. column which begin⟨s⟩ with "The use intended" &c — in the words "application of *this* argument" instead of "this" read "their."[4]

———

In the 3d. column of the 1st. page, 7th. paragraph, instead of "organizable," read "cognizable."[5]

———

In the last column of the 1st. page 4th. paragraph 3d. line for "would" read "could."[6]

———

In the 1st. column of the 2d. page 7th. paragraph for "Minor" read "Mirror." In the same sentence instead of "&c" complete the translation.[7]

———

In the 2d. column of the 2d. page 2d. paragraph, 4th. line strike out "uniform" before "course."[8]

———

In the 3d. column of the 2d. page 4th. paragraph for "strangest" read "strongest.⟨"⟩[9]

ALS, Henry Wheaton Papers, NNPM.

1. *An Anniversary Discourse Delivered before the New-York Historical Society . . . December 28, 1820* (New York, 1821).

2. *A Digest of the Decisions of the Supreme Court of the United States* (New York, 1821).

3. See Opinion, 3 Mar. 1821 and n. 2.

HENRY WHEATON

Oil on canvas by Robert Hinckley. Date unknown but probably from the time Wheaton became Supreme Court reporter. *Courtesy of Office of the Curator, Supreme Court of the United States.*

4. See Opinion, 3 Mar. 1821 and n. 3.
5. See Opinion, 3 Mar. 1821 and n. 5.
6. See Opinion, 3 Mar. 1821 and n. 7.
7. See Opinion, 3 Mar. 1821 and nn. 10, 11.
8. See Opinion, 3 Mar. 1821 and n. 13.
9. See Opinion, 3 Mar. 1821 and n. 18.

To Henry Wheaton

My dear Sir   Richmond June 2d. 1821

The opinion of the Supreme court in the case of Cohens vs. The Commonwealth of Virginia is attacked with a degree of virulence superior even to that which was employed in the Bank question. Among other Calumnies the Judges are charged with giving an opinion on a case not before them, & even with "feigning" a case for the purpose [of] ushering prematurely on the public their political dogmas.[1] As it is desirable that the truth should always appear, I wish it to appear in this instance. When this judgement was rendered Cohens prayed an appeal which was refused. The fact appears on the record. This was a decision that the judgement of the court was final, for in Virginia every cause which can be carried before a superior tribunal can be carried thither by appeal.

I do not know whether this fact is stated in your report of the case. If it be not I hope it is not too late to make an asterisk at that part of the opinion which states it to be the judgement of a court of the last resort & insert in a note some such words as these, "Cohens prayed an appeal from this judgement but it was refused on the principle that there was no higher tribunal which could take cognizance of the case.["][2]

The old *friend* of the court seems inflamed with more than a double portion of ire. I am dear Sir with much regard & esteem, your obedt

J MARSHALL

ALS, Henry Wheaton Papers, NNPM.

1. Spencer Roane's "Algernon Sidney" essay in the Richmond *Enquirer* of 29 May 1821 contained the charge of feigning a case (*John P. Branch Historical Papers of Randolph-Macon College*, II [June 1906], 93).

2. See the note at 6 Wheat. 376.

Coates v. Muse
Opinion and Decree
U.S. Circuit Court, Virginia, 4 June 1821

Margaret Coates, a British subject and executrix of William Coates (surviving partner of William Gray & Company), filed her bill in chancery in November 1817 against Elliott Muse, surviving administrator of Hudson Muse and executor of Thomas Muse. The bill was brought to revive an 1811 decree of the federal court obtained by Coates against Hudson Muse's administrators. Marshall's opinion contains a concise narrative of the proceedings in this suit up to the interlocutory decree of 4 June 1821 (bill in chancery [filed 14 Nov. 1817], Coates v. Muse, U.S. Cir. Ct., Va., Ended Cases [Unrestored], 1823, Vi; U.S. Cir. Ct., Va., Ord. Bk. XI, 55, 118).

In 1805, the plaintiff in this cause, instituted her suit in this Court, against Thomas Muse and Elliott Muse, who were administrators, with the will annexed, of Hudson Muse, deceased, and also, his principal devisees and legatees, to obtain payment of a considerable sum of money, due from Hudson Muse, in his lifetime, to the plaintiff's testator. Others of the legatees of Hudson Muse, were also made parties, but against them, no decree was ever given. The estate of Hudson Muse, except the sums which were disbursed in the payment of debts, and some small portions of the legacies, which had been paid, the amount of which is not ascertained, was retained in the hands of the administrators. Their accounts were referred, and the commissioner reported, that the sum of $7493 76, remained in the hands of the administrators, for which sum, a decree was pronounced on the 3d of June, 1811.[1]

In 1817, the plaintiff filed her bill in this Court, for the purpose of reviving this decree, and carrying it into effect, against Elliott Muse, as executor of Thomas Muse, and surviving administrator of Hudson Muse.

Elliott Muse, also, departed this life, without answering this bill, upon which, in June 1818, a bill of revivor was filed against Zachariah Crittenden, the administrator of the estate of Elliott Muse, deceased, and Robert Blakey and Harry Gaines, the administrators, with the will annexed, de bonis non, of Thomas Muse, and against Richard Corbin, the executor of John T. Corbin, who was a surety in the administration bond of Thomas and Elliott Muse, executed by them, as administrators of Hudson Muse.[2]

In May 1819, the defendants, Harry Gaines, and Robert Blakey, administrators of the estate of Thomas Muse, unadministered by Elliott Muse, filed their answer, stating, that on the books of Elliott Muse, the estate of Thomas Muse is debited with its proportion of the debt now claimed, and the whole is stated to be settled with W. C. Williams, the attorney for the plaintiff: that they had understood, that Elliott Muse executed a mortgage to W. C. Williams, for the security of the debt which, through negligence, was never recorded. They, therefore, claimed to be discharged.[3]

In July 1819, Zachariah Crittenden, administrator of Elliott Muse, deceased, filed his answer, stating, that he had fully administered, before any knowledge of the decree rendered in favour of the plaintiff.[4]

At the May Term of this Court, 1820, the Court directed the defendants, Gaines and Blakey, to settle the account of the administration of Thomas Muse, of the estate of Hudson Muse, deceased, and also, an account of their own administration of the estate of Thomas Muse. The Court also directed the defendant, Crittenden, to settle the account of the administration of Elliott Muse, of the estate of Hudson Muse, and his own administration, of the estate of Elliott Muse, before one of the commissioners of this Court.[5]

In October 1820, due notice having been given to the defendants, the commissioner proceeded to execute this decretal order, and the defendants having failed to attend, he reported the proportions, by which the original decree ought to be charged on the estates of Thomas and Elliott Muse. His report charges $5155 02, part of this decree, on the estate of Thomas Muse, and $2338 74, the residue thereof, on the estate of Elliott Muse. This report was filed on the 14th of October, 1820. It states the principles on which the commissioner proceeded, in thus apportioning the debt due to the plaintiff, and also states some other matters, supposed by him to shed some light on the situation of the defendants, with regard to each other. At the November Term, 1820, this report was confirmed, and the matter thereof decreed, no counsel appearing for the defendants.[6]

In January 1821, Robert Blakey, one of the administrators of Thomas Muse, deceased, applied to one of the judges of this Court, for an injunction to stay proceedings on this decree, so far as respected the estate of Thomas Muse, praying that the decree might be opened, and the plaintiff have the relief to which he might be decided to be entitled. The injunction was granted, to continue to the first day of this Term, and the whole case now came on to be decided on its merits.[7]

In his bill for an injunction, the plaintiff states sundry errors in the proceedings and decree, for which he thinks it ought to be opened, and set aside, and also, excuses his non-attendance on the commissioner, and his neglect of the case in this court. The errors alleged, are,

1st. That the decretal order for an account, did not direct an account of the administration of the estate of Thomas Muse, by Elliott Muse.

2d. That the commissioner has made his report *ex-parte*, not being authorized so to do, by the order under which he acted.

3d. That the court acted on the report during the term to which it was made, instead of leaving it to the next term for exceptions.

4th. That the decree is not warranted by the report, since it takes no notice of a sum reported to be due from the estate of Elliott Muse, to that of Thomas Muse, to an amount equal to the whole sum due to the plaintiff.

These errors as assigned, will be severally considered.

1st. An account of the administration of Elliott Muse, of the estate of Thomas Muse, ought to have been directed.

That this account might have been directed, especially as all the parties were before the court, will not be denied. That it ought to have been directed, is not so obvious. If Elliott Muse, as administrator of Thomas Muse, is indebted to that estate, he is not distinguishable, so far as respects the claim of the plaintiff, from any other debtor. Although, in a suit against the representatives of an original debtor, the subject may be pursued further than those representatives, I know of no case in which it has been decided, that the plaintiff is bound to do so.[8] In this particular case, the plaintiff, in her bill, has not required, that this administration account should be settled.

It is impossible to say what delays might attend its settlement; and though the plaintiff would be bound to submit to these delays, had she made any demand on the representatives of Elliott Muse, in virtue of his administration of the estate of Thomas Muse, it would be unreasonable to impose them on her, should they be considerable, when she makes no such demand. In the bill praying the injunction, this supposed error is more relied on, because, as is alleged, the defendants, in their answer, demand such account. Had this demand been really made, it would probably have been attended to, so far as was consistent with a just regard to the rights of the plaintiff, but might have been disregarded without error. In such a case, the court would be regulated by circumstances. But I understand the answer very differently. I can discover in it no claim for this account; nor was it claimed at the hearing. It would have been rather an extraordinary order, had this Court directed an administration account to be taken, which was neither required by the plaintiff or defendant, and did not appear to be essential in the cause.

2d. The report, itself, being made by the commissioner *ex-parte*, is considered as a nullity, because it was not authorized by the decretal order.

Undoubtedly, the decretal order directs the account to be made up by the defendants. They are to be the actors, and the order does not direct the commissioner to proceed *ex-parte*, on their failing to appear. Of the propriety of proceeding *ex-parte*, under such an order, without notice, therefore, to the defendants, I am not perfectly satisfied. Undoubtedly, the court would, on motion, have allowed the defendants, or either of them, to repair their fault, especially if their non-attendance could be excused, as it is in this case; and would feel much disposed, even after the report was acted on, to let in a just defence, if in its power.

3d. The court is also supposed to have erred, in taking up the report at the first term, contrary to its own rule.

I believe no positive rule has been made on this subject. Perhaps one ought to have been made. There has been a practice, and the court ought, undoubtedly, to respect its own practice. That, to the best of my recollection is, to permit original reports, in any degree complex, to lie to a second Term for consideration and exception. This is generally done on the application of one of the parties. In plain cases the report has frequently, I might say commonly, been taken up at the first Term. I cannot pronounce it an error to take up a report at the first Term; but I would listen with great favour to any objections made to a report so taken up, and to any excuse for not having made those objections in the proper time, if the cause were in a situation to allow me to listen to them. This is, undoubtedly, a case in which the report would have been permitted to lie, if desired.

4th. The fourth error assigned is in the decree. It is, that the whole sum is not decreed against the estate of Elliott Muse, since that estate appears to be indebted to the estate of Thomas Muse, in a larger sum than the plaintiff claims from both.

The representative of Elliott Muse was not required to settle his administration of the estate of Thomas Muse, nor did he attempt to settle it. The representatives of those two estates were not directed to settle accounts between them, nor has either of them made the attempt. The commissioner, however has, as a volunteer, reported the inventory and appraisement of the estate of Thomas Muse, and has supposed his executor to be indebted to the full amount, whatever debts he may have discharged; and that, without regard to the answer of the defendants, his administrators, in which they admit themselves to be in possession of part of that very estate. If the court had acted on the presumption, that this debt was actually due, its decree would have been equally without example, and without excuse.

A much more serious objection to the decree has been made in argument. The report, and, consequently, the decree affirming it, is said to be erroneous in this, that it has adopted a principle in apportioning the debt, which is not authorized by any testimony before the commissioner. He has charged each administrator with the amount of his own purchase at the sale of the estate, and has divided the residue of the debts equally between them.

I think this objection to the report, and the decree, well founded.

Thomas and Elliott Muse considered themselves in the character of devisees and legatees, as well as administrators of Hudson Muse. They acted together, so far as the Court can perceive, in the collection and payment of moneys. There is nothing unreasonable in the supposition, that they arranged between themselves their claims upon the estate of Hudson Muse, and that each retained in his own hands, computing his particular debt, as much of the estate as the other. If this is not extremely improbable, and is not contradicted by testimony, the situation in which the cause stood when it came before the commissioner, a situation in which it was placed by the parties themselves, required, that this should be assumed as the basis of the report and of the decree.

Thomas and Elliott Muse were acquainted with their own transactions. They must be supposed to have understood their own situation with the estate, and with each other. Possessing this understanding, and called upon to settle their administration account, the report states a balance in their hands, for which a decree is rendered, binding them equally. Had they been liable for this debt in different proportions, the Court would have decreed against them severally, and according to their proportions. But they permit a report, stating a balance in the hands of both, and a decree upon that report, binding them equally. This decree constitutes a joint debt, of which either paying the whole, could recover a moiety from the other. In the absence of all testimony, showing that this decree ought to be satisfied in unequal proportions, Thomas or Elliott Muse, having satisfied it, could have called on the other for contribution, and this demand could not have been repelled by light presumptions. I am, therefore, of opinion, that the decree, in the actual state of the testimony, ought to have been revived equally, and that the representatives of each of the parties, at least in the first instance, ought to have been subjected only to a moiety of it.

Upon these principles the decree ought to have made against the representatives of Thomas Muse for $3746 88, with the interest which accrued thereon. If it is final, and beyond the reach of the Court, it ought to stand enjoined for the residue. If the court may now open it, the reasons for doing so, which are stated in the bill, and have been noticed in this opinion, and the excuse alleged in the bill for not appearing before the commissioner, are I think, sufficient to justify its being opened, and to induce the Court now to make the order, which would have been made on the application of the party at the last term.

I think, upon authority, the decree may be now opened. The case of Templeman v. Steptoe, reported in 1st Munford 339, goes far in showing that this decree is not final.[9] I had been rather inclined to think otherwise on the reason of the thing, but on that point, I give no opinion. I think the authorities quoted at the bar, and especially that from 1st Ves. 205,[10] and that in Ambler 89,[11] are strong authorities for showing that a court of equity, may, on sufficient circumstances, open a decree, and let in the real merits of the cause, which have been excluded by any excusable misapprehension of the party, or irregularity, or error of the court. I shall follow those precedents in this case, and shall open the decree, and refer the accounts back to the commissioner, taking care to guard the plaintiff against unreasonable delay.

[Decree]

Coats surviving exx.
v
Muses Admrs. & al

This cause came on this day to be heard on the papers read ⟨on⟩ the former hearing and on the bill of the defendant Robert Blakey admr. &c of Thomas Muse decd. which was also considered as a petition for a rehearing and was argued by counsel. On consideration whereof, the court being satisfied that the decree pronounced at the last term is erroneous in apportioning on the estate of Thomas Muse a larger part of the debt due to the plaintiff than ought to be charged on that estate, and being also satisfied with the excuse made by the said Robert Blakey for his non attendance on the commissioner and for his failure to make his objections to the report on its return to this court, doth open & set aside the decree made in this cause at the last term, and doth refer the case to one of the commissioner[s] to execute the order made in May 1820; and he is farther directed to receive any proper evidence which may be offered to show that any part of the debt claimed by the plf. has been paid, or that it ought to be apportioned ⟨on⟩ the estates of their intestates respectively by a different rule from that adopted in his report of October 1820. And the Commr. is directed to proceed ex parte if either of the defendants shall fail to attend. The Commr. is directed to make his report to the next term.[12]

Printed, John W. Brockenbrough, *Reports of Cases Decided by the Honourable John Marshall . . .* , I (Philadelphia, 1837), 531–38. Decree, AD, Coates v. Muse, U.S. Cir. Ct., Va., Ended Cases (Unrestored), 1823, Vi.

1. A copy of this decree is in the case papers (Coates v. Muse). See also U.S. Cir. Ct., Va., Ord. Bk. VIII, 334.

2. Bill of revivor, [filed June 1818] (Coates v. Muse). One who was granted administration of an estate not fully settled was called an administrator *de bonis non* ("of the goods not already administered").

3. Answer of Gaines and Blakey, 27 May 1819 (Coates v. Muse).

4. Answer of Crittenden, 27 May 1819 (Coates v. Muse).

5. Decree (in JM's hand), [25 May 1820]; copy of decree, 25 May 1820, and notice of commissioner's proceedings, 22 July 1820 (Coates v. Muse).

6. Decree of 19 Dec. 1820, U.S. Cir. Ct., Va., Ord. Bk. XI, 55.

7. Bill of injunction, 30 Jan. 1821 (Coates v. Muse). JM's autograph endorsement granting the injunction appears at the foot of the bill.

8. At this point, according to Brockenbrough, JM subjoined the following note: "It has been determined in this Court, on full consideration, I think in a suit against Johnson's Representatives that he is not bound to do so." The reference is to Corbet v. Johnson, 1 Brock. 77; *PJM*, VI, 383–91.

9. Templeman v. Steptoe, 1 Munf. 339 (Va. Court of Appeals, 1810).

10. Kemp v. Squire, 1 Ves. sen. 205, 27 Eng. Rep. 984 (Ch., 1749).

11. Cunyngham v. Cunyngham, Amb. 89, 27 Eng. Rep. 55 (Ch., 1750).

12. See the further opinions and decrees in this case at 12 June 1822 and 18 Dec. 1823.

Backhouse v. Jett's Administrator
Opinion and Decree
U.S. Circuit Court, Virginia, 6 June 1821

The object of this equity suit was to recover a debt owed by the estate of Thomas Jett to the late John Backhouse, a subject of Great Britain. Backhouse's administratrix had obtained a judgment at law for $3,400 in the federal court in June 1799, but the jury also found that William Storke Jett, Jett's son and executor, had "fully administered" the assets of the estate. A few years later Backhouse's representatives filed a bill in equity against the executor and other legatees of the late Thomas Jett, alleging property in their possession belonging to the estate of which the jury had no knowledge at the time of the law trial. An amended bill filed in July 1817 brought into issue the validity of a deed of gift made by Thomas Jett in June 1783 (two years before his death) to William Storke Jett, conveying half of his lands, twenty-one slaves, and half of his other personal property. After William Storke Jett filed his answer to this bill in November 1818, the court at the June 1819 term ordered the commissioner to prepare a report. To this report, which was filed in December 1820, both parties entered exceptions. Marshall gave his opinion and decree on 6 June 1821 (U.S. Cir. Ct., Va., Ord. Bk. III, 242; V, 180–81, 268; VII, 257; VIII, 76–77; IX, 23, 406, 420; XI, 120; pleadings and other case papers, Backhouse v. Jett, U.S. Cir. Ct., Va., Ended Cases [Unrestored], 1849, Vi).

Backhouse

v

Jetts admr. &c

In this case the plf. had instituted a suit on the common law side of the court to which the defendant pleaded the general issue and fully administered. The first was found for the plf. & the second for the defendand and judgement was rendered for the plf. to be satisfied out of the assetts of his testator when they should come to his hands to be administered.[1] This bill is filed alleging that assetts were in the hands of the Admr. at the time the verdict was given which were not known to the plf., & were not shown to the jury, & that assetts have since come to the hands of the Admr. which are liable for this debt. The bill also asserts a claim on the real estate upon the principle of Marshaling assetts.[2] The accounts were referred to a commissioner, and his report has been excepted to by both parties. ¶1

The plaintiff excepts, because the Commissioner has given to an ex-parte report made by the county commissioners to the county court of Westmoreland while this suit demanding an account was depending in this court the same effect as would be allowed to such report had it been made before the institution of this suit.[3] ¶2

This exception is sustained. While a suit for an account is depending, neither of the parties ought to be permitted to change their relative situation, by a proceeding without the knowledge or the participation of the other. The commissioner therefore ought to have required vouchers for this account. It is said that the deposition of Mr. Campbell is a sufficient voucher for the most considerable item in it. The objection made to this deposition is that this debt was not mentioned in the account which was taken before the commrs. in 1798, nor in the answer filed in this cause.[4] ¶3

These omissions certainly throw some doubt over the claim for this credit, & require that it should be sustained by clear testimony, but they do not conclusively negative the right to it. When an admr. supposes himself to have fully administered the assetts in his hands, he may be careless about adding to the sum he has overpaid; and when a plaintiff himself comes into a court of equity after a verdict against him on the plea of fully administered to show assetts at that time in the hands of the ¶4 admr., he cannot be permitted to contest the right of the admr. to show the disbursement of those assetts. I shall however reserve the decision on this claim till the report shall come in.

¶5 The principle controversy between the parties respects a number of slaves comprized in a deed of gift made in his life time by Thomas Jett the original debtor, to the defendant his son, for his establishment in life. This deed being voluntary is said to be fraudulent as to creditors, and the plf. claims the slaves & their hire from the death of the donor. The defendant contends that he is liable only for the slaves now alive, for the price of such as have been sold, and for interest, & hire, if at all, only from the filing of the bill in which the claim is made.

¶6 The commr. has charged the admr. with the value of all these slaves & interest on this sum. Several exceptions have been made to this item of the account, and the instructions of the court for regulating the conduct of the commissioner have been required.

¶7 The plf contends

1st. That these slaves were assetts in the hands of the administrator.
2d. That a person holding under a voluntary deed is liable for profits.
If the first point be decided in favor of the plf. it will determine the question, for it has never been doubted that an admr. is liable for the profits which have been made on the assetts in his hands.

¶8 Are slaves then, which are given by the owner in his lifetime, assetts in the hands of his representative, if required for the payment of debts?

¶9 If this was a case of the first impression it would be decided by the words of the act of our state legislature which makes such deeds of gift void against those only who may have been injured by them.[5] As between the parties they are to all intents & purposes valid. Wm. S. Jett, so far as respected any claim to be set up by Thomas Jett, was the owner of these slaves; and if this be true, they could not be assetts in the hands of the representative of Thomas Jett. But our statute is in a great degree copied from that of England & so far as it is copied Virginia is supposed to have adopted with the statute the settled English construction of it. It is therefore proper to examine the english cases on this point.

¶10 The counsel for the plf. relies much on Roberts on Frauds v. 2. p 592–3.[6] Roberts says "But wherever a man makes a fraudulent gift of his goods & chattels & dies indebted, the rule upon the 13th. of El. ch 5. has always been to construe the gift as utterly void against all his creditors & the debtor to have died in full possession with respect to *their* claims, so that the effects are just as much assetts in the hands of the personal representatives as to creditors as if no such attempt to alien them had been made."

¶11 It is admitted that Roberts lays down the rule in broad & explicit terms. But very little attention to what immediately follows will be sufficient to show that his expressions are very unguarded; and that, if his proposition is true in any case it is only in the case of the donor's retaining possession. This was the point secondly determined in Bethel v Stanhope Cr. El 810.[7]

In Bethel v Stanhope the Donor died in possession and the defendant had intermeddled with the goods so as to become exr. in his own wrong before admn. was granted to him. After admn. granted he delivered the goods to the donee who was the daughter of the Donor. The court determined 1st. that the defendant might be sued as exr. & 2d. that the goods which had been in his possession, were assetts, & remained such notwithstanding the delivery to the donee. ¶12

In addition to the very essential fact that the Donor, in this case died in possession of the goods, there was a clause in the deed that it should be void upon the payment of 20/ & the jury expressly find that it was made by covin to defraud his creditors. As covin implies participation in the actual fraud on the part of the donee, it is presumed that she could not have recovered these goods in a suit against the Donor or his admr. He was therefore in possession of goods which he might lawfully retain, & which were assetts in his hands for the payment of debts. He could no more divest himself of these assetts or of his liability for them to creditors by delivering them to a donee not having a legal right to demand them, than by delivering them to a legatee. ¶13

Roberts adds "To give substantial effect to this construction the voluntary donee is considered as liable to be charged as exr. *de son tort* if he take possession of the goods after the decease of the donor."[8] ¶14

Now to me it seems difficult to reconcile this determination with the idea that these goods are assetts in the hands of the rightful exr. If any other person than the donee take them from the possession of the exr. he is a trespasser, & not an exr. de son tort unless he claims to take them as exr. or does other acts of an exr. This is expressly determined in Reads case 5th. Co. 33.[9] It seems to me that charging the donee in this case as exr. de son tort, when another person would not be so charged for the same act, instead of proving that they are assetts in the hands of the rightful exr., goes far to prove the contrary. Reads case contains another principle which is decisive on the general question where the possession has been parted with by the Donor. The court says "when the defendant takes the goods before the rightful exr. hath taken upon him or proved the will, he may be charge⟨d⟩ as exr. of his own wrong, for the rightful exr. shall not be charged but with the goods which come to his hands after he takes upon him the charge of the will." ¶15

Now if the exr. shall not be charged with goods of which the testator died possessed until they are reduced to actual possession, he shall not a fortiori be charged with goods of which his testator did not die possessed, but which he had given away in his life time. But to return to Roberts. He says that where the goods are taken by the donee after admn. granted to another he may be charged as exr. *de son tort* "and this," he adds, "seems to be a rule much in favor of the rightful exr. or admr. who cannot excuse himself upon the statute of Elizabeth from delivering up the subject of his testator or intestates fraudulent gift to the donee if he demand it."[10] ¶16

¶17   Now this proposition appears to me to be in direct opposition to that before laid down by the same author. If under the statute, the exr. is obliged to surrender the thing given to the donee even where the donor dies in possession and the thing is in his hands, he is not afterwards chargeable with the same property as assetts, & a fortiori he cannot be charged with it if it never came to his hands, but was delivered to the donee in the life time of the testator.

¶18   This last doctrine of Mr. Roberts is completely sustained by Hawes v Leader Cr. J. 271.[11] In that case the Donor died in possession & the Donee sued the admr. who pleaded that the gift was fraudulent & that his testator was indebted & did not leave other assetts sufficient to pay his debts. The plf. demurred & the court gave judgement in his favor.

¶19   This case seems to me to be entirely decisive of the whole question. If the admr. could not maintain his own possession against the Donee, it is very clear that he could not defeat the possession of the Donee; and if he could not, it is equally clear that the law cannot consider the goods as assetts in his hands.

¶20   Mr Stannard also quoted 1 Maddox 218 & 2 Term 587.[12] But Maddox goes no further than to say that the goods "shall still be considered as a part of the Donors estate for the benefit of his creditors";[13] that is, as I understand him, they shall be so considered in the hands of the Donee; and the case in 2d. Term only determines that the Donee may be considered as *exr de son tort.*

¶21   I think then it is very clear that according to the English cases as well as on the words of the statute, these slaves are not assetts.

¶22   2d. This leads to the enquiry into the extent of the liability of the Donee.

¶23   It is not denied that this is a case free from any charge of covin.[14] There is no fraud in fact, or bad faith on the part of the donee. I think there was none on the part of the Donor for the case presents no reason for supposing that the deed was made in contemplation of insolvency or with a view to defraud creditors. It is made two years before the death of the testator, & before the date of his will & it is not pretended that he was at the time in bad health. He does not appear to have been pressed by creditors, nor does the admn. account exhibit debts of which he might be particularly apprehensive. There are no judgements, or even bonds; there is nothing to induce a suspicion that he was not in good credit or that he doubted his ability to pay any claim which might be brought against him. In this situation he gives half his estate to his only son for his establishment in life. The policy of the law very properly declares this gift void as to creditors, but looking at the probable views of the parties at the time, there appears to be no moral turpitude in it. In such a case, is the Donee responsible for more than the slaves themselves including their issue now in existence, & their profits from the time they were claimed by creditors, and for the money actually received for those which have been sold, and for interest on that money from the same time? Is he responsible for profits which accrued before the creditor made his demand?

There is some difficulty in this question considered meerly on princi- ¶24 ple. The donee has title against all the world except against creditors. He has a title defeasible by creditors only. It is good against the Donor and his exrs. Where a person having no title holds the property of another the profits belong to that other; but in this case the slaves are not the property of the creditors. They have a claim upon them for satisfaction of their debts but no title in them. Profits in the hands of an exr. are liable for debts because they form a part of the estate of the testator, & the exr. receives them as trustee for that estate. But the donee is not a trustee for the estate of the testator; & it is not clear that he is a trustee for the creditors, since he has always held the property in his own right. It is by no means clear upon principle, where the title is not to the thing itself, but to have it sold in satisfaction of a debt, that this title can extend to the profits previously made of that thing by a bona fide possessor.

It might be expected that these questions had frequently arisen under a ¶25 statute passed in the reign of Elizabeth & had been long settled. But I have been able to find no case in which it has arisen; & I am the more inclined to think it never has been made because the gentlemen concerned in this cause would I think have found the case had it existed. In Partridge v Gop Ambler 596. a gift of money to daughters was declared void & directed to be refunded but no claim appears to have been made for interest.[15]

Viner in his first volume page 186 pl. 9. lays down the broad & general ¶26 principle that a bona fide possessor receives the profits as his own. But I should be much better satisfied could I see the case itself, & the reasoning on which the decision was made.[16]

In the absence of decisions in cases of personal property, those which ¶27 have been made respecting the profits of real estate have been resorted to on both sides, & gentlemen, reasoning from analogy, have applied the law in such cases to voluntary gifts of chattels. It has been affirmed & denied that heirs devisees & all persons holding real estates as voluntiers, are accountable to creditors for profits.

The case of Davies v Top 1. Browns chy. rep 524 has been relied on as ¶28 showing that the heir is accountable for profits.[17]

The report of that case is remarkably confused & unsatisfactory. John ¶29 Top died in April 1778. The bill was brought for an account & application of the personal estate not specially bequeathed, to the payment of debts; and in case the personal estate should not be sufficient, to have the deficiency raised by sale or mortgage of the real estate.

The cause was heard at the Rolls in Feb. 80. when it was directed that ¶30 the real estate should be sold to make up any deficiency in the personal estate; and it was declared that if the real estate should not be sufficient, the rents & profits should be applied to make up the deficiency.

There are several parts of this decree as stated which appear to me to ¶31 be very extraordinary; but I shall not notice them because they do not apply to the question before the court, though they certainly bring the whole case into some doubt. But the decree so far as it respects rents & profits is expressed in general terms not declaring whether the rents & profits shall be computed from the death of the testator or from the filing of the bill. In the particular case it could not have been of much consequence, for the cause was heard at the Rolls in less than two years after the death of the testator which leaves it probable that no profits accrued between the death of the testator & the filing of the bill.

¶32   It does not appear certainly from the opinion of the Chancellor whether this case was affirmed or reversed: And in his opinion not a syllable is said on that part of it which respects profits. The principle question, that on which the parties were desirous of obtaining the opinion of the court appears to have been whether after purchased lands which descended to the heir, or specific legacies & lands specifically devised but charged with debts & legacies, should be first liable for those debts. The complexion of the case gives some reason for the opinion that the question of profits was in fact of no importance & was not raised in the bill. This case I think leaves that question where it was found.

¶33   The cases in 2d. Adkyns are so obscurely reported as to give no decisive information on the subject. In Simms v Urry 2 Ch. ca. 225 the Chancellor decreed profits only from the time of pronouncing the decree.[18]

¶34   Baron Westons case as cited in 1st. Vern. 174 was this.[19] Baron Weston brought debt on a bond against the heir, but for three descents the heir continued an infant so that the parol demurred.[20] The guardia⟨n⟩ received the profits of the estate & converted them to her own use. The Baron brought an action agt. her as admr. of the children but did not succeed. In the principal case the counsel admitted that profits could not be demanded during minority.

¶35   In Waters v Ebral 2. Ver. 606. it was determined that a guardian was not compellable to apply the profits of a wards estate to the payment of bond debts.[21]

¶36   In the case of Chambers & al v Harvest & al Moseley 124 the question was whether the heir should account for profits from the time of filing the bill or only from the decree; & it was determined that he should account from the time of filing the bill.[22]

¶37   In 6th. Vezey 93 The Chancellor says "Where there has been an adverse possession, and upon an application to this court upon grounds of equitable releif the plf. appears entitled to an account of rents & profits, if there has been a meer adverse possession, without fraud concealment, or an adverse possession of some instrument, without which the plf could not proceed, the court has said the account shall be taken only from the filing of the bill, for it is his own fault not to file it sooner."[23]

¶38   In 7th. Vezey 546 the account of rents & profits was restrained to the time of filing the bill.[24]

These two cases from Vezey are not cases where the heir is made liable ¶39
for the debt of the Ancester. They are cases of title which is much stronger.
Even in them the account has been restrained, where there was nothing
to prevent the plf. from having proceeded, to the time of filing the bill.

In the case of Shettelworth v Neville 1 Term 454 which was an action of ¶40
debt against the heir Ashhurst says "till the possession is recovered against
him (the heir) he is entitled to the rents & profits; & he is entitled to
receive them till judgement is given against him.["][25]

At common law the heir who had aliened before action brought might ¶41
plead that he had nothing by descent at the time of suing out the writ or
filing the bill. Had the profits been assetts, this plea could not have been
maintained. The profits therefore were not assetts. The statute of the 3d.
& 4th. of W. & M. which has rendered the heir in cases of alienation liable
for the value of the land does not make him liable for the profits, or for
interest on the money.[26] It is to be fairly presumed that the statute has
adopted the rule of the court of chancery.

Upon the best consideration I can give to the cases I am well satisfied ¶42
that chancery does not make an heir responsible for profits accrued
before the filing of the bill, & I think the analogy between real & personal
estate in this respect is a strong one.

This question was well considered in Munfords case & decided against ¶43
the claim to profits. I regret that the opinion then given has been
mislaid.[27]

The plfs counsel has relied on a case reported in 5th. Munf. 492.[28] In ¶44
the construction of a state statute the courts of the Union have uniformly
adopted the rule of decision given by the state courts. If therefore the
court of Appeals had decided that under our statute of frauds a donee
was responsible for profits I should have followed the precedent however
erroneous I might have thought it. But the case to which the plf. has
referred is not a case under the statute. It is not the case of a creditor; but
of a person having title to the slave recovered.

I think the defendant W. S. Jett is responsible for the slaves now alive at ¶45
their present value or for the slaves themselves & for profits from the filing
of the amended bill which claims them, and for the money actually received for those which have been sold with interest thereon from the same
time. And the report is to be made up in conformity with this opinion.

[Decree]

Backhouse
v
Jett &c.

This cause came on to be heard on the bill & amended bill answers,
exhibits depositions, & the report of the commissioner and the exceptions of the parties to that report & was argued by counsel on consider-

ation whereof this Court doth allow the exceptions both of the plaintiff and defendant and doth recommit the report with directions not to admit any account taken before Commissioners in the country subsequent to the institution of this suit further than the same shall be supported by vouchers or evidences. And the court doth farther direct the commisioners to charge the defendant with the present value of such of the slaves contained in the deed of the 10th. day of June 1783 in the amended bill mentioned & their issue, as are now in possession of deft. & with the profits thereon from the   day of July in the year 1817 when the amended bill in this cause was filed and also with the profits of those who may have died since the said   day of July 1817, from that day to the time of their death, and also with the price of the slaves contained in the said deed or of their issue, who may have been sold, or with the value of those otherwise disposed of at the time when disposed of together with interest on such price or value, to be calculated from the said   day of July 1817. And the Commissioner is directed to perform the order of the 5th. day of June 1819 — with the additional instructions herein given.[29]

AD, Marshall Judicial Opinions, PPAmP; printed, John W. Brockenbrough, *Reports of Cases Decided by the Honourable John Marshall . . .* , I (Philadelphia, 1837), 504–16. Decree, AD, Backhouse v. Jett, U.S. Cir. Ct., Va., Ended Cases (Unrestored), 1849, Vi. For JM's deletions and interlineations, see Textual Notes below.

1. This was an action of assumpsit brought by Rebecca Backhouse, John Backhouse's administratrix, against William Storke Jett, Thomas Jett's executor. Judgment was rendered on 4 June 1799 (U.S. Cir. Ct., Va., Ord. Bk. III, 242).

2. A creditor by bond could satisfy his claim out of the personal or real estate of his debtor. If he exhausted the personal estate, however, a simple contract creditor (such as Backhouse) was allowed in equity to stand in place of the bond creditor and recover from the real estate. This was the principle of marshaling assets (*PJM*, V, 148–49; VIII, 55–56).

3. This exception to the commissioner's report, signed by plaintiff's counsel Robert Stanard, is in the case papers. Commissioner Thomas Ladd's report relied on two administration accounts on Jett's estate taken by commissioners appointed by the county court of Westmoreland, one dated 22 Sept. 1798, the other dated 18 May 1818. The plaintiff objected to the latter account as made "ex parte, without any notice, to the plaintiff and while this Suit was depending" (Backhouse v. Jett).

4. In his answer to the amended bill, William Storke Jett claimed a credit for £450 paid to the estate of Archibald Campbell in 1788. This sum was omitted in the 1798 administration account, explained Jett, because he "was not then prepared with Vouchers to support the charge but now has it in his power to establish the same." The commissioner approved this credit in his report of Dec. 1820 (answer of William Storke Jett, 11 Sept. 1818; commissioner's report, 5 Dec. 1820; deposition of John Campbell, 16 Nov. 1820 [summarized in 1 Brock. 504–5], Backhouse v. Jett).

5. Virginia's act "to prevent fraud and perjuries," enacted in 1785 (*Revised Code of Va.*, I, 372–73).

6. William Roberts, *A Treatise on the Construction of the Statutes, . . . Relating to Voluntary and Fraudulent Conveyances* (Philadelphia, 1807), 592–93.

7. Ibid., 593; Bethel v. Stanhope, Cro. Eliz. 810, 78 Eng. Rep. 1037 (K.B., 1599).

8. Roberts, *Treatise on Voluntary and Fraudulent Conveyances*, 593. An executor *de son tort* ("of his own wrong") is one who takes on an executorship without any legal authority.

9. Read's Case, 5 Co. Rep. 33, 77 Eng. Rep. 103 (C.P., 1604).

10. Roberts, *Treatise on Voluntary and Fraudulent Conveyances*, 592–93.

11. Hawes v. Leader, Cro. Jac. 270, 79 Eng. Rep. 232 (K.B., 1611).

12. Henry Maddock, *A Treatise on the Principles and Practice in the High Court of Chancery* (3d Am. ed.; 2 vols.; Hartford, Conn., 1827); Edwards v. Harben, 2 T.R. 587, 100 Eng. Rep. 315 (K.B., 1788).

13. JM paraphrased Maddock, *Treatise on the Principles and Practice of the High Court of Chancery*, I, 275: "If one, *indebted at the time*, makes a mere voluntary Conveyance to a Child, and dies indebted, it is still considered as part of his Estate for the benefit of his Creditors."

14. "Covin" is the legal term for a secret conspiracy or agreement between two or more persons to defraud another.

15. Partridge v. Gopp, Amb. 596, 27 Eng. Rep. 388 (Ch., 1758).

16. Charles Viner, *A General Abridgment of Law and Equity* . . . (22 vols.; n.p., 1742–53), I, 186.

17. Davies v. Topp, 1 Bro. C.C. 524, 28 Eng. Rep. 1276 (Ch., 1780).

18. Sims v. Urry, 2 Chan. Cas. 225, 22 Eng. Rep. 920 (Ch., 1676).

19. Baron Weston's case was cited in Creed v. Colville, 1 Vern. 172, 174, 23 Eng. Rep. 395, 396 (Ch., 1683).

20. A parol demurrer was a suspension of proceedings during the minority of an infant.

21. Waters v. Ebrall, 2 Vern. 606, 23 Eng. Rep. 996 (Ch., 1707).

22. Chambers v. Harvest, Mosely 124, 25 Eng. Rep. 307 (Ch., 1729).

23. Pulteney v. Warren, 6 Ves. 73, 93, 31 Eng. Rep. 944, 954 (Ch., 1801).

24. Pettiward v. Prescott, 7 Ves. 541, 546, 32 Eng. Rep. 218, 220 (Ch., 1802).

25. Shetelworth v. Neville, 1 T.R. 454, 457, 99 Eng. Rep. 1194, 1195 (K.B., 1786).

26. This statute (reenacted in Virginia in 1726) made lands passing by devise as well as by descent to the heir liable for bond debts in which the heir was expressly bound (*PJM*, V, 125 n. 10).

27. Mutter's Ex. v. Munford, 1 Brock. 266, 285 n.; *PJM*, VIII, 51, 59, 60 n. 31. At the end of his opinion given in 1814 in this case, JM wrote: "This cause came on afterward to be argued on the question whether the heir was liable for profits received before the filing of the bill: and the Court determined that he was not; but that opinion is lost." This opinion apparently was rendered sometime between 1816 and 1820, a period for which the order books are missing.

28. Baird v. Bland, 5 Munf. 492 (Va. Court of Appeals, 1817).

29. Pursuant to this interlocutory decree, the commissioner made another report, which resulted in another interlocutory decree, given on 23 Dec. 1826, recommitting the report. The case was not finally concluded until 1849 (U.S. Cir. Ct., Va., Ord. Bk. XII, 147; U.S. Cir. Ct., Va., Index to Ended Causes, 1790–1860, Vi).

Textual Notes

Title	l. 3	Jetts ~~exr~~ admr. &c
¶ 1	l. 1	this ~~cause~~ ↑case↓ the
	l. 6	filed ~~for the discovery of~~ ↑alleging that↓ assetts ↑were↓ in
	l. 7	time ↑the verdict was given↓ which
	l. 8	& ~~for the discovery of~~ ↑that↓ assetts ~~which~~ have
¶ 2	l. 1	has ~~received~~ given
	l. 4	report ~~of~~ had
¶ 3	l. 2	parties ~~would~~ ↑ought to↓ be
¶ 4	l. 3	admr. ~~has~~ supposes
¶ 5	l. 2	made ↑in his life time↓ by
	l. 5	their ~~profits~~ hire

	l. 7	interest, ~~of~~ & hire,
	l. 8	the ~~time institution~~ filing
¶ 6	l. 3	court ~~as to the~~ ↑for↓ regulating
¶ 8	l. 1 beg.	~~Is persona~~ Are
	l. 1	the ~~testato~~ owner
	l. 2	his ~~ex~~ ↑representative,↓ if
¶ 9	l. 3	those ↑only↓ who
	l. 3	them. ~~as~~ ↑As↓ between
	l. 8	copied ~~the~~ Virginia
¶10	l. 1	relies ↑much↓ on
¶11	l. 1	down ↑the rule↓ in
	ll. 3–4	his ~~position~~ ↑proposition↓ is
	ll. 4–5	possession. [*erasure*] ~~He says~~" This was the point [*erasure*] ↑secondly↓ determined
¶12	l. 3	him. [*erasure*] ↑After↓ admn.
	ll. 4–5	determined ↑1st.↓ that
¶13	ll. 4–5	the ↑actual↓ fraud
	l. 6	the ↑Donor or his↓ admr.
¶14	l. 1 beg.	Roberts ~~proceeds to~~ adds
¶15	l. 9	exr., ~~proves~~ ↑goes far to prove↓ the contrary. Reads case ~~settles~~ contains
¶16	l. 5	taken ~~he~~ by
¶17	ll. 1–2	that ↑before↓ laid
	l. 6	came to ↑his↓ hands,
¶18	l. 2	271. ~~as well as by Reads case~~ In
	l. 5	his [*erasure*] ↑favor.↓
¶21	l. 2	the [*erasure*] ↑words↓ of
¶23	l. 1	that ↑this↓ is a
	ll. 2–3	was ~~known~~ ↑none↓ on
	ll. 3–4	for ~~the~~ supposing
	l. 7	health. [*erasure*] ↑He↓ does
	l. 16	themselves ↑including their issue↓ now
¶24	l. 3	a ~~property~~ ↑title↓ defeasible
	l. 5	the ~~property is~~ ↑slaves are↓ not
	l. 7	exr. ~~remain~~ ↑are↓ liable
	l. 11	right. ~~In this view of the question the act of limitations presents some difficulties which would deserve to be considered. But~~ It is
	ll. 13–14	profits ↑previously↓ made
¶25	l. 1	that ~~this~~ ↑these↓ questions
	ll. 5–7	existed. ↑In Partridge v Gop Ambler [*erasure*] 596. a gift of money to [*erasure*] daughters was declared void & directed to be refunded but no claim appears to have been made for interest.↓
¶27	l. 3	gentlemen, ~~have~~ reasoning
	l. 4	of ~~goods &~~ chattels.
	l. 6	creditors ~~as~~ ↑for↓ profits.
¶29	l. 4	should ~~be deficient~~ ↑not be sufficient,↓ to
¶30	l. 4	up ~~such~~ ↑the↓ deficiency.

¶31 l. 8 the ~~rolls~~ ↑Rolls↓ in
¶32 l. 1 beg. ~~Wh~~ It does not appear ↑certainly↓ from
l. 6 specific ~~debts~~ ↑legacies↓ & lands ~~charged~~ specifically
l. 9 the ↑question of↓ profits ~~were~~ ↑was↓ in
¶34 l. 6 the ~~principle~~ ↑principal↓ case
¶35 l. 1 Ver. ↑606.↓ it
¶38 l. 1 beg. In 7th. ~~Term~~ ↑Vezey↓ 546
¶40 l. 1 Neville ↑1 Term 454↓ which
¶41 l. 5 has ~~sub~~ rendered
¶43 ll. 1–2 case & ↑decided against the claim to profits.↓ I
l. 2 given ~~to which this conforms~~ has
¶44 l. 3 the ↑rule of↓ decision

To Joseph Story

Dear Sir   Richmond June 15th. 1821

A question has occurred in the course of this term which I have taken under advisement for the purpose [of] enquiring whether it has been decided by my brethren. It is this. **A** & **B** trading under the firm of A B & Co. were indebted to the U.S. on bonds for duties. They made an assignment of all their social effects to secure certain creditors of the firm. **A** had private property to a considerable amount which he afterwards conveyed to secure his individual creditors. The question is whether the first conveyance was an act of insolvency within the act of Congress so that the priority of the U.S. attached on the social effects, or whether the act of insolvency was not committed until the execution of the second deed. The case arises on a contest between the creditors secured by the two deeds, each contending that the claim of the U.S. should be satisfied by the other. Had the second deed never been executed would the first have amounted to an act of insolvency on the part of the firm? If the case has ever occurred in your circuit I shall be glad to know how it has been decided. If it has never occurred you will oblige me by stating your opinion on it if you have one.[1]

The opinion of the supreme court in the lottery case has been assaulted with a degree of virulence transcending what has appeared on any former occasion. Algernon Sydney is written by the gentleman who is so much distinguished for his feelings towards the supreme court, & if you have not an opportunity of seeing the Enquirer I will send it to you. There are other minor gentry who seek to curry favor & get into office by adding their mite of abuse, but I think for coarseness & malignity of invective Algernon Sidney surpasses all party writers who have ever made pretensions to any decency of character. There is on this subject no such thing as a free press in Virginia; and of consequence the calumnies & misrepresentations of this gentleman will remain uncontradicted & will

by many be beleived to be true. He will be supposed to be the champion
of state rights instead of being what he really is the champion of dismem-
berment. With great regard & esteem, I am dear Sir yours &c

J MARSHALL

I am anxious to know whether that amendm⟨ent to⟩ the constitution on
which Mr. Webster & yourself were so distinguished has been approved or
rejected by your sapient people.[2]

ALS, Story Papers, MHi.

1. After writing to Story and to Washington on this day, JM apparently changed his mind
and decided the case of U.S. v. Shelton. See Opinion and Decree, 15 June 1821.

2. At the Massachusetts Constitutional Convention of 1820–21 an amendment was proposed to change the basis for representation in the Senate from taxable property to
population. Story and Daniel Webster joined forces to defeat the amendment. When the
convention's proposed amendments were submitted to the people in Apr. 1821, the one
pertaining to the Senate and House of Representatives was defeated. The result was that
the Senate continued to be apportioned according to taxation, as provided in the constitution of 1780 (Merrill D. Peterson, ed., *Democracy, Liberty, and Property: The State Constitutional Conventions of the 1820's* [Indianapolis, Ind., 1966], 11–17, 77–108; Story to JM,
27 June 1821).

To Bushrod Washington

My dear Sir   Richmond June 15th. 1821
    I have not heard from you since you set out for Philadelphia, but I hope
your health has not at any rate been injured by your attention on your
circuit duties.
    A case has occurred in this circuit which I have taken under advise-
ment for the purpose of enquiring whether it has also occurred in other
circuits. **A** & **B** merchants & partners were indebted to the U.S. on duty
bonds. They made an assignment of all their social effects for the security
of creditors of the firm. **A** individually was in possession of property to a
considerable amount. Some time afterwards he assigned this property
for the benefit of his private creditors. Was the first deed an act of insolvency as to the firm so as to attach the priority of the U.S. on the effects of
the firm? or did this priority not attach till the execution of the second
deed. The question arises between the creditors under the different
deeds, each endeavouring to throw the debt due to the U.S. on the other.
    Has this question arisen in your circuit, & if so, how has it been de-
cided. If it has not arisen what think you of it?
    You have probably seen Algernon Sidney & can be at no loss for the
author. There is probably but one man in the United States who could or
would write such pieces. If you have not seen them I recommend them

to you as being an excitement to stagnating spirits as powerful as the essence of chian[1] to a palate which has lost its discriminating power. Yours truely

J MARSHALL

ALS, Marshall Papers, ViW. Addressed to Washington at Mount Vernon; postmarked Richmond, 15 June. Endorsed by Washington.

1. Cayenne. Above this word, JM inserted an alternate spelling: "kian."

United States v. P. T. Shelton & Company
Opinion and Decree
U.S. Circuit Court, Virginia, 15 June 1821

Philip T. Shelton and Walter Shelton, partners in the firm of P. T. Shelton & Company, became indebted to the United States for duties on goods imported by the firm, amounting to $2,500. The bonds executed by the company remaining unpaid, U.S. Attorney Robert Stanard (1781–1846) filed suit in August 1819. The preceding April the Sheltons had conveyed the company's property to trustees for the benefit of certain creditors. By a subsequent deed of trust, executed in April 1820, Walter Shelton conveyed his private real and personal property to secure payment to certain creditors. In addition to the Sheltons, the defendants included the various trustees and creditors named in the two deeds of trust. The United States claimed priority of payment out of the funds provided in both deeds. Marshall rendered his opinion and decree on 15 June 1821 (subpoenas, 7 Aug. 1819, 24 June 1820; bill in chancery, [ca. Aug. 1819]; amended bill in chancery, [filed June 1820]; deed of trust, 26 Apr. 1819; deed of trust, 12 Apr. 1820, U.S. v. Shelton, U.S. Cir. Ct., Va., Ended Cases [Unrestored], 1821, Vi; U.S. Cir. Ct., Va., Ord. Bk. XI, 155–56; *Richmond Portraits*, 188–89).

The United States
v
P. T. Shelton & Co.

In this case P. T. Shelton & Co. consisting of P. T. Shelton & Walter ¶1 Shelton being indebted to the United States for duties, made a voluntary assignment of all their effects for the payment of their debts. W. Shelton was in possession of some estate in his private character which he afterwards conveyed for the payment of his private debts.

The United States have filed their bill claiming priority out of the social ¶2 fund, & have also in a supplemental bill claimed priority out of the private fund. The controversy is between the creditors under the first & the last deed. Those under the first deed contend that its execution was not an act of insolvency in as much as one of the partners remained solvent.

The creditors under the second deed insist that the claim of the United States, if it can now be asserted ought to be charged on the first deed.

¶3   Some other questions have been made in the cause, but they are contingent questions, depending on the manner in which the first shall be decided.

¶4   The act of Congress gives a preference to the U.S. "in all cases of insolvency." And these "shall be deemed to extend as well to cases in which a debtor, not having sufficient property to pay all his or her debts, shall have made a voluntary assignment thereof, for the benefit of his or her creditors," "as to cases in which an act of legal bankruptcy shall have been committed."[1]

¶5   P. T. Shelton & Co. executed their bond to the U.S. as partners for a partnership debt. In that character they were the "debtor" of the U.S. In that character they had not "sufficient property to pay all their debts." In that character they "made a voluntary assignment of all their property for the benefit of their creditors." This would I think have been "an act of legal bankruptcy," under the act of Congress passed afterwards on the subject,[2] as well as under the bankrupt laws of England, & would probably have constituted an act of bankruptcy under any state law which might exist at the time. Of this however I am not certain. I cannot therefore say positively that the question whether this assignment is an act of insolvency under the act of Congress, derives any illustration from the reference it makes to "an act of legal bankruptcy"; though I am incline⟨d⟩ to think it does. But be this as it may, I am disposed to think that on the meer reason of the case, it is a fair exposition of the words of the act of Congress to consider it as an act of insolvency. It was an alienation of that whole fund which was immediately, & in the first instance chargeable with this debt. Had a commission of bankruptcy been sued out the debt of the U.S. being a partnership debt would have been paid out of the social fund; and recourse would not have been allowed against the private fund, until the social fund was exhausted, or shown to be inadequate to the satisfaction of the debt. It seems to be the dictate of justice that partnership transactions should be charged in the first instance on the partnership fund, & private transactions on the private fund where there is not enough for the payment of all.

¶6   I shall therefore direct the trustees under the first deed to pay the debt due to the U.S. with liberty to apply to the court should that fund prove insufficient.

[Decree]

The United States
    v
P. T. Shelton & Co & al

This cause came on to be heard on the bill amended bill, answers, exhibits & testimony read in the cause and was argued by counsel; on consideration whereof this court is of opinion that the indenture of the 26th. day of april in the year 1819 in the original bill mentioned being an assignment of all the social effects of P. T. Shelton & Co the debtors of the United States in their character as partners & joint traders is an act of insolvency within the true spirit & meaning of the act of Congress, upon which the claim of the United States to priority of payment bound the partnership effects in the hands of the assignees; & it is therefore decreed & ordered that John Enders & Henry Clarke the acting trustees under the said deed do out of the proceeds of the property assigned to them pay to the United States the sums due from the said P. T. Shelton & Co on the duty bonds mentioned in the bills to wit $337.63. with interest from the 30th. day of July 1819 $337.63. with interest from the 30th. Septr. 1819. $337.63. with interest from the 30th. of Novr. 1819 $196.03 with interest from the 5th. Septr. 1819; $196.03 wit⟨h⟩ interest from the 5th. of Novr. 1819; $196.04 with interest from the 5th. of January 1820; $308.26 with interest from the 30th. Septr. 1819; $308.26 with interest from the 30th. Novr. 1819 and $308.26 with interest from the 30th. of January 1820. And liberty is reserved to the United States to apply to this court should their debt not be satisfied out of the fund in the hands of the defendants John Enders & Henry Clarke. And it is ordered that those defendants do also out of the same fund pay to the United States their costs.

AD, Marshall Judicial Opinions, PPAmP; printed, John W. Brockenbrough, *Reports of Cases Decided by the Honourable John Marshall . . .* , I (Philadelphia, 1837), 517–19. Decree, AD, U.S. v. Shelton, U.S. Cir. Ct., Va., Ended Cases (Unrestored), 1821, Vi. For JM's deletions and interlineations, see Textual Notes below.

1. JM quoted from sec. 65 of the 1799 act to regulate the collection of duties (*U.S. Statutes at Large*, I, 627, 676–77).
2. A federal bankruptcy statute was enacted in 1800 and repealed in 1803 (ibid., II, 19).

Textual Notes

¶ 1 l. 2	Shelton ~~made a voluntary as being indebted~~ being
¶ 4 l. 2	these ~~cases~~ "shall
¶ 5 l. 7	subject, ↑as well as under the bankrupt laws of England,↓ & would
ll. 11–12	reference ↑it makes↓ to
l. 14	the ~~thing~~ case,
l. 15	It ~~as~~ ↑was↓ an
ll. 17–18	U.S. ↑being a partnership debt↓ would
¶ 6 l. 2	court ~~to pay~~ should

To Edward C. Marshall

My dear Son   Richmond June 24th. 1821

I received to day your letter of the 12th. or 14th. I do not know which.[1]

I am glad to hear that Doctor Peyton has a prospect of obtaining a gentleman of abilities for his school & am entirely willing that you should remain with him another year.[2] If you employ your time to the best advantage I am persuaded that you may derive great benefit from devoting to the earlier studies another year; & think it probable that your education may be more complete than it would be should you enter the sophomore class this autumn.

Had you expressed to your mother a month or two past your want of shirts, she would have got them ready to send up by Mr. Page or Miss Pickett, but they are gone & it is not probable that another opportunity will offer till I come up in August. You ought to recollect that making of shirts like every thing else requires some thing more than a mere order for their production. Had you given your mother notice in March or April of your wants she would have procured the linnen & have endeavoured at least to have them made up; but if she were now to purchase the linnen it would take three or four weeks to make the shirts & then we should have to wait for an opportunity to send them. You may be assured that the way to have your wants supplied is to foresee them. It is probable that I may bring you shirts in August.

You wrote to your mother for a straw hat & I procured one which I have sent by Miss M. Pickett. She promises to leave it at the court house either at Mr. Picketts or Mr. Colstons. You would perhaps do well to go for it.

If you can get the books you want at alexandria, it will be well to do so. If you cannot let me know it in time that I may endeavor to carry them up with me.

I am very sorry to hear that you are afflicted with sore eyes. Your mother recommends it to you to get the small twigs of sassafras which have young pith, to strip of[f] the outer bark & then split the twigs & cut them into tolerably short pieces & put them in a cup of water & stand there ⟨for⟩ an hour or so when the water will become a jelly. Bath your eyes in this jelly & ⟨she⟩ thinks it will be of great service to th⟨em.⟩ I am my dear Son your affectionate Father

J Marshall

Your mother who is now very unwell complains of your writing to her so seldom.

ALS, ViHi. Addressed to Marshall at "Gordons Dale / near Salem / Fauquier"; postmarked Richmond, 25 June.

1. Letter not found. Edward Carrington Marshall (1805–1882), JM's youngest son, graduated from Harvard College in 1826 and married Rebecca Courtenay Peyton in 1829. He

led a life of farming in Fauquier County and served four terms in the Virginia legislature during the 1830s (Paxton, *Marshall Family*, 103–4).

2. Chandler Peyton (1769?-1827), a physician, evidently operated a school at Gordonsdale, his estate near the village of Salem (now Marshall) in Fauquier. He belonged to a different branch of the Peyton family from that of Edward C. Marshall's future wife (Horace Edwin Hayden, *Virginia Genealogies* . . . [Wilkes Barre, Pa., 1891], 478–79, 538–40; H. C. Groome, *Fauquier during the Proprietorship: A Chronicle of the Colonization and Organization of a Northern Neck County* [Richmond, Va., 1927], 102, 206–7).

To William S. Cardell

Sir   Richmond June 25th 1821

I had the pleasure of receiving in due course of the mail, your letter of the 15th. inst.,[1] informing me of the honor conferred on me by the American Academy of language and Belles Lettres, in electing me one of their honorary members.[2]

Do me the favor, Sir, to convey my acknowledgements to the society for this distinguished & highly valued mark of their attention; and to accompany these acknowledgements with the expression of my fears that I shall disappoint the expectations under which the election was made, and that it will not be so much in my power as it is in my will, to contribute those aids which may be expected from a member, whose wishes for the prosperity of the institution are very strong, however feeble may be his efforts.

The objects of the society are national, & it will, I trust, receive the countenance of the nation. Inattention in a great, a free, & an enlightened people to their own literature & their own language, would, in the present state of the world, indicate a carelessness respecting matters of high interest, a disregard of the opinion of those whose opinion is most valuable, of which the united states, I hope, will not give an example.

The English language is also ours; and the attempt to change it would be more than Quixotism. The attempt will be to preserve and to improve it. It is a great subject in which the two nations have a common property, and their efforts to maintain it ought to be common. Present and temporary circumstances — the present state of society — give to the european portion of the commonwealth of letters some right to take the lead. But Americans ma⟨y⟩ cooperate in the joint work, and may exercise their own judgement on the performance of their fellow laborers, as well as on their own.

Much may I think be expected from the society which ⟨the⟩ literary gentlemen of New York have the honor to originate. Much in every view which has been taken of it. Were its only good, the tendency it will have to preserve a sameness of language throughout our own wide spreading country, that alone would be an object worthy of the public attention. At present, the intermingling of classes, the intercommunication of well educated persons with those whose improvement is very limited, the removals from one neighborhood, & from one state, to another distant neighborhood, & another state, the intimate intercourse thus kept up between all ranks, & the different parts of our extensive empire, all contribute to preserve an identity of language throughout the United States, which can find no example in other parts of the world.

As our population becomes more dense, these causes will diminish in their operation; and, without some standard which all will respect, and to which all may appeal, it is not probable that our language will escape those casualties, & those deteriorations, to which all seem to be exposed.

I have delayed my acknowledgement of your letter for the purpose of obtaining a private conveyance as the pecuniary contribution of a member is enclosed.[3]

Accept my thanks for the politeness of ⟨your⟩ communication & beleive me to be with great resp⟨ect⟩, Your Obedt. Servt

J Marsha⟨ll⟩

ALS, Miscellaneous Manuscripts, NHi. Addressed to Cardell as "Cor. Sec. of the Am. Ac. of Lang. & Belles Lettres / New York." Endorsed by Cardell.

1. Letter not found.
2. Cardell (1780–1828), a Connecticut native who attended Williams College, founded the American Academy of Languages and Belles Lettres in the fall of 1820. Its officers included John Quincy Adams as president, Justices Livingston and Story as vice presidents, and a number of other statesmen, lawyers, clergymen, physicians, and educators. Members were divided into three classes: resident, corresponding, and honorary. The original honorary members were John Adams, Thomas Jefferson, James Madison, James Monroe, John Jay, Charles C. Pinckney, and John Trumbull. JM was among a new group of honorary members that included Charles Carroll of Carrollton, the Marquis de Lafayette, and Rufus King. The Academy evidently survived for about three years (Cardell to Jefferson, 11 Jan. 1821, with Cardell's printed circular, dated 1 Oct. 1820, Jefferson Papers, DLC; Cardell to Madison, 12 Jan. 1821, Madison Papers, DLC; Cardell to Story, 25 June 1821, Story Collection, MiU-C; Allen Walker Read, "American Projects for an Academy to Regulate Speech," *Publications of the Modern Language Association*, LI [1936], 1141–79; Dennis E. Baron, *Grammar and Good Taste: Reforming the American Language* [New Haven, Conn., 1982], 101–15).
3. JM contributed one hundred dollars (Read, "American Projects," 1154 n. 44).

From Joseph Story

Dear Sir   Salem June 27. 1821.

I had the pleasure a few days since to receive your letter of the 15th instant. The question which you propound has never occurred in my circuit, & of course my mind has never been called upon to weigh it with deliberation. I have however turned it in my mind since I received your letter & am very willing to submit to your better judgment my present opinion.

I think that the first conveyance by the Partners of all their partnership effects constituted an insolvency within the act of Congress, so as to give the U.S. a priority of payment. My reason is that the debt of the U.S. was a partnership debt & not a private debt of either of the partners; & that the *firm* are in contemplation of law in their *partnership character* the debtor, & the assignment of all the partnership effects is an assignment of all the property of the debtor within the meaning of the act of Congress. It is an assignment of all that fund which the law appropriates in the first instance in discharge of the partnership debts; & the firm is truly as well as technically insolvent, if that fund is insufficient to pay the partnership debts. I take it to be true that under the English Bankrupt Law, (& probably for the like reason under our late Bankrupt Law) such a general assignment of all the partnership effects would constitute an act of bankruptcy by the partnership, notwithstanding one of the partners might have other private property & might even be solvent as to his private debts. And in Bankruptcy the joint debts are always first paid out of the joint effects before the separate creditors are permitted to come in; & so e converso the separate creditors come in first against the separate estate. This must be upon the ground that the joint property is the primary & natural fund for the payment of joint debts, & the private individual property of the partners is merely collateral security in aid of that fund.

From what I have stated it follows, that if the second deed had never been executed by one of the partners, conveying his private property, in my opinion the first would have been a clear act of insolvency within the law. But even if I were of different opinion on this point I do not know whether it would alter the decree I should make in the case. For in marshalling the assets I should probably follow the general rule adopted on this subject viz require the partnership debts in the first instance to be paid out of the partnership funds & the private debts out of the private funds; & as by the execution of the second deed a complete insolvency would have arisen within the act of Congress I should apply the joint effects in the first instance to the discharge of the joint debt of the U.S. & give the US. the full benefit of the priority of payment out of them. I say I should probably follow that course, because at present I see no objection to it. If one partner should die insolvent, would a Court of equity permit a *joint* creditor to proceed against his separate funds for payment before the joint fund was applied for & exhausted?

Such, my dear Sir are my present opinions on what I consider a very interesting question. Allow me to add.

Si quid novisti rectius
Candidus imperti; si non, his utere mecum.[1]

As to the decision of the Supreme Court in Cohens v Virginia I believe it meets with general approbation among our professional gentlemen. I have not heard of any diversity of opinion respecting it among any of our party lawyers. The people here are disposed to place confidence in Courts; & when they decide after full argument, they are generally satisfied. But on subjects like this we are as yet inoculated with no disease. Massachusetts is attached to the Union & has no jealousy of its powers; & no political object to answer in crying up "state rights." We should dread to see the government reduced as Virginia wishes it, to a confederacy; & we are disposed to construe the constitution of the U.S. as a *frame of government* & not as a petty charter granted to a paltry corporation for the purpose of regulating a fishery or collecting a toll. The opinion of our best lawyers is unequivocally with the Supreme Court, heartily & resolutely. They consider your opinion in Cohens v Virginia as a most masterly & convincing argument, & as the greatest of your judgments. Allow me to say that no where is your reputation more sincerely cherished than here; & however strange it may sound in Virginia, if you were known here only by this last opinion, you could not wish for more unequivocal fame.

I never see the Enquirer & should be glad to read the attacks which have been made upon the Court, if you think they would not make me too angry. The truth is that the whole doctrine of Virginia on the subject of the constitution appears to me so fundamentally erroneous, not to say absurd, that I have a good deal of difficulty in reading with patience the elaborate attempts of her political leaders to mislead & deceive us. Hitherto her attacks have not been very successful. But I own I am not without my fears for the future. The attacks are insidious — often popular — & not infrequently plausible. Her weight in the Union & the infatuation of her statesmen on this subject, together with the absolute suppression of a free press on the other side there, may ultimately lead to serious consequences. She may combine the temporary interests of other states with her own, & by espousing their quarrels, & assuming to be their champion, lead them astray, as she has already led Ohio. It is not possible to foresee how far her abominable heresies may extend. As a *republican* & a lover of the Union I look with alarm upon her opinions & conduct. I would rather allow her the exclusive possession of the Executive power for a half century than witness the prevalence in other states of any of her new constitutional dogmas. If they prevail, in my judgment there is a practical end of the Union. I trust in God however that the Supreme Court will continue fearlessly to do its duty; & I pray that your invaluable life may be long preserved to guide us in our defence of the Constitution. Will you excuse me for saying that your appointment to the Bench has in my judgment more contributed under providence to the preservation of the true principles of the constitution than any other circumstance in our domestic history. I say this with more deep feeling from having been most painfully drawn to the subject by reading a copy of a letter written last year to a gentleman in this State by Mr Jefferson. That gentleman sent to Mr Jefferson a copy of a work called "The Republican" containing as I believe, for I never read it, political essays on the general principles of our Govt.[2] Among other things the work dwelt on the importance of the Judiciary, its independence, & tenure of office during good behaviour, & its right to decide constitutional questions in the last resort. Mr Jefferson takes particular notice of these last topics — in the most direct terms denies the right of the Judges to decide constitutional questions — declares the nature of the tenure of their office to be sufficiently dangerous — alludes in a manner not to be misunderstood to the usurpation of Judges in attem⟨pt⟩ing to control the Executive with a pointing to Marbury v Madison & endeavours to establish that the people are the only proper judges of violations of constitutional authority & by changes in the course of elections are alone competent to apply the proper remedy. If, he says, it be objected they are not sufficiently enlightened to exercise this duty with discretion, the remedy is to enlighten them the more. The letter is long & I quote its contents, because it is exposed in a public bookstore to every body's perusal, as a recommendation of the work; & I must say that its obvious design is, as far as his influence extends, to prostrate the judicial authority & annihilate all public reverence of its dignity.[3] There never was a period of my life when these opinions would not have shocked me; but *at his age* & in these critical times they fill me alternately with indignation & melancholy. Can he wish yet to have influence enough to destroy the Government of his Country?

In answer to your question as to the conduct of the people of Massachusetts in adopting the amendments proposed by the convention I would state that here as every where else popular feelings & local interests & religious jealousies among different sects have prevented the adoption of a few of our best amendments. The Senate stands upon the old basis apportioned according to property. The amendment sent out to the people incorporated this with a new mode of corporate representation in the *House*, which would greatly diminish the latter. As the vote was to be taken upon the proposition as a whole, & the proposed alteration very essentially diminished the representation of *smal⟨l⟩ towns*, & subjected them to some inequalities, it was rejected. All those, who were in favour of the old representation in the House voted against it. All those, who wished the representation to be apportioned solely on population, voted against it. All those who wished, as all the Demagogues did that the *Senate* should be apportioned on population instead of property, be the House what it may, voted against it. And so the proposed amendment fell by this combination of interests proceeding upon the most opposite principles. I fear we shall have trouble yet on this subject; for, as by the present representation of the House the *country* has a decided & permanent ascendency, its natural interest will be to change the basis of the Senate to population & thus to acquire a like ascendency over ⟨the⟩ *Seaboard* in that body also. Even in respect to local interests this will be a serious evil for the tendency is to keep the whole weight of taxation on the commerce & wealth of the seaboard. I think however there will at present be strength to resist the attempt: but considering the popular cant & popular prejudices I have some fears that we shall not have wisdom enough to maintain ourselves upon the present decided basis that protects property. The truth is that we have yet much to learn as to the nature of free governments; & it will be matter of surprise if in our rage for experiments to ascertain with what weakness in its institutions the government may possibly go on — & stop & go on — we should not shipwreck the cause of liberty. I endeavour to hope for the best — but there are many painful forebodings about us.

I have a copy of the Debates of our Convention for you which I shall send you by the first private opportunity.[4] I hope also that some Salem vessel will go hence to Richmond, as I wish to send you a quintal of our best dumb fish.[5] I have no doubt that an opportunity will occur & I shall send you in the true spirit of cookery a written direction how to cook the fish — which is as essential as the fish itself. I am with the highest respect, Your much obliged friend

JOSEPH STORY

ALS, Marshall Papers, ViW. Addressed to JM in Richmond; postmarked Salem, 3 July.

1. Horace, *Epistles*, Bk. I, Ep. VI, ll. 67–68: "If you know something better than these precepts, pass it on, my good fellow. If not, join me in following these." Story omitted "istis" after "rectius" (H. Rushton Fairclough, trans., *Horace: Satires, Epistles and Ars Poetica* [Cambridge, Mass., 1978], 290, 291).

2. William Charles Jarvis (d. 1836) of Pittsfield, Massachusetts, was the author of *The Republican; or, A Series of Essays on the Principles and Policy of Free States* (Pittsfield, Mass., 1820). He served in the Massachusetts legislature during the 1820s (J. E. A. Smith, *The History of Pittsfield, Massachusetts, from the Year 1800 to the Year 1876* [Springfield, Mass., 1876], 403).

3. Jefferson to Jarvis, 28 Sept. 1820, in Paul Leicester Ford, ed., *The Works of Thomas Jefferson* (12 vols.; New York, 1904–5), XII, 161–64. See Dumas Malone, *Jefferson and His Time*, VI: *The Sage of Monticello* (Boston, 1981), 353–55. The letter was also published in the Richmond *Enquirer*, 20 Nov. 1821, from a Massachusetts newspaper.

4. *Journal of Debates and Proceedings in the Convention of Delegates Chosen to Revise the Constitution of Massachusetts* (Boston, 1821).

5. Winter cod, caught between February and May, were known as dumb, or dun, fish. The best dumb fish were found in the Isles of Shoals, off the New Hampshire coast (Lorenzo Sabine, *Report on the Principle Fisheries of the American Seas* [Washington, D.C., 1853], 113–14; George Brown Goode, comp., *The Fisheries and Fishery Industries of the United States* [8 vols. in 7; Washington, D.C., 1884–87], sec. 2, II, 681–82).

To Joseph Story

My dear Sir   Richmond July 13th. 1821

I had yesterday the pleasure of receiving your letter of the 27th. of June by which I am greatly obliged. I shall decide the case concerning which I enquired in conformity with your opinion. The law of the case I have thought very doubtful, the equity of it is I think pretty clear.[1]

Your kind expressions respecting myself gratify me very much. Entertaining the truest affection & esteem for my brethren generally, & for

yourself particularly, it is extremely gratiful[2] to believe that it is recipro-
cated. The harmony of the bench will, I hope & pray, never be disturbed.
We have external & political enemies enough to preserve internal peace.

What you say of Mr. Jeffersons letter rather grieves than surprizes me. It
grieves me because his influence is still so great that many—very many
will adopt his opinions however unsound they may be, & however contradictory to their own reason. I cannot describe the surprize & mo[r]tifica-
tion I have felt at hearing that Mr. Madison has embraced them with
respect to the judicial department.[3]

For Mr. Jeffersons opinion as respects this department it is not difficult
to assign the cause. He is among the most ambitious, & I suspect among
the most unforgiving of men. His great power is over the mass of the
people & this power is chiefly acquired by professions of democracy.
Every check on the wild impulse of the moment is a check on his own
power, & he is unfriendly to the source from which it flows. He looks, of
course, with ill will at an independent judiciary.

That in a free country with a written constitution, any inteligent man
should wish a dependent judiciary, or should think that the constitution
is not a law for the court as well as the legislature, would astonish me if I
had not learnt from observation that, with many men, the judgement is
completely controuled by the passions. The case of the mandamus[4] may
be the cloak, but the batture is recollected with still more resentment.[5]

I send you the papers containing the essays of Algernon Sidney. Their
coarseness & malicnity would designate the author if he was not avowed.
The argument, if it may be called one, is I think as weak as its language is
violent & prolix. Two other gentlemen have appeared in the papers on
this subject. One of them is deeply concerned in pillaging the purchasers
of the Fairfax estate in which goodly work he fears no other obstruction
than what arises from the appellate power of the supreme court, & the
other is a hunter after office who hopes by his violent hostility to the
Union which in Virginia assumes the name of regard for State rights; & by
his devotion to Algernon Sidney, to obtain one.[6] In support of the sound
principles of the constitution, & of the Union of the States, not a pen is
drawn. In Virginia the tendency of things verges rapidly to the destruction of the government & the reestablishment of a league of Sove⟨reign⟩
States. I look elsewhere for safety. With very much esteem & affection, I
am dear Sir your

J MARSHALL

I will thank you for the copy of the debates

ALS, Story Papers, MHi. Addressed to Story in Salem, Mass.; postmarked Richmond,
1 3 July. Ms torn where seal was broken.

1. JM in fact had already decided the case of U.S. v. Shelton on 1 5 June.
2. JM meant to write "gratifying."

3. JM was misinformed. Madison privately criticized McCulloch v. Maryland and (to a lesser degree) Cohens v. Virginia, but he never questioned the role of the federal judiciary as the proper constitutional arbiter in cases that turned on the completing claims of federal and state power. He pointedly distanced himself from the views of Roane and Jefferson. See Drew R. McCoy, *The Last of the Fathers: James Madison and the Republican Legacy* (New York, 1989), 69–71, 99–103; Charles F. Hobson, *The Great Chief Justice: John Marshall and the Rule of Law* (Lawrence, Kans., 1996), 208–12.

4. Marbury v. Madison.

5. Livingston v. Jefferson. For this case, decided on circuit in 1811, see *PJM*, VII, 276–78.

6. JM referred to "Fletcher of Saltoun" and "Somers" (Peyton Randolph).

To Bushrod Washington

My dear Sir   Richmond July 13th. 1821

I thank you for the opinion you have been so good as to give me in the case on which I consulted you. I have from the first thought it doubtful but shall decide it in conformity with your opinion.

I have received your letter of the 3d. inst. & have enclosed the letters from Mr. Madison to Genl. ⟨Was⟩hi⟨n⟩gton in a packet addressed to you which I ⟨shall s⟩end by some ⟨safe?⟩ ⟨han⟩d.[1] I selected them last ⟨wi⟩nter for the purpose of giving them to you in Washington but I had not the pleasure of seeing you & forgot them.

The question whether a bill drawn in one state on a person residing in another state in the Union, is to be considered as an inland or a foreign bill, cannot arise in Virginia on a bill drawn in this state. The case is completely provided for by statute, & the bill is considered as inland.[2] I am a little surprized at its not being provided for in every state. I am equally surprized at its not being settled by the decisions of the court of the state in which the bill was drawn as one would suppose that the question had frequently occurred. In New York I percieve the decision is that the bill is inland.[3] Mr. Pendletons opinion is not direct but rather looks towards its being foreign.[4]

I should think the relation between the states ⟨as stro⟩ng as between E⟨ngland⟩ Scotland or ⟨Ireland?⟩ ⟨be⟩fore the Un⟨ion and I tend?⟩ to think stronger. What was a bill d⟨rawn upon⟩ one of these countries on the other before the ⟨Uni⟩on.

I cannot take such a view of the case as to form an opinion though I rather lean to the side of its being an inland bill.[5]

How does the question of damages stand? I am my dear Sir yours truely

J MARSHALL

I determined on great consideration that the master of a vessel lying in the port of one state the owners of which resided in a different state might hypothecate.[6] But the cases I think are not alike.

ALS, Marshall Papers, ViW. Addressed to Washington in Alexandria; postmarked Richmond, 13 July. Endorsed by Washington. Angle brackets enclose words obscured by tears in MS.

1. Letter not found. James Madison had corresponded with Bushrod Washington about obtaining either the originals or copies of the letters he had written to General Washington (*Index to the George Washington Papers* [Washington, D.C., 1964], ix-x).

2. In Virginia, bills of exchange drawn upon a person in another state had been considered inland bills since 1795. Justice Washington was then considering the case of Lonsdale v. Brown in the U.S. Circuit Court for Pennsylvania, which he decided at the Oct. 1821 term. He held that a bill drawn in New Orleans upon a person living in Pennsylvania was a foreign bill of exchange (Shepherd, *Statutes*, I, 366; Lonsdale v. Brown, 15 Fed. Cas. 855; *Niles' Weekly Register* [Baltimore], XXI [1821], 134).

3. Miller v. Hackley, a case decided by New York's Supreme Court of Judicature in 1810, was discussed by Washington in Lonsdale v. Brown (5 Johns. 375; Lonsdale v. Brown, 15 Fed. Cas. 859).

4. JM referred to Edmund Pendleton's opinion in the case of Warder v. Arell, decided by the Virginia Court of Appeals in 1796. Pendleton observed that "with respect to their municipal laws," the American states were "to each other foreign." Washington quoted this passage in his opinion (2 Wash. 282, 298; Lonsdale v. Brown, 15 Fed. Cas. 858, 859).

5. In 1829 the Supreme Court, with Washington delivering the opinion, ruled that such bills were to be considered foreign bills of exchange (Buckner v. Finley, 2 Pet. 586, 589).

6. Selden v. Hendrickson & Pryor (*PJM*, VIII, 378–84).

To Charles Miner

Sir   Richmond July 11th. [15]¹ 1821

I thank you very sincerely for your politeness & attention in forwarding to me "The Village Record" of the 11th., containing the proceedings of "The Washington Association in conjunction with the Washington guards," in West Chester on the 4th. of July, which I received this morning.²

Feeling deeply, as every American must, the great event commemorated on that day, throughout our nation; and considering the opinions expressed on it, as indicating, in no inconsiderable degree, the public feeling; I take an interest in what is said on that great anniversary, and was much gratified on reading your toast, & the truely American sentiments with which it was so handsomely introduced.³ I was the more gratified with those sentiments because the time is, I think, arrived, when the good & the wise are urged by the strongest motives of genuine patriotism, to assuage, by lenient applications, those asperities & jealousies between the States, which have been, I believe, excited without sufficient cause, & which too many are not unwilling still farther to irritate: Asperities & jealousies which may lead to consequences all must deplore when the time for preventing them shall have passed away.

I have seen no paper containing th⟨e⟩ proceedings of the 4th. of July with which I have been so highly pleased as with those of the Village

Record of the 11th. Accept my thanks for it & beleive me to be with great respect, Your obedt. Servt

J MARSHALL

ALS, Charles Miner Collection, PWbH. Addressed to Miner in West Chester, Pa.; postmarked Richmond, 15? July. Endorsed by Miner. Evidently misdated by JM (see n. 1).

1. This date is obviously incorrect, as shown by the acknowledgment of a West Chester newspaper of the 11th. JM probably wrote on 15 July, which appears to be the date on the postmark.

2. Letter not found. Miner (1780–1865), a newspaper editor and Federalist politician, was then proprietor of the *Village Record* of West Chester. He had previously served in the Pennsylvania legislature and from 1825 to 1829 was a member of the U.S. House of Representatives.

3. Miner's address introducing his toast was a call for attachment to the Union and an attack on anti-Southern prejudice in the wake of the Missouri crisis. The toast reads: "The United States — and the Citizens of the South — May our union be everlasting as our hills; and may mutual good will, freedom, and prosperity, like our rivers, flow through the land in perpetual streams" (reprinted in the Washington *Daily National Intelligencer*, 16 July 1821).

To John Quincy Adams

Sir   Richmond Septr. 6th. 1821

Yesterday, on my return from a visit to our mountain country, I recei⟨ved⟩ your letter requesting a report from the judicial department for the purpose of enabling the secretary of State to comply with the act of Congress directing him to report all the military & civil officers of the United States.[1]

As your letter does not state in particular what is required, but refers generally to the resolution of Congress, and as I am by no means sure that I understand the resolution correctly I take the liberty to ask a more full expression of your wishes on this subject.

I have doubted how far you consider the call on the heads of departments as applicable to the Chief Justice of the United States. In general the head of a department either appoints, or has some official connexion with, or controul over the subordinate officers of his department, which enables him to comply from his own knowledge or the means within his own possession, with the requisition to report their names, residence, &c. But the chief Justice stands in no such relation to the officers of the judicial department. They are in no degree dependent on him, make no communications to, or through him, & are in general totally unknown to him.

The Judicial officers consist of the associate Justices of the supreme court, the District Judges, the District Attornies the Marshals, & the Clerks. The Judges Attornies & Marshals being commissioned by the President, their names are already in the department of estate, but are unknown, except in a very limited degree, to the Chief Justice. The clerks are appointed by the several District Judges without any communication with the Chief Justice. Their intercourse is with the comptroller with whom they have constantly accounts to settle.

If your letter contemplates a report from the Chief Justice comprehending all these officers I will immediately set about collecting the necessary information, but its collection in time to report by the last of September is impossible. If your letter contemplates a report of the officers of the District in which I reside or of the cir⟨cuit⟩ which I attend, comprehending the several deputy Marshalls & Clerks, be pleased to say so, & it shall be forwarded without delay. With great respect, I am Sir your Obedt

J MARSHALL

ALS, RG 59, DNA. Addressed to Adams in Washington; postmarked Richmond, 7 Sept. Endorsed by Adams.

1. Letter not found. As Adams subsequently explained, this letter was a circular to "the Judicial Officers of the Union." Congress adopted a resolution in Apr. 1816 requiring the secretary of state to compile a register of federal civil, military, and naval officers every two years (Adams to JM, 12 Dec. 1821; *U.S. Statutes at Large*, III, 342).

To Joseph Story

My dear Sir   Richmond Septr. 18th. 1821

I had yesterday the pleasure of receiving your favor of the 9th.[1] I thank you for your Quintal of fish & shall try my possibles to observe your instructions in the cooking department. I hope to succeed; but be this as it may I promise to feed on the fish with an appetite which would not disgrace a genuine descendant of one of the Pilgrims.

I am a little surprized at the request which you say has been made to Mr. Hall, although there is no reason for my being so.[2] The settled hostility of the gentleman who has made that request to the judicial department will show itself in that & in every other form which he beleives will conduce to its object. For this he has several motives; & it is not among the weakest that the department could never lend itself as a tool to work for his political power. The Batture will never be forgotten. Indeed there is some reason to beleive that the essays written against the Supreme court were, in a degree at least, stimulated by this gentleman; and that, although the coarseness of the language belongs exclusively to the Author, its acerbity has been increased by his communications with the great Lama of the mountains. He may therefore feel himself in some measure required to obtain its republication in some place of distinction. But what does Mr. Hall purpose to do? I do not suppose you would willingly interfere so as to prevent his making the publication although I really think it is in form & substance totally unfit to be placed in his law journal. I really think a proper reply to the request would be to say that no objection existed to the publication of any law argument against the opinion of the Supreme court, but that the coarseness of its language, its personal & official abuse & its tedious prolixity constituted objections to the insertion of Algernon Sidney which were insuperable. If however Mr. Hall determines to comply with this request, I think he ought, unless he means to make himself a party militant, to say that he publishes that piece by particular request; & ought to subjoin the masterly answer of Mr. Wheaton.[3] I shall wish to know what course Mr. Hall will pursue.

I have not yet received the debates in your convention. Mr. Caldwell I presume has not met with an opportunity to send the volume.[4] I shall read it with much pleasure.

I have seen a sketch of your address to the Suffolk bar & shall be very glad to have it at large.[5] I have no doubt of being much gratified by the manner in which the subjects you mention are treated.

A deep design to convert our government into a meer league of States has taken strong hold of a powerful & violent party in Virginia. The attack upon the judiciary is in fact an attack upon the union. The judicial department is well understood to be that through which the government may be attacked most successfully, because it is without patronage, & of course without power, and it is equally well understood that every subtraction from its jurisdiction is a vital wound to the government itself. The attack upon it therefore is a marked battery aimed at the government itself.[6] The whole attack, if not originating with Mr. Jefferson, is obviously approved & guided by him. It is therefore formidable in other states as well as in this; & it behoves the friends of the union to be more on the alert than they have been. An effort will certainly be made to repeal the 25th. Sec. of the judicial act.

I have a case before me which cannot be carried up to the supreme court & which presents difficulties which appear to me to be considerable.[7] It is an action of debt brought by the U.S. for a forfeiture incurred by rescuing some distilled Spirits which had not been proceeded on by the Distiller according to law.

The declaration charges in the alternative that the defendants or one of them rescued or caused to be rescued &c.

It is clear enough that this would be ill in an indictment or information, but I am inclined to think it is cured by our statute of jeofails. The defendents insist that this statute does not apply to suits brought by the U.S. — but I think it does.

Another difficulty has puzzled me so much that I have taken the case under advisement with the intention of consulting some of my more experienced brethren.

The difficulty is this: At the trial the rescue was proved only by two depositions. Each contains the following ⟨ex⟩pressions. "On Novr. 17th.

1815, *agreeable to written & verbal instructions from Mr. William McKinly collector,* I" &c.

The defendants demurred to the testimony & the District co⟨ur⟩t gave judgement for the plaintiffs.

It is contended 1st. That there is no sufficient evidence that McKinly is collector. His commission ought to be produced & its absence cannot be supplied — but here is not even a direct averment that he is collector.

2d. The written instructions of the collector ought to be produced to show that the seizure was mad⟨e⟩ under his authority.

You are accustomed to these cases. Will you aid me with your advice? Yours truely & sincerely

J MARSHALL

ALS, Story Papers, MHi. Addressed to Story in Salem, Mass.; postmarked Richmond, 19 Sept.

1. Letter not found.

2. John E. Hall (1783–1829) was a Philadelphia lawyer and legal publisher. Between 1808 and 1817 he published six volumes of the *American Law Journal*. He had recently started a new publication, the *Journal of American Jurisprudence*. Jefferson had written Hall in Aug. 1821, suggesting that he reprint Roane's "Algernon Sidney" articles along with JM's opinion in Cohens v. Virginia. This project was never realized, for Hall's journal soon ceased publication (Dumas Malone, *Jefferson and His Time*, VI: *The Sage of Monticello* [Boston, 1981], 359).

3. Henry Wheaton wrote seven essays under the pseudonym "A Federalist of 1789," which appeared in the New York *American* in July and August of 1821. The essays have been reprinted in James E. Pfander, ed., "The Dangers of the Union. By Henry Wheaton," *Constitutional Commentary*, XIII (1995), 249–76, 355–80.

4. Elias B. Caldwell, clerk of the Supreme Court.

5. Story addressed the Suffolk [Massachusetts] Bar Association on 4 Sept. 1821 on the "Progress of Jurisprudence." A notice of this address appeared in the newspapers (see, for example, Washington *Daily National Intelligencer*, 14 Sept. 1821). The full address was printed in William W. Story, ed., *The Miscellaneous Writings of Joseph Story* (Boston, 1852), 198–241.

6. JM used strikingly similar phraseology in his 1819 essays defending McCulloch v. Maryland. See *PJM*, VIII, 288, 318.

7. See Jacob v. U.S., opinion, 11 Dec. 1821. Because the matter in dispute was less than two thousand dollars, this case could not be appealed to the Supreme Court, as provided by the Judiciary Act of 1789 (*U.S. Statutes at Large*, I, 84).

To Daniel Raymond

SIR: *Richmond, September* 25, 1821.

Your book on Political Economy was left for me while I was not at home, by an unknown person who did not give his name.[1] I found it enveloped in brown paper, and supposed it to be a volume left by the agent of some bookseller, who would call again in a few days. Being at the time much occupied with some intricate law cases, which had been sub-mitted to me for consideration during the session of the circuit court, I did not remove the envelope; and on the termination of my official duties I made an annual excursion to our mountains. It was not until after my return, some days past, that I took off the covering, and perceived the obligation you had conferred on me by transmitting me your valuable treatise. This explanation, I hope, will rescue me from the suspicion of having been regardless of this flattering evidence of your consideration.

I have read your 'Thoughts on Political Economy' with great attention and pleasure, and am gratified that an American has taken up the sub-ject. It is not less important than abstruse, and presents perhaps as many questions, the solution of which, on full investigation, will be different from our impressions on a first view, as any science whatever. You have thought upon it profoundly, and if I am not sure that every proposition you lay down is entirely accurate, I am convinced that many are, and that all deserve consideration.

Your opinion upon slavery, and especially on manumission, are deeply interesting to our southern states, and I wish they could engage that share of our serious reflection to which they are entitled.

Accept, sir, my thanks for this additional mark of your polite attention, which are not the less sincere for having been delayed; and believe me to be, with great respect, Your obedient servant,

J. MARSHALL.

Printed, Daniel Raymond, *The Elements of Political Economy*, I (Baltimore, 1836), vii-viii.

1. Raymond (1786–1849?), a Connecticut native, studied law at Tapping Reeve's law school in Litchfield and later settled in Baltimore. He gained fame for his *Thoughts on Politi-cal Economy* (Baltimore, 1820). This work also appeared in subsequent editions of 1823, 1836, and 1840. He rejected laissez-faire in favor of protectionism and government inter-vention as the policy best suited to the American economic system. He was also staunchly antislavery.

To Walter L. Fontaine

Dear Sir   Richmond Septr. 27th. 21
When I had last the pleasure of seeing you, you assured me that I should receive $700 from you either on your own account, or on account of Mr. Brown, in the course of this month.[1] In consequence of this as-surance I have made an engagement to pay about that sum, & have provided no other means for complying with my promise.

I do not write for the purpose of urging you to make any injurious exertion to raise this sum of money, because I am well convinced that you require nothing from me to induce you to pay as fast as you can with reasonable convenience, & I am not desirous of your paying faster; but I write because it is desirable to know with certainty what I may depend on. If the money is not to be received from you I must raise it in some other manner, probably by applying to the bank, which I am unwilling to do unless it be absolutely necessary.

My affairs are such that I always make arrangements to pay all the money I expect, &, as I am extremely unwilling to disappoint any person, it is material to me to be informed in time of any failure in the resources on which I depend. I am dear Sir very respectfully Your Obedt. Servt

J MARSHALL

ALS (advertised for sale by Joseph Rubinfine, West Palm Beach, Fla., 1994). Addressed to Fontaine "near New Canton" (Buckingham County); postmarked Richmond, 27 Sept.

1. See Fontaine to JM, 21 July 1820 and n. 1. According to accounts kept by both JM and Fontaine, JM received a payment of $500 on 11 Oct. 1821 (mortgage deed [in JM's hand], 18 June 1816 [advertised for sale by John Reznikoff, University Archives, Stamford, Conn., 1994]; account current [in Fontaine's hand], 1817–23 [owned by C. J. and Mary Ann Elder, Charlottesville, Va., 1990]).

To Walter L. Fontaine

Dear Sir   Richmond Novr. 20th. 1821

Two halves of notes of 100$ which you sent me are mismatched in consequence of which the Bank refuses to receive them. The one half is marked letter **D** No. 459 payable to Edward Fox. The other is marked letter **A** No. 92 dated the 8th. of Feby. 1812. Both halves are of the mother Bank of Virginia.

The Bank states a decision of the court of appeals that, if the holder of the other halves will make affidavit that he was the possessor of these halves & has lost them, he can compel a payment of the whole 200.$.[1] They therefore refuse to pay these unless you will make the affidavit required & give an indemnifying bond. If you divided these notes yourself it may possibly be in your power to get the other halves & send them down. The holder of them will be unable to get paid but by acting in consent with you. I shall be much obliged by your giving me the earliest intimation on this subject, that, if you can not command the other halves, I may enquire what is to be done. Very respectfully I am, dear Sir your obedt

J MARSHALL

ALS (advertised for sale by Joseph Rubinfine, West Palm Beach, Fla., 1994). Addressed to Fontaine in New Canton; postmarked Richmond, 20 Nov.

1. Probably Bank of Virginia v. Ward, decided by the Virginia Court of Appeals in 1818 (6 Munf. 166).

To Walter L. Fontaine

Dear Sir   [8 December 1821]

I have received your letter inclosing the half of a note of one hundred dollars & I now inclose you one of the halves before sent. I am dear Sir your obedt

J MARSHALL

ALS (advertised for sale by Joseph Rubinfine, West Palm Beach, Fla., 1996). Addressed to Fontaine in New Canton; postmarked Richmond, 8 Dec.

Jacob v. United States
Opinion
U.S. Circuit Court, Virginia, 11 December 1821

U.S. Attorney Robert Stanard filed a declaration in debt against John J. Jacob in the U.S. District Court in August 1818. Jacob, the owner of a boiler and four stills in Brooke County (in the panhandle region of present-day West Virginia), was charged with forcibly rescuing barrels of spirits seized by collectors for nonpayment of duties. At the trial the defendant demurred to the evidence, which consisted of the depositions of deputy collectors of internal duties. A jury found the defendant guilty subject to the court's opinion on the demurrer to the evidence. After the district court overruled the demurrer and gave judgment for the United States in October 1819, the defendant brought an appeal to the circuit court. The case presented certain difficulties, and Marshall took it under advisement to consult with Justice Story before giving his opinion on 11 December 1821 (proceedings in U.S. Dist. Ct., Richmond [copy], 22 Oct. 1819, Jacob v. U.S., Ended Cases [Unrestored], 1821, Vi; U.S. Cir. Ct., Va., Ord. Bk. XI, 184; JM to Story, 18 Sept. 1821).

Jacob
v
The U.S.

¶1   This is a writ of error to a judgement rendered in favor of the United States in the District court in an action of debt brought to recover a penalty alleged to be incurred by the defendant in violating some of the provisions of an act of Congress imposing duties on spirits distilled within the United States.[1] The defendant below demurred to the testimony & now insists that the judgment ought to be reversed because

1st. The declaration is insufficient in not alleging the offence with precision.

2d. The testimony is insufficient, because it does not show that the goods rescued were seized by an authorized officer.

1st. As to the sufficiency of the declaration.

It states the seizure & adds that "the defendant did forcibly rescue or ¶2 cause to be rescued from the said collectors or one of them the said spirits" &c.

The plf in error contends that this charge is too vague & that the ¶3 declaration instead of alleging in the alternative that he had committed one or another of several different offences, ought to have alleged specifically & singly the offence that he did commit.

The cases cited in argument prove conclusively that this error would ¶4 have been fatal in an indictment or information; but the counsel for the plf. has shown no case, & I can find none, in which it has been deemed fatal in an action of debt. He contends that in England an action of debt is not brought in such a case; but the books say expressly that where a penalty is given by a statute & no remedy for its recovery is expressly given, debt lies. He contends with more reason that where different remedies are allowed, the form of the remedy adopted, ought not to vary the case; nor ought a court to sanction, in one species of action for a penalty a more lax mode of proceeding than is allowed by the general principles which regulate suits for penal offences. If a precise charge would be required in an information, there can be no reason he contends for dispensing with this precision in an action of debt brought to recover the same penalty for the same offence. This is true in reason. But it is equally true in law that a statute applicable in its terms to particular actions cannot be applied by construction to other actions standing on the same reason. But the application of such statute to an action which it expressly comprehends, cannot, on that account, be denied.

Upon this principle, it is contended on the part of the United States ¶5 that the act of jeofails applies to this declaration & cures the fault which has been assigned in it.

The 32d. sec. of the judicial act enacts "that no summons &c or other ¶6 proceedings in civil causes, in any of the courts of the United States shall be abated arrested quashed or reversed for any defect or want of form, but the said courts respectively shall proceed & give judgement according as the right of the cause & matter in law shall appear unto them without regarding any imperfections" &c. except such as shall be alleged as causes of special demurrer.[2]

Is the defect in this declaration an error of substance or of form? The ¶7 act of congress v. 4th. p 730. Sec. 9. describes the offence in the very words of the declaration. The penalty is incurred by any person who shall "forcibly rescue or cause to be rescued any spirits &c after the same shall have been seized" by any collector.[3] The offence is equally consummated & the penalty equally incurred by ["]rescuing or causing to be rescued" from any collector whatever, any spirits &c which he had previously seized. It might have been more technically correct to have alleged the offense in the declaration with more precision, and this declaration might have been ill on a special demurrer. But if the defendant waives this exception by going to trial on the fact of rescue, the defect appears to me to be cured by the statute. The defect seems to me to be a defect of form whenever the defendant must of necessity be guilty of a breach of the law & have incurred the penalty for which the suit is brought, if the allegation in the declaration be true. This seems to me to constitute the difference between form & substance. The defendant has a right to insist on a precise statement of the offense with which he is charged, that he may know how to defend himself. This right is to be exercised by a special demurrer & may be waived. If instead of exercising it he prefers going to trial on the fact, & it be found against him, the only question of substance, as it seems to me which can arise upon the record is whether the fact be charged in such terms that, if committed, the penalty of the law must be incurred.

¶8   If then the 32d. Sec. of the judicial act applies to the case, the defendant comes too late with his exception to the declaration.

¶9   That section in its terms applies to all "civil causes in any of the courts of the United States.["] An action of debt for a penalty appears to me to be "a civil cause" under the 9th. section of the judicial act which defines the jurisdiction of the District courts.[4] But I am releieved from a critical examination of this question by the circumstance that, if it be not a civil cause this court has no jurisdiction over it. The 22d. Sec of the judicial act, under which this writ of error must be sustained, allows it only in "civil actions."[5] If then the 32d. Sec. of the act does not apply because this is not "a civil cause"; the writ of error must be dismissed for the same reason.

¶10   But the counsel for the plf. in error contends that the statute does not apply for another reason. In England, a statute is not supposed to relate to the crown unless the King be expressly named. I do not recollect that this principle, which is a branch of the royal prerogative, has ever been recognized in the courts of the United States, nor does it appear to me to be necessary to enquire, in this cause, how far the principle may be applicable in our government. I do not think it necessary to make the enquiry, because the judicial act does expressly comprehend the United States. It gives the courts of the union jurisdiction in suits brought by the United States. The question therefore is not whether a general statute not mentioning the United States shall comprehend them in its general provisions, but whether a statute made both for the United States & for individuals shall embrace the United States by provisions not particularly mentioning them, but which are adapted to them, & made in terms sufficiently comprehensive to include them.

¶11   This question is already settled in the supreme court.

¶12   The 26th. Sec. of the act directs that in all causes brought for a penalty annexed to articles of agreement &c the court shall render judgement in case of default, demurrer &c for so much as is due according to equity. This section does not mention the United States, but has been determined in the supreme court to extend to them. So in the cases to be carried by appeal or writ of error from an inferior to a superior tribunal, in the 21st. & 22d sec. of the act, the United States are not mentioned, but those sections have always been construed to comprehend their suits.

I think it then very clear that the 32d. Sec. of the judicial act extends to this case & cures the error, if there be one, in this declaration. This is a point on which I have never entertained a doubt. ¶13

The second question appeared to me at the argument to deserve serious consideration, & I reserved the cause in consequence of doubts which I then entertained upon it. Subsequent consideration has removed those doubts, & I now think the judgement of the district court correct on the demurrer to evidence as well as on the sufficiency of the declaration. ¶14

It was very properly observed by the attorney for the U.S. that a demurrer to evidence supposes that evidence to be already admitted. If the testimony be inadmissible, its admission may be opposed, & if the objection be improperly overruled the remedy is by a bill of exceptions. If instead of taking this course the party chuses to admit the evidence & to demur to its effect, he waives his objection to its admissibility, & places his cause on its sufficiency to establish the fact in controversy. The question whether it ought to be rejected as meer secondary evidence is no longer to be asked, and the caus⟨e⟩ rests upon the question whether, being admitted, it proves the fact in controversy. If a note or other ordinary instrument of writing have a subscribing witness, the paper cannot be proved even by a person who saw it executed, but if a witness who saw it executed be offered, & the party to the writing, instead of objecting to his being sworn, admits it & demurs to his testimony, the only question then seems to me to be whether his testimony be sufficient to convince the mind that the paper was executed by the person charged there with. ¶15

There is another principle also applicable to the case. The party who demurs is bound to admit every conclusion which the jury might rightfully draw from the testimony. Could the jury in this case have rightly concluded that this seizure was made by a collector of the internal revenue? It seems to me that the jury might very correctly draw this conclusion. The witness states that the plaintiff in error applied to McKinly as the collector for a license.[6] The conversation shows that the plf. in error had transacted business with him as collector. The witness in positive terms states him to be the collector. It is apparent that he acted as collector & was understood by the plaintiff in error to be invested with that office. ¶16

But had the defendant below excepted to the testimony instead of admitting it & demurring to it, I still think the question ought to be decided against him. ¶17

The rule that secondary evidence shall not be admitted where primary evidence is attainable, although a sound general rule, has been relaxed in some cases where general convenience has required the relaxation. The character of a public officer is one of those cases. That he has acted ¶18

notoriously as a public officer has been deemed *prima facie* evidence of his
character without producing his commission or appointment. In the trial
of the Gordons Leaches C. L. 585, this principle of evidence was sustained by all the Judges even in a case of Murder.[7] It is also laid down in
4 T. R. 366. 3 T. R. 635. Bevan q. t. v Williams[8] 3. Camp. 432[9] & Phillips'
law of evidence 170.[10]

¶19   The case at bar is I think completely within the principle of these cases.

¶20   The judgement of the District court is affirmed with costs.

AD, Marshall Judicial Opinions, PPAmP; printed, John W. Brockenbrough, *Reports of
Cases Decided by the Honourable John Marshall . . .* , I (Philadelphia, 1837), 522–28. For JM's
deletions and interlineations, see Textual Notes below.

1. This act was adopted on 21 Dec. 1814 (*U.S. Statutes at Large*, III, 152).

2. In referring to the "act of jeofails," JM meant this section of the Judiciary Act of 1789
(ibid., I, 91).

3. Ibid., III, 155. The edition of the laws JM cited was *Laws of the United States of America,
from the 4th of March, 1789, to the 4th of March, 1815* (5 vols.; Philadelphia and Washington,
1815).

4. Ibid., I, 76–77.

5. Ibid., 84–85.

6. JM referred to the deposition of John Gilfillin, taken on 19 Nov. 1818, a copy of which
was entered on the record as part of the demurrer to evidence (proceedings in U.S. Dist.
Ct., Richmond [copy], 22 Oct. 1819, Jacob v. U.S.).

7. King v. Gordons, 1 Leach 515, 168 Eng. Rep. 359 (Crown, 1789). JM cited the wrong
page number.

8. Berryman v. Wise, 4 T.R. 366, 100 Eng. Rep. 1067 (K.B., 1791); Radford qui tam v.
M'Intosh, 3 T.R. 632, 635, 100 Eng. Rep. 773, 775 (K.B., 1790); Bevan qui tam v. Williams,
3 T.R. 635 n., 100 Eng. Rep. 775 n. (K.B., 1776).

9. Rex v. Verelst, 3 Camp. 432, 170 Eng. Rep. 1435 (N.P., 1813).

10. S[amuel] M. Phillipps, *A Treatise on the Law of Evidence* (1st Am. ed.; New York, 1816; S
#38619), 170.

Textual Notes

¶ 1 l. 3	violating [*erasure*] ↑some↓ of	
l. 4	on ~~spiritous~~ ↑spirits↓ distilled	
l. 5	defendant ↑below↓ demurred	
ll. 7–8	alleging ~~any~~ ↑the↓ offence with ↑precision.↓	
¶ 3 ll. 2–3	that ~~the defendant~~ ↑he had committed↓ one	
ll. 3–4	specifically ↑& singly↓ the	
¶ 4 ll. 2–3	the ↑counsel for the plf.↓ has shown	
ll. 6–7	is ↑expressly↓ given,	
l. 8	are ~~given~~ ↑allowed,↓ the	
l. 8	remedy ↑adopted,↓ ought	
ll. 9–10	case; ~~&~~ ↑nor ought a court↓ to sanction, in one ~~mode of~~ ↑species of↓ action ↑for a penalty↓ a more	
l. 11	for ~~offences~~ ↑penal offences.↓ If	
l. 12	reason ↑he contends↓ for	
l. 14	true ↑in reason.↓ But	
l. 15	true ↑in law↓ that a statute applicable ↑in its terms↓ to	

ll. 16–18   actions ~~brought for the same~~ ↑standing on the same↓ reason.
                   ~~Then the act of limitations applies to as~~ ↑But the application
                   of such statute to an action which it expressly comprehends,
                   cannot, on that account, be denied.↓

¶ 7 ll. 5–6   consummated ↑& the penalty equally incurred↓ by

ll. 7–8   It ~~would~~ ↑might↓ have

ll. 20–21   question ↑of substance,↓ as it seems to me ~~of substance~~ which

¶10 l. 10   whether a [*erasure*] ↑general↓ statute

ll. 11–12   general ~~ex pre~~ provisions,

ll. 13–14   shall [*erasure*] ↑embrace↓ the United States by provisions
                   ↑not particularly mentioning them, but which are↓ adapted

¶12 l. 3   of ~~of~~ ↑default,↓ demurrer

l. 8   comprehend ~~the~~ ↑their↓ suits. ~~of the United States~~

¶14 l. 2   I ~~have~~ reserved

l. 4   district ↑court↓ correct

l. 5   on ↑the sufficiency of↓ the declaration.

¶15 l. 1   the ~~coun~~ ↑attorney↓ for

l. 4   be ↑improperly↓ overruled

l. 6   waives ~~its~~ ↑his↓ objection

ll. 8–9   is ~~waived~~ ↑no longer to be asked,↓ and

ll. 10–11   If ~~an~~ ↑a note or other ordinary↓ instrument

ll. 13–14   his ~~testimony~~ ↑being sworn,↓ admits it & demurs to ~~it~~ ↑his
                   testimony,↓ the

¶16 l. 2   is ~~about~~ ↑bound↓ to

l. 9   terms ~~stated~~ ↑states↓ him

¶17 ll. 1–2   of ~~add~~ ↑admitting↓ it

¶18 ll. 2–3   been ~~dispensed with where gene~~ ↑relaxed in some cases
                   where↓ general

From John Quincy Adams

Sir   Department of State, Washington 12. Decr. 1821

I have the honour to acknowledge the receipt of your Letter of the 19. Ultimo, informing me that you have received the 3d and 4th. and from the 6th. to the 15th., inclusive, Volumes, of the State papers of the 2nd. Session of the 16th. Congress.[1] The whole of the Documents of that Session, amount to 17. Volumes, which were put in five Packets, the Journals included; and it is the impression of the Clerk who is charged with that duty, in the Department of State, that they were all addressed to you. The manner of binding them from the Post Office here has been irregular, and it may have happened that the first Volumes of the set were forwarded the latest, so that it is thought possible, that you may, by this time, have received the entire number of Volumes. Should this not be the case, on your apprizing me of the deficiency, I will endeavour to have it supplied.

I embrace this occasion to advert, in answer to your Letter of the 6. of last September, which reached the Department during my absence from

Washington. It relates to information required for the Register of Officers &c, of the United States. In addressing a circular to the Judicial Officers of the Union, you were included, not from any want of knowledge of your own emoluments, residence &c. but from a hope that you would communicate a list of the judicial Officers in your circuit; more particularly of those in the Several Districts of North Carolina, respecting which the information has been heretofore defective. If it would not be too much trouble to you, an answer to this part of the enquiry, would still be acceptable. I am with great Respect, Sir, your obedient and very humble Servant.

JOHN QUINCY ADAMS

Letterbook copy, RG 59, DNA. Inside address to JM in Richmond.

1. JM to Adams, 19 Nov. 1821 (App. II, Cal.).

To Walter L. Fontaine

Dear Sir   Richmond Decr. 13th. .21

I have received your letter enclosing the second part of the bill for one hundred dollars & now transmit you the other half of the two odd halves you had previously sent me. I hope both halves will come safe to hand. I am dear Sir your obedt

J MARSHALL

ALS (owned by M. J. Sincock, Richmond, Va., 1975); photocopy of ALS, ViHi. Addressed to Fontaine in New Canton; postmarked Richmond, 14 Dec.

To John Quincy Adams

Sir   Richmond Decr. 18th. 1821

I have now the honor to acknowledge your letter of the 12th. inst. I had mistaken the figure 5 for 3 in my receipt for the documents which had reached me. I have from the 4th. to the 15th. inclusive. The 1st. 2d. & 3d have not come to hand.

The District Judge of North Carolina, Henry Potter, resides at Raleigh. The Marshal Beverly Daniel (I think his christian name is Beverly) resides also at Raleigh.[1] The Clerk of the court, Mr. Haywood, I do not recollect his christian name, but think it is Henry, resides at the same place;[2] as does Mr. Devereux, the Attorney for the district. If there are any clerks for the district courts on the sea coast, I do not know their names. Those I have mentioned are all native citizens, I believe of North Carolina.

In Virginia, the Judge of the Eastern District is Saint George Tucker who resides at Williamsburg, & is a native of the island of Bermuda. The marshal is John Pegram who resides in Dinwiddie & the post office to which his letters are directed is Dinwiddie court house.[3] The clerk of the court at Richmond is named Richard Jeffries who resides in Richmond, and the clerk of the lower District is Seth Foster who resides in Norfolk. These gentlemen are all natives of Virginia.

I do not know the name or residence of the Marshal or clerk of the western District.[4] I am Sir with very great respect, Your obedt. Servt

J MARSHALL

ALS, RG 59, DNA. Addressed to Adams in Washington. Postmarked Richmond, 19 Dec. Endorsed by Adams as received 23 Dec. On the cover Adams wrote: "Birth & Residence of the / Judges &a &a of his / Judicial Circuit."

1. Beverly Daniel had been U.S. marshal for North Carolina since 1808 (*Journal of the Executive Proceedings of the Senate* [3 vols.; Washington, D.C., 1828], II, 79).

2. William Henry Haywood, Sr. His son, William Henry Haywood, Jr., served in the U.S. Senate from 1843 to 1846.

3. John Pegram (1773–1831) had previously served in the Virginia General Assembly and briefly in the U.S. Congress. Pegram had been marshal since Apr. 1821 (U.S. Cir. Ct., Va., Ord. Bk. XI, 132–34; *Journal of the Executive Proceedings of the Senate*, III, 257, 264).

4. The marshal was Benjamin Reeder (*Journal of the Executive Proceedings of the Senate*, III, 186, 188).

To Bushrod Washington

My dear Sir   Richmond Decr. 27th. 1821

I had the pleasure this morning of receiving your favour of the 20th.[1] I am heartily rejoiced at hearing of any proposition to print a 2d. Edition of the Life of Washington as it is one of the most desirable objects I have in this life to publish a corrected edition of that work.[2] I would not on any terms, could I prevent it, consent that one other set of the first edition should be published, because it would so far obstruct the circulation of the 2d.; and it would be injustice to Mr. Wayne to publish a second without his full consent because after such publication it is probable that not another volume of the 1st. would sell. It is however material for Mr. Wayne to recollect that his copy right, if he has secured it only for 14 years, has expired, & that he must exercise his privilege of renewing it for the other 14 years if he thinks it worth asserting.[3] Should Mr. Wayne decline renewing his copy right I should hardly think it advisable to publish 1000 copies without previously securing the copy right for the amended work in 4 Volumes, if it can be done, because other printers would probably republish from the copy printed in New York.

We ought not to count on the same sum per volume which was received on the first edition. The printer cannot afford it. A 2d. large edition cannot be got off, and the profits of printing will of course be greatly diminished. I should think fifty cents per volume a liberal allowance, and that must be divided with Mr. Wayne should he decline being himself the printer.

I have gone through the corrections & have only to copy them over so as to make them inteligible to the printer. I can have them ready for the press faster than they will be required. With my sincere congratulations on your restoration to health, I am my dear Sir your affectionate frien⟨d⟩

J MARSHALL

ALS, Marshall Papers, DLC. Addressed to Washington at Mount Vernon; postmarked Richmond, 27 Dec. Endorsed by Washington.

1. Letter not found.

2. Caleb P. Wayne, the Philadelphia publisher of the first edition of the *Life of Washington*, apparently declined to undertake a second edition. The proposition discussed in this letter came from a New York printer, apparently William A. Mercein (Washington to Wayne, 14 Feb. 1822, NjMoHP; *Longwood's American Almanac, New-York Register, and City Directory* [New York, 1821], 306).

3. Wayne had renewed his copyright in 1817 (copyright, 31 May 1817, Dreer Collection, PHi).

From Philip Slaughter

Dear Sir   Springfield Culpeper Jany. 28. 1822

This letter will be handed to you by my particular friend Capt Wm. Ashby—the son of our old friend, & Brother officer, Capt John Ashby of the 3d. Virginia Continental Regiment.[1] The object of this letter is, to obtain your aid in geting Capt Wm. Ashbys son, George Strother Ashby, in, as a Cadet at West point.[2] Young Mr Ashby is in his Sixteenth year— Well grown — has had an Excellent English Education — is of an Amiable Disposition — Very Correct in his Deportment — & is in every Respect, a Very Worthy & Honorable young Man. From the Very High Respect I have for the parents of the young Man, I feel Very Solicitous for his Success. You are well acquainted with the Ashby family, & know them to be Worthy, Respectable, & Honorable Men — who possess great firmness, & Bravery, & are well Calculated to make good officers. Several of this young mans Uncles, Served in the Malitia during the late War, *as officers*, & all acquited themselves Well. Believe me to be with the highest Esteem & Respect, Yr. old friend

PHIL. SLAUGHTER.

ALS, RG 94, DNA. Inside address to JM. Filed with JM to John C. Calhoun, 16 Feb. 1822.

1. William Clarkson Ashby (1780–1841) of Culpeper County married Lucy Strother in 1805. His father, John Ashby (1740–1815) of Fauquier County, served in Thomas Marshall's regiment of the Virginia Continental Line during the Revolution (Thomas Arthur

Dicken, Jr., and Angus McDonald Greer, eds., *Early Churches of Culpeper County, Virginia: Colonial and Ante-Bellum Congregations* [Culpeper, Va., 1987], 54; Raleigh Travers Green, comp., *Genealogical and Historical Notes on Culpeper County, Virginia* [Baltimore, 1964], pt. II, 80; W. A. Crozier, ed., *The Buckners of Virginia and the Allied Families of Strother and Ashby* [New York, 1907], 249–59, 265; H. C. Groome, "General Turner Ashby and His Ancestry," *Bulletin of the Fauquier County Historical Society* [July 1922], 155–57).

2. George Strother Ashby (b. 1806?) wrote to Secretary of War Calhoun on 18 Apr. 1822 accepting a conditional appointment to West Point to begin in June 1822. In a postscript to this letter William Ashby gave his written consent for his son to bind himself to serve at the academy for five years (file of George S. Ashby, RG 94, DNA).

To [John C. Calhoun]

Dear Sir   Washington Feby. 16th. 1822

I am unwilling to be the channel through which any applications are made for situations in the gift of the Executive departments because I am sure they are so numerous as to be troublesome; but I cannot refuse to transmit you the enclosed letter with my assurance that the writer is entitled to entire confidence. I believe he is known to the President.

I am entirely unacquainted with the youth whose admission into the military academy is sollicited; but the family is brave, active, & inteligent. There is not one within the range of my observation to which I would sooner look for a good officer. With Capt. John Ashby the Grand Father, I was well acquainted. He was a good officer & is probably recollected by the President. With great respect & esteem, I am Sir your Obedt

J MARSHALL

ALS, RG 94, DNA. Filed with Philip Slaughter to JM, 28 Jan. 1822.

To Jedidiah Morse

Sir   Washington Feb. 21st. 1822

I have received your letter of the 16th. inst. accompanying a copy of the constitution of "A new society for the benefit of Indians organized, at the city of Washington," of which the Judges of the Supreme court of the United States, with other high officers of government, are, *ex officio*, Vice Presidents.[1]

From the most entire conviction of my inability to contribute in any manner to the success of this institution, I must decline the honor of being considered as one of its Vice Presidents. I am Sir with great respect, your obedt. Servt

J MARSHALL

ALS, Gratz Collection, PHi. Addressed to Morse in Washington. Endorsed by Morse.

THE OLD HOUSE OF REPRESENTATIVES
Oil on canvas by Samuel Finley Breese Morse, 1822. Justices Livingston,
Marshall, and Story are standing left of center in the rear of the portrait.
Samuel F. B. Morse was Jedidiah Morse's son. *Courtesy of Corcoran Art
Gallery, Washington, D.C.*

1. Letter not found. The Rev. Jedidiah Morse (1761–1826), a Congregational clergyman, achieved enduring fame as the author of *The American Geography*, first published in 1789. After leaving the pulpit in 1819, Morse took a great interest in missionary work among the Indians. The enclosure was a printed copy of the constitution of the society, which later adopted the name "American Society for Promoting the Civilization and General Improvement of the Indian Tribes in the United States" (*A New Society, for the Benefit of the Indians Organized at the City of Washington, February, 1822* [Washington, D.C., 1822]; *The First Annual Report of the American Society for Promoting the Civilization and General Improvement of the Indian Tribes in the United States* [New Haven, Conn., 1824]).

From James A. Hamilton

Sir   Washington March 8th 1822

I have the honor by direction of Mrs. Hamilton my mother to enclose to you an extract of a letter from Col Lear & an other from Col Pickering and to request if it should be found upon examination that the information they contain is correct permission to select from among Genl. Washington's papers such as will be useful in the Biography of my father or assist in writing his life and particularly all the Papers of which Genl Hamilton was the author.[1]

In order to relieve you from the toil of Searching for these papers I will with much pleasure at any time you will appoint go to Richmond or wherever the papers are to perform this Service. With very great respect, I am Sir, Yr obt hmbe Sevt

JAH

ALS (copy), Alexander Hamilton Papers, DLC.

1. James A. Hamilton (1788–1878), Alexander Hamilton's third son, was a lawyer and active participant in New York Democratic party politics. The enclosed extract of a letter from Tobias Lear has not been identified. The other extract was possibly a letter from Timothy Pickering to Hamilton, 4 Jan. 1821, in which Pickering inserted a memorandum of a conversation with JM concerning the correspondence between Alexander Hamilton and General Washington. In this conversation, which took place at Washington in Feb. 1811, JM (according to Pickering's memorandum) stated that "his reading of all the papers of Genl. Washington, had enabled him to form an opinion of General Hamilton and he then pronounced him the greatest man (or one of the greatest men) that had ever appeared in the United States" (Pickering to Hamilton, 4 Jan. 1821, Pickering Papers, MHi).

To James A. Hamilton

Sir   Washington March 9th. 1822

I have received your letter of yesterday.

I have always expressed freely the very high respect I felt for your Father while living, and for his memory since his decease, a respect which was certainly increased by his correspondence with General Washington. I shall participate with his warmest friends and admirers in the gratification to be derived from the justice which will, I doubt not, be done to his character & fame by his Biographer.

The papers of General Washington were placed in my hands for a particular purpose, &, beyond that purpose I have no controul over them. They are subject entirely to the disposition of his executor & near relation. I was requested some time past to send them back to Mount Vernon, & have sent a great part of them, among which, as well as I recollect, are those which belong to the period subsequent to the adoption of the constitution of the United States. Those which remain in my possession will be returned by the first opportunity. With great respect I am Sir, Your Obedt servt

J MARSHALL

ALS, Alexander Hamilton Papers, DLC; Tr, Beveridge-Marshall Papers, DLC. Addressed to Hamilton. Endorsed.

To Bushrod Washington

My dear Sir   Richmond Apl. 15th. 1822

I received your letter this morning[1] & immediately went to the cha[n]cery office & examined the papers in the case of Davenport v Thompson. The case is misstated in the report.[2] The bill was filed by J. D. Senr. & J. D. jr. & states that a certain D. D. mortgaged a tract of land to W. Thompson & discharged the whole amount of the mortgage money. That he afterwards conveyed the land with other tracts to Lewis & Ross to pay debts due to them respectively. That this tract was sold publickly at Hanover court house under the power contained in the trust deed & that James Davenport Senr. became the purchaser. That W. T. was present & did not allege any claim upon the land. That D. Davenport conveyed to the purchaser. That W. T. afterwards brought his bill to foreclose in Hanover court and that D D. wrote to the clerk admitting the whole ⟨sum?⟩ claimed in the bill to be due. That the court entered up an order against D. D. but left the case open as to J. D. senr. That afterwards in 1783 the court gave an absolute decree of foreclosure although J. D. had never answered. Under this decree the land was sold & J. D. jr. became the purchaser for £213.64 for which sum he gave his bond. J. D. Senr. announced his title at the sale & refuses to give up the land. J. D. jr. complains he cannot get title nor possession &c.

If you feel any farther difficulty in the case & will explain it to me I will with much pleasure endeavour to remove it; but I presume you will find none.

I congratulate [you] on your prospect of a short term, though you will I suppose pay for it in the fall. Do not trust my certificate of stock to the mail. If you have not a secure hand keep it till I see you in February. I am dear Sir with much esteem & regard, your

J MARSHALL

ALS, Marshall Papers, DLC. Addressed to Washington at Mount Vernon; postmarked Richmond, 18 Apr. Endorsed by Washington.

1. Letter not found.
2. Thompson v. Davenport was decided by the Virginia Court of Appeals in 1792 (1 Wash. 125). The case had begun in the High Court of Chancery as Davenport v. Thompson. Washington was then preparing a new edition of his reports (Bushrod Washington, *Reports of Cases Argued and Determined in the Court of Appeals of Virginia* [2d ed.; Philadelphia, 1823]).

To Littleton W. Tazewell

Dear Sir   Richmond May 19th. 1822
    With some difficulty I have procured notice to be delivered that your deposition will be taken on the 23d. of this month at your office in the suit of Burwells admr. & al v Willis' admrs. concerning which I spoke to you in Washington.[1] I have only received the notice to day though it was given early in April. I enclose you a commission & must beg the favor of you to prepare your deposition & if no person should attend to it, to have the deposition properly certified and taken on the 23d. & enclosed to the clerk of the court of chancery setting in Fredericksburg under cover to me.[2]
    I have written to General Taylor to attend to this business but he may be out of town &, if so, there is no person to whom I can apply.[3] Mr. Blair has spoken to Mr. Tabb but Mr. Blair is out of Richmond & Mr. Tabb is totally unknown to me.[4] If therefore Genl Taylor should be out of town I must hope that you will not refuse to send for magistrates & have the necessary steps taken. With great respect & esteem, I am dear Sir your obedt

J MARSHALL

ALS, Marshall Papers, ViW. Addressed to Tazewell in Norfolk; postmarked Richmond, 19 May. Endorsed by Tazewell.

1. The case of Burwell's Administrator et al. v. Willis's Executor et al. was pending in the Fredericksburg Superior Court of Chancery. The plaintiffs were John H. Blair, administrator of Nathaniel Burwell and of Ann Rich Burwell, and Claudia Burwell Marshall. Claudia Marshall (1804–1884) was the wife of JM's son, James K. Marshall. Her mother, Ann Rich Burwell, was the daughter of Francis Willis of Whitehall in Gloucester County (Burwell v. Willis, File 43, Office of the Clerk, Fredericksburg Circuit Court, Fredericksburg, Va.; Fredericksburg Superior Court of Chancery, Ord. Bk. I, 1814–18, 128, 234 [microfilm], Vi; Paxton, *Marshall Family*, 101–3; William Carter Stubbs, *Descendants of Mordecai Cooke . . . and Thomas Booth . . .* [New Orleans, La., 1923], 31).
2. Tazewell's deposition concerned a legal case he had handled years earlier when prac-

ticing in the Williamsburg area. At that time Tazewell represented a creditor of Francis Willis, who before the Revolution had mortgaged the Whitehall estate to secure a large debt owed by his father (deposition of Littleton W. Tazewell, Burwell v. Willis).

3. Robert B. Taylor (1774–1834) graduated from the College of William and Mary in 1793, studied law, and became an eminent practitioner in his native Norfolk. As a brigadier general of the state militia, he participated in the defense of the city during the War of 1812. He served several terms in the state legislature and was a member of the Virginia Convention of 1829. In his later years he was a judge of the General Court. Taylor was a defendant in this suit in his capacity as executor of Dr. John Willis, son and executor of Francis Willis (Lyon G. Tyler, ed., *Encyclopedia of Virginia Biography* [5 vols.; New York, 1915], II, 188–89; Stubbs, *Descendants of Mordecai Cooke*, 31; deposition of Littleton W. Tazewell, Burwell v. Willis).

4. Tabb was evidently John Tabb, a Norfolk alderman and justice of the peace, who had been commissioned to take Tazewell's deposition (deposition of Littleton W. Tazewell, Burwell v. Willis).

To Bushrod Washington

Dear Sir   Richmond May 28th. [1822]

I have not yet heard whether your session in Philadelphia is over & you have returned to Mount Vernon. I had supposed from your last letter that your term would be a short one, but not having heard of its being over, I doubt whether you may not be still engaged in Philadelphia.

I had some very perplexing questions in North Carolina where several suits are brought against the state bank. It will be necessary to form some rules respecting this matter. I determined that service on the President was sufficient & that it was not necessary to resort to the distringas to compel an appearance.[1] I suspect however that my decision will be reversed by your Honors.[2]

I am just about entering on the trial of five or six privates[3] who will I hope be all acquitted by the jury.[4] Their case presents the question whether a cruizing without a lawful commission, if there be no actual robbery or murder, is piracy?[5]

I shall be much obliged if you will countermand the order for a pipe of wine for Mr. Harvie. Mine I hope to receive but he seems rather disposed to chuse for himself. The mistake respecting his wish was made by myself.

As soon as the court is over I shall enter on the perusal of the letters. I am dear Sir your

J Mars⟨ha⟩ll

ALS, Miscellaneous Manuscripts, NHi. Addressed to Washington at Mount Vernon; postmarked Richmond, 28 May. Endorsed by Washington. MS torn where seal was broken.

1. A writ of distringas directed a sheriff to distrain upon the goods and chattels of a defendant in order to compel appearance. This writ was issued when it was impracticable to serve a summons on the defendant personally. It was also issued in equity proceedings to compel the appearance of a corporation.

2. JM was possibly referring to Bank of the U.S. v. State Bank of North Carolina, and Solomon and Moses Allen v. State Bank of North Carolina (U.S. Cir. Ct., N.C., Min. Bk., 15 May, 14 Nov. 1822). According to the Supreme Court dockets, no case from the North Carolina circuit was filed in the Supreme Court for the 1823 term or for several terms thereafter.

3. JM meant "pirates."

4. An indictment for piracy had been brought against five crewmen of the schooner *Moscow* at the May term of the U.S. Circuit Court at Richmond. The schooner had been taken prize by the *Hornet* the preceding October between Santo Domingo and Cuba and brought into Norfolk. The captured vessel was described as having "a mixed crew of blacks and Spaniards — nineteen in number." Of the five indicted as pirates, four were "Creoles of Colombia" and the fifth Italian. Their names as recorded by the court clerk were Joseph Martines, Juan de la Crux, Joseph Bostaide, Cayeton Paloma, and Miguel Jamines. They all spoke Spanish and required an interpreter. The court assigned three lawyers to defend them (U.S. Cir. Ct., Va., Ord. Bk. XI, 215, 217; Washington *Daily National Intelligencer*, 1 Dec. 1821; Richmond *Enquirer*, 31 May 1822).

5. On this day a jury acquitted the five crewmen, and the court ordered them to be returned to Norfolk. The testimony of the midshipman who brought in the prize was regarded as being so weak that U.S. Attorney Robert Stanard declined further prosecution. The *Moscow* claimed to have been taken by a Colombian privateer and was cruising under a commission from the privateer. Citing a recent decision of the Supreme Court, Stanard stated that it would be "necessary to prove that some act had been committed at sea which would amount to felony or larceny on land, to constitute piracy" but that no such act had been proved. JM "in substance" then remarked "that however a vessel found armed and cruising without authority from any nation, and evidently intent on plundering any vessel she might fall in with might be considered a pirate before an opportunity offered to commit any depredation — yet in such a case as this, where the vessel and crew claimed to belong to the Colombian government, and to be sailing under a regular commission, and produced something like proof of it, it was necessary, to authorise a conviction for piracy, to show that some act of piracy had actually been committed — but that as nothing like that had been proved, it would be necessary for the jury to find a verdict of acquittal." The jury then acquitted "without a moment's consultation, and in less than an hour after the trial commenced" (U.S. Cir. Ct., Va., Ord. Bk. XI, 224; Richmond *Enquirer*, 31 May 1822).

Furniss, Cutler, & Stacey v. Allan & Ellis
Opinion
U.S. Circuit Court, Virginia, 1 June 1822

The plaintiffs, British merchants, brought an action of assumpsit against Richmond merchants John Allan and Charles Ellis for recovery of $10,000. Counsel for the plaintiffs, Daniel Call, left a memorandum with the clerk of the court directing him to file the suit. In filling out the writ of capias and in copying the declaration, the clerk mistakenly wrote "Stany" for "Stacey." At the March 1822 rules in the clerk's office, the defendants, in addition to pleading the general issue denying the claim, filed a demurrer stating that the persons bringing the action were "not the same persons named as plaintiffs in the said declaration." On the plaintiffs' refusal to join in the demurrer, the clerk entered an office judgment for the defendants at the May rules. Marshall's opinion of 1 June 1822 was on the plaintiffs' motions to dismiss the demurrer and proceed to trial on the general issue and to amend the error that had given rise to the demurrer (U.S. Cir. Ct., Va., Ord. Bk. XI, 238; Furniss v. Allan & Ellis, declaration [Mar. 1822]; demurrers and plea of defendants, 7 Mar. 1822, U.S. Cir. Ct., Va., Ended Cases [Unrestored], 1822, Vi).

Furniss &c

v

Allen & Ellis[1]

In this case,[2] the defendants demurred to the plaintiffs declaration, ¶1 and assigned as special cause of demurrer matter in abatement. They also pleaded the general issue. The plaintiff took issue on the plea, but refused to join in demurrer. For this cause judgement was entered at the rules for the defendants, but the clerk has, notwithstanding, set the cause down among the writs of enquiry.[3] The plf. now moves to strike out the demurrer & proceed to trial on the issue. He also moves to amend the error which is assigned as cause of demurrer because it is a mistake of the clerk.

This motion is sustained by the allegation that the demurrer ought not ¶2 to have been received by the clerk: and consequently admits of no enquiry into its sufficiency farther than is necessary to determine on the right to offer it.

It was offered at a time when the right to plead was complete, and ¶3 under a law which authorizes the defendant to plead as many several matters both of law & fact as he may think necessary for his defence.[4]

From the comprehensive letter of this law there would be some diffi- ¶4 culty in excluding any plea which the defendant might offer at the time when he had a right to offer it. The sufficiency of the plea is not submitted to the clerk. He cannot judge of it. Consequently it would seem, he must receive it if it be tendered in proper time.

But the plaintiffs contend that there is in the nature & fitness of things ¶5 an objection to the allowance of inconsistent matter to be pleaded in the same cause which must enter into the construction of the act of assembly, & controul, or at least influence the meaning of its words. There is they say this inconsistency in a demurrer to the whole declaration & a plea to the whole. The demurrer confesses all the facts & the plea denies them all.

But a demurrer confesses those facts only which are sufficiently ¶6 pleaded; and the plea, as the plea of non assumpsit, though it admits nothing is not false though many of the facts alleged in the declaration be true. It amounts to pleading double but not to a positive inconsistency. I cannot however admit that it is beyond the power of the legislature to pass an act allowing inconsistent pleas, or that a court can disregard such an act.

The plaintiffs counsel supports his argument by reference to several ¶7 English authorities, to all which it may be observed that the law which governs the practice in England is different from that which governs the practice in Virginia. The statute of the 4th. & 5th. of Anne Ch. 16 allows the defendant to plead several matters only with the leave of the court. The English statute gives to the court a controuling power over the admission of the plea: The Statute of Virginia gives the court no such controuling power. In the exercise of this controuling power the courts of England have prescribed rules by which they will be governed in granting or refusing an application to plead different matters. But the courts of Virginia can prescribe no such rules. The law declares that the defendant may plead as many several matters of law & fact as he pleases withou⟨t⟩ making any application to the court necessary. The defendant in England is when he first pleads, in the same situation as to a double plea that the defendant in Virginia is after his right to plead depends on the favour of the court.[5]

¶8   But the cases quoted to show that the demurrer is not good, do not show that, even in England, it ought not to be received, if tendered in proper time. In 5th. B. 459 it is said "If a defendant demur in abatement, the court will notwithstanding give a final judgement, because there cannot be a demurrer in abatement."[6]

¶9   This does not prove that the demurrer itself shall be rejected, but that it shall be received, & the judgement upon it be final. A judgement on pleas in abatement, or on a demurrer to a plea in abatement is not final; but, on a demurrer which contains matter in abatement it shall be final, because a demurrer cannot partake of the character of a plea in abatement. Salk 220 is quoted by Bacon & is to the same purport, indeed in the same words.[7] These cases show that a demurrer, being in its own nature a plea to the action, and being even in form a plea to the action, shall not be considered as a plea in abatement, though the special causes alleged for demurring be matter of abatement. The court will disregard those special causes, and considering the demurrer independently of them, will decide upon it as if they had not been inserted in it.

¶10   These cases go far to show that the court would overrule this demurrer; and decide the cause against the party demuring not that it should be expunged from the pleadings.

¶11   1st. Tidd 419 "if the defendant plead in abatement["] &c.[8]

¶12   These cases show that if a plea in abatement be tendered when it is not receivable, the plf. may proceed as if no plea had been offered, or he may move the court to strike it out. It is obvious that they do not apply directly to the case at bar. This demurrer was receivable when it was tendered.

¶13   But the counsel brings his case within their reasoning by considering the demurrer as a plea in abatement. Now this it cannot be. The cases cited from Bacon & Salkeld show that a demurrer can not be in abatement. The court therefore can consider this only as a general demurrer; and of course it was offered in proper time.

¶14   Tidd 429 shows that where a defendant is under a Judges order to plead issuably, & pleads a plea which is not issuable, or puts in a sham demurrer the plf. may consider it as a meer nullity.[9]

But these defendants were not under a Judges order to plead. They ¶15 were not acting under the guidance of the court, but acting, by authority of the law of the land, according to their own judgement. Had they permitted a writ of enquiry to be entered against them, & the term at which it might be set aside to pass away; or had they been in a situation in which they could not plead but under the direction of the court, this doctrine would certainly be applicable to the case. At present I think it is not.

Tidd 434 shows that the court will set aside irregular proceedings.[10] ¶16 But this is not an irregular proceeding. It is perfectly regular. The demurrer was offered in proper time; and, though it may not be sustainable, it must be considered. Any plea in bar may be unsustainable; but it is not on that account to be discarded without being considered.

The cases cited from the term reports only confirm the doctrines of ¶17 Tidd.[11]

In Ewers practice 210 it is said "But if the demurrer be frivolous only to ¶18 put off the trial or for delay of the proceedings, they will not allow of such a demurrer, nor cause the other party to join, But will give judgement against the party upon his frivolous demurrer.["][12]

It would require a person more conversant with the English practice ¶19 than I am to understand precisely the bearing of this dictum. The court must examine the declaration to determine whether a demurrer be frivolous. Although the special causes assigned for demurring may be frivolous, the demurrer itself may be substantial. But be this as it may the rule is inapplicable to this case & perhaps to the practice of this country. The demurrer according to our practice can produce no delay, cannot put off the trial of the cause. Had the plfs. joined in demurrer & it had appeared to be frivolous, a writ of enquiry would have been awarded & executed immediately; or the issue would have been tried without allowing a continuance. A frivolous demurrer therefore in this case could not put off the cause or occasion any delay. I do not know what delays, according to the practice of England, a frivolous demurrer may occasion. But this doctrine is founded on the controuling power of the courts of England over pleading, a power which the courts of this country do not possess.

If the demurrer in this case was receivable, and I think it was, the ¶20 refusal to join in it was a discontinuance which is provided for in the act of assembly. The plfs. must be non suited. This proceeding however is now under the direction of the court & the cause may certainly be reinstated.

I come now to consider the application to amend. ¶21

I have no doubt of the power of the court to allow amendments in all ¶22 cases of clerical misprision where there is any thing to amend by, but I had doubted whether the memorandum of counsel was a document by which an amendment could be made.

The cases cited by Mr. Call have in a great measure removed those ¶23 doubts & I am inclined to permit an amendment of the writ. An amendment to the declaration will be allowed also, but not on the ground of clerical misprision. To copy a declaration in order to file it is no part of the duty of the clerk. He acted as the agent of the plfs attorney. It is to be considered as a declaration drawn & filed by the attorney himself. In every such case the amendment will be allowed; but it is a new declaration & the defendants are allowed to plead de *novo*.

¶24   This motion involves no question about the recognizance of the bail. I do not at present percieve how that recognizance can avail the party, but I do not understand that the motion extends to it.[13]

AD, Marshall Judicial Opinions, PPAmP; printed, John W. Brockenbrough, *Reports of Cases Decided by the Honourable John Marshall* . . . , II (Philadelphia, 1837), 15–19. For JM's deletions and interlineations, see Textual Notes below.

1. Although the suit papers and order book entries for this case consistently refer to the Richmond merchants as "Allan & Ellis," the company was usually styled "Ellis & Allan." John Allan (1780–1834), a native of Scotland, formed his partnership with Charles Ellis in 1800. Allan was the adoptive father of author and poet Edgar Allan Poe (1809–1849). See *Richmond Portraits*, 3–5.

2. Brockenbrough omitted the first paragraph of the opinion but summarized it in his statement of the case.

3. A judgment entered "at the rules" was an office judgment. Office judgments requiring a jury sworn by a writ of inquiry to assess damages were placed on the regular court docket. Although in this case the office judgment had been for the defendants and no writ of inquiry was issued, the clerk "set the cause down" with other writ of inquiry cases. On proceedings at the rules, see *PJM*, V, xxxix-xl.

4. JM referred to a law first enacted in Virginia in 1788, which allowed a defendant to plead as many matters of law or fact necessary to his defense without having to apply to the court (Hening, *Statutes*, XII, 745; *Revised Code of Va.*, I, 510).

5. On the English statute of 1705, which relaxed the common law rule against "double pleading," and the 1788 Virginia law, see *PJM*, V, xli-xlii, 39–40 n. 3. Under the Virginia law, a defendant could plead and demur to the same declaration.

6. Bacon, *Abridgment*, V, 459. A plea in abatement did not go to the merits of the cause but was entered for some defect in the writ or declaration.

7. The marginal note in Bacon cites Dominique v. Davenant, Salk. 220, 91 Eng. Rep. 195 (K.B., 1704).

8. William Tidd, *The Practice of the Court of King's Bench* (2d Am. ed.; 2 vols.; New York, 1807), I, 419.

9. Ibid., 429.

10. Ibid., 434.

11. A canceled passage identifies these cases as Doughty v. Lascelles, 4 T.R. 520, 100 Eng. Rep. 1152 (K.B., 1792); Buddle v. Willson, 6 T.R. 369, 372, 101 Eng. Rep. 601 (K.B., 1793); Hutchinson v. Brown, 7 T.R. 298, 101 Eng. Rep. 985 (K.B., 1797).

12. The quoted passage is from Samson Euer, *A System of Pleading* . . . (London, 1771), 186. JM evidently used a later edition of this work.

13. The case continued on the clerk's rule docket from June through September. The plaintiffs then withdrew the suit, which was accordingly dismissed at the Nov. 1822 term (Shepherd & Leslie to Daniel Call, 19 Oct. 1822, Furniss, Cutler, and Stacey v. Allan and Ellis; U.S. Cir. Ct., Va., Ord. Bk. XI, 265).

Textual Notes

¶ 1 l. 2   abatement. ~~He~~ ↑They↓ also
l. 6   The ~~plfs~~ ↑plf.↓ now ~~move~~ ↑moves↓ to
ll. 7–8   error ~~for~~ which
¶ 4 l. 1 beg.   ~~Under~~ ↑From↓ the
l. 4   Consequently ↑it would seem,↓ he
¶ 5 l. 1   plaintiffs ~~contends~~ ↑contend↓ that
ll. 4–5   There is ~~he says~~ ↑they say↓ this
l. 6   demurrer ~~he says~~ confesses [*erasure*] ↑all↓ the
¶ 6 l. 2   and ~~an issue,~~ ↑the plea,↓ as
l. 3   many ~~or all~~ ↑of↓ the
l. 4   positive ~~consistency~~ ↑inconsistency.↓ I
¶ 7 l. 10   application ~~for~~ ↑to↓ ~~file~~ plead
¶ 8 l. 1 beg.   ~~I will however examine some of these authorities. Tidd 419 29.34 6 Term 372. A plea in abatement received at an improper time. 4 T. 520 & 7th. do. 298 prove that the plf. may sign judgement if the plea be offered where it is not receivable. The plf has a right to consider it as a nullity & to proceed as if it had not been offered. But this demurrer was offered in proper time. The plaintiff does not deny this but says it is not good at any time because it is a demurrer in abatement which is not good. This objection goes to the sufficiency of the demurrer, to the judgement which the court ought to give on it, not to the power of the clerk to receive or reject it. Let it be admitted that the defendant cannot avail himself on demurrer of matter in abatement, yet this demurrer goes also to the whole merits. It is a general as well as a special demurrer; and though the matter specially assigned as error may be naught, yet the demurrer remains general.~~
¶ 9 l. 6   is [*erasure*] ↑to↓ the [*erasure*] ↑same↓ purport,
l. 8   action, ~~if~~ ↑and↓ being
¶ 10 ll. 1–2   demurrer; ↑and decide the cause against the party demuring↓ not
¶ 14 ll. 2–3   issuable, ↑or puts in a sham demurrer↓ the
¶ 15 ll. 3–4   permitted [*erasure*] ↑a↓ writ
l. 5   or ~~if~~ ↑had↓ they
¶ 18 ll. 2–3   proceedings, ↑they will not allow of such a demurrer,↓ nor
¶ 19 ll. 12–13   delay. ↑I do not know what delays, according to the practice of England, a frivolous demurrer may occasion.↓ [*erasure*] ↑But↓ this
¶ 23 ll. 2–3   An ~~allowance to amend~~ ↑amendment to↓ the
l. 7   but [*erasure*] ↑it↓ is

From William Gaston

Dear Sir   Newbern June 12th. 1822

The Bearer of this letter, Mr. Bryan, is solicitous of the honour of being made known to you.[1] He is making a short excursion to the North, and is unwilling to pass thro' Richmond without that gratification. Allow me to take the liberty of introducing him to you, with an assurance of his great personal worth, and of his high promises of future usefulness.

I am always glad of an occasion to declare the sentiments of respect esteem and affection with which I have the honour to be, Sir, Truly your's

WM: GASTON.

ALS, William Gaston Papers, Southern Historical Collection, NcU. Addressed to JM in Richmond; noted as conveyed by "Mr. Bryan."

1. John Herritage Bryan (1798–1870) of New Bern graduated from the University of North Carolina in 1815, studied law in Gaston's office, and was admitted to the bar in 1819. He later served in the state senate and was a member of the U.S. House of Representatives from 1825 to 1829. After leaving the House, he remained active in Whig politics in his home state (William S. Powell, ed., *Dictionary of North Carolina Biography*, I [Raleigh, N.C., 1990], 255–56; J. Herman Schauinger, *William Gaston, Carolinian* [Milwaukee, Wis., 1949], 112–13).

Coates v. Muse
Opinion
U.S. Circuit Court, Virginia, 12 June 1822

In consequence of Marshall's interlocutory decree of 4 June 1821, a commissioner in chancery made a further report in this case on 1 December 1821. This report produced another interlocutory decree on 19 December 1821, in which the court, "reserving to a future day its decision on the ultimate responsibility of the parties defendants," ordered Elliott Muse's administrator to pay the plaintiff $3,700 out of the estate's assets. The administrator, Zachariah Crittenden, then moved to set aside this decree. In support of this motion Crittenden submitted the record of two suits pending against him as Elliott Muse's administrator in the state superior court of chancery at Williamsburg. Marshall ruled on the motion on 12 June 1822 (Coates v. Muse, opinion and decree, 4 June 1821; decree [in JM's hand], Coates v. Muse, U.S. Cir. Ct., Va., Ended Cases [Unrestored], 1823, Vi; U.S. Cir. Ct., Va., Ord. Bk. XI, 205, 228; proceedings in the Superior Court of Chancery, Williamsburg, Coates v. Muse).

The first question which arises in this cause is: In what proportion was the debt due to the plaintiff, originally chargeable on the estate of Thomas and Elliott Muse?

By the decree of this Court, at the May Term, 1811, Thomas and Elliott

Muse, administrators of Hudson Muse, deceased, were directed to pay to the plaintiff, the sum of $7493 76, that being the amount of the assets of Hudson Muse in their hands, to be administered.

This decree is not expressed to be made by consent of parties; but there is much reason to believe that such was the fact. In general, one executor is not liable for the acts of his co-executor, and it is certain that this Court would not have made a joint decree against the defendants, had not an acquiescence in such decree been expressed; or had not the Court understood, that there would be so much difficulty in ascertaining their respective liabilities before a commissioner, that the defendants preferred making the adjustment between themselves. But, whatever may have been the motive for the decree, its effect certainly was to charge Thomas and Elliott Muse equally. It cannot, however, be doubted, that if, on an application to carry this decree into execution, it should be shown to the Court, that the defendants were unequally indebted to the estate of the deceased, the decree would be revived against each, according to his liability. The commissioner has supposed, that this inequality of liability is proved by the fact, that Thomas and Elliott Muse, were debtors in unequal sums, for purchases made at the sale of Hudson Muse's estate. He supposes, that precisely the same amount of debts was collected by each, and that Thomas Muse is chargeable beyond Elliott Muse, in the sum which his purchases exceed those made by Elliott Muse. This supposition, the Court considers as inadmissible, because the defendants would have resisted a joint decree, had they divided the outstanding debts, without regard to their individual debts; and, because also, it is most probable, especially since they considered themselves as entitled to the estate of Hudson Muse, that each collected as much of the outstanding debts, as would place him on an equality with the other. The fact, then, that they purchased unequally at the sale, does not authorize any inference, opposed to the decree of 1811.

The entry made by Elliott Muse, as representative of Thomas Muse, is undoubtedly satisfactory evidence, that he did not think the estate of Thomas Muse liable to him beyond the sum charged to it; but does not, perhaps, sufficiently prove, that the estate of Thomas Muse was indebted in that sum. That entry shows the extent of Elliott Muse's claim, when he supposed himself entitled to the decree, but cannot demonstrate the justice of that claim. The sum charged to the estate of Thomas Muse, however, exceeds so little a moiety of the decree, with interest, as to make this an unimportant inquiry. I shall consider Thomas and Elliott Muse, as originally liable for this decree in moieties.

The second question, depends upon the construction of the "act concerning partitions, and joint rights, and obligations."[1]

Soon after the decree was pronounced, Thomas Muse died; and the question is, whether the decree survived, so that his representatives were discharged at law; or, whether it might have been revived as against them.

At common law, the rule undoubtedly is, that a judgment or decree against two persons, is joint and not several, that it survives against the survivor, and cannot be enforced, at law, against the representatives of the deceased; nor in equity, farther than those representatives are equitably bound, in consequence of being equitable debtors. But the legislature of Virginia, has enacted, that, "The representative of one jointly bound with another, for the payment of a debt, or for performance or forbearance of any act, or for any other thing, and dying in the lifetime of the latter, may be charged by virtue of such obligation, in the same manner as such representatives might have been charged, if the obligors had been bound severally, as well as jointly."

The question is, whether this section of the act, extends to judgments and decrees, or is confined to obligations, created by the act of the party bound.

This question, as I understand, is now, for the first time, raised in a court of justice.

It is always, with much reluctance, that I break the way, in expounding the statute of a state; for the exposition of the acts of every legislature is, I think, the peculiar and appropriate duty of the tribunals, created by that legislature. Although, if a case depending on a statute, not yet construed by the appropriate tribunal, comes on to be tried, the judge is under the necessity of construing the statute, because it forms a part of the case, yet he will yield to this necessity, only where it is real, and when the case depends upon the statute. The reluctance with which he yields to it is increased, when, as in this case, the language of the act is sufficiently ambiguous to admit of different constructions among intelligent gentlemen of the profession. In such a case, he will be particularly anxious to avoid giving a first construction; and will avoid it, if the case can be otherwise decided.

"The representative of one jointly bound with another," is the subject of the act; and this description is, certainly, broad enough to comprehend a person bound by act of law, as well as one who is bound by his own act. The statute proceeds: "May be charged, by virtue of such obligation, in the same manner as such representatives might have been charged, if the obligors had been bound severally, as well as jointly."

These words may be considered as restraining the general term used in the first part of the sentence. It is true, that the words "such obligation," referring, directly, to the words "one jointly bound with another," may very naturally have been used in a sense co-extensive with the first words, and may, without violence, or departure from their usual sense, be understood to designate any obligation, whether created by the act of law or of a party; but the subsequent words produce more difficulty. The representatives of the person dying first, are to be charged in the same manner as they might have been charged "if the obligors had been bound severally, as well as jointly."

The word "obligors," in the last part of the sentence, was certainly intended to be co-extensive with the words "one jointly bound with another," in the first part of it. These different words were, unquestionably, introduced by the legislature, to describe the same persons and the same obligation; but the word "obligors" seems to me to designate, exclusively, those who bind themselves, the actors, in creating an obligation. Those bound by a judgment or decree, are never, I think, denominated obligors. The following words add strength to this construction. They are to be charged, as if the obligors had been bound "severally as well as jointly." Now, a judgment never, and a decree very rarely, binds severally as well as jointly. A judgment, or decree, against two, is a joint, and never a joint and several judgment or decree; unless, indeed, in a decree, this quality be particularly expressed.

These phrases in the section, which are entirely adapted to obligations created by the act of the party, satisfy me, that such obligations, alone, were in the mind of the legislature, when the law was framed; and I should feel no difficulty in saying, that its provisions ought to be limited to them, were it not that the obvious and general intention of the act would be defeated by this construction.

The obvious intention of the act is, that all obligations, which are joint in their terms, should be several, as well as joint, in their legal operation and effect. This policy is beneficial and just to creditors, because they are not defrauded, by the death of one of the obligors, of any part of the security for which they originally stipulated; and it is justice to the obligors themselves, because it leaves the representatives of each, bound to precisely the same extent to which the original obligor probably intended to bind himself. The legislature stops short, without effecting its object, if the provision does not apply to the judgment, as well as to the contract on which that judgment is founded. It would be strange, if, in severing that which the parties themselves had made joint, the legislature had intended to leave the law in such a state as still to join, by its own operation, that which the parties had severed, or that which the act was made for the purpose of severing. If the legislature, when framing this law, had been asked: "Do you intend, that a judgment shall bind those jointly, and not severally, who had bound themselves severally, as well as jointly; or that the judgment shall be joint on contracts which this legislature intended to sever?" The answer, it is probable, would have been in the negative. It may, then, be urged with plausibility, and, perhaps, with truth, that this is a case in which the literal construction of an act is opposed to its spirit, and would defeat, in part, the object of the legislature. That it is a case in which words of some ambiguity are used, which, construed according to their common acceptation, would not reach a case within the mischief intended to be provided against.

I feel the force of this reasoning, but my general rule of construction, and I think it a good one, is to adhere to the letter of the statute, taking the whole together; and I would not readily depart from that rule in this case. It is, however, no weak argument in favour of the more liberal construction, that no mischief can come from its adoption, and the consequence of a contrary construction, would, I think, be the multiplication of suits. Creditors would bring, in many instances, as many actions as there are parties to the contract on which they sue. Without expressly adopting either construction I shall inquire whether the one or the other may not lead to the same result.

If the act of assembly so changes the law, that this decree may be revived against the representatives of Thomas Muse, then those representatives would be clearly liable for one moiety of it; but if, in consequence of transactions subsequent thereto, or of circumstances not known to the Court when it was pronounced, the representatives of Thomas Muse ought to recover from those of Elliott Muse, the sum they pay to the plaintiff, or any part of it, then the Court would decree, in the first instance, that the estate of Elliott Muse should pay to the plaintiff, the sum for which they would be liable to the estate of Thomas Muse, provided that might be done without delaying the plaintiff, or in any manner prejudicing him.

If the decree survives, and could not be regularly revived against the representatives of Thomas Muse, still the original *equity* of the plaintiff against him for a moiety of the decree, would not be destroyed. This equity may indeed be rebutted by equitable circumstances; but those circumstances must, I think, derive some of their force from the conduct of the creditor. Transactions between the debtors alone, might be a reason for decreeing in the first instance against the estate of one of them, but not for such a postponement of the rights of the creditor as would materially injure him.

We should be brought, then, to the same result in whichever way the statute be construed, unless there are transactions between the parties, which ought to postpone the decree, as against the estate of Thomas Muse, under one construction, and not under the other.

His counsel contends that there are such circumstances.

On the death of Thomas Muse, Elliott Muse qualified as his executor, and has died greatly indebted to his estate. It is contended that as the representatives both of Thomas and Elliott Muse are before the court, and as the representatives of Elliott Muse, will be accountable to those of Thomas Muse, for the estate of Thomas Muse wasted by Elliott Muse, that this Court will decree directly against those representatives, so far as they are liable to the representatives of Thomas Muse. This is undoubtedly the course of justice, and the course of the Court, so far as it can be conformed to, without delays and perplexities injurious to the creditor. In a plain case, the Court will never hesitate to decree directly against a party, who is ultimately responsible. But in a case where great delay must be encountered to establish this ultimate responsibility, the Court does not think itself at liberty to impose these delays and difficulties on the creditor.

If Elliott Muse were still living, and the report of the commissioner were to be confirmed, the Court could not hesitate to decree against him to the full amount of the debt, for he is shown to be the debtor of Thomas Muse in a still larger sum. But Elliott Muse is dead, and his representatives are responsible under any construction of the laws of Virginia, so far only as assets have come to their hands. Whether they are responsible to that extent, or not, depends upon the construction of the 60th section of the act, (1 Rev. Co. ch. 104) for regulating the conduct of executors and administrators,[2] and on the operation of a paper given to Elliott Muse by William C. Williams, then the attorney for the plaintiff.[3]

The words of the act of assembly are, "The executors or administrators, of a guardian, of a committee, or of any other person who shall have been chargeable with, or accountable for, the estate of a ward, an idiot or a lunatic, or the estate of a dead person, committed to their testator or intestate, by a court of record, shall pay so much as shall be due from their testator or intestate, to the ward, idiot, or lunatic, or to the legatees or persons entitled to distribution, before any proper debt of their testator or intestate."[4]

The question is, whether the priority given by this section, extends to creditors, or is confined to the claims of the ward, idiot, &c. and legatees or distributees of the deceased.

In the case of a ward, or of an idiot or lunatic, the question cannot well arise; and I am not sure that this circumstance may not in some degree, affect the construction of the act, in its application to the case of legatees and distributees, who are thus connected in the same provision with the ward, and the idiot or lunatic.

There are, however, some considerations, which powerfully oppose this construction of the act.

The executor, or administrator, holds the estate of his testator, or intestate, as a trustee, first for creditors, and, then, for legatees, or distributees. This rule is so intermingled with all the principles of our law, its observance is so imperiously exacted by the most sacred injunctions of justice and morals, that the legislature cannot be supposed to impair it, unless the language be such, that the construction is inevitable. Express words, only, can change the order which debts and legacies, or distributive shares hold to each other. The executor of an executor, is often the executor of the first testator. The debt due from his immediate, to his original testator, represents the property converted by that immediate testator, to his own use, and is assets in his hands, first, to satisfy the claim of the creditors of the first testator, and then, the claims of legatees. In a contest between those creditors and legatees, all our experience, all our legal education, every thing we derive from observation or instruction, informs us, that the creditors must prevail. In such a state of things, the priority of a legatee over a creditor of the last testator, is, by an implication so necessary as to be inevitable, the priority of a creditor of the first testator, whose claim is so superior in dignity, to that of the legatee, as to enable him to wrest the property from the legatee, after it shall be delivered to him.

The case is not materially varied, if the representative of the administrator, or of the last testator, be not also the representative of the first.

If an executor or administrator die, indebted to the estate of his testator, or intestate, that debt charges his estate in the hands of his representative. It is a debt, the dignity of which depends upon the law. This debt, in the regular course of things, is to be sued for, by the representative of the original testator. When it comes to the hands of that representative, it is assets to be paid in the course of administration, first to creditors, and then to legatees, or distributees. The law must be very clear, and very positive, indeed, which would make a difference between these assets, and those which had remained unchanged, and which came to his hands, as they came to the hands of the first representative. If we examine the section under consideration, it makes no such difference. It does not say, that the executor or administrator, shall pay to the legatees, or distributees, so much as shall be due from their testator, or intestate, before any other debts whatever. It does not reverse the long established order of things, and give a preference under any circumstances, to a man's legatees, or distributees, over his own creditors; but declares, that the executors, or administrators of any person, "who shall have been chargeable with, or accountable for," "the estate of a dead person, committed to their testator, or intestate, by a court of record, shall pay so much as shall be due from their testator, or intestate, to the legatees, or persons entitled to distribution, before any proper debt of their testator, or intestate."

The words, "to the legatees, or persons entitled to distribution," are not connected with the word "pay," but with the word "due." The law does not command, that payment shall be made to the distributees, or legatees, but, generally, that payment shall be made of what is "due to the legatees, or distributees of the dead person," "before any proper debt of their testator, or intestate." Payment shall be made, to whom? The act does not tells us, but the answer must be, to the person authorized by law to receive it. This person is the representative of the original testator, in whose hands this debt becomes assets, not distinguishable from other assets; not more liable than other assets to the claims of legatees, or distributees, nor less liable to the claims of creditors; for the law does not give any priority, except over the proper debts of the last testator, or intestate.

For these reasons, I think it impossible to resist the conviction, that this section gives a priority to debts due to the estate of a dead person, committed to the hands of the last decedent in his lifetime, over the proper debts of such decedent, but interferes no farther with the subject.

If, then, this suit had been instituted by the representative of Thomas

Muse, against the representative of Elliott Muse, the defendant could not, if the foregoing reasoning be just, have resisted the claim, by setting up the payment of the proper debts of his testator, but would have been liable, in like manner, as if the suit had been instituted by the legatees, or distributees of Thomas Muse, against the present defendants.

Is the defence the stronger, when made to a suit brought by the creditors? I think it is not.

The right of the creditors to bring the suit, cannot be questioned. It is every day's practice, and has not been controverted in this case. If the right to sue be admitted, and the act of assembly, as has been already shown, attaches the superior dignity it gives, to the debt, and not to the character of the plaintiff, it follows, that if the debt be still due, and its priority has not been lost by any act of the creditor, it is of superior dignity to any proper debt of Elliott Muse, and the assets, which have been disbursed in the payment of such debts, have been wasted, and must still be accounted for, by the representative of Elliott Muse.[5]

Printed, John W. Brockenbrough, *Reports of Cases Decided by the Honourable John Marshall...*, I (Philadelphia, 1837), 540–50.

1. *Revised Code of Va.*, I, 359.
2. Ibid., 375.
3. The note by William C. Williams, dated 13 Mar. 1813, was reproduced and discussed in JM's third and final opinion in this case (Coates v. Muse, Opinion, 18 Dec. 1823).
4. *Revised Code of Va.*, I, 389.
5. The court overruled Crittenden's motion and then amended its decree of 19 Dec. 1821 to make the administrator personally liable for the sum owed the creditor in case there were no assets of Elliott Muse's estate to pay the debt (U.S. Cir. Ct., Va., Ord. Bk. XI, 228).

Hopkirk v. Page
Opinion
U.S. Circuit Court, Virginia, 12 June 1822

The original plaintiffs in this equity suit, which was filed in the federal court sometime before 15 December 1817, were the executors of Joseph Hornsby and others. James Hopkirk, surviving partner of the British firm of Speirs, Bowman & Company, joined the suit in December 1819 as a creditor of the estate of William Byrd III, who had died heavily indebted during the Revolutionary war. Hopkirk's claim consisted of two bills of exchange drawn by Byrd in July 1774 and in November 1775, both of which were protested and not accepted for payment. William Byrd Page (ca. 1788–1828) of Frederick County, executor of Mary Byrd (William Byrd's widow and executrix), filed his answer in June 1820. Marshall delivered his opinion on 12 June 1822 (U.S. Cir. Ct., Va., Rec. Bk. XVI, 316, 363–76, 389, 398; Richmond *Enquirer*, 9 Sept. 1828; J. E. Norris, ed., *History of the Lower Shenandoah Valley* [Chicago, Ill., 1890], 570–71).

Hopkirk surviving partner &c

v

Page exrs. of Byrd

¶1   This suit is brought to obtain payment of two bills of exchange drawn by the late William Byrd of Virginia on Robert Cary & Co merchants of London, the one in the year 1774, & the other in 1775.[1] These bills were regularly protested; but the defendant makes several objections to paying them. The first to be considered is that no notice of their non payment & protest was given either to William Byrd in his life time, or to his representatives since his death.

¶2   The plf. contends that this notice was unnecessary because the drawer had no funds in the hands of the drawee.

¶3   Although this application, in consequence of the state of the fund to which the plaintiff must resort, it consisting of equitable assetts, is made to a court of equity, it is admitted to be a law case depending entirely on legal principles. It requires an attentive consideration of the question how far the want of funds of the drawer in the hands of the drawee discharges the holder of a bill of exchange from the necessity of giving notice to the drawer of its dishonor.

¶4   The rule requiring this notice was, for a long time, supposed to be general, and Mr. Justice Blackstone in his commentaries lays it down without any exception.[2] The first case in which an exception was admitted, is Bikerdike v Bollman decided in Novr. 1786, and reported in 1st. D & E. In that case the court stated that if it be proved by the holder that "from the time the bill was drawn till the time it became due, the drawee never had any effects of the drawer in his hands," notice to the drawer is not necessary. The reason given is that he had *no right to draw*, and *could not be injured* by not receiving notice. An additional observation made by one of the Judges is that to draw in such a case "is a fraud in itself."[3]

¶5   It does not appear from the report of this case, nor is there any reason to beleive that there were any running accounts between the parties. The whole complexion of the case, and the reasons assigned by the Judges for their opinions, negative this idea. It is simply the case of a debtor drawing a bill on his creditor without a prospect of its being paid. In such a case notice is declared by the court to be unnecessary.

¶6   It is remarkable that in this case altho' the principle is expressly asserted by both the Judges, each declares that the case would be decided in the same way on a different principle.

¶7   In Goodall & others v Dolly, decided in 1787, the judgement was against the holder of the bill for want of notice, but, in giving his opinion, Mr. Justice Buller recognizes the principle established in Bikerdike v Bollman.[4]

¶8   In Rogers v Stephens, 2 Term. 713. decided in 1788, the law is said to be settled that no effects of the drawer in the hands of the drawee excuses the holder from the necessity of giving notice.[5] Yet it is remarkable that, in this case, all three of the Judges rely very much on a subsequent assumpsit made by the drawer.

In Gale v Walsh 5 Term 239, decided in 1793, the principle appears to be recognized, but a rule to show cause why a new trial should not be granted for this cause, was discharged because the fact did not exist in the case.[6] ¶9

These are the earliest cases on this point. It has occurred very frequently in subsequent cases, and the principle seems to be firmly established, but, as the question has come forward in different forms & been viewed under different aspects, the principle has been greatly modified, and is no longer laid down in the general terms which were carelessly used on its introduction. It has been found necessary to define its extent with more precision, and to state the rule with more accuracy. It was percieved that in the course of commercial dealing, it would frequently occur that a person might draw a bill with the best reasons for beleiving that it would be honored, although, in fact, he might have, at the time, no funds in the hands of the drawee; and that all the reasons for requiring notice would apply in such a case, with the same force as if the bill had been drawn on actual funds. In Legge v Thorpe 12 East 177 Le Blanc & Bayley Justices stated the principle laid down in Bikerdike vs Bollman & afterward adhered to, in these terms; they said "That the court, in that case, looking to the reason for which notice was required to be given, laid down the rule, *not generally*, that where the drawer had no effects in the hands of the drawee at the time (which perhaps might turn out to be the case upon a future settlement of accounts between them) no notice of the dishonour should be given; but that it need not be given where the drawer *must have known* at the time that he had *no effects* to answer the bill, and *could* have no reason to expect that his bill would be honored."[7] ¶10

In Blackhan v Doren 2 Campbell 503 Lord Ellenborough said "If a man draw upon a house with whom he has no account, he knows that the bill will not be accepted, he can suffer no injury from want of notice of its dishonour, and therefore he is not entitled to such notice. But the case is quite otherwise where the drawer has a fluctuating balance in the hands of the drawee."[8] ¶11

In Walwyn v St Quintin 1. Bos. & Pul. 654, one of the strongest cases in the books in favor of dispensing with notice Eyre Ch. J. said "But it may be proper to caution bill holders not to rely on it as a general rule, that if the drawer has no effects in the acceptors hands notice is not necessary. The cases of acceptances on the faith of consignments from the drawer not come to hands, and the case of acceptances on the ground of fair mercantile agreements, may be stated as exceptions, and there may possibly be many others."[9] ¶12

In Brown & al v Maffey 15th. East Lord Ellenborough said "The doctrine of dispensing with notice of the dishonor of a bill has grown almost ¶13 entirely out of the case of Bikerdike v Bollman. That decision dispensed with notice to the drawer where he knew before hand that he had no effects in the hands of the drawee, and had no reason to expect that the bill would be paid when it became due. But that exception must be taken with some restrictions, which, since I sat here, I have often had occasion to put on it: as where the drawer, though he might not have effects at the time of the drawing of the bill in the drawees hands, has a running account with him, and there is a fluctuating balance between them, and the drawer has reasonable ground to expect that he shall have effects in the drawees hands when the bill becomes due. In such cases I have always held the drawer to be entitled to notice because he draws the bill upon a reasonable presumption that it will be honored."[10]

¶14   In Rucker & al v Hiller 16th. East 43. Lord Ellenborough said "Where the drawer draws his bill in the bona fide expectation of assetts in the hands of the drawee to answer it, it would be carrying the case of Biker-dike v Bollman farther than has ever been done, if he were not at all events entitled to notice of the dishonor. And I know the opinion of my Lord Chancellor to be that the doctrine of that case ought not to be pushed farther. The case is very different where the party knows that he has no right to draw the bill. There are many occasions where a drawee may be justified in refusing from motives of prudence to accept a bill, on which notice ought nevertheless to be given to the drawer; and if we were to extend the exception farther, it would come at last to a general dispen-sation with notice of the dishonor in all cases where the drawee had not assetts in hand at the very time of presenting the bill; and thus get rid of the general rule requiring notice, than which nothing is more conve-nient in the commercial world. A bona fide reasonable expectation of assetts in the hands of the drawee has been several times held to be sufficient to entitle the drawer to notice of the dishonour, though such expectation may ultimately fail to be realized." And in the same case Bayley J. said "The general rule requires notice of the dishonour to be given in due time to the drawer; and it lay upon the plaintiffs to show that he could not possibly be injured by the want of it. It would be somewhat hard to call upon the drawer towards the end of six years after the bill given; and when he objected that he had no notice of the dishonour, to tell him that he had no effects in the drawees hands at the time when the bill was presented, though they might have come to his hands the very day after, and the drawer might have settled his accounts with the drawee on the presumption that the bill was paid.["][11]

¶15   This subject was considered by the Supreme court of the United States in the case of French v The Bank of Columbia reported in 4th. Cranch. In that case it was said "to be the fair construction of the English cases that a person having a *right to draw* in consequence of engagements between himself & the drawee, or in consequence of consignments made to the drawee, or from any other cause, ought to be considered as drawing upon funds in the hands of the drawee, and therefore as not coming within the exception to the general rule."[12]

Where the drawer is continually making consignments to the drawee, ¶16 and continually drawing on those consignments, his conduct may be essentially affected by knowing that any of his bills have been protested. He may stop *in transitu*, or he may suspend farther consignments. It may be as material to his interest to place no more funds in the hands of the drawee in such a case, as to withdraw the funds previously placed in his hands. Notice may be as important to him in the one case as in the other, and there seems to be the same reason for requiring it.

Supposing the rule to be that every person having *a right to draw*, or ¶17 having reason to believe that his bill will be honored, is entitled to notice. I will proceed to apply the principle to the facts of this case; and in doing so, I shall consider the two bills separately.

On the 19th. of July 1774 William Byrd drew on Robert Cary & Co. in ¶18 favor of Edward Brisbane for the sum of £353.6. This bill was indorsed by Edward Brisbane to Alexande[r] Speirs & by him to the company. On the 26th. day of November 1774 it was protested for non payment.[13] The first information that appears to have been given of this protest to Colonel Byrd or his representatives was the institution of this suit in 1819. The exr. of Byrd resists its payment for the want of notice; and the plaintiff alleges that notice was unnecessary because the drawer had no effects at the time in the hands of the drawee. To support this allegation he relies on several letters written by Robert Cary & Co to William Byrd which have [been] exhibited by the exr. on his requisition.

The defendant objects to this testimony that the letters are the meer ¶19 allegations of Robert Cary & Co. & do not contain a full statement of the correspondence between the parties, or of their accounts: that Colo. Byrd may not have acquiesced in the accounts transmitted with these letters or in the statements they contain, although from the loss of papers, the death of parties, & the great lapse of time, the letters containing his objections cannot now be produced.

The general rule is that a long acquiescence in letters containing accounts is prima facie evidence of an acquiescence in their contents; and ¶20 there is the less reason for excepting this case from the rule because the letters of R. C. & Co. from Novr. 73 to Oct. 75 do not notice any objection on the part of W. B. to any of the accounts which one of those letters says was annually transmitted to him.

The letter from R. C. & Co to W. B. dated the 10th. of Novr. 73 encloses ¶21 an account current showing a balance due R. C. & Co. of £616.9.5. This letter gives notice of the completion of a contract for the sale of Byrd's english estate, says the money is to be paid the 5th. of april, that they shall immediately afterwards take up the whole of his bills, & say that they have referred Farrell & Jones to him to determine whether they s[h]all pay a debt of about £800 claimed by F & Js.[14]

¶22   The next letter is dated the 13th. of May 1774. It states the receipt of 5000£ on account of the estate which had been sold & the expectation of receiving the farther sum of £11500 on the same account. It states the payment of debts to the amount of £5544.7.4. & gives a list of other debts due from B to the amount of £11577. The letter concludes with saying that by Greenlands estimate the produce of the estate will not exceed £15500 out of which great charges are to be deducted. From this sketch, the letter proceeds "you will be able to judge how the account may stand & what bills must be returned."[15]

¶23   It is observable that among the debts paid are several bills of exchange which had been long protested, one of them as early as feby. 68. This fact shows an understanding by which bills were held up after protest in the expectation that they would be paid by the drawee notwithstanding the protest. In such a case, if no notice be given the law seems to be that the holder looks to the drawee, not to the drawer, for payment.

¶24   The next letter of the 5th. of Aug. 74 states that there are many bills which must be returned after paying all the money received on account of the English estate. This letter speaks of a farther sum for a half years rent accruing before the purchaser took possession to be received after Michael Mass. This would be £371.4.6. There is too a subsequent letter of the 14th. of March 75 which mentions a farther receipt of £448.12.1 on account of the english estate.[16]

¶25   Colonel Byrd appears to have drawn to the full amount of his English estate; so far as R. C. & Co. had stated the money to have been received; and if the transactions between the parties had gone no farther, these letters would furnish strong reasons for the opinion that in July 1774 he acted at least incautiously in drawing the bill under consideration. But there were other transactions between the parties. Colo. Byrd held a large estate in Virginia; and the usage of the considerable planters to ship their tobacco to London merchants & to draw on their consignments, is of general notoriety. In their letter of 17th. of Novr. 1774 R. C. & Co say "We shall in the disposal of your tobacco hope to render you a safe & pleasing tale."[17]

¶26   In a letter of the 10th. of Feby. 1775 is an account of sales of 15 hoxheads of tobo. shipped in a vessel commanded by Capt. Power; and there is also notice taken of a mortgage on the estate sold to Mrs. Otway, for which no claimant had appeared, but for which Mrs. Otway had retained a considerable sum in her hands. The letter says "we were compelled to settle the conveyance in the manner we did, yet at the same time it no ways precluded you from recovering your part of this other mortgage if no claimants." The letter shows that Colo. Byrd had written on this subject & had manifested the expectation of receiving a farther sum on this account. The letter also mentions the payment of some small orders given by Byrd.[18]

It may be considered as probable from these letters that Colo. Byrd was ¶27
not perfectly satisfied with the sums retained on account of charges on
the estate, & expected more money from it.

A letter of the 20th. of June 1775 states the payment of a draft drawn by ¶28
Colo. Byrd in favor of Hornsby for £75 & their payment for his honour of
another draft on Farrell & Jones for the same sum.[19]

The last letter is dated the 2d. of october 75. It mentions the payment ¶29
of several little drafts as desired by Colo. Byrd "which are mentioned in
an account current inclosed["] but the account itself does not appear. It
shows a balance as the letter says of £0.16.11 in favor of Colo. Byrd.[20]

From this review of the letters in the cause, it is obvious that Colo. Byrd ¶30
was much pressed for money, that he was sanguine in his calculations of
the sums to be y[i]elded by his estate in England, that he drew upon that
fund by anticipation, and to an amount greater perhaps than was strictly
justifiable. It is also apparent that a considerable part of the money for
which the estate sold, was retained for incumbrances, some of which were
questionable, and there is reason to beleive that he questioned them. It is
also apparent that there were running transactions between the parties;
and that the holders of his bills were in the habit of retaining them, & of
receiving payment long after protest. That he made shipments of tobacco
in the time is unquestionable, but the amount of his shipments is uncertain. His letters are not produced. They would throw much light on this
transaction. The letter giving notice of this particular draft might, &
probably would, show the idea on which it was drawn, & the calculations
of the drawee. It might be drawn on an actual consignment of tobacco, or
it might be drawn on a calculation that some thing farther might be
yielded by those items of the English estate which the letters show had not
been finally adjusted. These calculations may have been erroneous; but if
they were made, the bill was not drawn with a knowledge that it would not
be honored, and therefore notice of its dishonor was necessary.

The court will not presume that these calculations were made; the ¶31
court will not presume that the letter of advice which usually accompanies a bill of exchange, did show that the drawer calculated on his bills
being honored; but the court cannot presume the contrary; and it is to be
recollected that when a protested bill is held up for a great length of time
without notice, the whole *onus probandi* is thrown on the holder. He must
prove every thing; and nothing is required from the drawer.

The case furnishes strong reason for the opinion that this bill was not ¶32
returned to Virginia but was held up by Speirs Bowman & Co. in the
expectation of its being paid by R. C. & Co. It was drawn on the 19th. of
July 1774 & protested for non payment on the 26th. day of November of
the same year. Another bill for £213.15. drawn on the 4th. of July 1774 in
favor of Speirs Bowman & Co. & protested on the 9th. of Novr. 74 was
returned to Colonel Byrd & was taken up. These bills drawn by the same

person, & held by the same house, at the same time, would probably have been returned by the same vessel, had they been both returned. The circumstance that one was drawn in favor of Spiers Bowman & Co. & the other in favor of Brisbane an agent of the company & indorsed by him to a member of the co. & by that member to the co. would not account for the appearance of one bill without the other, if both were returned. They were both the property of the same company, both due by the same person, both in possession of the company at the same time, and would probably have been both returned, if they were both returned, by the same vessel. The bill said not to be originally drawn in favor of the S. B. & Co. would probably have been transmitted to the same agent to whom the other bill was transmitted. The appearance of the one bill without the other is then a strong circumstance in favor of the opinion that the bill retained was held up in England in the expectation of its being paid by the drawee. In estimating the probabilities of the circumstances & prospects under which the bill was drawn, this fact is entitled to some consideration.

¶33   We have no regular accounts, we have no statements of the consignments made by Byrd to R. C. & co. We know that their connexion was of long standing, that there was a considerable degree of mutual kindness & confidence, that Byrd was in the habit of shipping tobacco to R. C. & Co. that there may have been a shipment at the very time this bill was drawn, that money was paid for Byrd by R. C. & Co. after this bill was protested, that a bill of £75 was taken up for his honor, and that in october 1775 the balance of £616.9.5 which stood against him in Novr. 1773 was converted into a balance of 0.16.11 in his favor. We have not all the intermediate accounts & we do not know how this balance may have fluctuated. Add to this that the bill is not said to have been protested for want of effects.

¶34   Under all these circumstances I cannot say that this bill was drawn with a knowledge that it would be protested; & that notice of the protest could not be necessary. I cannot say that it was a fraud upon the payee by giving him a bill which the drawer knew would not be paid.

¶35   If the *onus probandi* lay on the drawer of the bill, the case would be clearly against him; but, as it lies entirely on the holder, whose laches[21] are without a precedent in a court of law or equity, I think he has not made out a case of complete justification, on which he can entitle himself to a decree for the bill drawn on the 19th. of July 1774.

¶36   The second bill was drawn on the 26th. of Novr. 75 for £246.3.7. & protested on the 26th. day of June 1776.[22] It was drawn after the commencement of hostilities in Virginia; & before it was protested, all intercourse between the two countries was interdicted. Under these circumstances notice is not to be expected & ought not to be required. I, at first, doubted whether a bill which, for a great length of time is held under circumstances which dispense with notice does not lose its commercial character & become an ordinary debt. But on reflection I am satisfied that this idea cannot be sustained; and that, to charge the drawer, notice of the dishonour of his bill ought to be given within a reasonable time after the removal of the impediment. The question therefore on this bill also is, were the circumstances under which it was drawn such as to dispense with notice? Was it drawn without reasonable ground for an expectation that it would be paid?

It may reasonably be supposed that on the 26th. of November, the letter of the 2d. of October, which came by the last packet to New York, was received. In attempting to show that notice of the dishonour of this bill was unnecessary because the drawer had no effects in the hands of the drawee, the holder is met *in limine*[23] by the fact that this letter shows a balance in his favor of £0.16.11; and the exception under which the plf. withdraws himself from the general rule is that the drawer had at the time *no* effects in the hands of the drawee. If we may depart from the letter of the exception, there is no point at which to stop; and if notice may be dispensed with when a small sum is in the hands of the drawee, it may also be dispensed with when a large sum is in his hands, provided that sum be one cent less than the bill is drawn for. ¶37

I am aware of this argument but think it more perplexing than convincing. There are many questions in which no precise line can be marked, which must depend on sound legal discretion, and where the case itself must be decided by a jury, or by the court acting on the principles which ought to regulate a jury. The sound sense and justice of the exception is that where a drawer knows he has no right to draw, and has the strongest reason to beleive his bill will not be paid, the motives for requiring notice of its dishonour do not exist, & his case comes within the reason of the exception. Where all transactions between parties have ceased, and there is nothing to justify a draft but a balance of one penny, it would be sporting with our understanding to tell us that a creditor for this balance who should draw for £1000, would be in a situation substantially different from what he would be in, were he the debtor in the same sum. The true enquiry appears to me to be whether the connexion between W. B. & R. C. & Co remained such as to justify a hope that his bill would be honored, and to afford any shadow of justification for drawing it. ¶38

I think it as demonstrable as any proposition of this sort can be that he knew this bill would not be paid. ¶39

He had no funds in the hands of the drawee except £0.16.11 and no prospect of having any. He had made no shipment of tobacco by the last vessel & R. C. & Co. speak of the fact with some resentment. In their letter of June 75, they had mentioned sending a vessel to Virginia chartered at a high price, in which they expected consignments of tobo. from their friends & among others from Colo. Byrd. In their letter of the 2d. of October they say "When Power came in we were in hopes you would have afforded him some assistance, but we observe the high price in the country was the cause of the disappointment and no compliment to our charter. However if we are no losers, we are not beholding to our friends for it.["] ¶40

¶41   With respect to the Mortgage for which it had been supposed that the mortgagee was dead without a representative, he says "it is feared the representative is found but be this as it may["] he adds, the estate will be always liable "and therefore without a proper indemnity little can be expected. What indemnity you may offer we know not, but we shall not engage for our own parts." After mentioning the payment of some bills they add "but for paying any more or raising money on the uncertainty of the mortgage, we shall not attempt.["]

¶42   With this letter before him, Colonel Byrd must have drawn, I think, with a moral certainty that his bill would be dishonored: and if in any case a holder can be excused for not giving notice, this is that case. There was an end of all consignments, of all intercourse between the parties; there were no funds to withdraw, & no remittances to stop. The want of notice could be no injury to him. This case seems to me to come within the exception of Bikerdike & Bollman as modified in the subsequent cases.

¶43   This brings me to the consideration of the other objections made by the defendant to the payment of this bill.

¶44   He contends that after such a lapse of time payment must be presumed.

¶45   Admitting the doctrine of presumption to be the same in respect of a bill as of an instrument under seal, of which I am not confident, still it is not a positive rule depending absolutely like the statute of limitations, on length of time; but is the meer creature of reason, resting on probabilities. The creditor may meet this presumption & rebut it by accounting for the time which has been permitted to elapse and by showing the improbability that his debt has been paid.

¶46   He has I think met & completely rebutted it in this case. The bill was protested in England on the 26th. of June 1776 & Colo. Byrd died in 1777 or 1778. In the meantime war raged between the two countries; all intercourse between them was unlawful; and Colo. Byrds circumstances were too much embarassed to admit of a suspicion that he would be eager in his search for those creditors who could make no legal demand upon him. It is then almost certain that this debt was not paid by him in his life time.

¶47   The chief argument in support of this presumption is founded on the time which has elapsed since his death without any demand on his representatives. The plaintiff ascribes this to the insolvency of his estate; but to this it is answered that a suit has been brought in 1803 for a different claim by the same agent who was in possession of these bills. A bill was then filed claiming £70.19.10 as a debt due from W. B. & Co for dealings at their store in Manchester, and £15.9.6½ a debt due from W. B. for dealings at their store in Petersburg.[24] If the insolvency of the estate did not prevent this suit, it cannot have prevented a suit on the bills.

¶48   The plaintiff assigns two reasons for this suit by which he attempts to repel the inference which has been drawn from it. One is that though W. B. was supposed to be insolvent, W. B. & Co were not so. The other, that this suit was only preparatory to an application to the British commissioners sitting under the treaty of 1802.[25]

Neither of these reasons is satisfactory. The suit does not seek for satisfaction from the effects of W. B. & Co, nor does it even charge that W. B. was the surviving partner of that Co. or even had any of its property in his hands. It charges him meerly as a member of the company & seeks for satisfaction out of his private estate which is alleged to be in the hands of his exx. or of his trustees. But this reason, were it more consistent with the fact would not apply to the claim against him as an individual. ¶49

To account for this we are told that it was necessary to establish the debt in order to justify an application to the British commissioners. But surely it was not less necessary to establish the claim on this bill than on an open account. The production in 1804 or afterwards of a protested bill without notice to the drawer of its dishonor, or proof of a single attempt to obtain payment of it could never be received by the commissioners as a valid claim on the British government. ¶50

But if these bills were held up in order to be laid before the commissioners why were they not laid before that board? Is not the fact that no application has ever been made on them to the commissioners a proof that this is not the cause which prevented the institution of suits on them in this country? ¶51

If it be said that they have been laid before the commissioners, I ask what has been the fate of the application? Has it been rejected in consequence of the laches of the holder, or has it been successful? ¶52

But there is no reason to beleive that the suit in 1803 was brought with any other view than to recover the money it demanded, and the question recurs, why were not these bills put in suit also? ¶53

It has been said that they were overlooked by the agent. ¶54

But this is not credible. There is an indorsement on the envelope which contained them in his handwriting; and it must be supposed that bonds bills & notes were not thrown in confusion among general books & papers but were carefully preserved & listed, & that they would be immediately inspected by the agent to whom their collection was confided. ¶55

Must it then be presumed that the agent beleived them to be paid? ¶56

The reasons against this presumption so far as respects a payment made by Colo. Byrd have already been stated. The reasons against their having been paid by his representatives are still stronger. Their accounts are all preserved and this credit is not claimed. ¶57

How could the agent have received an impression that they were paid? He must have received it from the papers themselves, from the entries on the books, or from direct communication made by S. B. & Co. ¶58

But the papers contain no indications of payment. The books I am told contain none. And is it reasonable to suppose that the plaintiff would send the bills to be collected & write to the agent that nothing was due on them? We must impute negligence to the agent or beleive that he was of ¶59 opinion that the debt was not recoverable at law. The last opinion however does not necessarily imply his conviction that it had been paid. The bills were not accompanied with any proof of notice, and he could obtain none. Without this proof, & without any evidence that the drawer had no right to draw, he might have thought the claim desperate; but this does not create a presumption that he beleived it to be paid.

¶60   I think, on a consideration of the circumstances of the case, that the presumption of payment is completely rebutted.

¶61   I am next to consider an objection which goes to the right of the plaintiff to sustain this action, even admitting that the right to bring it exists in some person.

¶62   In 1813, a contract was entered into between the plaintiff and W. C. W. a citizen of Virginia by which the former conveyed to the latter all his debts in this country & authorized him to sue for them either in his own name or in the name of the present plaintiff.[26] It is contended that these bills passed by this assignment; and that, the whole legal & equitable interest being in another, no suit on them can be maintained by the plaintiff.

¶63   On the part of the plf. it is answered that this instrument, being made *flagrante bello*, is void, and that no action can be sustained on it even after peace.

¶64   As this may possibly become a question between the parties to the instrument I would not give an opinion on it unless it should be necessary in this cause. I am rather disposed to think it is not necessary.

¶65   Bills of exchange are transferrable, not by force of any statute, but by the custom of merchants. Their transfer is regulated by usage, and that usage is founded in convenience. It appears to me that it would be extremely inconvenient to separate the evidence of ownership from the bill itself, and I think there is no usage to justify such separation. Nothing can be more anticommercial than the idea of transferring a negotiable paper by a deed transferring a vast number of bills, bonds, notes, & accounts. Such an instrument may very properly be considered as conveying the equitable interest, the right to receive the money, but cannot be considered as a negotiation of the bill upon mercantile principles, or according to mercantile usage, so as to authorize the holder to sue in his own name. The books treat of no such mode of transfer. The person to whom a bill is transferred is never denominated an assignee. He is always termed an indorsee. Upon this ground I am of opinion that in this case a suit could not be maintained in the name of W. C. W. Were this even doubtful, the instrument now relied on contains an authority to sue in the name of the plaintiff & may therefore fairly be considered as not being intended to have the legal effect of an assignment but to operate as an agreement authorizing W. C. W. to exercise all the powers of ownership in the name of the plf. But I rely on the principle that a bill of exchange is not by the custom of merchants transferrable by such an instrument as is produced in this case.

But the defendant contends that admitting the suit to be maintainable ¶66
in the name of the plaintiff still W. C. W. ought to be a party, because in a
court of equity all persons concerned in interest must be parties.

I do not think the rule applies to such a case as this. ¶67

All persons having distinct interests must undoubtedly be brought be- ¶68
fore the court; but where the interest of one person is involved in that of
another, and that other possesses the legal right so that the interest may
be asserted in his name it is not I think always necessary to bring both
before the court.

Thus a trustee may sue without naming cestui que trust as a party; an ¶69
exr. or Admr. may sue without naming legatees, or distributees. And the
obligee in a bond where it is not by law assignable may sue, or the equitable
assignee may sue in his name without being named himself as a party. This
may I think be done in a court of equity as well as a court of law. The person
having the equitable interest, if the suit be not really brought for his
benefit, may insist on being made a party, & the court will direct it; but I do
not think the omission of persons in this situation any objection to the suit.

Had this suit been brought by W. C. W. Hopkirk must have been made ¶70
a part[y], but I do not think W. C. W. a necessary party to a suit in the
name of Hopkirk.

I am of opinion that the plf. is entitled to a decree for £246.3.7 sterling ¶71
with interest thereon at the rate of ten per centum per annum for eighteen months, and with interest on the whole sum at the rate of five per
centum per annum either from the expiration of 18 months, or from the
time that this claim was asserted in court, according to the manner in
which the act in the revisal of 1748 which regulates this transaction has
been construed.[27] I shall give the five percent only from the assertion of
the demand in court unless by a reference to the records of the general
or district court it can be shown that the law has been expounded to allow
interest from the expiration of the 18 months.

AD, Marshall Judicial Opinions, PPAmP; printed, John W. Brockenbrough, *Reports of
Cases Decided by the Honourable John Marshall . . .*, II (Philadelphia, 1837), 23–42. For JM's
deletions and interlineations, see Textual Notes below.

1. The first bill had been endorsed to Speirs, Bowman & Co.; the second had been drawn
in the company's favor. On this Glasgow firm, see *PJM*, VII, 325–26.

2. Blackstone, *Commentaries*, II, 469.

3. Bickerdike v. Bollman, 1 T.R. 405, 410, 99 Eng. Rep. 1164, 1167 (K.B., 1786). "D & E"
stands for Durnford and East, the reporters of Term Reports.

4. Goodall v. Dolley, 1 T.R. 712, 714, 99 Eng. Rep. 1336, 1337 (K.B., 1787).

5. Rogers v. Stephens, 2 T.R. 713, 100 Eng. Rep. 384 (K.B., 1788).

6. Gale v. Walsh, 5 T.R. 239, 101 Eng. Rep. 134 (K.B., 1793).

7. Legge v. Thorpe, 12 East 171, 177, 104 Eng. Rep. 68, 70 (K.B., 1810). JM quoted from
Judge Le Blanc's opinion. Judge Bayley used similar language.

8. Blackhan v. Doren, 2 Camp. 503, 504, 170 Eng. Rep. 1232 (N.P., 1810).

9. Walwyn v. St. Quintin, 1 Bos. & Pul. 652, 655, 126 Eng. Rep. 1115, 1117 (C.P., 1797).

10. Brown v. Maffey, 15 East 216, 221, 104 Eng. Rep. 826, 828 (K.B., 1812).

11. Rucker v. Hiller, 16 East 43, 44–45, 104 Eng. Rep. 1005–6 (K.B., 1812).

12. French v. Bank of Columbia, 4 Cranch 141, 156 (1807). JM's opinion for the Court cited many of the English cases discussed in the present opinion.

13. Copy of the bill of exchange and protest (U.S. Cir. Ct., Va., Rec. Bk. XVI, 406–7).

14. Robert Cary & Co. to William Byrd, 10 Nov. 1773 (ibid., 411–12). On the Bristol firm of Farell & Jones, see *PJM*, V, 264–65.

15. Letter of 13 May 1774 (U.S. Cir. Ct., Va., Rec. Bk. XVI, 412–14).

16. Letters of 5 Aug. 1774 and 14 Mar. 1775 (ibid., 417, 425).

17. Letter of 17 Nov. 1774 (ibid., 419–20). The record book copy of the letter has "sale" instead of "tale."

18. Letter of 10 Feb. 1775 (ibid., 421–22).

19. Letter of 20 June 1775 (ibid., 426).

20. Letter of 2 Oct. 1775 (ibid., 427).

21. A legal term for neglect or failure to assert a right or claim.

22. Copy of the bill and protest (U.S. Cir. Ct., Va., Rec. Bk. XVI, 408–9).

23. At very beginning.

24. The suit mentioned Page's answer had been brought in the U.S. Circuit Court and was dismissed by agreement of the parties at the May 1805 term (U.S. Cir. Ct., Va., Rec. Bk. XVI, 372; U.S. Cir. Ct., Va., Ord. Bk. V, 94).

25. JM referred to the Convention of 1802 by which the U.S. agreed to make a lump sum payment of £600,000 sterling to Great Britain in satisfaction of debts owed by American citizens to British subjects (John Bassett Moore, *International Adjudications*, III [New York, 1931], 349–56).

26. A contract appointing William C. Williams, a Richmond lawyer, as agent to collect the debts of Speirs, Bowman & Co., was dated 15 Sept. 1813 (U.S. Cir. Ct., Va., Rec. Bk. XVI, 462–64).

27. An act for "ascertaining the damage upon protested bills of exchange" (Hening, *Statutes*, VI, 85–87).

Textual Notes

¶ 1	l. 3	& ↑the other↓ in 1775.
	l. 4	the ~~defendants~~ ↑defendant↓ makes
	l. 5	of [*erasure*] ↑their↓ non
¶ 3	l. 5	funds [*erasure*] ↑of↓ the
¶ 4	l. 1 beg.	The rule ~~that this~~ ↑requiring↓ this
	l. 4	Bollman ↑decided in Novr. 1786, and↓ reported
	ll. 6–7	drawee [*erasure*] never
	l. 9	by ~~th~~ ↑not↓ receiving notice. ~~The rea~~ An
	l. 10	that " to
¶ 5	l. 5	prospect ~~that it would be~~ ↑of its being↓ paid.
¶ 6	l. 2	Judges, ~~they both~~ ↑each↓ declares
¶ 7	ll. 1–2	Dolly, ↑decided in 1787,↓ the judgement was ~~in favor of the~~ ↑against the↓ holder
	l. 3	Buller [*erasure*] ↑recognizes↓ the
¶ 8	l. 1	decided [*erasure*] ↑in↓ 1788,
¶ 9	l. 1	239, [*erasure*] ↑decided↓ in 1793,
¶10	ll. 5–6	were ↑carelessly↓ used
	l. 11	that [*erasure*] ↑all↓ the reasons
	l. 13	funds. ~~In Blackhan v Doran 2. Camp. 503 Lord Ellenborough said "If a man draw upon a house with whom he has no account, he knows that the bill will not be accepted.~~ In

l. 14   Bikerdike ↑vs↓ Bollman
l. 15   to, [*erasure*] ↑in↓ these
ll. 15–16   in ~~Bikerdike~~ that case,
¶12 l. 1 beg.   In ~~th~~ ↑Walwyn↓ v St Quintin
¶13 l. 5   the ~~drawer~~ ↑drawee,↓ and had
¶14 l. 8   occasions where ~~the~~ ↑a↓ drawee
l. 19   Bayley [*erasure*] ↑J.↓ said
l. 26   the ~~draw~~ drawee
¶15 ll. 1–2   States ~~in the case~~ in
l. 3   fair ↑construction↓ of the
¶16 l. 3   that ↑any of↓ his
ll. 4–5   may ↑be↓ as ~~materially~~ ↑material↓ to
ll. 6–7   placed in ~~the~~ ↑his↓ hands. ~~of the drawee~~ Notice may be as ~~ess~~
                 important
¶18 l. 4   protested ↑for non payment.↓ The first
l. 11   exr. on ~~the~~ ↑his↓ requisition.
¶20 l. 2   is ↑prima facie evidence of↓ an
¶21 l. 3   the ↑completion of a contract for the↓ sale
¶22 l. 3   farther [*erasure*] ↑sum↓ of
¶23 l. 5   case, ↑if no notice be given↓ the law
¶24 l. 2   money ↑received↓ on account
¶25 ll. 2–3   estate; ↑so far as R. C. & Co. had stated the money to have
                 been received;↓ and
l. 4   in ~~Novr.~~ ↑July↓ 1774
l. 8   merchants ↑& to draw on their consignments,↓ is
¶26 l. 1 beg.   In ~~th~~ ↑a↓ letter
l. 2   shipped ~~by P~~ ↑in a↓ vessel
l. 4   which ~~the~~ ↑no↓ claimant
¶27 l. 3   expected ↑more money from it,↓
¶28 l. 2   favor of [*erasure*] ↑Hornsby↓ for
¶29 l. 2   several ~~sums~~ ↑little↓ drafts
l. 2   Byrd ~~but these drafts themselves are not stated & speaks of~~
                 "which
¶30 l. 5   that ↑a considerable part of the↓ money
l. 11   is [*erasure*] ↑unquestionable,↓ but
l. 13   transaction. ~~The~~ The letter
l. 19   made, [*erasure*] ↑the↓ bill
l. 20   honored ↑, and therefore notice of its dishonor was
                 necessary.↓
¶32 l. 12   would ~~be no inducement~~ not
¶33 ll. 10–11   fluctuated. ↑Add to this that the bill is not said to have been
                 protested for want of effects.↓
¶35 l. 2   holder, ~~of the bill,~~ whose
¶36 ll. 1–2   £246.3.7. [*erasure*] ↑&↓ protested
¶37 ll. 6–7   the ↑plf.↓ ~~justifies~~ withdraws
l. 11   hands, ~~wh~~ ↑provided↓ that
¶38 l. 6   knows ~~his~~ ↑the↓ has no
l. 13   debtor [*erasure*] ↑in↓ the
l. 14   the ~~connect~~ ↑connexion↓ between

	l. 16	it. I think ↑I think↓ it
¶40	l. 4	of the June 75,
	l. 4	vessel chart to
¶41	l. 4	little is to ↑can↓ be
¶42	l. 2	bill wou would be
¶47	l. 4	1803 [*erasure*] ↑for↓ a different
¶48	l. 1	plaintiff attempts to assigns
	ll. 1–2	he repels ↑attempts to repel↓ the
¶49	l. 3	or had ↑even↓ had
	l. 7	claim for ↑against↓ him
¶50	l. 4	production ↑in 1804 or afterwards↓ of
¶51	ll. 2–3	no demand of application
¶60	l. 1	of these ↑the↓ circumstances ↑of the case,↓ that
¶61	l. 1	an objections ↑objection↓ which
¶62	ll. 5–6	legal ↑&↓ equitable↓ interest
¶63	ll. 2–3	on it ↑even↓ after peace.
¶64	l. 2	I [*erasure*] ↑would↓ not
¶65	l. 12	The bill person
	l. 13	denominated the ↑an↓ assignee.
	l. 20	not [*erasure*] ↑by↓ the
¶68	l. 1 beg.	All parties All persons
	ll. 4–5	bring [*erasure*] ↑both↓ before
¶69	l. 4	without naming being named ↑himself↓ as
¶71	l. 4	expiration [*erasure*] ↑of 18↓ months
	ll. 5–6	according [*erasure*] ↑to↓ the manner in ↑which↓ the

United States v. Mann
Opinion
U.S. Circuit Court, Virginia, 12 June 1822

In December 1820 the U.S. Circuit Court ordered William Mann, former deputy marshal of the Virginia district, to return an execution issued by the court in the case of U.S. v. Foushee and Ritchie. Mann was subsequently ordered to pay the money arising on the execution into the Richmond branch of the Bank of the United States. In January 1822 an attachment was issued against him for not paying the money—amounting to $1,700. The case was argued on 3 June 1822 by U.S. Attorney Robert Stanard and by Robert G. Scott (1791–1870) and Daniel Call, representing Mann. Marshall pronounced judgment on 12 June (U.S. Cir. Ct., Va., Ord. Bk. XI, 76, 87, 97, 164, 195, 214, 223, 229, 264; attachment, 10 Jan. 1822, U.S. v. Mann, Ended Cases [Unrestored], 1832, Vi; "Cases in the Courts of the United States, 25 February 1813-November 1824," No. 3, p. 156, Tucker-Coleman Papers, ViW; Thomas M. Owen, *History of Alabama and Dictionary of Alabama Biography*, IV [Chicago, 1921], 1511–12).

The United States
v
Mann

This is a motion on the part of the United States to commit William ¶1
Mann late deputy Marshal of this district on an attachment for not paying
over a sum of money levied by him on an execution issued from this court
on a judgement obtained by the United States; and a motion on the part
of the said Mann to discharge the said attachment because the United
States are indebted to him in a larger sum for fees due to him as deputy
Marshal which fees the treasury department has refused to pay.

The deputy Marshal has exhibited a long account for fees against the ¶2
United States, many items of which are substantiated beyond controversy.
His counsel contends that his account is clearly supported to an amount
exceeding the sum claimed by the United States. The court will not
enter into a minute examination of the particulars of this account, because should the principle be established in favor of allowing the credits
claimed, their amount may, in such a case as this, be the proper subject
for a reference to a commissioner; and, should this principle be rejected,
the examination will become useless.

Nothing can be more clear than the right of the officer to receive his ¶3
fees for services performed for the United States. In equity & justice, the
claim is founded on service actually rendered. This just & equitable claim
is recognized by the acts of Congress which regulate its [a]mount. The
law fixes the sum to which the marshal shall be entitled for those services
which the law requires him to perform, and makes no distinction between the suits of the United States and those of an individual. The
demand of the Marshal then on the United States for his fees of office, is
as clear both in law & equity, as his demand would be against any individual for whom the same services were performed. The United States have
not sought to discriminate in this respect between themselves & other
suitors. They have not required their officers to labour for the government gratuitously. The law acknowleges the obligation of the U.S. to pay
for services rendered, in common with all others for whom the same
services may be rendered.

The United States are not, it is true, subject to those coercive measures ¶4
which may be employed against an individual; but the duty is the same,
and the theory of the law is that this duty will be respected. Officers are
appointed for the liquidation of these claims, and appropriations are
made for their payment. The law is violated when these are disregarded.

The treasury department may certainly prescribe its own rules for the ¶5
adjustment of such claims; and those rules, if reasonable, will be respected. The dependent situation of the officers who claim, will, in general, secure their respect; and the desire for the preservation of that

harmony which ought to exist between the departments, will secure that of the court. But when these rules go to a total denial of justice, to an absolute refusal to allow a just & legal claim, a court cannot, if it has jurisdiction of the subject, disregard the rights of the party.

¶6   It may be convenient, and may conduce to the regularity of these accounts, to the course established for them in the proper department of the treasury, to require that the officer, in suits against public debtors, should receive his fees out of the money made by an execution. In the ordinary course of things, this may be reasonable, and the officers of the court acquiesce in it. But if the United States do not proceed to judgement, or if they do not place the execution in the hands of the officer; if they receive the money through a different channel, or make any arrangement by which the officer is deprived of all means by which his claim can be satisfied otherwise than by a direct resort to the treasury, on what principle can his application to the treasury be resisted? He has performed Services for the government for which the law entitles him to a certain remuneration, and gives the government a power to reimburse itself from the individual against whom a judgement for costs is rendered. The claim against the individual is in favor of the government, not of the officer. The government settles this claim, and either receives the fees of the officer or relinquishes them. On what pretext can the claim of the officer on the government be rejected?

¶7   The clearest principles of equity & of law require that it should not be rejected; and, if a court be permitted to take jurisdiction of the subject, it cannot be disregarded without disregarding also the soundest principles of law.

¶8   In an action brought by an individual against an officer for money made by an execution, the officer would we think be at liberty to show that the individual was indebted to him & would be at liberty to set off such debt. Were it doubtful whether such an off set would be allowable in every case, it cannot we think be doubted that it would be allowed in many cases. If, for example an officer had earned fees to a large amount from an individual, and were to stop the whole of them out of a particular execution, no court would over rule his claim.

¶9   If instead of an action, an attachment be resorted to the law, is we think the same. The duty of the officer is to bring the money into court; and should he fail to perform this duty, it is a contempt for which the court will attach him. But this attachment will not be enforced if he shows sufficient cause against it. It will not be enforced if he shows that he has paid the money to the plaintiff. Neither will it be enforced we think if he shows that he stands in relation to the plaintiff in the same situation as if he had paid to him the identical money made by the execution.

¶10   We will not now enquire into the course which ought to be pursued with an officer who speculates on the situation of a plaintiff, & procures the assignment of demands against him; but we think that a direct demand of the officer in his own right upon the plaintiff, for which he is entitled to an immediate satisfaction in money, clears the contempt, & ought to arrest the attachment. The argument is the stronger, if the creditor, from any cause, cannot be coerced to pay this demand.

These are principles which would govern in a case between individuals. ¶11 Their application to a case of the United States has been doubted. That doubt appears to us to be removed by the opinion of the Supreme court in the case of the United States against Wilkins reported in 6th. Wheaton. In that case the court, speaking of the discounts allowed by the act of the 3d. of March 1797 Ch. 74 in suits brought by the United States says "There being no limitation as to the nature & origin of the claim for a credit which may be set up in the suit we think it a reasonable construction of the act that it intended to allow the defendant the full benefit at the trial of any credit whether arising out of the particular transaction for which he was sued, or out of any distinct & independent transaction, which would constitute a legal or equitable set off, in whole or in part of the debt sued for by the United States."[1]

The attorney for the United States would withdraw the case at bar from ¶12 this opinion because it was given in a case of contract & in a suit regulated in some measure by the act of Congress which it expounds. But we think the opinion applies substantially to this case. On examining the act referred to, we percieve that it gives no right whatever to use any discount but regulates & restrains a right recognized as already existing. The words of the law are not that in such a suit the defendant shall be allowed to give equitable or legal discounts in evidence but that the cause shall be tried unless the defendant shall make oath "that he is equitably entitled to credits" &c and that "no claim for a credit shall be admitted upon trial but such as shall appear to have been presented to the accounting officers of the treasury" &c.[2]

These words apparently give no right whatever, but recognize a preexisting right. And if it was a preexisting right, it existed in other cases as ¶13 well as in those which were contemplated by this act.

The opinion of the supreme court then in the case of the United States ¶14 against Wilkins is we think expressly in point; and we are governed by it in this case. We think that Mr. Mann is entitled to sett off the fees earned by himself for which the U.S. are liable & that so far an attachment ought not to go against him. If there be any doubt respecting the amount, a commissioner must report upon it to the court.[3]

AD, Marshall Judicial Opinions, PPAmP; printed, John W. Brockenbrough, *Reports of Cases Decided by the Honourable John Marshall . . .* , II (Philadelphia, 1837), 9–13. For JM's deletions and interlineations, see Textual Notes below.

1. U.S. v. Wilkins, 6 Wheat. 135, 144 (1821). JM quoted Story's opinion for the Court.
2. This was the 1797 act concerning the settlement of accounts between the U.S. and receivers of public money (*U.S. Statutes at Large*, I, 514–15).

3. The court ordered the attachment to be suspended on Mann's depositing sum of $293 and court fees. In the meantime commissioners of the court were to state and report the claims of Mann against the U.S. The case remained on the docket another ten years pending completion of a final report on Mann's claims (U.S. Cir. Ct., Va., Ord. Bk. XI, 264; XII, 106, 402; U.S. Cir. Ct., Va., Index to Ended Causes, 1790–1860, Vi).

Textual Notes

¶ 2 l. 1	The ↑deputy↓ Marshal
l. 2	many ~~arti~~ ↑items↓ of
ll. 2–3	controversy. ~~The~~ ↑His↓ counsel
l. 7	claimed, ~~be established~~ their
¶ 5 l. 1 beg.	~~It is reasonable that~~ The
l. 2	of ~~those~~ ↑such↓ claims;
ll. 2–3	will [erasure] ↑be↓ respected.
l. 6	court. ~~W~~ ↑But↓ when
¶ 6 ll. 10–11	treasury, ↑on what principle can his application to the treasury be resisted?↓ He
ll. 13–14	reimburse [erasure] ↑itself↓ from
¶ 9 l. 1	be [erasure] ↑resorted↓ to
¶11 l. 5	court, ~~says~~ speaking
¶12 l. 2	given ~~under~~ in
ll. 4–5	case. ~~If~~ ↑On examining↓ the act referred to, ~~be examined,~~ we
¶13 l. 1 beg.	~~The last words which are quoted from~~ These

To James Monroe

Sir   Richmond June 13th. 1822

I have received the copy of your message to Congress on the subject of internal improvements which you did me the honor to transmit me, and thank you for it. I have read it with great attention and interest.[1]

This is a question which very much divides the opinions of inteligent men; and it is not to be expected that there will be an entire concurrence in that you have expressed. All however will I think admit that your views are profound, and that you have thought deeply on the subject. To me they appear to be most generally just.

A general power over internal improvement, if to be exercised by the Union, would certainly be cumbersome to the government, & of no utility to the people. But, to the extent you recommend, it would be productive of no mischief, and of great good. I despair however of the adoption of such a measure.[2] With great respect and esteem, I am Sir your Obedt

J MARSHALL

ALS, Monroe Papers, DLC. Addressed to the president and franked; postmarked Richmond, 13 June. Endorsed by Monroe.

1. On 4 May 1822 Monroe vetoed a bill for improving the Cumberland Road, which authorized the federal government to construct turnpikes and collect tolls. He accompanied his message with a lengthy pamphlet, "Views of the President of the United States on the subject of Internal Improvements." After exhaustively reviewing the arguments for and against, the president concluded that the Constitution did not vest Congress with a general power over internal improvements. He recommended a constitutional amendment as the best means to settle the question (Stanislaus Murray Hamilton, ed., *The Writings of James Monroe* [7 vols.; New York, 1898–1904], VI, 216–84).

2. In addition to JM, two other Supreme Court justices replied to Monroe's message. Story, like JM, was circumspect, refusing to express an opinion on the constitutional question, which might "come for discussion before the Supreme Court." Johnson, however, candidly expressed his nationalist views on this subject. Moreover, he couched his reply in the formal language of an advisory opinion, claiming that "his Brother Judges" had "instructed" him "to make the following Report."

According to Johnson, the justices could scarcely "conceal or disavow" their true opinion, which was that the decision in McCulloch v. Maryland "completely commits them on the subject of internal improvement, as applied to Postroads and Military Roads." He recommended that the president have the Court's opinion in the bank case "printed and dispersed through the Union." For accounts of this curious episode, see Charles Warren, *The Supreme Court in United States History* (2 vols.; Boston, 1926), I, 595–97; Donald G. Morgan, *Justice William Johnson, the First Dissenter* (Columbia, S.C., 1954), 122–24.

To Bushrod Washington

My dear Sir   Richmond June 17th. 1822

On the same day that I wrote to you a few hours after sending my letter to the post office I received yours marked the 26th. of May.[1] I must apologize if I can for having so long omitted to answer it.

When I read it I supposed it would require an attentive perusal of the record in the case of Reynolds & Wallers exrs.[2] to satisfy your enquiries and as I was then engaged in a very weighty cause & thought the term would not be of long continuance I put by the letter & postponed the enquiry to the close of the session. It was of much longer duration than I expected & at its termination which was on wednesday last I was charged with a long record containing several intricate points which I have just settled. As soon as this business was finished I went to the chancery office to attend to yours & was a little surprized at finding that I might have completed it at any time in five minutes.

There is no mistake in your report of the case. The chancellors decree does not contain the error for which it is reversed. After setting aside the contract & directing the restoration of the certificate with interest he adds "or if that certificate cannot be restored deliver to the plaintiff other certificates of the same kind and of equal value, with like interest." The chancellor makes no provision for the event of there being no other certificates of the same kind & of equal value, & therefore the court of appeals supposes that in that case the appellant must have paid the nominal amount in specie. But this inference is not drawn by the Chancellor, &

the fact was that there were other certificates of the same kind & of equal value in abundance. Had there been another court to which the cause might have been carried the chancellors decree woul⟨d I⟩ think have been affirmed.

I reproach myself for not having looked earlier into this case since your enquiry could have been so readily answered, & assure you that I feel at all times great pleasure in rendering you any service in my power.

I regret your indisposition & hope your health is by this time perfectly restored. With sincere & affectionate esteem, I am your

J MARSHALL

ALS, Marshall Papers, DLC. Addressed to Washington at Mount Vernon; postmarked Richmond, 18 June. Endorsed by Washington. MS torn where seal was broken.

1. Letter not found. JM had written to Washington on 28 May.
2. Reynolds v. Waller, a case originating in the Virginia High Court of Chancery and decided by the Court of Appeals in 1793, had been reported in the first edition of Washington's reports (1 Wash. 164). Washington was then revising his reports (see JM to Washington, 15 Apr. 1822 and n. 2).

To Bushrod Washington

My dear Sir   Richmond July 6th 1822

I have received your letter respecting the wine & beg you to take no farther trouble about it than to request Mr. Cazenove, if the wine comes by Alexandria, to send both pipes to me, & to direct the bills to be both presented to me.[1]

I am just returned from an excursion I am regularly under the necessity of making into the country with Mrs. Marshall to avoid the noisy festivities of the 4th. of July, & am looking over the letters.

Do you not think it advisable to copy the letters of interest to all persons not in the army, as well as to the governors &c of States? I scarcely think that the letters to the Governors alone will make two volumes. Should you have more copies taken, I wish you would suggest to the copyist that he plays the devil by beginning almost every word with a capital. I set out at first with my knife to erase the capitals & to substitute the modest small letters which belong to the words, but found the task so laborious that I would really prefer copying over the whole again. There is not a single s. scarcely even in the middle of a word which is not a capital — and there are very few K's E's B's Cs M's D's & W's, to say nothing of the others but what claim the same privilege. I know it was usual to employ these great letters in many instances where small ones are now written; but it never was usual to begin every word adjective as well as substantive in this manner, & if the General's letters appear so in the book, I am sure they must have been miscopied.

You have said nothing to me about any arrangement you may have made respecting the printing, nor about the 2d. ed. of the life &c, your

J MARSHALL

ALS, Miscellaneous Manuscripts, NHi. Addressed to Washington at Mount Vernon; postmarked Richmond, 10 July. Endorsed by Washington "to be ansd."

1. Letter not found. Antoine Charles Cazenove was an Alexandria merchant (*PJM*, VII, 245 and n. 6).

To James M. Marshall

My dear brother   Richmond July 9th. 1822
    I have searched the journals of the house of Delegates & find that the bill for confiscating the estate of Lord Fairfax passed that house in January 1786. It was lost in the Senate.[1] Whether it was negatived or lost meerely from the multiplicity of business, it being sent up at the close of the session, I am unable to say, as the journals of the senate are not here, but in the custody of Mr. Hansford, the Clerk, who resides in King George.[2] If you wish to make any enquiries into this subject, Charles Marshall will probably pass near Mr. Hansford on some visit to his Father in law & may make them for you.[3] The bill was sent up to the senate on the 11th. of Jany. 1786. I presume however your object cannot be effected as the bill passed the house of Delegates. The act of compromise itself is an act of disclaimer on the part of the State.[4]
    I have wished to impress on your son before the argument of this cause one consideration which appears to me to be of great weight.[5]
    Although Judge White will, of course, conform to the decision of the court of appeals against the appellate jurisdiction of the Supreme court, & therefore deny that the opinion in the case of Fairfax & Hunter is binding, yet he must admit that the supreme court is the proper tribunal for expounding the treaties of the United States, & that its deci[si]ons on a treaty are binding on the state courts, whether they possess the appellate jurisdiction or not.[6] Thus the exposition of a british court of an act of Parliament, or of any foreign court of a foreign edict, are considered as conclusive. No court in any case will controvert it. Thus the exposition of any state law by the courts of that state, are considered in the courts of all the other states, and in those of the United states, as a correct exposition, not to be reexamined. The only exception to this rule is where the statute of a state is supposed to violate the constitution of the United States, in which case the courts of the Union claim a controuling & supervising power. Thus any construction made by the courts of Virginia on the statute of descents or of distribution, or on any other subject, is admitted as conclusive in the federal courts, although those courts might have decided

differently on the statute itself. The principle is that the courts of every government are the proper tribunals for construing the legislative acts of that government. Upon this principle the Supreme court of the United States, independent of its appellate jurisdiction, is the proper tribunal for construing the laws & treaties of the United States; and the construction of that court ought to be received every where as the right construction.

The Supreme court of the United States has settled the construction of the treaty of peace to be that lands at that time held by British subjects were not escheatab[l]e or grantable by a state. The case of Hunter & Fairfax is very absurdly put on the treaty of 94 but other cases have put the same construction on the treaty of peace. I refer particularly to Smith v The State of Maryland 6th. Cranch[7] Jackson v Clarke 3 Wheaton[8] & Orr v Hodgson 4 Wheaton.[9] The last case is explicit & was decided unanimously, Judge Johnson assenting.[10] This being the construction of the highest court of the government which is a party to the treaty is to be considered by all the world as its true construction unless Great Britain, the other party, should controvert it. The court of appeals has not denied this principle. The dicta of Judge Roane respecting the treaty were anterior to this constitutional construction of it.[11]

I fear it will not be in my power to be at Happy creek before the 6th. of August. I shall probably reach Fauquier about that time. If I can get up sooner I will see you. I shall make another visit to Cumberland & purpose returning by Mr. Colstons.[12] It is not impossible that I may pass a night at Bath. I am my dear brother your affectionate

J MARSHALL

The effect of the principle I have stated is that we hold not under the compromise but under the treaty, and the question is what does the compromise take from us?

ALS, William Keeney Bixby Collection, MoSW. Addressed to James Marshall at "Happy creek / near Front Royal / Frederick County"; postmarked Richmond, 10 July.

1. This was the bill "for disposing of certain lands within the Northern Neck," which passed the House of Delegates on 11 Jan. 1786. The Senate rejected it on 16 Jan. (*Journal of the House of Delegates of the Commonwealth of Virginia [Oct. 1785]* [Richmond, Va., 1828], 137; *Journal of the Senate of the Commonwealth of Virginia [Oct. 1785]* [Richmond, Va., 1827], 6, 92). Concerning this bill, James Madison, a member of the House of Delegates at the time, remarked that it had been "brought in by Mr. [John Francis] Mercer for seizing & selling the deeded land of the late lord Fairfax on the ground of its being devized to aliens. . . ." Madison further noted that the bill "was opposed as exerting at least a legislative interference in and improper influence on the Judiciary question" but that "being of a popular cast," it passed the House "by a great majority. In the Senate it was rejected by a greater one, if not unanimously" (Madison to Thomas Jefferson, 22 Jan. 1786, in Robert A. Rutland et al., eds., *The Papers of James Madison*, VIII [Chicago, 1973], 478–79).

2. Theodosius Hansford (1768–1824) was clerk of the Virginia Senate from 1802 until his death (George Wesley Rogers, *Officers of the Senate of Virginia, 1776–1956* [Richmond, Va., 1959], 126).

3. Charles C. Marshall had recently married Judith Steptoe Ball of Lancaster County. Her father, William L. Ball, was then a member of Congress (Paxton, *Marshall Family*, 147–48).

4. On the compromise act of 1796, see Marshall and the Fairfax Litigation, Editorial Note, *PJM*, VIII, 108–21.

5. Thomas Marshall (1796–1826), oldest son of James M. Marshall, was then practicing law in Winchester. The case he was to argue before Judge Robert White of the Frederick County Superior Court of Law was evidently an ejectment involving the Fairfax title (Paxton, *Marshall Family*, 138–39).

6. Fairfax's Devisee v. Hunter's Lessee, 7 Cranch 603 (1813). The Virginia Court of Appeals refused to obey the Supreme Court's mandate in this case and denied that court's appellate jurisdiction over state courts. This decision, in turn, was reversed by the Supreme Court (Hunter v. Martin, 4 Munf. 1 [1815]; Martin v. Hunter's Lessee, 1 Wheat. 303 [1816]; *PJM*, VIII, 116–18).

7. Smith v. Maryland, 6 Cranch 286 (1810).

8. Jackson v. Clarke, 3 Wheat. 1 (1818).

9. Orr v. Hodgson, 4 Wheat. 453 (1819).

10. In his opinion for the Court, Justice Story declared that the sixth article of the peace treaty of 1783 completely protected titles of British subjects from forfeiture by escheat proceedings on account of alienage. Justice Johnson had dissented in Fairfax's Devisee v. Hunter's Lessee (4 Wheat. 459, 462–63 [1819]; 7 Cranch 628–32 [1813]).

11. JM referred to Judge Roane's opinion in Hunter v. Fairfax's Devisee, decided by the Virginia Court of Appeals in 1810 (1 Munf. 223–32).

12. Rawleigh Colston, JM's brother-in-law and business partner, resided at "Honeywood," near Martinsburg in Berkeley County (now W.Va.). The purpose of JM's trip to Cumberland, Md., is not known.

To Martin Marshall

My dear Nephew   Richmond Septr. 23d. 1822

I have received your letter of the 5th. removing the mistake under which I had been respecting my claim on Mr. Davies' estate.[1] I certainly had supposed from your former communication on the subject that all difficulty in the way of receiving the money was removed. This mistake is to be ascribed to another. I had taken it for granted that the suit was brought in the federal circuit court. The delay which you mention is I presume unavoidable, & I do not wish any application to the exrs. to make a payment which the laws do not require & which may probably be inconvenient to the estate. What I regard more than the delay is the state of your currency. I do not understand your law on the subject, but am apprehensive that when the payment is made, should it ever be made, it will not be in money, but in your worthless paper.[2] You will oblige me by letting me know how the claim stands & what is my prospect from it. I do not understand from your letter whether the judgement will be available or not; whether it binds the land or not; & if not, whether there is any prospect of its being satisfied out of the personal estate. If it cannot be so satisfied must a new suit be brought to charge the land, or is any proceeding to be founded on the present judgement in order to charge them? I am entirely unacquainted with the provisions made on this subject by your legislature.

If the personal estate will not pay the debt & a suit must be brought against the heirs to charge the real estate, would it not be advisable to bring that suit in the federal court? I submit the management of the business entirely to you & only suggest this for your con⟨si⟩deration.

I have mentioned to my sister Taylor what you say respecting her lands & she desires you to act according to your own judgement.

I am extremely sorry to hear of the death of my Nephew T. McClung.[3] I hope my sister and the rest of our friends are well.

William has had a dangerous attack but is recovering from it. He speaks of going this winter to the south.[4] Your Aunt wishes to be remembered & sa⟨ys⟩ she will be very glad to see you t⟨his⟩ winter. I am my dear Nephew your affectionate

J MARSHALL

ALS, ICN. Addressed to Martin Marshall in Washington, Mason County, Ky.; postmarked Richmond, 23 Sept.

1. Letter not found. "Davies" was probably the late Joseph Hamilton Daveiss (1774–1811), a Kentucky lawyer who had been prominently involved in sounding the alarm against the "Spanish Conspiracy" in 1806. Daveiss was the first husband of JM's sister Nancy (Paxton, *Marshall Family*, 78).

2. In Dec. 1820 the Kentucky legislature passed a law that property seized for debt payment could not be sold by the courts for less than three-fourths of its value, unless the plaintiff agreed to accept payment in Bank of Kentucky or Bank of the Commonwealth notes. Kentucky paper was worth only half of its face value by May 1822 (George Dangerfield, *The Awakening of American Nationalism, 1815–1828* [New York, 1965], 208; Arndt M. Stickles, *The Critical Court Struggle in Kentucky, 1819–1829* [Bloomington, Ind., 1929], 25–27; Sandra F. VanBurkleo, "Relief Crisis," in John E. Kleber et al., eds., *The Kentucky Encyclopedia* [Lexington, Ky., 1992], 762–63).

3. Thomas McClung (b. 1800?) was the son of William McClung and Susan Tarleton Marshall (Paxton, *Marshall Family*, 73).

4. Probably William Marshall, Martin Marshall's cousin (*PJM*, VIII, 155, 156 n. 4).

To St. George Tucker

Dear Sir   Richmond Novr. 23d. 1822

I received this morning your letter mentioning your indisposition which I always regret, but particularly now, because I am told that the parties are very urgent for a trial.[1] I am in hopes that your health will admit of your coming up early in the next week. If it should not, the cause must of course be continued.[2] With great esteem I am dear Sir, Your obedt

J MARSHALL

ALS, Tucker-Coleman Papers, ViW. Endorsed by Tucker.

1. Letter not found.

2. The case alluded to was evidently one in which JM could not sit. It may have been Taylor v. Priddy, which was tried by Tucker alone between 5 and 11 Dec. (U.S. Cir. Ct., Va., Ord. Bk. XI, 291–95).

To [Hugh Mercer?]

Dear Sir   Richmond Decr. 4th. 1822

Enclosed you will receive the papers you placed in my hands.[1] I am truely sorry for the trouble which has been given you in consequence of my supposing that I might have it in my power to save both trouble & expence to the families of two highly valued friends. I am dear Sir with great respect & esteem, Your Obedt

J MARSHALL

ALS, Clay Papers, DLC. Identity of recipient based on conjectural evidence (see n. 1).

1. The enclosures evidently concerned a friendly suit in chancery between the heirs of Cyrus Griffin and John Tayloe Griffin, arising from a devise in the will of Francis Peart of Woodford County, Ky. Mercer (1776–1853), a resident of Fredericksburg and son of the Revolutionary general of the same name, was married to a daughter of Cyrus Griffin. He had asked JM to arbitrate this dispute, no doubt to save the expense of a suit. As Mercer later wrote to Henry Clay, JM had been "very guarded & concise, in his reasons for declining to arbitrate the Business for us." Unable to settle the matter by arbitration, Mercer retained Henry Clay to bring suit in the U.S. Circuit Court for Kentucky. This suit eventually came to the Supreme Court in 1824 and was decided without argument at the 1826 term, JM giving the opinion of the Court (John F. Goolrick, *The Life of General Hugh Mercer* [New York, 1906], 106–7; Mercer to Clay, 11 Mar. 1823, in James F. Hopkins, ed., *The Papers of Henry Clay*, III [Lexington, Ky., 1963], 393–96; Walker v. Griffin's Heirs, App. Cas. No. 1251, U.S. Sup. Ct. Dockets; 11 Wheat. 375–80).

Pendleton v. United States
Opinion
U.S. Circuit Court, Virginia, 16 December 1822

Philip Pendleton was surety on a performance bond executed by Michael McKewan and Daniel Harragan as contractors to supply rations to troops stationed in Virginia and Maryland for the year 1802. In October 1822 the United States obtained a judgment in the U.S. District Court against Pendleton's executors, Philip C. Pendleton and David Hunter. The defendants tendered a bill of exceptions objecting to the court's admission of certain evidence, which was overruled by Judge Tucker. The case then came by writ of error to the circuit court. Marshall delivered his opinion on 16 December 1822 (proceedings in U.S. District Court [copy], 8 Apr. 1822, U.S. v. Pen-

dleton's Executors, U.S. Cir. Ct., Va., Ended Cases [Unrestored], 1824, Vi;
U.S. Cir. Ct., Va., Ord. Bk. XI, 296–97).

Pendleton &c exrs. of Pendleton
v
The United States

¶1   This is a writ of error to a judgement of the district court obtained by
the U.S. v The plfs. in error for the sum of $496.08 with interest from the
30th. of Septr. 1808.

¶2   Philip Pendleton, the testator of the plaintiffs, had become bound to
the U.S. as security for Michael McKewan & Daniel Harrigan who were
contractors to furnish rations to the troops in Virga. & Maryland for the
Ye⟨ar⟩ 1802. This suit is brought for the balance of monies unaccount⟨ed⟩
for, which was in their hands on the last day of Decr. of that year. The
breach assigned in the declaration is the non payment of $1159.89 ["]be-
ing the balance due from the said McKewan & Harragan on the 31st. day
of Decr. 1802."[1]

¶3   In support of this action the attorney for the United States offered in
evidence a certificate from the Treasury department certified by the
Comptroller on the 23d. day of October 1821[2] stating that, on a settlement of the accounts of Michael McKewan and Daniel Harrigan late
contractors for supplying the troops stationed in Maryland and Virginia
they are chargeable.

¶4   "To balance remaining in their hands for monies advanced from the
22d. of October 1801 to the 6th. of Jany. 1803 per report No. 15129
                                                    1159.89["]

The same paper contains the following credits
         on the 30th. of June 1808   230
         on the 30th. Septr. —   306   536
                                                        _____

         Leaving due to the United States $ 623.89

This paper was objected to by the counsel for the defendants & was
rejected by the court because it claimed a gross sum of $1159.89 for
monies advanced up to the 6th. of Jany. 1803 to McKewan & Harragan,
whereas the defendants were liable only for monies advanced up to the
last day of Decr. 1802.

¶5   The attorney for the United States then offered in evidence an affidavit
made by the defendant Philip Pendleton Decr. 1st. 1818 for the purpose
of obtaining a continuance in which he states among other things that
during the pendency of the suit & prior to the year 1810 he with the
other security in the bond caused sundry payments to be made to an
amount about equal to the sum stated to be due after deducting there-

from a sum of $392.54 or thereabouts which was obviously as he thinks an unjust charge against the sureties. The vouchers for these payments were placed with other documents in the hands of Mr. Williams a gentleman then practising at this bar, who is since dead.[3] After the death of Mr. Williams a judgement was obtained without any appearance for the defendant for upwards of 2000$. which on his motion was set aside & a new trial granted. The affidavit then states that a search was made among the papers of Mr. Williams which resulted as he is informed in finding a statement made by Mr. Hay the then attorney for the U.S. admitting the incorrectness of the charge as against the sureties, a certificate of the Treasurer of the U.S. as to the payment of $160 on or about the 31st. day of October 1803. & a letter from the affiant to Mr. Williams dated the 20th. of April 1809 in which he says "I send you two receipts & a letter evidencing the payment of $696 of the judgement.["] These papers the affiant says are, as he is informed, mislaid and he prays a continuance for the purpose of endeavouring to replace them.

The attorney for the United States also offered to read a letter from   ¶6
William Simmonds, to Michael McKewan in these words

> Department of war Accou⟨n⟩tants office Jany. 15. 1803
> Sir
> I have to acknowledge the receipt of yours of the 10th. inst. with the papers referred to, the whole of which have been admitted and your accoun⟨ts as contractor for⟩ the year 1801 & of yourself & Daniel Harr⟨agan for the⟩ year 1802, finally closed leaving a ⟨balance⟩ due to the U.S. in each to wit

	should by
⟨from⟩ yourself as contractor for Virga. for the year 1802 —	$408.76
⟨from⟩ yourself & D. H. & contractors for V. & M for 1802 —	$767.35
	1176.11

for which you are to make immediate payment to the U.S.

> Sighned Wm. Simmons

The counsil for the defendant objected to the admission of the account from the Treasury department & of the letter from Mr Simmons, which objection the court overruled, "being of opinion that the document from the Treasury department was capable of being explained to the satisfaction of the jury by reference to the letter from William Simmons to Michael McKewan which letter was found by the attorney for the U.S. this day among the papers filed in this cause in this court, & because from inspection of the same the court is satisfied that the same was probably brought into court many years ago & has remained among the papers in this cause as being produced originally by the said Michael McKewan an original party in the cause to whom the same is directed." To this opinion the counsel for the defendant excepted, and the judgement is now before this court on writ of error.

¶7   The letter from Simmons to McKewan, not being authenticated in the form prescribed by the act of Congress, derives no aid from that act, and the question concerning its admissibility is consequently dependent on general principles of law.[4]

¶8   The record contains no evidence that Michael McKewan was ever a party to this cause. The declaration is against the exrs. of Philip Pendleton decd. who was one of the Securities of McKewan & D Harragan. I must presume from the statement of the Judge of the District court that a suit was originally brought against all the parties to the bond, & that on the death of Philip Pendleton, one of the obligors this suit was brought against his exrs. and that this paper was found in the original suit.

¶9   It is not stated by the Judge nor does it in any manner appear that a trial ever took place as against McKewan, that this paper was ever read in evidence, or that it was filed with the permission of the court. In what light then is this letter to be considered? I am by no means satisfied that it is not the paper of McKewan which he would be at liberty to withdraw at his own pleasure, & would not be compellable to use. If seized by the attorney for the United States, he could not use it as evidence offered by McKewan, but as a letter addressed to & received by him. But if I am wrong in this, still it only establishes the amount of the claim against McKewan & Harragan, & does not show with sufficient precision that the sureties were liable for the whole of that claim. The documents show that, on the books of the Treasury, the sums for which the sureties are not liable, are blended with those for which they are liable, and that the whole is claimed from them. The account certified by the comptroller claims for monies advanced to the contractors up to the 6th. of January 1803 without specifying the dates at which the several advances were made or showing how much was advanced after the last day of Decr. 1802. The letter of the war accountant is dated after the 6th. day of January 1803 & states a balance to be due varying from that contained in the account certified by the comptroller but omits to state that it was wholly due for advances made on or prior to the last day of Decr. 1802. It is said that an inference may be fairly drawn from a comparison of these accounts that the balance claimed in the letter of Mr. Simmons was due for advances for which the sureties are responsible. But inferences may be drawn either way & this is not a case which ought to be left to uncertain inferences. The books of the Treasury ought to show with precision & certainty the several periods at which the money was advanced & an abstract from those books would be evidence in the cause. A court ought not to reason on a letter not explicit & draw from it doubtful inferences when the party requiring this course has in his possession testimony which would dispel every doubt.

¶10   If the letter does not show, when accompanied by the account certified by the comptroller, that all the money it claims was advanced before the 1st. of Jany. 1803, then no acquiescence in it by McKewan, no admission of its verity, implied or expressed can affect the security. McKewans admissions show only his own liability; but if that is more extensive than the liability of his securities, they cannot be affected by admissions which apply to the claim against him generally, without discriminating between those parts of it which affect the sureties, & those which do not.

Upon these reasons I am of opinion that the letter of Simmonds does not explain with the requisite clearness the account certified by the comptroller, & ought not to have been admitted. ¶11

I am not unmindful of the allegation made by the attorney for the United States, that the papers which would explain this transaction are burnt & cannot be produced. But this fact is not stated in the bill of exceptions & cannot be noticed. I can no more take it into consideration than I can the indorsement on the letter controverting the sum it claims, & consequently destroying every implication arising from its being considered as the paper of McKewan. I must consider it as a paper equivocal in itself produced by a party in possession of testimony which is unequivocal. The judgement must be reversed.[5] ¶12

AD, Marshall Judicial Opinions, PPAmP; printed, John W. Brockenbrough, *Reports of Cases Decided by the Honourable John Marshall . . .* , II (Philadelphia, 1837), 75–80. For JM's deletions and interlineations, see Textual Notes below.

1. The suit had commenced in the U.S. District Court at Richmond in 1803 or soon thereafter. The declaration was filed by then U.S. Attorney George Hay (proceedings in U.S. District Court [copy], 8 Apr. 1822, U.S. v. Pendleton's Executors).
2. Copies of the certificate and other evidence submitted by U.S. Attorney Stanard were entered on the defendants' bill of exceptions and made part of the record of the case (ibid.).
3. William C. Williams.
4. JM referred to the 1797 act concerning the settlement of accounts between the U.S. and receivers of public money (*U.S. Statutes at Large*, I, 512–13).
5. JM set aside the verdict of the district court and ordered a new trial in the circuit court. At the May 1824 term the U.S. obtained a verdict and judgment against Pendleton's executors for $623.89, with six percent interest from 1 Jan. 1803 (U.S. Cir. Ct., Va., Ord. Bk. XI, 296–97, 348, 447, 492–93).

Textual Notes

Title l. 1	Pendleton ↑&c↓ ~~exr.~~ ↑exrs.↓ of Pendleton
¶ 1 l. 1	error ~~obta~~ to
¶ 2 l. 3	rations ↑to the troops in Virga. & Maryland↓ for
l. 5	Decr. [*erasure*] ↑of↓ that year.
l. 7	due ~~by~~ ↑from↓ the
¶ 3 ll. 3–4	settlement of ↑the↓ accounts
ll. 4–5	Harrigan ↑late↓ contractors
ll. 5–6	Virginia ~~a balance is found against them for mon~~ they
¶ 4 l. 9	court ~~& was rejected~~ because
¶ 5 l. 9	placed ↑with other documents↓ in
l. 11	Williams a [*erasure*] ↑judgement↓ was

	l. 12	for ~~the~~ upwards of ~~two~~ 2000$. which on ~~the~~ ↑this↓ motion ~~of the~~ was
	l. 13	made ~~into~~ ↑among↓ the
	l. 16	charge ~~ag~~ ↑as↓ against the sureties, & a certificate
¶ 6	l. 2	Simmonds, ~~(then accountant of (the War De)partment)~~ to Michael
	l. 18	of ~~these~~ ↑the↓ account
	l. 19	from ~~the~~ Mr
	l. 26	papers ~~& has remained among the papers~~ in
	l. 28	directed." ~~to~~ ↑To↓ this
¶ 7	l. 1	Simmons [*erasure*] ↑to↓ McKewan,
¶ 8	l. 4	the ~~District~~ Judge ↑of the District court↓ that
¶ 9	l. 8	as a [*erasure*] ↑letter↓ addressed
	ll. 15–16	January ↑1803↓ without
	l. 18	the ~~comptroller~~ ↑war↓ accountant
	l. 21	made ↑on or↓ prior
¶10	ll. 7–8	discriminating ↑between↓ those
¶11	ll. 1–3	Simmonds ↑does not explain with the requisite clearness the account certified by the comptroller, &↓ ought not to have been admitted. ~~& does n~~
¶12	l. 2	would [*erasure*] ↑explain↓ this

To Joseph Gales

Dear Sir   Richmond Decr. 19th. 1822

   Mrs. Martyr who lives in my family has just received a letter informing her that her son Richard who is a journeyman in your office, is ill of a pleurisy.[1] He is a young man about whose welfare I am sollicitous & I will thank you to direct a physician to attend him, if that is not already done. I will take care that he shall be paid. Very respectfully I am, your Obedt

J MARSHALL

ALS (formerly owned by the late Theodore Sheldon, Chicago, Ill.; advertised for sale by Mercury Stamp Co., Inc., New York, N.Y., 1970). Addressed to Gales in Washington; postmarked Richmond, 19 Dec. Endorsed by Gales.

1. Frances Martyr was a housekeeper and companion to Mary Marshall (Frances Norton Mason, *My Dearest Polly* [Richmond, Va., 1961], 285).

Scott and Lyle v. Lenox
Opinion
U.S. Circuit Court, Virginia, 26 December 1822

James B. Scott and James Lyle brought this suit for the benefit of Scott, Irvine & Company and of Archibald Freeland. Scott (1773–1861), a prominent merchant of the town of Manchester (across the James River from Richmond), was receiver for Archibald Freeland, a fellow merchant of that town who had lost his fortune through bad investments. In October 1819 Freeland executed a deed of trust to Scott and Lyle for the benefit of Scott, Irvine & Company, conveying fifteen half-acre lots and appurtenances in Manchester. Previously, in June 1818, the British firm of Heron, Lenox & Company had obtained a decree against Freeland in the federal court, part of which was permanently enjoined in June 1820. By a writ of elegit issued in July 1820 Samuel Lenox, the surviving partner of the British firm, came into possession of a moiety (one half) of the fifteen Manchester lots. In the present action the plaintiffs charged Lenox with committing "waste" as tenant by elegit — specifically, for removing and selling screws from buildings erected for a tobacco factory and stemmery. The defendant filed a demurrer and entered plea of "no waste" on 27 November 1822. Marshall ruled on the demurrer on 26 December (*Richmond Portraits*, 186–87; declaration, [Oct. 1822]; pleas, [27 Nov. 1822], decree [copy], Heron, Lenox & Co. v. Freeland, 9 June 1818, Scott and Lyle v. Lenox, U.S. Cir. Ct., Va., Ended Cases [Unrestored], 1822, Vi; U.S. Cir. Ct., Va., Ord. Bk. XI, 275–76, 306–7).

Scott & Lyle

v

Lenox

This is a demurrer to a declaration in an action of waste; and the only question is — can the action be maintained against a tenant by elegit.[1] ¶1

Could the court be guided solely by considerations of the reason & policy of the law, the argument of the counsel for the plf. would certainly have great weight; but it is a case of strict authority & by authority my opinion will be regulated. ¶2

The register contains the form of a writ of waste against a tenant by elegit; and the Register is admitted to be a book entitled to great respect. Its authority on this particular point, is however in some degree diminished by the circumstance that the Editor has placed this note in the Margin. "Quære if it be maintainable by the law against him."[2] Fitzherbert, in his natura brevium, says that this writ is in the register & that it stands with reason that this action should lie, but adds that some say the debtor shall not have this action because he may have account.[3] ¶3

The plf also relies on a case reported in the year books & decided the 21 of Ed. 3.[4] That was a sci. fa.[5] sued out by the person whose lands had been delivered on a Recognizance, praying that the tenant might receive ¶4 the money due & restore the land. He also suggested that the tenant had cut trees growing in a wood delivered to him, & prayed for a writ to compel him to answer for the cutting aforesaid. The writ was granted.[6]

¶5   The counsel for the plaintiff assumes that this was a writ of waste. But the case does not say so; nor does it furnish any thing which will justify this inference. A writ to compel a tenant to answer for Cutting trees, is not, necessarily, a writ of waste. The writ was awarded, but I do not find any decision on the cause. A similar case came on at the Trinity term in the same year when the Judges said it would be advisable for the plaintiff to strike the cutting of the trees out of his writ as he might bring trespass on the case for that injury.[7] The writ in the Register then & the opinion of Fitzherbert, are the only authorities in support of the action.

¶6   In support of the Demurrer the counsel for the defendant has cited 1st. Inst. 54. a. where Lord Coke says "no action of waste lyeth against a Guardian in socage, but an account or trespass; nor against tenant by statute staple, &c or Elegit.["][8]

¶7   It is unnecessary to speak of the high respect which is due to the opinions of my Lord Coke, especially on subjects of this sort. He was particularly conversant in all the antient decisions, and was well acquainted with the writs in the Register; with their reason, & with the authority on which they were founded. He understood too all the antient opinions & doctrines on this subject.

¶8   In the Dean & Chapter of Worcesters case 6th. Co 37, it was contended at the bar that the lease was void under the statute of the 13th. of El. Ch. 10 "because it was made for the lives of others, in which case it might happen that there might be an occupant who would not be subject to waste; no more than tenant by statute merchant, or Tenant by elegit &c." It was admitted by the court that the Dean & chapter are restrained to make leases dispunishable of waste but it was resolved that an occupant is punishable for waste because he has the estate of the lessee for life, and is therefore within the statute of Glocester; "but tenant by statute Merchant, statute staple, or elegit do not hold for life or years & therefore they are not of the statute."[9]

¶9   Two objections have been made to the authority of this case.
1st. The question was not a point in the cause, & the opinion therefore is a meer obiter dictum.
2d. This dictum goes no farther than to deny that the action is given by the statute of Gloster.
To the first objection I answer that although the opinion expressed by a court on a principle stated in argument as analogous to that contended for in the cause be not of equal authority with a decision on the very point in issue, yet, in such a case as this, it is of great weight.

¶10   It was the usage of the court in the time of Lord Coke to decide the collateral points of law which were stated in argument & considered by the Judges as bearing on the main question. Those points were argued, and were deliberately considered and settled. In this case it was contended at the bar that an occupant was not punishable for waste; no more than a tenant by elegit. The court resolved that an occupant was punishable for waste, which was the very point in controversy, though a tenant by elegit was not; and took the distinction between the two tenants. Certainly when a principle is stated at the bar as acknowledged law, & is declared by the court to be law, it deserves great respect, though it may not have all the authority of an express decision on the very point in issue.

2d. To the 2d. objection it is to be observed, that the proposition made ¶11 at the bar was general that the action was not maintainable. Of course it was not maintainable either at common law or by the statute. The court assents to this proposition, & gives as a reason that it is not within the statute. The inference is that by the admission of all it was not maintainable at common law; and to show the truth of the general proposition that the action could not be sustained, it was necessary to state only that it was not given by the statute.

In 2d. Inst. p 299 Lord Coke says "At the common law waste was ¶12 punishable in three persons viz tenant in dower, tenant by the curtesy & the guardian.["]¹⁰

It is argued that although tenant by elegit is not comprehended in this ¶13 enumeration, Lord Coke is not to be understood as denying that the action might be maintained independent of any statute, because the estate did not exist at common law but was created by statute. When created, it is contended, the principles of the common law give the action, because the estate is created by act of law & not by the act of the pa⟨r⟩ty.

This argument is not without its weight; but it is opposed by other rea- ¶14 sons which seem to me to be entitled to greater consideration. When we consider the fullness with which Lord Coke discusses every question on which he treats we cannot resist the conviction that, had he supposed the action was maintainable on the principles of the common law he would have said so, & not have left the student to draw the very strong inference against the action which his words justify. But his opinion on this point is expressly declared in his ⟨1⟩st. inst. in the passage already cited.

If this action cannot be maintained at the common law it depends ¶15 entirely on our act of Assembly. That act seems to have been intended to comprehend the whole subject since it enumerates the persons against whom the action lay at common law.¹¹ If a tenant by elegit be comprehended in this act it must be under the words "tenant for years." It has been contended at the bar that tenant by elegit is a tenant for years because that is certain which may be rendered certain, and when the land is delivered to him at a certain annual¹² to be held till it discharges a certain sum, he is a tenant for a certain number of years which may be computed with exactness.

Were this a case of the first impression I should incline strongly to this ¶16 opinion. I do not clearly percieve the distinction between the tenant who holds land at 10$ per an. until he shall receive $100 and a lease for ten years if J. S. shall so long live. The tenancy by elegit is determinable within the time by the payment of the money & the estate for ten years is determinable within the time by the death of J. S. But the question is as completely settled as a question of law can be settled by authority. Lord Coke in his commentary on the statute of Gloster says that tenant by elegit is not within it, because he is not a tenant for years. All the books concur in this opinion. There is not I beleive a dictum against it.

¶17   I think the demurrer must be sustained.

AD, Marshall Judicial Opinions, PPAmP; printed, John W. Brockenbrough, *Reports of Cases Decided by the Honourable John Marshall . . .*, II (Philadelphia, 1837), 59–63. For JM's deletions and interlineations, see Textual Notes below.

1. On the writ of elegit, see *PJM*, V, l.

2. The *Register of Writs* (*Registrum Omnium Brevium*) was a collection of common law writs dating from the medieval period. It circulated first in manuscript and then appeared in various printed editions beginning in 1531 (S. F. C. Milsom, *Historical Foundations of the Common Law* [2d ed.; Toronto, 1981], 37; Sir William Holdsworth, *A History of English Law*, II [1936; London, 1971 reprint], 512–25, 636–40). JM probably consulted the last edition of this work, *Registrum Brevium tam Originalium, quam Judicialium* (London, 1687), 75, translating the editor's marginal note from law French.

3. *La Novel Natura Brevium* by Anthony Fitzherbert (d. 1538), a justice of the Court of Common Pleas, was first published in 1534. JM undoubtedly used the edition containing Matthew Hale's commentary: *The New Natura Brevium of the Most Reverend Judge Mr. Anthony Fitzherbert* (8th ed.; London, 1755), 134.

4. The "year books" were the law reports of the medieval period. The first standard printed edition of the year books appeared in 1679 and consisted of eleven parts (Holdsworth, *History of English Law*, II, 525–31). The case discussed by JM was reported in *Le Second Part de les Reports des Cases en Ley* (London, 1679), which contains reports from the seventeenth through the thirty-ninth year of Edward III. The reports for each year are separately paginated.

5. On the writ of scire facias, see *PJM*, V, 156 n. 7.

6. This appears to be case number six, 21 Edw. III, Hilary term, 1347 (*Le Second Part de les Reports des Cases en Ley*, 2–3).

7. Probably case number twenty-one, 21 Edw. III, Trinity term, 1347 (ibid., 26).

8. Edward Coke, *The First Part of the Institutes of the Laws of England; or, A Commentary upon Littleton . . .*, I (16th ed.; London, 1809), 54a.

9. The Dean and Chapter of Worcester's Case, 6 Co. 37a, 37b, 77 Eng. Rep. 307, 308 (K.B., 1605).

10. Edward Coke, *The Second Part of the Institutes of the Laws of England . . .* (2 vols.; London, 1797), I, 299.

11. Virginia's "act concerning Waste," enacted in 1792, specified "any tenant by the curtesy, tenant in dower, or otherwise for term of life or years," as subject to an action of waste (*Revised Code of Va.*, I, 462–63).

12. JM omitted "rent."

Textual Notes

¶ 1 l. 2   can [*erasure*] ↑the↓ action
¶ 2 l. 1   guided ↑solely↓ by
l. 3   & ~~to~~ ↑by↓ authority

¶ 3 l. 4   the ~~editor~~ ↑Editor↓ has
    ll. 5–8   him." ↑Fitzherbert, in his natura brevium, says that this writ is
                        in the register & that it stands with reason that this action
                        should lie, but adds that some say the debtor shall not have
                        this action because he may have account.↓
¶ 4 l. 1   case [*erasure*] ↑reported↓ in
    l. 2   Ed. [*erasure*] ↑3.↓ That
    l. 6   granted. ∓
¶ 5 l. 1   plaintiff ~~takes it for granted~~ ↑assumes↓ that
    ll. 4–9   waste. ~~These are the authorities relied on in support of the
                        action~~ ↑The writ was awarded, but I do not find any decision
                        on the cause. A similar case came on at the Trinity term in
                        the same year when the Judges said it would be advisable for
                        the plaintiff to strike the cutting of the trees out of his writ as
                        he might bring trespass on the case for that injury. The writ in
                        the Register then & the opinion of Fitzherbert, are the only
                        authorities in support of the action.↓
¶ 6 l. 1   counsel [*erasure*] ↑for↓ the
    l. 3   an ~~acccount~~ ↑account↓ or
¶ 8 l. 5   statute ~~staple,~~ ↑merchant,↓ or Tenant
¶10 ll. 2–3   points ↑of law↓ which were stated in argument ↑& considered
                        by the Judges↓ as bearing
¶12 l. 1   law ~~rent~~ ↑waste↓ was
¶14 l. 2   to ~~out weigh it~~ be entitled
    l. 8   his [*erasure*] ⟨1⟩st.
    l. 8   cited. ∤
¶15 l. 1 beg.   ~~In Virginia~~ If

Gaines v. Span
Opinion
U.S. Circuit Court, Virginia, [28 December 1822?]

This equity suit had its origins in the ambiguous testamentary arrangements made by Camm Garlick (d. 1782) of King and Queen County. Camm Garlick made two wills, the first of which he executed in May 1780 before leaving to visit his uncle Edward Garlick in Bristol, England. On arrival in England he learned that his uncle had died and bequeathed him a legacy of six thousand pounds sterling. In December 1781, while in England, Camm Garlick made a second will, in which he left pecuniary legacies to his son Samuel and daughters Sarah and Mary, to be paid out of the money left to him by Edward Garlick. Soon thereafter Camm Garlick died in Portugal, where he had gone on account of poor health. The second will appointed Benjamin Pollard and the Reverend Thomas Hall, who were in England with Camm Garlick at the time, executors and guardians for the special purpose of collecting and paying out the money bequeathed to Garlick's children. Pollard, who in 1783 entered into a partnership with Bristol merchant Samuel Span for the purpose of trading in Virginia, invested funds from Garlick's estate in this firm, styled Benjamin Pollard & Company. John and Samuel Garlick, Camm Garlick's brothers and general executors appointed under the first will, also joined the company. In the aftermath of the company's failure, two suits were filed. The first, begun in 1799 in the state chancery court, was brought by Camm Garlick's legatees against John and Samuel Garlick and Benjamin Pollard in their capacity as executors. The second, begun in 1803 in the U.S. Circuit Court, was brought by Samuel Span's executors against the same defendants in their capacity as surviving partners of Benjamin Pollard & Company. In 1816 Span's executors obtained a decree in the federal court for a large sum. In 1820, by a consent decree in the state chancery court, the administrator of one of Camm Garlick's executors was directed to pay specific sums to each of Camm Garlick's daughters. The daughters, Sarah Gaines and Mary Tunstall, then brought a bill in the U.S. Circuit Court to assert their superior claim to the fund set aside for Span's executors under the 1816 decree. In June 1822 the court directed a commissioner to make a report stating the accounts between the parties. The exact date of Marshall's opinion is uncertain. Although Brockenbrough places it at the May 1823 term, when the court issued a final decree, the opinion clearly belongs to an earlier, provisional decree. The only decree between the order of June 1822 for a commissioner's report and the final decree of June 1823 was issued on 28 December 1822 (2 Brock. 83–88; Beverley Fleet, ed., *Virginia Colonial Abstracts* [Richmond, Va., 1946], XXVIII, 88–96; Malcolm Hart Harris, *Old New Kent County* [2 vols.; West Point, Va., 1977], II, 771–74; U.S. Cir. Ct., Va., Ord. Bk. XI, 244–45, 247, 316–17, 353–56; U.S. Cir. Ct., Va., Rec. Bk. XI, 1–122).

¶1   ⟨. . .⟩ To support this allegation it would be necessary to prove that Mary Garlick was entitled to so much of this debt as her account with Baynham amounted to.[1] If she is not so entitled, it is nothing more than the receipt of a demand on Mary Garlick as so much money. In that case John Garlick would be chargeable with this account in like manner as if he had received the money. I percieve no evidence tending to show the right of Mary Garlick to any part of this debt, & therefore think the whole stands properly charged to John Garlick.

¶2   The next difference which I shall notice is the debt due from Benjamin Pollard. The plaintiffs claim to charge John & Samuel Garlick with this debt as Guardians of the infant children of Camm Garlick or as his exrs. They contend that it was in the power of J & S. G.[2] to collect the money due from Pollard; their omission to do which is gross negligence, which renders them liable for the money lost.[3]

¶3   This claim depends on two questions.
1st. Were J & S. G. testamentary Guardians of the children of C. G.?
2d. Were they bound as exrs. to collect the debt due from Pollard?
1st. Were they testamentary Guardians of the infant children of Camm Garlick?

¶4   His will made in Virginia empowers & directs his wife "to clothe maintain & educate his children in the best manner that the estate given to her will admit" and desires her "to consult his exrs." thereinafter named "as to the mode of their education."

It is admitted that a guardian may be appointed without using the ¶5 term, and that no form of words is prescribed: but to appoint a guardian by implication the powers essential to the office ought to be conferred. In this will no power is given over the persons or estates of th⟨e⟩ orphans to J. & S. G. These remain with the mother who is only to consult his exrs. as to the education of his children. She may follow or reject their advice, & they have no authority to enforce it. Nothing can be more clear than that they are not appointed Guardians in this will.

In his additional will made in England he ratifies & confirms the will ¶6 made in Virginia, gives a legacy of 50£ per annum to his wife, and directs "that the Guardians by his said former will appointed shall by their bond of a sufficient penalty" &c "secure to be paid to his said wife for her life, out of the monies coming to their hands or which they shall be in the receipt of for the use of or in trust for his said children, the said annuity or yearly sum of fifty pounds."

This is said to be a recognition of their character as guardians, and an ¶7 appointment of them by implication to that office.

This is a point on which I have felt no inconsiderable difficulty. The ¶8 two papers making in point of law but one will, and the last ratifying, confirming, & establishing the first, I have supposed that they might be considered as if written on the same paper, at the same time; and as if the words of the last recited clause had been "my will is that the guardians of my children herein by me above appointed, shall by their bond" &c. Had this been the fact, it would have been very certain that the testator understood his words as appointing a guardian; and although the powers of a guardian were in reality conferred on his wife, & not on his exrs., the inference would have been very strong that the words of the last clause must refer to his exrs. & not to his wife because the persons he supposed himself to have appointed were directed to give bond & to pay money to his wife. The allusion to his exrs. is almost as strong as if he had named them; and had he done so had the language of such a will been "It is my desire that my brothers J & S. G. whom I have herein before appointed Guardians of my children, shall by their bond &c secure to be paid to my said wife" &c, it would be difficult to resist the argument that such language would amount to an actual appointment.

The subsequent clause too appointing Benjamin Pollard & the Rever- ¶9 end Thomas Hall guardians of the persons & estates of his children until the legacies bequeathed to them in England could be collected and paid to their guardians appointed by his first will would, under the same view of the case, afford an argument equally strong in favor of the construction for which the plaintiffs contend. I was the more disposed to yield to this construction from percieving that the chancellor who decided the cause in the state court, treated J & S. G. as guardians. Had this point been directly made & directly determined by him, the leaning of my own judgement to the contrary opinion would probably have yielded to my respect for his decision. But the point was not directly made. The report was not excepted to on this account; and the parties seem to have proceeded on the idea that J & S. G. were to be considered as guardians, and were in that character liable for Pollards debt.

¶10   Taking this view of the decree I have felt it to be my duty to consider the question uninfluenced by the proceedings in the state court.

¶11   I do not think the case can be considered as if the two papers formed in point of fact as well as law, one instrument. Had the provisions of the first will been before the testator when he wrote the last, the subsequent clauses could not have been founded on ignorance or forgetfulness of what he had before written, but would have shown his construction of the clause referred to. They would have shown his opinion that the words he had previously employed were competent to the appointment of Guardians for his children, & that he employed them with that intent. In such a case there would be great force in the argument requiring the court to construe those words as the testator himself obviously construed them. But in the case at bar we have no reason to suppose that the will made in Virginia was in possession of C. G. when he made his will in England. It rested only in his memory. We have therefore no right to suppose that the words used in it, were used in a sense which they will not bear; we can only suppose that he was under a mistake respecting it; that he had no distinct recollection of it; that he supposed it to contain an appointment of exrs. when it contained no such appointment.

¶12   I can find no case which decides that anything passes by words used clearly under such mistake. In Wright & Wivell 4 Ba. Abr. 290. reported in 3 Lev. 2 Vent. & Moor **A** devised to his wife 600£ to be paid to J. S. for the payment of lands he purchased from him, & are already settled on her for her jointure; the lands were not settled on her; and adjudged, in favor of the heir, they did not pass by implication.[4] The testator certainly supposed the lands were settled; but this mistake did not give the wife a right to them.

¶13   So in the same book page 339. the following passages are cited from Godolphin 282.[5] "If a man says *out of the 100£ which I bequeathed A I give* **B** *£50*; this is a good bequest of the £50 to **B** because only a false demonstration in an immaterial circumstance, which shall not vitiate the legacy; but in this case **A** takes nothing; for words of diminution shall never be construed to give a legacy by implication. But if the demonstration be totally false, as if the testator says *I bequeath to* **A** *the £100 which I have in my chest*, and there is not any money in the chest, the legacy is void.["]

¶14   So in the case at bar a direction that money shall be paid to the persons who were, in a former will, appointed the guardians of his children, when no persons were so appointed, is a plain mistake, & can give no rights to those whom we may suppose the words allude to. Had his brothers been named, so as to render it absolutely certain that they were the persons to whom he alludes, this meer mistake would not I think, under the authorities which have been quoted, or on general principles, have amounted to an appointment; their not being named would render it still more unjustifiable to put the construction on the will which is required by the plaintiff.

If the words themselves be analysed, nothing can be extracted from them indicating an intention in the testator to appoint; they meerly show the mistaken idea that he had made an appointment. This was completely an error in his recollection, and the court cannot, I think, supply the defect. ¶15

It is contended that they acted as Guardians & this fact is supposed to show their understanding of the will, & to have some influence on its construction. ¶16

The proof that they acted as Guardians is I think equivocal. Had the appointment been explicit, the evidence would be sufficient to show their acceptance of the office; but no regular appointment having been made the evidence does not I think make out a clear case of their acting as Guardians. ¶17

Several witnesses depose a general understanding, founded on the care they took of the infants & their property, that they were the guardians; but I think no fact, except signing a direction to the clerk to issue a marriage license for one of the young ladies, is proved which is not entirely compatible with the relation in which they stood to the family, admitting them not to think themselves Guardians. ¶18

The testator had devised his whole estate to his wife during the minority of his children charging her with their maintenance & education. There was then no estate for the Guardians to manage. It did not belong to the children during their infancy, but to their mother. If their uncles attended to it, such attention could neither make them Guardians nor make the estate their property. It was an attention to be expected from their connexion with the family, and they would have been chargeable with want of natural affection had they refused it.[6] ¶19

To the authority to the Clerk to issue a marriage license they sign their names but do not add their character as Guardians. This cannot make them Guardians; and, although it would amount to an acceptance of the guardianship had they been appointed, it is dated in June 1798, before which time Pollard had become insolvent. ¶20

But supposing J. & S. G. to have been the guardians of the infant children of C G. are they responsible in that character for Pollards debt? ¶21

A guardian is undoubtedly responsible for all the estate of the ward real or personal which comes to his hands, but is he responsible for monies which he might but did not collect, and which, in strict legal language, never formed a part of the wards estate? ¶22

¶23   A legacy is not a part of the estate of the legatee until the executor assents to it. As a part of the personal estate of the testator it is cast by law on the exr. who has a right to retain it till debts are paid. I have seen no case in which a guardian is charged with a legacy until he has received it. I do not know that this point has ever been settled in the courts of the state. Were I of opinion that J & S. G. were really to be considered as testamentary Guardians, I should think it necessary to look into this point before I should feel myself justified in saying that they were chargeable with this legacy.

¶24   If J & S. G. are not chargeable with Pollards debt as Guardians, we are next to enquire whether
2d. They are chargeable as executors.

¶25   This depends, I think, on the English will, and on the character held by Pollard under that will.

¶26   That J. & S. G. were general executors, and that they are liable for this debt if it was their duty to collect it, & if they had the right & the power to coerce its payment, are, I think, propositions not to be questioned. The whole enquiry then is, was it their duty to collect it, and could they coerce its payment?

¶27   The clauses of the will which relate to this subject are those in which B. P. & T. Hall are appointed Guardians of his children, & exrs. of his will. They are in these words. "And I do hereby appoint the said Benjamin Pollard & the revd. Thomas Hall Guardians of the persons & estate of my said children during & until such time as the several sums of money by me herein before bequeathed can be paid for their use & benefit into the hands of the several persons by me nominated & appointed Guardians of the persons & estates of my said children under the said will & disposition by me made & executed prior to my departure from America as aforesaid." "And I hereby appoint the said B. P. & T. H. joint exrs. in trust of this my will.["]

¶28   The legacies to which the plaintiffs were entitled were in the hands of B. P. either as their guardian, or as executor.

¶29   Let it be that the money was held by him as Guardian. Have the exrs. a right to sue the Guardian for money of the ward which came lawfully to his hands, if it be not required for the debts of the testator? I believe he has no such right. I am persuaded such a suit would be of the first impression.

¶30   But, on coming to America B. P. ceased to be Guardian, & was bound to pay over the money to those who were entitled to receive it. But who were entitled to receive it? Not the exrs. I think, because it had been paid by them to the Guardian for the use of the infants, & had consequently become a part of their estate. The testator had shown his intention that the exrs. in Virginia should not receive it, for he directed specially that the money should be paid to the Guardians in Virginia. Had the exrs. been really Guardians, they would have received the money as guardians

& not as executors. Had the Guardians & exrs. been different persons, the money would have been payable to the Guardians, not to the exrs. — if not required for debts.

But suppose the exrs. entitled to receive this money, would this circumstance attach responsibility to J. & S. G? B. P. who was in possession of it, was also an exr. If he is to be considered as a general exr., the law is clear that one exr. cannot sue another, and that one exr. is not liable for money in the hands of another. The question whether he is to be considered as general exr., or, if not, what limitations are imposed on his power, depends on the will. The words are "And I hereby appoint the said B. P. & T. H. joint exrs. in trust of this my will." The particular paper which contains this appointment, contains also a reference to, & a confirmation of, the former will. The two papers make one instrument, & constitute one will in law, & I should feel some difficulty in determining the question whether B. P. was not exr. in Virginia as well as in England; whether he was exr. of the whole will or of that particular paper only, which was executed in England. ¶31

But let it be conceded that he was to execute that part of the will only which was made in England. What is the extent of his power & what the relation in which he stood to the exrs. in Virginia & to the legatees of C. G.? ¶32

He was an exr. in trust of the English will. His power & duty under that will was to settle the affairs of C. G. in England, collect the money due to him, & pay it to the Guardians of his children in Virginia. The Guardians were to become trustees of the money for the benefit of the infants. The beneficial interest then was from the commencement in the infants. The exrs. & guardians in England were trustees for them. B. P. continued to be exr. for the purposes of the trust. He received the money as exr. & trustee, & retained those characters till the trust was executed. If then the money was in his hands as Guardian, & the exrs. had a right to collect it, B. P. might be considered as exr. of that part of the will, & being in possession of the money, his coexecutors had no power over it. ¶33

If this money which he collected is to be considered as remaining in his hands as exr., a part of the foregoing reasoning applies directly to the question. He was, it must be admitted unfaithful to his trust as exr. in trust. But he still retained that character & could not divest himself of it till the trust was executed. The children & not the exrs. were the *cestui que trust*. The children & not the exrs. could coerce its execution. The exrs. therefore cannot be responsible for its non execution. ¶34

I feel myself constrained to say that the representatives of J. & S. G. are not chargeable with Pollards debt.[7] ¶35

The plaintiff also claims $274.25 for money paid by Benjamin Pollard to John Garlick as exr. of C. G. which sum is omitted in the account stated according to the directions of the defendant. ¶36

In the account raised by B. P. against the estate of C. G. this sum is charged as being paid to the order of J. G. If this debt due from Pollard ¶37 was due to the legatees & not to the exrs. of C. G. a payment to the exrs. was a mispayment which cannot charge their securities & is not a debt of superior dignity. This objection therefore is allowed.

¶38   The next point of difference between the parties respects the debt due from Carter Braxton.

¶39   That debt is lost & the sole object of enquiry is whether the exrs. might, by using due diligence have collected it.[8]

¶40   The money was advanced in England to the sons of Carter Braxton by Camm Garlick & the debt was certainly known to the exrs. in the summer of 1783. Mr. Braxtons circumstances were at that time much embarassed & he was probably insolvent, but he was in possession of a large estate & considerable sums were obtained from him by some means. Whether the exrs. could have obtained payment of this debt is very doubtful. Under such circumstances my mind rather leans to the opinion that the exrs. ought not to be charged with it. But, in the suit brought by the legatees of C. G. in the state court an exception was taken to this item of the report which was overruled by the Chancellor. His decision bound the parties; and although the amount of the decree was afterwards fixed by consent, the consent was not given until the chancellor had overruled this exception & decided on this item. My respect for his opinion & my sense of its real obligation in this case settle the doubts I should otherwise have entertained on this point.

¶41   The plaintiffs also claim for the profits of C. G's. estate in Virginia; but the objections to this claim are insurmountable. It was relinquished in the state.[9] J. & S. G. were not Guardians. The infants had no estate. It was willed to their mother during their infancy, & if J. & S. G. interfered with it, their agency was in behalf of the mother & cannot be considered in this suit.

¶42   From the report of the Commissioner made at the instance of the plaintiffs is to be deducted Pollards debt so much of Brooks debt as exceeds £60.2.6 sterling with interest thereon the sum paid by B. P. to the order of J. G. in favor of Temple & the whole of the sum allowed for the profits of the Virginia estate, and the commissioner is directed to reform his report in these particulars & return the same to the court in order to a final decree.[10]

AD, Marshall Judicial Opinions, PPAmP; printed, John W. Brockenbrough, *Reports of Cases Decided by the Honourable John Marshall...*, II (Philadelphia, 1837), 88–95. First sheet of MS missing. Brockenbrough omits first two paragraphs and concluding seven paragraphs. For JM's deletions and interlineations, see Textual Notes below.

1. Mary Garlick was Camm Garlick's widow (Harris, *Old New Kent County*, II, 772). The original suit papers have been lost or destroyed since Brockenbrough published his report.
2. Here and throughout the opinion these initials stand for John and Samuel Garlick.
3. After summarizing this paragraph in a headnote, Brockenbrough begins JM's opinion at this point.
4. Bacon, *Abridgment*, IV, 290. Bacon's marginal note cites Wright v. Wivell, 3 Lev. 259, 83

Eng. Rep. 679, 2 Vent. 57, 86 Eng. Rep. 306 (K.B., 1689). Bacon's cite of "Moor 31," if intended to refer to Sir Francis Moore's reports of cases during the reign of Elizabeth I, is evidently an error.

5. Ibid., 339. Bacon's marginal note cites John Godolphin, *The Orphan's Legacy, Or, A Testamentary Abridgment in Three Parts* (3d ed.; London, 1685), 282.

6. The following notes on the Garlick family are based on records from the case in the state chancery court at Williamsburg and transcribed before a fire destroyed the chancery papers: "Camm Garlick's widow and children lived on the estate of 'old Mrs. Garlick' in King William Co. 'expensively and genteelly.' A 'chariot' was imported for them and they were 'supplied liberally and genteelly from the stores,' and 'considerable expence incurred in the education of Camm Garlick's children.' They had hogs and corn from Heartquake plantation, five times as much corn 'from Bewdley, the seat of Samuel Garlick,' and also from 'old Mrs. Garlick's plantation in King Wm.,' which plantation belonged to Samuel Garlick after her death. Her home place after her death was to be Camm Garlick's" (Fleet, ed., *Virginia Colonial Abstracts*, XXVIII, 91).

7. Brockenbrough ends the opinion at this point.

8. An abstract of an affidavit given by William Fleming Gaines in 1806 states that "Camm Garlick advanced in England 500 pounds to Carter Braxton, deceased, for his sons, Corbin and Carter, which debt is still unpaid and is considered lost on account of the insolvency of the estate of Carter Braxton." Robert Pollard testified at the same time that " 'it would have been very difficult to collect anything from Carter Braxton, Esq., deceased' in 1784 or 1785 as he was very much in the habit of executing deeds of mortgage and trust about that time and his property of every description was encumbered" (Fleet, ed., *Virginia Colonial Abstracts*, XXVIII, 90).

9. Presumably JM meant that this claim had been relinquished in the case heard in the state chancery court.

10. The court issued a final decree on 14 June 1823 (U.S. Cir. Ct., Va., Ord. Bk. XI, 353–56).

Textual Notes

¶ 1	ll. 4–5	case ↑John↓ Garlick
¶ 2	l. 2	charge ~~the exrs.~~ John
¶ 3	l. 1	on ~~t~~ ↑two↓ questions.
¶ 4	l. 1	His ~~Virginia~~ will
¶ 5	l. 2	to [*erasure*] ↑appoint↓ a guardian
	l. 4	estates of [*erasure*] ↑th⟨e⟩↓ orphans
	l. 6	to ~~their~~ ↑the↓ education
¶ 6	l. 2	Virginia, ↑gives a legacy of 50£ per annum to his wife,↓ and
¶ 8	l. 5	recited [*erasure*] ↑clause↓ had
	ll. 7–8	understood ~~himself to have employed~~ ↑his↓ words
¶11	ll. 1–2	papers ~~were~~ ↑formed↓ in point
	l. 10	testator ↑himself↓ obviously
	l. 12	in ~~Virginia~~ ↑England.↓ It
¶12	l. 1	that [*erasure*] ↑anything↓ passes
	l. 2	Wivell ~~3~~ ↑4↓ Ba.
¶14	l. 1	bar a ~~devise beque~~ direction
	l. 4	may ~~conjecture~~ suppose
	l. 5	named, ~~the wo~~ so
	l. 6	alludes, [*erasure*] ↑this↓ meer
¶15	l. 3	mistaken [*erasure*] ↑idea↓ that
¶18	l. 3	no fact, ~~excepting~~ ↑except↓ signing

¶19 l. 6   estate ~~the~~ ↑their↓ property. ~~of the infants~~ It

¶20 l. 3   would ~~be~~ ↑amount to↓ an acceptance

¶26 l. 2   debt ↑if it was their duty to collect it, &↓ if

　　　l. 3   payment, ~~is~~ ↑are,↓ I think, propositions ~~which are~~ not

　　　l. 4   is, ↑was it their duty to collect it, and↓ could

¶27 l. 1   are ~~those that~~ ↑those↓ in

　　　l. 2   & ~~that in which~~ exrs.

¶28 l. 1   plaintiffs ~~was~~ ↑were↓ entitled

¶29 l. 2   money ↑of the ward↓ which

　　　l. 3   not ~~necessary for~~ ↑required for↓ the

¶30 ll. 2–3   it. ↑But who were entitled to receive it?↓ Not

　　　l. 4   Guardian ~~of the infants for their use~~ ↑for the use of the infants,↓ &

　　　ll. 7–8   exrs. & ↑been really↓ Guardians

　　　ll. 9–11 executors. ~~So clearly was it the intention of the testator that this money should not pass into the hands of his exrs. in Virginia, that he directs his legatees, if his Virginia estate~~ ↑Had the Guardians & exrs. been different persons, the money would have been payable to the Guardians, not to the exrs. — if not required for debts.↓

¶31 ll. 2–3   B. P. ~~in whose hands the money was~~ ↑who was in possession of it,↓ was

　　　ll. 5–6   whether ~~they are~~ ↑he is↓ to be considered as general ~~exrs~~ ↑exr.,↓ or,

　　　l. 6   on ~~their~~ his power

¶33 l. 6   exrs. ↑& guardians↓ in England were ~~the~~ trustees

　　　l. 8   executed. ~~If he was unfaithful in its execution~~ If

　　　l. 10   B. P. ~~was~~ ↑might be considered as↓ exr.

　　　l. 11   money, [*erasure*] ↑his↓ coexecutors

¶34 l. 1   money ~~still rem~~ which he collected is ~~be~~ ↑to↓ be

　　　l. 3   question. ~~As exr. &~~ He was,

　　　l. 7   execution. ~~I feel~~

¶35 l. 1   the ~~exrs.~~ representatives

¶36 l. 2   Garlick & ↑as↓ exr.

¶37 ll. 2–5   If this ~~entry be correct, the orders must have been drawn by J. G. as executor. In the report on which the decree of the Chancellor in the state court was founded, this item was introduced & no exception was taken to it. The testimony proves that J. G. received this money as exr. & I know not how an objection to charging him with it in that character can be sustained. It has been said that B. P. had no right to apply the effects of B. P. & Co. to the payment of the~~ ↑this individual↓ ~~debts. But if he has so applied them, the receiver of the money cannot set up~~ ↑make↓ ~~this defense, nor can any person make it for him.~~ ↑debt due from Pollard was due to the legatees & not to the exrs. of C. G. a payment to the exrs. was a mispayment which cannot charge their securities & is not a debt of superior dignity. This objection therefore is allowed.↓

¶40 l. 1 beg.   [*erasure*] ↑The↓ money

ll. 4–5   but ↑he was in possession of a large estate &↓ considerable
l. 11   the ~~sum~~ ↑amount↓ of
¶41 l. 3   state. ~~S &~~ J. & S. G.
¶42 l. 2   debt ↑so much of Brooks debt↓ as
ll. 3–4   thereon ↑the sum paid by B. P. to the order of J. G. in favor of
             Temple↓ & the

United States v. Nelson and Myers
Opinion
U.S. Circuit Court, Virginia, 28 December 1822

This was an action of debt on a performance bond executed during the War
of 1812 by Lt. John Archer, a regimental paymaster of the U.S. Army, and
signed by Thomas Nelson and Samuel Myers as sureties. Nelson and Myers
entered their pleas in May 1819. A jury returned a special verdict on 25 May
1822, on which the court took time to consider. The unusual circumstances
of this case are fully explained in Marshall's opinion, given on 28 December
1822 (U.S. Cir. Ct., Va., Ord. Bk. XI, 14, 98, 217–18, 317; bond, 1 Sept.
1812; pleas of Nelson and Myers, 28 May 1819; special verdict, [25 May
1822], in U.S. v. Nelson and Myers, Ended Cases [Unrestored], 1822, Vi).

The United States
    v
Nelson & Myers

John Archer was appointed pay master of the 20th. regt. of infantry in   ¶1
the army of the United States. The defendants Nelson & Myers agreed to
become his securities & to execute such bond as was required by law. A
printed paper in the usual form prepared for official bonds to be given by
paymasters was presented to, & was executed by, them. At the time of its
execution & delivery, all those parts which are usually written, including
the penalty, the names of the obligors, & the date, were blank. John
Archer the principal, had not executed it.

This blank bond was afterwards filled up in the absence of the said   ¶2
Nelson & Myers, without their knowledge & without any authority from
them, other than is implied from their having executed the said paper
with the intention to bind themselves as the sureties of the said Archer,
and with full knowledge of the object of the said bond. The Jury further
find "that the paper so as aforesaid signed sealed & delivered was accepted by the proper authorities of the United States as the official bond
of the said Archer, & of the defendants as his sureties."

The defendants pleaded a special *non est factum*,[1] & the jury has found   ¶3
the facts & referred to the court the question whether this be the deed of
the defendants.

¶4   At the common law all instruments under seal were considered as deeds. Every contract not under seal was considered as a parol contract. To the consummation of every deed the solemnity of a delivery is indispensable. Until delivery, the writing does not become the deed of the party who has sealed it. It is also necessary to the validity of a deed that it be in writing (C. L. 35. 6) Shep. Touchstone p 55.[2] These two circumstances must concur, or there is no deed binding on the party whose seal is affixed to the paper.

¶5   The rule requiring that the deed should be written implies necessarily that it binds no farther than the writing binds. Perkins sec. 118 says "If a common person seal an obligation or any other deed without any writing in it, & deliver the same unto a stranger, man or woman, it is nothing worth; notwithstanding the stranger make it to be written that he who sealed & delivered the same unto him is bound unto him in £20.["][3]

¶6   There are many other authorities to the same effect. It would be useless to quote them, because the principle is not denied. In the case now under consideration, there being no sum of money mentioned in the bond, the defendants were no more bound by the instrument they had executed at the time of its execution, than if the paper had been all blank. The United States could not have availed themselves of the bond in its then condition. The whole question then is whether the defendants have authorized any other persons to fill up this bond in such manner as to create an obligation which did not exist when it was delivered.

¶7   It is found by the jury that the defendants executed this bond with a knowledge that it was to be received as an official bond, & with an intention to bind themselves as sureties for the said John Archer, as pay master, by their sealing & delivery of it: but that no special authority was given to any person to fill it up, nor any authority whatever other than is implied from their sealing & delivering the paper.

¶8   Does this act authorize any person whatever to insert the penalty & other written parts in the bond, and does it make the writing, in its present form, their deed?

¶9   If this question depended on those moral rules of action which, in the ordinary course of things, are applied by courts to human transactions, there would be not much difficulty in saying that this paper ought to have the effect which the parties, at the time of its execution, intended it should have. But there are certain technical rules growing out of the state of things when many of our legal principles originated, which are firmly engrafted on the law; and still remain a part of it, though the circumstances in which they had their birth are totally changed. Perhaps every distinction between a sealed & an unsealed instrument is of this description. But the distinction and the rules which are founded on it, have taken such fast hold of the law that they can be separated only by the power of the legislature. Till that power shall interpose, courts must respect the rules as they are found in adjudged cases. Those cases must be referred to in order to determine whether this be the deed of the defendants.

In the case stated in Perkins the inference to be fairly drawn from the sealing & delivery of a paper on which nothing was written is that the person to whom it was delivered was authorized to write over the signature & seal, if not any obligation he pleased, an obligation for some certain thing previously agreed on by the parties, and that the person making the instrument confided in him to whom this implied authority was given for its faithful execution. It means this or it means nothing. Yet the obligation written over this signature was declared to be of no validity. It follows that the sealing & delivery of a paper does not imply an unlimited power to write even what had been previously agreed on by the parties. Shepherd in his Touchstone, p 55. referring to this section of Perkins says "The agreement must be all written before the sealing & delivery of it, for if a man seal & deliver an empty piece of paper or, parchment, albeit he do withal give commandment that an obligation or other matter shall be written in it, and this be done accordingly yet this is no good deed.["]⁴   ¶10

This declaration, if it be law, is conclusive with respect to a paper which is sealed & delivered as the act & deed of the party but which at the time of the sealing & delivery, has nothing written in it. I proceed to those cases in which an obligation is written on the paper which is incomplete at the time & is afterwards made complete or in any manner varied.   ¶11

The case of Markham v Gonaston which is reported in Cros. El. & Moor, was argued at great length & considered by the court.⁵ That case depended on the question whether an obligation executed with blanks for the Christian name & place of residence of a person named in it became void by filling up those blanks. The point was argued in three different suits. The first was brought against Fox on an obligation made by Sir F. W & said Fox; &, upon the plea of *non est factum* being pleaded the plaintiff became non suited. The party injured then brought an action on the case against the person who made the alteration, who pleaded that he had written the obligation by the command of Sir F. W with those blanks in it. That it was, in this state executed by Fox: That the blanks were then filled up by order of Sir F. W. with the assent of Fox after which Sir F. W. executed the obligation. This plea was held ill on demurrer, and the court said that the alteration was material & that it avoided the bond.   ¶12

Moor in his report of this case says note that the plf. afterwards brought a new action on the obligation against Fox who pleaded the special matter & concluded that it was not his deed. The plaintiff replied that it was filled up with the assent of both the obligors; and upon demurrer it was adjudged for the plaintiff in B. R.   ¶13

The note in Moor does not give us the words of the replication, but the term assent certainly implies an assent expressed, and the special plea of   ¶14 the person who made the alteration, as appears in Croke was that the alteration was made by order of one of the obligors with the assent of the other.

¶15   Hargrave & Butler in their notes on C. L. quote this case in the following terms.[6] "Obligation with a condition to save harmless against Tracy with a blank. A stranger after delivery fills up the blank with a christian name by consent of the obligor, yet adjudged to avoid the deed because material. But if the addition is not material, as the addition of a county, and it be by a stranger, it doth not avoid the deed, though, if by the party himself, it doth avoid it."

¶16   In the case of Zouch v Clay reported in 1 Ventris & 2d. Lev. the defendant pleaded that at the time of his executing the bond there was a blank in it which was afterwards filled up with the name of another obligor & so it is not his deed.[7] The plea was held ill. Ventris says the court considered the insertion of the name of a new obligor as not affecting the person who had previously executed the obligation — it remaining the same as to him. Levenz, in his report of the case, says that the name was inserted with the consent of all the obligors, & therefore the obligation was still binding.

¶17   In these cases the obligation was complete although the blanks had never been filled up. The alteration did not create nor enlarge the obligation, nor vary it to the injury of the obligor. They do not therefore contradict the law as laid down in Perkins & Shepherds Touchstone. In the case put by them, the obligation if it exists, is created by the writing inserted after delivery. In the subsequent cases which have been noticed, the obligation was complete when it was delivered. The alteration was in the words, not in the obligation, of the instrument, and that alteration was made by the assent of parties. I understand this to be an assent to the specific alteration, & to be an assent not implied but expressly given.

¶18   A case has been cited from 5th. Mass. rep., decided by a Judge whose opinions deserve to be greatly respected, and whose decisions must always have much influence with any court in which they are quoted.[8] The case is this.

¶19   An official bond was prepared for Crooker, with a blank for the name of the surety. Cushing afterwards agreed to become surety, & executed the bond. The blank was filled up with his name, in his absence; and then Crooker also executed it. Cushing pleaded non est factum to this bond; but it was determined to be his deed.

¶20   No person will controvert this decision. The alteration was immaterial, and, not being made by the obliger himself, could not on any sound principle of law, affect the instrument. But a principle is laid down in the opinion which goes much farther than the decision. Judge Parsons lays down the general rule that any material alteration will avoid the bond, but states as an exception to this rule, an alteration made by consent of parties. He adds that "the party executing the bond, knowing that there are blanks in it, to be filled up by inserting particular names or things, must be considered as assenting that the blanks may be thus filled after he has executed the bond."

Any distinction between an express and implied assent in a case where ¶21 the implication is so strong as it must be where a blank is to be filled of course "with a particular name or thing," is here denied. In such a case there is undoubtedly good sense in the opinion which rejects this distinction; but I am not certain that it is sustained by law. He who adds to the obligation of another must do so by the authority of that other; and I know of no case in which as respects a deed, such authority is implied in a court of law, certainly of none when not even the person is designated by whom the authority is to be executed.

But the proposition laid down by the very able Judge who gave this ¶22 opinion does not necessarily extend to the case at bar. He lays down his principle in a case "where a blank is to be filled by inserting particular names or things." That is where the blank can be filled up only in one manner. But this principle does not apply to a blank to be filled up with a sum of money, which sum is not precisely fixed.

It is also observable that in reviewing the cases on which he founds his ¶23 opinion, the Judge takes no notice of Perkins or Shepherd;[9] and the case before him, as well as that which he supposes in giving his opinion, was not produced by a paper which was blank, or of no obligation whatever when delivered. A blank of such vital importance that the paper, while it remained, was a nullity, does not seem to have been in his view. For this reason too, whatever authority may be ascribed to the opinion of Judge Parsons, and no person acknowledges his authority more willingly than myself, its application to the case at bar may well be doubted.

In Russel v Langstaffe, Doug. 496, it is determined by the court that ¶24 the "indorsement on a blank note is a letter of credit for an indefinite sum."[10] The same principle is asserted by this court in Violett v Patton 5th. Cranch 151.[11] If these decisions apply to sealed instruments, they decide the cause now before the court; for the presumption is at least as strong that the defendants intended, when they executed this bond, to allow the blank to be filled with such sum as the government would require in the official bond of a regimental paymaster, as that the person who signs a blank paper intends to give indefinite credit to the person who receives it. They would too completely overturn the principles laid down in the old books.

But there are certain differences in law between sealed & unsealed ¶25 instrument(s) which make it difficult to apply the principles of one species of co⟨ntr⟩act to the other. All unsealed instruments being considered as verbal contracts, they require neither writing nor delivery. They were never governed by those technical rules which are founded on the necessity of writing & delivery. General & liberal principles therefore which are laid down in such cases, cannot safely be applied to sealed instruments, unless the courts have expressed the intention so to apply them.

¶26   But the case on which most reliance is placed, is that of Speake & others v. The United States 9th. Cranch 28.[12] Speake, Beverly & Eliason had executed an embargo bond; and afterwards the name & seal of Eliason were removed and those of Ober substituted in their place. To an action brought on this bond the defendant Beverly pleaded that this alteration was made "without his consent, license, or authority." The plaintiff replied "that the alteration was made with the assent, and by the concurrent license, direction, and authority of all the defendants and of the said Ebenezer Eliason.["] The defendant demurred to this plea, & the court overruled his demurrer. On appeal to the Supreme court the judgement was affirmed.

¶27   The pleadings present the case of an express authority to make the alteration, and the only questions were whether this express authority could avail the obligee, & whether it could be given by parol. Whatever previous difficulty might have existed on this point, there is none now. The case of Speake against the United States has settled them. But that case goes no farther. It does not decide that an obligation may be created originally by virtue of an authority which is not expressly given but is implied from the sealing & delivery of a paper which in its existing state can avail nothing. This point does not appear to have been ever decided in the case of a sealed instrument. The case of Speake v The United States, in determining that parol evidence of such assent may be received, undoubtedly goes far towards deciding it; and it is probable that the same court may completely abolish the distinction, in this particular, between sealed & unsealed instruments. In this place I do not feel authorized to disregard it. In the English courts, from which the rules applicable to this subject are derived, the distinction is still maintained in a case which bears some analogy to this. The right of one partner to bind another so far as respects the business of the trade & the partnership property is unquestioned. Yet if a partner affix a seal to the instrument by which he pro⟨mises⟩ in the name of the company to pay money, the English Judges, with what propriety I shall not now say, have determined that the company is not bound by it.

¶28   I say with much doubt, & with a strong belief that this judgement will be reversed, that the law on this verdict is, in my opinion with the defendants.

AD, Marshall Judicial Opinions, PPAmP; printed, John W. Brockenbrough, *Reports of Cases Decided by the Honourable John Marshall . . .* , II (Philadelphia, 1837), 66–75. For JM's deletions and interlineations, see Textual Notes below.

1. "Not his deed" was the general issue, or denial, pleaded to an action of debt on a bond. In this instance the defendants pleaded a special denial reciting the fact that the blanks had been filled up in their absence (pleas of Nelson and Myers, 28 May 1819, U.S. v. Nelson and Myers).

2. Edward Coke, *The First Part of the Institutes of the Laws of England; or, A Commentary upon Littleton . . .* , I (16th ed.; London, 1809), 35b-36a; William Sheppard, *Touchstone of Common Assurances* (7th ed.; London, 1820), 54.

3. John Perkins, *A Profitable Book, Treating of the Laws of England: Principally as They Relate to Conveyancing* (1827; New York and London, 1978 reprint, from 15th ed.), sec. 118.

4. Sheppard, *Touchstone of Common Assurances,* 54.

5. Markham v. Gonaston, Cro. Eliz. 676, 78 Eng. Rep. 866; Moo. K.B. 547, 72 Eng. Rep. 749 (K.B., 1598).

6. Coke, *Institutes: Commentary upon Littleton,* III, Note 221 (keyed to ibid., I, 35b). Francis Hargrave and Charles Butler were the editors of the edition of Coke used by JM. Their notes were published in the third volume, which was entitled *Notes on Lord Coke's First Institute, or Commentary upon Littleton.*

7. Zouch v. Clay, 1 Vent. 185, 86 Eng. Rep. 126; 2 Lev. 35, 83 Eng. Rep. 441 (K.B., 1672).

8. Smith v. Crooker, 5 Mass. 538, 539 (1809). The chief justice of Massachusetts from 1806 to 1813 was Theophilus Parsons (1750–1813).

9. Parsons cited Zouch v. Clay and Markham v. Gonaston.

10. Russel v. Langstaffe, 2 Doug. 514, 516, 99 Eng. Rep. 328, 329 (K.B., 1780), quoting Lord Mansfield.

11. Violett v. Patton, 5 Cranch 142, 151 (1809), where JM cited Russel v. Langstaffe.

12. Speake v. U.S., 9 Cranch 28 (1815).

Textual Notes

¶ 1 l. 7 penalty, & the
¶ 2 l. 2 Myers, ~~& was executed by Archer. This was done~~ without
    l. 5 bond. & The ~~paper~~ Jury
    l. 8 said ~~archer~~ ↑Archer,↓ &
¶ 3 l. 1 pleaded ~~the~~ ↑a↓ special
    ll. 1–2 found ~~a special verdict referring the law~~ ↑the facts & referred↓ to
¶ 4 ll. 3–4 delivery ~~was~~ ↑is↓ indispensable. [*erasure*] ↑Until↓ delivery,
    l. 4 writing ~~did~~ ↑does↓ not
    l. 5 who ~~had~~ ↑has↓ sealed it.
    l. 6 (C.L. 35. 6) ↑Shep. Touchstone p 55.↓ These
¶ 5 l. 2 farther than [*erasure*] ↑the↓ writing
¶ 6 l. 6 The ~~united~~ ↑United↓ States
    l. 9 When ~~the bond~~ ↑it↓ was delivered.
¶ 7 l. 2 was ~~intended as~~ ↑to be received as↓ an
¶ 8 l. 1 act ~~make the~~ authorize
¶ 9 l. 1 those ↑moral↓ rules of action ~~by~~ which,
    l. 3 not ↑much↓ difficulty
    l. 13 cases. ~~They~~ ↑Those cases↓ must
¶10 l. 7 execution. ↑It means this or it means nothing.↓ Yet
    ll. 9–10 imply ~~a po~~ ↑an↓ unlimited
    ll. 13–15 deliver ~~a blank~~ ↑an empty piece of paper or, parchment,↓ albeit he do withal give ~~command~~ ↑commandment↓ that an obligation ↑or other matter shall↓ be
¶12 l. 2 was ~~repeatedly~~ argued
    ll. 2–3 case ~~was~~ depended
    l. 5 argued ↑in↓ three
    ll. 6–7 first ~~suit~~ was brought ~~on the~~ ↑against Fox on an↓ obligation ↑made by Sir F. W & said Fox;↓ ~~against Fox~~ &, upon
    ll. 8–9 suited. ~~The pla He then instituted a suit a~~ ↑The party injured then brought an action on the↓ case

	l. 10	command of ~~one of the obligors~~ ↑Sir F. W↓ with
	l. 11	executed by ~~the other obligor~~ ↑Fox:↓ That
¶13	l. 1 beg.	~~Moore~~ ↑Moor↓ in
	l. 1	says ↑note↓ that
¶16	l. 8	therefore ↑the obligation↓ was
¶17	ll. 2–3	create ~~the alteration~~ ↑nor enlarge the obligation,↓ nor
	ll. 5–6	obligation ↑if it exists,↓ is created by the writing ↑inserted after delivery.↓ In the ~~ea~~ ↑subsequent↓ cases
	ll. 7–8	the ~~writing~~ ↑words,↓ not in
¶18	l. 3	court ~~to~~ ↑in↓ which
¶19	l. 1	prepared ↑for Crooker,↓ with
	l. 2	of [erasure] ↑the↓ surety.
	l. 2	become ~~security~~ ↑surety,↓ & executed
	ll. 3–4	then ~~Cushing~~ ↑Crooker↓ also
¶20	l. 5	general ~~principle~~ ↑rule↓ that
¶21	l. 6	do [erasure] ↑so↓ by the
	l. 7	which ↑as respects a deed,↓ such
	ll. 8–9	when ~~no~~ ↑not even the↓ person is designated by whom ~~it~~ ↑the authority↓ is
¶23	l. 7	too, ~~the~~ whatever
¶24	l. 1 beg.	~~A question bearing some analogy to this also came on before the very respectable court of New York.~~ In Russel
	l. 1	496, [erasure] ↑it↓ is
	l. 2	credit ~~for~~ ↑for↓ an
	l. 4	these ↑decisions↓ apply
	ll. 5–6	is ↑at least↓ as strong
	l. 8	require ~~from~~ ↑in the official bond of↓ a
¶25	ll. 4–5	delivery. ↑They ~~were~~ were never governed by↓ those
	l. 6	delivery. ~~never applied to them.~~ General
¶26	l. 5	the ~~defendants~~ ↑defendant Beverly↓ pleaded
	l. 7	made ↑with the assent, and↓ by the
¶27	ll. 2–3	only ~~question was~~ ↑questions were↓ whether this express authority ↑could avail the obligee, & whether it↓ could
	l. 5	settled ~~it~~ ↑them.↓ But
	l. 9	been ↑ever↓ decided
	l. 18	the ↑partnership↓ property
¶28	l. 1	strong ~~belif~~ ↑belief↓ that

To Jaquelin A. Marshall

My dear Son   Richmond Jany. 15th. 23

I have received your letter[1] informing me of the application of Capt. Moorehead for money & fear that the old gentlemans expectations are more sanguine than the state of facts will justify.[2] A letter I had previously written on the subject reached you I presume within a day or two after yours; but as I did not then know the precise quantity of land I had purchased I now write again respecting it. One hundred & ninety one ⅜ acres at 6$ is $1148.25. I paid Capt. Moorehead $100. There is now due $1048.25. I have assumed to pay the debt due by judgement to Smith & Ricard, which, including interest & costs amounts I am told to about $1000. Capt Moorehead estimates it at $700, but I must have the estimate of Smith & Ricard. They will not credit me for payments made to him. I shall write by James to Mr. Smith & request him to inform you what is the precise sum for which he looks to me. Capt. Moorehead ought to bring this in writing to you before he asks you to pay him money. The difference between $1048.25 and the sum I must pay Smith & Ricard Capt. Moorehead is entitled to & I wish him to recieve it. Tell McCormack I am much pressed for money & hope he will be punctual. I hope Mrs. Dodd has returned her administration account.[3] This business ought to be closed.

I have undertaken to pay your legacy and send you the account which shows that I shall have to pay you $2318.⟨42.⟩ James has the money & will settle with you immediately for his bond. Your brother Tom owes me $170 or thereabouts which he will pay you. Your own debt to me must be deducted, & I will pay you the balan⟨ce⟩ as soon as possible. It shall not be very long before you receive the money.

The Reverend Mr. Blair, the bosom friend & companion of Mr. Buchanan was not long behind him. His funeral took place last sunday & the town testified its respect for him by one of the largest processions I ever saw.[4] These two gentlemen have not left two better men behind them. Mr. Blair died very poor and has left, I fear a distressed family.

Your brother left us the other day for Westover. The family are all well. If the district should not be changed, about which there is some doubt, he will be at the courts in February.[5] Your mother is as usual. Our love to yourself Eliza & the children.[6] I am my dear Son your affectionate Father

J MARSHALL

Dr. J. A. Marsh⟨all⟩			
Jany. 1st. 1823	⟨706.66⟩		J. Buchanan
By your bond ⟨. . .⟩	⟨300⟩		
By int from 1st. Jany. 1822 ⟨. . .⟩		⟨8.25⟩	To you by a 3333.33
By bond of J K. Marshall assigned to you	300		
By int from the 15th. July 1822 . . .	8.25		
By bond of J Marshall assigned —	1000		
By int. from the 15th. Oct. 1822	14.37½		
By bond of J Marshall assigned —	1000		
By int. from the 15th. Oct. 1822 —	14.37½		
By part bond of J. Marshall	289.67		
	3333.33		

$$\begin{array}{r} 2318.42 \\ \text{I send you } 480\$ \text{ by James which reduces my debt to} \quad \underline{480.} \\ 1838.42 \end{array}$$

$$\begin{array}{r} 706.66 \\ \underline{308.25} \\ 1014.91 \\ \underline{480.00} \\ 1464.91 \end{array}$$

ALS, Collection of Linda Ball Olson, Beaufort, S.C. Addressed to "Doctor Jaquelin A. Marshall."

1. Letter not found. Jaquelin A. Marshall was then living in Fauquier County.

2. Probably George Morehead, a Fauquier landowner, with whom JM executed articles of agreement in Sept. 1825 (ADS, Collection of Mrs. James R. Green, Markham, Va., 1971).

3. In 1828 JM executed a lease to Ann Dodd for land in Fauquier County (Irwin S. Rhodes, *The Papers of John Marshall: A Descriptive Calendar* [2 vols.; Norman, Okla., 1969], II, 320).

4. The Rev. John D. Blair, minister of the Presbyterian church on Shockoe Hill, died on 10 Jan. He and the Rev. John Buchanan, who died in 1822, were Richmond's "two parsons," beloved for their benevolence and conviviality (Richmond *Enquirer*, 11, 14 Jan. 1823; George Wythe Munford, *The Two Parsons; Cupid's Sports; The Dream; and The Jewels of Virginia* [Richmond, Va., 1884]).

5. Thomas Marshall, whose wife's family lived at Weyanoke (near Westover) in Charles City County, was a Federalist candidate for Congress (see JM to Mary W. Marshall, 11 Apr. 1823 and n. 4).

6. Jaquelin A. Marshall married Eliza Clarkson in 1819 (Paxton, *Marshall Family*, 99).

To Robert Mayo and William A. Bartow

GENTLEMEN —   *Richmond, Jan. 26, 1823.*

I have received your Circular Address, in behalf of the "Juvenile Library Company of the city of Richmond," with a card annexed in which you do me the honour to associate me with gentlemen of the first literary character in our country, whose views you solicit on the subject of education.[1]

I am truly flattered by this distinction, and should feel great pleasure in complying with your request could I persuade myself that it is in my power to say any thing new or valuable on this interesting topic. But I have been accustomed to take only general views of the subject; and it is too vast and complex to be properly treated by one whose attention has not, heretofore, been particularly directed towards it, and who is now too much occupied by arduous public duties, as well as private business, to give it the consideration it deserves.

Your fellow-citizens are greatly indebted to you for the enlightened zeal with which you have engaged in an undertaking of the deepest interest to the community. To establish a good system for the education of youth, is certainly among the most meritorious efforts of patriotism; but it is an object which, I fear and believe, the legislative power alone can accomplish.[2] Our Eastern brethren have engrafted the principle of general instruction on their original establishments. It has grown with their growth, and is incorporated with the very essence of their political existence. Public opinion co-operates with law to cherish their institutions. I would hope that the experiment might be equally successful in Virginia were similar means employed. Should your commencement seem to give this direction to public sentiment, you will receive a rich reward in the consciousness of having rendered much real good to your country.[3] With great respect, I am gentlemen, Your obed't serv't,

J. MARSHALL.

Printed, *An Address in Behalf of the Juvenile Library Company of the City of Richmond* (Richmond, Va., 1823), 15–16.

1. The enclosed circular was *An Address in Behalf of the Juvenile Library Company of the City of Richmond* (Richmond, Va., 1823), dated 8 Jan. 1823. This twelve-page imprint was accompanied by a "card," dated 20 Jan. 1823 and signed by Robert Mayo and William A. Bartow, who had been appointed by the library company's board of directors to solicit donations "in books or money" from the citizens of Richmond. The card was addressed to "eminent" gentlemen of the city, seeking their support for the library company and soliciting "a commendatory line in its behalf." Mayo (1784–1864) was graduated from the University of Pennsylvania Medical School in 1808 and practiced in Richmond from 1808 to 1830. Bartow (1794–1869) had been a bookseller and printer in New York City before moving to Richmond (John Howard Brown, ed., *Lamb's Biographical Dictionary of the United States*, V [Boston, 1903], 426; George L. McKay, *A Register of Artists, Engravers, Booksellers, Bookbinders, Printers & Publishers in New York City, 1633–1820* [New York, 1942], 9).

2. The juvenile library was to be part of a larger system of public education outlined in the address. The plan called upon counties and cities to establish local literary funds to purchase books for the library, to provide rooms to house the library and a school for the instruction of youth free of tuition fees and charges for books, and to pay a qualified person to superintend the library and instruction of the students (*An Address in Behalf of the Juvenile Library Company of the City of Richmond*, 8–9).

3. A subsequent imprint of the circular address, now expanded to eighteen pages, included JM's testimonial letter along with those from other prominent Richmond citizens. Below JM's letter Mayo and Bartow subjoined this: "It is due to the liberality of Judge Marshall, to say, that in a private conversation with him, he has also authorised us to expect a donation for the benefit of the Company, which accounts for his not mentioning that subject in his letter." Mayo also published JM's letter in his *Political Sketches of Eight Years in Washington* (Baltimore, 1839), 47.

To Mary W. Marshall

My dearest Polly   Washington, Jany [February][1] 4th. 1823

I arrived at this place yesterday between ten & eleven & am now sitting by a fine wood fire in one of the best rooms in the city about to tell my beloved wife what a comfortable Journey I have had & how well I am now situated. The roads were better than I have ever found them at this season of the year, & we accomplished our Journey each day a very little after dark. Last winter I got into Alexandria after eleven at night, & this winter about seven. One stage sooner & the roads would not have been nearly so good; one stage later & they would have been bad, for on Monday morning we found the ground covered with a wet snow which dissolved rapidly & will make them very deep. It is the first time that I have been fortunate in my day of setting out.

When I reached Fredericksburg I found that James[2] had left no instructions at the stage office respecting the trunk, & I brought it with me to Alexandria, &, as Mr. Ashby is not now in the town or in business, I left it with Mr. Massie.[3] I found my unkle Keith in his bed very unwell, though rather getting better.[4] I was very glad that I went to see him though it was early in the morning & in a wet snow because he had been enquiring for me & seemed much gratified at the call. My aunt is much better but was not up.[5]

We paid our visit yesterday to the President whom we found in good health but a year older I think than he was last winter, & looking very serious.

Mr. Washington has been very unwell. I have not yet asked him how it happens that he did not write to me, but I have no doubt it is to be ascribed to his apprehension respecting his health.

I have not yet seen or heard anything concerning Richard Martyr.

Soon after dinner yesterday the French Chargé d'affaires called upon us with a pressing invitation to be present at a party given to the young couple, a gentleman of the French legation & the daughter of the secretary of the navy who are lately married.[6] There was a most briliant illumination which we saw and admired, & then we returned.

Mr. Johnson is not arrived & Mr. Todd is too sick to come. I very much fear that we shall lose him. Today we should set in to close business were it not that Mr. Wirt is unfortunately very sick. This I regret very much for his own sake, & some thing on a public account. Farewell my dearest Polly. I am ever your affectionate

J MARSHALL

Tr, Beveridge-Marshall Papers, DLC.

1. Evidently a transcription error. Internal evidence clearly establishes that JM wrote this letter in February, just after arriving in Washington for the session of the Supreme Court.
2. James Keith Marshall.
3. Possibly Turner Ashby and John W. Massie, who were Alexandria merchants (T. Michael Miller, comp., *Artisans and Merchants of Alexandria, Virginia: 1780–1820* [2 vols.; Bowie, Md., 1991], I, 15, 325).
4. The aged James Keith of Alexandria was the eldest brother of JM's mother. He died at the age of 90 in Oct. 1824 (*Alexandria Gazette*, 17 Oct. 1824).
5. Elizabeth Contee Keith (1745–1827), wife of James Keith (*Alexandria Gazette*, 7 June 1827).
6. The French chargé d'affaires was the Comte de Menou. On 23 Jan. Charles de Bresson

(1798–1847), secretary to the French legation, married Catharine Livingston Thompson, eldest daughter of Secretary of the Navy Smith Thompson (Charles Francis Adams, ed., *Memoirs of John Quincy Adams*, VI [Philadelphia, 1875], 22–23; *Daily National Intelligencer*, 25 Jan. 1823).

Notes on Arguments
U.S. Supreme Court, 12–13 February 1823

EDITORIAL NOTE

In the document below Chief Justice Marshall recorded arguments in three cases heard in the Supreme Court on 12 and 13 February 1823: *Buel* v. *Van Ness*, *Williams* v. *United States*, and *Nicholas* v. *Anderson*. At least one sheet of the original is missing, for the notes on the surviving sheet begin with the concluding portion of the arguments in *Buel* v. *Van Ness*.

Buel v. *Van Ness* was a writ of error to the Supreme Court of Vermont, Chittenden County. Samuel Buel, who had served as customs collector from 1811 to 1813, sued Cornelius P. Van Ness, his successor as collector, in the state court for money arising on a forfeiture of illegally imported fur and wine. The seizure and forfeiture occurred while Buel was collector, but the money was paid to Van Ness after he became collector. After the state court ruled for Van Ness, Buel, claiming a right under a federal law, obtained a writ of error as prescribed by section 25 of the Judiciary Act of 1789. The appeal was argued in the Supreme Court on 12 February 1823 by John Sergeant for Buel and William Wirt for Van Ness. The principal point at issue was whether the Supreme Court properly had jurisdiction in this case under section 25 of the Judiciary Act of 1789.[1]

Williams v. *United States*, an unreported case, began in the U.S. District Court for Maryland. James Williams in October 1815 had executed a bond to secure import duties as surety for Charles F. Kalkman. The United States obtained a judgment against Kalkman and Williams on this bond in December 1816. Kalkman was arrested and taken into custody, but in February 1818 was discharged by President Monroe pursuant to an act of March 1817 for the relief of persons imprisoned for debts due to the United States. When the United States sought to revive the judgment against Williams, the surety pleaded that the discharge of Kalkman operated in law to discharge him as well. The United States demurred to this plea and the court sustained the demurrer. The case first went to the Supreme Court in August 1818, but the writ of error was dismissed on 9 March 1819 as having been directed to the U.S. District Court. It was filed again in February 1820 and argued on 13 February 1823 by William H. Winder for Williams and Attorney General Wirt for the United States.[2]

The parties in *Nicholas* v. *Anderson* were Philip N. Nicholas, acting in his capacity as attorney general of Virginia, and Richard C. Anderson, of Kentucky. Nicholas filed a bill of equity in the U.S. Circuit Court for Kentucky under a special act of the Virginia legislature authorizing an agent to proceed in the name of the state attorney general to recover money paid to Anderson as principal surveyor of lands given to Revolutionary veterans. Anderson had been appointed in virtue of a 1783 act, which among other things provided that all persons holding military land warrants by assignment should pay the surveyor one dollar for every one hundred acres as a fund for paying contingent expenses. The bill charged that Anderson had refused to account for this money. The court upheld the defendant's demurrer to this bill in November 1818. The appeal was filed in the Supreme Court in January 1821 and argued on 13 February 1823 by Wirt for Nicholas and by Isham Talbot (1773–1837), a U.S. Senator from Kentucky, for Anderson.[3]

1. Buel v. Van Ness, App. Cas. No. 1019; U.S. Sup. Ct. Dockets, Buel v. Van Ness, App. Cas. No. 1019; 8 Wheat. 312–19; *U.S. Statutes at Large*, I, 85–86.

2. Williams v. U.S., App. Cas. No. 939; Williams v. U.S., App. Cas. No. 1048; U.S. Sup. Ct. Dockets, Williams v. U.S., App. Cas. Nos. 939, 1048; U.S. Sup. Ct. Minutes, 9 Mar. 1819, 13 Feb. 1823.

3. Nicholas v. Anderson, App. Cas. No. 1083; U.S. Sup. Ct. Dockets, Nicholas v. Anderson, App. Cas. No. 1083; 8 Wheat. 365–68.

The act of Congress aims at one policy — the preservation of the powers of the federal government its constitution laws & treaties & those claiming under them, from claims against them.[1]

3 Cranch 3 268- 4 Cranch 382 5 Cranch 92	Decision in favor of the party claiming under the act of Congress[2]
6th	This assumpsit & it appears that the plf. was not the only person entitled.
Mr. Sergeant	
1st.	The form sent by the Clerk of this court under the authority of an act of Congress. The clerk of the circuit court cannot vary it.
2. V. 302	forms of the writ to be sent by the clerk of the circuits Whatever authority is given to the clerk of the supreme court to issue writs of error is given to the clerks of the circuits.[3]
3.	This objection the same as to the 1st. point. That which the court is presumed to know need not be pleaded nor proved by witnesses. The law of a state is neither to be pleaded nor proved.
4th.	The sum. The counsel has lost sight of the distinction between what regulates the writ & regulates the court
5th.	The case of Mathews v Zane in 4th. Cranch in point
6th.	If the verdict be defective the judgement must be reversed & sent back.[4]

Williams
The US
Winder

The general principle is that the creditor discharges the surety by altering the relation of the parties. Even a suspension agt. principal releases the surety—Much more a release

---

5th B abr	A discharge or release of one obligor is a release of
Release G	both[5]
6 Term 525	In case of a joint judgement the discharge of one from execution discharges both.[6]
1 Gal. 36	The law under which principal was discharged existed at time of contract. This release affects the rights of the surety who is deprived of his right to stand in the place of the US.[7]
Act of 1817 ch 14.	Under which the President acted.
v 3.54.	The act of 98. difft. from that of 17.[8]
———	If the P. under this law discharges a principal without making the terms which may [be] required by the surety, it ought as in the case of a private creditor, to discharge the surety

The Atty. Genl. Reads the act to show how far it affects a judgement. The discharge releases the person not the judgement.

———	Questions whether at com. law the discharge of the
5 Co. 86	principal person discharges security. Questions whether at com. law the body is satisfaction[9]

5 East 147	Where a principal is discharged under an insolvent
1. Wash. 95	law the surety is not discharged. It would be so if
2 Sir WBl 1235.	body was satisfaction.[10]

4 Bur. 2482	not the case of two debtors but of one.
7 Term 420	The first judgt. was discharged by the new agree-
2 East 244	ment. The action ought to be not on the original
1. Term 557	judgt. which was discharged but only upon agreement.[11]

	Is this discharge any disadvantage to the surety? Would his detention in prison have benefited the surety?
v.3. p 197. Sec 65.	He does not lose any advantage.[12]

Winder

The President by a discharge under the act of 1817 takes from the surety, especially in a case of conveyance for other creditors, of the priority secured by the act of 98.[13]

Atty. Genl of Virga.

v

Richard Anderson

Mr. Wirt

Ch. rev. 210   Virga. considers Mr. Anderson as an officer of Virga. &
is so stated in the bill.[14] Demurrer admits the fact.

The authority given to the superintendants has expired. The surveyor who has received large sums of money under an act of Virga. is called to account for it.

An act of assembly has passed in Virga. authorizing the Atty. Genl. to proceed

---

The argument is that the deputation being no longer existing the money belongs to the surveyor.

Virga. does not claim this money beneficially but as trustee.

In virtue of her sovereignty may claim the power to superintend the exn. of such law.

Resulting trust to the grantor.

Corporate body endowed for a given purpose which fails the fund reverts.

Mr. Talbot

The state of Virga. has no colour or pretext of claim to demand this money for herself or as trustee.

All the expenses borne by the assignees & as an additional fund to releive those who held in their own right.[15]

AD, Wheaton Papers, NNPM.

1. The MS begins in the middle of Wirt's argument for the defendant in Buel v. Van Ness. In the fifth of six enumerated points, Wirt discussed section 25 of the Judiciary Act of 1789 (8 Wheat. 316–18).

2. Wirt cited the following cases: Gordon v. Caldcleugh, 3 Cranch 268 (1806); Matthews v. Zane, 4 Cranch 382 (1808); Matthews v. Zane's Lessee, 5 Cranch 92 (1809).

3. The reference is to section 9 of the 1792 act regulating processes in U.S. courts (U.S. Statutes at Large, I, 275, 278). Here and below the edition of laws JM cited in the notes is Laws of the United States of America, from the 4th of March, 1789, to the 4th of March, 1815 (5 vols.; Philadelphia and Washington, 1815).

4. On 18 Feb. 1823 Justice Johnson for the Court sustained the Court's jurisdiction and directed that the state court's judgment be reversed and entered for Buel (8 Wheat. 319–25).

5. Bacon, Abridgment, V, 702.

6. Clarke v. Clement and English, 6 T.R. 525, 101 Eng. Rep. 683 (K.B., 1796).

7. Hunt v. U.S., 1 Gall. 32, 36, 12 Fed. Cas. 948–50 (U.S. Cir. Ct., Mass., 1812).

8. The references are to an act for the relief of persons imprisoned for debts due the U.S., enacted in June 1798, and a supplementary act, enacted in Mar. 1817 (*U.S. Statutes at Large*, I, 561–62; III, 399).

9. Blumfield's Case, 5 Co. Rep. 86, 77 Eng. Rep. 185 (K.B., 1596).

10. Nadin v. Battie and Wardle, 5 East 147, 102 Eng. Rep. 1025 (K.B., 1804); Taylor v. Dundass, 1 Wash. 95 (Va. Ct. App., 1792); Hayling v. Mullhall, 2 Black. W. 1235, 96 Eng. Rep. 728 (C.P., 1778).

11. Vigers v. Aldrich, 4 Burr. 2482, 98 Eng. Rep. 301 (K.B., 1769); Tanner v. Hague, 7 T.R. 420, 101 Eng. Rep. 1054 (K.B., 1797); Blackburn v. Stupart, 2 East 243, 244, 102 Eng. Rep. 362 (K.B., 1802); Jaques v. Withy, 1 T.R. 557, 99 Eng. Rep. 1249 (K.B., 1787).

12. The 1799 act to regulate the collection of duties, section 65, provided that a surety paying an insolvent's bond to the U.S. would have the same priority of payment as enjoyed by the U.S. (*U.S. Statutes at Large*, I, 676).

13. On 21 Feb. 1823 the Court again (as in 1819) quashed the writ of error as having been directed to the U.S. District Court (U.S. Sup. Ct. Minutes, 21 Feb. 1823).

14. The citation is to an act for surveying lands given by law to officers of the state and Continental lines, enacted at the Oct. 1783 session of the Virginia General Assembly (Hening, *Statutes*, XI, 309). The abbreviation stands for the compilation known as the "Chancellors' Revisal," officially entitled *A Collection of All Such Public Acts of the General Assembly . . . of Virginia* (Richmond, Va., 1785), which contained the statutes and convention ordinances enacted from 1768 through June 1783. A facsimile edition has been published as *The First Laws of the State of Virginia* (Wilmington, Del., 1982).

15. On 24 Feb. 1823 Justice Story for the Court affirmed the circuit court's decree (8 Wheat. 368–70).

Johnson v. McIntosh
Opinion
U.S. Supreme Court, 28 February 1823

EDITORIAL NOTE

Until the Cherokee cases of the 1830s, *Johnson* v. *McIntosh* was the Marshall Court's most important statement about the legal rights of Native Americans who lived within the territorial limits of the United States. Although in form a land title dispute between white American parties, the case elicited from Chief Justice Marshall a probing inquiry into the nature of the Indian tribes' title to the lands they occupied. In this respect the opinion became an influential precedent in the formation of federal Indian law that has also been cited in other jurisdictions in cases concerning the rights of indigenous peoples.[1] Behind the decision was a long history (dating from before the Revolution) of the efforts of land companies to obtain legal recognition of titles acquired by direct purchase from the Indians.

Plaintiffs Joshua Johnson and Thomas J. Graham were citizens of Maryland and devisees of Thomas Johnson (1732–1819), a prominent Maryland politician who had been the state's first governor and later served briefly as associate justice of the U.S. Supreme Court. In the years immediately preceding the outbreak of the War of Independence, Thomas Johnson joined with other speculators from Pennsylvania and Maryland (but whose numbers also included Lord Dunmore, Virginia's last royal governor) in purchasing land in the Illinois country. At the time this land lay within the chartered limits of the colony of Virginia. Two companies were involved in this speculation: the Illinois Land Company, which in July 1773 purchased two tracts from the Illinois Indians, and the Wabash Land Company, which in October 1775 purchased two tracts from the Piankeshaw Indians. The plaintiffs claimed Thomas Johnson's undivided share of the two tracts acquired by the Wabash Land Company in 1775.[2]

Some years later, in 1803 and in 1805, the United States purchased by treaty with the same tribes much of the land they had previously sold to the land companies.[3] In July 1818 William McIntosh obtained a patent from the United States that fell within the lines of the Wabash purchase of 1775. To contest McIntosh's possession of this land Johnson and Graham brought an ejectment in the U.S. District Court of Illinois. Like all ejectments the case proceeded on an agreed statement of facts, upon which, in December 1820, Judge Nathaniel Pope gave judgment for McIntosh. The plaintiffs obtained a writ of error and brought their case to the Supreme Court in February 1821. The appeal was argued over four days in February 1823 by Robert G. Harper and Daniel Webster for the plaintiffs and William H. Winder and Henry M. Murray for the defendants.[4]

In bringing their ejectment in the federal courts, the plaintiffs (who represented the interests of the land companies) were transferring their case to a judicial forum after failing over the course of thirty-five years to obtain confirmation of their titles by Congress. As early as 1780 the two companies that had purchased the Illinois lands joined together as the Illinois and Wabash Land Company and presented an application to the old Congress of the Confederation. Supreme Court justice James Wilson served as president of the company and signed two memorials submitted to Congress in 1791 and 1797. The company presented further petitions in 1804 and 1810. Harper, who argued the 1823 case in the Supreme Court, served as the company's agent in drawing up the 1810 memorial.[5]

The company staked the validity of its title to the Illinois lands on the premise that the Indian tribes were the "lawful possessors of the soil, who, being free and independent, . . . had, . . . an absolute and indefeasible right to sell and convey the same to any persons or companies whomsoever." It offered various corollary arguments as well: that the charters issued by the British government to establish colonies in North America were never intended to divest the Indians of their property in the soil, that the British and colonial governments had always treated the tribes as independent nations and as absolute owners of their land, and that the British king (by the Proclamation of 1763) had no authority to prevent the Indians from selling land or British subjects from purchasing it from the Indians.[6]

Although asserting its full legal and equitable title to the lands, for "reasons of policy and public good" the company was willing to compromise. It proposed to surrender all its lands to the federal government, provided that the United States reconvey one-fourth of the lands to the company. In making this offer (subsequently modified), the company admitted that the government's measures "for the defence and settlement of the neighboring country" had "greatly enhanced the value of this property" and that it might "be inconvenient to the public for individuals to hold so large a body of land."[7] Congress, however, spurned the company's generosity, declaring that unauthorized purchases from Indians by private individuals did not vest a lawful title. The purchases of 1773 and 1775, said Congress, were made in direct violation of the British crown's Proclamation of 1763, which expressly prohibited purchases from Indians inhabiting the territory beyond the Alleghenies. Independent of the effect of the Proclamation, the purchases were contrary to the settled policy that required "concomitant assent or subsequent sanction of the Government" to render an Indian conveyance valid — a rule that in Congress's opinion was "a part of the law of the land."[8]

In the Supreme Court Harper and Webster restated the case presented in the company's memorials to Congress. Identifying the essential issue as whether the right of purchasing from Indians was "competent to *individuals*" or belonged exclusively to the government, they insisted that the purchasers' rights under the deeds of 1773 and 1775 were unaffected by the Proclamation of 1763 and that there was no express law of Virginia in force at the time prohibiting individuals from purchasing lands from Indians.[9] On the other side, Winder and Murray contended that the settled policy and law of the "civilized" states of Europe "denied the right of the Indians to be considered as independent communities, having a permanent property in the soil, capable of alienation to private individuals." This right was also incompatible with the theory that all land titles in America ultimately derived from the British crown through the principle of "discovery," by which England and other European nations claimed sovereignty and the right of the soil over the North American continent. Indians were a "subject" people under the jurisdiction of the United States, nomadic inhabitants who had never acquired any "proprietary interest" in the territory "they wandered over."[10]

Marshall delivered the Court's opinion on 28 February, nine days after arguments concluded. His unrivaled knowledge of land law acquired through his law practice and his experience as a purchaser of the Fairfax estate, his intimate familiarity as a lawyer and legislator with the land companies' claims to extensive tracts in the west, his background as a historian — all conspired to make the chief justice the logical choice to write the Court's opinion in *Johnson*. Much of the opinion is taken up with a historical recital of various colonial charters, patents, grants, treaties, and legislative acts for which his own *Life of Washington* provided a convenient reference. As a Congressman in 1800 Marshall had conducted a similar investigation in a report on Connecticut's cession of the Western Reserve.[11] The subject was again fresh in his mind in 1823, for he was then revising the introductory part of the *Life of Washington*, published separately in 1824 as a *History of the American Colonies*. As a judge, Marshall had briefly considered the nature of Indian title in *Fletcher* v. *Peck* (1810), which he cited in *Johnson*. In addition, the theory of Indian title he set forth in *Johnson* had been adumbrated as early as 1791 by Judge Pendleton of the Virginia Court of Appeals in a case in which Marshall's father was plaintiff.[12]

The opinion affirmed the lower court's ruling in favor of McIntosh, holding that the title acquired by purchase from the Indians in 1775 could not be sustained in the courts of the United States. Such a decision was no surprise, for it conformed to a long-settled policy, dating from the early colonial period, governing land titles and relations with the Indians. The close attention the Court bestowed upon this question, said Marshall, "was more required by the magnitude of the interest in litigation, and the able and elaborate arguments of the bar, than by its intrinsic difficulty."[13]

Johnson exhibited in full measure the chief justice's gift for rationalizing and synthesizing a historical record that was sometimes ambiguous and even contradictory. To decide the case, Marshall elaborated a theory of an Indian "title of occupancy," which he distinguished from the British crown's "ultimate absolute title." The crown's claim to absolute title in the soil of North America was founded on the principle of discovery, according to which the discovering nation asserted against all other European nations its exclusive right to acquire territory from the native inhabitants and to establish settlements. The crown and its successor, the government of the United States, claimed under the discovery doctrine the sole right to "extinguish" (by purchase) the Indian title of occupancy and to convey absolute title in the soil to individuals. Such a title could not be acquired by direct purchase from Indians. In asserting absolute title, European governments assumed the right to grant the soil even while it remained in possession of the natives. The greater part of the opinion was devoted to demonstrating recognition of these principles in the historical record from discovery to the present.

Although the rights of Indians were not directly at issue in this case, the enduring significance of *Johnson* is the theory of Indian title Marshall applied to decide the rights of white litigants. His opinion has been censured for "effectively" denying American Indians "recognizable full legal title to their ancestral homelands" and as embodying legal principles and rhetoric that would give "future acts of genocide . . . a rationalized, legal basis."[14] Such a reading grossly misconstrues the meaning of the opinion and fails to appreciate the extent to which the chief justice placed Indian property rights on a firm legal foundation. As he did on other occasions, Marshall paid due homage to the principles of natural justice while grounding his decision largely in actual practice and positive law. If in this case he could not satisfactorily reconcile the principles of American land law with the higher claims of natural law, the resulting decision was by no means incompatible with a fully protected Indian right to the soil and with a large measure of Indian sovereignty as well. The chief justice left no doubt that Indian rights were based not merely on "abstract justice" but firmly embedded in American law.[15]

While sustaining McIntosh's title, Marshall largely eschewed reasoning and rhetoric that portrayed the Indians as an inferior people virtually destitute of any proprietary rights. True, the chief justice did refer to the Indians as "fierce savages, whose occupation was war, and whose subsistence was drawn chiefly from the forest." At the same time, however, he was unable to suppress a tone of apology, even embarrassment, in his narrative of relations between "primitive" native societies and "civilized" European states. He spoke of the "pompous claims" of Europe to North America and the "extravagant . . . pretension of converting the discovery of an inhabited country into conquest." However fantastic the notion that discovery conferred absolute title to the soil, he had to acknowledge that this principle and its corollary, that Indians were mere occupants "incapable of transferring the absolute title to others," had become the law of the land. This restriction, so contrary "to natural right, and to the usages of civilized nations," was nevertheless "indispensable" to the American system of settlement and "adapted to the actual condition of the two people." It could therefore, "perhaps, be supported by reason, and certainly cannot be rejected by Courts of justice."[16] Clearly, Chief Justice Marshall experienced no little discomfort in announcing these principles as the law he had to apply to this case.

Despite the denial of absolute title in the Indians, *Johnson* gave due recognition to an Indian right of occupancy that was to be respected by American courts. This right, moreover, was in practical terms scarcely distinguishable from a "fee simple" interest, for the Court's holding imposed no restriction on the tribes' right to sell their land. Indeed, read carefully, the opinion was fully compatible with the notion of Indian sovereignty and independence. The discovery principle, Marshall explained, was never asserted to deny the right of the original inhabitants to occupy the soil and was never understood to vest fee simple title in the discovering nation. Discovery conveyed nothing more than a right to acquire the Indian title of occupancy. It was an agreement among European nations to divide up the right to extinguish Indian title. It did not affect or in any way limit the internal nature of that title.[17]

Marshall in effect validated an Indian land tenure system that was distinct from the federal and state systems. The denial of Johnson's claim did not mean that Indian tribes were restricted to selling their land only to the federal government. They were perfectly free to sell land to individuals, though the title conveyed was the Indian title of occupancy. This title would be held under the law of the tribe, which retained the power to annul the grant if it chose. If the tribe annulled the grant, said Marshall, "we know of no tribunal which can revise and set aside the proceeding."[18] In the case at hand the Court's refusal to sustain the white claimant's interest under purchase from the Indians in no way impugned the legality of the Indian title. Rather, it recognized the tribe's sovereign right of eminent domain to abolish the vested rights of individual purchasers of tribal lands. The Indians themselves defeated Johnson's claim when they subsequently ceded their territory to the United States without reserving the particular tract.

1. Howard R. Berman, "The Concept of Aboriginal Rights in the Early Legal History of the United States," *Buffalo Law Review*, XXVII (1978), 643 and n. 28, citing a 1971 Australian case, Milirrpum v. Nabalco Pty. Ltd. On Johnson v. McIntosh as a precedent in Australia, see L. J. Priestley, "Communal Native Title and the Common Law: Further Thoughts on the Gove Land Rights Case," *Federal Law Review*, VI (1974), 151–52.

2. 8 Wheat. 550–57, 560–61; Clarence Walworth Alvord, *The Illinois Country, 1673–1818* (1922; Chicago, 1965 reprint), 301–2; Jack M. Sosin, *Whitehall and the Wilderness: The Middle West in British Colonial Policy, 1760–1775* (Lincoln, Nebr., 1961), 231–35.

3. Alvord, *Illinois Country*, 416–17; ASP, *Public Lands*, II, 111; ASP, *Indian Affairs*, I, 687, 704–5.

4. Johnson v. McIntosh, Record on Appeal, 1–12, App. Cas. No. 1105; U.S. Sup. Ct. Minutes, 15, 17–19 Feb. 1823.

5. Alvord, *Illinois Country*, 384–86; ASP, *Public Lands*, I, 27, 72–73, 160–61; II, 108–20. The company also presented its case in printed pamphlets: *An Account of the Proceedings of the Illinois and Ouabache Land Companies* (Philadelphia, 1796; Evans #30618 [reprinted, with additions, Philadelphia, 1803; S #5193]); *Memorial of the United Illinois and Wabash Land Companies to the Senate and House of Representatives* (Baltimore, 1810; S #21552). One last attempt by the company to obtain a hearing by Congress appears to have been made in 1816. See *Memorial of the United Illinois and Wabash Land Companies, to the Senate and House of Representatives* (Baltimore, 1816; S #39145), 48.

6. ASP, *Public Lands*, I, 72; II, 112.

7. Ibid., I, 73; II, 116.

8. Ibid., II, 253.

9. 8 Wheat. 562–67 (quotation at 563).

10. 8 Wheat. 567–71 (quotations at 567, 569–70).

11. *PJM*, IV, 115–17; ASP, *Public Lands*, I, 94–98; Priestley, "Communal Native Title and the Common Law," 170.

12. Marshall v. Clark, 4 Call 272–73.

13. Opinion, 28 Feb. 1823 (300, below).

14. Robert A. Williams, Jr., *The American Indian in Western Legal Thought: The Discourses of Conquest* (New York, 1990), 313, 317.

15. J. Youngblood Henderson, "Unraveling the Riddle of Aboriginal Title," *American Indian Law Journal*, V (1977), 87–96; Berman, "The Concept of Aboriginal Rights," 642–56; Milner S. Ball, "Court Constitution, Indian Tribes," *American Bar Foundation Research Journal*, I (1987), 23–29.

16. Opinion, 28 Feb. 1823 (293–94, below).

17. Henderson, "Unraveling the Riddle of Aboriginal Title," 90–91.

18. Opinion, 28 Feb. 1823 (295, below).

OPINION

The plaintiffs in this cause claim the land, in their declaration mentioned, under two grants, purporting to be made, the first in 1773, and the last in 1775, by the chiefs of certain Indian tribes, constituting the Illinois and the Piankeshaw nations; and the question is whether this title can be recognised in the Courts of the United States?

The facts, as stated in the case agreed, show the authority of the chiefs who executed this conveyance, so far as it could be given by their own people; and likewise show, that the particular tribes for whom these chiefs acted were in rightful possession of the land they sold. The inquiry, therefore, is, in a great measure, confined to the power of Indians to give, and of private individuals to receive, a title which can be sustained in the Courts of this country.

As the right of society, to prescribe those rules by which property may be acquired and preserved is not, and cannot be drawn into question; as the title to lands, especially, is and must be admitted to depend entirely on the law of the nation in which they lie; it will be necessary, in pursuing this inquiry, to examine, not singly those principles of abstract justice, which the Creator of all things has impressed on the mind of his creature man, and which are admitted to regulate, in a great degree, the rights of civilized nations, whose perfect independence is acknowledged; but those principles also which our own government has adopted in the particular case, and given us as the rule for our decision.

On the discovery of this immense continent, the great nations of Europe were eager to appropriate to themselves so much of it as they could respectively acquire. Its vast extent offered an ample field to the ambition and enterprise of all; and the character and religion of its inhabitants afforded an apology for considering them as a people over whom the superior genius of Europe might claim an ascendency. The potentates of the old world found no difficulty in convincing themselves that they made ample compensation to the inhabitants of the new, by bestowing on them civilization and Christianity, in exchange for unlimited independence. But, as they were all in pursuit of nearly the same object, it was necessary, in order to avoid conflicting settlements, and consequent war with each other, to establish a principle, which all should acknowledge as the law by which the right of acquisition, which they all asserted, should be regulated as between themselves. This principle was, that discovery gave title to the government by whose subjects, or by whose authority, it was made, against all other European governments, which title might be consummated by possession.

The exclusion of all other Europeans, necessarily gave to the nation making the discovery the sole right of acquiring the soil from the natives, and establishing settlements upon it. It was a right with which no Europeans could interfere. It was a right which all asserted for themselves, and to the assertion of which, by others, all assented.

Those relations which were to exist between the discoverer and the natives, were to be regulated by themselves. The rights thus acquired being exclusive, no other power could interpose between them.

In the establishment of these relations, the rights of the original inhabitants were, in no instance, entirely disregarded; but were necessarily, to a considerable extent, impaired. They were admitted to be the rightful occupants of the soil, with a legal as well as just claim to retain possession of it, and to use it according to their own discretion; but their rights to complete sovereignty, as independent nations, were necessarily diminished, and their power to dispose of the soil at their own will, to whomsoever they pleased, was denied by the original fundamental principle, that discovery gave exclusive title to those who made it.

While the different nations of Europe respected the right of the natives, as occupants, they asserted the ultimate dominion to be in themselves; and claimed and exercised, as a consequence of this ultimate dominion, a power to grant the soil, while yet in possession of the natives. These grants have been understood by all, to convey a title to the grantees, subject only to the Indian right of occupancy.

The history of America, from its discovery to the present day, proves, we think, the universal recognition of these principles.[1]

Spain did not rest her title solely on the grant of the Pope. Her discussions respecting boundary, with France, with Great Britain, and with the United States, all show that she placed it on the rights given by discovery. Portugal sustained her claim to the Brazils by the same title.

France, also, founded her title to the vast territories she claimed in America on discovery. However conciliatory her conduct to the natives may have been, she still asserted her right of dominion over a great extent of country not actually settled by Frenchmen, and her exclusive right to acquire and dispose of the soil which remained in the occupation of Indians. Her monarch claimed all Canada and Acadie, as colonies of France, at a time when the French population was very inconsiderable, and the Indians occupied almost the whole country. He also claimed Louisiana, comprehending the immense territories watered by the Mississippi, and the rivers which empty into it, by the title of discovery. The letters patent granted to the Sieur Demonts, in 1603, constitute him Lieutenant General, and the representative of the King in Acadie, which is described as stretching from the 40th to the 46th degree of north latitude; with authority to extend the power of the French over that country, and its inhabitants, to give laws to the people, to treat with the natives, and enforce the observance of treaties, and to parcel out, and give title to lands, according to his own judgment.

The States of Holland also made acquisitions in America, and sustained their right on the common principle adopted by all Europe. They allege, as we are told by Smith, in his History of New-York,[2] that Henry Hudson, who sailed, as they say, under the orders of their East India Company, discovered the country from the Delaware to the Hudson, up which he sailed to the 43d degree of north latitude; and this country they claimed under the title acquired by this voyage. Their first object was commercial, as appears by a grant made to a company of merchants in 1614; but in 1621, the States General made, as we are told by Mr. Smith, a grant of the country to the West India Company, by the name of New Netherlands.

The claim of the Dutch was always contested by the English; not because they questioned the title given by discovery, but because they insisted on being themselves the rightful claimants under that title. Their pretensions were finally decided by the sword.

No one of the powers of Europe gave its full assent to this principle, more unequivocally than England. The documents upon this subject are ample and complete. So early as the year 1496, her monarch granted a commission to the Cabots, to discover countries then unknown to *Christian people*, and to take possession of them in the name of the king of England. Two years afterwards, Cabot proceeded on this voyage, and discovered the continent of North America, along which he sailed as far south as Virginia. To this discovery the English trace their title.

In this first effort made by the English government to acquire territory on this continent, we perceive a complete recognition of the principle which has been mentioned. The right of discovery given by this commission, is confined to countries "then unknown to all Christian people"; and of these countries Cabot was empowered to take possession in the name of the king of England. Thus asserting a right to take possession, notwithstanding the occupancy of the natives, who were heathens, and, at the same time, admitting the prior title of any Christian people who may have made a previous discovery.

The same principle continued to be recognised. The charter granted to Sir Humphrey Gilbert, in 1578, authorizes him to discover and take possession of such remote, heathen, and barbarous lands, as were not actually possessed by any Christian prince or people. This charter was afterwards renewed to Sir Walter Raleigh, in nearly the same terms.

By the charter of 1606, under which the first permanent English settlement on this continent was made, James I. granted to Sir Thomas Gates and others, those territories in America lying on the seacoast, between the 34th and 45th degrees of north latitude, and which either belonged to that monarch, or were not then possessed by any other Christian prince or people. The grantees were divided into two companies at their own request. The first, or southern colony, was directed to settle between the 34th and 41st degrees of north latitude; and the second, or northern colony, between the 38th and 45th degrees.

In 1609, after some expensive and not very successful attempts at settlement had been made, a new and more enlarged charter was given by the crown to the first colony, in which the king granted to the "Treasurer and Company of Adventurers of the city of London for the first colony in Virginia," in absolute property, the lands extending along the seacoast four hundred miles, and into the land throughout from sea to sea. This charter, which is a part of the special verdict in this cause, was annulled, so far as respected the rights of the company, by the judgment of the Court of King's Bench on a writ of *quo warranto*; but the whole effect allowed to this judgment was, to revest in the crown the powers of government, and the title to the lands within its limits.

At the solicitation of those who held under the grant to the second or northern colony, a new and more enlarged charter was granted to the Duke of Lenox and others, in 1620, who were denominated the Plymouth Company, conveying to them in absolute property all the lands between the 40th and 48th degrees of north latitude.

Under this patent, New-England has been in a great measure settled. The company conveyed to Henry Rosewell and others, in 1627, that territory which is now Massachusetts; and in 1628, a charter of incorporation, comprehending the powers of government, was granted to the purchasers.

Great part of New-England was granted by this company, which, at length, divided their remaining lands among themselves; and, in 1635, surrendered their charter to the crown. A patent was granted to Gorges for Maine, which was allotted to him in the division of property.

All the grants made by the Plymouth Company, so far as we can learn, have been respected. In pursuance of the same principle, the king, in 1664, granted to the Duke of York the country of New-England as far south as the Delaware bay. His royal highness transferred New-Jersey to Lord Berkeley and Sir George Carteret.

In 1663, the crown granted to Lord Clarendon and others, the country lying between the 36th degree of north latitude and the river St. Mathes; and, in 1666, the proprietors obtained from the crown a new charter, granting to them that province in the king's dominions in North America which lies from 36 degrees 30 minutes north latitude to the 29th degree, and from the Atlantic ocean to the South sea.

Thus has our whole country been granted by the crown while in the occupation of the Indians. These grants purport to convey the soil as well as the right of dominion to the grantees. In those governments which were denominated royal, where the right to the soil was not vested in individuals, but remained in the crown, or was vested in the colonial government, the king claimed and exercised the right of granting lands, and of dismembering the government at his will. The grants made out of the two original colonies, after the resumption of their charters by the crown, are examples of this. The governments of New-England, New-York, New-Jersey, Pennsylvania, Maryland, and a part of Carolina, were thus created. In all of them, the soil, at the time the grants were made, was occupied by the Indians. Yet almost every title within those governments is dependent on these grants. In some instances, the soil was conveyed by the crown unaccompanied by the powers of government, as in the case of the northern neck of Virginia. It has never been objected to this, or to any other similar grant, that the title as well as possession was in the Indians when it was made, and that it passed nothing on that account.

These various patents cannot be considered as nullities; nor can they be limited to a mere grant of the powers of government. A charter intended to convey political power only, would never contain words expressly granting the land, the soil, and the waters. Some of them purport to convey the soil alone; and in those cases in which the powers of government, as well as the soil, are conveyed to individuals, the crown has always acknowledged itself to be bound by the grant. Though the power to dismember regal governments was asserted and exercised, the power to dismember proprietary governments was not claimed; and, in some instances, even after the powers of government were revested in the crown, the title of the proprietors to the soil was respected.

Charles II. was extremely anxious to acquire the property of Maine, but the grantees sold it to Massachusetts, and he did not venture to contest the right of that colony to the soil. The Carolinas were originally proprietary governments. In 1721 a revolution was effected by the people, who shook off their obedience to the proprietors, and declared their dependence immediately on the crown. The king, however, purchased the title of those who were disposed to sell. One of them, Lord Carteret, surrendered his interest in the government, but retained his title to the soil. That title was respected till the revolution, when it was forfeited by the laws of war.

Further proofs of the extent to which this principle has been recognised, will be found in the history of the wars, negotiations, and treaties, which the different nations, claiming territory in America, have carried on, and held with each other.

The contests between the cabinets of Versailles and Madrid, respecting the territory on the northern coast of the gulf of Mexico, were fierce and bloody; and continued, until the establishment of a Bourbon on the throne of Spain, produced such amicable dispositions in the two crowns, as to suspend or terminate them.

Between France and Great Britain, whose discoveries as well as settlements were nearly contemporaneous, contests for the country, actually covered by the Indians, began as soon as their settlements approached each other, and were continued until finally settled in the year 1763, by the treaty of Paris.

Each nation had granted and partially settled the country, denominated by the French, Acadie, and by the English, Nova Scotia. By the 12th article of the treaty of Utrecht, made in 1703,[3] his most Christian Majesty ceded to the Queen of Great Britain, "all Nova Scotia or Acadie, with its ancient boundaries." A great part of the ceded territory was in the possession of the Indians, and the extent of the cession could not be adjusted by the commissioners to whom it was to be referred.

The treaty of Aix la Chapelle, which was made on the principle of the *status ante bellum*, did not remove this subject of controversy. Commissioners for its adjustment were appointed, whose very able and elaborate, though unsuccessful arguments, in favour of the title of their respective sovereigns, show how entirely each relied on the title given by discovery to lands remaining in the possession of Indians.

After the termination of this fruitless discussion, the subject was transferred to Europe, and taken up by the cabinets of Versailles and London. This controversy embraced not only the boundaries of New-England, Nova Scotia, and that part of Canada which adjoined those colonies, but embraced our whole western country also. France contended not only that the St. Lawrence was to be considered as the centre of Canada, but that the Ohio was within that colony. She founded this claim on discovery, and on having used that river for the transportation of troops, in a war with some southern Indians.

This river was comprehended in the chartered limits of Virginia; but, though the right of England to a reasonable extent of country, in virtue of her discovery of the seacoast, and of the settlements she made on it, was not to be questioned; her claim of all the lands to the Pacific ocean, because she had discovered the country washed by the Atlantic, might, without derogating from the principle recognised by all, be deemed extravagant. It interfered, too, with the claims of France, founded on the same principle. She therefore sought to strengthen her original title to the lands in controversy, by insisting that it had been acknowledged by France in the 15th article of the treaty of Utrecht. The dispute respecting the construction of that article, has no tendency to impair the principle, that discovery gave a title to lands still remaining in the possession of the Indians. Whichever title prevailed, it was still a title to lands occupied by the Indians, whose right of occupancy neither controverted, and neither had then extinguished.

These conflicting claims produced a long and bloody war, which was terminated by the conquest of the whole country east of the Mississippi. In the treaty of 1763, France ceded and guaranteed to Great Britain, all

Nova Scotia, or Acadie, and Canada, with their dependencies; and it was agreed, that the boundaries between the territories of the two nations, in America, should be irrevocably fixed by a line drawn from the source of the Mississippi, through the middle of that river and the lakes Maurepas and Ponchartrain, to the sea. This treaty expressly cedes, and has always been understood to cede, the whole country, on the English side of the dividing line, between the two nations, although a great and valuable part of it was occupied by the Indians. Great Britain, on her part, surrendered to France all her pretensions to the country west of the Mississippi. It has never been supposed that she surrendered nothing, although she was not in actual possession of a foot of land. She surrendered all right to acquire the country; and any after attempt to purchase it from the Indians, would have been considered and treated as an invasion of the territories of France.

By the 20th article of the same treaty, Spain ceded Florida, with its dependencies, and all the country she claimed east or southeast of the Mississippi, to Great Britain. Great part of this territory also was in possession of the Indians.

By a secret treaty, which was executed about the same time, France ceded Louisiana to Spain; and Spain has since retroceded the same country to France. At the time both of its cession and retrocession, it was occupied, chiefly, by the Indians.

Thus, all the nations of Europe, who have acquired territory on this continent, have asserted in themselves, and have recognised in others, the exclusive right of the discoverer to appropriate the lands occupied by the Indians. Have the American States rejected or adopted this principle?

By the treaty which concluded the war of our revolution, Great Britain relinquished all claim, not only to the government, but to the "propriety and territorial rights of the United States," whose boundaries were fixed in the second article. By this treaty, the powers of government, and the right to soil, which had previously been in Great Britain, passed definitively to these States. We had before taken possession of them, by declaring independence; but neither the declaration of independence, nor the treaty confirming it, could give us more than that which we before possessed, or to which Great Britain was before entitled. It has never been doubted, that either the United States, or the several States, had a clear title to all the lands within the boundary lines described in the treaty, subject only to the Indian right of occupancy, and that the exclusive power to extinguish that right, was vested in that government which might constitutionally exercise it.

Virginia, particularly, within whose chartered limits the land in controversy lay, passed an act, in the year 1779, declaring her "exclusive right of pre-emption from the Indians, of all the lands within the limits of her own chartered territory, and that no person or persons whatsoever, have, or ever had, a right to purchase any lands within the same, from any

Indian nation, except only persons duly authorized to make such purchase; formerly for the use and benefit of the colony, and lately for the Commonwealth." The act then proceeds to annul all deeds made by Indians to individuals, for the private use of the purchasers.[4]

Without ascribing to this act the power of annulling vested rights, or admitting it to countervail the testimony furnished by the marginal note opposite to the title of the law, forbidding purchases from the Indians, in the revisals of the Virginia statutes, stating that law to be repealed, it may safely be considered as an unequivocal affirmance, on the part of Virginia, of the broad principle which had always been maintained, that the exclusive right to purchase from the Indians resided in the government.

In pursuance of the same idea, Virginia proceeded, at the same session, to open her land office, for the sale of that country which now constitutes Kentucky, a country, every acre of which was then claimed and possessed by Indians, who maintained their title with as much persevering courage as was ever manifested by any people.

The States, having within their chartered limits different portions of territory covered by Indians, ceded that territory, generally, to the United States, on conditions expressed in their deeds of cession, which demonstrate the opinion, that they ceded the soil as well as jurisdiction, and that in doing so, they granted a productive fund to the government of the Union. The lands in controversy lay within the chartered limits of Virginia, and were ceded with the whole country northwest of the river Ohio. This grant contained reservations and stipulations, which could only be made by the owners of the soil; and concluded with a stipulation, that "all the lands in the ceded territory, not reserved, should be considered as a common fund, for the use and benefit of such of the United States as have become, or shall become, members of the confederation," &c. "according to their usual respective proportions in the general charge and expenditure, and shall be faithfully and *bona fide* disposed of for that purpose, and for no other use or purpose whatsoever."[5]

The ceded territory was occupied by numerous and warlike tribes of Indians; but the exclusive right of the United States to extinguish their title, and to grant the soil, has never, we believe, been doubted.

After these States became independent, a controversy subsisted between them and Spain respecting boundary. By the treaty of 1795, this controversy was adjusted, and Spain ceded to the United States the territory in question. This territory, though claimed by both nations, was chiefly in the actual occupation of Indians.

The magnificent purchase of Louisiana, was the purchase from France of a country almost entirely occupied by numerous tribes of Indians, who are in fact independent. Yet, any attempt of others to intrude into that country, would be considered as an aggression which would justify war.

Our late acquisitions from Spain are of the same character; and the negotiations which preceded those acquisitions, recognise and elucidate the principle which has been received as the foundation of all European title in America.

The United States, then, have unequivocally acceded to that great and broad rule by which its civilized inhabitants now hold this country. They hold, and assert in themselves, the title by which it was acquired. They maintain, as all others have maintained, that discovery gave an exclusive right to extinguish the Indian title of occupancy, either by purchase or by conquest; and gave also a right to such a degree of sovereignty, as the circumstances of the people would allow them to exercise.

The power now possessed by the government of the United States to grant lands, resided, while we were colonies, in the crown, or its grantees. The validity of the titles given by either has never been questioned in our Courts. It has been exercised uniformly over territory in possession of the Indians. The existence of this power must negative the existence of any right which may conflict with, and control it. An absolute title to lands cannot exist, at the same time, in different persons, or in different governments. An absolute, must be an exclusive title, or at least a title which excludes all others not compatible with it. All our institutions recognise the absolute title of the crown, subject only to the Indian right of occupancy, and recognise the absolute title of the crown to extinguish that right. This is incompatible with an absolute and complete title in the Indians.

We will not enter into the controversy, whether agriculturists, merchants, and manufacturers, have a right, on abstract principles, to expel hunters from the territory they possess, or to contract their limits. Conquest gives a title which the Courts of the conqueror cannot deny, whatever the private and speculative opinions of individuals may be, respecting the original justice of the claim which has been successfully asserted. The British government, which was then our government, and whose rights have passed to the United States, asserted a title to all the lands occupied by Indians, within the chartered limits of the British colonies. It asserted also a limited sovereignty over them, and the exclusive right of extinguishing the title which occupancy gave to them. These claims have been maintained and established as far west as the river Mississippi, by the sword. The title to a vast portion of the lands we now hold, originates in them. It is not for the Courts of this country to question the validity of this title, or to sustain one which is incompatible with it.

Although we do not mean to engage in the defence of those principles which Europeans have applied to Indian title, they may, we think, find some excuse, if not justification, in the character and habits of the people whose rights have been wrested from them.

The title by conquest is acquired and maintained by force. The conqueror prescribes its limits. Humanity, however, acting on public opinion, has established, as a general rule, that the conquered shall not be wantonly oppressed, and that their condition shall remain as eligible as is compatible with the objects of the conquest. Most usually, they are incorporated with the victorious nation, and become subjects or citizens of the government with which they are connected. The new and old members of the society mingle with each other; the distinction between them is gradually lost, and they make one people. Where this incorporation is practicable, humanity demands, and a wise policy requires, that the rights of the conquered to property should remain unimpaired; that the new subjects should be governed as equitably as the old, and that confidence in their security should gradually banish the painful sense of being separated from their ancient connexions, and united by force to strangers.

When the conquest is complete, and the conquered inhabitants can be blended with the conquerors, or safely governed as a distinct people, public opinion, which not even the conqueror can disregard, imposes these restraints upon him; and he cannot neglect them without injury to his fame, and hazard to his power.

But the tribes of Indians inhabiting this country were fierce savages, whose occupation was war, and whose subsistence was drawn chiefly from the forest. To leave them in possession of their country, was to leave the country a wilderness; to govern them as a distinct people, was impossible, because they were as brave and as high spirited as they were fierce, and were ready to repel by arms every attempt on their independence.

What was the inevitable consequence of this state of things? The Europeans were under the necessity either of abandoning the country, and relinquishing their pompous claims to it, or of enforcing those claims by the sword, and by the adoption of principles adapted to the condition of a people with whom it was impossible to mix, and who could not be governed as a distinct society, or of remaining in their neighbourhood, and exposing themselves and their families to the perpetual hazard of being massacred.

Frequent and bloody wars, in which the whites were not always the aggressors, unavoidably ensued. European policy, numbers, and skill, prevailed. As the white population advanced, that of the Indians necessarily receded. The country in the immediate neighbourhood of agriculturists became unfit for them. The game fled into thicker and more unbroken forests, and the Indians followed. The soil, to which the crown originally claimed title, being no longer occupied by its ancient inhabitants, was parcelled out according to the will of the sovereign power, and taken possession of by persons who claimed immediately from the crown, or mediately, through its grantees or deputies.

That law which regulates, and ought to regulate in general, the relations between the conqueror and conquered, was incapable of application to a people under such circumstances. The resort to some new and different rule, better adapted to the actual state of things, was unavoidable. Every rule which can be suggested will be found to be attended with great difficulty.

However extravagant the pretension of converting the discovery of an inhabited country into conquest may appear; if the principle has been asserted in the first instance, and afterwards sustained; if a country has been acquired and held under it; if the property of the great mass of the community originates in it, it becomes the law of the land, and cannot be questioned. So, too, with respect to the concomitant principle, that the Indian inhabitants are to be considered merely as occupants, to be protected, indeed, while in peace, in the possession of their lands, but to be deemed incapable of transferring the absolute title to others. However this restriction may be opposed to natural right, and to the usages of civilized nations, yet, if it be indispensable to that system under which the country has been settled, and be adapted to the actual condition of the two people, it may, perhaps, be supported by reason, and certainly cannot be rejected by Courts of justice.

This question is not entirely new in this Court. The case of *Fletcher* v. *Peck*, grew out of a sale made by the State of Georgia of a large tract of country within the limits of that State, the grant of which was afterwards resumed. The action was brought by a sub-purchaser, on the contract of sale, and one of the covenants in the deed was, that the State of Georgia was, at the time of sale, seised in fee of the premises. The real question presented by the issue was, whether the seisin in fee was in the State of Georgia, or in the United States. After stating, that this controversy between the several States and the United States, had been compromised, the Court thought it necessary to notice the Indian title, which, although entitled to the respect of all Courts until it should be legitimately extinguished, was declared not to be such as to be absolutely repugnant to a seisin in fee on the part of the State.[6]

This opinion conforms precisely to the principle which has been supposed to be recognised by all European governments, from the first settlement of America. The absolute ultimate title has been considered as acquired by discovery, subject only to the Indian title of occupancy, which title the discoverers possessed the exclusive right of acquiring. Such a right is no more incompatible with a seisin in fee, than a lease for years, and might as effectually bar an ejectment.

Another view has been taken of this question, which deserves to be considered. The title of the crown, whatever it might be, could be acquired only by a conveyance from the crown. If an individual might extinguish the Indian title for his own benefit, or, in other words, might purchase it, still he could acquire only that title. Admitting their power to change their laws or usages, so far as to allow an individual to separate a portion of their lands from the common stock, and hold it in severalty, still it is a part of their territory, and is held under them, by a title dependent on their laws. The grant derives its efficacy from their will; and, if they choose to resume it, and make a different disposition of the land, the Courts of the United States cannot interpose for the protection of the title. The person who purchases lands from the Indians, within their territory, incorporates himself with them, so far as respects the property purchased; holds their title under their protection, and subject to their laws. If they annul the grant, we know of no tribunal which can revise and set aside the proceeding. We know of no principle which can distinguish this case from a grant made to a native Indian, authorizing him to hold a particular tract of land in severalty.

As such a grant could not separate the Indian from his nation, nor give a title which our Courts could distinguish from the title of his tribe, as it might still be conquered from, or ceded by his tribe, we can perceive no legal principle which will authorize a Court to say, that different consequences are attached to this purchase, because it was made by a stranger. By the treaties concluded between the United States and the Indian nations, whose title the plaintiffs claim, the country comprehending the lands in controversy has been ceded to the United States, without any reservation of their title. These nations had been at war with the United States, and had an unquestionable right to annul any grant they had made to American citizens. Their cession of the country, without a reservation of this land, affords a fair presumption, that they considered it as of no validity. They ceded to the United States this very property, after having used it in common with other lands, as their own, from the date of their deeds to the time of cession; and the attempt now made, is to set up their title against that of the United States.[7]

The proclamation issued by the King of Great Britain, in 1763, has been considered, and, we think, with reason, as constituting an additional objection to the title of the plaintiffs.

By that proclamation, the crown reserved under its own dominion and protection, for the use of the Indians, "all the land and territories lying to the westward of the sources of the rivers which fall into the sea from the west and northwest," and strictly forbade all British subjects from making any purchases or settlements whatever, or taking possession of the reserved lands.

It has been contended, that, in this proclamation, the king transcended his constitutional powers; and the case of *Campbell* v. *Hall*, (reported by *Cowper*,) is relied on to support this position.[8]

It is supposed to be a principle of universal law, that, if an uninhabited country be discovered by a number of individuals, who acknowledge no connexion with, and owe no allegiance to, any government whatever, the country becomes the property of the discoverers, so far at least as they can use it. They acquire a title in common. The title of the whole land is in the whole society. It is to be divided and parcelled out according to the will of the society, expressed by the whole body, or by that organ which is authorized by the whole to express it.

If the discovery be made, and possession of the country be taken, under the authority of an existing government, which is acknowledged by the emigrants, it is supposed to be equally well settled, that the discovery is made for the whole nation, that the country becomes a part of the nation, and that the vacant soil is to be disposed of by that organ of the government which has the constitutional power to dispose of the national domains, by that organ in which all vacant territory is vested by law.

According to the theory of the British constitution, all vacant lands are vested in the crown, as representing the nation; and the exclusive power to grant them is admitted to reside in the crown, as a branch of the royal prerogative. It has been already shown, that this principle was as fully recognised in America as in the island of Great Britain. All the lands we hold were originally granted by the crown; and the establishment of a regal government has never been considered as impairing its right to grant lands within the chartered limits of such colony. In addition to the proof of this principle, furnished by the immense grants, already mentioned, of lands lying within the chartered limits of Virginia, the continuing right of the crown to grant lands lying within that colony was always admitted. A title might be obtained, either by making an entry with the surveyor of a county, in pursuance of law, or by an order of the governor in council, who was the deputy of the king, or by an immediate grant from the crown. In Virginia, therefore, as well as elsewhere in the British dominions, the complete title of the crown to vacant lands was acknowledged.

So far as respected the authority of the crown, no distinction was taken between vacant lands and lands occupied by the Indians. The title, subject only to the right of occupancy by the Indians, was admitted to be in the king, as was his right to grant that title. The lands, then, to which this proclamation referred, were lands which the king had a right to grant, or to reserve for the Indians.

According to the theory of the British constitution, the royal prerogative is very extensive, so far as respects the political relations between Great Britain and foreign nations. The peculiar situation of the Indians, necessarily considered, in some respects, as a dependent, and in some respects as a distinct people, occupying a country claimed by Great Britain, and yet too powerful and brave not to be dreaded as formidable enemies, required, that means should be adopted for the preservation of peace; and that their friendship should be secured by quieting their alarms for their property. This was to be effected by restraining the encroachments of the whites; and the power to do this was never, we believe, denied by the colonies to the crown.

In the case of *Campbell* against *Hall*, that part of the proclamation was determined to be illegal, which imposed a tax on a conquered province, after a government had been bestowed upon it.[9] The correctness of this decision cannot be questioned, but its application to the case at bar cannot be admitted. Since the expulsion of the Stuart family, the power of imposing taxes, by proclamation, has never been claimed as a branch of regal prerogative; but the powers of granting, or refusing to grant, vacant lands, and of restraining encroachments on the Indians, have always been asserted and admitted.

The authority of this proclamation, so far as it respected this continent, has never been denied, and the titles it gave to lands have always been sustained in our Courts.

In the argument of this cause, the counsel for the plaintiffs have relied very much on the opinions expressed by men holding offices of trust, and on various proceedings in America, to sustain titles to land derived from the Indians.

The collection of claims to lands lying in the western country, made in the 1st volume of the Laws of the United States, has been referred to; but we find nothing in that collection to support the argument. Most of the titles were derived from persons professing to act under the authority of the government existing at the time; and the two grants under which the plaintiffs claim, are supposed, by the person under whose inspection the collection was made, to be void, because forbidden by the royal proclamation of 1763.[10] It is not unworthy of remark, that the usual mode adopted by the Indians for granting lands to individuals, has been to reserve them in a treaty, or to grant them under the sanction of the commissioners with whom the treaty was negotiated. The practice, in such case, to grant to the crown, for the use of the individual, is some evidence of a general understanding, that the validity even of such a grant depended on its receiving the royal sanction.

The controversy between the colony of Connecticut and the Mohegan Indians, depended on the nature and extent of a grant made by those Indians to the colony; on the nature and extent of the reservations made by the Indians, in their several deeds and treaties, which were alleged to be recognised by the legitimate authority; and on the violation by the colony of rights thus reserved and secured.[11] We do not perceive, in that case, any assertion of the principle, that individuals might obtain a complete and valid title from the Indians.

It has been stated, that in the memorial transmitted from the Cabinet of London to that of Versailles, during the controversy between the two nations, respecting boundary, which took place in 1755, the Indian right to the soil is recognised. But this recognition was made with reference to their character as Indians, and for the purpose of showing that they were fixed to a particular territory. It was made for the purpose of sustaining the claim of his Britannic majesty to dominion over them.

The opinion of the Attorney and Solicitor General, Pratt and Yorke, have been adduced to prove, that, in the opinion of those great law officers, the Indian grant could convey a title to the soil without a patent emanating from the crown.[12] The opinion of those persons would certainly be of great authority on such a question, and we were not a little surprised, when it was read, at the doctrine it seemed to advance. An opinion so contrary to the whole practice of the crown, and to the uniform opinions given on all other occasions by its great law officers, ought to be very explicit, and accompanied by the circumstances under which it was given, and to which it was applied, before we can be assured that it is properly understood. In a pamphlet, written for the purpose of asserting the Indian title, styled "*Plain Facts,*" the same opinion is quoted, and is said to relate to purchases made in the East Indies.[13] It is, of course, entirely inapplicable to purchases made in America. Chalmers, in whose collection this opinion is found, does not say to whom it applies;[14] but there is reason to believe, that the author of *Plain Facts* is, in this respect, correct. The opinion commences thus: "In respect to such places as have been, or shall be acquired, by treaty or grant, from any of the Indian princes or governments, your majesty's letters patent are not necessary." The words "princes or governments," are usually applied to the East Indians, but not to those of North America. We speak of their sachems, their warriors, their chiefmen, their nations or tribes, not of their "princes or governments."[15] The question on which the opinion was given, too, and to which it relates, was, whether the king's subjects carry with them the common law wherever they may form settlements. The opinion is given with a view to this point, and its object must be kept in mind while construing its expressions.

Much reliance is also placed on the fact, that many tracts are now held in the United States under the Indian title, the validity of which is not questioned.

Before the importance attached to this fact is conceded, the circumstances under which such grants were obtained, and such titles are supported, ought to be considered. These lands lie chiefly in the eastern States. It is known that the Plymouth Company made many extensive grants, which, from their ignorance of the country, interfered with each other. It is also known that Mason, to whom New-Hampshire, and Gorges, to whom Maine was granted, found great difficulty in managing such unwieldy property. The country was settled by emigrants, some from Europe, but chiefly from Massachusetts, who took possession of lands they found unoccupied, and secured themselves in that possession by the best means in their power. The disturbances in England, and the civil war and revolution which followed those disturbances, prevented any interference on the part of the mother country, and the proprietors were unable to maintain their title. In the mean time, Massachusetts claimed the country, and governed it. As her claim was adversary to that of the proprietors, she encouraged the settlement of persons made under her authority, and encouraged, likewise, their securing themselves in possession, by purchasing the acquiescence and forbearance of the Indians.

After the restoration of Charles II., Gorges and Mason, when they attempted to establish their title, found themselves opposed by men, who held under Massachusetts, and under the Indians. The title of the proprietors was resisted; and though, in some cases, compromises were made and in some, the opinion of a Court was given ultimately in their favour, the juries found uniformly against them. They became wearied with the struggle, and sold their property. The titles held under the Indians, were sanctioned by length of possession; but there is no case, so far as we are informed, of a judicial decision in their favour.

Much reliance has also been placed on a recital contained in the charter of Rhode-Island, and on a letter addressed to the governors of the neighbouring colonies, by the king's command, in which some expressions are inserted, indicating the royal approbation of titles acquired from the Indians.

The charter to Rhode-Island recites, "that the said John Clark, and others, had transplanted themselves into the midst of the Indian nations, and were seised and possessed, by purchase and consent of the said natives, to their full content, of such lands," &c. And the letter recites, that "Thomas Chifflinch, and others, having, in the right of Major Asperton, a just propriety in the Narraghanset country, in New-England, by grants from the native princes of that country, and being desirous to improve it into an English colony," &c. "are yet daily disturbed."

The impression this language might make, if viewed apart from the circumstances under which it was employed, will be effaced, when considered in connexion with those circumstances.

In the year 1635, the Plymouth Company surrendered their charter to the crown. About the same time, the religious dissentions of Massachusetts expelled from that colony several societies of individuals, one of which settled in Rhode-Island, on lands purchased from the Indians. They were not within the chartered limits of Massachusetts, and the English government was too much occupied at home to bestow its attention on this subject. There existed no authority to arrest their settlement of the country. If they obtained the Indian title, there were none to assert the title of the crown. Under these circumstances, the settlement became considerable. Individuals acquired separate property in lands which they cultivated and improved; a government was established among themselves; and no power existed in America which could rightfully interfere with it.

On the restoration of Charles II., this small society hastened to acknowledge his authority, and to solicit his confirmation of their title to the soil, and to jurisdiction over the country. Their solicitations were successful, and a charter was granted to them, containing the recital which has been mentioned.

It is obvious, that this transaction can amount to no acknowledgment, that the Indian grant could convey a title paramount to that of the crown, or could, in itself, constitute a complete title. On the contrary, the charter of the crown was considered as indispensable to its completion.

It has never been contended, that the Indian title amounted to nothing. Their right of possession has never been questioned. The claim of government extends to the complete ultimate title, charged with the right of possession, and to the exclusive power of acquiring that right. The object of the crown was to settle the seacoast of America; and when a portion of it was settled, without violating the rights of others, by persons professing their loyalty, and soliciting the royal sanction of an act, the consequences of which were ascertained to be beneficial, it would have been as unwise as ungracious to expel them from their habitations, because they had obtained the Indian title otherwise than through the agency of government. The very grant of a charter is an assertion of the title of the crown, and its words convey the same idea. The country granted, is said to be "our island called Rhode-Island"; and the charter contains an actual grant of the soil, as well as of the powers of government.

The letter was written a few months before the charter was issued, apparently at the request of the agents of the intended colony, for the sole purpose of preventing the trespasses of neighbours, who were disposed to claim some authority over them. The king, being willing himself to ratify and confirm their title, was, of course, inclined to quiet them in their possession.

This charter, and this letter, certainly sanction a previous unauthorized purchase from Indians, under the circumstances attending that particular purchase, but are far from supporting the general proposition, that a title acquired from the Indians would be valid against a title acquired from the crown, or without the confirmation of the crown.

The acts of several colonial assemblies, prohibiting purchases from the Indians, have also been relied on, as proving, that, independent of such prohibitions, Indian deeds would be valid. But, we think this fact, at most, equivocal. While the existence of such purchases would justify their prohibition, even by colonies which considered Indian deeds as previously invalid, the fact that such acts have been generally passed, is strong evidence of the general opinion, that such purchases are opposed by the soundest principles of wisdom and national policy.

After bestowing on this subject a degree of attention which was more required by the magnitude of the interest in litigation, and the able and elaborate arguments of the bar, than by its intrinsic difficulty, the Court is decidedly of opinion, that the plaintiffs do not exhibit a title which can be sustained in the Court of the United States; and that there is no error in the judgment which was rendered against them in the District Court of Illinois.

Judgment affirmed, with costs.

Printed, Henry Wheaton, *Reports of Cases Argued and Adjudged in the Supreme Court of the United States . . .* , VIII (New York, 1823), 571–605.

1. For the following historical recitation, JM probably consulted George Chalmers, *Political Annals of the Present United Colonies, from Their Settlement to the Peace of 1763*, I (London, 1780). He had used Chalmers's work as a principal source in composing the introductory part of the *Life of Washington* (*PJM*, VI, 235).

2. William Smith, *The History of the Province of New-York, from the First Discovery* . . . (Albany, N.Y., 1814).

3. The correct year for the Treaty of Utrecht is 1713.

4. Hening, *Statutes*, X, 97–98. Counsel for the plaintiff contended that this act should be considered as repealed because it was not included in the 1794 revisal of Virginia's laws (8 Wheat. 565–66).

5. JM quoted from the 1781 Virginia act ceding the Northwest Territory (Hening, *Statutes*, X, 566).

6. Fletcher v. Peck, 6 Cranch 142–43; *PJM*, VII, 240–41.

7. By a treaty of 30 Dec. 1805, the Piankeshaws ceded to the U.S. the lands contained in the 1775 deed, within which Johnson's claim lay (*ASP, Indian Affairs*, I, 704–5).

8. Campbell v. Hall, 1 Cowp. 204, 98 Eng. Rep. 1045 (K.B., 1774).

9. The "conquered province" was Grenada, which had been captured by the British during the Seven Years' War. See the discussion of this case and Lord Mansfield's opinion in Robert A Williams, Jr., *The American Indian in Western Legal Thought: The Discourses of Conquest* (New York, 1990), 300–303.

10. The collection of claims to western lands was included in the first volume of an 1815 edition of U.S. laws. The claim of the Illinois and Wabash Company was stated to be "derived solely from Indian purchases made in 1773 and 1775, by unauthorized individuals. Exclusively of other considerations, such purchases were expressly forbidden by the proclamation of 1763, of the king of England" (*Laws of the United States of America, from the 4th of March, 1789, to the 4th of March, 1815* [5 vols.; Philadelphia and Washington, 1815], I, 459).

11. The controversy between the Mohegan Indians and the colony of Connecticut was omitted in Wheaton's summary of arguments but figured prominently in the Illinois and Wabash Land Company's memorials to Congress. The tribe claimed that it had been deprived of certain tracts reserved by treaty with the colony. The case was heard by several royal commissions beginning in 1703 and was finally decided by the British Privy Council in 1773 (*An Account of the Proceedings of the Illinois and Ouabache Land Companies* [Philadelphia, 1796; Evans #30618], 47–48; *ASP, Public Lands*, II, 112–13; Joseph H. Smith, *Appeals to the Privy Council from the American Plantations* [New York, 1950], 422–42).

12. Charles Pratt (later Lord Camden) and Charles Yorke (later Baron Morden) were, respectively, Attorney General and Solicitor General of England in 1757, when their celebrated opinion was given. As JM correctly surmised, this opinion was originally drawn in response to a question about India on behalf of the East India Company. Under circumstances that have not been fully explained, an edited and truncated version of the opinion came into the hands of American land speculators in the early 1770s. This version, which eliminated all references to India and the East India Company, appeared to support the proposition that grants by North American Indians to private companies vested property in the soil. The edited opinion figured prominently in the formation of the Illinois Company in 1773 and was quoted in the various memorials submitted by the Illinois and Wabash Land Company to Congress. In those memorials the opinion was erroneously stated to have been given in Aug. 1772 (*An Account of the Proceedings of the Illinois and Ouabache Land Companies*, 34; *ASP, Public Lands*, II, 114). The best account of this documentary episode is in Jack M. Sosin, *Whitehall and the Wilderness: The Middle West in British Colonial Policy, 1760–1775* (Lincoln, Nebr., 1961), 229–35, 259–67.

13. *Plain Facts: Being an Examination into the Rights of the Indian Nations of America, to Their Respective Countries* (Philadelphia, 1781). The author of this pamphlet was Samuel Wharton of Pennsylvania, a prominent speculator in western land (Sosin, *Whitehall and the Wilderness*, 261).

14. George Chalmers, *Opinions of Eminent Lawyers on Various Points of English Jurisprudence, Chiefly concerning the Colonies, Fisheries, and Commerce of Great Britain* (Burlington, Vt., 1858), 206–7. Chalmers printed the edited version and gave no date. He included it in a section entitled "How far the King's subjects, who emigrate, carry with them the Law of England."

15. For the full opinion, as given in 1757, see Sosin, *Whitehall and the Wilderness*, 230.

To Jaquelin B. Harvie

Dear Sir   Washington March. 8th. 1823

I received your letter on the 3d. of March the day on which Congress rose.¹ Mr. Williams was in the Senate & did not come into court.² I addressed a letter to him requesting the information you desire & received an answer informing me that he had placed my letter in the hands of the delegate from Florida who would answer it.³ I have waited till now for his letter & have not received. I shall wait on him if he does not write immediately & will inform you what he says when I come . . .

Fragment of AL[S?], Marshall Papers, ViW. Addressed to Harvie in Richmond; postmarked Washington, 8 Mar. Bottom portion of MS cut off.

1. Letter not found.
2. Sen. John Williams of Tennessee was a member of the Supreme Court bar and argued the case of Danforth v. Wear at the Feb. 1823 term (9 Wheat. 673).
3. Letters not found. Florida's territorial delegate to Congress for the 1822–23 session was Joseph Marion Hernandez (1793–1857).

To Mary W. Marshall

My dearest Polly   Warrenton Apl. 11th. 1823

I am thus far on my way to the Doctors & purpose proceeding on my journey after dinner.¹ I have had a comfortable travel of it though I found the road about Elk run excessively bad. There has been a vast deal of rain on this side of Richmond all the way; a good deal more I think than we had. I did not find Mr. Skinker² at home, in consequence of which I came last night to General Blackwells.³ I found my old friend quite well but almost blind, which he ascribes to reading by candlelight. Tom was at Genl Blackwells in the course of the day a few hours before me on his electioneering business. From what I can learn the election will be close & is very doubtful, more doubtful than I had supposed it to be from what I heard in Richmond. Tom will lose some federal votes who had en-[ga]ged themselves before his being known as a candidate.⁴

I have just returned from Mr. Bells but did not find him at home. I have requested him to bring his papers to court.

I must repeat my requests that you will ride regularly & market liberally. Farewell my dearest Polly, Your ever affectionate

J MARSHALL

ALS, Marshall Papers, ViW; Tr, Claudia Hamilton Mason Notebook, Collection of H. Norton Mason, Richmond, Va. Addressed to Mrs. Marshall in Richmond; postmarked (by hand) Warrenton, 13 Apr.

1. JM was on his way to the Fauquier home of his son, Jaquelin A. Marshall, the "Doctor."

2. Possibly William Skinker, a descendant of Samuel Skinker, an early grantee of land in the Pignut Ridge region of Fauquier (Fairfax Harrison, *Landmarks of Old Prince William: A Study of Origins in Northern Virginia* [Berryville, Va., 1964], 261, 318, 553).

3. "General Blackwell" was probably John Blackwell, who died soon thereafter (*Fauquier Historical Sociey Bulletin* [July 1924], 351, 497).

4. Thomas Marshall was a Federalist candidate for Congress in the district composed of Fauquier and Culpeper Counties. He lost to Republican John S. Barbour of Culpeper County by forty-three votes (Richmond *Enquirer*, 6 May 1823).

To Bushrod Washington

My dear Sir   Richmond May 3d. 1823

Yesterday on my return from the upper country I found your letter of the 8th. of April & immediately deposited with the clerk of the district court the copy of the title of your reports.[1]

I am very glad to hear that Mr. Small will undertake the printing you wished to put into his hands & think the terms you mention quite satisfactory.[2]

I had gone through the corrections of the life of Washington & arranged the work into four volumes; the first to contain a history of all which precedes the appointment of General Washington to the command of the army; the 2d. & 3d. to comprehend his birth his part in the French war, & the history of the war of the Revolution after his appointment to the command of the American army. The 4th. to comprehend the matter now contained in the 5th. but somewhat abridged. The volumes will be about the present size if printed in the same type, if in a smaller the editor can calculate much better than myself at the reduction which will take place. I should be unwilling to redu[c]e the type so much as to make the reading irksome. Mr. Small however will decide on this point. The last volume will be somewhat reduced, but not in proportion to the other parts of the work. I am quite willing as I told you to take on myself the risk of the first volume & shall be glad to know what the expense will be.

I did not recover my health sufficiently to set in to close reading till I went to the upper country & shall in a few days set out for North Carolina, after which comes the long term in Richmond. I shall however proceed with as much dispatch as is in my power in reading the letters. I will let you know what progress I make & shall be glad to hear from you again, if this reaches you in Philadelphia respecting the publishing the 2d. ed. of the Life. I am dear Sir sincerely & affectionately, your

J MARSHALL

ALS, NHi. Addressed to Washington in Philadelphia (crossed out and addressed in unknown hand to Alexandria, District of Columbia); postmarked Richmond, 3 May. Endorsed by Washington.

1. Letter not found. Bushrod Washington, *Reports of Cases Argued and Determined in the Court of Appeals of Virginia* (2d ed.; Philadelphia, 1823).

2. The second edition of Washington's reports was printed by Abraham Small, who in 1824 published JM's *History of the Colonies Planted by the English on the Continent of North America . . . (PJM,* VIII, 141 n. 5).

United States v. Maurice
Opinion
U.S. Circuit Court, Virginia, 22 May 1823

U.S. Attorney Robert Stanard brought an action of debt at the May 1822 term on a performance bond executed by James Maurice and his sureties, William Sharp, Thomas Reilly, and Thomas Williamson. The bond, executed in August 1818, was in the penalty of twenty thousand dollars, conditioned on Maurice's faithful discharge of his duties as an agent for fortifications. The defendants Sharp, Reilly, and Williamson submitted five pleas as well as a demurrer to the declaration. The United States demurred to part of the defendants' second plea and to the fifth plea. Marshall's opinion, given on 22 May 1823, dealt with the matters of law arising upon the demurrers. The circumstances of the case and the various pleadings are fully discussed in the opinion (capias, declaration, pleas, and demurrers, U.S. v. Maurice, Sharp, Reilly, and Williamson, Ended Cases [Unrestored], 1823, Vi; U.S. Cir. Ct., Va., Ord. Bk. XI, 320).

⟨This is an action of debt brought upon a bond executed on the eighteenth day of August, 1818, in the penalty of twenty thousand dollars, with the following condition: "Whereas the said James Maurice has been appointed agent for fortifications on the part of the United States, now, therefore, if the said James Maurice shall truly and faithfully execute and discharge all the duties appertaining to the said office of agent, as aforesaid, then the above obligation to be void, &c." The breach assigned in the declaration is, that large sums of money came to the hands of the said Maurice, as agent of fortifications, which he was bound by the duties of his office faithfully to disburse and account for, a part of which, namely, forty thousand dollars, he has, in violation of his said duty, utterly failed to disburse to the use of the United States, or account for; wherefore, &c.

The defendants, the sureties in the said obligation, prayed oyer of the bond, and of the condition, and then demurred to the declaration. The plaintiff joined in the demurrer.

The defendants also pleaded several pleas, on some of which issue has been made up, and others, demurrer has been joined.

The first point to be considered is the demurrer to the declaration.

The defendants insist that the declaration cannot be sustained, because the bond is void in law, it being taken for the performance of duties of an office, which office has no legal existence, and consequently, no legal duties. No violation of duty, it is said, can take place, when no duty exists.

Since the demurrer admits all the facts alleged in the declaration, which are properly charged, and denies that those facts create any obligation in law, it must be taken as true that James Maurice was in fact appointed an agent of fortification on the part of the United States; that he received large sums of money in virtue of that appointment, and has failed to apply it to the purpose for which he received it, or to account for it to the United States.

As the securities certainly intended to undertake that Maurice should perform the very acts which he has failed to perform, and as the money of the nation has come into his hands on the faith of this undertaking, it is the duty of the Court to hold them responsible, to the extent of this undertaking, unless the law shall plainly interpose its protecting power for their relief, upon the principle that the bond creates no legal obligation. Is this such a bond? The first step in this inquiry, is the character of the bond. Does it, on its face, purport to be a mere official bond, or to be in the nature of a contract? This question is to be answered by a reference to the terms in which its condition is expressed. These leave no shadow of doubt on the mind. The condition refers to no contract — states no undertaking to perform any specific act — refers to nothing — describes nothing which the obligor was bound to do, except to perform the duties of an officer. It recites that he was appointed to an office, and declares that the obligation is to be void if he "shall truly and faithfully execute and discharge all the duties appertaining to the said office." Of the nature of those duties no information whatever is given. Whether the disbursement of public money does or does not constitute a part of them, is a subject on which the instrument is entirely silent.

The bond, then, is, on its face, completely an official bond, given, not for the performance of any contract, but for the performance of the duties of an office, which duties were known, and had been prescribed by law, or by persons authorized to prescribe them.

In his declaration, the attorney for the United States has necessarily taken up this idea, and proceeded on it. In his assignment of breaches, he states that the said James Maurice had been appointed agent of fortifications, and alleges that he had not performed the duties of the said office, nor kept the condition of his bond, but that the said condition is broken in this, that while he held and remained in the said office, divers large sums of money came to his hands, as agent of fortifications, which he was bound by the duties of his office faithfully to disburse and account for; a part of which, forty thousand dollars, he has, in violation of his said duty, utterly failed to disburse or account for. On this breach of his official duty, which is alleged to constitute a breach of his bond, the action is founded. No allusion is made to any other circumstance whatever as giving cause of action.

The suit then is plainly prosecuted for a violation of the duty of office, which is alleged to constitute a breach of an official bond. The Court must, on this demurrer, at least, so consider it, and must decide it according to those rules which govern cases of this description. This being a suit upon an official bond, the condition of which binds the obligors only that the officer should perform the duties of his office, it would seem that the obligation could be only co-extensive with these duties. What is their extent? The defendants contend that no such office exists; that James Maurice was never an officer, and, of consequence, was never bound by this bond to the performance of any duty whatever.

To estimate the weight of this objection, it becomes necessary to examine the Constitution of the United States, and the acts of Congress in relation to this subject.

The Constitution, art. 2, sec. 2, declares, that the President "shall nominate, and, by and with the advice and consent of the Senate, shall appoint ambassadors, &c.," "and all other officers of the United States, whose appointments are not herein otherwise provided for, and which shall be established by law."

I feel no diminution of reverence for the framers of this sacred instrument, when I say that some ambiguity of expression has found its way into this clause. If the relative "*which*," refers to the word "appointments," that word is referred to in a sense rather different from that in which it had been used. It is used to signify the act of placing a man in office, and referred to as signifying the office itself. Considering this relative as referring to the word "offices," which word, if not expressed, must be understood, it is not perfectly clear whether the words "which" offices "shall be established by law," are to be construed as ordaining, that all offices of the United States shall be established by law, or merely as limiting the previous general words to such offices as shall be established by law. Understood in the first sense, this clause makes a general provision, that the President shall nominate, and by and with the consent of the Senate, appoint to all offices of the United States, with such exceptions only as are made in the Constitution; and that all offices (with the same exceptions) shall be established by law. Understood in the last sense, this general provision comprehends those offices only which might be established by law, leaving it in the power of the executive, or of those who might be entrusted with the execution of the laws, to create in all laws of legislative omission, such offices as might be deemed necessary for their execution, and afterwards to fill those offices.

I do not know whether this question has ever occurred to the legislative or executive of the United States, nor how it may have been decided. In this ignorance of the course which may have been pursued by the government, I shall adopt the first interpretation, because I think it accords best with the general spirit of the Constitution, which seems to have arranged the creation of office among legislative powers, and because, too, this construction is, I think, sustained by the subsequent words of the same clause, and by the third clause of the same section.

The sentence which follows, and forms an exception to the general provision which had been made, authorizes Congress "by law to vest the appointment of such inferior officers as they think proper, in the President alone, in the courts of law, or in the heads of departments." This sentence, I think, indicates an opinion in the framers of the Constitution, that they had provided for all cases of offices.

The third section empowers the President "to fill up all vacancies that may happen during the recess of the Senate, by granting commissions which shall expire at the end of their next session."

This power is not confined to vacancies which may happen in offices created by law. If the convention supposed that the President might create an office, and fill it originally without the consent of the Senate, that consent would not be required for filling up a vacancy in the same office.

The Constitution then is understood to declare, that all offices of the United States, except in cases where the Constitution itself may otherwise provide, shall be established by law.

Has the office of agent of fortifications been established by law?

From the year 1794 to the year 1808, Congress passed several acts, empowering the President)[1] to erect fortifications, & appropriating large sums of money to enable him to carry these acts into execution. No system for their execution has ever been organized by law. The legislature seems to have left this subject to the discretion of the executive. The President was consequently at liberty to employ any means which the constitution & laws of the United States placed under his controul. He might, it is presumed, employ detachments from the army, or he might execute the work by contract in all the various forms which contract can assume. Might he organize a corps consisting of labourers, managers, paymasters, providers &c with distinct departments of duty prescribed & defined by the executive, & with such fixed compensation as might be annexed to the various parts of the service? If this mode of executing the law be consistent with the constitution, there is nothing in the law itself to restrain the President from adopting it. But the general language of the law must be limited by the constitution, & must be construed to empower the President to employ those means only which are constitutional. According to the construction given in this opinion of the 2d. sec. of the 2d. art. of that instrument, it directs that all offices of the United States shall be established by law; & I do not think that the meer direction that a thing shall be done without prescribing the mode of doing it, can be fairly construed into the establishment of an office for the purpose, if the object can be effected without one. It is not a necessary or even a fair inference from such an act, that Congress intended it should be executed through the medium of offices, since there are other ample means by which it may be executed, and since the practice of the government has been for the legislature, wherever this mode of executing an act was intended, to organize a system by law, & either to create the several offices expressly, or to authorize the President in terms, to employ such persons as he might think proper for the performance of particular services.

¶2   If then the agent of fortifications be an officer of the United States in the sense in which that term is used in the constitution, his office ought to be established by law, and cannot be considered as having been established by the acts empowering the President generally to cause fortifications to be constructed.

¶3   Is the agent of fortifications an officer of the United States? An office is defined to be "a publick charge or employment"; and he who performs the duties of the office is an officer. If employed on the part of the US he is an officer of the U.S. Although "an office" is "an employment," it does not follow that every employment is an office. A man may certainly be employed under a contract express or implied to do an act or perform a service without becoming an officer. But if a duty be a continuing one, which is defined by rules prescribed by the government & not by contract; which an individual is appointed by government to perform, who enters on the duties appertaining to his station, without any contract defining them; if those duties continue though the person be changed; it seems very difficult to distinguish such a charge or employment from an office, or the person who performs its duties from an officer.

¶4   If it may be converted into a contract, it must be a contract to perform the duties of the office of agent of fortifications, & such an office must exist with ascertained duties or there is no standard by which the extent of the condition can be measured.

¶5   The army regulations are referred to in acts of Congress passed previous & subsequent to the execution of the bond under consideration. A copy of those regulations, purporting to be a revisal made in the war office in September 1816, conformably to the act of 24th. April 1816, has been laid before the court & referred to by both parties. These regulations provide for the appointment, & define the duties, of the agents of fortifications.

¶6   They are to be governed by the orders of the engineer department in the disbursement of the money placed in their hands. They are to provide the materials & workmen deemed necessary for the fortifications; and they are to pay the laborers employed. In the performance of these duties they are directed to make out 1st. an "abstract of articles purchased," 2d. an "abstract of labour performed["] 3d. an "abstract of pay of mechanics" & 4th. "an abstract of contingent expenses."

¶7   These duties are those of a purchasing quartermaster, commissary, & paymaster. These are important duties. A very superficial examination of the laws will be sufficient to show that duties of this description, if not performed by contract, are performed by persons who are considered as officers of the United States, whose offices are established by law.

If then we look at the bond & declaration we find in both every charac-   ¶8
teristic of an office bond. If we look at the army regulations, the only
additional source of information within our reach, we find the duties of
an agent of fortifications to be such as would make him an officer of the
United States. Is the office established by law?

The permanent agents mentioned in the act of the 3d. of March 1809   ¶9
ch 19, Sec. 3 & 4 are those who are appointed "either for the purpose of
making contracts, or for the purchase of supplies, or for the disbursement in any other manner of moneys for the use of the military establishment, or of the navy of the United States."[2] If this act authorizes the
appointment of such agents & virtually establishes their offices, it cannot
I think, in correct construction, be extended to other persons than those
who are employed in some manner, in disbursing money "for the use of
the military establishment or navy of the United States." "The military
establishment" is a term which seems to be well defined in the acts of
Congress, & to be well understood; & I do not think the act can be
construed to comprehend an agent of fortifications.

In the act of March 3d. 1813 ch 517 sec 5 it is made the duty of the   ¶10
Secretary of war "to prepare general regulations better defining & prescribing the respective duties & powers in the adjutant General, inspector
General, quartermaster general, and commissary of ordnance departments, of the topographical engineers, of the aids of Generals, & generally of the general & regimental staff; which regulations when approved
by the President of the United States, shall be respected & obeyed until
altered or revoked by the same authority."[3]

The exclusive object of this section is I think the regulation of existing   ¶11
offices: I do not think it can be fairly construed to extend to the establishment of office. Yet if, under this act, subordinate agencies or offices have
in fact been introduced, such offices may be established by subsequent
acts of Congress.

The act of the 24th. April 1816 "for organizing the general staff &   ¶12
making farther provision for the army of the United States" sec. 9 enacts
"that the regulations in force before the reduction of the army be recognized, as far as the same shall be found applicable to the service, subject
however to such alterations as the secretary of war may adopt with the
approbation of the President."[4]

A legislative recognition of the actually existing regulations of the   ¶13
Army must be understood as giving to those regulations the sanction of
law; & the subsequent words of the sentence authorize the secretary of
war to alter those regulations with the approbation of the President. Such
alterations have also the sanction of the act of 1816.

This subject appears to have been taken up by the Secretary.   ¶14

A pamphlet entitled "army regulations, revised conformably to the act   ¶15
of the 24th. of April 1816," has been laid before the court as authentic, &
has been appealed to by both plaintiff and defendants as being the same

regulations which are approved & adopted by the act of the 2d. March 1821. Ch 13.⁵

¶16 These regulations direct the appointment of agents of fortifications & define their duties. They purport to have been revised in the war office in September 1816. If the provision they contain respecting agents of fortifications formed a part of the Army regulations prior to the act of 24th. of April 1816; it is recognized by that act. If that provision was first introduced in September 1816, it may, if approved by the President, be considered as an alteration authorized by that act. The question whether this alteration has been approved by the President, is perhaps a question of fact, not properly examinable on this demurrer.

¶17 When I consider the act of 24th. April 1816 & this revisal in the war office, in connexion with the act of the 2d. of March 1821 adopting the revisal of September 1816, under the name of "General regulations of the army" compiled by Major General Scott,⁶ (for they are represented as being the same regulations) I feel much difficulty in saying that the office of agent of fortifications was not established by law when this bond was executed. I am the more incline[d] to give this opinion because I am persuaded that this cause must be carried before a tribunal which can make that certain which was before uncertain, & because, by overruling the demurrer to the declaration the other questions of law which occur in the cause, & which would be arrested by sustaining the demurrer to the declaration, will all be brought before the Supreme court.⁷

¶18 The defendants pleaded several pleas to the declaration. The second plea is that the defendant James Maurice performed the condition of his bond up to the 26th day of September 1820, on which day a new bond was executed in pursuance of the act of the 15th. of May 1820, "providing for the better organization of the Treasury department." The plaintiff takes issue on that part of the plea which alleges performance up to the 26 of Septr. 1820, & demurs to the residue. The act under which this new bond was executed, gives a new & summary remedy against officers of the United States who had received public money for which they had failed to account, & against their sureties; & contains a proviso "That the summary process herein directed shall not affect any surety of any officer of the United States, who became bound to the United States before the passing of this act; but each & every such officer shall, on or before the 30th. day of Septr. next give new & sufficient sureties for the performance of the duties required of such officer."⁸ The defendants contend that this new & sufficient bond was a substitute for the old one, & discharged the sureties to the original obligation, so far as respects subsequent transactions.

¶19 The plaintiff contends that the bond is cumulative; and that the sureties to the first obligation continue bound for any subsequent, as well as for any preceding, default of the officer.

¶20 There is certainly no express declaration of the act on this subject and, if the second bond operates a discharge of the first, this effect is produced by implication only. Yet the implication is very strong in favor of this construction.

The sole object of the law is to obtain sureties against whom the new & ¶21 summary remedy it gives might be used. To obtain additional security does not appear to have been one of the motives for which it was passed. The direction that the sureties should be "new & sufficient" countenances the opinion that they were to be solely relied on for the subsequent transactions of the officer. If no additional security was intended to be demanded, if the sole object of the law was to coerce the giving of sureties against whom this new remedy by distress might be used, it seems reasonable to think that the legislature supposed the new sureties to be alone responsible for the subsequent conduct of the officer.

It could not escape the consideration of the legislature that the same ¶22 friends who became bound in the first bond might probably become bound in the second, thinking themselves discharged from the first. But friends may be willing to become bound in a penalty within their resources, or to an amount to which the officer can secure them, & very unwilling to become bound in double that sum. The officer may be able to give security in a penalty of $25000, & totally unable to give security in the penalty of $50000. The government fixes the penalty in which an officer shall give bond & sureties, & is regulated in fixing that penalty by all the considerations which belong to the subject. It ought not to be considered as augmenting that penalty unless the means used for augmenting it are plain direct & intelligible. In this case, if the same sureties execute the new bond, they are liable to a double penalty by an act not clearly understood to have that effect. If these are new sureties to the new bond, the attention of the old sureties may be diverted from watching the conduct of the officer, & they may even be induced to relinquish liens on property, in order to enable the officer to find his new sureties. If the course of legislation on the subject has been such as to furnish to the original sureties reasonable ground for the opinion that they were discharged from all liability for the subsequent conduct of the officer, & reasonable ground for the implication that such was the intention of the legislature, and I think it has, such ought to be the construction of the act. This demurrer therefore is overruled.

The 5th. plea is that J. M. was never legally appointed, but was on the ¶23 1st. day of Aug. 1818 appointed, by the secretary of war, agent of fortifications for Norfolk Hampton roads & the lower part of the Chesapeak bay without any provision of law whatever authorizing & empowering him to make such appointment, & directly contrary to the act entitled an act &c approved the 3d. of March 1809.

To this plea there is a demurrer. ¶24
The first question arising on this demurrer respects the validity of this appointment made by the secretary of war.

¶25   It is I think too clear for controversy that appointments to office can be made by the heads of departments, in those cases only, which congress has authorized by law; & I know of no law which has authorized the secretary of war to make this appointment. There is certainly no statute which directly & expressly confers the power; and the "Army regulations" which are exhibited as having been adopted by Congress in the act of the 2d. of March 1821, declares that agents of fortifications shall be appointed, but not that they shall be appointed by the secretary of war. If this mode of appointment formed a part of the regulations previous to the revision of Septr. 1816, that is a fact which might or might not be noticed if averred in the pleadings. The court is not informed of its existence by this demurrer. It must therefore be supposed not to exist; & J. M. cannot be considered as regularly appointed agent of fortifications.

¶26   This brings us to the question in the cause on which I have felt, & still continue to feel, great difficulty.

¶27   The appointment of J. M. having been irregular, is this bond absolutely void, or may it be sustained as a contract entered into by a person not legally an officer, to perform certain duties belonging to an office?

¶28   If the office had no existence it has been already stated that a bond to perform its duties generally could create no obligation; but, since the office does exist, the condition refers to something certain, by which the nature & extent of the undertaking of the obligors may be determined. It is an undertaking that J. M. shall perform the duties appertaining to the office of agent of fortifications; and this undertaking is in the nature of contract. If this contract does not bind the parties according to its expressed extent, its failure must be ascribed to some legal defect or vice inherent in the instrument.

¶29   It is contended that the bond is void because 1st. there is an inability on the part of the United States to make any contract not previously directed by statute.

¶30   The United States is a government, and consequently a body politic & corporate, capable of attaining the objects for which it was created, by the means which are necessary for their attainment. This great corporation was ordained & established by the American people, & endowed by them with great powers for important purposes. Its powers are unquestionably limited: but, while within those limits, it is as perfect a government as any other, having all the faculties & properties belonging to government, with a perfect right to use them freely in order to accomplish the objects of its institution. It will certainly require no argument to prove that one of the means by which some of these objects are to be accomplished is contract. The government therefore is capable of contracting, & its contracts may be made in the name of the United States.

¶31   The government acts by its agents, but it is neither usual nor necessary to express, in those contracts which meerly acknowledge the obligation of an individual to the United States, the name of the agent who was employed in making it. His authority is acknowledged by the individual when he executes the contract, and is acknowledged by the United States when the government asserts any right under that contract. I do not mean to say that there exists any estoppel on either party. I only mean to say that a contract executed by an individual & received by the government, is *prima facie* evidence that it was entered into between proper parties.

So with respect to the subject of the contract. Without entering on the ¶32 enquiry respecting the limits which may circumscribe the capacity of the United States to contract, I venture to say that it is coextensive with the powers & duties of the government. Every contract which subserves to the performance of a duty may be rightfully made.

The constitution, which has vested the whole legislative power of the ¶33 union in Congress, has declared that the President "shall take care that the laws be faithfully executed." The manner in which a law shall be executed does not always form a part of it. The acts on the subject of fortifications furnish an apt example of this proposition. A power not limited or regulated by the words of the acts, has been given by the legislature to the executive, to construct fortifications; & large sums of money have been appropriated to the object. It is not & cannot be denied that these laws might have been carried into execution by means of contract. Yet there is no act of Congress expressly authorizing the executive to make any contract in the case. It is useless & would be tedious to multiply examples; but many might be given to illustrate the truth of the proposition. It follows as a necessary consequence that the duty & of course the right to make contracts may flow from an act of Congress which does not, in terms, prescribe this duty. The proposition then is true that there is a power to contract in every case where it is necessary to the execution of a public duty.

It remains to enquire whether it be indispensable to the validity of a ¶34 contract, that it should express the circumstances under which it was made so precisely & distinctly, as to show the motives which induced it, & the objects to be effected by it.

This is certainly often done; &, in many cases, conduces to a clear ¶35 understanding of the intention of the parties, and of the obligations which the instrument creates. But it is not universally practiced, would be often inconvenient, and is necessary, I think, only so far as may be requisite to explain the nature of the contract.

We know too well that persons entrusted with the publick money are ¶36 often defaulters. It is not, I believe, doubted that the law raises an assumpsit to pay the money which the defaulter owes. An overpayment is sometimes made by mistake. Is not the receiver liable to the United States? Yet there is no act of Congress creating the assumpsit in either case. I presume it will not be denied that a declaration charging that the defendant was indebted to the U.S. for money had & received to their use, & that, being so indebted, he assumed & promised to pay it, would be sufficient, without setting forth at large all the circumstances of the character in which, & the objects for which, the money was received.

¶37   If the law would raise an implied assumpsit which would be binding, I cannot concieve that an express assumpsit would be less so; nor can I concieve that such express assumpsit, more than the implied assumpsit, need detail the various circumstances on which its validity might depend.[9] These would be matter of evidence.

¶38   In any case where an assumpsit would be valid, the government may certainly take a bond, & I percieve no reasons why sureties may not also be demanded. It is the duty of the government to collect debts due to it, however they may have accrued; & it results from this duty that the means of securing & collecting the publick money may be used. Sureties may therefore be required to the bond demanded from the debtor. The instrument itself is an admission that it is given for a debt; and it is contrary to all our received opinions to require that it should show how the debt was contracted. Anything which destroys its validity may undoubtedly be shown in pleading; but a bond given to the United States is, I think, *prima facie* evidence of debt & would be sustained on demurrer.

¶39   So if money be committed to the care of any person for a legitimate object; bond & security may on the same principle be required with condition that he shall account for it.

¶40   The jurisdiction of a limited court must undoubtedly appear on the record; but I do not think that the same rule applies to contracts. Infants, fêmes covert, idiots, persons under duress, are not bound by their contracts. But their disability must be shown by pleading, & it need not appear in any contract that the parties to it are not liable to these disabilities. Every contract which is legal on its face & imports a consideration is supposed to be entered into on valid consideration, & to be obligatory, if the parties be ostensibly able to contract, until the contrary is shown; and the same rule applies I think to a government which is capable of making contracts.

¶41   2d. It is also contended that this bond is void because it is entered into on a consideration which is either forbidden by express law, or contrary to the general policy of the law.

¶42   The plea refers to the act, passed on the 3d. of March 1809 "to amend the several acts for the establishment & regulation of the treasury, war, & navy departments."

¶43   I have already said that I do not consider the prohibitions of this act as comprehending agents of fortifications, because they do not belong to the military establishment; nor do their employments relate to it. It is unnecessary to enter into any argument in support of this opinion, because it is of no importance to the point under consideration. The effect, if the act applied to the office, would be to show that the appointment of J. M. was not legal; and that effect is produced by the construction I have given to the constitution. I consider the appoint[ment] of J. M. to the office of agent of fortifications by the secretary of war as invalid; but the question, is the bond void on that account, still remains to be considered. It was undoubtedly intended as an office bond, & was given in the confidence that J. M. was legally appointed to office. If the suit were instituted to punish him for neglect of duty in the nature of *non user*, or for any other failure which could be attributed in any degree to the illegality of his appointment, I should be much disposed to think the plea a good bar to the action. But this suit is brought to recover the money of the United States which came to the hands of J. M. in virtue of his supposed office, and which he has neither applied to the purpose for which he received it, nor returned to the treasury. In such a case neither J. M. nor those who undertook for him, can claim any thing more than positive law affords them.

The plea does not controvert, but must be understood to confess, the ¶44 material facts charged in the declaration. It must be understood to confess that the money of the U.S. came to the hands of J. M., as agent of fortifications, that it was the duty of such agent to disburse it for the use of the United States in the manner prescribed by the army regulations, or to account for it, that he has failed to do either, & that they were bound for him in this respect. Admitting these things, they say it is a bar to the action brought for the money that his appointment was illegal.

If the bond contained no reference to the appointment of J.M. as agent ¶45 of fortifications, if its condition stated only that certain sums of money had been delivered to him to be disbursed under the directions of the principal engineer in the purchase of materials for fortifications, & in the payment of laborers, its obligation, I presume, would not be questioned. It would be a contract which the United States might lawfully make.

If, instead of specifying the particular purposes for which the money ¶46 was received, the condition of the bond refers to a paper which does specify those purposes, I know of no principle of reason or of law which varies the obligation of the instrument from what it would be if containing that specification within itself. That is certain which may be rendered certain, and an undertaking to perform the duties prescribed in a distinct contract, or in a law, or in any other known paper prescribing those duties, is equivalent to an enumeration of those duties in the body of the contract itself.

This obligation is an undertaking to perform the duties appertaining ¶47 to the office of agent of fortifications. Tho⟨se⟩ duties were prescribed in the Army regulations, & were such as any individual might lawfully undertake to perform. The plea does not allege that the thing to be done was unlawful, nor does it allege that the illegality of the appointment to office constituted any impediment to a performance of the condition of the bond. Were it even improper to disburse the money receivd, in the manner intended by the contract, it could not be improper to return it. There

can be nothing unlawful in the engagement to return it. The obligation
to return it, as in every other case of money advanced by mistake, is one
which, independent of all express contract, would be created by the law
itself. So far as respects the r[e]ceiver himself he would be bound by law
to return the money not disbursed, & if he would be so bound, why may
not others be bound with him for his doing that which law & justice
oblige him to do?

¶48   Admitting the appointment to be irregular, to be contrary to the law &
to its policy, What is to be the consequence of this irregularity? Does it
absolve the person appointed from the legal & moral obligation of accounting for public money which has been placed in his hands in consequence of such appointment? Does it authorize him to apply money so
received to his own use?

¶49   If the policy of the law condemns such appointments, does it also
condemn the repayment of the monies received under them? Had this
subject been brought before the legislature, & the opinion been there
entertained that such appointments were illegal, what would have been
its probable course? The secretary of war might have been censured; an
attempt might have been authorized to make him ultimately responsible
for the money advanced under this illegal appointment; but is it credible
that the bond would be declared void? Would this have been the policy of
those who make the law? Let the course of congress in another case
answer this question.

¶50   It is declared to be unlawful for any member of congress to be concerned in any contract made on the part of the United States, & all such
contracts are declared to be void.[10] What is the consequence of violating
this law & making a contract against its express provisions? A fine is
imposed on the violater; but does he keep the money received under the
contract? Far from it. The law directs that the money so received shall be
forthwith repaid; & in case of refusal or delay, "every person so refusing
or delaying together with his surety or sureties shall be forthwith prosecuted at law for the recovery of any such sum or sums of money advanced as aforesaid." If then this appointment be contrary to the policy
of the law, the repayment of the money received under it is not, and a suit
may I think be sustained to coerce such repayment on the bond given for
that purpose.

¶51   The cases cited by the defendants do not, I think, support the plea.

¶52   Collins v Blantern 2 Wilson 341 was a bond given the consideration of
which was illegal.[11] It was to compound a prosecution for a criminal
offence. It was to induce a witness not to appear & give testimony against
a person charged with the commission of a crime. The court determined
that the bond was void & that the illegal consideration might be averred
in the plea though not appearing in the condition. It is only wonderful
that this could ever have been doubted.

¶53   The case of Paxton v Popham 9th. East 408 & the case of Pole v Harrobin reported in a note in page 416 are both cases in which bonds were given for the payment of money for the performance of an act which was contrary to law.[12] These cases differ in principle from that at bar. This bond was not given to induce the illegal appointment, or for any purpose in itself unlawful. The appointment had been made, & the object of the bond was to secure the regular disbursement of or otherwise accounting for, public money advanced for a lawful purpose. The bond then was not, I think unlawful, though the appointment was.

The case of Nares & Pepys v Rowles 14th. East 510 was a suit on a bond ¶54 given by a collector & his sureties for the due collection & payment to the Receiver General of certain duties assessed under an act of Parliament.[13] The duties were collected but not paid to the Receiver General in consequence of which the collector was displaced & suit brought against one of the sureties in the bond. The defense was that the duties were not in law demandable, & this defense was founded on an ambiguity in the language of the act. The argument turned chiefly on the words of the statute; but the counsel for the plaintiffs contended also that, supposing the act not to impose the taxes, yet the bond would not be void, for such a security might well be taken, that the duties which were actually collected should not be lost, but might be preserved to be paid over to those who should be found ultimately entitled to receive the money. It was competent for him to enter into a bond to pay over voluntary payments made to him, although he might not have been able to enforce payment of the rates from those who might refuse.

In answer to this argument it was said that unless the act gave authority ¶55 to assess & collect the duties, he was no collector, & could not be subject to any obligation for not paying money over to the plaintiffs in that character, which was obtained by extortion.

The court seemed inclined to this opinion: but determined that the ¶56 taxes were imposed & assessed according to law, & therefore gave judgement for the plaintiffs.

The impression which may at first blush be made by this case will be ¶57 effaced by an attentive consideration of it. If the money collected was not due by law, the plaintiffs could have no right to receive it, and had consequently no cause of action against the defendant. The money sued for was not their money, but the money of the individuals from whom it had been unlawfully collected. The bond to collect & pay over this money to the receiver General was a bond to do an unlawful act. The contract would have been clearly against law. In giving his opinion on this point the Chief Justice said "Looking at the condition of this bond as it appears upon the record, I cannot say that if the rates were collected without any authority, the collector could be called upon to pay them over; because he would be answerable to the individuals from whom ⟨he⟩ had received the money, and would be entitled to retain it for his own indemnity."[14]

The case at bar is in principle entirely different from that of Nares & ¶58

Pepys v Rolles. This is not money obtained illegally from others & therefore returnable to them, but is the money of the United States drawn out
of the public treasury. The person holding it, is not "entitled to retain it
for his own indemnity" against the claims of others, for there are no
others who can claim it.

¶59 　　The justice of this case requires, I think, very clearly, that the defendants should be liable to the extent of their undertaking, & I do not think
the principles of law discharge them from it. I am therefore of opinion
that the demurrer to this plea ought to be sustained & that judgement on
it be rendered for the plaintiff.[15]

AD, Marshall Judicial Opinions, PPAmP; printed, John W. Brockenbrough, *Reports of
Cases Decided by the Honourable John Marshall...*, II (Philadelphia, 1837), 97–118. First sheet
of MS missing; text within angle brackets supplied from Brockenbrough. For JM's deletions
and interlineations, see Textual Notes below.

1. The surviving portion of the MS begins here.
2. *U.S. Statutes at Large*, II, 536.
3. Ibid., 819.
4. Ibid., III, 298.
5. Ibid., 615.
6. Ibid., 616.
7. There was no appeal of this case to the Supreme Court.
8. *U.S. Statutes at Large*, III, 592–93. Concurrently with this case, the U.S. instituted an
identical action for debt against Maurice and his sureties on the second bond, executed on
26 Sept. 1820. The sureties on this bond were Sharp, Reilly, and Eugene Higgins. As in the
first case, the defendants entered pleas and a demurrer to the declaration; and the plaintiff
demurred to one of the defendants' pleas (capias, declaration, pleas, and demurrers, U.S.
v. Maurice, Sharp, Reilly, and Higgins, Ended Cases [Unrestored], 1823, Vi).
9. An action of general assumpsit could be brought on an implied contract. Special
assumpsit could be used on an express contract (*PJM*, V, 22).
10. JM referred to an 1808 act "concerning public contracts" (*U.S. Statutes at Large*, II,
484–85).
11. Collins v. Blantern, 2 Wils. K.B. 341, 95 Eng. Rep. 847 (K.B., 1767).
12. Paxton v. Popham, 9 East 408, 103 Eng. Rep. 628 (K.B., 1808); Pole v. Harrobin, 9
East 416, 103 Eng. Rep. 632 n. (K.B., 1782).
13. Nares and Pepys v. Rowles, 14 East 510, 104 Eng. Rep. 697 (K.B., 1811).
14. 14 East 518, 104 Eng. Rep. 700.
15. On 30 May a jury returned a verdict for the U.S. on the issues joined, and the court
awarded judgment for $25,000. On the same day the court, after ruling on the demurrers,
gave judgment for the U.S. for $20,000 on the second bond (U.S. Cir. Ct., Va., Ord. Bk. XI,
333–34).

Textual Notes

¶ 1 l. 5	the ~~Executive~~ ↑executive.↓ The
l. 7	States ~~left~~ placed
ll. 9–10	contract ~~may~~ ↑can↓ assume.
ll. 10–11	of ~~mana~~ labourers, managers, paymasters, ~~&c~~ providers
l. 14	nothing ↑in the law itself↓ to
l. 22	office ↑for the purpose,↓ if

l. 27	executing ~~a law an~~ ↑an act↓ was
l. 28	the ↑several↓ offices
l. 29	President [*erasure*] ↑in↓ terms,
¶ 2 l. 4	the ~~president~~ ↑President↓ generally
¶ 3 ll. 3–4	officer. ↑If employed on the part of the US he is an officer of the U.S.↓ Although
ll. 7–8	continuing ↑one,↓ which
l. 11	defining ~~those duties; (~~ ↑them;↓ if
l. 13	who ~~fills~~ performs
l. 13	officer. ~~It is laid down by the Judges in the case of ——— in Carthew that he is a publick officer who hath any duty concerning the publick; and he is not the less a publick officer where his authority is confined to narrow limits, because~~
	~~——— But it has been already observed that the bond (illegible) which this suit is interested, if considered~~ ↑viewed↓ ~~on its face (illegible) itself must be considered as an office bond. It has [the cha?]racteristic of an office~~ ↑such a↓ ~~bond. If however the laws, or any (illegible) government is assumable by~~ ↑into↓ ~~which the↓ court could look changed the character of the employment so that the agent of fortifications ought not to be considered an officer of the United States I should be much inclined, at least to endeavour to view~~ ↑treat↓ ~~this bond according to the intent of the parties when it was executed.~~
¶ 4 l. 1 beg.	↑If it may be converted into a contract ↑to p↓, ↑but↓ it must be a contract to perform the duties of the office of agent of fortifications, & such an office must exist with ascertained duties or there is no standard by which the extent of the condition can be measured.↓
¶ 5 l. 2	to ↑the↓ execution
l. 4	of ~~1816~~ 24th.
ll. 5–6	regulations ↑provide for the appointment, &↓ define
¶ 6 l. 5	to ~~keep~~ ↑make out↓ 1st.
¶ 7 ll. 1–2	quartermaster, ~~& of a~~ ↑commissary, &↓ paymaster.
l. 2	A ~~slight~~ very
l. 3	that ~~offices~~ ↑duties↓ of
¶ 9 l. 1	agents ~~appo~~ mentioned
ll. 1–2	1809 ↑ch 19, Sec. 3 & 4↓ are
l. 5	the [*erasure*] ↑navy of↓ the
l. 10	defined in ~~our laws &~~ ↑the↓ acts
l. 11	think ~~it~~ ↑the act↓ can
¶10 l. 3	powers ~~of~~ ↑in↓ the adjutant ~~general~~ ↑General,↓ inspector
l. 4	of ~~ordinance~~ ordnance,
¶13 l. 4	the [*erasure*] ↑approbation↓ of
¶14 l. 1	have ~~engaged the attention of~~ ↑been taken up by↓ the Secretary.
¶15 l. 1	regulations, " revised
ll. 3–4	same ↑regulations↓ which
¶16 ll. 2–3	war [*erasure*] ↑office↓ in September

l. 3   the ~~provisions~~ ↑provision↓ they
ll. 3–4   fortifications ~~was~~ formed
l. 6   the [*erasure*] ↑President,↓ be
¶17 l. 3   1816, ~~as being~~ under
l. 7   I ↑am↓ the more
l. 8   before ~~that~~ ↑a↓ tribunal
l. 11   cause, ~~will)~~ ↑& which↓ would
¶18 l. 6   alleges ~~the~~ performance
l. 8   was ~~given~~ executed,
ll. 9–10   which they ↑had↓ failed
l. 10   contains ~~this~~ ↑a↓ proviso
ll. 16–17   & ~~that~~ ↑discharged↓ the
¶21 l. 1   obtain ~~security~~ ↑sureties↓ against
ll. 5–6   for ↑the↓ subsequent
l. 7   to ~~obtai~~ coerce
l. 9   to ~~suppose~~ ↑think↓ that
¶22 ll. 5–6   & [*erasure*] ↑very↓ unwilling
l. 9   give [*erasure*] ↑bond↓ & sureties,
l. 12   & ~~inteligible~~ ↑intelligible.↓ In
ll. 16–17   liens [*erasure*] ↑on↓ property, ~~which may have been given them~~ in
l. 18   to ~~induce~~ furnish
l. 22   ought ~~I think~~ to be
¶23 ll. 3–4   bay ~~with~~ ↑without↓ any
¶24 l. 2   respects [*erasure*] ↑the↓ validity
¶25 l. 3   no [*erasure*] law
l. 6   exhibited [*erasure*] ↑as↓ having
l. 9   appointment ~~was~~ formed
l. 10   the ~~act~~ revision
ll. 10–11   which ~~ought to be~~ ↑might or might not be noticed if↓ averred
¶26 l. 2   feel, ~~most~~ ↑great↓ difficulty.
¶27 ll. 2–3   not ~~reall~~ legally
¶28 ll. 1–2   that ~~the~~ ↑a↓ bond ↑to perform its duties generally↓ could
l. 7   parties ~~to it~~ according
¶29 l. 1   because ↑1st.↓ there
¶30 ll. 1–2   body ↑politic &↓ corporate, capable of attaining the ~~ends~~ objects
l. 8   freely ↑in order↓ to accomplish
¶31 l. 1   The ~~governments~~ ↑government↓ acts
l. 8   contract ↑executed by an individual &↓ received
¶33 l. 5   fortifications [*erasure*] ↑furnish↓ an
ll. 13–14   duty ↑& of course the right↓ to
¶35 l. 2   understanding ↑of the intention of the parties, and↓ of
ll. 4–5   may be ~~necessary~~ ↑requisite↓ to
¶36 l. 2   law ~~implies~~ ↑raises↓ an
ll. 3–5   owes. ↑An overpayment is sometimes made by mistake. Is not the receiver liable to the United States?↓ Yet
ll. 5–6   creating ~~this~~ ↑the↓ [*erasure*] ↑assumpsit↓ ↑in either case.↓ I
¶37 l. 4   need ~~express)~~ ↑detail↓ ~~the various~~

¶38 l. 5   of ~~coll~~ ↑securing↓ & collecting the [*erasure*] ↑publick↓ money

¶39 l. 1 beg.   ↑So if money be committed to the care of any person for a legitimate object; bond & security may on the same principle be required with condition that he shall account for it.↓

¶40 l. 1   a ~~cou~~ ↑limited↓ court

    ll. 1–2   the ~~pleadings;~~ ↑record;↓ but

    l. 5   parties [*erasure*] ↑to↓ it are

    ll. 6–7   face ↑& imports a consideration↓ is

    l. 7   supposed to ↑be↓ entered

¶42 l. 1   The ~~act referred to in the plea~~ ↑plea refers to the act,↓ passed

    l. 3   departments." ~~I have~~

¶43 l. 4   argument ~~to show the correctness~~ ↑in support of↓ of this

    ll. 13–14   any ↑other↓ failure

    l. 18   purpose ~~of~~ ↑for↓ which

¶44 ll. 2–3   declaration. ↑It must be understood to confess↓ that

    l. 3   J. M., ~~that it was~~ as agent

    l. 7   this [*erasure*] ↑respect.↓ Admitting

¶45 ll. 3–4   disbursed ↑under the directions of the principal engineer↓ in the

¶46 l. 6   an [*erasure*] ↑undertaking↓ to perform ~~certain~~ ↑the↓ duties

¶47 l. 14   bound [*erasure*] ↑with↓ him

¶48 l. 3   appointed [*erasure*] ↑from↓ the

    l. 5   apply ~~such~~ ↑money↓ so

¶49 l. 9   Let ~~this~~ ↑the↓ course

¶50 l. 3   are [*erasure*] ↑declared↓ to

    l. 4   contract [*erasure*] ↑against↓ its

    l. 5   under ~~under~~ the

¶52 l. 1   Blantern 2 [*erasure*] ↑Wilson↓ 341

¶53 l. 7   disbursement ↑of↓ or otherwise

    l. 8   The ~~condition of the~~ bond

¶54 ll. 4–5   in [*erasure*] ↑consequence↓ of which

    l. 12   preserved ~~in order to pay them~~ ↑to be paid over to those↓ who

¶57 ll. 1–2   be ~~worn off~~ ↑effaced↓ by an

¶58 l. 4   holding ↑it,↓ is not

¶59 ll. 1–2   defendants ~~in this case~~ should

To St. George Tucker

My dear Sir   Richmond May 27th. 1823

    I have received your letter of the 24th. & regret very much to hear of your indisposition.[1] It woud have given me great pleasure to have seen you & to have had your aid in the business of the court, but ill health is an obstacle not to be surmounted. There are three ejectments in which though neither myself nor any of my connexions are interested I cannot sit because the Fairfax title is implicated on them. This is however the first term & they may I presume lie over till the next when you may be in better health.[2] With sincere wishes that this may be the case I am dear Sir your

J MARSHALL

ALS, Tucker-Coleman Papers, ViW. Addressed to Tucker in Williamsburg; postmarked Richmond, 28 May. Endorsed by Tucker.

1. Letter not found.
2. The three ejectments were Martin's Lessee v. Blessing, Martin's Lessee v. Peters, and Martin's Lessee v. Abbott. They were decided in favor of the plaintiff at the Nov. 1823 term, Judge Tucker sitting alone (U.S. Cir. Ct., Va., Ord. Bk. XI, 396–400, 400–401, 401–2).

To Bushrod Washington

My dear Sir   Richmond May 28th. 1823
    I did not receive your letter of the 22d. till yesterday.[1]
    I recollect but very indistinctly to have seen among the papers of Genl. Washington a letter from some foreigner respecting lands or to have seen Genl. Washingtons answer to the letter I forget which. I am now much occupied in court, &, when the term is over, will examine for the letter.
    Did you not request me to send the papers remaining in my possession by the steam boat? If you did am I to send them to Alexandria or to Mount Vernon?
    I have been reflecting on printing a second edition of the life & suppose there might be some embarassment in the accounts were the printing of the 1st. vol to be distinct from that of the others. I would therefore propose, instead of taking the expence & profit of that volume on myself, that it should be printed at the risk of the editor but that all compensation for the copy right should be relinquished upon it. I presume Mr. Wayne can have no objection to this as that volume seems to be rather considered as a weight on the rest. For myself I am indifferent about profit on any part of the 2d. edition being only anxious that the work should be made worthy of the subject & the authors. I am dear Sir yours &c

J MARSHALL

I will attend to the subjects of your letter in a few days when the press of business is a little over.

ALS, NHi. Addressed to Washington at Mount Vernon, "near Alexandria"; postmarked Richmond, 29 [28?] May. Endorsed by Washington as received on 14 June.

1. Letter not found.

To Joseph Story

My dear Sir   Richmond June 1st. .23

I have to thank you for the paper containing a list of the studies to be pursued by the different classes in the college at Cambridge.[1]

This will probably be presented to you by my youngest son Edward who purposes entering college this fall. As my wish is that he should enter in the Sophomore class for which I hope he is or will be fitted, I send him on before the time of entering the college that he may prepare himself for that class by studying under some private tutor, & I will thank you, should you be in Boston on his arrival, to advise him respecting the person to whom he should apply & respecting his place of boarding, should you be able to do so without farther enquiry & without, in any manner, distracting your attention from your official duties. I should prefer his immediately taking a room in college & boarding there, but presume this cannot be allowed until he is admitted as a scholar.[2]

I am entirely ignorant of the fees for tuition & of the times when they are expected to be paid, whether quarterly, half annually, or yearly. In this uncertainty I send you a draft on the branch bank of the United States at Washington, payable next month, for 100$. which may be negotiated, I presume, in the manner in which you negotiate your own salary, & will thank you to inform me respecting college fees, board &c. It will be my choice to pay in advance where I can do so with convenience. I have heard it suggested that one of the rules of college requires that the money for students should be deposited with one of the Professors? Is this so? If it is I will thank you to recommend one of them to me. You see I avail myself without hesitation of your kind offer to make use of you in this business which, to me, is a very interesting one.[3]

I have given some money to my son for the purpose of supporting him till he enters college, but probably not enough. I will therefore thank you, after receiving the amount of my draft, to furnish him as he may require. After his arrival in Boston I shall receive such intelligence respecting the state of things there as will enable me to do precisely what is necessary. I will not encourage expensive habits in my son, but I do not wish to treat him over parsimoniously.

The court is now in session at this pla⟨ce⟩ & will probably continue so for a week or ten days. We shall probably adjourn about the same time. With affectionate esteem, I am dear Sir your

                                              J MARSHALL

ALS, MH-Ar. Addressed to Story in Salem, Mass.; noted as conveyed by "E. C. Marshall." Endorsed in unknown hand "June 23. 1823 / Chf Justice Marshall / to Judge Story / of his Son for College."

1. The enclosure may have been *A Statement of the Course of Instruction, Terms of Administration, Expenses, &c. at Harvard University* (Cambridge, Mass., 1823). Story may also have sent a newspaper containing this information.

2. Edward Carrington Marshall entered Harvard College as a member of the class of 1826. In Apr. 1824 he was listed as occupying room number fifteen of Massachusetts Hall. In August of that year he (along with five others) was "admonished for a Festive Entertainment." For an Aug. 1825 "Exhibition" he was assigned (with two others) to hold a "Conference" on "Pastoral, Epic, and Dramatic Poetry." A final entry in the faculty records, for 29 Aug. 1826, notes that Marshall (and three others) were "restored to their standing and recommended for a degree" (College Papers [2 Apr. 1824], XI, 2; Faculty Records [Aug. 1824, 1 July 1825, 29 Aug. 1826], X, 75, 91, 126, MH-Ar). Of the three sons JM sent to Harvard, Edward was the only one to graduate (see PJM, VIII, 81–82 and n. 1, 83–84 and nn.).

3. As indicated by the endorsement, Story forwarded JM's letter to the college.

Bank of the United States v. Dandridge
Report
U.S. Circuit Court, Virginia, 6 June 1823

This suit commenced in the U.S. Circuit Court in September 1820. The plaintiffs, the president and directors of the Richmond branch of the Bank of the United States, sued on a performance bond executed by Julius B. Dandridge, former cashier of the bank, and six other persons who acted as his sureties. The lengthy declaration set forth numerous counts of misfeasance and nonfeasance by Dandridge between February 1817 and February 1820, when he was forced to resign. With Dandridge himself not presenting a defense, the principal issue was the liability of the sureties to this bond, which had evidently remained in Dandridge's possession for some time after he entered upon his duties as cashier. In addition to the general issue of "not his deed" submitted by one of the sureties, the defendants entered a number of special pleas, the most important of which was that the bond had never been approved and accepted by the president and directors according to the act of Congress incorporating the bank. Counsel for the plaintiffs contended that possession of the bond and the suit upon it was sufficient evidence for the jury to infer the delivery of the bond and its acceptance. As he explained in letters to Story and Washington, Marshall was at first inclined to favor the plaintiffs but "changed that first impression on reflection." After a jury was sworn on 3 June, counsel on 4 and 5 June argued the defendants' motion to exclude the bond as evidence. Marshall gave his opinion on 6 June (Bank of the U.S. v. Dandridge, U.S. Cir. Ct., Va., Ended Cases [Unrestored], 1833, Vi; Bank of the U.S. v. Dandridge, Record on Appeal, App. Cas. No. 1283; JM to Story, 2 July 1823; JM to Washington, 12 July 1823; U.S. Cir. Ct., Va., Ord. Bk. XI, 339–40, 341, 342, 342–43).

The following decision is a very important one, from the consequences which it involves in all similar cases — No bond given to any Bank is considered as binding on its obligors, until it has been accepted by the corporation, and its acceptance made a matter of record:

The case of the BANK *of the United States* against their former Cashier, Julius B. Dandridge, and his securities, came on for trial last week, before the Federal Court for this district; the Chief Justice of the U. States, presiding — and was finally closed yesterday.

This was an action brought upon a bond in the penalty of $50,000 *charged* to have been given by Dandridge to the Bank, for the faithful discharge of his duty as Cashier of their Office of Discount and Deposite at the city of Richmond. The bond has subscribed to it the names of Julius B. Dandridge, Carter B. Page, Wilson Allen, James Brown jun. Thomas Taylor, Harry Heth and Andrew Stevenson; and there are *wafer* or *wax* seals to each name, except Mr. Allen's, to which a scroll is affixed. There were many special pleas and demurrers. Mr. Stevenson pleaded *separately*, and among other pleas, that of *non est factum;* and set forth the circumstances under which the bond was *signed* by him. He alleged, that although his name appeared last on the face of the bond, it was in fact first *subscribed* by him: That it was not sealed, or witnessed as to him, or *delivered* by him as his deed; but was returned, after being signed, to the principal obligor, to get other persons to join as his securities, and then to be returned, and if approved, to be completed: That this was never done, and that the seal which now appeared to his name, was not put by himself. There was also a special plea, setting forth, that the said bond was not delivered as the act and deed of any of the obligors, before the several malfeasances and nonfeasances assigned, as the breach of the condition, in the declaration; and that the said bond and the securities named in it were never received and approved by the Board of Directors, according to the act of Congress, and the rules, by-laws and regulations of the Bank.

Upon these pleas, as well as others, issues were joined. After the jury were sworn, the plaintiff's counsel offered the bond, and proved the hand-writing of Andrew Stevenson, (there being no *subscribing* witness as to him, but as to all the other obligors) — and relied on this, as presumptive evidence, of a *sealing* and *delivery* by him, and of its being his deed.

The counsel for Mr. Stevenson thereupon moved the court, to exclude the bond from going to the jury, upon these grounds: 1st, That possession of a bond, and proof of handwriting alone were not sufficient, in any case, to presume a *sealing* and delivery, which were essential to every deed; and 2ndly, That if this be the law as between *individuals;* yet in this case, the bare possession of the bond and bringing suit on it, would not be *sufficient;* but that they must shew acceptance and approval, by the records of the corporation, before the bond could be submitted to the jury.

These questions were ably argued on Wednesday and Thursday last by the counsel on both sides, (Messrs. Stanard and Call being counsel for the bank, and Messrs. B. W. Leigh, John Wickham, and Chapman Johnson,[1] for the defendants; the order, in which these gentlemen's names are here placed, being the order in which those on each side respectively addressed the court.) After the argument concluded, the court took time to deliberate.

On Friday morning, the Chief Justice delivered a very long and elaborate opinion. Upon the 1st point, he decided, that according to the established rules of evidence, possession of a bond and proof of the handwriting of the obligor (where there was no subscribing witness to its execution,) might be left to the jury, to presume a *sealing* and delivery by the obligor: but, that this did not apply to corporations: That, without ascribing to these artificial bodies, all the qualities and disabilities annexed by the common law to ancient institutions of this sort, yet it was to be conceded, that they were in their corporate capacities, the mere creatures of the act which gave them existence; deriving their powers from that act, and capable of executing them in the manner only, which the act authorized: That the forms and solemnities required by law, must be pursued, and to dispense with the formalities which this required for valuable purposes, and to enable these *artificial* bodies to act in a manner essentially different from that prescribed for them by the Legislature, was *inadmissible:* The bond was, therefore, in this case not to go to the jury, and *accordingly was excluded.* An exception was taken to this opinion of the court; and the jury found a general verdict for the defendants.

The counsel for Mr. Allen made and argued also this question before the court, viz. whether in the courts of the United States, a *scroll* was a seal — which the Judge decided was valid under the statute of Virginia.

It is of course not known, whether the Bank will take the case to the Supreme Court of the United States; or, acquiesce in the opinion of the Chief Justice. Their counsel have put it in their power to adopt either course, (which they may prefer,) by filing the bills of exceptions.[2]

Printed, *Enquirer* (Richmond, Va.), 10 June 1823.

1. Chapman Johnson (1779–1849) studied law at the College of William and Mary and obtained his license in 1802. After moving to Staunton, he began a distinguished career in law and politics. From 1810 to 1826 he represented the Staunton district in the state senate. At the Virginia Convention of 1829–30, Johnson championed apportioning representation on the basis of the white population.

2. After the court gave formal judgment for the defendants on 10 June, counsel for the bank tendered several bills of exceptions that had the effect of placing on the record the bond as well as the voluminous evidence of the former cashier's misconduct and negligence. The case was filed in the Supreme Court in January 1824. JM correctly predicted to Story that he would be overruled, adding that the judge "who draws the opinion must have more ingenuity than I have if he draws a good one." The author of the Court's 1827 opinion of reversal was Story. JM, dissenting, chose at this time to set for at length "the reasons and the imposing authorities" that produced his 1823 opinion in the circuit court (U.S. Cir. Ct., Va., Ord. Bk. XI, 347; Bank of the U.S. v. Dandridge, App. Cas. No. 1283; JM to Story, 2 July 1823; 12 Wheat. 64, 90).

From Joseph Story

My dear Sir   Salem June 22. 1823.

I had the pleasure of receiving your letter by your son, Mr Edward C. Marshall, a few days since. It was on the eve of my departure to hold the Circuit Court in Rhode Island & of course I had but a short opportunity of conversing with him, or of giving a personal attention to his business. This I regretted; but I took occasion on our going to Boston to introduce him to several gentlemen there, & I also wrote a letter to the President of the College commending him to his care, & requesting him to engage a tutor &c for him preparatory to his entering the university.[1] I have now the pleasure to inform you, that he is at Cambridge residing in a private boarding house under the instruction of two of the Tutors of the College; & that he writes me he is quite satisfied with his situation. The Commencement takes place in August, after which rooms in the College are assigned to the scholars; & after his matriculation I do not doubt, that he will have one assigned to him & Mr. Henning.[2] I shall personally attend to this myself. His expences in the intermediate period will of course be considerably larger than afterwards. I will take care that his wants are properly supplied; but I believe the arrangement now made that the Steward of the College is to superintend the expences of the Students, will diminish any particular care on this head. As to the mode of payment the expences, I believe the Bills are rendered quarterly, & of course advances are not required. But I shall soon go to Cambridge & adjust with the Steward the best means of supplying your son with every needful thing.

In the mean time I wish you to understand that I do not feel it any burthen or trouble to attend to his concerns & that I shall take great pleasure in aiding him in all ways within my power. I hope he will view me as a friend interested in his advancement; & short as has been our acquaintance I am greatly pleased with his demeanour, & character. I hope to have more claims upon him hereafter.

You need give your self no particular care as to the means of paying the advances. From time to time I will send you the accounts as I r⟨e⟩ceive them, & you can pay them as best suits your own convenience. I followed your request by handing your son as much money as he thought necessary for his present expences; & I do not think, that he will be likely to exceed, what you would deem discreet.

I observe that you have decided a very important case as to the responsibility of the sureties of Cashier of the Branch B'k of the UStates.[3] I should be very happy to see a copy of the opinion; & have been looking for it in print. The decision is of vast interest to every corporation in the Union; & I incline to think, that it would in the end have a salutary tendency by inducing greater caution.

My own circuit Courts have been some what laborious; & I am afraid that in some few cases my Brethren will have the trouble to revise my opinions. At least I shall be glad for their instruction on some difficult points.

I feel deep anxiety as to the successor of our lamented friend, Judge Livingston. I have heard strange rumours on the subject.[4] If the President does not make a very excellent appointment he is utterly without apology, for there never was a more enlightened Bar, from which to make the best selection.

I hope you will not take it to be a remark of course, that I wish you a long enjoyment of health. In the present state of the Court & the Country I may be permitted to say that I deem your lif⟨e in⟩valuable. With great respect, I am Dear Sir, Your most obliged friend & servant

JOSEPH STORY

ALS, Marshall Papers, ViW. Addressed to JM in Richmond; postmarked Salem, 23 June. MS torn where seal was broken.

1. The president of Harvard College was John Thornton Kirkland.

2. Edmund W. Hening was the son of William Waller Hening, the law reporter and compiler of Virginia's early statutes. He entered with the class of 1826 but left Harvard in 1824 (Faculty Records [1823–24], X, 57–58, 64, MH-Ar).

3. Bank of the U.S. v. Dandridge, Report, 6 June 1823.

4. Justice Brockholst Livingston died on 18 Mar. 1823. President Monroe soon thereafter offered to nominate Smith Thompson to fill Livingston's seat, but Thompson postponed giving a definite answer until he could determine whether he was a viable presidential candidate. Daniel Webster had reported to Story in April that if Thompson refused the appointment, the two leading candidates were the eminent New York jurists James Kent and Ambrose Spencer. Webster added that Sen. Nathaniel Macon of North Carolina had also been mentioned to the president. By this time, as well, Story likely had heard the rumor that Monroe was considering appointing Martin Van Buren. The previous year Van Buren, seeking to build a North-South Republican political coalition, had traveled to Richmond and paid a visit to Spencer Roane. Webster was correct in predicting that Thompson would ultimately accept the judicial appointment (Charles Warren, *The Supreme Court in United States History* [2 vols.; Boston, 1926], I, 587–94; Harry Ammon, *James Monroe: The Quest for National Identity* [New York, 1971], 513–14; Donald B. Cole, *Martin Van Buren and the American Political System* [Princeton, N.J., 1984], 116–17; Donald M. Roper, *Mr. Justice Thompson and the Constitution* [New York, 1987], 23–26).

To Bushrod Washington

My dear Sir   Richmond June 25th. [1823]

The court which has just terminated has furnished some business for your Honors at Washington. I have had some new & intricate questions on one of which, that goes up to the Supreme court, I decided on reflection differently from my first impression. That judgement will probably be reversed.[1]

I have not been able to lay my hands on the papers you mention. I do not recollect more than a letter mentioning some claim through Genl. Oglethorpe & without knowing the name & the date of the letter it cannot be found without examining every bundle. The best mode of search will be by looking at Genl. Washingtons letters to foreigners, for he must have acknowledged the receipt of that addressed to him. I will attend to your request respecting the books & papers.

I forgot in the letter I wrote to you respecting General Washingtons letters to say that you have not sent me the package containing those I had copied. I have gone through those you sent me & think it will be necessary to go through them again, to separate all the pamphlets & arrange them in the order in which they are to be published. In doing this I must have those which were copied at this place for the purpose of giving them their proper place. It is desirable that you should send them as soon as you have a safe opportunity. I cannot read the christian name of the Mr. Herbert to whose care I am to consign the trunks of papers.[2] I have purchased the laws but have not had an opportunity to send them.

I am extremely anxious to hear about the 2d. edition of the life. I have prepared it & will thank y⟨ou to⟩ keep me informed respecting it. I am very desirous that it should be published, but it cannot I think be broken & cannot be comprized in less than four volumes unless I go again through the whole & change it essentially. Hereafter the Civil administration may be published separately; Your

J MARSHALL

If you can find the letter of Mr. Jefferson to the President of the 11th of July '93 respecting the little Democrat, I wish you would send me a copy.[3] Perhaps there may be cabinet papers of that date. I know there are many letters respecting the vessel.

ALS, NHi. Addressed to Washington at Mount Vernon; postmarked Richmond, 27 June. Endorsed by Washington.

1. Bank of the U.S. v. Dandridge, Report, 6 June 1823.

2. Probably Maurice Herbert of Alexandria (ca. 1796–1830) (*Alexandria Gazette*, 26 July 1830). See JM to Washington, 6 Aug. 1823 and n.

3. The *Little Democrat* was a captured British ship that French minister Edmond Genêt had outfitted in Philadelphia as a French privateer. Jefferson's letter of 11 July 1793 was a response to the president's exasperated message of the same day about the French minister's conduct. This incident and other actions in defiance of American neutrality prompted the U.S. to ask for Genêt's recall (Harry Ammon, *The Genet Mission* [New York, 1973], 80–81, 86–93, 127–28). JM discussed the *Little Democrat* affair in his *Life of Washington*, citing Jefferson's letter in a way that implied the secretary of state was gullible in dealing with Genêt. See the *Life of George Washington* ... (2d ed.; 2 vols.; Philadelphia, 1838), II, 270–73.

To Joseph Story

My dear Sir   Richmond July 2d. 1823

I had the pleasure a few days past of receiving your letter of the 22d. of June & am greatly obliged by your friendly attention to my son. I am sorry that he misunderstood me so far as to request an advance of money from you when you could not have funds of mine in your hands. I gave him what I hoped would be sufficient for all his purposes until he should enter college but told him, should I be mistaken respecting the amount of his expenditures to apply to you. I did not suspect that his application would be made till the month of August.

The case concerning the securities of the cashier of the Bank goes to the Supreme court & will probably be reversed.[1] I suppose so because I conjecture that the practice of banks has not conformed to my construction of the law. The Judge however who draws the opinion must have more ingenuity than I have if he draws a good one.

The main question respects the validity of the bond on which the suit was instituted. It was signed at different times and left in possession of the cashier, certainly I suppose in the expectation that he would forward it to the proper place. The plea of non est factum[2] was put in among other pleas & the plaintiff proved the signature of the obligors, & relied on the possession of the bond & the suit on it as evidence to be left to the jury of its delivery & acceptance.

The cause was argued with very great ability, and it was contended that this would not be sufficient in any case — but if in general — not in this case.

I held very clearly that in the case of an individual obligee the evidence would authorize the jury to infer delivery, but not in the case of the bank of the United States.

The incorporating act requires that before the cashier shall be permitted to enter on the duties of his office he shall give bond with security to be approved by the board of directors for the faithful performance of its duties. I had no doubt that the suit upon the bond was evidence of its acceptance, & consequently of its being approved, if that fact could be established by parol evidence; but I was of opinion that it could not be so established. The board of directors, I thought, could only speak by their record. They cannot speak or act as individuals speak or act. They speak & act by their minutes. Their approbation & acceptance of the bond could not be expressed otherwise than officially on their minutes, & no other evidence than the minutes could establish the fact. I therefore did not permit the bond to go to the jury.

The question was entirely new & I was at first rather in favour of the plaintiffs. But in so lax a manner was this business conducted as to show very clearly that the cashier was in the full performance of his duty before the bond was executed, & to leave it very doubtful whether the breaches

assigned were not committed before the bond passed out of the possession of the cashier. There was reason to believe that it had never been
seen by the board of directors till he was removed from office, if then. It
was impossible not to foresee that if the bond went to the jury questions
would immediately arise on the time of its commencing obligation. The
date could not be the guide because it was not executed at its date. If the
time when it was signed by the last obligor should be insisted on, it was
obvious that it had not then been seen or approved by the directors nor
was it accepted by them. The delivery therefore could not be complete. If
the time when it came to the possession of the directors were to be taken,
it probably never came to their possession. These difficulties produced a
close examination of the point, the result of which was a perfect conviction that the minutes of the board could alone prove the acceptance of
the bond. I did not doubt that the board of Philadelphia might have
authorized the board at Richmond to accept the bond, but such authority ought to appear by the minutes of the board at Philadelphia.

I shall bow with respect to the judgement of reversal but till it is given I
shall retain the opinion I have expressed. With great & affectionate esteem, I am your

J MARSHALL

You alarm me respecting the successor of our much lamented friend. I
too had heard a rumour which I hoped was impossible. Our Presidents I
fear will never again seek to make our department respectable.

ALS, Story Papers, MHi. Addressed to Story in Salem, Mass.; postmarked Richmond,
2 July.

1. Bank of the U.S. v. Dandridge, Report, 6 June 1823.
2. This plea ("not his deed") was the general issue, or denial, in an action of debt on a
bond.

To St. George Tucker

My dear Sir   Richmond July 7th. [1823]
The packet from the consul of Portugal which accompanies this was received on the 3d. just as I was about to convey my poor wife into the country to escape the noisy rejoicings of the 4th. I send it now for your consideration.[1] I ride out every afternoon & will call to day or tomorrow as will
be most convenient to you for the purpose of determining what we shall
do. With the truest wishes for your health & happiness I am dear Sir, Your

J MARSHALL

ALS, Tucker-Coleman Papers, ViW. Addressed to Tucker. Endorsed by Tucker.

1. The packet from the Portuguese consul no doubt concerned the case of the U.S. v. Manuel Catacho, for which JM and Tucker held a special court at Norfolk in October. See Order, 11 July 1823; Charge to Grand Jury, 27 Oct. 1823.

United States v. Manuel Catacho
Order
U.S. Circuit Court, Richmond, Virginia, 11 July 1823

To the Clerk of the court of the United States for the fifth circuit and district of Virginia.

Whereas a petition has been presented to us by a certain Manuel Castacho who stands committed to jail by the Mayor of Norfolk borough on a charge of piracy, requesting that a special court may be directed for his trial, which said petition is supported by an affidavit stating that material testimony now in his power may be lost before the regular session of the court, We, taking the said petition into consideration do hereby direct a special session of the circuit court for the fifth circuit and District of Virginia to be holden at the court house in the borough of Norfolk on Monday the 27th. day of October next for the trial of the said Manuel Castacho; of the time and place of holding which special court you are hereby required to give notice in one of the papers published in the said borough of Norfolk; in conformity with the act of Congress passed on the 2d. day of March 1793 entitled "An act in addition to the act entitled 'An act to establish the judicial courts of the United States.[' "][1] Given under our hands this 11th. day of July in the year 1823

J MARSHALL CH. J OF THE U.S.
S: G: TUCKER, JUDGE OF THE
U:S: COURT FOR THE EASTERN
DISTRICT OF VIRGINIA

ADS, U.S. v. Catacho, U.S. Circuit Court, Va., Ended Cases (Unrestored), 1823, Vi.

1. *U.S. Statutes at Large*, I, 333, 334.

To Bushrod Washington

My dear Sir   Richmond July 12th. 1823

I received your letter expressing your wish to know the principle decided in the case of the Bank of the U.S. v Dandridge's securities.[1] The case will be carried before the Supreme court, & I am very glad of it, as the law on the subject ought to be settled.

The act incorporating the Bank directs that every cashier of a Branch

Bank shall before he enters on the duties of his office give bond with security to be approved by the President & Directors in a penalty not less than $50000 for the faithful performance of his duty.

This bond is in the penalty of $50000, & the plea of non est factum was pleaded. On the trial of this issue the signature of the Obligor was proved and the plaintiff at first rested his cause on this testimony. The defendants insisted that this would not be sufficient in any case, but if in general sufficient, would not be so in this case, the plaintiff being the Bank of the United States.

The cause was argued at great length & with great ability. I was of opinion that in the case of an individual obligee, the possession of the bond & the suit upon it were prima facie evidence that the bond was delivered ⟨an⟩d received by him; but that it was otherwise in the case of ⟨the⟩ Bank of the U.S.

I thought the assent of the Bank Directors indispensable to the completion of the bond, and that consent I thought could be given only at the board, and could be proved only by the minutes of their proceedings. The board must keep a record of all their proceedings, they can speak or act only in writing, and their proceedings can be proved only by their record. I found it impossible to comprehend how the board could act, or how its acts could be proved otherwise than by its record.

My first impression was different, but I changed that first impression on reflection. My mind was forcibly attracted to the point by the nature of the testimony. The bond was executed by the obligors at different times and remained in possession of Mr. Dandridge who was performing the duties of the office before it was signed by the last obligor. The breaches were some of them very probably committed before it was fully executed, certainly before it was seen by the obligees. Indeed the probability was that it was never seen by them until Mr. Dandridge was removed from office. It was easy to foresee that if the bond went before the jury I should be required to say when it became obligatory & what breaches it covered. It could not take effect from its date because its execution was at a subsequent period & it was not then received. What then was the criterion ⟨o⟩f its obligation? The more I thought on the subject the more ⟨wa⟩s I convinced that the acceptance of the bond must be proved by the minutes of the board, & I stopped it on its way to the jury.

I had no doubt but that the board of the mother bank might empower the board of the Branch Bank to approve & receieve the bond, but the minutes were as essential to the establishment of this fact as of the approbation & reception by themselves.

I have reflected a good deal on the subject of the Life & have come to the conclusion to separate the introduction from the other volumes & to publish a small edition of it at my own risk if I may be permitted to do so by Mr. Wayne & yourself without being charged with the copy right. As it is considered rather as an incumbrance on the residue of the work I presume there will be no objection to this. If I may be permitted to do so, I will thank you to enquire of Mr Small on what terms I can get 500, or 1000 copies printed & in boards; and on what terms bound in the usual way.

You have given no answer to my enquiries respecting that part of the corresponden⟨ce that⟩ was copied in Richmond & left with you. ⟨I ask?⟩ you to notice this subject & also to say in what arrang⟨e⟩ment the letters ought to be published. Is not the order of their dates to be preferred to the books from which they are copied? If so a new arrangement of them all must be made.

With the best wishes for your health and happiness. I am my dear Sir yours affectionately

J MARSHALL

If I separate the introduction the life will consist of three volumes.

ALS, Marshall Papers, DLC. Addressed to Washington at Mount Vernon; postmarked Richmond, 12 July. Endorsed by Washington.

1. Letter not found.

To Bushrod Washington

My dear Sir   Richmond Aug. 6th. 1823
I have received the box of letters by the steam boat.

I have this day shipped on board the Schooner John Capt. Burk six trunks & a box containing all the manuscript books & papers which were in my possession. I have also sent the journals of the old Congress,[1] Ramsays history of the revolution[2] & some volumes of the Remembrancer,[3] & the life of Putnam by Humphries.[4] I received also Gordons history of the war but, cannot find it.[5] I have no recollection of having sent it to you with the papers formerly transmitted, but as I cannot suppose that any person would take it & am unable to find it I hope that I may have sent it. If you have it not I must repeat my search.

You have not noticed that part of my former letter which asks your opinion on the propriety of arranging the letters according to their dates. I am my dear Sir with esteem & affection, Your

J MARSHALL

I had been so alarmed about the successor to our lamented brother Livingston that I am truely rejoiced to find Mr. Thompson is appointed.

ALS, NjMoHP. Addressed to Washington in Alexandria, "To be opened in the absence of Mr. Washington / by Maurice Herbert esquire"; postmarked Richmond, 8 Aug. Endorsed by Washington.

BUSHROD WASHINGTON

Oil on canvas by unknown, ca. 1820–1829. *Courtesy of Harvard Law Art Collection, Cambridge, Massachusetts.*

1. *Journals of Congress. Containing the Proceedings from Sept. 5, 1774 to the 3rd day of November 1788* (13 vols.; Philadelphia, 1778–88).

2. David Ramsay, *The History of the American Revolution* (2 vols.; Philadelphia, 1789).

3. [John Almon and Thomas Pownall], *The Remembrancer, Or Impartial Repository of Public Events* (17 vols.; London, 1775–84).

4. David Humphreys, *Memoirs of the Life, Adventures, and Military Exploits of Israel Putnam* (New York, 1815).

5. William Gordon, *The History of the Rise, Progress, and Establishment, of the Independence of the United States of America . . .* (4 vols.; London, 1788).

To Bushrod Washington

My dear Sir   Richmond Aug. 12th. 1823

Soon after receiving the box containing the correspondence copied at this place I commenced a careful reperusal of it & have just finished that part which concerns the old war of 1754. I find that the last letter is dated the 25th. of July 1758 & consequently breaks off in the midst of the interesting transactions which preceded the capture of fort Du Quêsne. Before I made this discovery I had packed up all the books & sent them to you so that it is not in my power to supply this chasm. The last letter is to Colo. Bouquet & I am not certain that the whole is copied as I have only one page without the signature of Genl. Washington.[1] I must beg the favor of you to have the residue of the letters copied, beginning with that of the 29th. of July 1758 to Colo. Bouquet, lest I should not have the whole of it. It will not do to publish this part of the correspondence without completing it.

I have received your letter of the 4th. & hope Mr. Wayne will concur in allowing me to publish the Introduction to the life in a separate volume, distinctly from the life itself.[2] I would not ask it if I did not believe that it would be expensive rather than profitable; and if I did not suppose that its connexion with the main work, by adding to its size & cost would be a weight upon it. I therefore propose not to connect it even in its publication, with the main work. I wish to publish a few copies & to do it first, because (excuse this vanity & keep it to yourself) I think it is so much improved that its publication may probably be useful to what is to follow. I wish [to] print 500 or 1000 copies & will furnish in the first instance the money to purchase the paper. If Mr. Wayne gives his consent I could wish to know immediately from Mr. Small on what terms he would print this number of copies, making the advance for the paper. We will correspond on this subject while you are in Philadelphia on the fall circuit. I shall not wish any subscription paper to be used as I am willing to incur the risk of the publication, my object being to do ju⟨stice⟩ to my own reputation in this work. With the best wishes for your health & with true esteem & affection, I am your

J MARSHALL

ALS, Marshall Papers, DLC. Addressed to Washington at Mount Vernon by "way of Alexandria"; postmarked Richmond, 13 Aug. Endorsed by Washington: "To be attended to when / I return from Phila."

1. Henry Bouquet (1719–1765) was a Swiss-born soldier of fortune who received a British commission in 1755. He was second-in-command of Gen. John Forbes's 1758 campaign against Fort Duquesne.

2. Letter not found.

To Stephen Girard

Sir   Richmond Septr. 25th. 1823

You will be surprized at receiving this letter from me, who, being personally unknown to you, can have no solid pretensions to your confidence. The gentleman however by whom it will be delivered, beleives that you will credit any fact I may assert, and, as he is my near connexion & intimate friend, I cannot refuse to comply with his request to state such circumstances as may promote his views and are within my own knowledge.

Mr. Harvie is a gentleman of strict honour & unquestionable integrity, who possesses a considerable estate.[1] In the seductive times which have gone by, he was imprudent enough to contract debt, which now oppresses him, & which, in the great changes property has undergone, he cannot pay without making immense & ruinous sacrifices. He is therefore desirous of negotiating a loan which may discharge claims which press upon him, & enable him to sell property on terms less injurious than if it should be forced into the market at the present moment. The state of the money market in Virginia makes it impossible to negotiate such a loan here; and he is informed that you would probably not be disinclined to advance him the sum he wants on receiving ample security for the repayment of the principal, and of the interest, at such times as may be stipulated. The object of this letter is to assure you of my entire convictio⟨n⟩ that every representation Mr. Harvie may make to yo⟨u⟩ respecting the security he offers will be perfectly true, & that the laws of Virginia interpose no obstacle to th⟨e⟩ inforcement of any specific lien on land. I am Sir very respectfully, Your Obedt.

J MARSHALL

ALS, Stephen Girard Papers, PPAmP. Addressed to Girard in Philadelphia and noted as conveyed by "Mr. Harvie." Endorsed as received 30 Sept. and answered 6 Oct.

1. Jaquelin B. Harvie, JM's son-in-law.

To Joseph Story

My dear Sir   [Richmond 26 September 1823][1]

Being entirely uncertain at what time & to what amount advances for my son may be expected, I have taken the liberty once more to trespass on your goodness so far as to send you a check on the branch of the Bank at Washington for $150. I hope it may be passed without difficulty or trouble through the branch at Boston, or through your bank at Salem, in the same manner as your drafts for your own salary are passed. Should there be any discount upon it, that of course is chargeable on the draft. I could have remitted this draft or a bill directly to my son, but I sent him a bill in August for $100, & my sons, in the north, have such an aptitude for spending money, that I am unwilling to tempt Edward by placing too much in his hands.

Our brother Johnson, I percieve, has hung himself on a democratic snag in a hedge composed entirely of thorny state rights in South Carolina, and will find some difficulty, I fear, in getting off into smooth open ground.

You have I presume seen his opinion in the national Intelligencer, & could scarcely have supposed that it would have excited so much irritation as it seems to have produced.[2] The subject is one of much feeling in the south. Of this I was apprized, but did not think it would have shown itself in such strength as it has. The decision has been considered as another act of judicial usurpation; but the sentiment has been avowed that if this be the constitution, it is better to break that instrument than submit to the principle. Reference has been made to the Massacres of St. Domingo, and the people have been reminded that those massacres also originated in the theories of a distant government, insensible of, & not participating in the dangers their systems produced. It is suggested that the point will be brought before the Supreme court, but the writer seems to despair of a more favorable decision from that tribunal since they are deserted by the friend in whom their confidence was placed.

Thus you see fuel is continually adding to the fire at which the *exaltées* are about to roast the judicial department. You have, it is said, some law in Massachusetts not very unlike in principle to that which our brother has declared unconsti⟨tutional.⟩ We have its twin brother in Virginia, and a ca⟨se was?⟩ brought before me in which I might have considered its constitutionality had I chosen to do so; but it was not absolutely necessary, &, as I am not fond of butting against a wall in sport, I escaped on the construction of the act.[3] Farewell. I am my dear Sir with affectionate esteem, your

J MARSHALL

ALS, Story Papers, MHi. Addressed to Story in Salem, Mass.; postmarked Richmond, 27 Sept. MS torn where seal was broken.

1. The dateline appears to have been cut off. At the top center of the MS someone wrote "[Sept. 26. 1823]."

2. On 7 Aug. 1823 Justice Johnson on circuit in South Carolina decided the case of Elkison v. Deliesseline (8 Fed. Cas. 493). Adopting an expansive reading of the commerce clause, Johnson ruled that South Carolina's Negro Seamen Act, which required detention in jail of free black sailors while their ships lay in port, was unconstitutional. The opinion was published as a pamphlet and widely reprinted in the newspapers, including the *Daily National Intelligencer* on 8 Sept. The decision provoked heated controversy that was played out in the Charleston newspapers during September and October (Donald G. Morgan, *Justice William Johnson, the First Dissenter* [Columbia, S.C., 1954], 192–202).

3. JM alluded to the case of the Brig Wilson v. U.S. See Opinion, ca. 22 May 1820. Sections 64 and 65 of Virginia's "Act reducing into one, the several acts concerning Slaves, Free Negroes, and Mulattoes" prohibited free blacks from entering Virginia's ports, and set penalties for violators (*Revised Code of Va.*, I, 437–38). These two sections were first enacted in 1793.

To Caleb P. Wayne

Dear Sir   Richmond Septr. 29th. 1823

On my return to this place from an excursion to our mountains I received your letter of the 10th. and am much obliged by the trouble you have taken in making the enquiries I wished from Mr. Small.[1] The subject of a second edition of the book I have written is one about which I feel a good deal of interest without the most remote view to further pecuniary advantage. My object is to separate entirely that part of the work which is peculiarly the life of Washington from that which is purely historical & to publish with the introduction that part of the second volume which comprizes the controversy between the two countries anterior to the appointment of Genl. Washington to the command of the armies. That was the original plan of the work; but as it was then supposed to contain too much matter for one volume, that part of it was transferred to the second & forms the 2d. & 3d. Chapters of the 2d. vol. I have gone through the whole & have reduced the history of the war including also Braddocks war as it has been termed in this country, to two volumes. I am willing to publish the introductory, or meerly historical part, (about 1000 copies) at my own risk. The fate of that volume will determine you as to the propriety of hazarding the others.

I am truely sorry to hear of the accident which has befallen you & hope that you have recovered from it. Very respectfully I am Sir, Your Obedt

J MARSHALL

ALS, NjMoHP. Addressed to Wayne in Philadelphia; postmarked Richmond, 29 Sept. Endorsed.

1. Letter not found.

From Stephen Girard

Sir! Philada 6th Oct 1823

On the 30th. ultimo, I had the honor to receive your letter of the 25th. of that month from the hands of your friend Mr Harvey who has communicated me the object of his journey to this City, although it would have been very pleasing to me to meet the views of a Gentleman who is your near relation, present circumstances together with my several branches of business, which require all my funds has prevented me to comply with his request. I have the honor to be with great respect, Your obt Servt.

Letterbook copy, Stephen Girard Papers, PPAmP. Inside address to JM.

To Bushrod Washington

My dear Sir Richmond Oct. 11th. 1823

I returned from the upper country too late to answer your letter of the 29th of August previous to your proceeding on your circuit.[1]

The copies which I mentioned to you may be carried to Washington in Feb. when they may be placed with the others which I shall endeavour to carry with me. Meanwhile I shall try to arrange them as we both think most advisable. It cannot be made complete, but I shall endeavour so far to complete it as to free it from any striking impropriety.

I think with you that repetitions ought to be avoided & that letters without interest may be omitted. Apparent inaccuracies should certainly be corrected. Whether they may have been produced by the negligence of the original copyer, or have escaped the General in the hurry of writing, is perhaps not very material. There is I think no motive for preserving them.

I have received a letter from Mr. Wayne, for which I am greatly obliged to him, enclosing a memorandum from Mr. Small of the expence of publishing 1000 copies of the Introduction, but I am so ignorant of the technical language of the craft that I do not understand it.[2] I propose to have the Introduction published in good type, such for instance as the first edition, on paper about the same size & quality; 33 or 34 lines to the page, about 500 pages or rather more. I am willing to advance money to buy the paper, & leave the publisher to make the residue of the money out of the books if it can be done in a reasonable time — if not I will pay it. I wish to know what will be the cost of 1000 volumes, distinguishing the price of the paper from the other part of the work. I wish the book to be bound in the most usual manner — say as the Life of Washington is bound. About 500 copies may be bound first & the residue when there shall be a demand for them should that ever be. I shall make enquiries in

Baltimore & perhaps elsewhere but shall give Mr. Small the preference unless his terms should be much higher than the terms of others. Your

J MARSHALL

ALS, Marshall Papers, DLC. Addressed to Washington at Philadelphia; postmarked Richmond, 11 Oct. Endorsed by Washington.

1. Letter not found.
2. Probably Wayne's letter of 10 Sept. 1823 (not found), which JM acknowledged in his letter to Wayne, 29 Sept. 1823.

To Joseph Story

My dear Sir   Richmond Oct. 12th. 1823

By the Libra Capt. Snow, I send you two barrels of our family flour which the Captain has promised to deliver at the store of E & E Reid Long wharf No. 37. in Boston. Your name is marked on the heads of the barrels & I hope you will receive them safely. They are part of the stock laid up for my own use, and, though not quite so white as we usually make flour of that description, in consequence of the dryness of the wheat when ground, will, I trust, be found very good.

Our country has been unusually sickly. The autumnal fevers have not only been more frequent, but have been also more fatal than common. I hope our climate is not about to assume permanently the character it wears at present. In the East, I hope you have no other fever than the political one which seems to have infected all parts of the Union. Farewell. With affectionate esteem, I am your

J MARSHALL

ALS, Story Papers, MHi. Addressed to Story in Boston; postmarked Richmond, 13 Oct.

From John Lowell

Sir,   Roxbury, near Boston, Octo. 25. 1823.

I am fully aware of the extreme delicacy & responsibility of the measure I am about to take. No man living has an higher, a purer sense of the dignity of the judicial office — of the impropriety eith⟨er⟩ previously or subsequently to any decision, of approaching privately the administrators of the Laws, the only body in which well regulated liberty depends, for its ultimate security. Yet there may be cases, in which an appeal to the members of the most venerable tribunal may be justified. If their opinions are wantonly & wickedly misrepresented to the defamation of *Individuals*, I can scarcely perceive any difference except in degree between such a case, & a wanton & wicked misrepresentation of their opinions with intent to bring that venerable tribunal itself in to disrepute with the publick. An opinion delivered by you as the organ of the Supreme Court has in my opinion been so maliciously perverted, to blast the reputation of *one of the witnesses in that Court*.[1] It matters not whether it has produced *all* the intended effects. If fifty four years of virtue have been a shield, you will perceive that they have not been a sufficient one to secure the individual from that licentiousness constantly increasing in our country & which threatens the extinction of our liberties. Never intermingling in questions of *local* or *Presidential* elections, & devoting his whole leisure to Agriculture & its advancement, he had hoped, that he might be permitted to enjoy a quiet old age. The inclosed papers will shew to you that this blessing has been denied to him. It was strangely & improperly believed that his friends the earliest movers in our revolution in this state & the most strenuous supporters of the *Constitution* of the United States, when its acceptance was doubtful, were not altogether cordial in the nomination of Mr Adams for the Presidency. Always exposed to obloquy for their zealous, & constant defence of the true principles of a free government, as administered by Washington, the old stories were revived, & *my father*, dead 20 years since, was by an Editor of that party accused of being a *Tory & Refugee*. It was distinctly stated that he *fled to Halifax*.[2] This was, at that time, by our laws, High Treason, & you will not condemn a son — an *oldest* son — almost an only son (for my brother Dr. Lowell is a clergyman) for undertaking his *defence*. For this act of filial duty, signed *openly* by me, I was accused of *perjury* in the case of Holker versus Parker, in equity, & your opinion was maliciously & corruptly mutilated & my own testimony *much more* mutilated, to support the charge. It is not the first time, as you will see by the enclosed papers.[3]

Now it will naturally occur to you, what is it that Mr Lowell wants? what is the object of laying this subject in which I have no concern, before *me*?

I reply, in the first place — not to give you pain, or trouble — not to excite a doubt in your mind as to my own c⟨on⟩viction of your *unquestionable impartiality*. The veneration which my father, Mr Ames, Mr Cabot & all my friends had taught me to feel for you, as well as my own personal knowledge of your character as a statesman, an impartial & fearless historian, & as an upright magistrate was not in the *slightest* degree impaired by the circumstance of your differing from Chief Justice Parsons & myself on the legal questions in the Case of Holker.[4] Nay more, I openly said, that sitting in your place, with the *evidence* before you, I should have decided precisely as the Court did; the *new* evidence *now* published may tend to shew how embarrassing & how imperfect is the condition of a Supreme Court of Appeals, unable to sift testimony on the *stand*, & when depositions are exhibited to them taken *ex parte*.[5]

My only object is, to *vindicate myself*, & to shew to one, who must feel in his *own* bosom the value of *private* character, to what we are exposed.

What would any man of conscious integrity feel, if the *mutilated* opinion, of the most venerated judge were arrayed before the publick, improperly & iniquitously arrayed, as proofs of a conviction on the part of that *Judge* that he was a *perjured man?* ⟨In the⟩ south I am unknown. In the North I have been ⟨the b⟩utt of unprincipled men for having fearlessly ⟨perfo⟩rmed the part of a good citizen in expressing my opinions, declining for twenty years office, of all sorts, to which I had been appointed in early life, & which I had been again solicited to accept. But if our republic is destined to survive a few generations, *private character* must be *fearlessly upheld*, & modest services have some claim to general protection. Judge Story, who was c⟨o⟩unsel in the case of Ho⟨lker⟩ & did not for that reason, sit in the cause, although divided from me in political opinion, has openly & honorably given the negative to these calumnies. I have the honor to be, with unfeigned respect, yr hble Svt.

JOHN LOWELL.

ALS, Marshall Papers, ViW. Addressed to JM in Richmond; postmarked Boston, 26 Oct. MS torn where seal was broken.

1. The case was Holker v. Parker, decided by the Supreme Court in 1813. Much of JM's opinion for the Court dealt with a deposition given by Lowell, who had been John Holker's attorney in earlier proceedings brought by Holker against Daniel Parker in the U.S. Circuit Court for Massachusetts. A judgment for Holker, based on an arbitration award, was rendered at the Oct. 1799 term of the U.S. Circuit Court at Boston. In 1807 Holker and his trustees brought a suit on the chancery side of this court to set aside the law judgment. The circuit court dismissed this suit in Oct. 1811, and Holker appealed to the Supreme Court. The Supreme Court reversed the lower court's decree and remanded the case for further legal proceedings (Holker v. Parker, App. Cas. No. 512; 7 Cranch 436–56).

2. On 27 Sept. 1823 an article in the *Independent Chronicle and Boston Patriot* stated that John Lowell, Sr., was " 'a Tory and Refugee.' " John Lowell, Jr., wrote two articles vindicating his father's memory for the Boston *Daily Advertiser* of 29 Sept. and 1 Oct.

3. A piece in the *Independent Chronicle* of 4 Oct. insinuated that the younger Lowell committed perjury in Holker v. Parker. Lowell's defense against this charge appeared in the *Daily Advertiser* on 7 and 9 Oct. In those pieces he recounted that the charge of perjury in Holker v. Parker had first appeared in the *Independent Chronicle* in 1814. Lowell sued Davis C. Ballard, editor of the paper, for libel, but before trial Ballard published a retraction.

4. Theophilus Parsons had represented Daniel Parker in the original case brought by Holker against Parker in the U.S. Circuit Court for Massachusetts in the 1790s.

5. The *Daily Advertiser* on 9 Oct. published an affidavit given by Rufus G. Amory. Amory served with Parsons as cocounsel and swore that Holker's absence from court compelled Lowell to accept a $5,000 settlement. Holker had thirty days to reject the settlement but took no action. Amory further swore that James Lloyd, cocounsel with Lowell, approved of Lowell's conduct.

United States v. Manuel Catacho
Charge to Grand Jury
U.S. Circuit Court, Norfolk, Virginia, 27 October 1823

I stated to the Jury that this, being a special court called for a single case, its jurisdiction was confined to that case.

That the Grand Jury being a part of the court its regular powers had the same limits.

That the court was called for the trial of an individual charged with piracy & the duty of the jury would be singly to enquire whether the prisoner was guilty or innocent of that charge. The court therefore had only to inform the jury what in law was piracy.

That Piracy consisted in cruizing on the high seas without a lawful commission & committing any murder or robbery. If the act was committed every person on board was guilty unless the accused could show that he acted under coercion.[1]

AD, Tucker-Coleman Papers, ViW. Endorsed by Tucker: "Judge Marshal's charge / to the Grand-Jury, on a / Case of piracy. / Octo: 27. 1823 / In the Case of / Manuel Catacho / otherwise called / Manuel Cartacho." Another endorsement in unknown hand: "A special Jury of respectable freeholders who / are not engaged in navigation or Importation of foreign merchandise."

1. After deliberating "about two hours" the grand jury returned "a *True Bill*." Albert Allmond, Catacho's attorney, then moved for a petit jury *de medietate linguæ* ("of the half-tongue"), in which half the jurors were to be citizens and the other half to be foreigners. Such juries could be ordered under state law, but there was no federal law to this effect. The court took this motion under advisement and granted it on 30 Oct. As he subsequently confided to Story, JM was inclined to disallow the motion but acceded to Judge Tucker's opinion. The mixed jury of citizens and foreigners returned a verdict of guilty on 31 Oct., but recommended clemency " 'in consideration of some circumstances stated in the evidence, which although they had no bearing on the question of the prisoner's guilt, were of a nature to interest the feelings of humanity in his favor.' " On 1 Nov. the court sentenced Catacho to death by hanging, setting 5 Dec. as the execution date. He was subsequently discharged by a pardon from President Monroe (Washington *Daily National Intelligencer*, 1 and 5 Nov. 1823; U.S. Cir. Ct., Va., Ord. Bk. XI, 360–63; *Revised Code of Va.*, I, 266; JM to Story, 24 Nov. 1823; *Niles' Weekly Register* [Baltimore], XXV [1823–24], 160; Richmond *Enquirer*, 11 Dec. 1823).

To Mary W. Marshall

My dearest Polly   Norfolk Oct. 31st. 1823

I have the mortification to tell you that it will not be in my power to come up till tuesday. The case will not be finished till saturday.

I had a very pleasant sail down the river and got into Norfolk about eight.[1] I board in a very agreeable house & am treated by the gentlemen of the town with a degree of kindness & attention which exceeds even what I had expected. Yet I am much disappointed at not being able to return as soon as I had hoped. I am my dearest Polly your ever affectionate

J MARSHALL

ALS, Marshall Papers, ViW. Addressed to Mrs. Marshall in Richmond. "STEAM BOAT" stamped on cover.

1. JM traveled to Norfolk on the steamboat *Potomac*, arriving on the evening of 26 Oct. (Washington *Daily National Intelligencer*, 30 Oct. 1823).

To [John Lowell]

Sir   Richmond Novr. 6th. 1823

Yesterday, on my return to this place after a short absence, I received your two letters of the 25th. & 28th. of October.[1] I was equally concerned and surprized at the information that any opinion of the supreme court, especially one delivered by myself, should be the foundation of so serious a charge against any gentleman as that which has been brought against you. It has never been my habit, in any situation, much less when acting under the high responsabilities of office, to make insinuations against the characters of those of whom I was not compelled to speak unfavorably. It was therefore matter of astonishment to me to learn that I had deliberately and unnecessarily uttered expressions which could be construed into the imputation of a crime of the deepest die against a gentleman who, though not known to me personally was known by reputation to great advantage. I turned, without reading the papers inclosed in your letter to the opinion itself, and was not a little releived at finding that it did not in any manner justify the inference which seems to have been drawn from it. Its language is very intelligible & conveys I think the idea it was intended to convey. The award was set aside because it was not beleived to be the judgement of the arbitrators on the real case, but on a supposed compromise between the parties by their counsel. In stating the ground on which the opinion that the arbitrators did so proceed was made up, there is no insinuation that your testimony was disregarded or discredited. On the contrary, the declaration is unequivocal that it is supported by the facts and circumstances detailed in your deposition.

The opinion speaks for itself. No explanatory comment upon it is necessary; and one from me might perhaps be deemed improper.

With the gentlemen to whom you refer as your friends and connexions, it was my pride and my happiness to be on terms of some intimacy, and they have always been placed in my estimation, among the most distinguished patriots of our country.

ADf, Marshall Papers, ViW.

1. Letter of 28 Oct. not found.

To Joseph Story

My dear Sir   Richmond Novr. 24th. 1823

I had the pleasure of receiving your letter of the 19th. of october and am greatly obliged by your kind attention to the affairs of my son.[1] My remittances will hereafter be made directly to Mr. Higginson.[2] I have received a letter from that gentleman in which he credits me for only one of the sums paid by you to Judge Davis.[3] This mistake he has I presume corrected before this time.

In the Pennsylvania cause I have come with very considerable doubt, to a conclusion different from yours & therefore hope you will prepare your opinion. Should the court concur with you I shall be far from regretting it for my opinion in this case is not one of those in which I feel such confidence as to regret its not prevailing.[4]

I have had two applications lately for a jury *de medietate lingua*. The first was a case of robbing the mail. I sat alone, and rejected the application on a hasty view of the judicial act.[5] The second was on the trial of a person charged with Piracy and the District Judge sat with me.[6] I still inclined to my first opinion, but the District Judge was very clear in favor of the application. We were told by the bar that the same question had occurred in New York & that Judge Thompson had directed the Jury *de medietate*.[7] Being unwilling in a capital case to reject the application of the prisoner by a division of the court, where I felt doubt myself, & where an associate Justice had determined the question in favor of the application I concurred in directing the jury. It is a point on which the practice ought certainly to be uniform & I propose to suggest it to the Judges in February next. If you have not already considered and determined it, I wish you would turn it in your mind. With very great esteem and regard, I am dear Sir your Obedt

J MARSHALL

ALS, Story Papers, MHi. Addressed to Story in Salem, Mass.; postmarked Richmond, 24 Nov.

1. Letter not found.

2. Stephen Higginson (1770–1834), a Harvard graduate and Salem merchant, served as steward of Harvard College from 1819 to 1827 (Joshua L. Chamberlain, ed., *Harvard University: Its History, Influence, Equipment, and Characteristics* [Boston, 1900], 109).

3. John Davis (1761–1847) was judge of the U.S. District Court for Massachusetts from 1801 to 1841. He also sat with Justice Story on the U.S. Circuit Court.

4. Probably Kirk v. Smith, which came by writ of error to the U.S. Circuit Court for Pennsylvania. The case, which concerned the operation of certain laws on the manor lands of the Penn family, was continued "for advisement" to the 1824 term. JM gave the opinion of the Court, Justice Johnson dissenting (9 Wheat. 241, 256, 294).

5. Possibly a reference to the cases of Patrick Carroll, John Daugherty, and William Kelly, who were charged with misdemeanor for attempting to rob the U.S. mail near Petersburg in Dec. 1822. They were convicted and sentenced at the May 1823 term (Richmond *Enquirer*, 3 June 1823; U.S. Cir. Ct., Va., Ord. Bk. XI, 321, 324–25, 331).

6. U.S. v. Manuel Catacho, Charge to Grand Jury, 27 Oct. 1823 and n. 1.

7. The case heard by Judge Smith Thompson on circuit in New York has not been identified. Thompson had just begun his tenure as a Supreme Court justice, replacing the late Brockholst Livingston.

Mankin v. Chandler & Company
Opinion
U.S. Circuit Court, Virginia, 5 December 1823

Isaiah Mankin, a Baltimore merchant, sued John and William Chandler, merchants trading under the name of John Chandler & Company, on a note given by the company to Jacob Walsh of Baltimore in October 1818. Walsh subsequently assigned the note to Mankin. The defendants filed a plea of payment in November 1822 and a second special plea in December 1823. The second plea interposed a chancery decree of the Westmoreland County Court issued in April 1822 by which Chandler was ordered to pay the same debt in satisfaction of a debt owed by Walsh to Thomas Rowand. The case in the county court was a "foreign attachment," an action by which a creditor could proceed against the property of an absent or non-resident debtor. Marshall's opinion of 5 December 1823 was on the sufficiency of the plaintiff's demurrer to this special plea (U.S. Cir. Ct., Va., Ord. Bk. XI, 275, 382, 395; pleas [with record of proceedings in Westmoreland County Court], Mankin v. Chandler & Co., U.S. Cir. Ct., Va., Ended Cases [Unrestored], 1823, Vi).

Mankin assee. of Walsh

v

John Chandler & Co.

This is an action of debt brought by the plaintiff as assignee of Walsh on a note given by the defendants to Walsh on the 10th. of October 1818. ¶1

The defendants plead in bar a decree made by the county court of Westmoreland sitting in chancery, in a suit brought by Thomas Rowand a creditor of the said Walsh against the said Walsh & the defendant John Chandler to attach the effects of the said Walsh in the hands of the said Chandler and subject them to the payment of the debt due from Walsh to Rowand. ¶2

The record of the proceedings in that suit forms a part of the plea, and shows that the note was assigned anterior to the answer of the defendant and that he had notice of the assignment. The decree directs the defendant John Chandler to pay to Thomas Rowand out of the note given by John Chandler & Co. to Walsh the sum which was shown to be due from Walsh to Rowan; and the decree was enforced before the service of process in this cause. ¶3

¶4   To this plea the plaintiff has demurred, and the defendants have joined in demurrer.

¶5   It is admitted that the decree of the county court of Westmoreland is erroneous, and would unquestionably be reversed if carried before a superior tribunal. But this court can take no notice of its errors. While it remains in force, it binds the subject as conclusively as it would do had it been affirmed in the highest court of the country. The question is, can it affect the rights of the plaintiff in this cause; for if it can, [it] concludes them.

¶6   In support of the demurrer it is argued that this decree cannot be given in evidence in this cause, as the plain[tiff] is neither a party nor a privy, it not being alleged that the assignment or notice of it was subsequent to the attachment.

¶7   The rule relied on by the plf. is familiar to every gentleman of the profession, and has not been controverted; but the defendants counsel insists that this is a case to which that rule does not apply, because it is not within the ordinary jurisdiction of a court of chancery, but a case of which that court takes cognizance by virtue of a statute and is in its nature a proceeding *in rem,* and not *in personam.* It is he says a sentence on the thing itself and not a decree against the person; and that in all cases of this description, the subject matter is bound by the sentence, and the title of those who are not particularly before the court is as entirely decided as the title of those who are. In support of this rule he refers to the effect of decisions in the courts of Admiralty, and in the court of exchequer in England, which courts entertain suits *in rem* to which all the world are said to be parties.

¶8   The principle on which the defendants rely is as little to be questioned as that asserted by the plaintiff. The whole enquiry is to which class of cases does that under consideration belong? what is the nature of a proceeding *in rem?* and in what does its specific difference from an ordinary action consist? Is every action in which a specific article is demanded a proceeding *in rem.* If it were, a writ of right which demands land, of detinue, which demands a personal chattel, would be a proceeding *in rem* to which all the world would be parties and by which the rights of all would be bound. But this, all know, is not the law. What then is the rule by which cases of this description are to [be] ascertained?

¶9   I have always understood that where the process is to be served on the thing itself, and where the meer possession of the thing by the service of that process and making proclamation authorizes the court to decide upon it, without notice to any individual whatever, it is a proceeding in rem to which all the world are parties. The rule is one of convenience and of necessity. In cases to which it applies it would often be impossible to ascertain the person whose property is proceeded against, and it is presumable that the person whose property is seized, is either himself attentive to it, or has placed it in the care to some person who has the power, and whose duty it is to represent him and to assert his claim. Such claim may be asserted; but the jurisdiction of the court does not depend on its assertion. The claimant is a party whether he speaks or is silent, whether he asserts his claim or abandons it.[1]

A Thus in the case of Scott v Shearman & others 2 W.B. 977 which was an action of trespass against the officer who had seized goods which were condemned in the court of Exchequer, Judge Blackstone says the sentence of condemnation is conclusive evidence in a case in which no notice was given to the owner in person who was not a party to the suit because "the seizure itself is notice to the owner, who is presumed to know whatever is become of his own goods. He knew they were seized by a revenue officer. He knew they were carried to the Kings ware house. He knew or might have known that by the course of law, the validity of that seizure would come on to be examined in the court of exchequer and could be examined no where else. He had notice by the two proclamations according to the course of that court. He had notice by the writ of appraisement which must be publickly executed on the spot where the goods were detained. And having neglected this opportunity of putting in his claim, and trying the point of forfeiture, it was his own laches and he shall forever be concluded by it."[2]

¶10

But in every case where parties are necessary to give the court cognizance of the cause, the decree, the judgment, or the sentence, binds those only (with some few exceptions standing on particular principles) who are parties or privies to it. If a party is necessary, it follows that the party should be one who has the real interest; and to secure this, the interest of persons who are not parties, cannot be affected. This is understood to be as true with respect to cases in the courts of Admiralty and of the exchequer, as in courts of common law and chancery. If a case be cognizable in either of those courts in consequence of a seizure which vests the possession, and of a general proclamation of that fact, every person is a party to the proceeding, and his interest is bound by the sentence; but in a case in which the law requires that parties should be brought before the court, the sentence binds those only who are parties.

¶11

If this be the rule, it remains only to examine the act of assembly which gives this remedy in order to ascertain its character.

¶12

The law enacts that, ["]if in any case which hath been or shall be hereafter commenced for relief in equity, in any superior court of chancery or in any other court, against any defendant or defendants who are out of this country, and others within the same, having in their hands effects of or otherwise indebted to such absent defendant or defendants, or against any such absent defendant or defendants having lands or tenements within the Commonwealth, and the appearance of such absentees be not entered" &c "in all such cases, the court may make any order" &c. The act then proceeds to make publication equivalent to service of the process, so far as is necessary to enable the court to decree in the cause.[3]

¶13

¶14   The process then given by the act of assembly in the particular case is not against the thing but the person. It is in a suit brought against a defendant not residing in the country, and having effects within it, that this proceeding is allowed. And of course the foreign defendant must be named in the subpœna and in the bill. The questions to be decided by the court in every such case are, is the foreign defendant indebted to the plaintiff, and are the attached effects his property. The plaintiff must establish both these facts, and the defendants may controvert them. It is then a case which, by the very words of the law, is a suit between parties, by which the rights of the individuals before the court are to be examined and determined. The law substitutes a publication for service of process on the absent defendant, which shall give the court jurisdiction over the cause, and enable it to make a decree for the payment of the debt which is chargeable on his effects in the hands of the garnishee. No reason can be assigned why this decree should bind a person who is not party or a privy to it which does not apply to every case. No reason can be given for the rule which does not apply to this case.

¶15   It is, we are told, excessive oppression, that a court of justice should decree a man to pay a sum of money, and after enforcing its decree, compel him to pay the money a second time to another person. This is admitted: but it is also oppression to decree the money of A to B. Every illegal & unrighteous judgement of a court is oppression. The law presumes no such judgement to be given. But, if it be given, the law deems it more reasonable that the loss should fall on the person who was a party to the suit, who could assert his rights, and controvert the decision than on him who was not a party to it, and who had no opportunity of controverting it. Had Mankin been a party to the suit in Westmoreland county court the decree would have bound him had it been as iniquitous as it now appears to be. But not being a party the rule of law protects him from its operation.

¶16   It has been truely said that our law respecting foreign attachments is founded on the same proceeding in london which is established by custom. Some inconsiderable difference exists as to the manner of proceeding against the absent defendant which has no bearing on the question arising in this case. As to that question, the law is the same. The case of McDaniel & al v Hughes 3d. East 366 goes fully into the law on this subject.[4] In that case as in this a decree of the court was pleaded in bar to an action brought by the foreign defendant himself against his debtor, and in that case too a demurrer was filed to the plea. It was contended in Argument "that three parties are necessary in a foreign attachment, the plaintiff, the defendant, and a garnishee. The plaintiff must prove his debt; the defendant must have due notice of the process against him; and the garnishee must be in the actual possession of [that property of] the defendants which is to be attached."[5] The law as laid down for the plaintiff was not controverted: but it was insisted that according to the custom the return of nihil authorized the attachment. And of this opinion was the court, and for this reason the demurrer was overruled. The person who claimed the property was, in that case, a party to the suit, and such proceedings were had against him as according to the custom, authorized the court to pronounce judgement in the case. He was precisely in the same situation as the plaintiff in this case would have been had he been named as a defendant in the subpœna & been included in the publication. Had this essential circumstance been wanting in the case of McDaniel v. Hughes, it is apparent from the whole report, that the demurrer must have been sustained.

Upon the best examination I have been able to make of the cases which have been cited as well as upon principle, I am perfectly satisfied that a foreign attachment is not to be considered as a proceeding *in rem* but as a suit by a plaintiff against defendants, and that decree in such case is within the general rule of being conclusive evidence only ⟨ag⟩ainst parties and privies. The demurrer therefore is sustained.[6] ¶17

AD, Marshall Judicial Opinions, PPAmP; printed, John W. Brockenbrough, *Reports of Cases Decided by the Honourable John Marshall . . .*, II (Philadelphia, 1837), 125–31. For JM's deletions and interlineations, see Textual Notes below.

1. Here JM wrote the letter "A" to indicate the place where a passage written on a separate sheet should be inserted.
2. Scott v. Shearman, 2 Black. W. 977, 979, 96 Eng. Rep. 575, 577 (C.P., 1775).
3. JM quoted from Virginia's act "directing the method of proceeding in courts of equity against absent debtors" (*Revised Code of Va.*, I, 474).
4. M'Daniel v. Hughes, 3 East 367, 102 Eng. Rep. 638 (K.B., 1803).
5. 3 East 371, 102 Eng. Rep. 640.
6. After JM sustained the plaintiff's demurrer, overruling the second special plea, the case went to a jury on the plea of payment. On 6 Dec. verdict for plaintiff, $627.04, with interest from 22 Apr. 1821 (U.S. Cir. Ct., Va., Ord. Bk. XI, 408).

Textual Notes

¶ 1 l. 2   a ~~bond~~ ↑note↓ given
¶ 2 l. 6   Rowand. ~~This decree orders the payment of defendant John Chandler to pay to Thomas Rowand~~ ↑out of this bond due to Walsh by J.C. & Co↓ ~~the sum due by Walsh to Rowand; and~~ ↑the plea states that↓ ~~the payment has been enforced before the service of the process in this suit. To this plea the plf. has demurred and the defendant has joined in demurrer.~~
¶ 3 l. 1 beg.   ~~On the part of the plain~~ The record
    l. 4   note ~~due~~ given
    l. 6   to Rowan [*erasure*]; and
¶ 6 l. 2   in ~~this~~ evidence
¶ 7 l. 6   *personam.* ~~In all cases of this character, he contends~~ It is
¶ 8 l. 6   a ~~real action for~~ writ
¶ 9 l. 3   process ↑and making proclamation↓ authorizes
    l. 4   upon ↑it,↓ without

l. 6	would ~~seldom~~ ↑often↓ be
l. 8	is ↑seized, is↓ either
ll. 11–12	on [*erasure*] ↑its↓ assertion.
¶10 l. 1	977 ~~Jud~~ which
l. 4	evidence ~~of property against all the world~~ in a case in which ↑it was alleged that↓ no
¶11 l. 4	follows ~~Thus in a case cogniza~~ that
l. 6	interest of ~~parti~~ ↑persons↓ who
l. 7	in ~~Admir~~ the
l. 12	but ~~if~~ in
l. 13	parties. ~~If the~~
¶12 l. 1 beg.	~~If this be the~~ If
ll. 1–2	assembly ~~on~~ which ↑gives↓ this
¶14 l. 3	country, ~~that~~ and
l. 9	law, ↑is↓ a suit
ll. 10–11	be ~~ascertained~~ ↑examined↓ and determined. ~~No reason can be assigned~~ ↑The law substitutes a publication↓ for
l. 15	not ~~a~~ party
¶15 ll. 9–10	of ~~op~~ controverting
¶16 ll. 1–2	our ~~act~~ ↑law respecting↓ foreign attachments is ~~pr~~ founded
l. 8	action ~~of debt~~ brought
l. 10	three ~~things~~ ↑parties↓ are
l. 14	down ~~by~~ ↑for↓ the
¶17 l. 4	by ↑a↓ plaintiff
ll. 4–5	is ~~aga~~ ↑within the↓ general ~~prin~~ rule ↑of being conclusive↓ evidence

To Bushrod Washington

My dear Sir   December 6th 1823

I was extremely sorry to learn from your last that you were again indisposed.[1] This has been generally the most sickly season I have ever known, but I will hope that the frosts have had a favourable influence on your health as they have had on that of most others. You were certainly right to return, and I hope your endeavours to meet your brethren in February will succeed.

I must remind you of the chasm in that part of the correspondence copied by me which I mentioned in a former letter. In looking over the copied letters for the purpose of final arrangement I find there is another chasm arising from the loss of a few sheets which must I think have taken place at Mount Vernon. It is the copy of those letters which were written just before the capture of Fort duquêsne. The last letter I have is to Colonel Bouqet[2] of the 28th of July 1758, and of that I have only the first part. It ends with the words, "if my presence could be dispensed with for a day or two of which you are the best judge."

It will be necessary to copy the residue of this letter, as well as the other letters of 1758 & bring them with you to Washington. I hope you will also have copied the few letters which I omitted & of which I wrote to you last summer. With the best wishes for your health & happiness, I am my dear Sir yours truely

J MARSHALL

ALS, NHi. Addressed to Washington at Mount Vernon; postmarked Richmond, 6 Dec. Endorsed by Washington.

1. Letter not found.
2. Henry Bouquet.

To James Monroe

Dear Sir   Richmond December 9th. 1823

I received yesterday the message of the President to Congress, franked by yourself.[1] Allow me to express the grateful sentiment with which I acknowledge this mark of polite attention, and this evidence of your recollection of times which are long passed away. I shall not forget it.

I have read with interest and attention the comprehensive view which you have taken of our affairs, and think with you that we cannot look on the present state of the world with indifference.[2] With great and respectful esteem, I remain your Obedt

J MARSHALL

ALS, Monroe Papers, DLC.

1. Letter not found.
2. Among the various subjects discussed in the president's message to Congress of 2 Dec. 1823 were the principles that came to be known as the Monroe Doctrine (James D. Richardson, ed., *A Compilation of the Messages and Papers of the Presidents, 1789–1897* [11 vols.; Washington, D.C., 1896–99], II, 207–20).

To Joseph Story

My dear Sir   Richmond Decr. 9th. 1823

I had the pleasure yesterday of receiving your letter of the 24th. ultimo & congratulate you on passing through your circuit in such good health & spirits.[1] Our brother Washington was so unwell as to be under the necessity of adjournning the court at Philadelphia without going through the docket. I am still engaged at this place in a sort of dilatory way, doing very little, and still having something to do. A case was argued yesterday which I would send to the supreme court if I could, but I cannot. The Pilot, an american vessel was captured by Pirates & converted into a piratical cruizer. She was then recaptured by one of our squadron under Commodore Porter, after a sharp action. She was brought into Norfolk, libelled as prize, & claimed by the original owner.[2] The attorney for the captors abandoned the claim as prize, and asked salvage. This claim was resisted on the ground that the capture was not within the act of 1800,[3] because that applies only to recaptures from an enemy of the United States, not to recaptures from a Pirate. It was insisted too that the act of 1819[4] does not give salvage for a recapture made by a national ship, because, although an american vessel recaptured by a merchantman or private vessel is to be brought in, yet such vessel recaptured by a national ship is not to be brought in. As there is no salvage given by statute, the claim it was said must rest upon general law. It was admitted that according to that law salvage is due for a vessel recaptured by a private ship, but not for a vessel recaptured by a national ship, because the nation owes protection to all its people, and it is a part of the duty of the national force to afford this protection. In the present case it was one of the objects of the expedition. It was said that the general dicta that salvage is due for recaptures made from Pirates must be limited to such as are made by private ships or by the public ships of some other nation than that of the recaptured vessel.

The council for the recaptors relied chiefly on the general principle that by the law of nations, or by the general Maritime law salvage is due for all vessels recaptured from pirates.

The District Judge gave salvage & the owners have appealed. I do not know that the question has ever arisen in any of the courts of the United States. Perhaps your information may be more extensive, and I will thank you to give it to me. If the case has not been decided you will greatly oblige me by your sentiments on it, as I know that you are more *au fait* on these questions than I am. The sooner I hear from you, provided you are satisfied in the case, the better.[5]

I have read the correspondence to which you refer and regret its publication extremely.[6] I feel great respect for Mr. Adams, and shall always feel it whatever he may do. The extreme bitterness with which he speaks of honourable men who were once his friends, is calculated to mortify and pain those who remain truely attached to him. A comparison of the language he applies to gentlemen of high character in Massachusetts with that which, in the early part of the correspondence, he applied to those who were always his enemies and gross calumniators, who cannot even now treat him with decency, inspires serious reflections. We can only say non est qualis erat.[7]

I think I can *guess*, although not born north of the Hudson, what you hint at respecting the Presidential election; but I shall be as careful not to commit my *guess* to paper as you are respecting your scheme.

Farewell. Providence I hope will cont⟨in⟩ue to take care of us. With affectionate esteem, I am dear Sir your obedt

J MARSHALL

ALS, Story Papers, MHi. Addressed to Story in Salem, Mass.; postmarked Richmond, 9 Dec.

1. Letter not found.
2. The case involving the schooner *Pilot* was Chesapeake Insurance Co. v. U.S., an appeal from an 8 Nov. 1823 decree of the U.S. District Court at Norfolk. David Porter (1780–1843), a prominent officer of the U.S. Navy, was then commander-in-chief of the West India Squadron, which was engaged in suppressing piracy.
3. "An Act providing for Salvage in cases of Recapture" (*U.S. Statutes at Large*, II, 16–18).
4. "An Act to protect the commerce of the United States, and punish the crime of piracy" (ibid., III, 510–14).
5. JM decided this case on 15 June 1824 (U.S. Cir. Ct., Va., Ord. Bk. XI, 463–64).
6. *Correspondence between the Hon. John Adams . . . and the late Wm. Cunningham, Esq., Beginning in 1803 and Ending in 1812* (Boston, 1823; S #11528), in which Adams bitterly attacked Thomas Jefferson and many Federalist leaders in Massachusetts. William Cunningham, Jr., a Jackson supporter, published the correspondence after his father's death in an effort to embarrass John Quincy Adams (Joseph E. Ellis, *Passionate Sage: The Legacy of John Adams* [New York, 1993], 137–38, 183).
7. Non est qualis erat (he is not what he was).

Maxwell v. Call
Opinion
U.S. Circuit Court, Virginia, 16 December 1823

This chancery suit commenced in the Richmond City Hustings Court and was transferred to the U.S. Circuit Court in November 1823 on the petition of Walter Dun, a defendant who was a citizen of Ohio. The case arose from the will of Robert Means, who had died in 1808 having appointed Daniel Call and Robert Graham his executors. The will directed the executors to sell the estate and invest the proceeds in public securities or in bank stock. After the payment of certain legacies, the residuary estate was to be divided into four equal parts and given to Means's brothers and sisters. The complex provisions of the will spelling out the ways in which the estate was to be distributed on the happening of various contingencies are discussed in the opinion below. The complainants were William M. Maxwell, son of a sister of the testator, Elizabeth Kerr, a sister and only surviving sibling of the testator, and Robert Kerr, son of Elizabeth Kerr. In addition to Call, who had undertaken the major burden of the executorship, and Dun, who was Graham's executor, the other defendants were specific legatees of the testator. After answers were filed, Marshall gave the following opinion accompanying an interlocutory decree on 16 December 1823 (proceedings of Richmond City Hustings Court, [22 Nov. 1823], in Maxwell v. Graham's Executor et al., U.S. Cir. Ct., Va., Ended Cases [Unrestored], 1824, Vi; U.S. Cir. Ct., Va., Ord. Bk. XI, 374, 417).

Maxwell & al
v
Call exr. of Means & al.

¶1   This suit is brought for one moity of the residuary estate of Robert Means deceased which the plaintiffs claim under his will. The testator directs his whole estate to be sold and the proceeds to be invested in stock at the discretion of his executors. After several legacies he directs the residue to be divided into four equal parts, and gives the dividends or interest of one of the said parts to his sister Nancy Maxwell during her life; and after her death he gives the principal of the said fourth part to all and every of the children of the said Nancy Maxwell who may attain to the age of twenty one years; In case of infancy the children to be maintained &c on the dividends; but if the said Nancy Maxwell should die without leaving any issue of her body alive at the time of her death, or all such issue of her body should die before attaining to the age of twenty one years, then he gives the principal of the said fourth part in the same manner and to the same persons as the other three fourths are given. The other three fourths are given, one to his brother William Means for life and afterwards to his children, one to his brother George Means for life, and afterwards to his children, and the other to his sister Elizabeth Means for life and afterwards to her children in the same words as are used in the bequest to Nancy Maxwell and to her children. Then comes the following clause. "But if the said Nancy Maxwell, William Means, George Means, and Elizabeth Means should all die without leaving any issue of the body of either of them alive at the time of the death of the survivor of them, or if such issue should all die before attaining the age of twenty one years as aforesaid, then I desire the said stock to be divided into three equal parts, to be disposed of as follows" &c.[1]

¶2   Nancy Maxwell in the will mentioned is dead leaving the complainant William M. Maxwell her only child, who has attained his age of twenty one years. George Means and William Means died intestate and without issue in the life time of Nancy Maxwell. Elizabeth Means intermarried with William Ker who is since dead. She is a plaintiff in the bill and the infant plaintiff Robert Kerr is her only child.

¶3   The complainant William M Maxwell claims two fourths of the said stock, and prays that a moity of the lands may be conveyed to him instead of its remaining in the hands of the exr. to be sold as directed in the will. He contends that on his attaining his age of 21 years, & the death of his mother, his rights became absolute by the happening of the contingency on which the legacy was to vest, and that he is also entitled to one moity of the shares of George & William Means immediately, and to the whole property should Elizabeth Ker die without leaving any child alive, or should that child die before attaining his age of 21 years. If this be not the true construction of the will, he insists the limitation over is too remote and is therefore void.[2]

The exr. resists this claim, and contends that the limitation over is not too remote, and that nothing vests absolutely in the legatees until the death of Elizabeth Ker who is the survivor of the four legatees for life.   ¶4

Considering the bequests to the children of each of the testators brothers and sisters separately, without taking into view the effect which the ultimate limitation in remainder may have on them, it is very clear that the portion alloted to the children of Nancy Maxwell would vest absolutely in the plaintiff William M. Maxwell. His mother is dead, he is her only child, and he has attained his age of twenty one years. The contingencies mentioned in this part of the will have all happened, and the title of William M. Maxwell to one fourth of the fund is complete, so far as it depends on this part of the will.   ¶5

The legacies to the children of George and William Means can never take effect, they being both dead without issue. It becomes therefore necessary to enquire whether the two fourths devised to the children of these two brothers be disposed of during the life of the surviver of the testators sisters in the clause which gives the whole property over if there be no issue of any of the brothers and sisters living when that event takes place, or whether there be an intestacy for that time; and in making this enquiry the court will also consider the influence which this clause may have on the preceding bequests.   ¶6

The words are "but if the said Nancy Maxwell George Means William Means, and Elizabeth Means should all die without leaving any issue of the body of either of them alive at the time of the death of the surviver of them, or if such issue should all die before attaining the age of twenty one years as aforesaid, then I give the said stock" &c.   ¶7

It is very clear that this limitation over must take effect with respect to the whole property at the same time, and on the happening of the same event. No interest can vest in the remainderman under this clause, in the stock devised to the children of George and William until it also vests in the stock devised to Nancy Maxwell and Elizabeth Means. It is entire[ly] unimportant whether these words create cross remainders among the four families of the legatees until the death of the surviver and the happening of the contingency on which the ultimate limitation is made to depend, or the testator is intestate until that contingency happens, with respect to those two fourths, because the property passes for that time to the plaintiffs under either construction. The real and only enquiry is into the effect of the last clause on the whole of the property in any event which can now happen.   ¶8

The interest is given to Nancy Maxwell for her life, the principal is given to such of her children as may attain to the age of twenty one years. If the clause stopped here the remainder would vest in every child who   ¶9 should attain the age of twenty one, to open and let in others who should afterwards attain that age. The will proceeds, but if the said Nancy Maxwell should die without leaving any issue of her body alive at the time of her death, or all such issue of her body should die before attaining to the age of twenty one years, then the property is given over.

¶10   The word issue is known to comprehend in its usual sense, all issue to the latest time. Nancy Maxwell is not dead without issue of her body, although she may have no child living, so long as any of her descendant[s] in the direct line remain. Is there any thing in this will to confine the meaning of the term to children? I think there is nothing. The will is penned with great attention to technical language, and it is not to be presumed that technical words are used without a knowledge of their meaning and an intention to use them in their legal sense. The term "children" is abandoned in this part of the will for "issue" because the latter word conveyed the meaning of the testator. If he intended that, if Nancy Maxwell should have children who should die under twenty one leaving children, those last mentioned children should represent their parents, and take the property given to their parents, he has used the very words which would produce this effect. No intent is discovered by the words of the will or in the relations of the parties to alter the legal construction of these words.

¶11   I proceed next to consider the last clause.

¶12   "But if the said Nancy Maxwell, George Means, William Means and Elizabeth Means should all die without leaving any issue of the body of either of them alive at the time of the death of the survivor of them, or if such issue should all die before attaining the age of twenty one years as aforesaid, then I desire" &c.

¶13   The word issue is unquestionably used in this clause in the same sense in which it is used in the particular bequests to the children and families of each of his brothers and children. If on the death of the surviver of his brothers & sisters, there should be no child of either of them living but should be grand children, they would not all be dead without issue and the remainder would not take effect. The only difficulty I have ever felt in the case remains to be considered. It depends on the meaning of the words "if *such* issue should all die before attaining the age of twenty one years.["] Does the word such restrict the issue which may take to those which are living at the death of the surviver, or may the issue of such issue take. If for example, on the death of Elizabeth Ker, the surviver of the testators brothers and sisters, the issue of all of them should be under the age of twenty one, if no one of the issue then living should attain the age of twenty one but should leave issue that do attain that age, would such issue take? or would the property pass to those in remainder. According to a literal interpretation of the words, it would pass to those in remainder; but I think the will discloses enough to show that this was not the intent of the testator.

Three of his brothers and sisters had certainly no children at the date ¶14
of the will. The testator therefore could have no affection for them but as
the descendants of his brothers and sisters. In this view his desire to
provide for them would extend to the whole family & not be limited to
their children, or to such issue as might happen to be living at the death
of the survivor to the exclusion of those who might be born afterwards.
He obviously prefers all the descendants of his brothers sisters to the
more remote relations who are the remaindermen. To provide for those
descendants per stirpes is his primary intent.[3] The provision for the more
remote relations is postponed till the extinction of the issue of his brothers and sisters. This primary intent, I think, though with some doubt,
must prevail, and if all the issue alive at the death of the survivor should
be under age & should die under age leaving that issue, I think such issue
would take. If I am correct in this the remainder is too remote because it
is limitted to take effect on a contingency which may not happen during a
life in being or twenty one years afterwards.[4]

If I am correct in this the plaintiffs are entitled & I percieve no objec- ¶15
tion to directing a conveyance of the lands instead of leaving them to be
sold by the exr. it being understood that the terms on which such conveyance shall be made are adjusted between the parties.[5]

AD, Marshall Judicial Opinions, PPAmP; printed, John W. Brockenbrough, *Reports of
Cases Decided by the Honourable John Marshall . . .*, II (Philadelphia, 1837), 119–24. For JM's
deletions and interlineations, see Textual Notes below.

1. In the event of this contingency, the estate was to go to the children of relatives in
Ireland (copy of Robert Means's will, Maxwell v. Graham's Executor et al.).
2. The term "limitation over" includes any estate in the same property created or contemplated by the conveyance, to be enjoyed after the first estate granted expires or is
exhausted. For example, in an estate devised to A for life with remainder to the heirs of his
body, the remainder is a "limitation over" to such heirs. In the present case Robert Means
devised his residuary estate to his siblings and their children. At the same time he provided
that if his siblings died without issue alive at the time of the death of the last survivor of
them, or if such issue died before reaching twenty-one, then the estate was "limited over" to
the children of the testator's Irish relatives.
3. *Per stirpes* (by roots or stocks; by representation). The descendants could assert their
rights not as particular individuals but as representatives of deceased ancestors.
4. JM alluded to the rule against perpetuities, by which the vesting of an estate could not
be postponed beyond a reasonable period, defined as a life in being plus twenty-one years
(see *PJM*, V, 542–43).
5. The court accordingly decreed that William M. Maxwell was entitled to one moiety of
the principal of the residuary estate of Robert Means and that Elizabeth Kerr was entitled
during her life to the profits of the other moiety and the principal to be disposed of to her
issue attaining the age of twenty-one. Both moieties were subject to the executor's claim for
commissions, disbursements, and charges and to an annuity bequeathed to another legatee. The decree also ordered Call to render an account of his administration of the estate to
commissioners, who were to make a report upon which a final decree could be made. The
court approved the commissioners' report and issued a final decree in June 1824 (U.S. Cir.
Ct., Va., Ord. Bk. XI, 417–18, 478–80, 484).

Textual Notes

¶ 1 ll. 9–10　　years; ↑In case of infancy the children to be maintained &c
　　　　　　　　on the dividends;↓ but
l. 16　　his ~~issue~~ ↑children,↓ one to
l. 17　　his ~~issue~~ ↑children,↓ and the
l. 18　　her ~~issue~~ ↑children↓ in the
l. 20　　Nancy ~~maxwell~~ ↑Maxwell,↓ William
¶ 2 ll. 3–4　　Means ~~are died~~ ↑died intestate and↓ ~~with~~ ↑without↓ issue
ll. 5–6　　bill [*erasure*] ↑and↓ the ↓infant↓ plaintiff
¶ 3 l. 7　　shares ~~on~~ ↑of↓ George
¶ 4 l. 3　　of ~~the~~ Elizabeth
¶ 6 l. 1　　legacies to ~~George an~~ the
ll. 4–5　　disposed of ↑during the life of the surviver of the testators
　　　　　　　sisters↓ in the
¶ 8 l. 3　　vest ↑in the remainderman↓ under
l. 4　　William [*erasure*] ↑until↓ it
l. 12　　the last ~~above~~ clause
¶ 9 l. 1　　The ~~pr~~ ↑interest↓ is given
¶10 l. 9　　for ~~that of~~ "issue"
¶12 l. 2　　Elizabeth ~~means~~ ↑Means↓ should
¶13 l. 6　　effect. "The
l. 12　　brothers and ~~children~~ ↑sisters,↓ the

Coates v. Muse

Opinion

U.S. Circuit Court, Virginia, 18 December 1823

On the 4th day of June, 1821, the Court, considering a bill filed in January 1821, as being both a bill enjoining the decree rendered at the November Term, 1820, and a petition for a rehearing, opened the decree rendered in November 1820, and referred the accounts to the commissioner for a resettlement, with instructions to settle, also, the administration of the estate of Thomas Muse, by Elliott Muse.[1]

In December 1821, the commissioner made his report, which was taken up a few days thereafter, and a decree pronounced, directing Z. U. Crittenden, administrator, &c., of Elliott Muse, deceased, out of the assets of his testator, in his hands to be administered, to pay the plaintiff the sum of $3731 32, with interest on $3171 42, from the 20th of November, 1821, till paid; and the Court reserved, to a future day, its decision on the ultimate responsibility of the parties.

In May Term, 1822, the said defendant, Z. U. Crittenden, administrator, &c., produced two records of suits, pending against him as administrator, in the state court, in Williamsburg, on claims of the highest dignity, and prayed, that the interlocutory decree of the preceding Term, might be set aside. The Court overruled this motion, and directed that decree to be satisfied out of the private estate of the said Crittenden, if assets of his intestate could not be found.[2]

The cause comes on again to be heard on all the papers, and it is contended by the defendant, Crittenden, administrator, &c., of Elliott Muse, that the original decree, pronounced, in 1811, against Elliott Muse and Thomas Muse, administrators of Hudson Muse, has lost its dignity, as against the representatives of those defendants, in consequence of a receipt and agreement, in these words: "Elliott Muse, Esq., has adjusted with me, by securing the same to be paid, the amount of the decree against the administrators of Hudson Muse, deceased, and is entitled to the benefit of the decree, as to that part of the debt, but not as to the house and lot in Urbanna, which is the fund for payment of the residue of the plaintiff's demand."

"WM. C. WILLIAMS,

"18th March, 1813.   Attorney for plaintiff."[3]

It was admitted before the commissioner, by the agent for the plaintiff, that a deed of trust or mortgage was, about this time, executed by the said Elliott Muse, to secure the payment of the decree, but that the said deed was held by the plaintiff's attorney, was never recorded or enforced; and it is admitted by Z. U. Crittenden, that Elliott Muse afterwards sold the land.

The principle on which the decree of November 1820, was opened in May Term 1821, was that the decree of May 1811, ought to be apportioned equally on the estates of Elliott and Thomas Muse, unless the representatives of one of those estates, could show that the other ought to be charged with more than a moiety of that decree. That principle is still believed to be correct.

The accounts, as now exhibited to the court, furnish no evidence on this subject, other than two entries on the books of Elliott Muse, as executor of Thomas Muse, in which he credits himself as follows.

"1813, *March 9th.*

To cash in discharge of testator's proportion of decree, Coates's Executrix v. Muse's administrators, including interest and costs of suit, ...$2411 54½

"*June 19th.*

To amount of your proportion of a balance not charged in a former account of a decree in fed. ct. Muse's administrator v. Coates's executors, ...$1602 90"

The respective liabilities of Elliott and Thomas Muse, having been known only to themselves, this is the only testimony now attainable on this point. The entries of Elliott Muse cannot increase the liability of Thomas Muse, but may diminish it. If, therefore, these two sums which were obviously intended to comprise Thomas Muse's part of the decree be less than a moiety of the decree with interest and costs, these entries amount to an admission on the part of Elliott Muse, that the estate of Thomas Muse was not liable farther, and that he ought himself to pay the residue. This conclusion is rendered irresistible, by the circumstance, that at the date of the last entry, Elliott Muse considered the whole decree as being transferred to him by the paper of the 18th of March, 1813, executed by the attorney of the plaintiff, and of course, charged the estate of his testator with the whole sum for which it was liable on the decree.

The deed of trust, which is supposed to be referred to in this paper of the 18th of March, 1813, is prepared in blank in one handwriting, and afterwards filled up in another. It is dated the 18th day of March, 1811, three months before the decree was rendered, and is filled up to John Gray, agent for the plaintiff. It was, obviously from the expressions of the deed, filled up in the year 1813, before the 3d of June, and was probably filled up and executed on the 18th of March, 1813, when the receipt or assignment was executed.

This deed having never been recorded, and Elliott Muse having sold the land, and received the money, for which he has never accounted, it is obvious, that he must remain liable to the plaintiff in the same sum as if this transaction had never taken place. Were Elliott Muse alive and solvent, there could be no difficulty in decreeing him to pay the whole sum. But he is dead insolvent, and the whole difficulty of the case consists in determining, how far the representative of Elliott Muse is chargeable with a devastavit for having paid debts of inferior dignity to the decree of the 3d of June, 1811.

A decree is not, in law, assignable, but is like any other chose in action, transferrable for a valuable consideration, and a court of equity will support the transfer. If, therefore, the estate of Thomas Muse, had been represented by any other than Elliott Muse, and such representative had, without knowledge of the fraud, paid his part of the decree to Elliott Muse, this Court would unquestionably have sustained the payment. But as no money was really paid by the estate of Thomas Muse, nor any injury sustained by his estate, in consequence of this credit in his account by Elliott Muse; as the person committing the fraud was the representative of Thomas Muse, it seems unreasonable to deprive the creditor of his recourse against Thomas Muse, for so much as was equitably due from his estate. Had Elliott Muse never made this entry in his accounts, it would be admitted, that the liability of Thomas Muse remained; and I cannot think, that this entry changes his liability, unless it should appear that he has sustained an injury from it.

The question of dignity is unimportant in this part of the case, because the estate of Thomas Muse is solvent.

In a suit instituted in a court of chancery for the state, an account was taken of the administration of Elliott Muse, of the estate of Thomas

Muse, and the balance reported against the executor, is $314 54¾. But this report is understood to credit the executor for the sum charged, as being paid to the executor of Coates. Those sums are, therefore, to be added to this balance, and they will leave Elliott Muse indebted to the estate of Thomas Muse, in the full sum now claimed by the plaintiff from the estate of Thomas Muse. This debt, from the representative of Elliott Muse, to the estate of Thomas Muse, is, undeniably, a debt of the first dignity.

It is contended, on the part of the representative of Thomas Muse, that as all the parties are before the Court, the representative of Elliott Muse, ought to be decreed to pay to the plaintiff, the sum due from the estate of Thomas Muse: and the Court is of that opinion. The plaintiff, therefore, is in the place of a representative of Thomas Muse, as to that part of the decree, and is in virtue of the rights of that representative, a creditor of the highest dignity. Z. U. Crittenden, the administrator of Elliott Muse, deceased, will, therefore be directed to pay to the plaintiff, the sum of $, that being the sum the plaintiff has a right to demand from the estate of Thomas Muse, and which is due to that estate, from the representative of Elliott Muse.

The decree which ought to be pronounced against Z. U. Crittenden, the administrator of Elliott Muse, deceased, for the residue of the decree of the 3d of June, 1811, remains to be considered. It is contended by the plaintiff, that the whole transaction between William C. Williams, the attorney of the plaintiff, and Elliott Muse, on the 18th of March, 1813, ought to be considered as a nullity, in consequence of the fraud committed by Elliott Muse, in selling the mortgaged property, and converting the money to his own use.

I cannot concur in this opinion.

There is certainly no positive evidence of the concurrence of the plaintiff's agent, in the arrangement of the 18th of March, 1813, but when it is recollected, that the name of that agent is introduced into the deed of mortgage, that the agent himself, states the deed to have been executed, about the time the paper of the 18th of March was signed, that there must have been a free course of communication between the attorney at law, and the agent, I must conclude, that the agreement of the 18th of March, was made with the knowledge and consent of the agent. The effect of that agreement was, to take the deed of mortgage in satisfaction of the decree, and to transfer the decree itself, so far as relates to the question now before the Court, to Elliott Muse. The motives for making this arrangement were, at the time, satisfactory to both parties, and the Court has no right to suppose they were inadequate. The contract was, then, at the time, a fair and valid contract, the obligation of which, neither could controvert.

Had an attempt been made, immediately to enforce the decree of 1811, the Court would not have enforced it; and if the plaintiff could have proceeded without the aid of the Court, she would have been enjoined. Had the deed been recorded, or had Elliott Muse abstained from selling the property, the plaintiff could never, in the face of the agreement of March 1813, have proceeded on the original decree. She could only have proceeded on the mortgage. Had the mortgaged property been insufficient to satisfy the decree, the plaintiff could not have proceeded against Elliott or Thomas Muse, or their representatives, for the sum remaining unsatisfied. The neglect of the plaintiff to record her mortgage, and the fraud of Elliott Muse, in selling the property, and misapplying the money, leave Elliott Muse responsible on the deed of Mortgage, but not on the original decree. The debt, therefore, is a debt by specialty only; and as the suits instituted in the state court, are for debts of higher dignity, than a debt by specialty, the claim of the plaintiff, for the debt due from Elliott Muse must be postponed, to the claims of some of the plaintiffs in the state court.[4]

The decree of the third of June, 1811, comprehended the sum of £429 9s., equal to $1431 50, not then collected, but in suit. This sum was considered as assets in hand, because the parties expressed a confidence, that it would be collected, and because the counsel for the plaintiff assured the Court, of an arrangement being made, by which the decree would not be enforced, till this money should be received. Under these representations, the Court gave, improperly, a decree for the whole sum, as if the assets had been in the hands of the administrators. If this money has not been collected; and if the failure to collect it, arises from no default of the administrators — if due diligence has been used, this error in the decree of 1811, ought not to prejudice them, but ought now to be corrected.[5]

Printed, John W. Brockenbrough, *Reports of Cases Decided by the Honourable John Marshall...*, I (Philadelphia, 1837), 552–58.

1. See Coates v. Muse, Opinion and Decree, 4 June 1821.
2. See Coates v. Muse, Opinion, 12 June 1822.
3. The original of this note is on the verso of a copy of the decree of 3 June 1811. Below the note is a witness's certification, dated 20 Nov. 1821, that the handwriting was that of the late William C. Williams (Coates v. Muse, U.S. Cir. Ct., Va., Ended Cases [Unrestored], 1823, Vi).
4. Executors and administrators were required to pay the debts of their testators according to rules of priority. A "specialty" debt, or a debt due by special contract under seal (such as a bond), was of lesser dignity than a debt of record, such as a court judgment or a debt due by an executor or administrator to a decedent's estate. The suits against Elliott Muse's administrator in the state chancery court at Williamsburg were for the recovery of debts of record (*PJM*, V, 127 n. 1; proceedings in the Superior Court of Chancery, Williamsburg, Coates v. Muse).
5. For the lengthy formal decree, see 1 Brock. 558–60; U.S. Cir. Ct., Va., Ord. Bk. XI, 433–35. A copy of the decree, with JM's notation "To be entered" and signature, is in the case papers (Coates v. Muse).

To Henry Clay

Dear Sir   Richmond Decr. 22d. 1823

Your favour of the 11th. reached me in due time and I can assure you that its perusal gave me no "trouble."[1] With an abatement, which I dare say you are prepared to expect, that is — that few non residents of Kentucky will concur with the citizens of that state in opinion, either on their laws respecting the occupants of lands, or what is miscalled their "relief system," I had a sort of half way disposition to think with you on several points, till that section of my mind which was disposed to arrange itself with you was completely routed by Mr. Johnsons proposition in the senate. That gentleman, I percieve has moved a resolution requiring a concurrence of more than a majority of all the Judges of the supreme court to decide that a law is repugnant to the constitution.[2]

It is the privilege of age to utter *wise sayings* somewhat like proverbs, in the shape of counsel, as a substitute for that powerful and convincing argument which it has lost the faculty of making; but this privilege is more than countervailed by another which is possessed and generally exercised by the middle aged as well as the young — it is to disregard entirely the wise sayings of the old. When I exercise my privilege, I am not quite so old or so unreasonable as to suspect that you are not in perfect readiness to exercise yours also.

But for the apothegm. If I do not come to it quickly you will think I waste more time in preparing for it than it is worth after being introduced. I will say then at once that it is among the most dangerous things in legislation to enact a general law of great and extensive influence to effect a particular object; or to legislate for a nation under a strong excitement which must be suspected to influence the judgement. If the mental eye be directed to a single object, it is not easy for the legislator, intent only on that object, to look all around him, and to percieve and guard against the serious mischief with which his measure may burn. I am perhaps more alive to what concerns the judicial department, and attach more importance to its organization, than my fellow citizens in the legislature or executive, but let me ask if serious inconvenience is not to be apprehended from a very numerous supreme court? It ought not to be too small; but the one extreme is as much to be avoided as the other.

Let me ask too, and I put the question very seriously, if a regulation requiring a concurrence of more than a majority of all the Judges to decide any case, ought not to be well considered in all its bearings, before its adoption? To say nothing of the influence of such a rule on the business of the court, let me ask your attention to the enquiry whether it accords with the spirit of the constitution? If it goes to defeat an object which the constitution obviously designs to accomplish, I need not say to you that, although the judiciary may be bound by it, a conscientious legislator can never assent to it. It is I think difficult to read that instrument attentively without feeling the conviction that it intends to provide a tribunal for every case of collision between itself and a law, so far as such case can assume a form for judicial enquiry; and a law incapable of being placed in such form can rarely have very extensive or pernicious effects.

If this be the obvious intention of the constitution, can the legislature withdraw such cases from that tribunal without counteracting its views and defeating its objects? If congress should say explicitly that the courts of the union should never enter into the enquiry concerning the constitutionality of a law; or should dismiss for want of jurisdiction, every case depending on a law deemed by the court to be unconstitutional; could there be two opinions respecting such an act? And what substantial difference is there between such a law, if law it may be called, and one which makes the decision to depend on an event which will seldom happen? What substantial difference is there between withdrawing a question from a court, and disabling a court from deciding that question? Those only, I should think, who were capable of drawing the memorable distinction as to tenure of office, between removing the Judge from the office, and removing the office from the Judge, can take this distinction.[3]

That the measure proposed in the senate has this tendency is not, I presume, doubted by any person; that it will very often have this effect practically is, I think, as little to be questioned. When we consider the remoteness, the numbers, and the age of the Judges, we cannot expect that the assemblage of all of them, when they shall amount to ten, will be of frequent recurrence. The difficulty of the questions, and other considerations, may often divide those who do attend. To require almost unanimity, is to require what cannot often happen, and consequently to disable the court from deciding constitutional questions.

A majority of the court is according to constant usage and the common understanding of mankind as much the court, as the majority of the legislature is the legislature; and it seems to me that a law requiring more than a majority to make a decision as much counteracts the views of the constitution as an act requiring more than a majority of the legislature to pass a law.

But I will detain you no longer with my prosing & will only add that I am with great respect & esteem, your obedt. Servt

J MARSHALL

ALS, Gilder Lehrman Collection, NNPM. Addressed to Clay in Washington and franked; postmarked Richmond, 23 Dec. Endorsed by Clay.

1. Letter not found.

2. On 10 Dec. Sen. Richard M. Johnson of Kentucky introduced a resolution instructing the judiciary committee to "inquire into the expediency" of establishing three additional circuits, thereby increasing the number of Supreme Court justices from seven to ten, and of

amending the Judiciary Act to require the concurrence of at least seven justices in cases involving the validity of state laws or acts of Congress. This resolution was adopted on 15 Dec. and referred to the committee. The context for Senator Johnson's proposal was the intense anti-Court sentiment in Kentucky generated by the decisions in Green v. Biddle of 1821 and 1823, which invalidated Kentucky's occupying claimant laws. On the reargument of the case in 1822, Clay had defended the validity of those laws, but the Court upheld its former ruling. The second decision particularly rankled, for it was believed to have been made by a minority of three of the seven justices — Story, Washington, and Duvall. JM did not sit, Livingston and Todd were absent because of illness, and Johnson delivered a separate concurrence (8 Wheat. 1; Charles Warren, *The Supreme Court in United States History* [2 vols.; Boston, 1926], I, 636–41, 663–64; G. Edward White, *The Marshall Court and Cultural Change, 1815–35*, the Oliver Wendell Holmes Devise History of the Supreme Court of the United States, III-IV [New York, 1988], 641–44).

3. JM alluded to Congress's repeal (in 1802) of the Judiciary Act of 1801.

To Charles Hammond

Dear Sir[1]   Richmond Decr. 28th. 1823

I recieved some time past your printed argument in the case of Sullivan and others against the Bank of the United States, and a day or two afterwards, your letter of the 4th. instant which was intended to accompany it.[2] I have read the argument with that pleasure which I always feel in reading or hearing one in which the subject is discussed with real ability, whether I concur or not in opinion with the person who makes it. This is certainly exempt from anything like the charge of Jacobinism or disrespect to the court, and is at the same time, I think, less vulnerable than a certain report to which you allude, which however was far from being deficient in vigour.[3] If Judge Washington will not consent to receive it; absolutely & unconditionally as an argument, it must be read over in court, & he must view it in the light of notes, and as a substitute for those which might be taken by himself.

I abstain scrupulously from all intermedling in the election of President; but as your letter on that subject was undoubtedly intended to be seen, I have shown it to some gentlemen who will not fail to communicate its contents to others.[4] A resolution is now before our house of Delegates recommending a congressional caucus. It may probably pass; but not without some considerable opposition. It is supported by the friends of Mr. Crawford who undoubtedly constitute a majority of the assembly and I believe of the state.[5] I rather conjecture that Mr. Clay is the second man with Virginia. I however know too little of public opinion to say anything about it which deserves attention. For myself I can say that I consider Mr. Clay as an enlightened Statesman who has ever since his mission to Europe acted on a system which displays enlarged and liberal views; and I think him entitled to particular credit for having brought the Missouri conflict to a pacific termination. I shall be perfectly content with the choice of the nation whoever he may be. With great respect and esteem, I am Sir your Obedt

J MARSHALL

ALS, Hammond Papers, OHi. Addressed to Hammond in Cincinnati; postmarked Richmond, 29 Dec. Endorsed "Judge Marshall's / Friendship."

1. Charles Hammond (1779–1840) was a prominent Ohio lawyer, legislator, and newspaper editor. Although a Federalist and later a Whig, Hammond opposed the Bank of the United States.

2. Letter not found. The printed enclosure was Hammond's *State of the Case and Argument from the Appellants, in the Case of the Bank of the United States, versus the Auditor and Treasurer of the State of Ohio, in the Supreme Court of the United States* (Cincinnati, Ohio, 1823; S #12751). The case of Osborn (Ohio auditor) and Sullivan (Ohio treasurer) v. the Bank of the U.S. was then pending in the Supreme Court. It had originally been scheduled for argument at the 1823 term but was continued. Hammond presented his oral argument in the Supreme Court in Feb. 1824 (U.S. Sup. Ct. Dockets, App. Cas. No. 1135; 9 Wheat. 744–95).

3. The report alluded to may be that drafted by Hammond in Dec. 1820 as chairman of a joint committee of the Ohio legislature. The report strenuously protested against the Bank's suit against the state auditor, alleging that it was a suit against a state in violation of its constitutional rights (*Report of the Joint Committee of Both Houses of the General Assembly . . . on the Proceedings of the Bank of the United States, against the Officers of State, in the United States Circuit Court* [Columbus, Ohio, 1820; S #2592]; Charles Warren, *The Supreme Court in United States History* [2 vols.; Boston, 1926], I, 535–36).

4. In October Henry Clay had written to Hammond urging him to inform his Richmond correspondents that public sentiment in the West was decidedly unfavorable to William H. Crawford's presidential candidacy. "The Chief Justice would be a good person to address," Clay suggested, adding: "He thinks highly of you I know, and you could employ as an occasion to write him that of transmitting a Copy of your argument in the Bank case" (Clay to Hammond, 29 Oct. 1823, in James F. Hopkins, ed., *The Papers of Henry Clay*, III [Lexington, Ky., 1963], 504–7).

5. The House of Delegates adopted the resolution in favor of a congressional caucus to nominate a presidential candidate on 23 Dec. In past elections and again in 1824 Republicans employed this nominating system, though it was falling into disuse. Those Republican congressmen participating in the Feb. 1824 caucus that chose Crawford numbered only about a quarter of the total (Richmond *Enquirer*, 27 Dec. 1823; George Dangerfield, *The Awakening of American Nationalism, 1815–1828* [New York, 1965], 22–23, 212–14).

APPENDICES

Appendix I
Opinions Delivered by Chief Justice John Marshall
in the U.S. Supreme Court
1820–1823

The calendar below lists in chronological order all the opinions delivered by Chief Justice Marshall from the 1820 term through the 1823 term of the Supreme Court. All forty-six opinions were cases of appellate jurisdiction, six of which came up by certificate of division and the rest by appeal or by writ of error. For a brief discussion of federal appellate procedure under the judicial statutes of 1789, 1802, and 1803, see the *Papers of John Marshall*, VI, 537–38.

In addition to the date of the opinion and the name of the case, the calendar provides the following information: the citation to the printed report, the type of appeal, the name of the court of origin, the appellate case number, and the date(s) of arguments by counsel. This information has been compiled from the printed reports and the Supreme Court minutes, dockets, and appellate case files belonging to Record Group 267 in the National Archives. The style of the case is that used by the reporter Henry Wheaton, unless other sources indicate that he was mistaken. The existence of an original manuscript opinion in Marshall's hand is also noted.

1820

14 February	McClung v. Ross, 5 Wheat. 117–26. Error to U.S. Circuit Court, E. Tenn. Appellate Case No. 901. Argued 10 Feb. 1820.
18 February	United States v. Wiltberger, 5 Wheat. 93–105. Certificate of division from U.S. Circuit Court, Pa. Appellate Case No. 1018. Argued 14, 15 Feb. 1820.
24 February	United States v. Klintock, 5 Wheat. 149–52. Certificate of division from U.S. Circuit Court, Ga. Appellate Case No. 1029. Argued 14–15 Feb. 1820.
8 March	Wallace v. Anderson, 5 Wheat. 292. Error to U.S. Circuit Court, Ohio. Appellate Case No. 1009. Argued 6 Mar. 1820.
10 March	Loughborough v. Blake, 5 Wheat. 317–25. Error to U.S. Circuit Court, D.C. Appellate Case No. 921. Argued 7 Mar. 1820.
13 March	Blake v. Doherty, 5 Wheat. 360–67. Error to U.S. Circuit Court, W. Tenn. Appellate Case No. 903. Argued 1–2 Mar. 1820.
14 March	Handley's Lessee v. Anthony, 5 Wheat. 375–85. Error to U.S. Circuit Court, Ky. Appellate Case No. 927. Argued 4, 6 Mar. 1820.
15 March	Lyle v. Rodgers, 5 Wheat. 405–11. Error to U.S. Circuit Court, D.C. Appellate Case No. 951. Argued 11 Mar. 1820.
16 March	Owings v. Speed, 5 Wheat. 420–24. Error to U.S. Circuit Court, Ky. Appellate Case No. 961. Argued 13 Mar. 1820.
16 March	Conn v. Penn, 5 Wheat. 425–28. Appeal from U.S. Circuit Court, Pa. Appellate Case No. 962. Argued 14 Mar. 1820.

16 March   United States v. Lancaster, 5 Wheat. 434. Error to U.S. Circuit
            Court, Pa. Appellate Case No. 949. Argued 10 Mar. 1820.

1821

9 February   Mechanics' Bank of Alexandria v. Withers, 6 Wheat. 107–9.
              Error to U.S. Circuit Court, D.C., Alexandria. Appellate Case
              No. 969. Argued 8 Feb. 1821.

12 February   Thatcher v. Powell, 6 Wheat. 119–27. Error to U.S. Circuit
              Court, W. Tenn. Appellate Case No. 827. Argued 2 Feb. 1819.

12 February   Mayhew v. Thatcher, 6 Wheat. 130. Error to U.S. District Court,
              La. Appellate Case No. 968. Argued 10 Feb. 1821.

12 February   Farmers and Mechanics' Bank of Pennsylvania v. Smith, 6
              Wheat. 134–35. Error to the Supreme Court of Pa., Eastern
              District. Appellate Case No. 976. No date found for argument.

22 February   Young v. Bryan, 6 Wheat. 151–52. Error to U.S. Circuit Court,
              W. Tenn. Appellate Case No. 1073. Argued 22 Feb. 1821.

3 March   Cohens v. Virginia, 6 Wheat. 375–430. Error to Quarterly
              Session, Borough of Norfolk, Va. Appellate Case No. 1068.
              Argued 13, 19–20 Feb. 1821.

5 March   Cohens v. Virginia, 6 Wheat. 440–47. Error to Quarterly
              Session, Borough of Norfolk, Va. Appellate Case No. 1068.
              Argued 2 Mar. 1821.

8 March   Willink v. Hollingsworth, 6 Wheat. 251–59. Certificate of
              division from U.S. Circuit Court, Md. Appellate Case No. 998.
              Argued 23–24 Feb. 1821.

12 March   Bartle v. Coleman, 6 Wheat. 476–81. Error to U.S. Circuit Court,
              D.C., Alexandria. Appellate Case No. 982. Argued 8 Mar. 1821.

13 March   Bowie v. Henderson, 6 Wheat. 518–19. Appeal from U.S.
              Circuit Court, D.C., Alexandria. Appellate Case No. 1010.
              Argued 12 Mar. 1821.

13 March   United States v. Daniel, 6 Wheat. 546–49. Certificate of division
              from U.S. Circuit Court, S.C. Appellate Case No. 1093. Argued
              6 Mar. 1821.

14 March   Brashier v. Gratz, 6 Wheat. 529–41. Appeal from U.S. Circuit
              Court, Ky. Appellate Case No. 1008. Argued 10 Mar. 1821.

16 March   Goszler v. Corporation of Georgetown, 6 Wheat. 593–98.
              Appeal from U.S. Circuit Court, D.C. Appellate Case No. 1022.
              Argued 14 Mar. 1821.

1822

12 February   Newson v. Pryor's Lessee, 7 Wheat. 8–13. Error to U.S. Circuit
              Court, W. Tenn. Appellate Case No. 1012. Argued 6 Feb. 1822.

12 February   Tayloe v. T. & S. Sandiford, 7 Wheat. 14–22. Error to U.S. Circuit
              Court, D.C. Appellate Case No. 1028. Argued 6 Feb. 1822.

12 February   Taylor's Lessee v. Myers, 7 Wheat. 23–26. Certificate of division
              from U.S. Circuit Court, Ohio. Appellate Case No. 1043.
              Argued 15 Mar. 1821.

18 February   Bayley v. Greenleaf, 7 Wheat. 49–58. Appeal from U.S. Circuit
              Court, D.C. Appellate Case No. 1027. Argued 11 Feb. 1822.

1 March   Bouldin v. Massie's Heirs, 7 Wheat. 147–57. Appeal from U.S.
               Circuit Court, Ohio. Appellate Case No. 1106. Argued 21 Feb.
               1822.
1 March   Matthews v. Zane's Lessee, 7 Wheat. 202–11. Appeal from Ohio
               Supreme Court, Muskingum County. Appellate Case No. 1056.
               Argued 20 Feb. 1822.
2 March   Hoofnagle v. Anderson, 7 Wheat. 212–18. Appeal from U.S.
               Circuit Court, Ohio. Appellate Case No. 1087. Argued 25 Feb.
               1822.
7 March   Blount's Lessee v. Smith, 7 Wheat. 272–83. Error to U.S. Circuit
               Court, W. Tenn. Appellate Case No. 1074. Argued 23 Feb. 1822.
12 March   Crocket v. Lee, 7 Wheat. 523–28. Appeal from U.S. Circuit
               Court, Ky. Appellate Case No. 1053. Argued 6–7 Mar. 1822.
16 March   The Gran Para, 7 Wheat. 486–89. Appeal from U.S. Circuit
               Court, Md. Appellate Case No. 1098. Argued 20 Feb. 1822.
20 March   The Monte Allegre and the Rainha de los Anjos, 7 Wheat. 520–
               22. Appeal from U.S. Circuit Court, Md. Appellate Case Nos.
               1102, 1103. Argued 14 Mar. 1822.
20 March   Blight's Lessee v. Rochester, 7 Wheat. 543–51. Error to U.S.
               Circuit Court, Ky. Appellate Case No. 981. Argued 15–16 Mar.
               1822.
21 March   The Irresistible, 7 Wheat. 551–52. Appeal from U.S. Circuit
               Court, Md. Appellate Case No. 1104. Argued 20 Mar. 1822.
21 March   Holbrook v. Union Bank of Alexandria, 7 Wheat. 555–56.
               Appeal from U.S. Circuit Court, D.C., Alexandria. Appellate
               Case No. 1137. Argued 20 March 1822.
22 March   Marbury v. Brooks, 7 Wheat. 572–81. Error to U.S. Circuit
               Court, D.C. Appellate Case No. 1060. Argued 21–22 Mar. 1822.

                                    1823

5 February   Siglar and Nall v. Haywood, 8 Wheat. 679–80. Error to U.S.
               Circuit Court, E. Tenn. Appellate Case No. 1006. Argued 4 Feb.
               1823.
13 February   Sexton v. Wheaton, 8 Wheat. 238–52. Appeal from U.S. Circuit
               Court, D.C. Appellate Case No. 1115. Argued 4–5 Feb. 1823.
28 February   Johnson and Graham's Lessee v. McIntosh, 8 Wheat. 571–605.
               Error to U.S. District Court, Ill. Appellate Case No. 1105.
               Argued 15, 17–19 Feb. 1823.
1 March   The Mary Ann, 8 Wheat. 385–90. Appeal from U.S. District
               Court, La. Appellate Case No. 963. Argued 10–11 Feb. 1823.
4 March   The Sarah, 8 Wheat. 394–95. Appeal from U.S. District Court,
               La. Appellate Case No. 1082. Argued 1 Mar. 1823.
14 March   Hunt v. Rousmanier's Administrators, 8 Wheat. 201–16. Appeal
               from U.S. Circuit Court, R.I. Appellate Case No. 1151. Argued
               1 Mar. 1823.
14 March   Hugh v. Higgs, 8 Wheat. 697–98. Error to U.S. Circuit Court,
               D.C. Appellate Case No. 1125. Argued 7 Mar. 1823.
14 March   Gracie v. Palmer, 8 Wheat. 699–700. Error to U.S. Circuit
               Court, Pa. Appellate Case No. 1130. Argued 5–6, 7 Mar. 1823.

Appendix II
Calendar of Miscellaneous Papers
and Letters Not Found

Beginning with Volume VI, the editors adopted a policy of presenting calendar summaries in a separate appendix. Any inconvenience resulting from this separation is more than offset, they believe, by keeping the main body of the volume reserved for documents selected for printing in full. In this volume calendar entries have been prepared for proforma correspondence with Secretary of State John Quincy Adams, in which the secretary transmits copies of printed public documents and requests acknowledgment of receipt; letters and certificates drawn for various purposes; and other routine documents such as a special verdict, fire insurance declaration, and power of attorney. Entries have also been prepared for letters not found whose contents are at least partly known from extracts or summaries in the catalogs of auction houses and autograph dealers. Most of these letters, if extant, would be printed in full.

All calendar entries begin with the dateline in italics, followed by information (in parentheses) describing the document and its location. The contents of the document are then stated in summary style; however, extracts from letters not found are quoted in full. Where necessary, footnotes have been subjoined to calendar entries.

Certificate for the Prestons

2 February 1820, Richmond (ADS, KyLoF). States his belief that the Preston brothers "possess property to a great amount."[1]

1. JM's statement was appended to a longer certificate drawn up and signed by John Coalter and Henry St. George Tucker giving detailed information on the assets of the brothers Francis, James, and John Preston, who were applying for a loan from the Bank of the United States.

To [William S. Cardell?]

17 March 1820, Washington (printed extract of ALS, Walter R. Benjamin Autographs, Inc., *Collector* [May 1907], 80; also listed in Merwin-Clayton Sales Co. [New York, 1906]). " 'Whatever may serve to make early and correct impressions respecting our language on the minds of our children is of manifest utility. The earlier these impressions are made the deeper and more lasting they will be,' etc."[1]

1. The addressee was probably William S. Cardell, who was then trying to organize a "National Philological Academy." This was the forerunner of the American Academy of Language and Belles Lettres, which Cardell founded in the fall of 1820 (Cardell to James Madison, 4 Mar. 1820; Madison to Cardell, Mar. 1820, Madison Papers, DLC; JM to Cardell, 25 June 1821).

From James L. Edwards

27 March 1820, Washington (letterbook copy, RG 15, DNA). Clerk of War Department Pension Office informs JM that John Laws has been added to the pension rolls.[1]

1. On Laws, see *PJM*, I, 6 and n. 3; VIII, 403.

From John Quincy Adams

26 May 1820, Washington (letterbook copy, RG 59, DNA). Secretary of state transmits copy of laws passed during the late session of Congress.

To Charles Carter

12 September 1820, Richmond (summary of ALS, Walter R. Benjamin Autographs, Inc., *Collector* [Apr. 1946], 85). JM advises Carter, fearing lawsuit by bank, of lenient and understanding attitude of bank directors.

To John Quincy Adams

8 November 1820, Washington (ALS, RG 59, DNA). Acknowledges receipt of volumes of state papers containing reports to the House of Representatives from the first session of the Sixteenth Congress.

Special Verdict

7 December 1820, Richmond (AD, Martin v. Redd et al., U.S. Cir. Ct., Va., Ended Cases [Unrestored], 1820, Vi). Recites the facts and circumstances of the Fairfax proprietorship of the Northern Neck and the surveys and deeds under which the plaintiff, claiming under the Fairfax title, and the defendants, claiming under a grant from the Commonwealth of Virginia, assert title to a tract of land in Fauquier County.[1]

1. This was an ejectment for 931 acres in Fauquier County, brought in the name of Philip Martin against Joseph Redd, Thomas Humes, and Thomas Nelson, tenants in possession of the premises. The disputed tract was among the lands sold by Denny Fairfax to James Marshall in 1797 and subsequently partitioned among the members of the Marshall syndicate. With JM not sitting, Judge Tucker decided for the plaintiff on 14 Dec. 1820. Noting the strong similarity between this case and that between David Hunter and Denny Fairfax, Tucker referred to the opinions of Judge William Fleming in the Virginia Court of Appeals and of Justice Story in the Supreme Court (confirming Tucker's own 1794 judgment in the Winchester District Court) "as fully containing the grounds of my opinion in the present Case" (U.S. Cir. Ct., Va., Ord. Bk. XI, 25–28, 39; Tucker, "Cases in the Courts of the United States, 25 February 1813-November 1824," No. 3, p. 154, Tucker-Coleman Papers, ViW; *PJM*, VIII, 108–21).

To Unknown

16 March 1821, [Washington] (summary of ALS, James F. Drake, Catalog No. 103 [1917], 18). JM writes on business matters.

From John B. Armistead

19 May 1821, Fredericksburg (ALS, Bounty Warrants, Vi). Armistead writes on behalf of John Laws, asking JM to certify to governor and council of Virginia his recollections of Laws's Revolutionary war service.[1]

1. At the foot of the letter JM wrote and signed a certificate stating that Laws had faithfully served three years in his regiment of the Continental Line. See also James L. Edwards to JM, 27 Mar. 1820 (App. II, Cal.).

To Martin Marshall

22 May 1821, Richmond (summary of ALS, Thomas F. Madigan, Catalog [Nov. 1928], 74; also listed in *American Book-Prices Current in 1933* [New York, 1934], 602). Requests nephew to straighten out legal matters involving lands along the Ohio River belonging to Jane Marshall Taylor.

To John Quincy Adams

19 November 1821, Richmond (ALS, RG 59, DNA). Acknowledges receipt of the journals and documents of the second session of the Sixteenth Congress.

Remarks on the Death of William Pinkney

[26 February 1822, Washington] (printed, *Daily National Intelligencer* [Washington, D.C.], 27 Feb. 1822). In response to a motion by Robert G. Harper to adjourn the Supreme Court to honor the memory of William Pinkney, JM on behalf of the Court remarks: "We all lament the death of Mr. PINKNEY, as a loss to the profession generally, and most especially to that part of it which is assembled in this room. We lament it, too, as a loss to our country. We most readily assent to the motion which has been made, and shall direct an adjournment until to morrow at twelve."

To John Quincy Adams

22 July 1822, [Richmond] (noted as missing in Register of Miscellaneous Letters Received, RG 59, DNA). Recommends Landon Carter as secretary of legation.

To John Quincy Adams

27 July 1822, [Richmond] (noted as missing in Register of Miscellaneous Letters Received, RG 59, DNA). Acknowledges receipt of printed laws.

To John Quincy Adams

27 August 1822, Richmond (ALS, RG 59, DNA). Acknowledges receipt of the acts of the second session of the Sixteenth Congress and the 1820 census.

To John Quincy Adams

4 November 1822 [Richmond] (noted as missing in Register of Miscellaneous Letters Received, RG 59, DNA). Acknowledges receipt of Wheaton's Supreme Court reports.

To John Quincy Adams

18 November 1822, Richmond (ALS, RG 59, DNA). Acknowledges receipt of the additional census of Alabama.

Fire Insurance Declaration

29 November 1822, Richmond (DS [printed form], Records of the Mutual Assurance Society of Virginia, Vi). JM declares for fire insurance on four buildings situated on his square of four lots in the city of Richmond: dwelling house ($5,000), office ($800), laundry ($100), and kitchen ($800).[1]

1. This is a printed form (No. 4621), with blanks filled in by special agent William H. Allen and signed by JM (also signed by the agent and by two freeholders affirming the appraisal). Beneath the form is a plat showing the locations and dimensions of the insured buildings. These are the same buildings shown on JM's 1815 declaration, except that the 1822 declaration no longer shows a smokehouse between the kitchen and dwelling house. The 1822 declaration shows a second story added to the kitchen (*PJM*, VIII, 399).

Certificate for Jasper Graham

5 December 1822, Richmond (DS, Legislative Petitions, Richmond City, 1822–23, Vi). In support of Jasper Graham's petition to be allowed to reside in Virginia, JM and five others attest that they know Jasper and that he is "a proper object for the indulgence of the legislature."[1]

1. The document signed by JM was drawn by Philip N. Nicholas and was one of several certificates accompanying the petition. In his will John Graham of Richmond emancipated

his slaves, Jasper and his wife Mary, and stated that he presumed Jasper would be allowed to remain in Virginia. Graham explained that he had purchased Jasper before the 1806 act forbidding emancipated slaves from remaining in Virginia and that his purchase was conditioned upon Jasper's eventual emancipation. The petition, after first being rejected by a committee, was eventually approved by the House of Delegates, but a bill for the purpose was evidently not enacted into law (extract of will accompanying petition of Jasper Graham, Legislative Petitions, Richmond City, 1822–23, Vi; *Revised Code of Va.*, I, 436; *Journal of the House of Delegates of the Commonwealth of Virginia [1822–23]* [Richmond, Va., 1822], 27, 36, 48).

To [Thomas Mann Randolph?]

[Ca. December 1822, Richmond] (ALS, Executive Communications, Vi). Writes on behalf of Mr. Underwood whom he has known for many years "during some of which he wrote in the Land office." Thinks him intelligent and "very capable of performing the duties of a Clerk."

Power of Attorney

2 February 1823, Washington (ADS, PP). JM appoints Benjamin Watkins Leigh of Richmond as attorney to subscribe his name as maker or endorser of any promissory note given by Edward Colston and James Marshall or James M. Marshall "for the purpose of securing to the President Directors and company of the Bank of the United States the payment of a debt due from Nimrod Farrow, or from the estate of Turner Dixon deceased, or for any other purpose whatever."

Certificate

19 May 1823, Richmond (printed extract of ADS, Parke-Bernet, *Autographs & Manuscripts* [New York, sale of 27–28 Oct. 1959], 64). JM certifies to taking the deposition of Patrick McGuire to be used in the case of Harry Heth's Executor v. John Mason in the U.S. Circuit Court for the District of Columbia, county of Washington.

To Martin Marshall

25 June 1823, Richmond (summary of ALS, Stan V. Henkels, Auction Catalog [Philadelphia, 1932], item #1208). Writes on business and legal matters.

Certificate for Baptist African Church

3 December 1823, Richmond (DS, Legislative Petitions, Richmond City, 1822–23, Vi). In support of a petition submitted by ninety-two "persons of Colour" of Richmond requesting that a law be passed to erect a house of worship to be called the Baptist African Church, JM subscribes to the following statement: "My limited acquaintance in Richmond prevents my knowing many of the petitioners. The few I do know I beleive enti[r]ely respectable & think their petition reasonable."[1]

1. The certificate was drawn by James Pleasants, Jr., and signed by two others besides Pleasants and JM. It was one of several certificates accompanying the petition. Although a committee reported favorably on the petition and presented a bill, the House of Delegates postponed the measure indefinitely on 13 Dec. 1823 (*Journal of the House of Delegates of the Commonwealth of Virginia [1823–24]* [Richmond, Va., 1823], 17, 39, 47).

INDEX

In addition to persons and subjects, this index includes the titles of all cases mentioned in the documents and in the accompanying annotation. Persons are identified on pages cited below in italics. If a person has been identified in an earlier volume, the volume number and page reference follow the name in parentheses.

Abatement: plea in, 206, 208 n. 6
Adams, John (III, 476 n. 1), 174 n. 2, 354, 355 n. 6
Adams, John Quincy, 174 n. 2, 355 n. 6; letter from, 193–94; letters to, 46, 182–83, 194–95, 375, 376, 377; secretary of state, 46, 47 n. 1, 104 n. 1
Adams, Robert, 65 n. 1, 68
Addington, Henry (Viscount Sidmouth), 52 n. 2
Administrator. See Executor and administrator
Admiralty: case in, 31–40; jurisdiction, 11 n. 2, 77–78, 86 n. 2
"Algernon Sidney." See Roane, Spencer, writes as "Algernon Sidney"
Allan, John, 204, 208 n. 1
Allan & Ellis. See Furniss, Cutler, & Stacey v. Allan & Ellis
Allen v. State Bank of North Carolina, 204 n. 2
Allmond, Albert, 344 n. 1
Almeida, Joseph, 31
Almon, John: Remembrancer, 334
Ambler, Edward, 60 n. 4
Ambler, John (I, 122 n. 9), 59–60 and nn.
Ambler, Mary, 60 n. 4
Ambler v. Macon, 60 and n. 4
American Academy of Languages and Belle Lettres, 173–74 and n. 2, 374 n. 1
American Society for Promoting the Civilization of the Indian Tribes, 197, 200 n. 1
Ames, Fisher, 342
Amiable Isabella, The, 25–28 and nn., 101, 102 n. 1
Amory, Rufus G., 343 n. 5
Amos, William, 97

Anderson, Richard C. (I, 166 n. 7), 275–76, 278
Anderson & Wilkins v. Tompkins, 53–58
Anry, Henry, 45 n. 1
Archer, John. See United States v. Nelson and Myers
Armistead, John B., 376
Ashby, George Strother, 196, 197 n. 2, 197
Ashby, John, 196 and n. 1, 197
Ashby, Lucy Strother, 196 n. 1
Ashby, Turner, 274 and n. 3
Ashby, William Clarkson, 196 and n. 1, 197 n. 2
Assumpsit, 313–14, 318 n. 9
Atkins v. Hill, 23, 25 n. 20

Backhouse, John. See Backhouse v. Jett's Administrator
Backhouse, Rebecca. See Backhouse v. Jett's Administrator
Backhouse v. Jett's Administrator, 156–67
Bacon, Matthew: Abridgment, 19, 24 n. 10, 131, 142 n. 13, 206, 208 nn., 256, 260 n. 4, 261 n. 5, 277
Bainbridge, William (VIII, 181 n. 2), 3 and n. 1
Baird v. Bland, 163, 165 n. 28
Balcarce, Antonio Gonzales, 100 n. 1
Ball, Judith Steptoe (VIII, 156 n. 3), 241 n. 3
Ball, William L., 241 n. 3
Ballard, Davis C., 342, 343 n. 3
Bank of the United States v. Dandridge, 324–26, 327, 328, 330–31, 332–33
Bank of the United States v. State Bank of North Carolina, 204 n. 2
Baptist African Church, 378–79
Barbecue Club, 30 n. 2
Barbour, John S., 303 n. 4

Barbour, Philip P., *107*, 108
Barnes, James, 96
Baron Weston's Case, 162, 165 n. 19
Barry v. Rush, 23, 25 n. 20
Bartow, William A., 272–73 and nn.,
    273 *n. 1*
Batture controversy, 179, 183
Bayley, Sir John (judge of King's Bench),
    219, 220
Bell, Mr. (of Fauquier County), 302
Benjamin Pollard & Company. *See* Gaines
    v. Span
Benjamin Rush (U.S. ship), 5
Berry, Isaac, 95
Berryman v. Wise, 192 and n. 8
Bethel v. Stanhope, 158–59
Bevan v. Williams, 192 and n. 8
Bible Society of Virginia, 30 and n. 2
Bickerdike v. Bollman, 218, 219, 220, 226
Bills of exchange, 180, 181 nn.; case con-
    cerning, 217–32
Black, James A., 45 and nn.
Blackburn v. Stupart, 277, 279 n. 11
Blackhan v. Doren, 219
Blackstone, William: *Commentaries*, 19, 24
    n. 10, 130, 218; judge of Common Pleas,
    349
Blackwell, John (I, 22 n. 5), 302, 303 n. 3
Blair, John D. (II, 398 n. 84), 30 and n. 2,
    271, 272 n. 4
Blair, John H., 202 and n. 1
Blake, James H. *See* Loughborough v.
    Blake
Blakey, Robert. *See* Coates v. Muse
Blumfield's Case, 277, 279 n. 9
Bond, Joshua B., 18
Bostaide, Joseph, 204 n. 4
Bouquet, Henry, 336, *337 n. 1*, 352
Bracton, 130, 142 n. 12
Braxton, Carter (I, 370 n. 62), 260,
    261 n. 8
Bresson, Charles de, 274 and *n. 6*
Brig Penobscot v. United States, 80,
    86 n. 4
Brig Wilson v. United States, 31–40, 338,
    339 n. 3
Brown, William. *See* Robertson v. Miller
Brown v. Maffey, 219–20
Bryan, John Herritage, 210 and *n. 1*
Buchanan, John (I, 313 n. 11), 30 n. 2,
    271, 272 n. 4
Buckingham County, Va.: JM sells land in,
    62 and n. 1, 186–87, 187, 188, 194

Buddle v. Willson, 207, 208 n. 11
Buel, Samuel, 275
Buel v. Van Ness, 275, 276
Bullard v. Bell, 101, 102 n. 3
Buller, Francis (judge of King's Bench),
    218
Burwell, Ann Rich, 202 n. 1
Burwell, Nathaniel, 202 n. 1
Burwell's Administrator v. Willis's Executor,
    202 and nn.
Bush, Wilson, 38 and n. 9
Bussard, Daniel. *See* Bussard v. Levering
Bussard v. Levering, 17, 18, 22, 25 n. 18
Butler, Charles, 266, 269 n. 6
Byrd, Mary, 217
Byrd, William III (II, 102 n. 7). *See* Hop-
    kirk v. Page

Cabot, George, 342
Cagne, Hugh, 96, 97, 98
Caldwell, Elias B., 184, 185 n. 4
Calhoun, John C.: secretary of war, 63, 197
    n. 2, 197
Call, Daniel (II, 111 n. 9): lawyer, 204, 207,
    232, 325. *See also* Maxwell v. Call
Campbell v. Hall, 295, 296–97
Cardell, William S., 173–74, *174 n. 2*,
    374 and n. 1
Carroll, Charles, 174 n. 2
Carroll, Patrick, 346 n. 5
Carter, Charles, 375
Catacho, Manuel. *See* United States v.
    Manuel Catacho
Cazenove, Antoine Charles (VII, 245 n. 6),
    238, 239 n. 1
Chacon, Pablo, 89
Chalmers, George: *Opinions of Eminent
    Lawyers*, 298, 301 n. 14; *Political Annals*,
    300 n. 1
Chambers v. Harvest, 162
Chandler, John. *See* Mankin v. Chandler &
    Company
Chandler, William. *See* Mankin v. Chandler
    & Company
Chapels, William, 45 n. 1
Chaytor, James. *See* Santissima Trinidad
    and St. Ander, The
Chesapeake Insurance Company v. United
    States, 353–54, 355 n. 2
Chickahominy farm (JM's), 104, 105
Chitty, Joseph: *Treatise on Criminal Law*,
    19, 24 n. 9; *Treatise on Pleading*, 19, 24
    n. 9

Circuit Court, U.S., North Carolina, 28 n. 1, 203, 204 n. 2

Circuit Court, U.S., Virginia: admiralty case in, 31–40; case concerning action of waste, 249–53; case concerning U.S. marshal, 232–36; cases concerning sureties, 243–48, 263–70, 304–21; constitutional case in, 304–21; decedent's estates cases in, 150–56, 156–67, 210–17, 253–63, 355–60, 360–64; equity cases in, 48–52, 53–58, 69–76, 150–56, 156–67, 169–71, 210–17, 217–32, 253–63, 355–60, 360–64; nonintercourse cases in, 40–44, 76–89; piracy cases in, 30 n. 1, 44–45 and nn., 46, 47 and n. 1, 203, 204 nn., 344, 354, 355 n. 2; prize case in, 89–101; special session of, 344 and n. 1

JM's Opinions in: Anderson & Wilkins v. Tompkins, 53–57; Backhouse v. Jett's Administrator, 157–64; Bank of the U.S. v. Dandridge (report), 325–26; Brig Wilson v. U.S., 31–38; Coates v. Muse, 151–56, 210–17, 360–64; Furniss v. Allan, 205–8; Gaines v. Span, 254–60; Gallego v. U.S., 40–43; Hopkirk v. Page, 218–29; Jacob v. U.S., 188–92; Mankin v. Chandler, 347–51; Maxwell v. Call, 356–59; Pendleton v. U.S., 244–47; Robertson v. Miller, 69–75; Santissima Trinidad, 90–100; Scott and Lyle v. Lenox, 249–52; Thompson v. U.S., 77–86; U.S. v. Mann, 233–35; U.S. v. Maurice, 304–18; U.S. v. Nelson and Myers, 263–68; U.S. v. Shelton, 169–71; Wilson v. LeRoy, 48–52

Clark v. Graham, 101, 102 n. 2

Clarke v. Clement and English, 277, 279 n. 6

Clarke v. Hackwell, 19, 24 n. 9

Clay, Henry, 243 n. 1, 367–68 and n. 4; letter to, 365–67

Coalter, John, 47, *48 n. 1*, 374 n. 1

Coates, Margaret. *See* Coates v. Muse

Coates, William. *See* Coates v. Muse

Coates v. Muse, 150–56, 210–17, 360–64

Cohen, Jacob, 106

Cohen, Mendez, 106

Cohen, Philip, 106

Cohens v. Virginia, 101; argued in Supreme Court, 108; background of, 106–8; first opinion in, 113–41; Jefferson and, 111–12; JM comments on reaction to, 150, 167–68, 168–69, 179; Massachusetts approves of, 175–76; publication of opinion in, 142, 143, 148; second opinion in, 143–46; significance of, 108–10; Virginia's reaction to, 107–8, 110–12, 142 n. 10, 150, 167–68, 168–69, 179

Coke, Edward: *Institutes*, 19, 24 n. 10, 131, 142 n. 13, 250–51, 252, 264, 266, 269 n. 6

Collins v. Blantern, 316

Colston, Mr., 172

Colston, Edward (VII, 247 n. 8), 378

Colston, Rawleigh (I, 300 n. 40), 60 and n. 3, 240, 241 n. 12

Conn v. Penn, 30 n. 1

Constitution, U.S.: commerce clause, 33–34; Eleventh Amendment, 75 n. 7, 109–10, 129–32; "exclusive legislation" clause, 13, 16, 138–41; judiciary article, 106, 108–9, 109, 110, 115–16, 117–18, 121–29; nature of, 116–17, 120, 312; power of appointment under, 306–7; power to lay direct taxes under, 13–17; rules for construing, 118, 122–23, 123–24, 134–37; supremacy clause, 116–17

Convention of *1802*, 227, 230 n. 25

Corbet v. Johnson, 156 n. 8

Corbin, John T. *See* Coates v. Muse

Corbin, Richard. *See* Coates v. Muse

Courts, U.S.: jurisdiction of, 5–11 and n. 2, 75 and n. 7, 77–78, 86 n. 2, 115–41. *See also* Circuit Court, U.S., North Carolina; Circuit Court, U.S., Virginia; Supreme Court, U.S.

Covin, 159, 160, 165 n. 14

Cowper, John (II, 248 n. 3), 52 n. 5

Crawford, William H., 367, 368 nn.

Creed v. Colville, 165 n. 19

Crittenden, Zachariah. *See* Coates v. Muse

Crux, Juan de la, 204 n. 4

Cunningham, William, Jr., 355 n. 6

Cunyngham v. Cunyngham, 155, 156 n. 11

Currie, Edward, 94, 96

Dagworthy, John, 66, 67 n. 3

Dandridge, Julius B. *See* Bank of the United States v. Dandridge

Daniel, Beverly, 194, 195 n. 1

Daugherty, John, 346 n. 5

Daveiss, Joseph Hamilton, 241, *242 n. 1*

Davenport v. Thompson. *See* Thompson v. Davenport

Davies v. Topp, 161–62
Davis, John (seaman), 94–95, 96
Davis, John (U.S. judge), 346 and *n. 3*
Davis, William P., 38 n. 2
Decedent's estates: cases concerning,
    150–56, 156–67, 210–17, 253–63,
    355–60, 360–64
De Lovio v. Boit, 11 n. 2
Demurrer, 205–7; to evidence, 191
Dennison, Gideon, 18
Dennison, Jerusha, 18
Devereux, Thomas P. (VIII, 180 n. 2), 194
Dickson, Robert. *See* Thompson and Dickson v. United States
District of Columbia. *See* Washington, D.C.
Distringas, writ of, 203 and n. 1
Dodd, Ann, 271, 272 n. 3
Dominique v. Davenant, 206, 208 n. 7
Doughty v. Lascelles, 207, 208 n. 11
Duke, Basil (VIII, 101 n. 2), 12 n. 2, 62
Duke, Charlotte Marshall (VIII, 101 n. 2),
    12 n. 2
Duke, Nathaniel Wilson, 12 and *n. 2*
Dun, Walter, 355
Durfey, Bailey, 45 n. 1
Duvall, Gabriel (VII, 256 n. 7), 366 n. 2

Edwards, James L., 375
Elegit, writ of, 249–52
Eliza (brig), 17–18
Elkison v. Deliesseline, 338, 339 n. 2
Ellenborough, Edward Law, Baron (chief
    judge of King's Bench), 219, 219–20
Ellis, Charles, 204, 208 n. 1
Embuscade, L' (French privateer), 98, 101
    n. 20
Emmet, Thomas A., 107
Enquirer (Richmond): publishes attacks
    on Cohens v. Virginia, 107, 111, 112, 142
    n. 10, 150 and n. 1, 167, 176, 179
Error, writ of, 131–32
Escheat, 70–71, 75 n. 4
Esdaile v. Sowerby and Meller, 22, 25 n. 17
Euer (Ewer), Samson: *System of Pleading*,
    207, 208 n. 12
Evidence: demurrer to, 191; rules of,
    191–92
Executor and administrator, 211, 215–16,
    364 n. 4; *de bonis non*, 156 n. 2; *de son
    tort*, 159, 160, 164 n. 8
Eyre, Sir James (chief judge of Common
    Pleas), 219

Fairfax, Denny Martin (II, 141), 60 n. 1,
    69 n. 2, 375 n. 1
Fairfax, William, 63, 64 n. 2, 65, 66, 67
Fairfax lands: bill concerning, 239, 240
    n. 1; compromise concerning title
    to, 239, 240, 241 n. 4; Leeds Manor,
    59–60; litigation concerning, 69 and
    n. 2, 239–40, 241 nn., 375 and n. 1
Fairfax's Devisee v. Hunter's Lessee, 239,
    240, 241 nn.
Federalist, The, 110, 134, 135–36
"Federalist of *1789*, A." *See* Wheaton,
    Henry, writes as "A Federalist of
    1789"
Fitzherbert, Anthony: *New Natura Brevium*,
    249, 252 n. 3
Fleming, William (I, 142 n. 7), 375 n. 1
Fleta, 130, 142 n. 12
"Fletcher of Saltoun," 111, 113 n. 24, 142
    n. 10, 179, 180 n. 6
Fletcher v. Peck, 281, 294
Fontaine, Walter L., 62 n. 1; letter from,
    62; letters to, 186–87, 187, 188, 194
Foster, Seth, 195
Fox, Messrs., 62
Franklin (U.S. ship), 103 n. 1
Frauds, statute of, 158–61
Freeland, Archibald, 249
French v. Bank of Columbia, 220–21
Fry, Joshua, 66, 67 n. 2
Fuller, John, 45 n. 1
Furniss, Cutler, & Stacey v. Allan & Ellis,
    204–9

Gaines, Harry. *See* Coates v. Muse
Gaines, Sarah. *See* Gaines v. Span
Gaines, William Fleming, 261 n. 8
Gaines v. Span, 253–63
Gales, Joseph, 142 and *n. 1*, 143, 248
Gales & Seaton: proprietors of Washington
    Daily National Intelligencer, 142, 143
Gale v. Walsh, 219
Gallego, Joseph, *40; see also* Gallego,
    Richard & Company v. United States
Gallego, Richard & Company v. United
    States, 40–44
Garland, Samuel, 69
Garlick, Camm, 253; *see also* Gaines v.
    Span
Garlick, Edward. *See* Gaines v. Span
Garlick, John. *See* Gaines v. Span
Garlick, Mary. *See* Gaines v. Span
Garlick, Samuel. *See* Gaines v. Span

Gaston, William (VIII, 217 n. 1), 210
Genêt, Edmond, 101 n. 20, 329 n. 3
Gilliat, John, 40
Girard, Stephen (IV, 326 n. 2), 337, 340
Godolphin, John: *Orphan's Legacy*, 256,
  261 n. 5
Goodall v. Dolley, 218
Gordon, William: *History of the Indepen-
  dence of the U.S.*, 334
Gordon v. Caldcleugh, 276, 278 n. 2
Graham, Jasper, 377 and n. 1
Graham, John, 377 n. 1
Graham, Mary, 377 n. 1
Graham, Robert, 355
Graham, Thomas J. *See* Johnson v.
  McIntosh
Grange (British ship), 98, 99, 101 n. 20
Great Britain, 45 n. 1, 366 n. 2; Conven-
  tion with U.S. (1802), 227, 230 n. 25
    Statutes: 6 Edw. I (1278; Statute of
    Gloucester), 250–52; 13 Eliz. I, c. 5
    (1571), 158–61; 13 Eliz. I, c. 10 (1571),
    250; 3 Wm. III, c. 14 (1691), 163, 165
    n. 26; 4 and 5 Anne, c. 16 (1705), 206,
    208 n. 5
Griffin, Cyrus (I, 134 n. 4), 243 n. 1
Griffin, John Tayloe (V, 105 n. 13),
  243 n. 1
Grotius, Hugo, 148
Guerrière (U.S. ship), 3 and n. 2, 102, 103
  n. 2

Hale, Matthew: "Treatise on Customs," 19,
  24 n. 9
Hall, John E., 183–84, *185 n. 2*
Hall, Thomas. *See* Gaines v. Span
Hamilton, Alexander (II, 119 n. 9), 200
  and n. 1, 200–201
Hamilton, Elizabeth, 200
Hamilton, James A., 200 and *n. 1*,
  200–201
Hammond, Charles, 113 n. 21, 367–68,
  368 n. 1
"Hampden." *See* Roane, Spencer, writes as
  "Hampden"
Hansford, Theodosius, 239, *240 n. 2*
Hargrave, Francis, 266, 269 n. 6; *Law
  Tracts*, 19, 24 n. 9
Harper, Robert G. (IV, 48 n. 6), 280, 281
Harragan, Daniel. *See* Pendleton v. United
  States
Harris, John, 95
Harrison v. Jackson, 56, 57, 58 n. 3

Harvie, Jaquelin B. (II, 321 n. 5), 63 and
  nn., 203, 302, 337, 340
Hawes v. Leader, 160
Hawkes v. Saunders, 23, 25 n. 20
Hawkins, William: *Pleas of the Crown*, 19,
  24 n. 10
Hay, George (I, 94 n. 3), 245, 247 n. 1
Hayling v. Mullhall, 277, 279 n. 10
Haywood, William Henry, Sr., 194,
  195 n. 2
Haywood, William Henry, Jr., 195 n. 2
Hening, Edmund W., 327, *328 n. 2*
Henry, John, 93
Herbert, Maurice, 329 and n. 2
Hernandez, Joseph Marion, 302 and *n. 3*
Heron, Lenox & Company, 249
Heth's Executors v. Mason, 378
Higgins, Eugene, 318 n. 8
Higginson, Stephen, 346 and *n. 2*
*History of the Colonies Planted by the English
  on the Continent of North America*, 281,
  304 n. 2
Holker, John. *See* Holker v. Parker
Holker v. Parker, 341–43 and nn., 345
Hollen, The, 19, 24 n. 8
Hopkins, John (V, 535 n. 3), 59
Hopkirk, James. *See* Hopkirk v. Page
Hopkirk v. Page, 217–32
Horace: *Epistles*, 175, 178 n. 1
Hornet (U.S. ship), 204 n. 4
Hornsby, Joseph, 217
Humes, Thomas, 375 n. 1
Humphreys, David (III, 133 n. 7): *Life of
  Israel Putnam*, 334
Hunt v. United States, 277, 279 n. 7
Hunter, Alexander, 96
Hunter, David (V, 229), 243, 375 n. 1
Hunter v. Fairfax's Devisee, 240, 241 n. 11
Huntress, Ivory, 31
Hutchinson v. Brown, 207, 208 n. 11

Illinois Indians, 280
Illinois Land Company, 280
Independencia del Sud (ship). *See* Santissima
  Trinidad and St. Ander, The
Indians: Illinois, 280; land titles of (*see*
  Johnson v. McIntosh); Mohegan,
  297, 301 n. 11; Piankeshaw, 280, 295,
  301 n. 7; religion of, 29 and n. 1
Ingersoll, Charles J.: argues Supreme
  Court cases, 5, 18, 19, 21–22
International law, 147–48; case in,
  89–101

Irresistible (ship), 44–45 and nn.
Irwin (Irvine), Hugh, 93

Jackson, John George, 12 and *n. 1*
Jackson, Luke, 45 n. 1
Jackson v. Clarke, 240
Jacob (slave), 105
Jacob, John J. *See* Jacob v. United States
Jacob v. United States, 184–85 and n. 7, 188–93
James, Daniel, 96
James Dykes & Company. *See* Wilson v. LeRoy, Bayard & McEvers
Jamines, Miguel, 204 n. 4
Jaques v. Withy, 277, 279 n. 11
Jarvis, Samuel F., 29 *n. 1*; *Discourse on Indian Religion*, 29 and n. 1
Jarvis, William Charles, *178 n. 2*; *The Republican*, 176–77
Jay, John (I, 33 n. 3), 174 n. 2
Jefferson, Thomas (I, 116 n. 5), 174 n. 2, 329 and n. 3, 355 n. 6; and batture controversy, 179, 183; and Cohens v. Virginia, 111–12; JM criticizes, 179, 183–84; opinion of federal judiciary, 112; Story criticizes, 176–77
Jeffries, Richard, 195
Jett, Thomas. *See* Backhouse v. Jett's Administrator
Jett, William Storke. *See* Backhouse v. Jett's Administrator
John & Adam (ship), 40
John Chandler & Company, 347
Johnson, Andrew, 38 and n. 10
Johnson, Chapman, 325, *326 n. 1*
Johnson, Joshua. *See* Johnson v. McIntosh
Johnson, Richard M., 112, 365, 366 n. 2
Johnson, Thomas, 279, 279–80
Johnson, William, 237 n. 2; Supreme Court justice, 240, 241 n. 10, 274, 278 n. 4, 366 n. 2; U.S. Circuit Court judge, 338, 339 n. 2
Johnson v. McIntosh: argued in Supreme Court, 280, 281; background of, 279–81; opinion in, 284–300; significance of, 279, 281–83
Johnston (Johnson), Peter, 45 n. 1, 46
Jones, J. William, 43 n. 5
Jones, Walter, 107; argues Supreme Court cases, 13, 18, 22–23
Jones v. Shore's Executor, 19, 20, 24 n. 8
Judicial review, 366
Judiciary, federal. *See* Courts, U.S.

Judiciary Act of *1789*: section 9, 77–78, 86 n. 2, 190; section 22, 185 n. 7, 190; section 25, 110, 116, 136, 138, 184, 276, 278 n. 1; section 32, 189–91
Judiciary Act of *1801*, 366, 367 n. 3
Jurisdiction, federal. *See* Courts, U.S., jurisdiction of
Jury: *de medietate linguæ*, 344 n. 1, 346
Juvenile Library Company of Richmond, 272–73 and nn.

Kalkman, Charles F., 275
Keith, Elizabeth Contee, 274 and *n. 5*
Keith, James (I, 139 n. 4), 274 and n. 4
Kelly, William, 346 n. 5
Kemp v. Squire, 155, 156 n. 10
Kent, James, 328 n. 4
Kentucky, 241, 242 n. 2, 366 n. 2
Kerr, Elizabeth. *See* Maxwell v. Call
Kerr, Robert. *See* Maxwell v. Call
Key, Francis Scott, 18, 22
King, Rufus, 174 n. 2
King v. Gordons, 192 and n. 7
Kirk v. Smith, 346 and n. 4
Kirkland, John Thornton (VI, 196 n. 2), 327, 328 n. 1
Kyd, Stewart: *Treatise on Awards*, 23, 25 n. 21

Lafayette, Gilbert du Motier, Marquis de (I, 317 n. 26), 174 n. 2
Lancaster, Thomas. *See* United States v. Lancaster
Law of Nations. *See* International law
Laws, John (I, 6 n. 3), 375, 376 and n. 1
Lawson, Oswald. *See* Thompson and Dickson v. United States
Lear, Tobias (VI, 38 n. 1), 200 and n. 1
Le Blanc, Simon (judge of King's Bench), 219, 229 n. 7
Lee, Henry (I, 110 n. 8), 3, 4 n. 1
Leeds Manor, 59–60
Legge v. Thorpe, 219, 229 n. 7
Leigh, Benjamin Watkins (VIII, 191 n. 2), 62 and n. 1, 325, 378
Lenox, Samuel, 249
LeRoy, Bayard & McEvers. *See* Wilson v. LeRoy, Bayard & McEvers
Levering, Aaron, 18
Levingston (Livingston), Daniel, 45 n. 1, 46
Lewis, John, 95
Life of George Washington, The, 3, 4 n. 1,

281; second edition, 63–64, 68 and nn., 195–96 and n. 2, 239, 303, 322, 329, 333–34, 336, 339, 340–41
Little Democrat (ship), 329 and n. 3
Livingston, Brockholst: death of, 328 and n. 4, 331, 334; Supreme Court justice, 174 n. 2, 347 n. 7, 366 n. 2
Livingston v. Jefferson, 180 n. 5
Lloyd, James, 343 n. 5
Lonsdale v. Brown, 181 nn.
Lotteries: in Washington, D.C., 106–7, 143–46
Loughborough v. Blake, 13–17
Lowell, John, Sr., 342, 343 n. 2
Lowell, John, Jr. (VIII, 33 n. 1): complains about Supreme Court opinion, 341–43 and nn., 345
Lufborough (Loughborough), Nathan. *See* Loughborough v. Blake
Lyle, James (of Philadelphia). *See* Lyle v. Rodgers
Lyle, James (of Virginia), 249
Lyle v. Rodgers, 17, 18, 22–24, 25 n. 22

McClung, Thomas, 242 and n. 3
McCulloch v. Maryland, 106, 111, 180 n. 3, 237 n. 2
M'Daniel v. Hughes, 350–51
McDonnel, Edward, 95, 96
Macdonough, Thomas, 3 and n. 2
McGuire, Patrick, 378
McIntosh, William. *See* Johnson v. McIntosh
McKewan, Michael. *See* Pendleton v. United States
McLane, Allen (VI, 347 n. 3), 3–4 and nn.
Macon, Nathaniel, 328 n. 4
Macon, Sarah, 60 n. 4
Macon, William H., 60 and n. 4
Maddock, Henry: *Treatise on High Court of Chancery*, 160, 165 n. 12
Madison, James (I, 141 n. 6), 174 n. 2, 179, 180 n. 3, 240 n. 1
Mankin, Isaiah. *See* Mankin v. Chandler & Company
Mankin v. Chandler & Company, 347–52
Mann, William. *See* United States v. Mann
Mansfield, William Murray, Lord (chief judge of King's Bench), 269 n. 1
Marbury v. Madison, 123, 177, 179; distinguished in Cohens v. Virginia, 126–27
Margaretta, The, 19, 21, 24 n. 8, 25 n. 15
Markham v. Gonaston, 265–66

Mars, The, 19, 24 n. 8
Marshaling assets, 157, 164 n. 2
Marshall, Agatha Smith (VIII, 147 n. 3), 61
Marshall, Charles C. (VIII, 66 n. 2), 239, 241 n. 3
Marshall, Claudia Burwell, 202 n. 1
Marshall, Edward C., 172 n. 1; attends Harvard, 323, 324 n. 2, 327, 330, 338, 346; letter to, 172–73
Marshall, Eliza Clarkson, 271, 272 n. 6
Marshall, Humphrey (I, 132 n. 6), 62
Marshall, James (1802–1880), 378
Marshall, James Keith (VII, 245 n. 5), 105, 202 n. 1, 271, 272, 274
Marshall, James M. (I, 169 n. 4), 3, 59–60 and nn., 69 and n. 2, 241 n. 5, 375 n. 1, 378; letter to, 239–41
Marshall, Jaquelin A. (I, 243 n. 3), 302, 303 n. 1; letter to, 270–72
Marshall, John: accounts with son, 271–72; advises B. Washington, 180; business affairs of, 62 and n. 1, 186–87, 187, 188, 194, 270–71; Chickahominy farm of, 104, 105; declines membership in philanthropic society, 197; declines to arbitrate dispute, 243 and n. 1; discusses cases, 167, 168, 184–85, 203, 328, 330–31, 332–33, 346, 353–54; discusses family matters, 62, 104, 105, 172, 242, 271, 302; drafts special verdict, 375; and Fairfax lands, 59–60, 69 and n. 2, 239–40, 375 and n. 1; fire insurance policy, 377; injured in fall from horse, 68; legal business of, 202, 241–42; member of American Academy of Languages, 173–74 and nn.; orders wine, 203, 238; prepares edition of Washington's correspondence, 58–59, 68, 102, 180, 238–39, 303, 322, 329, 334, 336, 340, 352–53; and publication of opinion in Cohens v. Virginia, 142, 143, 148; publishes *History of the Colonies*, 281, 304 n. 2; at ratifying convention of *1788*, 142 n. 10; recommends appointment, 197; reports on judicial department, 182–83, 194–95; revises *Life of Washington*, 63–64, 68, 195–96, 239, 303, 322, 329, 333–34, 336, 339, 340–41; seeks loan for son-in-law, 337, 340; sells bank stock, 65 n. 1; sells Buckingham land, 62 and n. 1, 186–87, 187, 188, 194; sends flour to Story, 341; sends son to Harvard, 323, 330, 338,

346; serves as executor, 62 and n. 1; slaves of, 105; Story praises, 176, 328; travels to Norfolk, 344–45; visits Fauquier, 302

Comments on: J. Adams, 354; Bank of the U.S. v. Dandridge, 328, 330–31, 332–33; Clay, 367–68; disunion sentiment in Virginia, 184; English language, 173–74, 374; A. Hamilton, 200 n. 1, 200–201; Hammond's argument, 367; international law, 147–48; Jarvis's *Discourse on Indian Religion,* 29; Jefferson, 79, 183–84; Johnson's opinion, 338; judicial review, 366; Kentucky relief laws, 241; Livingston's successor, 331, 334; Madison, 179; Miner's Fourth of July address, 181–82; Pinkney, 376; politics, 341, 354, 367–68; power over internal improvements, 236; proposal to reform Supreme Court, 365–66; public education, 272–73; Raymond's *Thoughts on Political Economy,* 185–86; reaction to Cohens v. Virginia, 150, 167–68, 168–69, 179; repeal of Judiciary Act of *1801,* 366; Roane, 150, 167–68, 168–69, 179, 184; social life in Washington, 105, 274; states' rights, 338; Story's address, 184; Supreme Court as expositor of federal law, 239–40; Wheaton's *Anniversary Discourse,* 147–48; Wheaton's *Digest of Supreme Court Decisions,* 148; Wheaton's essays, 184; wife's health, 104, 172

Chief Justice and U.S. Circuit Court Judge: charges grand jury, 344; construes acts of Congress, 5–11, 31–32, 34–38, 41–43, 78–84, 143–46, 170, 189–91, 235, 307–8, 309–11; construes army regulations, 308–9; construes articles of copartnery, 71–74; construes charter-party, 49–52; construes Virginia laws, 37–38, 74, 211–14, 215–16; construes will, 254–59, 357–59; disqualifies himself from sitting, 321; expounds Constitution, 13–17, 33–34, 108–10, 115–41, 306–7; notes on arguments (*see* Supreme Court, U.S., JM's notes on arguments in); opinions in Supreme Court (*see* Supreme Court, U.S., *JM's Opinions in*); opinions in U.S. Circuit Court, Virginia (*see* Circuit Court, U.S., Virginia, *JM's Opinions in*); sentences pirates, 44–45, 46; upholds appellate jurisdiction over state courts, 132–38

Citations of Authorities: Bacon, 131, 206, 256; Bayley, 219, 220; Blackstone, 130, 218, 349; Buller, 218; Chalmers, 298; Coke, 131, 250–51, 252, 264, 266; Ellenborough, 219–20; English cases, 56, 57, 155, 158–60, 161–63, 192, 206–7, 218–20, 226, 249–50, 256, 265–66, 267, 295, 296–97, 316–18, 349, 350–51; Euer (Ewer), 207; Eyre, 219; *Federalist,* 134, 135–36; Fitzherbert, 249; Godolphin, 256; Hargrave and Butler, 266; Le Blanc, 219; Maddock, 160; Parsons, 266–67; Perkins, 264, 265, 266, 267; Phillipps, 192; *Plain Facts,* 298; Pratt and Yorke, 297–98; *Register of Writs,* 249, 250; Roberts, 158–60; Sheppard, 264, 265, 266, 267; W. Smith, 286; Tidd, 206–7; U.S. cases, 51, 80, 99, 123, 126–27, 138, 220–21, 235, 266–67, 268, 294; Viner, 161; Virginia cases, 155, 163; Watson, 54

Legal Commentary on: action of waste, 249–52; assumpsit, 313–14; authority of English precedents, 158; bills of exchange, 180, 218–21, 224–25, 228; blank bonds, 264–68; claims of public officers, 233–35; commerce clause, 33–34; construing state laws, 163, 212; contracting power of U.S., 313–16; corporation powers of Washington, D.C., 143–46; demurrer to evidence, 191; "discovery" principle, 284–92; Eleventh Amendment, 129–32; escheat, 70–71; "exclusive legislation" clause, 138–41; executor and administrator, 211, 215–16; expatriation, 91; foreign attachment, 350–51; fraudulent conveyances, 158–63; Indian title of occupancy, 285, 290, 292–95, 296, 297–300; insolvency, 170; judicial power, 118; judiciary article, 115–16, 117–18, 121–29; jurisdiction of U.S. courts, 115–41; Marbury v. Madison, 126–27; national supremacy, 116–17, 133; nature of Constitution, 116–17, 120, 312; neutral rights, 90–93, 98, 99–100; parties to equity suit, 229; partnership, 54–57; pleading, 205–7; power of appointment, 306–7; power to lay direct taxes, 13–17; precedent, 99; proceeding *in rem,* 348–49; Proclamation of *1763,* 295–97; rights of creditors, 214–15, 215–17; rules for construing Constitution, 118, 122–23, 123–24,

134–37; rules of evidence, 191–92; separation of powers, 98–99; state sovereignty, 116–17, 129; statutory construction, 6, 212, 213–14; suit, 130–32; technical rules of law, 264–65, 267; writ of error, 131–32

Marshall, John (VIII, 126 n. 1), 3, 102–3

Marshall, Louis (II, 412 n. 41), 61 n. 1, 61–62

Marshall, Martin P. (VIII, 138 n. 1): letters to, 241–42, 376, 378

Marshall, Mary W.: health of, 104, 105 n. 2, 172; letters to, 104–5, 273–75, 302–3, 344–45

Marshall, Rebecca Peyton, 172 n. 1

Marshall, Thomas, 239, *241 n. 5*

Marshall, Thomas, Jr. (I, 125 n. 3), 64, 65 n. 1, 271, 272 n. 5, 302, 303 n. 4

Marshall, William (I, 334 n. 3), 60

Marshall, William (VIII, 156 n. 4), 242 and n. 4

Martin, Philip, 60 n. 1, 69 and *n. 2*, 375 n. 1

Martin v. Hunter's Lessee, 108, 138

Martin v. Redd, 69 and n. 2, 375 and n. 1

Martin's Lessee v. Abbott, 321–22 and n. 2

Martin's Lessee v. Blessing, 321–22 and n. 2

Martin's Lessee v. Peters, 321–22 and n. 2

Martines, Joseph, 204 n. 4

Martyr, Frances, 248 and n. 1

Martyr, Richard, 248, 274

Massachusetts: approves of Cohens v. Virginia, 175–76; Convention, 168 and n. 2, 177–78

Massie, John W., 274 and n. 3

Matthews v. Zane, 276, 278 n. 2

Matthews v. Zane's Lessee, 276, 278 n. 2

Maurice, James. See United States v. Maurice

Maxwell, William M. See Maxwell v. Call

Maxwell v. Call, 355–60

Mayo, Robert, 272–73 and nn., *273 n. 1*

Means, Robert. See Maxwell v. Call

Menou, Comte de (French chargé d'affaires), 274 and n. 6

Mercein, William A., 196 n. 2

Mercer, Hugh, 243 and *n. 1*

Mercer, John Francis (I, 114 n. 8), 240 n. 1

Miller, Boyd. See Robertson v. Miller

Miller v. Hackley, 180, 181 n. 3

Miner, Charles, 181–82 and nn., *182 n. 2*

Mirror of Justices, 130, 142 n. 12

Mohegan Indians, 297, 301 n. 11

Monroe, James (I, 39 n. 4), 174 n. 2; on constitutionality of internal improvements, 236, 237 n. 1; letters to, 103–4, 236–37; president, 18, 47 and n. 1, 103–4, 274, 328 n. 4, 353 and n. 2

Morehead, George, 270–71, 272 n. 2

Morse, Jedidiah, 197, *200 n. 1*

Moscow (schooner), 204 nn.

Moses Myers & Son. See Wilson v. LeRoy, Bayard & McEvers

Murdock, William, 105 and n. 3, 147

Murray, Adam. See Anderson & Wilkins v. Tompkins

Murray, Henry M., 280, 281

Murray, Mathew, 96

Muse, Elliott. See Coates v. Muse

Muse, Hudson. See Coates v. Muse

Muse, Thomas. See Coates v. Muse

Mutter's Executors v. Munford, 163, 165 n. 27

Mutual Assurance Society, 377

Myers, Samuel. See United States v. Nelson and Myers

Nadin v. Battie and Wardle, 277, 279 n. 10

Nares and Pepys v. Rowles, 317–18

Nelson, Peter, 45 n. 1

Nelson, Thomas (of Fauquier County), 375 n. 1

Nelson, Thomas. See United States v. Nelson and Myers

Nicholas, Philip N., 275–76, 278, 377 n. 1

Nicholas v. Anderson, 275–76, 278

Nonintercourse: cases concerning, 40–44, 76–89

Northern Neck. See Fairfax lands

Ogden, David B. (VIII, 178 n. 3), 107, 108, 110

Oglesby, Francis, 45 n. 1, 46, 47 n. 1

Oliver, Nariso Pares, 94, 101 n. 4

Orr v. Hodgson, 240

Osborn v. Bank of the United States, 367, 368 n. 2

Page, Mr., 172

Page, William Byrd, *217; see also* Hopkirk v. Page

Paloma, Cayeton, 204 n. 4

Parker, Daniel. See Holker v. Parker

Parsons, Theophilus, 266–67, *269 n. 8*, 342, 343 nn.

Partridge v. Gopp, 161
Patriot (schooner). *See* Thompson and Dickson v. United States
Patton v. Nicholson, 51, 52 n. 4
Paxton v. Popham, 316–17
Pearson v. Henry, 23, 25 n. 20
Peart, Francis, 243 n. 1
Peckner, John, 93
Pegram, John, 195 and *n. 3*
Pendleton, Edmund (I, 252 n. 7), 180, 181 n. 4
Pendleton, Philip. *See* Pendleton v. United States
Pendleton, Philip C. *See* Pendleton v. United States
Pendleton v. United States, 243–48
Perkins, John: *Conveyancing*, 264, 265, 266, 267
Perpetuities, rule against, 359 and n. 4
Peters, John, 5
Pettiward v. Prescott, 162, 165 n. 24
Peyton, Chandler, 172, *173 n. 2*
Peyton, Rebecca Courtenay. *See* Marshall, Rebecca Peyton
Phillipps, Samuel: *Treatise on the Law of Evidence*, 192 and n. 10
Phillips, Daniel, 45 n. 1
Piankeshaw Indians, 280, 295, 301 n. 7
Pickering, Timothy, 200 and n. 1
Pickett, Miss M., 172
Pickett, Mr., 172
Pilot (schooner), 353–54, 355 n. 2
Pinckney, Charles C. (III, 32 n. 9), 174 n. 2
Pinkney, William, 376; argues Supreme Court cases, 18, 24, 107, 108
Piracy: cases concerning, 30 n. 1, 44–45 and nn., 46, 47 and n. 1, 203, 204 nn., 344, 354, 355 n. 2
Pleading: abatement, 206, 208 n. 6; demurrer, 205–7; demurrer to evidence, 191
Pleasants, James, Jr., 379 n. 1
Plutarch's Lives, 65 and n. 2
Poe, Edgar Allan, 208 n. 1
Poitiaux, Michael B., *40*
Pole v. Harrobin, 316–17
Pollard, Benjamin. *See* Gaines v. Span
Pollard, Robert, 261 n. 8; *see also* Wilson v. LeRoy, Bayard & McEvers
Poole, Samuel G., 45 nn., 46, 47 n. 1
Pope, Nathaniel, 280
Porter, David, 354, *355 n. 2*
Potter, Henry, 194

Pownall, Thomas: *Remembrancer*, 334
Pratt, Charles, 297–98, 301 n. 12
Preston, Francis, 374 and n. 1
Preston, James, 374 and n. 1
Preston, John, 374 and n. 1
Prize: case in, 89–101; jurisdiction, 77–78, 86 n. 2
Pueyrredón, Juan Martín de, 92, 100 n. 1
Pulteney v. Warren, 162, 165 n. 23

Radford v. M'Intosh, 192 and n. 8
Ramsay, David: *History of the American Revolution*, 334
Randolph, Edmund (I, 127 n. 5), 113 n. 23
Randolph, Peyton, *113 n. 23*, 180 n. 6
Randolph, Thomas Mann, Jr. (V, 397 n. 1), 107, 378
Raymond, Daniel, *186 n. 1*; *Thoughts on Political Economy*, 185–86
Read's Case, 159
Redd, Joseph, 375 n. 1
Reeder, Benjamin, 195 n. 4
Reeve, Tapping, 186 n. 1
Register of Writs, 249, 250, 252 n. 2
Reilly, Thomas, 304, 318 n. 8
Rex v. Verelst, 192 and n. 9
Reynolds v. Waller, 237–38 and n. 2
Richard, John, 40
Richmond, Va.: Baptist African Church, 378–79; Barbecue Club, 30 n. 2; *Enquirer* (*see Enquirer* [Richmond]); Juvenile Library Company, 272–73 and nn.
Ritchie, Thomas: editor of Richmond *Enquirer*, 107, 111, 112, 142 n. 10
Roane, Spencer (I, 131 n. 2), 106, 142 n. 10, 328 n. 4; and Fairfax litigation, 240, 241 n. 11; writes as "Algernon Sidney," 111–12, 113 n. 25, 150 and n. 1, 167–68, 168–69, 179, 184, 185 n. 2; writes as "Hampden," 111
Robert Cary & Company. *See* Hopkirk v. Page
Roberts, William: *Treatise on Voluntary and Fraudulent Conveyances*, 158–60
Robertson, Archibald. *See* Robertson v. Miller
Robertson v. Miller, 69–76
Rodgers, John, 18
Rogers v. Stephens, 218–19
Rowand, Thomas, 347
Rucker v. Hiller, 220

Rules: proceedings in clerk's office, 205, 208 n. 3
Rush, Richard, 147 and *n. 1*
Russel v. Langstaffe, 267
Rutherforth, Thomas: *Institutes of Natural Law*, 19, 24 n. 9

St. Ander (ship). *See* Santissima Trinidad and St. Ander, The
Sales, Isaac, 45 n. 1
Santissima Trinidad (ship). *See* Santissima Trinidad and St. Ander, The
Santissima Trinidad and St. Ander, The, 89–101
Schooner Exchange v. McFadon, 99, 101 n. 22
Scott, Irvine & Company, 249
Scott, James B., 249
Scott, Robert G., 232
Scott and Lyle v. Lenox, 249–53
Scott v. Shearman, 349
Scruggs, Isham, 62
Selden v. Hendrickson, 180, 181 n. 6
Sergeant, John: argues Supreme Court cases, 5, 18, 19–21, 275, 276
Sharp, William, 304, 318 n. 8
Shelton, P. T., & Company. *See* United States v. P. T. Shelton & Company
Shelton, Philip T. *See* United States v. P. T. Shelton & Company
Shelton, Walter. *See* United States v. P. T. Shelton & Company
Sheppard, William: *Touchstone of Common Assurances*, 264, 265, 266, 267
Shetelworth v. Neville, 163
Sidmouth, Viscount. *See* Addington, Henry (Viscount Sidmouth)
Sidmouth license, 49–52 and n. 2
Sims v. Urry, 162
Skinker, Samuel, 303 n. 2
Skinker, William, 302, 303 n. 2
Slaughter, Philip (I, 324 n. 60), 196–97
Slaves, 105, 377 and n. 1
Small, Abraham: Philadelphia publisher, 303, 304 n. 2, 334, 336, 339, 340, 341
Smith, Joseph, 95
Smith, Thomas (of Fauquier County), 105 and n. 2
Smith, Thomas. *See* United States v. Smith
Smith, William: *History of New York*, 286, 301 n. 2
Smith & Ricard, 271
Smith v. Crooker, 266–67, 269 n. 8

Smith v. Maryland, 240
Smyth, Alexander, 107, 108
"Somers," 111, 113 n. 23, 179, 180 n. 6
South Carolina, 339 n. 2
Sovereign immunity, 108
Spain: treaty with U.S., 25–28 and nn., 91–92
Span, Samuel. *See* Gaines v. Span
Speake v. United States, 268
Speck, John H., 97–98
Speirs, Bowman & Company. *See* Hopkirk v. Page
Spencer, Ambrose, 328 n. 4
Stanard, Robert, 160, 164 n. 3, *169*, 325; U.S. attorney, 46 and n. 2, 169, 188, 204 n. 5, 232, 247 n. 2, 304
Stevenson, Andrew, 44, 45 and *n. 2*, 325
Story, Joseph, 112, 174 n. 2, 241 n. 10; address to Suffolk Bar, 184, 185 n. 5; on admiralty jurisdiction, 11 n. 2; advises JM, 174–75, 178; assists JM's son, 323, 330, 338, 346; criticizes Jefferson, 176–77; denounces Virginia's constitutional doctrines, 176; on insolvency, 174–75; letters from, 174–78, 327–28; letters to, 167–68, 178–80, 183–85, 323–24, 330–31, 338–39, 341, 346–47, 353–55; and Massachusetts Convention, 168 n. 2, 177–78; praises JM, 176, 328; quotes Horace, 175; on reaction to Cohens v. Virginia, 175–76; requests copy of JM's opinion, 327; sends fish to JM, 178, 183; Supreme Court justice, 235 n. 1, 237 n. 2, 279 n. 15, 326 n. 2, 366 n. 2, 375 n. 1; U.S. Circuit Court judge, 11 n. 2, 327–28
Strother, Lucy. *See* Ashby, Lucy Strother
Supreme Court, U.S.: appellate jurisdiction of, 108, 122–27, 132–38; calendar of JM's opinions in (1820–23), 371–73; constitutional cases in, 13–17, 106–42; criminal case in, 5–11; JM's notes on arguments in, 17–25, 275–79; library, 4; original jurisdiction of, 122–27; proposal to reform, 365–66 and n. 2
     JM's Opinions in: Cohens v. Virginia, 113–41, 143–46; Johnson v. McIntosh, 284–300; Loughborough v. Blake, 13–17; U.S. v. Wiltberger, 5–11
Surety: cases concerning, 243–48, 263–70, 304–21
Sydney, Stephen, 45 n. 1

Tabb, John, 202, 203 n. 4

Talbot, Isham, 276, 278

Tanner v. Hague, 277, 279 n. 11

Taylor, Jane Marshall (VIII, 140 n. 3), 61–62, 242, 376

Taylor, John (I, 110 n. 9): *Construction Construed*, 112

Taylor, Robert B., 90, 202, *203 n. 3*

Taylor, Thomas M., 61

Taylor v. Dundass, 277, 279 n. 10

Taylor v. Priddy, 242, 243 n. 2

Tazewell, Littleton W. (IV, 163 n. 9), 90, 202–3 and nn.

Templeman v. Steptoe, 155

Thomas, James, 45 n. 1

Thompson, Catharine Livingston, 274 and n. 6

Thompson, Smith, *12 n. 1*; appointed Supreme Court justice, 328 n. 4, 334, 347 n. 7; secretary of navy, 12 and n. 1, 102–3, 103, 274 n. 6; U.S. Circuit Court judge, 346

Thompson, William H. *See* Thompson and Dickson v. United States

Thompson and Dickson v. United States, 76–89

Thompson v. Davenport, 201–2 and n. 2

Tidd, William: *Practice of Court of King's Bench*, 206–7

Tindal v. Brown, 22, 25 n. 17

Todd, Thomas: Supreme Court justice, 101, 274, 366 n. 2

Toller, Samuel: *Law of Executors*, 23, 25 n. 19

Tompkins, John. *See* Anderson & Wilkins v. Tompkins

Tompkins & Murray. *See* Anderson & Wilkins v. Tompkins

Trumbull, John, 174 n. 2

Tucker, Henry St. George, 374 n. 1

Tucker, St. George (I, 148 n. 6): illness of, 69, 242, 321; letters to, 47–48, 69, 242–43, 321–22, 331–32; U.S. Circuit Court judge, 242, 243 n. 2, 321–22 and n. 2, 331, 332, 344 n. 1, 375 n. 1; U.S. District Court judge, 31, 38 n. 11, 76, 90, 195, 243, 346, 354

Tunstall, Mary. *See* Gaines v. Span

Underwood, Mr., 378

United States: Convention with Great Britain (1802), 227, 230 n. 25; treaty with Spain, 25–28 and nn., 91–92

Statutes: to amend charter of city of Washington (1812), 143–46; bankruptcy (1800), 170, 171 n. 2; census (1790), 20, 24 n. 11; concerning commercial intercourse (1810), 81, 82; embargo (1808), 19, 20, 24 n. 1, 24 n. 12; to fix the military peace establishment (1821), 310; judiciary (*see* Judiciary Act of *1789*; Judiciary Act of *1801*); to lay duties on spirits distilled within U.S. (1814), 188, 189; nonintercourse (1809), 78–84; nonintercourse (1811), 78–84; for organizing the general staff (1813), 309; for organizing the general staff (1816), 309–10; for organizing the Treasury Department (1789), 19; for organizing the Treasury Department (1820), 310–11; piracy (1819), 44, 45 n. 3, 354; to prevent importation of Negroes (1803), 33, 34–38 and n. 4; prize (1812), 84; providing for salvage in cases of recapture (1800), 354; for punishment of crimes (1790), 5–11; for punishment of crimes (1794), 93; to regulate collection of duties (1789), 20, 24 n. 12; to regulate collection of duties (1799), 19, 20, 24 n. 7, 24 n. 12, 31–32, 170, 171 n. 1, 175, 277, 279 n. 12; for regulating processes (1792), 276, 278 n. 3; for regulating Treasury, War, and Navy Departments (1809), 309, 314; for relief of persons imprisoned for debts due U.S. (1798), 277, 279 n. 8; for relief of persons imprisoned for debts due U.S. (1817), 277, 279 n. 8; to remit fines and forfeitures (1813), 40, 41–43; for remitting forfeitures (1790), 19, 24 n. 4; for remitting forfeitures (1792), 19, 21, 25 n. 14; for remitting forfeitures (1797), 19, 41–42; to repeal embargo (1814), 82, 84; for settling accounts between U.S. and receivers of public money (1797), 235 and n. 2, 246, 247 n. 4

United States v. Bevans, 11 n. 2

United States v. Foushee and Ritchie, 232

United States v. Lancaster, 17–19, 19–22, 25 n. 16, 30 n. 1

United States v. Mann, 19, 24 n. 10, 232–36

United States v. Manuel Catacho, 332, 344 and n. 1, 346

United States v. Maurice, 304–21

United States v. Nelson and Myers, 263–70

United States v. P. T. Shelton & Company, 167, 168, 169–71, 178, 180

United States v. Smith, 30 n. 1, 44–45 and nn., 46, 47 and n. 1

United States v. Wilkins, 235

United States v. Wiltberger, 5–11

Van Buren, Martin, 328 n. 4

Van Ness, Cornelius, 275

Vigers v. Aldrich, 277, 279 n. 11

Viner, Charles: *Abridgment*, 161

Violett v. Patton, 267

Virginia: Bible Society of, 30 and n. 2; constitutional doctrines of, 176; disunion sentiment in, 184; and election of *1824*, 367, 368 n. 5; law of bills of exchange in, 180, 181 nn.; reaction to Cohens v. Virginia, 107–8, 110–12, 142 n. 10, 150, 167–68, 168–69, 179

    Acts of Assembly: for ascertaining damage upon protested bills of exchange (1748), 229, 230 n. 27; civil procedure (1788), 205–6, 208 nn.; concerning partitions (1786), 211–14; concerning slaves, free Negroes, and mulattoes (1793), 338, 339 n. 3; concerning waste (1792), 251, 252 n. 11; concerning wills, intestacy, and distributions (1819), 215–16; to prevent fraud (1785), 158, 164 n. 5; to prevent migration of free Negroes (1793), 37–38; for proceeding against absent debtors (1819), 349, 350, 351 n. 3; releasing commonwealth's right to lands (1818), 74, 75 n. 6; for relief of creditors (1726), 165 n. 26; for surveying lands given to military officers (1783), 278, 279 n. 14

Virginia v. Ward, 187 and n. 1

Wabash Land Company, 280

Walker v. Griffin's Heirs, 243 n. 1

Walsh, Jacob, 347

Walwyn v. St. Quintin, 219

Ward, George A., *64 n. 1*, 65; letters to, 63–64, 66–68

Warder v. Arell, 180, 181 n. 4

Warrington, Lewis, 102, *103 n. 2*

Washington, Bushrod (II, 89 n. 6): advises JM, 180; illness of, 101–2, 104, 238, 274, 352; letters to, 30–31, 58–59, 64–66, 68, 101–2, 168–69, 180–81, 195–96,

201–2, 203–4, 237–38, 238–39, 303–4, 322, 328–29, 332–34, 334–36, 336–37, 340–41, 352–53; publishes reports, 303, 304 nn.; revises law reports, 201–2 and n. 2, 237–38 and n. 2; Supreme Court justice, 181 n. 5, 366 n. 2, 367; U.S. Circuit Court judge, 5, 25 n. 16, 30, 181 n. 2

Washington, D.C.: canal, 146, 147 n. 4; Congress' exclusive legislation over, 13, 16, 138–41; corporation powers of, 143–46; lotteries in, 106–7, 143–46; social life in, 105, 274

Washington, George, 3, 4 n. 2, 64, 65, 66–67; edition of correspondence of, 58–59, 68, 102, 180, 238–39, 303, 322, 329, 334, 336, 340, 352–53; papers of, 200, 201

Washington, Lawrence, 66–67, *68 n. 4*

Waste, action of: case concerning, 249–53

Waters v. Ebrall, 162

Watson, William: *Law of Partnership*, 54, 57 n. 1

Wayne, Caleb P. (IV, 314 n. 4): Philadelphia publisher, 68 and nn., 195–96 and nn., 322, 333, 336, 339, 340

Webster, Daniel, 168 and n. 2, 328 n. 4; argues Supreme Court cases, 110, 280, 281

Weems, Mason Locke (VI, 253 n. 2), 68 and n. 3

Wells, John, 107

Wharton, Samuel: *Plain Facts*, 298, 301 n. 13

Wheaton, Henry: *Anniversary Discourse*, 147–48; *Digest of Supreme Court Decisions*, 147, 148; letters to, 147–48, 150; Supreme Court reporter, 11 n. 2, 18, 148, 150; writes as "A Federalist of *1789*," 111, 184, 185 n. 3

White, Robert (VII, 187 n. 3), 239, 241 n. 5

Wickham, John (II, 36 n. 5), 325

William Gray & Company. See Coates v. Muse

Williams, James, 275

Williams, John, 4 and *n. 1*, 302 and n. 2

Williams, William C. (V, 240 n. 2), 228–29, 230 n. 26, 245, 361, 363, 364 n. 3

Williamson, Thomas, 304

Williams v. United States, 275, 277

Willis, Francis, 202 n. 1, 203 n. 3

Willis, John, 203 n. 3

Wilson, George, 48

Wilson (brig). *See* Brig Wilson v. United States

Wilson v. LeRoy, Bayard & McEvers, 48–52

Wiltberger, Peter. *See* United States v. Wiltberger

Winder, William H., 275, 277–78, 280

Wirt, William (VI, 477 n. 1): argues Supreme Court cases, 5, 13, 110, 275, 276, 277, 278; and case of The Amiable Isabella, 25–28; letters from, 3–4, 25–28, 29–30, 47; letter to, 46; U.S.

Attorney General, 30 n. 1, 46, 47, 274, 275

Woodrop Sims (ship). *See* Wilson v. LeRoy, Bayard & McEvers

Worcester's Case, The Dean and Chapter of, 250

Worthington v. Barlow, 23, 25 n. 20

Wright v. Wivell, 256

Year Books (law reports), 249–50, 252 n. 4

Yorke, Charles, 297–98, 301 n. 12

Zouch v. Clay, 266

Job #: 98993

Author name: Marshall Vol 9

Title of book: The Papers of John Marshall Vol 9

ISBN number: 0807824046